P9-BUI-432

PERFECT
MURDER

PERFECT
TOWN

PERFECT MURDER

PERFECT TOWN

Lawrence Schiller

HarperCollins*Publishers*

Copyright © by Lawrence Schiller and KLS Communications, Inc.

All rights reserved under International and Pan American Copyright Conventions. Printed in the United States of America.

Quotations from interviews by Lawrence Schiller and Charlie Brennan are copyright © 1997 and 1998 by KLS Communications, Inc.

Grateful acknowledgment is made to the following for permission to reprint previously published material and television broadcasts:

ABC: Brief excerpt from *ABC World News Tonight* on March 13, 1997. Used by permission of ABC News.

Associated Press: Excerpt from April 19, 1997, article pertaining to the Ramsey case. Copyright © 1997 by the Associated Press. Reprinted by permission of the Associated Press.

Boulder Weekly: Excerpt from May 15, 1997, article pertaining to the Ramsey case. Copyright © 1997 by the *Boulder Weekly*. Reprinted with permission of the *Boulder Weekly*.

Daily Camera: Excerpts from various articles from 1996 through 1998 pertaining to the Ramsey case and related matters. Copyright © 1996, 1997, 1998 by the *Daily Camera*. Reprinted by permission of the *Daily Camera*.

National Enquirer: Excerpts from various articles from 1997 and 1998 pertaining to the Ramsey case. Copyright © 1997, 1998 by the *National Enquirer*. Reprinted by permission of the *National Enquirer*.

NBC: Brief excerpt from the *Today* program and brief excerpt from the *Tonight* program. Used by permission of NBC.

Rocky Mountain News: Excerpts from various articles from 1996 through 1998 pertaining to the Ramsey case and related matters. Copyright © 1996, 1997, 1998 by the *Denver Rocky Mountain News*. Reprinted with permission of the *Denver Rocky Mountain News*.

The Denver Post: Excerpts from various articles from 1997 and 1998 pertaining to the Ramsey case and related matters. Copyright © 1997, 1998 by *The Denver Post*. Reprinted with permission of *The Denver Post*.

Time: Excerpt from "This Murder Is Ours," *Time* January 20, 1997, © 1997 Time Inc. Reprinted by permission.

No part of this book may be used or reproduced in any manner whatsoever without written permission except in the case of brief quotations embodied in critical articles and reviews. For information address HarperCollins Publishers, Inc., 10 East 53rd Street, New York, NY 10022.

HarperCollins books may be purchased for educational, business, or sales promotional use. For information please write: Special Markets Department, HarperCollins Publishers, 10 East 53rd Street, New York, NY 10022.

FIRST EDITION

ISBN 0-06-019153-8

99 00 01 02 03 ❖/RRD 10 9 8 7 6 5 4 3 2 1

To KATHY, MY FRIEND AND WIFE,
for the four loving years
we've shared together

AN APPRECIATION

To Charlie Brennan, my skillful colleague in interview and research,
for the year we labored side by side in Boulder,
feeling as devoted as family

"Evils that befall the world are not nearly so often caused by bad men as they are by good men who are silent when an opinion must be voiced."

AUTHOR'S NOTE

This work attempts to take the story of the murder investigation of Jon-Benét Ramsey out of the context of the newspaper reports and sound bites that have formed the nation's opinion of the case and place it into a more complete context.

This book is based on the memories of those interviewed, my own observations, reports, transcripts, and other documents I obtained during my research.

The passages that appear in the first person have been edited. Words, phrases, and even segments of the interviews on which the passages are based were removed and sentences rearranged to present the material in continuity. It was not done to make accounts more meaningful or to improve on what interview subjects said but to avoid duplication and confusing references and to make the transition from speech to print more fluent.

Lawrence Schiller
January 1999

CONTENTS

Dear Friends and Family,

It's been another busy year at the Ramsey household. Can't believe it's almost over and time to start again!

Melinda has graduated from the Medical College of Georgia and is working in Pediatrics ICU at Kennestone Hospital in Atlanta. John Andrew (2nd) is a Sophomore at the University of Colorado.

Burke is a busy fourth grader where he really shines in math and spelling. He played flag football this fall and is currently on a basketball binge! His little league team was #1. He's lost just about all of his baby teeth, so I'm sure we'll be seeing the orthodontist in 1997!

JonBenét is enjoying her first year in "real school." Kindergarten in the Core Knowledge program is fast paced and five full days a week. She has already been moved ahead to first grade math. She continues to enjoy participating in talent and modeling pageants. She was named "America's Royale Tiny Miss" last summer and is Colorado's Little Miss Christmas. Her teacher says she is so outgoing that she will never have trouble delivering an oral book report!

John is always on the go traveling hither and yon. Access recently celebrated its one-billion $$ mark in sales, so he's pretty happy! He and his crew were underway in the Port Huron to Mackinac Island yacht race in July, but had to pull out midway due to lack of wind. (Can you believe that?) But, his real love is the new "old looking" boat, Grand Season, which he spent months designing.

I spend most of my "free time" working in the school and doing volunteer work. The Charlevoix house was on the home tour in July and will likely appear in one of the Better Homes and Garden publications in 1997. On a recent trip to NYC, my friend and I appeared amid the throng of fans on the TODAY show. Al Roker and Bryant actually talked to us and we were on camera for a few fleeting moments!

We are all enjoying continued good health and look forward to seeing you in 1997! One final note...thank you to all my 'friends' and my dear husband for surprising me with the biggest, most outrageous 40th birthday bash I've ever had! We'll be spending my actual birthday on the Disney Big Red Boat over the new year!

Merry Christmas and much love,

The Ramseys

ACCESS CELEBRATES $1 BILLION MARK

A billion bucks. That's enough to make anybody celebrate.

So when Boulder-based computer distributor Access Graphics Inc. passed the $1 billion mark in 1996 revenues, it tossed a luncheon party at the Hotel Boulderado on Friday.

John Ramsey, president of Access Graphics, thanked about 300 employees at the gathering and told them it couldn't have happened without them.

Reaching the billion-dollar mark has come relatively quickly for Access, which was formed in 1989 from the merger of three companies: CAD Distributors Inc. of Boulder; CAD Sources Inc. of Piscataway, N.J,; and Advanced Products Group of Roswell, Ga.

—Tom Locke, business writer
Daily Camera, December 21, 1996

PART ONE

A Death in Paradise

"Do roses know their thorns can hurt?" JonBenét asked me that one morning. I was the landscaper at the Ramseys' home during the last two years of her life, and it was the kind of question I'd learned to expect from her.

I remember how intelligent JonBenét was. That's why I never talked to her as if she were just a little kid. I spoke to her pretty much as I would to an adult, the way I'm talking to you now. We would discuss evolution, the natural mutations that occur in plants, animals, even people.

So when she asked me about thorns, I told her, "They're a rose's shield. They allow roses to survive. They keep away animals who might eat them."

She would follow me all over the yard, finding something to do wherever I was working. I was happy to talk with her, and would answer her questions about anything and everything. All the topics you'd call natural science seemed to interest her.

"What is a year?"

"That's the length of time it takes for the earth to make one trip all around the sun."

"So I've been around the sun five times?"

"Right. And you've almost finished your sixth trip."

I added that I'd completed the journey twenty-seven times. That stopped her. So many trips, she exclaimed. Then she became lost in thought.

That same week in September, the needles were falling off the pine tree and the sap had started to drip. "Why does a tree do that?" she asked. I wasn't certain I knew exactly, but I tried to explain—scientifically. "The sun helps pull the sap up from the trunk to the leaves." Then I compared the sap to human blood, said the sap carries nourishment to the whole tree. Anyone could see she was excited to learn about these things.

The neighborhood kids would come by from time to time. JonBenét seemed to socialize with them just fine. Her brother, Burke, was three years older. He almost never said a word to me. Just played by himself in the backyard, completely occupied with his own projects. Next to the sandbox and swing, in the pea gravel area, he dug a system of canals.

3

Then he put a hose on top of the slide. The water poured down and spread perfectly throughout the elaborate waterway.

"Someday you're going to be an engineer?" I asked him.

"No," he said. Just a single word—no.

He always seemed to play alone.

Just then Patsy called from inside, "It's time to start your homework." I remember thinking, There's a mother who really cares about her children.

"Burke, come in and start your homework."

"OK, just a minute, Mom." It was like an old-fashioned TV show—Leave It to Beaver or Father Knows Best.

While I kept the gardens well-defined and tidy, as pristine as a golf course, JonBenét had her own projects. She would attach an exercise device to one ankle, and then, as it rotated several inches off the ground but parallel to it, she would hop with the other leg over the cord as it swung by. She'd keep this up for long periods on the back patio. And she was very good at it. It was kind of a cool thing—demanded good reflexes and coordination. I even thought of getting one for myself.

I figured her legwork was for the pageants. I could see the muscles becoming defined in her calves. I'd made a similar assumption when I saw her practicing the violin. I knew the competitions took a lot of preparation, but I never once saw her in makeup or costumes, never spotted her wearing anything but jumpers or jeans, or shorts and T-shirts.

I'd heard she was Little Miss Colorado, and I asked her if she was excited about winning the title.

"I really don't care about it," she said. It didn't seem to be a very big deal to her, or if it was, she certainly didn't let on. She seemed more interested in trips around the sun or the lifeblood of trees.

In early December of '96, I was raking the blanket of leaves under a maple, getting the property ready for winter.

"Don't pick the leaves up, please," JonBenét begged me. "Leave them for me to play with."

Well, I'm thinking, no way. My job is to pick them up, and that's what I'm going to do.

"Last year my dad and I did that."

And then she said quietly; "I really miss him. I wish he was around more."

"Where does he go?"

"I don't know. But sometimes he goes away for a long time."

"You really miss him?" I asked.

"Yeah, I really miss him a lot."

4

Then she started to cry, tears rolling down her cheeks.

I didn't know what to say—didn't know enough about the situation, didn't want to intrude or play counselor. It wasn't my place. I changed the subject and started to rake up the leaves.

A moment later, I saw JonBenét was scooping up the leaves from the top of the barrel and hurling them over her head into the wind. "Hey! Stop that!" I yelled.

"No, I want to play in 'em." She was being kind of bratty. She had a bit of smart aleck in her.

I grabbed the barrel and started running toward the compost pile. She chased after me, not about to give up her fun. I set the barrel down, and she dumped all the leaves out. That made me angry—almost. But before long I made a game out of it—it was fun for both of us.

That evening I left a big pile of leaves out front by the gutter for her to play with.

That was probably the last time I spoke to JonBenét. Six weeks later I took the morning paper from my front steps and saw it. I don't even remember now what the headlines said.

I wanted to go over to the Ramseys'. Later that day, I did drive by. It was crazy—media, police, yellow tape going all around the house. Just totally crazy. I didn't even try to go in. I kept driving.

—Brian Scott

1

On Thursday morning, December 26, 1996, at about 7:30 A.M., Pete Hofstrom, head of the felony division of the Boulder County district attorney's office, called Bill Wise, the first assistant district attorney, at home. The moment Wise heard Hofstrom's voice, he knew something serious had happened. Nothing else would warrant a call at that hour. Hofstrom said they had a report of a child kidnapping. The mother had called 911 at 5:52 A.M. There was a ransom note, which threatened that the child would be killed if the police were brought in.

Hofstrom told Wise he had asked the police when the FBI would be arriving, only to be told they hadn't even been called. Hofstrom had told the cops to notify the Bureau. Bill Wise could hear the frustration in his colleague's voice when he added that the police had asked him to join them at the crime scene. Hofstrom had to point out to them that in a kidnapping, the protocol was to set up a command post *away* from the victim's home, in case the perpetrators were monitoring the residence.

But the damage had already been done. The officer had told Hofstrom that marked police cars were parked in front of the home of John Ramsey, at 755 15th Street.

Earlier, Rick French, the first police officer to respond to the mother's 911 call, had immediately searched the house for the child and for any sign of forced entry, but he found nothing. Then he read the ransom note:

Mr. Ramsey,

Listen carefully! We are a group of individuals that represent a small foreign faction. We respect your bussiness [sic] but not the country that it serves. At this time we have your daughter in our possession. She is safe and unharmed and if you want her to see 1997, you must follow our instructions to the letter.

You will withdraw $118,000.00 from your account. $100,000 will be in $100 bills and the remaining $18,000 in $20 bills. Make sure that you bring an adequate size attache to the bank. When you get home you will put the money in a brown paper bag. I will call you between 8 and 10 am tomorrow to instruct you on delivery. The delivery will be exhausting so I advise you to be rested. If we monitor you getting the money early, we might call you early to arrange an earlier delivery of the money and hence a earlier delivery [the word *delivery* was written, then crossed out] pick-up of your daughter.

Any deviation of my instructions will result in the immediate execution of your daughter. You will also be denied her remains for proper burial. The two gentlemen watching over your daughter do not particularly like you so I advise you not to provoke them. Speaking to anyone about your situation, such as Police, F.B.I., etc., will result in your daughter being beheaded. If we catch you talking to a stray dog, she dies. If you alert bank authorities, she dies. If the money is in any way marked or tampered with, she dies. You will be scanned for electronic devices and if any are found, she dies. You can try to deceive us but be warned that we are familiar with Law enforcement countermeasures and tactics. You stand a 99% chance of killing your daughter if you try to out smart us. Follow our instructions and you stand a 100% chance of getting her back. You and your family are under constant scrutiny as well as the authorities. Don't try to grow a brain John. You are not the only fat cat around so don't think that killing will be difficult. Don't underestimate us John. Use that good southern common sense of yours. It is up to you now John!

Victory!

S.B.T.C.

By the time the second police officer got to the house, friends of the family, whom the child's parents had called, began to arrive. Meanwhile, four detectives were paged and assigned to the investigation, and three additional patrol officers were sent to the house. Even before the first detective arrived at the crime scene, police officers, family friends, and a victim advocate who had responded to an officer's page were wandering through the house trying to make sense of what had happened.*

---

*Victim assistance advocates serve crime victims but are employees of law enforcement. Their job is to minimize the victims' trauma. They are trained to recognize and meet the emotional needs of victims and/or their loved ones, whether it is to listen to their story or create an emotionally safe environment.

An hour before, at police headquarters, Sgt. Bob Whitson was the on-duty supervisor. In an emergency, Detective Sgt. Larry Mason was to be called at home to serve as acting commander. Mason's boss, John Eller, head of the detective division, was at home, officially on vacation. There was less than a skeleton crew working.

That morning, Detective Jane Harmer, who'd attended a seminar taught by the FBI's Child Abduction Serial Killer Unit, was also on vacation. Sgt. Whitson knew that Harmer had a copy of the Bureau's manual on procedures to follow in a kidnapping case, but he had no idea where she kept it. More than a year after the Boulder PD had sent Detective Harmer to the seminar, the department had not officially adopted the FBI protocol. They saw no need to make the agency's recommendations part of their own procedures. Sgt. Whitson knew that county sheriff's Lt. James Smith had also attended the FBI seminar. He phoned Smith, and half an hour later, the Boulder police had the FBI manual.

Hearing reports about the kidnapping ended Commander Eller's vacation. He wasn't happy about it; he had a house full of family and friends from back home in Florida. He was also annoyed to find out that nobody of substantial rank was on duty. In his irritation, the commander completely forgot he had approved Detective Mason to be on call at home.

Judging by what Eller heard from officers at the scene, the Ramseys appeared to be part of Boulder's elite. "Credible millionaires" was a phrase one officer used. Obviously, Eller felt, these were people you had to treat with respect, not people you wanted to offend.

The Ramseys lived in University Hill, a neighborhood that boasted many older, stately houses. A half mile or so east of their home was the University of Colorado campus. An equal distance to the west was the entrance to Chautauqua Park, with sweeping meadows, a hundred-year-old dining hall, cottages, and a rustic concert facility. Beyond that were the towering Flatirons and the foothills of the Front Range of the Rocky Mountains.

When Detective Linda Arndt arrived at the Ramsey house at 8:10 A.M. with fellow detective Fred Patterson, she found a crowd. Friends of the child's parents, Priscilla and Fleet White and Barbara and John

Fernie, were there, along with the family's minister, Reverend Rol Hoverstock. Patrol officers Rick French and Karl Veitch were also there with two victim advocates, Mary Lou Jedamus and Grace Morlock. Detective Arndt learned that the Ramseys had another child, nine-year-old Burke, who had been taken to the Whites' home by John Fernie and Fleet White.

The mother, Patsy Ramsey, was out of control. She kept saying she wanted to trade places with her daughter. "Please let her be safe. Oh please, let her be safe." She was tormented, incoherent. Her husband, John Ramsey, was saying he should have set the burglar alarm.

Arndt read the ransom note, which was written on white lined paper with a black felt-tipped pen. Then she ordered Officer Veitch to take it back to police headquarters, show it to the FBI, and book it into Property. John Ramsey was instructed to answer all telephone calls. When the kidnappers called, he was to say he couldn't get his hands on the ransom money until 5:00 P.M. At the same time, the police ordered a trap on the Ramseys' phone.*

Some officers went upstairs to check the bedroom of the missing child, whose name was JonBenét, for fingerprints. Detective Arndt began to question John Ramsey about whether he could think of anyone who might be involved in the kidnapping. Ramsey gave the detective the names of several ex-employees of his company, Access Graphics. Patsy Ramsey, who was sitting with Rev. Hoverstock in a corner, was at times confused and dazed. She mentioned to Arndt that her housekeeper, Linda Hoffmann-Pugh, had asked to borrow some money just a few days before. Linda had a key to the house and had major money problems. Patsy had made out a check for $2,000, and it was lying on the kitchen counter for Linda to pick up on her next scheduled cleaning day, December 27.

Later that morning, Patsy Ramsey would give the police copies of checks endorsed by Hoffmann-Pugh for handwriting comparison. The Ramseys' housekeeper would become the first suspect.

As the morning wore on, the victim advocates, Jedamus and Morlock, decided to go out and get bagels and fruit for everyone. With fewer people hovering around, Arndt noticed for the first time that Patsy and John rarely sat together.

---

* A phone *tap* provides direct access to a conversation so that it can be recorded or monitored. A phone *trap* collects data from the telephone company, which includes the telephone number called or caller ID and the names that are listed in association with the number.

When Larry Mason's pager went off at 9:45 A.M. he was at home, relaxing over a cup of coffee and a cigarette. Looking down, he read: "FBI agent is looking for Bob Whitson." Mason didn't stop to wonder why he had received a message for somebody else on his pager. He called police communications immediately and learned of the kidnapping. Light snow was on the ground when Mason left his home in Lyons for the twenty-five-minute drive to police headquarters in Boulder.

At headquarters, Mason met Special Agent Ron Walker, who had just arrived from the Denver FBI office with a four-man kidnapping team. The special agents were working with some police officers to set up phone taps and traps, which would give them immediate access to all incoming and outgoing calls at the Ramsey house. Agent Walker was treating the case as a kidnapping, but the ransom note was unusual. It made him wonder.

Walker was an experienced FBI profiler. He knew this was not the time to decide whether or not the ransom note was genuine. Certainly, the amount demanded was strange—not the usual round numbers. The reference to "a small foreign faction" was another red flag. How many ways would a group—foreign or not—divide up $118,000?

Then there was the length. At two and a half pages, it was the *War and Peace* of ransom notes. To Walker this suggested that the author might be trying to leave a false trail. Walker knew a ransom note required only a few sentences. We have your kid. It's going to cost you x millions. We will be in touch. Period.

At the house, the Ramseys gave the police some undeveloped film they'd recently taken. A few minutes later, it was taken to Mike's Camera on Pearl Street for processing and soon returned. The photos would be ready at noon.

Right before 10:00 A.M., alone, John Ramsey went downstairs to the basement, where Officer French had searched for his daughter. In the room where his son Burke's train set was kept, Ramsey found a broken open window. He closed it before going back upstairs.

When 10:00 A.M. came and went without a call from the kidnappers, John Ramsey became more distraught. He sat by himself nervously tapping his foot, leaning his face on one hand as if he was trying to figure something out. Patsy Ramsey kept repeating, "Why did they do this?"

At the detectives' request, John Ramsey provided a handwriting sample as well as shopping lists and writing pads that contained his and his wife's handwriting. One of the pads contained ruled white paper similar to the ransom note paper.

Just before 10:30 A.M., Detective Patterson ordered JonBenét's bedroom to be sealed. Then he and Detective Arndt decided to clear the house of nonessential persons. The six other police officers would leave. Patterson himself would return to headquarters to brief Commander Eller. Arndt, the Ramseys, the Whites, the Fernies, Rev. Hoverstock, and the two victim advocates would stay. They were all to remain on the first floor, in the rear study—behind the kitchen, breakfast, and dining room area. Before Patterson left, he declared the rest of the house off-limits to everyone.

Very soon after Patterson's departure, Arndt began to have trouble keeping everybody confined to the designated area. John Ramsey wandered out of sight. Arndt had to find him and lead him back into the study, leaving the others unsupervised. Meanwhile, Priscilla White was trying to keep her friend Patsy from fainting. She seemed to be in shock; she was vomiting and hyperventilating. Arndt was supposed to keep her eye on everyone and at the same time monitor the phone for a possible call from the kidnapper.

Half an hour after Larry Mason arrived at police headquarters, he was paged by Detective Arndt. She said she needed detective backup—urgently. She was now the only police officer in a fifteen-room, three-story house with nine civilians, all of whom were in emotional distress.

Arndt, with her caring and sympathetic style, was often able to turn reluctant victims into strong witnesses for the prosecution. Since 1994 she had specialized in sexual assault cases, and she was known for her compassion and listening skills. Arndt would never muscle someone to get what she wanted; she would use her kind demeanor to gain cooperation and information.

Mason tried to scare up some detectives to assist her, but the crew on duty the morning after Christmas was already spread thin on other assignments related to the case. For two hours and twenty-seven minutes, Linda Arndt was the only officer in the Ramsey house.

At first Mason couldn't understand why the officers on the scene hadn't secured the house earlier, separated the Ramseys, and questioned them individually. Then he learned that Commander Eller had ordered that the Ramseys be treated as victims, not suspects.

The Ramseys were an "influential family," Eller told Mason, who realized that this message must have affected the behavior of all the officers at the scene.

Very early Thursday morning, Gary Merriman, vice president of human resources at Ramsey's firm, Access Graphics, was already at his desk trying to finish some work in the postholiday lull.

"Hello, it's John," the voice said when Merriman answered his phone.

"Good morning. Merry Christmas," Gary said to his boss. There was a moment of silence. "What's wrong?" Merriman asked.

"My daughter's been kidnapped," Ramsey said.

"Oh my God. Which one?"

"JonBenét."

Less than an hour later, Detectives Jim Byfield and Michael Everett were in Merriman's office asking if anyone had ever made threats against the company. Did John Ramsey have enemies? Disgruntled employees? Merriman mentioned Jeff Merrick, an old friend of John Ramsey's who had been laid off, and Sandra Henderson, who owed Access Graphics a large sum of money.

As Merriman answered questions, he clung to the hope that JonBenét had just trotted over to a neighbor's house in her PJs and would be trotting home any minute to a scolding. His own son, only three, had once done exactly that—wandered over to a neighbor's house without telling anyone.

When the police left, they told Merriman not to talk to anyone, especially not the other employees.

In Denver, Tom Haney, chief of the patrol division of the Denver police, was discussing a case with several special agents from the FBI. The agents were obviously distracted. They kept listening to their hand-held radios as he tried to talk to them.

"Hey, what's the deal?" Haney finally asked.

"There's been a kidnapping in Boulder," one agent said. "It's kind of hinky, crazy. There's something wrong with this one. The amount of the ransom is a really weird number."

Just before noon, at Boulder police headquarters, Larry Mason suggested to John Eller that they get tracking dogs. If this was an abduction, the kidnapper might still be close by—in a canyon or in the Chautauqua Park area. Perhaps the Ramsey girl had been molested but was still alive.

Mason wanted to use Yogi, a tracking dog from the city of Aurora. Eller wanted to use Boulder's German shepherds. But the Boulder dogs worked from ground scent, Mason protested, and they were easily distracted. The dog Mason wanted was a bloodhound that in 1993 had backtracked nine miles to the base of Deer Creek Canyon and helped find the body of a kidnapped five-year-old girl. That child had been driven part of the way, and it was the kind of trail that might stymie a ground-tracking dog. The likelihood was that JonBenét Ramsey had been abducted in some kind of vehicle, and Yogi, Mason reminded Eller, was an air-scent dog and could handle the situation better.

"Did you learn that at the Academy?" Eller snapped. He was always baiting Mason for having attended the FBI academy in Quantico, Virginia.

Later in the morning the Ramseys' friends were still in the rear of the house consoling Patsy, who clutched a crucifix in her hands. Arndt, who didn't know that John Ramsey had gone down into the basement before 10:00 A.M., was still the only officer in the house. She was concerned for Ramsey when she saw him sitting alone in the dining room, head down and hands clasped together. He seemed despondent, totally withdrawn.

Everyone was waiting for the kidnappers to call.

A few minutes after noon, the victim advocates decided to leave for lunch. Their experience told them they could best serve the Ramseys if they maintained their own composure.

Just before 1:00 P.M., Arndt asked Fleet White and John Fernie to take John Ramsey on another tour of the house. She wanted to keep Ramsey busy. She also wanted him to check if anything was missing—anything that might have been taken along with JonBenét.

Fernie stayed upstairs while Ramsey led Fleet White down to the basement. In Burke's train room, they looked at the broken window. Ramsey told White that some months ago, he'd found himself locked out of the house and had broken the window, unlatched it, and climbed through.

Before they left the train room, they searched two closets near the entrance to the room. Then Ramsey, with White a few paces behind, turned right into the boiler room. At the rear was a door leading to what the family called the wine cellar, a windowless room with brick walls. Ramsey pulled the door open toward himself, stood at the threshold, and, peering to the left, into the darkness, saw a white blanket on the floor just as he reached for the switch on the wall to his right and turned on the light. Then he saw two little hands sticking out from under the blanket.

"Oh my God, oh my God," he cried.

JonBenét was lying on the floor, partly wrapped in a blanket. Her hands were extended over her head and appeared to be tied together. There was tape covering her mouth.

From a distance of about 12 feet, Fleet White saw Ramsey enter the wine cellar and turn out of sight to his left. As Ramsey cried out a second time, White followed him into the room.

By now Ramsey had ripped the tape off his daughter's mouth and was untying the cord from around one of her wrists. White knelt beside Ramsey and touched one of JonBenét's feet. The child was dead cold. A few moments later Ramsey picked up his daughter. Rigor mortis had set in and her body was rigid. Holding her by the waist like a plank of wood, he raced down the short hallway and up the basement stairs, yelling that JonBenét had been found. White followed from behind, shouting for an ambulance. It was 1:05 P.M.

As Ramsey emerged from the stairwell carrying his daughter, he turned and met Detective Arndt. JonBenét's hands were still extended above her head. A string hung from her right arm. Arndt ordered Fleet White to guard the door to the basement and not let anyone in. Ramsey placed JonBenét on the floor, right where he stood in the front hallway. Arndt could see that the child's lips were blue.

It was obvious that JonBenét was dead. Around her neck was a ligature with a small stick attached to one end. A similar ligature was around her right wrist. A circular red mark was visible at the base of her throat. On the palm of her left hand was a red ink drawing of a heart.

While the others rushed to the front of the house, Patsy Ramsey sat for a moment on a couch in the rear of the house looking out a window. She did not move despite all the shouting that JonBenét had been found. Finally, Barbara Fernie led her by the hand toward her daughter. Patsy threw herself on JonBenét's body. She pleaded with Rev. Hoverstock to bring her daughter back to life. Then she screamed, "Jesus, you raised Lazarus from the dead, please raise my baby!" Hoverstock led everyone in the Lord's Prayer. All the voices were lifeless with shock and despair. Patsy's voice was broken by sobs.

It was 1:12 P.M. when Detective Arndt grabbed a cellular phone in the kitchen and dialed 911. The operator dispatched the fire department and notified police communications, which transmitted the news to the officers working the case: a child's body had been found at the Ramsey house. Arndt moved JonBenét's body away from the front doorway to just inside the living room, at the foot of the Christmas tree. Then she paged Larry Mason and the victim advocates.

At police headquarters, Larry Mason got a page from the crime scene: "We've got a body."

"Oh fuck," Mason said, half aloud. "Ron, we don't have a kidnapping," he told Agent Walker. "It's a homicide. Do you want to go?"

"Of course." Walker knew that finding JonBenét's body in her own home meant there had probably never been a kidnapping.

In the Ramsey house, moments after Detective Arndt moved JonBenét's body, Fleet White decided to go back downstairs to the wine cellar where her body had been found. He had looked into the same room early that morning when he made a quick search of the house. Now that there was a light on, he saw clearly for the first time a white blanket in the center of the cement floor. A piece of black duct tape was lying on it. He picked up the tape, which felt sticky, and then placed it back on the blanket for the police. He looked around the room cluttered with paint cans, lumber and window screens, before he went back upstairs to guard the door.

Barry Weiss was the first of several officers to return to the Ramsey home. The next to arrive was Detective Michael Everett. He searched the basement to see if anyone was hiding there. He found no one. In the wine cellar, Everett discovered on the white blanket the piece of tape Fleet White had handled. Next to the blanket was a child-size pink nightgown with the word *Barbie* embossed on it.

When Rick French, the first officer on the scene after Patsy's report of a kidnapping, later saw the spot where the body had been found, he remembered his search of the house in the early morning. In the first minutes, French, seeing from where he stood that the door was latched shut, had thought there was no need to open it. Now he was baffled by his own decision. How hard would it have been to open the door? Had JonBenét still been alive when he stood just a few feet away and decided not to open the door? The thought devastated him.

Fifteen minutes after Detective Arndt's page, at around 1:30 P.M., Ron Walker entered the Ramseys' living room with Larry Mason and saw JonBenét's body lying at the foot of the Christmas tree. It hadn't yet been covered.

The room was empty, but they could hear the mother sobbing. She was at the rear of the house, surrounded by friends.

Mason and Walker went downstairs to the wine cellar, where they saw the white blanket, the duct tape, and the pink *Barbie* nightgown. Mason noticed that there was something about the crime scene—he couldn't put his finger on what it was—that made it look unnatural. In the train room he noticed a suitcase standing next to the wall, just under a broken window.

Mason knew there was no time to lose in clearing the house, securing the crime scene, and getting a search warrant. He decided he would move the Ramseys and their friends to the Holiday Inn at 28th and Baseline. He wanted everyone in separate rooms so that he could interview them independently.

In the study, however, another detective overheard John Ramsey talking on the phone to his private pilot. He was making plans to fly somewhere before nightfall. Moments later, Ramsey told Mason that he, his wife, and his son would be flying to Atlanta that evening. He said he had something really important to attend to. At first Mason thought Ramsey was planning to leave the country.

"You can't leave," Mason told him. "We have a lot of unfinished business here. We have to talk to you."

"OK," Ramsey said. He didn't protest.

"You're going to have to postpone that kind of stuff," Mason added. "You can't go."

Larry Mason had witnessed many SIDS★ deaths and fatal accidents to children, but he had never once seen a father as callous as Ramsey appeared to be. Still, the detective tried to withhold judgment. He knew he might be projecting his own emotions onto the situation—how *he* would act in Ramsey's place.

Ramsey then told Mason that he and Patsy wouldn't go to the Holiday Inn. He didn't seem defensive or adversarial—just stoic. Resigned, almost. His family would go to the home of their friends the Fernies. "Give us a day," Ramsey said quietly. "We just lost our child."

Mason consulted Arndt, who felt that every consideration should be weighed, then Eller. Everyone was still reluctant to push the parents. The family wasn't going anywhere, and besides, the department had to get organized. The police would wait to talk to the parents.

Minutes later, John Ramsey's older children from a previous marriage, John Andrew and Melinda, arrived. They had just flown in to Denver. Originally they were going to meet their father's private plane in Minneapolis that morning, and then the entire family would have continued on to their vacation home in Charlevoix, Michigan. But John Andrew had called his father from Minneapolis and learned about the kidnapping, and he and Melinda had taken a United Airlines flight to Denver. Now, outside in the early afternoon chill, Ramsey told his son and daughter that their little sister had been murdered. Minutes later, a patrol car escorted the Ramseys to the Fernies'.

After the family left, Detective Michael Everett, designated the lead crime scene investigator, and Larry Mason started to prepare a search warrant. By 1:50 the house was secured. Forty minutes later, Detective Arndt went to see the Ramseys at the Fernies' house, while Detective Patterson went to the Whites' house to speak with JonBenét's nine-year-old brother, Burke. Patterson confirmed what he had been told earlier—that the boy had slept through the events of the previous night.

When Larry Mason returned to police headquarters at midafternoon, he found John Eller upset that the FBI was still involved in the case. Eller had spent eleven years with the Dade County police before joining the Boulder PD as an administrator in 1979. He resented guys who

★ Sudden infant death syndrome.

hadn't come up from the street; they couldn't possibly know what he knew. Eller told Mason the Bureau was no longer needed.

In the case of a homicide where the dead child is found in the parents' home, the FBI's standard procedure is to investigate the parents first and then move outward in circles. The first circle of suspects would comprise the immediate family. Then would come people who had frequent access to the child—baby-sitters and domestic help. The next circle would contain the parents' friends and business associates. The outermost circle would be strangers. The technique was to avoid leaping over these concentric circles too quickly. For example, investigators shouldn't concentrate too early on a stranger, the least likely possibility. Agent Ron Walker hoped the Boulder police would do the job progressively and methodically. He also hoped they would ask for help from the FBI or the Colorado Bureau of Investigation, which had both the experience and the resources for a case like this.

But John Eller felt differently. He believed the Boulder detectives could handle the investigation alone.

Earlier, at 1:30 P.M., the phone in Gary Merriman's office at Access Graphics rang. It was John Ramsey. He seemed close to tears.

"We found her little body. She's been murdered," Ramsey said.

Merriman, too, began to cry.

When the police showed up at Merriman's office an hour later, for the second time that day, they grilled him. Who are you? What's your relationship to John Ramsey? Do you know of anybody with connections to a foreign country who might have a grudge against the company? Against Ramsey? Who are the key players at Access Graphics?

Merriman felt he had become a suspect. For the next five weeks, not only would the firm's computers be searched but as many as thirty employees would be questioned.

Later that evening, Merriman called Laurie Wagner, who had worked for Ramsey for ten years and was now vice president of worldwide market development. He told her what had happened, then he called the other executives. Some had already heard about JonBenét's death. Those who hadn't were horrified to find out.

At about 2:30 P.M. Pete Hofstrom called Bill Wise again to tell him that the DA's office now had a murder on its hands. Everyone was justifiably upset that Officer French hadn't found the body in his initial search of the Ramsey house early that morning. Hofstrom, who generally had a poor opinion of the Boulder police, told Wise he thought the police had lost control of the crime scene before the body was found by allowing so many people into the house.

Wise decided not to disturb his boss, Alex Hunter, the district attorney of Boulder County, who was on vacation in the Hawaiian Islands with his wife and two youngest children. Hunter was sure to call in within a day or two anyway. Wise would tell him then. There was no need for Hunter to rush back. For now, the police were in charge of the investigation.

By early afternoon, the Ramseys' property was surrounded by police cars and vans. Yellow police tape encircled the large brick house. Inside, the house was empty except for JonBenét's body, which was being guarded by an investigator for the coroner and a single police officer. The coroner would arrive only after the search warrant had been obtained. Outside, other police officers waited until the law allowed them to reenter the house. It would take the Boulder PD six hours to prepare a five-page search warrant and have it reviewed by the DA's office and signed by a judge. While the detectives huddled outside in the cold of the early evening, garlands and white Christmas bulbs lit up the snow on the lawn. A double row of red-and-white wooden candy canes bordered the front walk.

Meanwhile, the investigation continued elsewhere. The ransom note and the writing pads the Ramseys had voluntarily given to the police were sent to the Colorado Bureau of Investigation, which housed the state's forensic science lab.

It turned out that FBI special agent John Gedney knew the mother of one of JonBenét's schoolmates, Annie Smartt. In the late afternoon, Agent Gedney and Detective Jeff Kithcart went to see Mary Smartt and her husband, Bob, and asked if JonBenét had any unexplained absences from school. Mary didn't know of any.

At the same time, the Whites and the Fernies began to notify the Ramseys' other friends that JonBenét had died. Patsy told Pinky Barber, the mother of one of JonBenét's school friends, "Somebody came to my house and murdered my baby."

When Patsy's friend Pam Griffin got home in the early evening after exchanging some Christmas gifts at the Crossroads Mall in

Boulder, she found several frantic messages on her answering machine: "I need to talk to you. Call the Ramsey house." The voice sounded like Patsy Ramsey or one of her sisters, Polly or Pam.

Then there was a quieter message, almost a whisper, from Patsy's friend Priscilla White: "I can't talk to you about it over the phone—please call." Pam called Patsy's house and got her answering machine.

At dusk, the Ramseys picked up their son, Burke, from the Whites' house and brought him to the Fernies' place in the Shanahan Ridge development on Table Mesa, below the foothills. There was room for all of them to stay overnight. The victim advocates, who had gone with them to the Fernies', left at 5:00 P.M. Shortly afterward, Detective Arndt left too. One patrol officer was left behind for security.

Michael Bynum, John Ramsey's close friend and corporate attorney, who had been away snowshoeing, now arrived at the Fernies' house. As he walked in, the family was kneeling in the living room praying with Rev. Hoverstock. Around 7:00 P.M. John Ramsey went for a walk with John Fernie and Dr. Francesco Beuf, JonBenét's physician, who had brought over some medication for Patsy. When they returned a half hour later, Ramsey asked Bynum to represent him.

"I'm sorry, I'm so sorry," Ramsey told his friends over and over. Then, just after 8:00, he left alone to take a walk in the nearby foothills.

Earlier, at 7:00 P.M., Detectives Fred Patterson and Greg Idler knocked on the door of the Ramseys' housekeeper, Linda Hoffmann-Pugh. When she first saw the police, she thought something had happened to one of her children. They asked her to take a seat at the kitchen table, and then they took her husband, Merv, downstairs to the TV room. He wasn't allowed to leave the room—even to get a beer—unless an officer accompanied him.

In the kitchen, the police told the housekeeper that JonBenét had been murdered. She screamed and couldn't stop shaking. After Hoffmann-Pugh settled down, they asked her to print some words on a sheet of paper—*Mr. Ramsey, attaché, beheaded,* and the number *$118,000*—but Linda was too upset to write. Upon hearing the words, she assumed that JonBenét had been beheaded. She figured she and her husband were suspects.

The police spent three hours talking to the Pughs that night. Had Linda ever witnessed any signs of sexual abuse in the Ramsey household? Had JonBenét ever wet the bed? Had Linda seen semen, blood, or anything unusual on the child's bed? On anyone else's bed?

Hoffmann-Pugh confirmed for the police that the day after the Ramseys' December 23 Christmas party, she had called Patsy to ask for $2,000 that she desperately needed to pay the rent.

In the basement TV room, Merv Pugh told the police that the previous night he had fallen asleep on the couch in front of the TV and that Linda had said she went to sleep upstairs in their room. This morning, Pugh said, he had been up at 5:00 A.M. and the family had left the house at about 10:00.

Linda Hoffmann-Pugh would know for sure she was a suspect when the police returned the next day to search her house and fingerprint her. At a local doctor's office, she cried as the police yanked strands of hair from her head. As Linda gave saliva and blood samples, she wondered if JonBenét had been beheaded.

Meanwhile, Detective Jim Byfield had obtained a search warrant, and by 8:00 P.M. the police were allowed to begin searching the crime scene. Twenty minutes after they began, coroner John Meyer arrived. JonBenét's body was still lying at the foot of the lighted Christmas tree in the living room, but now she was covered with a blanket and a Colorado Avalanche sweatshirt. Meyer and his chief investigator, Patricia Dunn, noted the ligature around the child's neck and around one wrist. The cord around her neck had been pulled through a knot almost like a noose, and a broken, lacquered stick was tied to one end. They could also see a small abrasion or contusion on her right cheek, below her ear. Meyer had left the house by 8:30 P.M. Dunn stayed on to prepare the body for transport to the morgue.

At around 9:00 that evening, Patsy Ramsey lay down for a nap on an air mattress on the floor at the Fernies' home, while Fleet White and John Ramsey drove to Denver International Airport to pick up Ramsey's brother, Jeff, and his friend and broker, Rod Westmoreland. Patsy woke up an hour later. She discovered that her husband wasn't there, and she began to sob, asking anyone near her, "Why did they do this? Why did they do this?" Patsy's sisters, Pam and Polly, just in from Atlanta, arrived at the Fernies' house to find Patsy still on the mattress on the floor. A few minutes later, John arrived with his brother and Westmoreland.

At 10:00 P.M., Pam Griffin was watching the local news when they said something about the body of a little girl being found in a basement. When JonBenét's picture flashed on the TV screen, Pam grabbed her daughter, Kristine, told her guests she'd be back in a while, and drove to Patsy's house.

Pam and Kristine stood behind the yellow tape in the cold clear winter night and waited for Patsy to come outside. As they watched, a tiny black body bag was wheeled out on a stretcher. Pam asked about Patsy. Detective Larry Mason told her the Ramseys weren't there. Pam told Mason she was a friend of Patsy's—that she made beauty-pageant costumes for JonBenét. Mason asked her to come to police headquarters the next morning. Then Pam and Kristine left for their home in Longmont, twenty miles northeast of Boulder. No one had told them where Patsy was.

Earlier that day, Pete Hofstrom had assigned deputy DA Trip DeMuth to work with the police. DeMuth arrived at the Ramsey house in midafternoon and was soon troubled by the reluctance of the police to consider his advice on the preservation of evidence. Now, after spending only an hour and a half collecting evidence, the police announced that they were almost ready to release the house as a crime scene and return it to the Ramseys. DeMuth insisted that much more investigative work had to be done. In this huge house, the police had concentrated mainly on two rooms—the wine cellar and JonBenét's bedroom. When DeMuth found himself at an impasse with Commander Eller, he called his boss, Hofstrom, who phoned Eller immediately.

Eller made it clear to Hofstrom that he wanted the DA's office to get out of the crime-scene-analysis business. It was his call to make, Eller said, and if he said the police were finished at the Ramsey house, then they were finished. Twenty years earlier, in Dade County, Eller had been taught that a crime scene belonged to the police. A district attorney was there to give legal advice. Cops should never let prosecutors tell them who to interview or how to investigate. Those were tactical decisions, Eller had learned, and strictly police business.

Hofstrom, just as gruff and stubborn as Eller, bluntly explained to the commander how much work still had to be done at the crime scene. The officers and technicians hadn't even scratched the surface, he said. He wanted the entire house fingerprinted, shoeprint impressions taken, hair and fibers collected, drainpipes ripped out, floorboards removed. He wanted every drawer, every closet, every nook and cranny searched. The evidence, Hofstrom insisted, must be in a form that could be properly presented in court when the time came.

To Eller, the prosecutor's demands seemed a challenge to his authority. The commander made it clear once more that he was in charge. Hofstrom had better stay out of it or chaos would follow.

Commander Eller had been rotated into his job as head of the detective division only eleven months earlier, and he had never once directed a homicide investigation. Pete Hofstrom had twenty-three years behind him in the DA's office, fifteen of them as head of the felony division. In the last four years, he had overseen twenty-three murder cases in Boulder County.

Rather than argue any longer, Hofstrom went over Eller's head. He called police chief Tom Koby, who had been given periodic briefings since JonBenét's body was found. Late that night, Koby suggested to John Eller that he consider the recommendations of the DA's office very seriously and continue to search the scene. In the coming weeks it would become apparent that Eller could neither forgive nor forget Pete Hofstrom's questioning his skill, professionalism, and his authority.

In the end the police would continue their work at the crime scene for ten days, during which there would be constant disagreement between them and the DA's office. Hofstrom wanted three times what was needed—according to the cops. The police wanted half of what was necessary—according to Hofstrom. Differences of opinion between branches of law enforcement are to be expected, but nothing like this.

At 10:45 P.M. Larry Mason stepped outside the Ramseys' house and made an official statement to the two local reporters there. The TV crews had left earlier, to get on the air by 10:00. The dead child's name was JonBenét Ramsey, age six, said Mason. He refused to answer any questions.

Except for his terse statement, Mason had ignored the media throughout the evening. By 11:30, he found only Elliot Zaret from Boulder's *Daily Camera*. The *Camera* was holding the presses till Zaret filed a story. The reporter wanted to know exactly what had happened inside. Were there any signs of a break-in?

"I don't give a fuck about your First Amendment," Mason growled. "All I care about is solving this fucking case. I know what you journalists do—you're in everybody's face."

But Zaret persisted. He'd already been led astray once that evening, when the coroner's investigator, Patricia Dunn, told him that they had custody of the body, which suggested that the body had been removed when in fact it was still in the house.

"Nobody's telling me anything," Zaret said. "There's a dead little girl, and I don't know if there's a murderer on the loose. People reading the story tomorrow will be worried if they don't know."

Zaret asked Mason to talk to him off the record at least, then tell him what, if anything, he could print.

"What do you want to know?" Mason finally said.

"The cause of death."

"I can't tell you that."

"Was she shot?"

"No."

"Was she stabbed?"

"No."

"So she was strangled," Zaret said.

"I didn't say that. You can't print she was strangled."

"Can I print she wasn't shot or stabbed?"

"Yes. And if you burn me, I'm never going to say another word to you again."

Zaret printed only what they'd agreed on.

At 11:44 P.M., seventeen and a half hours after Linda Arndt was first paged, she was the last person to leave the Ramsey house.

At midnight that night, Dr. Beuf and his wife, Penny, were still at the Fernies' house, along with Patsy's friend Patty Novack, who had become her unofficial nurse. Patsy had to be helped even in the bathroom.

Finally, the Valium she had taken made Patsy drowsy. She fell asleep again on the living room floor. Two hours later she was awake again, sobbing, asking for Burke, asking if all the doors and windows were locked.

John Ramsey, lying on the sofa, slept fitfully. When he nodded off, his mask of stoicism vanished. He heaved with sobs.

2

Niki Hayden, a writer for the *Daily Camera*, was at her office late in the day on December 26 when her editor, Joan Zales, said to her: "I think the Ramsey family are members of your church."

Hayden was stunned. She looked at a picture of JonBenét that Zales was showing her, but she didn't recognize the child or recall the name.

"Would you know them if you saw them?" Zales asked.

"I don't think so."

Hayden thought she knew most everyone at St. John's Episcopal Church, but these people were strangers to her. She assumed they were very recent arrivals, though they weren't.

I've been married for almost thirty years, and I was originally trained as a teacher. Now I work for the Daily Camera. *When my husband and I moved here in 1982, I saw Boulder as a beautifully designed small town that had preserved its old buildings—a very human scale for pedestrians. It wasn't like living in New Jersey or New York, where you often feel dwarfed.*

Boulder was much more of a college town then than it is today. My first impression was that Boulder was a small city with intelligent people who liked small-town life. They could have made more money in a bigger place, but they wanted a real community. These were people who dedicated a portion of their lives to public service. I didn't ponder it deeply—I was immersed in changing diapers, learning to be a mom.

Today, I see less and less of that community spirit and much more of people who have escaped or retired from large cities and can pay people to run this city for them. They're not as involved. Today, we Boulder residents are not devoted to public service the way we once were. We've become more of an urban center.

Rol Hoverstock is pastor of St. John's. I knew him before he came to our church, before he was ordained. He owned a bicycle shop in town and he wanted to be a priest. When he left Boulder for his first parish in South Dakota, he was shaky, nervous, ill at ease in the pulpit. Then Father Jim—Jim McKeown—retired, and Rol was the congregation's unanimous choice to replace him. The priest who came back to us from South Dakota was a man who suddenly felt comfortable with what he was doing. I think of him as a country priest. He had a vision for our church as a family community. He really wanted a strong program for children. There's nothing I don't like about Rol.

—Niki Hayden

The next morning, Friday, December 27, everyone in the *Daily Camera*'s second-floor newsroom was scrambling to gather any scrap of information on the Ramseys. It was almost as busy as Election Day. The paper that morning led with an article about the murder of JonBenét.

MISSING GIRL FOUND DEAD

A 6-year-old Boulder girl reported kidnapped early Thursday was found dead in her parents' home later that afternoon. It is Boulder's first official homicide of 1996.

Police detectives and crime scene investigators began searching the house late Thursday after securing a search warrant. No details of what they had found were disclosed.

Although the official cause of death was not yet known, Police Chief Tom Koby said the case is considered a homicide. The child had not been shot or stabbed, said Detective Sgt. Larry Mason.

No arrest had been made as of press time, and police had no suspects, Mason said.

The Boulder County coroner's office refused to discuss details of the case, though an autopsy will be performed today, according to city spokeswoman Leslie Aaholm.

The child was the 1995 Little Miss Colorado and a student at Martin Park [sic] Elementary School, according to a family friend. Patsy Ramsey traveled around the country with JonBenét to attend her daughter's beauty contests. "They were so serious about this beauty queen stuff, but they never put any pressure on her. She was Little Miss Colorado in 1995," said Dee Dee Nelson-Schneider, a family friend.

"She had her own float in the Colorado Parade of Lights in December 1995, and Patsy walked along the side of the float the whole parade to make sure (JonBenét) was safe. That's how protective Patsy was."

—Elliot Zaret and Alli Krupski
Daily Camera, December 27, 1996

In the winter, when the aspen trees are bare, you can see the Front Range of the snow-covered Rockies from almost every street. Boulder, just twenty-six miles northwest of Denver, is an old-fashioned small town, with many brick and wood-framed houses dating from the 1930s. With a population of 96,000—one third of whom are affiliated with the University of Colorado—the town prides itself on its pretty neighborhoods. Boulderites like to think of themselves as having an excellent quality of life.

When you have lived for a while in the town, which is isolated by both municipal planning and topography, it isn't hard to lose a sense of how it looks from the outside. If you are a runner, however—and there are thousands of Boulderites who run—a five-mile jog up Flagstaff Road to the top of Flagstaff Mountain is one way to rediscover where you are.

In every direction you turn, you are faced with the facts of geography: to the southwest are the Flatirons, enormous slabs of rock that from some angles appear to prop up the snow-covered Rockies beyond; to the east, the vast flatlands of the Great Plains; to the west, the Continental Divide, dividing the country's two primary watersheds. Along the Divide, the Indian Peaks rise 13,000 feet above sea level. Off in the distance to the southeast, you can just make out a few of Denver's skyscrapers, where many Boulderites work five days a week. The rest are content with the pace of life in Boulder.

From the top of Flagstaff Mountain, you can see the tidy neighborhoods laid out in neat grids and, in the heart of town, the Pearl Street Mall, home to the Hotel Boulderado, shops with turn-of-the-century facades, and over a hundred restaurants. Parallel to the mall is Canyon Boulevard, once called Water Street because of the flooding that can occur when adjacent Boulder Creek explodes out of the foothills with springtime snowmelt. To the east lies the sprawling campus of the University of Colorado, easily distinguished by its many red sandstone roofs.

In Boulder, it's as if people are so intensely pursuing their own interests that they develop a kind of disregard for the general welfare. But the word community *itself implies care for the general welfare.*

I was the principal of High Peaks and Martin Park Elementary School, which shared a common property. In June 1996, I wanted to have the city build another speed bump on the west side of the schools. With the addition of High Peaks Elementary in the same building and the sudden influx of more cars, I was concerned about the kids who walked to school in this quiet neighborhood.

At a city council hearing in September or October of 1996, I was surprised at the number of people who protested. They said it would interfere with their bike riding. And yet a hundred yards from the school is a beautifully designed multimillion-dollar bike path running north and south along the creek. So it's not that the needs of bike riders have been ignored, just that bike riders were saying, "We don't like to slow down for speed bumps." But what about the children's safety? There was a real reluctance to address those needs.

That's what I have found missing in Boulder—a commitment to the general welfare that goes beyond "me" and "my own small world."

The day after JonBenét's body was found, I talked with some parents and realized how isolated they felt. All of them had either read about it in the morning paper or heard the news on TV, but there was no adequate way for them to share the loss with other parents who had a connection to this child. Throughout so much of history, whenever something bad happened, someone would knock on your door with the news and then come in and stay with you. But in talking to these parents, I felt the lack of natural community in Boulder. I decided I would open up the school so that parents, with or without their children, could gather with other families. It would be a place to talk and share their confusion and fears.

Then that morning I met with a group of therapists, the school psychologist, the school social worker, and several other professionals who volunteered. We decided that what really made this terrifying for kids is that JonBenét was killed in the sanctity of her own home. For kids, it would feel like their homes, their bedrooms. If JonBenét wasn't safe, they weren't safe. If JonBenét's parents couldn't protect her, how could their parents protect them?

I also decided early on that JonBenét's death would not become a school issue, apart from the fact that we would provide support for our children and their families. We wouldn't respond to media questions. The crime was an issue for the police, an issue for the Ramseys. I let the word out that the school would not participate in any media frenzy.

—Charles Elbot

★ ★ ★

At 8:00 A.M. on December 27, Gary Merriman convened an executive meeting in the small conference room in the offices of Access Graphics on the Pearl Street Mall. Gary Mann, president of the commercial systems group of Lockheed Martin, Access Graphics' parent company, had been notified. In a series of phone calls, Lockheed Martin specified a chain of command to handle essential business in John Ramsey's absence.

Ramsey's top people had gathered to manage the unmanageable. It was like the day John F. Kennedy was killed: nothing seemed normal. Nobody used the chair where Ramsey usually sat. Their job, Merriman said, was to make sure a billion-dollar business continued to operate. Very quickly they settled on a collaborative crisis team. It included Ross Churchill, Michael Minard, Laurie Wagner, Tom Carson, who was out of town, and Merriman. One of the division managers remarked that JonBenét's death would be a global story: "John's a rich guy. His daughter is a child beauty queen. They're going to attach dirty sex stuff to her death. It won't be about JonBenét. It's all about selling papers."

Everyone agreed that the business had to be isolated from the tragedy. They set up a procedure to keep clients and employees informed. As workers returned from the Christmas holidays, those who didn't already know would have to be told. Some were likely to feel helpless, outraged, or saddened. To employees at Access Graphics, JonBenét was not an abstraction—she was a real little girl. She'd visited the building. She had sat in her daddy's big chair. When she entered a room, it became brighter.

Then it hit Gary Merriman. Could the *Daily Camera* story about the company hitting a billion dollars in sales have anything to do with JonBenét's death? He was the one who had urged sending out the press release. John's picture had accompanied the article. Had he exposed the Ramsey family to some lunatic? Merriman would be tormented for months afterward by the thought that he might have inadvertently targeted JonBenét.

Lockheed Martin's Gary Mann said he'd keep in close contact for the next few weeks, but there wasn't much to add to what Merriman and his team were doing. Clearly, Lockheed Martin trusted the organization John Ramsey had built, but they also seemed to want to distance themselves from Ramsey's problems. JonBenét's death was none of Lockheed Martin's business. Mann told Carson, Churchill, Merriman, and Wagner were to report to him for the next ninety days. Wagner was appointed company spokesperson. Lockheed Martin had a succession plan in place if it turned out that one was needed. No one was irreplaceable to the corporation. Life had to go on.

Shortly after 8:15 A.M. on December 27, Dr. John Meyer entered the autopsy room at Boulder Community Hospital, accompanied by his medical investigators, Tom Faure and Patricia Dunn. Dunn had been at the Ramsey house the previous day and was Meyer's primary investigator on the case. For the autopsy, Detectives Linda Arndt and Tom Trujillo were on hand for the Boulder police; senior trial deputies Trip DeMuth and John Pickering were there for the DA's office.

Attendants unsealed a heavy white plastic bag, revealing Jon-Benét's body wrapped in a sterile white sheet. The child was placed on the steel autopsy table, whose slightly inclined subtray permitted fluids to drain into a sink-type apparatus. The sheet was removed and set aside as part of the evidence.

Meyer knew that in nine out of ten cases of a child's suspicious death, the perpetrator or an accomplice says that a bike fell on the victim or the child slipped in the bathtub—some accident is concocted to explain the victim's injuries. Meyer also knew, however, that good forensic pathology usually reveals the real cause of death.

JonBenét's body was just as Meyer had observed it twelve hours earlier in the Ramsey living room. Every stitch of her clothing, plus the ligatures on her right wrist and around her neck, remained in place. Paper bags had been sealed around her hands and feet to preserve any possible trace evidence.

Patricia Dunn took color slides for the coroner's office, while Detective Trujillo shot photos for the police department. Dunn shot 113 frames, documenting each stage of the procedure. Meyer dictated his observations into a tape recorder.

"The decedent is clothed in a long-sleeved white knit collarless shirt, the midanterior chest area of which contains an embroidered silver star decorated with silver sequins," Meyer began. "Tied loosely around the right wrist, overlying the sleeve of the shirt, is a white cord."

On the child's right sleeve, the coroner saw a brownish-tan stain about 2½ by 1½ inches in area, which seemed consistent with mucus from her mouth or nose.

"There are long white underwear with an elastic waistband containing a red-and-blue stripe." Meyer also noted urine stains on the underwear, in the crotch area, and at the front.

"Beneath the long underwear are white panties with printed rosebuds and the word *Wednesday* on the elastic waistband." The panties were also stained with urine. At the crotch, the coroner spotted several red spots that were each up to ½ inch in diameter.

Meyer then recorded the injuries that were visible with the body clothed. Beneath her right ear, at the point where the jawbone forms roughly a right angle, was a rust-colored abrasion about ⅜ by ¼ inch. There was pinpoint hemorrhaging on the upper and lower eyelids.

Meyer described the cord around the child's neck: "Wrapped around the neck with a double knot in the midline of the posterior neck is a length of white cord similar to that described as being tied around the right wrist." He cut through the cord on the right side of her neck and slipped it off.

"A single black mark is placed on the left side of the cut and a double black ink mark on the right side of the cut." Meyer stated these specifics in case it would be necessary to reconstruct the cord as evidence. He knew the police would want the knot left intact, to study the technique used to secure the ligature.

There were two tails of cord trailing from the knot. One was 4 inches long and frayed. The other was 17 inches long and had multiple loops secured around a wooden stick that was about 4½ inches long.

"This wooden stick," Meyer said, "is irregularly broken at both ends, and there are several colors of paint and apparent glistening varnish on the surface. Printed in gold letters on one end of the wood [stick] is the word *Korea*."

Fine blond hair, Meyer noted, was tangled in the knot of the cord around the child's neck as well as in the knot of the cord tied around the stick.

"The white cord is flattened and measures approximately ¼ inch in width. It appears to be made of a white synthetic material. Also secured around the neck is a gold chain with a single charm in the form of a cross."

Meyer then recorded a series of observations about a groove left in JonBenét's neck by the cord. In front, it was just below the prominence of her larynx. The coroner noted that the groove circled her neck almost completely horizontally, deviating only slightly upward near the back. At some points, the furrow was close to half an inch wide, and hemorrhaging and abrasions could be seen both above and below it. The groove included a roughly triangular abrasion, about the size of a 25-cent piece on the left side of the neck, that Meyer had seen when he first viewed the body at the Ramseys' house.

Continuing with the external examination, Meyer noticed—and Detective Arndt also observed—a number of dark fibers and hairs on the outside of JonBenét's nightshirt. Using forceps, Meyer lifted these for later microscopic analysis. Everyone in the room could also see strands of a green substance tangled in the child's hair. Arndt believed she'd seen the same thing the day before; it was probably some of the holiday garland decorating the spiral staircase that led downstairs from JonBenét's bedroom.

Meyer then removed her clothes and set the garments aside to be placed into evidence.

"The unembalmed, well-developed, and well-nourished Caucasian female body measures 47 inches in length and weighs an estimated 45 pounds," Meyer dictated. "The scalp is covered by long blond hair, which is fixed in two ponytails, one on top of the head secured by a cloth hair tie and blue elastic band and one in the lower back of the head secured by a blue elastic band. No scalp trauma is identified."

Meyer began an internal examination of the body.

An hour later on that same morning, December 27, Detectives Fred Patterson and Greg Idler began their first formal interview with Fleet White at Boulder police headquarters. By now the police knew that John Ramsey considered White a close friend—possibly his closest friend. The Whites had keys to the Ramseys' house.

White told the detectives that he and his wife, Priscilla, had invited relatives and friends from California to join them for the holidays. On December 22, Heather Cox, Priscilla's niece, and her husband, Bill, and the Whites had driven five hours to Aspen and spent the night. The next day they returned to Boulder, and the Whites attended the Ramseys' Christmas party with Priscilla's parents. JonBenét had hung up the guests' coats, White said. There were gingerbread houses for each family to decorate with gumdrops. On Christmas Day, the Whites were up early opening presents with their kids and Priscilla's parents. That afternoon at about 4:30, the Ramseys, with JonBenét and Burke, arrived at the Whites' house. They would join the Whites, the Coxes, and Allison Shoeny, Priscilla's sister, and her boyfriend, Cliff Gaston, for Christmas dinner. Afterward, the adults, along with the kids, played on the floor. Then some neighbors came over for Christmas caroling. Fleet White and the kids joined the group in singing. At around 9:30 P.M., White said, the Ramseys left, saying that they were going to drop off gifts for other friends, the Stines and the Walkers. By 11:00 White was in bed, he said. Priscilla and her sister talked in the kitchen until 2:00 in the morning. By then Cliff Gaston was asleep on the couch in the family room, and the Coxes were also asleep, in the Whites' daughter's room.

At 6:00 A.M. the telephone awakened Cliff Gaston. It was Patsy Ramsey. Priscilla took the call, and within minutes the Whites were dressed and on their way to the Ramseys' house. When they arrived, the police and John Fernie were already there. Patsy was on the floor, hysterical, and her husband was trying to comfort her. It was still dark outside.

White told the detectives that he had been there only a few minutes when he started to search the house. Alone, he went down to the basement, found some of the lights on, and started calling out Jon-Benét's name. It was so cluttered down there—with boxes stacked everywhere and shelves overflowing with odds and ends—that he could hardly see any open spaces where she might be. He started in Burke's train and hobby room, where he saw a suitcase sitting under a broken window. On the floor under the window, he found small pieces of glass. He placed some of them on the windowsill. Then he moved the suitcase a few feet to get a closer look at the window. White said he was sure the window was closed but unlatched. After he left the train room, he turned right, into the boiler room. At the back of the room, he said, he saw a door to what the Ramseys called the wine cellar. He turned the closed wooden latch and opened the door. The room was pitch-black, he said. He didn't enter, and he saw nothing. When he couldn't find a light switch, he closed the door and went back upstairs. He did not remember whether or not he relatched the door. Later, when White saw John Fernie, he told him that a window downstairs had been punched open. The police wondered why White had not seen JonBenét's body and later Ramsey had, since they both stood at the same spot after opening the door to the wine cellar.

At 6:45 A.M., White said, his wife called home and told her niece that JonBenét had been kidnapped. Her niece, Heather, woke the other adults in the house and told them why Fleet and Priscilla were with the Ramseys.

White told the police that the Ramseys decided to wake their son, Burke, at around 7:00 and move him to his house. Fleet White and John Fernie, with Burke in hand, first picked up the Fernies' children from their home and then took all the kids to the Whites', where his guests looked after them. Forty-five minutes later, the two men returned to the Ramseys'.

White remembered that just after 7:00, the Ramseys' pastor, Rev. Rol Hoverstock, arrived.

Meanwhile, Ramsey had called Rod Westmoreland, his friend and Merrill Lynch broker, at home in Atlanta and told him what had happened and that he needed cash. Westmoreland started to make arrangements to transfer money from one of Ramsey's cash management accounts—where he had over a million dollars—to a Boulder bank. Fleet White told the police that when the Lafayette branch of the bank opened, John Fernie went there to see about collecting the ransom money. During this time Ramsey was distressed, White said; the pain he observed in John was unmistakable. He'd never seen Ramsey this way, at the end of his rope. "He just put his head in his hands and cried and shook."

White also told the police that he and Ramsey went down to the basement again at about 1:00 P.M. and first went into Burke's train room, where they both looked at the broken window. Ramsey told White he had broken it to get into the house a few months earlier, when he came home one day without his house key. Then White described what had happened when John Ramsey found JonBenét's body. He couldn't forget seeing John standing in the doorway screaming, his back to White, the light being turned on and, when he entered the room himself, seeing Ramsey on his knees beside Jon-Benét. It all happened so fast, White said. He had no explanation for why he himself hadn't seen the body on his first trip to the basement.

At about 1:30 P.M., White said, his wife called home and told her niece that JonBenét had been found dead. White also said that around 3:00 P.M., he had called Ramsey's pilot to cancel a flight to Atlanta that John Ramsey had made arrangements for after finding his daughter's body. White told the pilot the Ramseys might not be allowed to leave that night because of the police investigation.

Around 4:00 P.M. Priscilla left the Fernies' house, where they'd all gone with the Ramseys, and returned home. White went home later, he said, and they told their children, Daphne and Fleet Jr., that Jon-Benét had gone to heaven. Later that night, White stopped by the Fernies' house on his way to Denver International Airport to pick up Jeff Ramsey, John's brother, and Rod Westmoreland. Ramsey asked to go along. The four men were back at the Fernies' home by around 11:00 P.M., White said.

3

I remember Boulder when there was no mall on Pearl Street, just a drug-store, some dress shops, and Valentine's Hardware. Valentine's had 20-foot ceilings, and you'd get a ladder out and climb up to find what you wanted. That was back in '71, when my wife and I moved to Boulder. I'm a CPA. And I've been a devoted member of St. John's and a member of its vestry ever since we arrived.

Boulder used to be a crossroads for teenagers and kids in their early twenties who were crossing the country—runaways, hitchhikers, activists, the whole spectrum. Our Father Jim created some havens for them. He got the parish involved in providing food and temporary housing. His one condition for their getting help was that they had to call their parents. He didn't ask anything beyond that.

Father Jim was the most open-minded person I ever met. He was an activist. He could reach all those young people marching through Boulder. He'd say, "This is who I am, and I'm not going to change. If you don't like it, go find another church." So in those days, St. John's actually lost a lot of parishioners.

These days, Rol says, "Look within this parish. Look at a lot of different members. Come join us and we'll work things out."

Not long ago we had one parishioner who took it upon herself to research the Catechesis of the Good Shepherd program. It's designed to teach four- and five-year-old children about the sacraments. It was quite an expensive thing, with lots of specially constructed child-sized furniture and icons and vessels. Hard work. Patsy and John decided to finance the entire project, which cost several thousand dollars. They were always generous in pledging.

Patsy was dynamic—to the point where she could be annoying. She absolutely could be. She was a take-charge person with very definite ideas. And she had this living angel. JonBenét was an actual angel. I don't remember ever seeing any child more beautiful. Always dressed stunningly. I heard about the murder on NPR radio.

—Robert Elmore

At 10:00 A.M. on Friday, December 27, Pam Griffin and her daughter, Kristine, a senior in high school, sat before a tape recorder in a small windowless room at police headquarters. Griffin told Larry Mason what she knew. She was the seamstress who made JonBenét's pageant costumes and Patsy's confidante about beauty pageants. Kristine was one of JonBenét's runway teachers.

The police wanted to know if she'd ever seen any inappropriate behavior between the Ramseys and JonBenét—anything abusive. Griffin said she hadn't. She had never even seen them discipline their children, she claimed. Pam told Mason that these were parents who didn't demand respect *from* their kids—it was they who respected their children. That was the best way she could describe the relationship. And then there was all the love in JonBenét's eyes when she spoke to her father. Everything he said was important to her, Griffin said. Mason then asked for information about child beauty pageants. JonBenét had won several, Griffin said. On the previous Sunday, December 22, she had performed at the Southwest Plaza as a pageant winner. Was JonBenét forced into the pageants, Mason wanted to know. Not that Griffin could see.

Then Kristine was interviewed. She gave much the same answers.

In 1995, four of us parents thought we could start a public elementary school that would work the way schools should. We wrote a 140-page proposal and got a lot of articles published in the local newspaper. We called it a focus school.

It took a marketing effort to convince parents to sign their kids up for a school that didn't have a building, didn't have teachers, didn't have physical materials to show. You have to remember that these kids are precious.

At one organizing meeting in someone's home, a man sat back and listened, listened carefully, and asked a few questions. Then he said thank you and left. That's how I met John Ramsey.

In the fall of 1995, High Peaks Elementary, our school, opened. Patsy enrolled Burke in the third grade. Hers was the first southern voice I'd heard in a long time—there aren't many southerners in Boulder. She was very overdressed for our little city. Her hair was always done, and she always wore city outfits and hats. Of course I didn't know then that she was recovering from chemotherapy and that her hair was still growing back.

High Peaks depended on volunteers for survival, and Patsy volunteered all the time. It wasn't long before we got to know each other. Nothing stopped Patsy from doing what needed to be done. John wasn't active at school. He traveled a great deal. He looked just like an ordinary guy. He could be in a room and never be noticed.

Around Valentine's Day of 1996, my daughter, Megan, met JonBenét for the first time. They were both in preschool. I remember the first time I saw them together—they looked so cute playing on the monkey bars.

That August, JonBenét entered kindergarten and Patsy kept volunteering. At the same time she was heading up an event for the University Women's Club. Around that time, John went to the Mayo Clinic for eye surgery.

Our kids started playing together, and they became close friends. JonBenét would come to our house to play, and I would drive Megan over there. Megan also really liked Burke. He was into computer games. That's how I got to see more of Patsy—twenty minutes here, thirty minutes there.

JonBenét seemed resentful that her father traveled so much. Not really angry, just sad. She really liked him a lot.

One day Megan told me she wanted to enter a beauty pageant. She'd learned about them from JonBenét. She liked the clothes, and she had been impressed by the crowns. I had to explain that everybody makes choices and that pageants were not something we were choosing to do. As soon as I told her that JonBenét had to sing and dance in front of a whole bunch of people during the competition, Megan's desire disappeared.

Patsy was very positive about pageants. She'd talk about the skills they give you—the poise, the self-confidence, and can-do attitude that stay with you for life.

The Ramseys lived a very lavish life. They went to the Olympics. Took vacations in Michigan and traveled all over. I wondered what JonBenét's life would be like when she grew up.

The day before Christmas, JonBenét was at our house playing with

Megan. The kids were talking about Santa, getting all excited. I asked Jon-
Benét if she had visited Santa Claus yet. She said, "Oh, Santa was at our
Christmas party the other night." Megan had seen Santa at the Pearl Street
Mall, so we talked about that.

Then JonBenét said, "Santa Claus promised that he would make a
secret visit after Christmas."

I thought she was confused. "Christmas is tonight," I told her. "And
Santa will be coming tonight."

"No, no," JonBenét insisted. "He said this would be after Christmas.
And it's a secret."

—Barbara Kostanick

By midmorning, December 27, reporters were canvassing the Ramseys' neighborhood. Almost everyone they talked to said the Ramseys
were extraordinary people who enjoyed a lifestyle far more affluent
than that of their friends and neighbors. They had moved to Boulder
from Atlanta in 1991. They owned a vacation place in Michigan and a
boat John Ramsey had built. Patsy was a former Miss West Virginia.
What struck most of the reporters was how little the people who
knew the Ramseys best were willing to say. One local reporter knew
John and Barbara Fernie through their church, but the Fernies told
him nothing. The Ramseys themselves were incommunicado. Their
close friends told the press that they were grieving.

Another local reporter visited St. John's Episcopal Church, which
was located at 14th Street and Pine in downtown Boulder. He'd been
married there, and Rol Hoverstock knew his daughter. He was welcomed to sit with his friends, the leaders of the congregation, just
outside the pastor's office, but they wouldn't tell him anything. The
reporters felt that this silence was creating a poor impression of Jon-
Benét's parents. What were they hiding?

After Detectives Patterson and Idler concluded their interview with
him around noon, Fleet White drove over to the Fernies' house to stay
with John and Patsy Ramsey. Later, at around 4:00 P.M., he went to
the office of Michael Bynum, Ramsey's corporate attorney, to talk to
him about the situation.

Meanwhile, at police headquarters, Commander Eller was meeting with officers in the detective division to compile a list of possible

suspects. The previous day they had put together a list of John Ramsey's employees and business associates. Brainstorming, they added to the list several housekeepers, acquaintances, and friends of the Ramseys as well as relatives and others—like baby-sitters—who'd had close contact with JonBenét.

John Ramsey's behavior after his daughter's body was found—together with national child homicide statistics, which showed that a large percentage of child murders are committed by fathers—made the Ramsey family automatic suspects. Ramsey's two older children had arrived from out of town after the body was found, but they too were added to the list. John Andrew Ramsey, a college student in Boulder who often stayed at his father's house, was under particular suspicion. The police would soon learn that the suitcase found under the broken window in the basement belonged to him.

The police would take weeks—and even months—checking and rechecking alibis and taking handwriting, fingerprint, blood, and hair samples from almost everyone known to have come in contact with JonBenét, as well as from those who had no known contact or motive to kill her. The initial list included over two dozen people, and it grew larger as the public provided further leads.

John Eller assigned thirty officers to the case. Larry Mason led the team in day-to-day field assignments, but he and Eller butted heads over who should be interviewed and when, and over how to prioritize the investigation. Mason, with a battered face and a prizefighter's compact body, stood no more than 5-feet-9 to Eller's 6-feet-1. The tension between the two men was obvious and palpable. Particularly galling to Mason was the dismissal of the FBI's investigators from the case. Mason had been a police officer for twenty-five years, and he knew how helpful the Bureau could be.

Larry Mason was a fourth-generation Coloradoan. His father, Allen, had been with the Boulder Fire Department, and he had an uncle who had been with the sheriff's department for thirty years. Another uncle was the first marshal in Jamestown, Colorado. Mason had joined the sheriff's department in 1972, a year when Boulder had witnessed another horrifying crime. Two eleven-year-old girls were kidnapped, sexually molested, and shot, then thrown into Boulder Canyon in the middle of winter. One girl survived and stumbled into the Gold Hill Café seeking help. The perpetrator, Peter Roy Fisher, had been caught and was still serving a life sentence.

On the afternoon of December 27, when Pam Griffin got home from her interview with Detective Mason, she found a telephone message from Patsy's sister Polly. "Patsy needs you right now!" Polly had left directions to the Fernies' house.

At the Fernies', Pam and Kristine found that Patsy was overdosing on Valium. She'd been taking the powerful tranquilizer every few hours and had probably lost track of the amount. Pam, a former registered nurse, touched Patsy's skin and realized she was dehydrated. She brought Patsy some water and made her drink it.

Later that afternoon, Kristine and Pam sat on either side of Patsy, holding her hands. "You know," Patsy said quietly to Pam, as if she were telling someone for the first time, "they've killed my baby." Pam noticed that Patsy used the word *they*.

"You need to brush your hair," Pam told her. "You need to lie down a little bit." But Patsy stood up to greet each new person who arrived, and as she did, tears streamed down her face. These friends, Pam observed, were entirely different from the people she and Patsy knew in common—their pageant friends. The people visiting her here were strangers to Pam. Hours later, Patsy finally took Pam's advice and lay down in the Fernies' bedroom.

Kristine went to the bathroom to get a cool washcloth for Patsy's forehead. While she was gone, Patsy reached up and touched Pam's face. "Couldn't you fix this for me?" she asked. Pam thought she was delirious. It was as if Patsy were asking her to fix a ripped seam. "Patsy said something like, 'We didn't mean for that to happen,'" Pam would say later.

After Patsy napped for almost an hour, Pam took her into the shower and washed her hair. Patsy was unable even to dry herself, and Pam wrapped a towel around her. Later, Pam couldn't say why, but she remembered feeling as if Patsy knew who killed JonBenét but was afraid to say.

Kristine, a former pageant winner, had been JonBenét's role model. Patsy in turn had become one for Kristine and had been planning to groom the girl for the Miss America pageant. That afternoon Patsy asked Kristine, "Why couldn't she have grown up? All Jonnie B ever wanted was to win a crown like yours."

While Patsy slept, Pam went downstairs. She found John in the living room holding Burke. To Pam, Ramsey seemed to be in a trance. His face was blank. His eyes were red. "I don't get it," he said over and over. Then he got up, walked outside, shook his head, and asked aloud, "Why?"

The next morning, Kristine brought one of her crowns to Patsy. It had been JonBenét's favorite.

In the early afternoon on Friday, December 27, a dozen or so reporters and photographers gathered in a ground-floor conference room in Boulder's Public Safety Building for the first press briefing on the Ramsey case. Formerly the telephone building, the two-story structure, which housed the Boulder Police Department, was located two miles from the Justice Center and downtown Boulder.

John Eller, a stranger to nearly all the reporters who jammed the room, seated himself at a table. Not the typical trim and fit officer, he held a few sheets of paper in his hands and was introduced by Leslie Aaholm, the city's press representative. To the journalists, Eller seemed depressed, tired, and obviously reluctant to address them. Pinned to a bulletin board behind his right shoulder was a picture of JonBenét Ramsey. She was wearing a pink pullover. Her shoulder-length hair and bangs framed a sweet face and a radiant smile.

Eller spoke softly—he sounded like a whispering Baptist preacher, according to one reporter—and didn't say much. He pointed out that his detectives were facing a "delicate and sensitive" investigation. "The death was clearly the result of a criminal act," he stated. No one had been identified or eliminated as a suspect yet.

The commander wouldn't tell reporters where in the basement JonBenét's body had been found, what she was wearing, or the condition of her body. He confirmed that she had been discovered by a family member, although he didn't say which one.

Reporters pressed him. Why didn't the police find her earlier if she was in the house?

"We had no reason to believe the child would be in the house at the time," Eller replied. "The initial efforts of the police were directed toward preparing to comply with the instructions in the ransom note."

So far, no reporters had spoken to the Ramseys, but they all knew that the family was staying with "friends." Eller stated that a police officer was staying with them for "security," and he revealed that his detectives had not yet conducted interviews with the family.

"The parents are going through a tremendous grieving process, we expect," was all Eller would say. "We're going to have to work our interviews and those kinds of things around it." While he said very little about the Ramseys themselves, reporters noted that Eller said the "victim's family was well connected with Boulder society."

As for JonBenét, he said, "It truly is a tragedy. This was a beautiful little girl, as you can see—very vibrant and, from what we can tell, very precocious and a wonderful child."

When reporters asked about the ransom note, Eller said little. He insisted the police hadn't ruled out the possibility that JonBenét might have been killed during a "bona fide" kidnapping. "We have no reason to believe that it was [a kidnapping] or not at this time," he explained. "It's too early in the investigation to start ruling things out." When reporters pressed for more details, Eller said only that the note had demanded money and referred to "future demands."

"The ransom note was a typical—if there is such a thing—kidnapping ransom note, the kind you'd find in any movie," he added.

After Eller concluded the press briefing, one reporter looked in his notebook. He'd jotted down the commander's description of the ransom note. He'd called it "typical" but in the same breath likened it to something in "any movie." What was Eller really saying? Was he unwittingly revealing something?

At Boulder Community Hospital, John Meyer concluded his autopsy at 2:20 P.M., and after the press conference, Eller was briefed by Detectives Arndt and Trujillo about the coroner's findings.

There was a linear fracture on the right side of the child's skull, running about 8½ inches from the front to above her right ear. Near the back of her skull, at one end of the linear fracture, there was a displaced rectangular section of skull, about ¾ by ½ inch. A heavy blow had caused the fracture.

The coroner had found small amounts of dried and half-dried blood at the entrance to JonBenét's vagina and reddening in the vaginal walls, most notably on the right side and toward the rear. What remained of the hymen was a rim of tissue running from the 10 o'clock to the 2 o'clock position. There was also an abrasion on the hymeneal orifice at about the 7 o'clock position.

During the autopsy, Meyer had told Arndt and Trujillo that JonBenét had suffered an injury consistent with vaginal penetration—digital or otherwise. In his opinion, she'd sustained some kind of genital trauma that could be consistent with sexual contact.

Arndt told Eller that before the internal examination began, Tom Trujillo had passed a black fluorescent lamp over JonBenét's naked body. This would reveal traces of semen—if there were any—not visible to the naked eye. The light revealed numerous traces of dark fibers scattered over her pubic area, similar to fibers found on the outside of JonBenét's outer garment. Under the black light, the coroner saw a residue on the child's upper thigh that could have come from semen, though residue from blood and even from certain kinds of soaps could appear the same way under the black light. Nevertheless, the detectives conjectured that they were semen traces.

In addition, JonBenét's underpants bore stains that appeared to be blood. The corresponding areas of her skin in the pubic area, however, showed no matching stains. The coroner told the police that the blood smears on the skin and the fibers found in the folds of the labia indicated that the child's pubic area had been wiped with a cloth. The blood smears also contained traces of fibers.

Eller knew the police had found no evidence that an intruder had entered the Ramsey home, and John Ramsey had said to Fleet White it was he who had broken the basement window—months earlier. Also, the police had found an intact spiderweb at that spot. It extended from the edge of the grate covering the window well outside the broken window to some nearby rocks. This seemed to confirm that nobody had entered through the broken basement window recently. Other doors and possible points of entry had been locked or covered by spiderwebs. Outside, much of the grass was topped with snow, and Sgt. Paul Reichenbach had noted in his report that there were no footprints. A south-facing door in the solarium showed a fresh pry mark near the deadbolt, but detectives had found no corresponding wood chips or splinters. They concluded that the door hadn't been breached. Pry marks were also found on the exterior door leading to the kitchen, but detectives told Eller the lock had been set from the inside. So far, no clear sign of forced entry had been found anywhere on the premises.

The Colorado Bureau of Investigation, which was studying the ransom note and the writing samples John Ramsey had given the police before JonBenét's body was found, called the Boulder PD with an initial finding: the ransom note had been written on paper torn from one of the pads that John Ramsey had given to Detective Patterson. The pad contained a sample of Patsy Ramsey's writing.

Given the apparent presence of semen on JonBenét's body, Eller concluded that he had no choice but to consider John Ramsey the most likely perpetrator. Now he knew that the parents had to be questioned without delay. The Ramseys were the prime suspects.

So long as the Ramseys were not taken into custody Eller knew they could be questioned without a *Miranda* warning,* and any admissions they made could be used as evidence. Later Eller admitted covering the case that he had always felt intimidated by the *Miranda* decision; *Miranda* warnings can turn the search for criminals into a fox hunt in which a clever suspect might escape capture, he said.

After the autopsy briefing, Eller ordered that John Ramsey's office at Access Graphics be sealed and an officer be posted until a legal search could be conducted. The Ramseys should be interviewed without delay, he told Mason and Arndt.

At 9:30 that evening, Detectives Mason and Arndt arrived at the Fernies' house to interview John and Patsy Ramsey. Patsy was heavily sedated. She was in shock, could barely talk, and couldn't sit up or stand. An interview was out of the question.

In the Fernies' living room, the detectives sat with John Ramsey, his brother, Jeff, and his friend and broker, Rod Westmoreland. Michael Bynum, Ramsey's lawyer, sat at the opposite side of the room but close enough to hear what Mason was saying. The detectives decided that under the circumstances, it would make more sense to schedule later interviews with the Ramseys. Earlier Mason had told Ramsey how important his and Patsy's contribution to the investigation would be. Now he said their assistance would be vital to finding their little girl's killer. Ramsey said he could not set a time and date for the interview. Arndt asked him a few questions, but his answers were so vague that the detectives soon left.

When the police left, Bynum and Westmoreland sat beside their friend, holding him as he wept. It was 2:00 in the morning before Ramsey fell asleep. A few minutes later he was up again, sobbing.

* Before any interrogation of a person taken into custody, the person must be warned 1) that he has a right to remain silent; 2) that any statement he makes can be used as evidence against him; 3) that he has the right to the presence of an attorney; 4) that if he cannot afford an attorney, one will be appointed for him prior to any questioning if he so desires; 5) that he may end the questioning at any time. The instruction stems from a case in which a suspect, Ernesto Miranda, was tricked into confessing by being told that he had been picked out of a lineup.

That night, John Meyer returned to the morgue. With the coroner was Dr. Andrew Sirotnak, an assistant professor of pediatrics at the University of Colorado's Health Sciences Center. The two men reexamined JonBenét's genitals and confirmed Meyer's earlier findings that there was evidence of vaginal injury. Meyer knew that JonBenét's death could be traced to strangulation and a blow to the head, but the facts surrounding the sexual assault of the child were unclear. In the event of a trial, the physical evidence about that would be open to interpretation.

4

On Saturday morning, December 28, seventy parents and children showed up at High Peaks Elementary School. The administrator had arranged for therapists to come in to talk to the kids and their parents. The school was in a U-shaped red brick building whose interior had been scrubbed clean and spruced up by dedicated parents. Now, many of these same adults gathered around the small tables in the library and talked in groups. Some of them were grateful to be temporarily separated from their children. It would give them a chance to express their own sadness and anxiety freely.

In the kindergarten classroom, children of various ages were gathered, some of them hyper, some of them relaxed, all of them full of questions. Charles Elbot, the principal, got their attention and then sat in one of the little chairs and read aloud from a book entitled *Lifetimes, the Beautiful Way to Explain Death to Children.*

> *All round us, everywhere, beginnings and endings are going on all the time. With living in between.*
>
> *Sometimes, living things become ill or they get hurt.*
>
> *Mostly, of course, they get better again but there are times when they are so badly hurt or they are so ill that they die because they can no longer stay alive.*
>
> *This can happen when you are young, or old, or anywhere in between.*

He told the children that there was no right or wrong way to feel at a time like this and that they should not be afraid to talk to their parents or teachers. "You need to know that tonight you should feel safe," he said. "What happened doesn't usually happen in Boulder."

"Yeah," one third grader responded, "JonBenét's parents would have told her that too."

"That's true," Elbot said. "But you need to understand it's a rare occurrence."

He told the children that this was like crossing the street—an accident can happen, but it's not likely to happen.

Elbot knew the children were terrified.

He suggested to them that they make some drawings. Jo-Lynn Yoshihara-Daly, the school's social worker, helped the younger children. Some of the kids painted pictures of JonBenét's family. Some drew JonBenét. Some added words to their pictures.

A few of us parents thought we should only tell our children that JonBenét died. Others thought we should say she had been murdered but not that she had been murdered in her own house. By Saturday morning there was a huge amount of speculation about the cause of JonBenét's death. Some parents had heard JonBenét was strangled. My daughter was in JonBenét's kindergarten class and hadn't heard anything. But some of the older children had seen news reports on TV.

The school psychologist told us he would tell the kids the facts that were known, but he assured us he wouldn't go near the subject of whether JonBenét was sexually assaulted. He would talk mostly about safety, about how you could feel safe. He wanted to focus on what the kids needed most.

The art therapy took forty-five minutes, maybe an hour. There were about twenty-five kids in two groups—younger children in one group, the older kids in another. Jo-Lynn dealt with the kindergartners.

The kids decided what had happened. They figured it out all by themselves. They drew pictures of JonBenét and her house. Then they came back to us parents with their drawings and their conclusions.

They said that JonBenét's family went to bed and forgot to make sure that all the doors were locked. Then a bad man had snuck in and murdered JonBenét. They decided that if a bad man came into their homes, they would have to make a lot of noise to scare him away. They decided they all wanted whistles. They said that no bad man could stand having a huge whistle blowing in his ear.

On the way home, I bought my daughter a whistle that she could hook to her pillow. She wanted her friends to have them too, so I bought whistles for them. Other parents I know got whistles for their kids. Our kindergarten kids latched on to the whistle idea pretty strongly.

For weeks, my daughter wouldn't go to sleep without the light on, the bedroom door open, and the whistle clipped to her pillow.

She didn't sleep through the whole night for months afterward.

Now I always make sure I turn on the house alarm that I hadn't used in two years. I don't think there's a night that's gone by since this happened that I haven't had our alarm on.

I was happy that my child grasped that whistle. It was something that gave her some comfort, some sense of power. You realize that it's absolutely futile, but you're never going to tell your child how futile it is.

—Barbara Kostanick

By Saturday morning, having been present at Mason and Arndt's abortive attempt at an interview the evening before, Michael Bynum realized that the police were targeting his friend and client John Ramsey. His instincts told him to make sure the Ramseys had every protection the law provided. Bynum, in his early fifties and a longtime resident of Colorado, was born in Arkansas and retained faint overtones of the South in his soft-spoken speech. Like so many who eventually settled in Boulder, he had attended the University of Colorado. Bynum also got his law degree at CU and worked briefly as a deputy DA in Boulder before becoming a specialist in business planning, acquisitions, and commercial transactions. Bynum had a saying: when it comes to murder, it doesn't matter if you're guilty or innocent—you need an attorney.

Shortly after noon that Saturday, without consulting John or Patsy, Bynum told Detective Arndt that the Ramseys would not give any more testimonial evidence without a criminal attorney present, and they would no longer share privileged information with the police. Since he was no longer a criminal attorney, Bynum called Bryan Morgan of Haddon, Morgan and Foreman in Denver, one of Colorado's top firms. By Saturday evening, the Ramseys had retained Morgan.

Arndt then checked with Pete Hofstrom in the DA's office about the non-testimonial evidence the police still wanted from the

Ramseys*. It was likely, Arndt knew, that according to court rulings, the Fifth Amendment and its protection against self-incrimination did not include physical evidence such as blood, hair, saliva, fingerprints, and handwriting samples.

Hofstrom then called Michael Bynum, who confirmed that although John and Patsy refused interviews at this time, the entire family—including Burke, John Andrew, and Melinda—would give blood, hair, fingerprint, and handwriting samples. Bynum agreed that Detectives Arndt and Kim Stewart could speak to John Ramsey's older children and his brother, Jeff, who were at the Fernies' house.

John Eller was unhappy with Bynum's position. The commander acknowledged that a suspect had the right to an attorney once he was arrested, but he thought the investigative process was hindered by the courts' liberal reading of the Sixth Amendment, which says that any person interviewed by law enforcement is entitled to counsel. For Eller, this court ruling was an unnecessary obstacle.

Just after noon on Saturday, Boulder County DA Alex Hunter, who had been in Hana, a remote area on the island of Maui, without a phone or pager for the last two days, checked in with first assistant DA Bill Wise and learned about the murder. Hunter, who had been the Boulder DA for twenty-five years, often read the business section of the *Daily Camera*, but he didn't recognize the family's name and didn't recall ever having met John or Patsy Ramsey. When Wise mentioned that Ramsey had hired private attorneys, Hunter wasn't surprised. A man as apparently wealthy as John Ramsey would automatically retain counsel. And if the victim's father had been Joe Schmo, Hunter knew that Boulder's proactive public defender's office would be right there advising Mr. Schmo just as John Ramsey's attorneys were now advising him.

Meanwhile, as Pete Hofstrom was talking to attorney Michael Bynum about the schedule for taking the Ramsey family's blood, hair, and handwriting samples, he received a call from the police. Eller wanted

---

* Case: *Schmerber* v. *California*, decided by the U.S. Supreme Court in 1966 [384 U.S. 757, opinion by Justice Brennan, 5-4 decision]. The Colorado Rules of Criminal Procedure [Rule 41.1] authorize any judge to issue an order requiring a person to supply such *non-testimonial* materials if there are reasonable grounds to believe the person committed a criminal offense. *Reasonable grounds* is a lenient standard, amounting to less than probable cause.

the Ramseys to give the police formal interviews before they left to bury JonBenét in Atlanta, which he had learned was their intention. Eller told Hofstrom that he would withhold the child's body until he got his interviews with the parents.

"You didn't get your statements in the first three days," Hofstrom told Eller bluntly. "You may not use this method to get your statements now. It's just not legal to withhold the body." It was obvious to everyone that the commander wanted to rectify the mistakes made in the first hours of the case. But holding the child's body hostage was unacceptable. "It's illegal. It's another mistake," Hofstrom said. Eller said nothing.

Hofstrom, balding, affable, and stocky, a former San Quentin prison guard, was exasperated by Eller's thinking. If he had been the commander's boss, he probably would have taken Eller off the case.

When Eller hung up after this unpleasant conversation with Hofstrom, he told Larry Mason he was going to withhold the body. "John, you can't do that," Mason protested. "You're violating their rights."

"I don't give a goddamn," Eller snapped. "You either get on board or get out."

Larry Mason could see that Eller had no idea how to handle this kind of investigation. His inexperience, bravado, and stubbornness were making a bad situation worse.

On Saturday afternoon at the Justice Center, while the Ramseys were providing their various samples, Michael Bynum learned of Eller's plan to withhold JonBenét's body until John and Patsy agreed to be interviewed. The lawyer took Pete Hofstrom aside and told him that whether or not his clients had killed their daughter, they were still JonBenét's parents. They had the right to bury their child. Bynum decided not to tell the Ramseys of Eller's plan for the time being.

When the police asked the coroner to hold JonBenét's body until they had interviewed the Ramseys, he refused. There was no reason for his office to maintain custody of the body, John Meyer said. The police department's legal adviser, Bob Keatley, agreed with Hofstrom and said so.

Hofstrom would never say it publicly, but he had now lost all confidence in John Eller. According to Larry Mason, Hofstrom was a strict judge of character. Eller had clearly failed to measure up.

At 5:40 P.M. a heavily sedated Patsy Ramsey gave the police her first handwriting samples on the second floor of the Justice Center, a sprawling two-story sandstone building that contains not only the county courts but the sheriff's department and the DA's and coroner's offices.

"Will this help find who killed my baby?" Patsy asked Detective Arndt. Then she added, "I did not murder my baby."

Meanwhile, Melinda Ramsey, John's twenty-five-year-old daughter from his first marriage, arrived at the Child Advocacy Center in the nearby town of Niwot. She had been called for a formal interview about her movements over the last few days. An hour later, her brother would be interviewed at the same place.

The Ramseys' attorneys and the police had agreed on this location as neutral territory. The police would have preferred to see them at headquarters, but since John Andrew and Melinda were cooperating without independent counsel, the detectives accepted the Child Advocacy Center as a reasonable compromise.

Detective Kim Stewart interviewed Melinda for almost two and a half hours. Detectives Ron Gosage and Steve Thomas questioned her brother from 6:00 to 8:00 P.M.

Twenty-year-old John Andrew was obviously upset, but he was composed enough to explain that he was a student at CU and had been in Boulder until December 19. Then he had gone to Atlanta to spend the first part of his vacation with his mother, Lucinda Johnson, and his sister and friends. Then the plan was to continue his vacation with his sister, father, stepmother, and their children. He said his father had arranged to meet him and his sister in Minneapolis at about 10:30 A.M. on December 26, and from there they would all continue to the house in Charlevoix, Michigan.

In the months that followed, the police would confirm that John Andrew, his mother, and her friend Harry Smiles had attended the Peachtree Presbyterian Church in Atlanta on Christmas Eve and that John Andrew had returned to his mother's home at 1:00 A.M.

Melinda, who worked at a hospital in Marietta, Georgia, finished her shift at about 7:00 A.M. on Christmas Day. That afternoon, John Andrew, Harry Smiles, Melinda, and her boyfriend, Stewart Long, exchanged gifts at Lucinda's home in Marietta. In the afternoon they all went across the street to a neighbor's for dinner.

Melinda and Stewart Long left the dinner party about 7:00 P.M., and Melinda started to pack for an early flight the next day. At 9:00 they went to visit Guy Long, Stewart's uncle, and after visiting other friends were home by midnight.

At about 8:30 P.M., John Andrew went to his friend Brad Millard's home in Marietta to play video games. After an hour, they left to catch a 10:30 show at the Town and Country Movie Theaters in Marietta with another friend, Chris Stanley.

John Andrew said that after the movie he went back to Brad Millard's house to get his car and arrived back at his mother's house at 1:00 A.M. The next morning he left his mother's house with Melinda, who had come there to pick him up. Together they boarded a flight to Minneapolis at 8:36 A.M. local time. That was forty-four minutes after Patsy called 911 to report that JonBenét was missing.

Could John Andrew, with one or more of the friends who provided his and his sister's alibis, have left Marietta, Georgia, flown to Boulder, Colorado, and returned in time to be seen by his sister's boyfriend, Stewart Long, at about 6:15 A.M. when John Andrew and Melinda left for the airport?

The police figured that John Andrew had a minimum of four and a half hours he could not account for—longer if he didn't stay to see the entire movie. It would have been longer still if he never went to the theater but went to an airport instead. That scenario would give John Andrew almost nine hours to get from Marietta to Boulder and back. Until all airline and private plane flights were checked, John Andrew Ramsey would remain a suspect.

Late on Saturday evening, December 28, DA Alex Hunter, who was still in Hawaii, called Bill Wise. He learned that the police had not only asked a heavily sedated Patsy Ramsey for a handwriting sample, they had asked her to copy out parts of the ransom note. She had become hysterical and could not complete it. Hunter agreed with the police procedure but was upset to hear from Wise that John Eller had tried to barter with the Ramseys—JonBenét's body in exchange for formal interviews with them.

The DA expected the police to follow the law and not jeopardize the integrity of the case. Hunter had always protected the constitutional rights of Boulder's citizens from overzealous police officers. To Hunter, Eller seemed to be such an officer.

UNEASE SETTLES OVER BOULDER
MYSTERY STILL SURROUNDS
CHILD'S SHOCKING DEATH

The gloomy mystery surrounding the strangulation of JonBenét Ramsey the day after Christmas has tarnished Boulder's reputation as a little slice of nirvana.

The investigation has mushroomed into one of the biggest in recent years here. More than 30 detectives and uniformed officers from Boulder Police Department and the Boulder County Sheriff's Department are participating. Combined, they represent nearly a third of the local police force.

In reality, Boulder's mellow reputation is a bit undeserved. According to 1994 statistics, the latest available, the city ranked as the fifth-most dangerous in Colorado, with 10.3 serious crimes per 1,000 residents.

Boulder officials objected that the data were misleading. . . . Many were crimes of passion or had domestic connections.

—Joseph Verrengia
Rocky Mountain News, December 29, 1996

On Sunday morning, after briefing Eller on the status of the investigation, Detectives Mason, Thomas, Gosage, and Arndt attended the memorial service for JonBenét at St. John's. Undercover officers videotaped everyone at the church. The police weren't taking any chances. Maybe the killer, like the arsonist who returns to watch the fire he set, was among those present.

On Sunday, December 29, I arrived at church late as usual. It was in the middle of the homily, so I sat in the balcony.

There was a lot of crying, and I started to feel this huge wave of emotion crashing down, this huge tragedy. I realized that many families with children knew this family. They knew this child.

The Ramseys were members of the church's Foyer Group, which was for couples new to the community who wanted to meet people. If you weren't involved in a group with the Ramseys, you might not know them. You see, Boulder doesn't have any overall social structure—just clubs and more informal groups.

That morning, Rol said he hoped this terrible thing could be resolved. And said it would never happen again.

After the service, almost everyone went to an adjoining building for coffee, as usual. One friend, Paula Schulte, said to me, "Maybe we can pull together as a church to help this family." I don't know why, but I answered that I couldn't see anything good coming from this thing.

—Niki Hayden

When I arrived at St. John's, I put my arms around Patsy's sister Pam, but I couldn't bring myself to talk to Patsy. Polly, Patsy's other sister, told me I had to go over and talk to her.

"Who could have done this to JonBenét?" Patsy asked.

"I wish I knew," I said. "Are you sure you had all the doors locked?"

"Yes, we are sure."

"Are you sure you pushed the button on the patio door?"

"We had all the windows and doors locked," Patsy said.

Before I could say another word, someone else was talking to Patsy. That was the last time I saw Patsy or John.

—Linda Hoffmann-Pugh

I knew where St. John's was because I had once gone to a wedding there. That Sunday, December 29, it was sunny but cold. Some of us from the school and the neighborhood went together. We were all crying. The service was unbearably sad—people were sobbing all over the church. Patsy was shrouded in black.

John spoke first. He told us he was wearing a medallion that Jon-Benét had won at her last pageant. He said that he often told his daughter the talent division was the most important because it was judged not on your appearance but on your achievements. The medallion he was wearing had been awarded to JonBenét for talent. He made it quite clear that he was not a fan of child beauty pageants. He thanked us all for coming, told us to remember we were all part of his family. He looked spaced out.

As I watched John speak, the gossip we were hearing about his possible involvement in JonBenét's death seemed ridiculous. Then Patsy's sisters spoke. They were more charismatic and evangelical in their approach to worship.

Bill McReynolds, who'd been the Santa at the Ramseys' Christmas party, got up to talk. He told us that JonBenét had given him fairy dust for his beard. He rambled and he was almost incoherent. He was so strange that some of us were uncomfortable.

When the service ended and Patsy stood up to get out of the pew, John helped her. Every step of the way, he told her, "I need you to be strong." She stopped beside me and put her arms around me and we cried. Most of the congregation was in tears.

We all went to the parish hall. There were silver pots of tea and cookies. Funeral stuff.

Outside, the media people were circling.

Eventually the Ramseys left for the airport and flew to Atlanta with JonBenét's body.

—Barbara Kostanick

After the service, Detective Steve Thomas, thirty-six, who had been transferred to the case from narcotics only the day before and still had long hair and a goatee, helped the Ramsey family into their waiting cars as photographers closed in. "Get rid of them!" John Andrew shouted to Thomas. When the detective asked one photographer to step back, he accused the officer of protecting a killer.

John Ramsey emerged from the church, and on his way to his car, he passed Thomas, whom he knew from the day before, when he had given blood and hair samples. Without looking directly at the detective, Ramsey shook his hand and said, "Thank you." Thomas caught Ramsey's eye and, looking squarely at him, said, "Good luck." As the motorcade pulled away, Thomas was left with an uneasy feeling about JonBenét's father. The detective had expected Ramsey to say, "Find the motherfucker" or "Bring the bastard to me." Instead he got a thank-you and a weak handshake. Maybe Thomas's reaction was due to frustration—the police had been unable to interview the Ramseys properly. The primary suspects were slipping out of their control, and the detectives were angry.

Several hours before the Ramseys left for Atlanta that Sunday, Detective Linda Arndt sent a fax to Bryan Morgan, the Ramseys' newly hired criminal attorney. It was two pages long:

> *I realize the Ramsey family will be out of state for an unknown amount of time after this afternoon. If it is possible, would you meet with John Ramsey, Patsy Ramsey, and Burke Ramsey and see if [the police] could get answers to*

any of these questions. I appreciate your assistance. I am available through Dispatch at the above pager number.

Det. Linda Arndt

Questions: JonBenét's immediate family
John, Patsy, and Burke Ramsey

What time did each of you go to your bedroom?
What time did each of you go to sleep?
Was your bedroom door open or closed?
Was there any TV or radio on when you went to bed?
What had JonBenét eaten before she went to bed?
Where, specifically, was the ransom note found?
What did Patsy do after she found the ransom note?
Who was the first person Patsy contacted after the note was found?
How did John find out that JonBenét was missing?
What interior house lights were on when the family went to bed?
What exterior lights were on when the family went to bed?
Who checked the doors and windows of the house to see if they were secure?
What was JonBenét wearing when she went to bed on Christmas night?
What time was the family planning on leaving the home on the morning of December 26th?
What time did each of you wake up on the morning of December 26th?
Did any of you get up during the night?

In the late afternoon of Sunday, December 29, a Lockheed Martin corporate jet left Jefferson County Airport, just south of Boulder, with the body of JonBenét and her family. Two hours later, Fleet White called Detective Arndt and asked her to retrieve JonBenét's favorite toy from her bedroom so the family could bury her with her Kitty. The day before, one of Patsy Ramsey's sisters had gone into the house with police permission and taken out an oil painting, several American Girl dolls, a portfolio of JonBenét's pageant photographs, a pageant medal with a blue ribbon, graduation photos of the older children, and a Bible from John Ramsey's desk, but she had missed JonBenét's stuffed cat, which Patsy had wanted retrieved.

Arndt did as she was asked and then delivered the toy to Priscilla White. The Whites would take it with them to Atlanta the next day.

On Monday, December 30, before the Whites and Fernies left Boulder for JonBenét's funeral in Atlanta, Linda Arndt interviewed Fleet White again.

White believed that an intruder had gotten into the Ramseys' house. "Somebody got into that house," he told Arndt. "I don't know how, but they got in. Somebody wanted to hurt that family and obviously hurt their daughter." White suggested that perhaps some beauty pageant mothers might have resented the Ramseys. A few hours later, Arndt and Detective Jane Harmer met with Fleet White again, this time with John Fernie, in Fernie's office. The Ramseys' friends were worried that John Andrew was a suspect, and they wanted everything possible to be done to clear his name promptly. An hour later, the Whites and the Fernies left for the Denver airport.

When Arndt returned to headquarters, she told Eller about her conversation with White and Fernie. Clearly, the Ramsey family was concerned about preserving John Andrew's and Melinda's presumption of innocence. Arndt suggested that maybe the department should make a public statement to pacify the Ramseys, that it might help the police get their cooperation. Eller agreed to the concept, but he said that at this early stage of the investigation, no one could be exonerated completely. That afternoon, at a scheduled press briefing, a police spokesperson said that both of John Ramsey's older children had been out of state at the time JonBenét was murdered but had not been eliminated as suspects. Forty minutes after the press conference ended, Arndt called the Ramseys in Atlanta and told them about the media briefing.

That same day, Eller placed Detective Sgt. Tom Wickman, who had a master's degree in psychology, in charge of the crime scene investigation. Of the thirty officers now working on the case, seventeen were detectives.

DA Alex Hunter would be in Hawaii for the next several days, but Bill Wise kept him informed. Some of the news was not good. Wise was troubled that John Ramsey had carried JonBenét's body upstairs and that evidence might have been contaminated. Also, he told Hunter, the media were starting to criticize the Boulder police for not having secured the crime scene.

5

Over the next several weeks, the police would reconstruct piecemeal the events leading up to the murder. They learned that on Christmas Eve, the Ramseys had dinner at Pasta Jay's restaurant on Pearl Street, then stopped by the Whites' house, and then drove around Boulder looking at Christmas lights before going home. After the children were in bed that night, John Ramsey went across the street to their neighbors the Barnhills', to pick up a bike he had been hiding in their basement. When he got home, he placed it under the Christmas tree in the living room. On Christmas morning, JonBenét and Burke gave gifts to their parents and each other, and in the early afternoon, JonBenét rode her new bicycle around the patio before the family went to the Whites' house for dinner. Fleet White, forty-seven, was retired, having made his money in the oil business. His daughter, Daphne, was the same age as JonBenét, and Fleet White Jr. was a year older. When the Ramseys left the Whites' house, they stopped off at their friends the Walkers' to drop off some presents and then stopped briefly at the home of the Stines, who were also friends. Glen Stine, forty-eight, was vice president for budget and finance at CU. The Stines' son, Doug, was about Burke Ramsey's age. Patsy talked to Susan Stine for about ten minutes. By that time, JonBenét was asleep in the backseat of the car.

During a conversation between John Ramsey and Detective Arndt on the morning of December 26, Ramsey said that the family arrived home at about 10:00 P.M. Christmas night. Ramsey parked their Jeep Cherokee next to their Jaguar in the garage, he said. According to a police report, he carried JonBenét, who was still asleep, upstairs to her room, where he took her shoes off and read to her. Patsy undressed her, remembered singing a bedtime song to her while she slept, and kissed her good night. Meanwhile, Burke was downstairs playing with a model he'd gotten for Christmas and didn't want to go to bed. John helped his son finish what he was doing and then took him upstairs and put him to bed before he himself retired

At about midnight, Scott Gibbons, a neighbor, looked out his kitchen window toward the Ramseys' house and saw a light on in the kitchen area. Sometime later, Adam Fermeire, another neighbor, who was up watching TV, said he didn't notice anything strange through the window that faced the Ramseys' house.

Diane Brumfitt, another neighbor, told Detective Barry Hartkopp on December 31 that on Christmas night she did not see a light on at the southeast corner of the Ramseys' house, though there had been a safety light in that spot for years. She remembered thinking that it was unusual. Melody Stanton, up the street at 738, told the police on January 3 that she was certain she had heard a child's scream at about 2:00 A.M. on the night of the murder. Her bedroom window, which looks toward the Ramsey house from across the street, had been partly open. When questioned by the police, Stanton said that there had been only one scream but it was horrifying. If it came from the child, she assumed the scream had awakened her parents.

Patsy Ramsey told Rick French, the first police officer to arrive at the scene on the morning of December 26, that her husband got up before her, at around 5:30 A.M., and took a shower. She got up a few minutes later, got dressed, and put on her makeup. From the third-floor master bedroom, she then went down the back spiral stairs, which were decorated with green garlands and red Christmas ribbons, and stopped on the second floor at a laundry area just outside JonBenét's room, where she washed a soiled jumpsuit of her daughter's in the sink.

The door to JonBenét's room was about 10 feet away, but Patsy said she didn't look in on her daughter. After doing this bit of laundry, she continued down the spiral staircase to the first floor. As she reached the bottom, Patsy saw three sheets of paper spread across one of the steps.

Patsy said she didn't remember but must have stepped over the papers, and police forensics later confirmed that no one appeared to have stepped on the ransom note. At the bottom of the stairs she turned around and, without picking up the papers, began to read them. After getting through a few lines, she realized the note was about JonBenét. She ran back upstairs, pushed open the door to her daughter's room, and found her bed empty.

Patsy screamed for her husband. Within seconds, John Ramsey reached the second floor. He was still in his underwear. Patsy told him there was a note downstairs that said JonBenét had been kidnapped. She ran to Burke's room, she said, turned on the light, and saw her son sleeping. Then she went downstairs, where she found her husband hunched over the three pieces of paper.

John told Officer French that as he read the pages, he realized someone had taken JonBenét. He had no idea where she was. It was still dark outside. Later Ramsey would tell a British TV interviewer that he knew he had to do something. But how could he close the airports and block the roads out of Boulder? Those were the first thoughts that went through his mind, he said. He soon realized that only the police could do what needed to be done.

Before he finished reading the ransom note, he told Patsy to call the police. Immediately afterward, Patsy called the Whites and Fernies and told them something terrible had happened. "Barbara, get over here as fast as you can," she said to her friend. Seven minutes after Patsy's call to 911, Officer French was at their front door.

John Fernie told the police that he was the first of the Ramseys' friends to arrive. His wife, Barbara, came later in her car. As Fernie drove over, he thought that John must have had a heart attack, since Patsy hadn't told his wife what had happened

Fernie parked his car in the alley behind the Ramseys' house and ran to the patio door on the south side, which he always used. It was locked. When he looked through the glass-paneled door, the lights were on and he could see some papers lying on the wooden floor. They were not facing him, but from where he stood, he could read the first few lines of one page. That was all he needed. He understood immediately that JonBenét had been kidnapped. Once inside the house, he read the entire ransom note. At first he thought it was bizarre, then later he saw it as perverse.

A few minutes later, John Ramsey tried to phone his pilot, Mike Archuleta, to tell him what had happened and learned that the pilot was already on his way to the airport for the Ramseys' scheduled flight to Michigan. When Archuleta returned Ramsey's call, Patsy answered. Archuleta told the police that Patsy had been hysterical, barely coherent. She was now being consoled by Barbara and John Fernie when a second officer, Karl Veitch, arrived. The police then paged Mary Lou Jedamus, a victim advocate.

By 6:45, three more officers—Barry Weiss, Sue Barcklow, and Sgt. Paul Reichenbach—had arrived. Now there were twelve people in the house, including five police officers, the Ramsey family, and their friends. John Ramsey told Officers French and Veitch that he believed the house had been locked when he went to bed.

Just after 7:00, Detective Fred Patterson, one of Boulder's most experienced officers, arrived at the Basemar Shopping Center, a mile from the Ramseys' home. He had arranged to meet Detective Linda Arndt, who was driving in from her home in Louisville. Arndt and Patterson were briefed by Reichenbach, who had come from the Ramsey home for this meeting.

Reichenbach told the detectives that there was light, crusty snow and frost on the Ramseys' lawn and he had seen no fresh footprints in the snow. The brick walkways were clear of snow. He had examined the exterior doors and windows and had seen no signs of forced entry. Other than that, all Reichenbach knew for sure was that there was a ransom note, the parents said the child was missing, and now they were praying. A short time later, when Arndt and Patterson arrived at the house, Fleet White and John Fernie had just returned from dropping Burke and the Fernies' kids off at the Whites' house.

Scott Gibbons, the Ramseys' next door neighbor, told police that at about 8:00 A.M. he saw the door on his side of the Ramseys' house open. But by then, anyone inside the house could have opened the door. A few minutes later, Officer Larry Burton found an earring at the curb directly in front of the Ramseys' house. It didn't seem to belong to anyone inside.

That morning, Officer Weiss noticed a heavy police-style flashlight on the Ramseys' kitchen counter. By the end of the day, none of the cops had claimed it, so it was taken into evidence. Sometime that morning, Detective Arndt found a paper bag with children's clothing next to the den door, and she moved it into the cloakroom.

Around noon, at police headquarters, Detective Jim Byfield received the first of several printouts listing the calls made to and from telephones the police had targeted. After the list was reviewed, additional phone traps were ordered.

During the next seven days, the police would trap calling information from phones belonging to suspects, neighbors, family friends, doctors, business associates, corporate offices, and public officials. Even the telephones at United Airlines Red Carpet airport lounges and the mortuary that held JonBenét's body were trapped. In all, there were traps on more than sixty-seven telephone numbers belonging to fifty-nine individuals, including Lt. Governor Gail Schoettler and her husband, Don Stevens, who knew John Ramsey from the days when they both attended Michigan State University.

After JonBenét's body was found, victim advocate Grace Morlock told detectives, John Ramsey said more than once that he didn't think the kidnapper meant to kill his daughter, because she was wrapped in her blanket. When Patsy saw her friend Susan Stine at the Fernies' house later that day, she kept asking, "Who would do this to my baby?" Susan responded, "I don't know."

The police interviewed Linda Hoffmann-Pugh for a second time on Friday, December 27, and they came with a tape recorder. The Ramseys' housekeeper told the police that the day after Thanksgiving, she, her daughter Ariana, and her husband were at the Ramseys' house washing the windows and getting the house ready for Christmas. Hoffmann-Pugh brought the Christmas decorations in from the garage but couldn't find the artificial trees that had been brought to the house from the Access Graphics storage hangar. There should have been a tree for the playroom and one for each of the five bedrooms. Hoffmann-Pugh even checked the basement, but she couldn't find them, so she continued cleaning the windows.

After they had washed the windows, Hoffmann-Pugh and her daughter started searching the house for the missing trees. She saw a closed door in the basement just past the boiler room, which she had never noticed before. She tried to open the door, but it was stuck shut, apparently from a recent painting. She pushed against it hard and it finally opened. Feeling around in the dark, she found a light switch on the wall to her right.

The room was full of trees, some still covered with last year's decorations, replicas of Burke's model airplanes and John Andrew's cowboy hats, boots, and red scarves. The next day the housekeeper had her older daughter, Tina, her son-in-law Mike, and her husband, Merv, take all the trees upstairs and place them in their proper rooms.

The police asked Hoffmann-Pugh if she had closed the door to that storage room securely. She didn't know. She couldn't even tell the police what the room looked like empty because she wasn't the last person to leave, she said.

When the police asked if she'd seen a broken window in the basement or had ever cleaned up broken glass from a broken window, she said she couldn't recall anything like that.

That same Friday, December 27, the police fingerprinted the housekeeper's entire family, including her daughters and sons-in-law.

★ ★ ★

On Monday morning, December 30, several of Sheriff George Epp's detectives met with him in his office at the Justice Center. Sheriff Epp had jurisdiction over the entire county, which included the city of Boulder. Even though the Boulder PD had primary responsibility for the city, the sheriff's department and the Boulder PD often loaned each other officers. The day after JonBenét's body was found, the Boulder police had requested four of Epp's detectives to work on the Ramsey case. Epp's officers had been involved with kidnappings in the past, including the Tracy Neef case, in which a child had been abducted from Bertha Hyde Elementary School and found dead near Barker Reservoir at the top of Boulder Canyon.

This morning Epp's detectives were upset with what they'd seen over the weekend. Eller, they said, wasn't organized. He wasn't running things efficiently. Some officers were just sitting around when they should have been canvassing the Ramseys' neighborhood. One of the detectives said that Eller's attitude was, We'll just vacuum up all the evidence, pull together everything, and give it to the DA to make a case out of it.

Epp was also troubled to learn that Larry Mason was working for Eller. Larry was the kind of cop who needed to be nurtured by his supervisor. But Eller's reputation was that he wouldn't accept input from anyone. Mason and Hofstrom could work well together, but Eller and Mason were bound to be trouble.

After the meeting with his detectives, Epp called police chief Tom Koby and offered his department's continued assistance. He had a couple of detectives available who wanted to help, he said.

"We're fine," Koby told him. "We can handle it ourselves."

A few weeks later, one sheriff's detective made T-shirts for his department, stenciled with WE'RE THE OTHER GUYS in bold letters. When the case dragged on, a second set of T-shirts appeared, bearing the slogan WHEN IT ABSOLUTELY, POSITIVELY HAS TO BE SOLVED OVERNIGHT.

That Monday afternoon, December 30, Pete Hofstrom received a letter from Bryan Morgan, one of the Ramseys' attorneys. A gracious gentleman in his midfifties with a passion for tough cases, Grady Morgan preferred to be known by his middle name as a tribute to his birthplace, Bryan, Texas. A proper defense, he believed, included addressing a client's emotional needs.

In his letter to Hofstrom, Morgan said he wanted to be informed in advance when it looked as if evidence might be destroyed by forensic tests. He asked for approval and participation in the tests of the physical evidence being provided by the Ramseys. Morgan also requested copies of the ransom note, the autopsy report, the affidavits for the search warrants, and copies of keys to the Ramsey house that were in the possession of the police.

Meanwhile, in Marietta, Georgia, Gary Mann, John Ramsey's boss at Lockheed Martin, attended the visitation service at the Mayes–Ward–Dobbins Funeral Home on Monday afternoon, December 30. Then he went to see Ramsey at the home of Patsy's parents, Don and Nedra Paugh, in Roswell. Mann, who stayed until 1:00 in the morning, was impressed with Ramsey's inner strength. He hoped that if he were ever faced with a tragedy of this magnitude, he could handle himself as well. Mann had worked with Ramsey for almost a year and knew he was deeply religious, with a good Christian foundation. Nevertheless, he wondered what it was in Ramsey's background that gave him such strength.

Three hours before JonBenét's funeral was to begin on Tuesday, December 31, the Boulder police asked the police in Marietta, Georgia, to take tracings and measurements of the child's hands at the funeral home.

At the Peachtree Presbyterian Church in Atlanta, mourners passed by JonBenét's open casket, where she lay with a pageant crown on her head and Kristine Griffin's crown in her hands. Some caressed her hair. Others kissed her cheek. In his eulogy, Reverend Frank Harrington, who had married John and Patsy in 1980 and had baptized Jon-Benét, told the congregation, "The mind cannot accept, and the heart refuses to grasp, the death of one so young, who is suddenly taken from us by the cruelty and malice of some unworthy person. . . . When a child is lost, one feels part of the future is gone."

Throughout the service, John stroked Patsy's back as they sat in the front row with Burke. Afterward, Patsy knelt and touched her face to the wooden casket. Just after noon, JonBenét was buried at the foot of a large dogwood tree in St. James Episcopal Cemetery in Marietta. John Ramsey cried, his grief as fresh as if he had just carried her lifeless body up the stairs from the basement.

After the funeral, about forty people went to the home of Patsy's parents in Roswell. Nedra Paugh noticed that everyone responded differently to her granddaughter's dreadful death. Some people cried. Some couldn't stop talking, it seemed. Some sat silently. Others had to make a great effort to compose themselves.

Nedra looked at John Ramsey sitting alone and saw a mature man who had endured other tragedies. He had lived through the death of his oldest child, Beth, who was killed in an auto accident in Chicago in 1992. When Patsy had been diagnosed with aggressive stage-four ovarian cancer in 1993 and the doctor said there was nothing that could be done, it was John who had said to her with conviction, "This too shall pass, and we will manage." It was John who had searched nationwide for the best treatment program, and a year later Patsy was declared cancer-free. Nedra remembered Patsy's doctor telling her, "Go have fun." Then John had his scare with prostate cancer just this past fall. The tests had proved negative. But now he was being cruelly tested again.

Nedra kept asking herself why such a horrifying thing should happen. All she could think was that someone had come in the middle of the night and killed her granddaughter. She had no idea who it could have been. She knew the police had a list—neighbors, enemies, disgruntled employees, the housekeeper, even poor old Santa Claus from the Christmas party. It could have been anyone.

What Patsy's sister Polly noticed at her parents' home was that Fleet White was quarreling angrily with her brother-in-law John. Patsy was standing to one side of them while Fleet hovered over John, telling him he had to go back to Boulder and help the police. It was wrong for him to hire his own investigators and criminal attorneys, said Fleet. His job was to cooperate with the police, not stonewall them. John's face reddened. It was obvious that he was embarrassed to have this conversation in front of his wife and family. But Fleet kept at him. What was this he'd heard about John contacting CNN for an interview? His daughter had just been buried! How could Patsy and John even think about going on television? Even if they wanted to respond to rumors that were going around, a TV appearance was unthinkable. By that point, Fleet had his hands at John's face, but John wasn't saying much. Then the room fell silent. The two friends separated, knowing they would never speak to each other again.

Fleet White's behavior seemed odd to some of the Ramseys' friends too. John Fernie felt uncomfortable speaking to Fleet, who seemed too focused on John's behavior. Others at the house felt that Fleet's behavior was so out of character for him that maybe he was involved somehow in JonBenét's death. Nedra, however, thought it was silly to judge anyone's conduct as inappropriate at a time like this. Who could act normally under these circumstances?

Meanwhile, in Boulder, Detectives Steve Thomas and Ron Gosage interviewed the Ramseys' neighbors Joe Barnhill, seventy-seven, and his wife, Betty, who lived across the street. The Barnhills had a key to the Ramseys' home, since they were taking care of JonBenét's dog, Jacques, a Bichon Frise. The detectives learned that the Barnhills had a boarder, Glenn Meyer, who lived in their basement.

Joe and Betty Barnhill had been guests at the Ramseys' Christmas party on December 23 and had chatted with Patsy's father, Don Paugh, a retired engineer. Paugh had worked as his son-in-law's first director of human resources at Access Graphics and still worked most of the time for John in Boulder, while Nedra, his wife, ran John's Atlanta office. Paugh told the Barnhills he had a new position at Access—manager of inventory tracking. The firm's market niche was "the Lincoln and Cadillac part of the industry," he said proudly.

Barnhill confirmed to police that at about 9:00 P.M. on December 24, John Ramsey had come to their house to pick up JonBenét's bicycle, a Christmas gift. The Barnhills said they were home the night JonBenét was killed. The police asked Joe for a handwriting sample, but his palsy made it impossible for him to give one. A week later he signed a waiver and his doctor confirmed Barnhill's illness to the police.

The detectives then interviewed the boarder, Glenn Meyer. He said that he had been at home on Christmas night and had watched television in the den with the Barnhills until 9:00 P.M. He then went downstairs to his basement room and spent the rest of the evening nursing a stomach flu. Meyer was also at the Ramseys' Christmas party, but he said he hadn't been introduced to Patsy or JonBenét.

"Do you mind taking a lie detector test?" Detective Thomas asked him. Meyer didn't, and on January 1, at 5:30 P.M., a polygraph test was administered. Most of the questions were about the Ramseys, and the examiner told him he had answered the questions truthfully. A few weeks later, Detective Thomas asked Meyer for several handwriting samples and took his fingerprints.

Now, the police decided, everyone who disliked John Ramsey for any reason had to be interviewed without delay.

While Thomas and Gosage were interviewing the Barnhills, Detective Carey Weinheimer met with Denise Wolf, John Ramsey's executive assistant at Access Graphics. She gave him the names of other employees who might have grievances.

Jeff Merrick was someone Ramsey had mentioned to the police on December 26. Ramsey had met Merrick in 1971, when they both worked as supervisors for AT&T in Columbus, Ohio. In 1994 Ramsey had found a job for Merrick with Access Graphics, but he didn't fit in. Ramsey tried him in different positions, and eventually he demoted him from director of distribution to director of security while letting him keep his six-figure salary. In March 1996, Ramsey could no longer justify Merrick's salary to Lockheed Martin and told Merrick he would have to take a large pay cut or leave by April 30. Merrick chose to leave. Later, he claimed the company owed him close to $118,000. He settled for half that amount, but one director of the company heard him say he was going to get Ramsey. Merrick then sent a long fax to Lockheed Martin, denouncing Ramsey for the way he dealt with employees.

On the afternoon of Tuesday, December 31, Detectives Patterson and Weinheimer interviewed Merrick at his home in Louisville, just fifteen minutes from the Ramseys' house. Merrick told the police that he and his wife, Kathy, had spent Christmas with Kathy's brother-in-law in Aurora and in the afternoon had visited their friends Dick and Diane Foote. The Merricks went home at about 8:00 and watched TV until they went to bed. His wife hadn't been feeling well, Merrick said. At 6:30 A.M. on December 26, he left for work in Littleton.

John Ramsey's former friend remained a suspect.

When Commander Eller debriefed his detectives that evening at police headquarters, he learned that they hadn't yet interviewed all the Access Graphics ex-employees on the list. Some were traveling, and others lived out of town. For the time being, the attention of the police would shift to the Ramsey family and their friends.

This New Year's Eve, John Eller would not be hosting his annual party for the rank-and-file officers of the department. He and most of them were working the Ramsey case.

6

During the final days of '96, I read about a little girl who had been mur-dered in Colorado—JonBenét Ramsey. I work in Atlanta for CNN as the network's Southeast correspondent. In the news business, it was the sort of story you'd quickly dismiss—it didn't have a national feel to it. But when it emerged that the child had been a beauty pageant queen, the story became sexier. That's what we played up.

It had a local angle for us too—the child was being buried in Marietta, Georgia, a suburb of Atlanta. On December 31, I was assigned to cover the church service. We call it "sidewalk" duty—watching people who come to pay their respects.

That same evening, New Year's Eve, I was at home with my family when the phone rang. Tom Johnson, the president of CNN, told me that the Ramseys had told CNN through a friend that they wanted to appear on national TV to explain why they weren't talking to the media and to discuss the suspicions that were being raised about their possible involve-ment. They were taking a beating in the Colorado papers and some of the national press, and they didn't like it. We scheduled the interview for late the next morning, New Year's Day. It would be a coup for CNN because the Ramseys had said nothing publicly since their daughter's death.

For security reasons, we decided that I'd go out to Patsy's parents' home and escort the Ramseys to CNN headquarters in Atlanta. I'd be interviewing them, and this way I could get a feel for them, and they might get a better sense of me.

During the taxi ride out to Roswell, I found myself ambivalent about doing the story. The news reports out of Denver seemed a little sordid. As a parent, I wasn't crazy about the prospect of confronting another parent about the death of a murdered child. But as a journalist, I knew that the story had some titillating elements.

First I met Jeff Ramsey, John's brother, and when John and Patsy came in, I offered my condolences. Patsy looked like she'd been crying for the last forty-eight hours, but you could see her personality through the grief.

John looked like an ordinary guy, but he was clearly subdued. As one of his friends later described him, "He's like wallpaper; he just sort of disappears sometimes."

Patsy, John, and Jeff sat in the back of the taxi while I joined the driver up front. John Ramsey responded to some of the few questions I asked during the forty-minute trip. There were awkward silences, long stretches where we all said absolutely nothing. Occasionally Jeff Ramsey would answer the questions I directed to John and Patsy.

Once we were in the sixth-floor conference room of the CNN Center, Jeff sat off to the side, lending moral support, as mikes and cameras were adjusted. I checked the eight to ten basic questions I had scribbled down. But in fact, I had no idea if the Ramseys were going to read a prepared statement or just take my questions. Distraught, seeming uncomfortable and a little frightened, the Ramseys nonetheless seemed ready. They sat there not as two individuals but as a couple.

My plan was to let them explain why they were talking to CNN since they'd been avoiding the media, then take them through the story chronologically. Like any newsman, I was afraid that after some question they might say, "Enough. I won't answer anything else," and walk out.

"Why did you decide to talk now?" I began.

"We have been pretty isolated . . . but we want to thank those people that care about us," John answered. "For our grief to resolve itself, we now have to find out why this happened."

I tried not to ask my questions in an accusatory tone. For all I knew, they were entirely innocent. Eventually I asked, "How did you happen [to find the body] in the basement?"

"One of the detectives asked me and my friend to go through every inch of the house to see if anything looked out of place. In one room in the basement—I opened the door—there were no windows in that room, and I turned the light on, and I—that was her."

From time to time Patsy would start to answer a question, and John would complete the sentence or the thought before Patsy could finish. He seemed to dominate the interview to a small but noticeable degree.

"Most laymen who don't understand would say, 'Why?'" I said. "Why [retain] an attorney?"

"It's not just the attorney," John replied. "We are also assembling an investigative team. I want the best minds this country has to offer to help us resolve this."

"Mrs. Ramsey, you found the note."

"I couldn't read the whole thing. I'd just gotten up. We had a back staircase and I always come down that staircase. The three pages [were] across the run of one of the stair treads. It was kind of dimly lit. I started to read it and it was addressed to John. 'We have your daughter'—it just wasn't registering. I don't know if I got further than that, and I immediately ran back upstairs and pushed open her door and she was not in her bed and I screamed for John."

John Ramsey said, "I read it very fast. I was out of my mind. It said, 'Don't call the police,' you know, that type of thing; I told Patsy to call the police immediately, and I think I ran through the house a bit. We checked our son's room; sometimes she sleeps in there."

Then Patsy continued: "We were just frantic, and I immediately dialed the police, 911, and [the operator] was trying to calm me down and I said our child had been kidnapped. I was just screaming, 'Send help, send help.' I dialed some of my very closest friends. 'Come quickly.' [Then] an officer was there. It seems like an eternity, but I know it was just minutes."

"Have the police interviewed you?" I inquired.

"I had questions all day the day of her death," Patsy replied. "For hours they asked us questions trying to get a chronology. I can scarcely recall exactly what happened. They were very compassionate, trying to help us help them. Boulder is a small, peaceful town, unlike Atlanta or New York or LA, where this, God forbid, is a much more frequent occurrence. This does not happen in Boulder."

Toward the end of the conversation, I broached the issue of their possible involvement: "The police said there is no killer on the loose. Do you believe it's someone outside your home?"

Patsy answered, "There is a killer on the loose."

John added, "Absolutely."

"I don't know who it is," Patsy continued. "I don't know if it's a he or a she. . . . But if I was a resident of Boulder, I would tell my friends to keep. . ."

Patsy started to cry.

"It's OK," John Ramsey said.

Then she continued, "Keep your babies close to you. There's someone out there."

Patsy's answer seemed dramatic, if not melodramatic. I was taken aback by it. But as a TV correspondent, I thought, Boy, there is a sound bite.

Then I began, "Speculation on talk shows will focus on you—"

"It's nauseating beyond belief," John cut in.

Then Patsy added, "America has just been hurt so deeply with this—the *tragic things that have happened. The young woman who drove her children into the water, and we don't know what happened with O. J. Simpson— America is suffering because [it has] lost faith in the American family."*

A minute later, speaking about JonBenét, Patsy said, "She'll never have to know the loss of a child. She will never have to know cancer or the death of a child."

"We learned when we lost our first child," Ramsey said, "that people would come forward to us and that sooner or later, everyone carries a very heavy burden in this life. And JonBenét didn't carry any burdens."

Soon afterward, I ended the interview. They had spoken for almost forty minutes, and it wasn't as if they were eager to leave. They'd done more than I had expected from a husband and wife who had just buried their daughter.

Then they took a taxi back by themselves.

When the interview aired that afternoon throughout the states, I added that John Ramsey had confirmed that duct tape was found on his daughter's mouth. Yet he said he didn't see cord around her neck—maybe because he panicked in picking up her body, screaming, running upstairs, hoping she was still alive.

—Brian Cabell

The interview took up half of the network's news broadcast and was a major scoop for CNN. By that evening, stations in Denver wanted Brian Cabell to go live from Atlanta to discuss the interview, and CNN's affiliates across the nation said they needed more footage of the Ramseys in Atlanta.

Reporters in Boulder and Denver started asking Cabell, "Why were the Ramseys afraid to face us here? Why did they talk to a reporter who hasn't really covered the case?" Cabell couldn't answer. He wondered the same thing.

Charlie Brennan, a reporter for the *Rocky Mountain News* who was assigned to cover the Ramsey story, was at a New Year's Day party when a law enforcement source alerted him to the CNN interview. Brennan switched channels from the football game he was watching and heard Patsy Ramsey say that a killer was loose. He thought immediately of Susan Smith, the South Carolina housewife who had accused a black man of carjacking and kidnapping her two little boys but was later found to have killed them herself.

Two days later, at a January 3 news conference, Boulder's mayor, Leslie Durgin, after consulting Police Chief Tom Koby, would say, "People have no need to fear that there is someone wandering the streets of Boulder looking for someone to attack. Boulder is safe."

JonBenét STRANGLED WITH CORD

SOURCE SAYS GIRL'S MOUTH TAPED SHUT; SEXUAL ASSAULT CONSIDERED A POSSIBILITY.

JonBenét Ramsey's killer placed duct tape over the 6-year-old's mouth and tightened a cord around her neck until she died. Authorities also found evidence that the killer may have sexually assaulted the little girl.

Patricia "Patsy" Ramsey, 39, JonBenét's mother, has also retained an attorney. Patrick J. Burke of Boulder will represent her.

—Charlie Brennan and Lynn Bartels
Rocky Mountain News, January 1, 1997

Late in the afternoon of January 1, Detectives Larry Mason, Steve Thomas, Tom Trujillo, Ron Gosage, and Jane Harmer left Boulder for Atlanta, where they had arranged to work out of the Roswell Police Department. The detectives had learned about Fleet White's heated arguments with John Ramsey, and they were shocked by the Ramseys' CNN interview. It seemed to contradict what they were being told—that the Ramseys were grieving and unavailable. The police had originally planned to leave for Atlanta the next day to check alibis and start background interviews with the Ramseys' extended family. Now, however, Commander Eller felt that someone in the household might be ready to talk, so he gave the detectives his own credit card to use for purchasing airplane tickets and ordered them to be in Atlanta by midnight.

The next morning, January 2, at 8:30 A.M., while Steve Thomas went to a Super Cuts to get rid of his goatee and long hair, vestiges of his stint in the narcotics division, Detectives Harmer and Trujillo interviewed Fleet and Priscilla White in their Atlanta hotel room. White now seemed to be replaying in his head everything he'd seen and experienced on December 26. Pacing, White told the officers what had happened at the Paughs'. Patsy's father, Don, had to intervene and get everyone to quiet down, White said. Now he was confused and wondered why he hadn't seen JonBenét's body in the wine cellar when he'd looked in earlier that morning and Ramsey had seen it hours later. After the interview, the Whites flew back to Boulder.

In Boulder that same morning, Detective Patterson met Gary Merriman in his Access Graphics office. Now, the questions focused on John Ramsey. "Did John do this?" "Did John feel . . .?" "Isn't it a fact that John resented JonBenét's being in pageants?"

"I don't find those questions legitimate," Merriman told Patterson.

Gary Merriman had spent fourteen years working in the criminal justice system as an institutional psychologist, including several years at the Florida Department of Corrections. He knew a leading question when he heard one.

Merriman had to keep reminding the detective that his knowledge of John Ramsey was limited to his conduct at the office. "I've never been in John's house," Merriman repeated. When the interview was over, he was photographed and fingerprinted. Merriman also agreed to give the police handwriting, hair, and blood samples.

Meanwhile, Pete Hofstrom had received a fax from Bryan Morgan. The attorney restated his objection to testing that would destroy physical evidence. Morgan noted that this would include tests of bodily fluids and secretions.

Hofstrom realized that the Ramseys' attorneys did not want to deal directly with the police and that he was becoming their go-between. He could only assume that John and Patsy Ramsey had been told about Eller's plan to withhold their daughter's body. Hofstrom felt that any cooperation the Ramseys gave the police would be highly guarded.

At midmorning on January 2, LaDonna Griego, a director of All Star Pageants, supplied ABC's Denver affiliate with JonBenét's December 17 All Star pageant video. Meanwhile, an amateur video of JonBenét's December 22 shopping mall appearance sponsored by America's Royal Miss popped up on local TV. Sunburst Pageants in Atlanta provided another television outlet with its video of JonBenét performing in a white Ziegfield Follies outfit.

That evening in households across the country, video clips of an angelic-looking six-year-old posturing suggestively in elaborate costumes appeared on network news programs. The televised images drew the public into a world that most Americans never knew existed. The CNN interview had made JonBenét's death a national issue. The pageant videos added a sexual element to the story, which would transfix the country.

One day in the spring of 1996, Pam Griffin, who had met Patsy and JonBenét at a pageant, telephoned Kit Andre, a dance instructor she knew. "I've got a great child for you," Pam said.

"Wonderful," Kit replied.

The following week, Patsy and JonBenét drove to Kit Andre's dance studio in Westminster, twenty minutes southeast of Boulder. Kit had danced in the Broadway companies of *Hello, Dolly!* and *Peter Pan* and had ballet credits in Paris and London, including a featured role under Dame Margot Fonteyn.

Patsy began by saying, "My little girl's name is JonBenét. I'd like her to learn to dance and sing."

Kit was impressed by Patsy. She was attractive and outgoing. However, JonBenét, who wore ordinary play clothes, was very plain-looking, she thought.

"Hello, JonBenét," Kit said. "How are you?"

JonBenét answered, "Hi," and smiled.

Patsy told Kit that JonBenét participated in pageants and she herself had been in pageants when she was younger. She'd brought an audiotape of music—"I Want to Be a Cowboy's Sweetheart."

There was no time for JonBenét to learn the basics of ballet or tap, but Patsy said they needed a song and dance by summer. "And whatever it takes, I'll pay for it," Patsy said. Private lessons were $100 each, Kit told her. That was no problem, Patsy replied.

The following week when JonBenét came in, she was dressed in shorts and sandals. Kit still didn't see anything special about her, though of course she wasn't made up and her hair wasn't styled.

"Can I join you?" Patsy asked.

Kit told her it would be better if she didn't, and Patsy stayed in the reception room.

Kit had three dance studios, mirrored and with 12-foot ceilings. She took JonBenét into the "small" one, which she used for private lessons—it was almost a thousand square feet.

First the two of them talked about music, then Kit played the audiotape Patsy had brought. She suggested a few movements to Jon-Benét—a little rhythm, then a few steps.

This child can dance, Kit thought. She's good.

"Now let's try this." A few more steps.

"Now try this," JonBenét said with a laugh, mimicking Kit.

The hour went by fast.

"How's she doing?" Patsy asked when the two of them emerged from the studio.

"She going to be wonderful," Kit said.

"Can she sing?"

"Well, not really," Kit admitted. "We're going to have to work on that."

"Can you see her tomorrow?"

Kit scheduled three lessons a week. Patsy was determined that JonBenét would be ready for the summer pageants.

During the third lesson, Patsy knocked on the studio door. "It will be better if I'm here," she insisted. "I've done this before."

Kit could see that she was miserable in the reception room and was eager to show her *exactly* how the routine should be staged.

Kit watched, and she thought that Patsy wasn't great but she was OK. She knew every note, every step, and every gesture. From that moment on, Kit couldn't get Patsy out of the studio.

As Kit taught JonBenét, Patsy would tap her feet, take notes about the movements, and then write down the words "I want to be a da-da-da cowboy" so that JonBenét could practice at home.

One day during the second week of lessons, Patsy got up and danced with JonBenét, showing Kit what she wanted. Side by side, mother and daughter. Suddenly Kit could see that Patsy wanted to be up there herself, wanted JonBenét to perform the way she longed to do. Kit now knew that she'd have to teach the song Patsy's way.

Finally Kit said, "Patsy, you're a pest. Teaching is my job. Sit down and be quiet."

Then one day Nedra, JonBenét's grandmother, showed up. She frequently came to Boulder to visit her family. Kit thought she was adorable—a small woman with a big personality. Nedra sat in a direc-tor's chair and couldn't stop talking about when Patsy was a little girl in the pageants and then when she was Miss West Virginia and com-peted in the Miss America pageant.

For her part, JonBenét was eager to learn and a quick study. Never once did she say, "I don't want to. I'd rather go play."

"You're going to be a star," Kit told her. "But if you want to be a star someday, you have to be a star right now."

Kit soon discovered that JonBenét had a wonderful personality. She understood how to gesture and use her shoulders as she danced. Kit was struck by how smart and talented she was. But she also understood that JonBenét was performing because her mother wanted her to, not because she wanted to. JonBenét wasn't one of those kids who had seen someone dance and decided, That's what I want to do.

JonBenét died that winter. I never saw her in a pageant. Never saw her in the cowboy costume. Never saw her do the routine I taught her until I saw that pageant video on TV.

I saw Patsy at the memorial service in Boulder. She was pathetic. She was nothing. She was all gone. And that was the first time I ever saw John Ramsey. He was talking about what had happened. Kind of matter-of-factly. Calmly. Patsy was crying in the chapel aisle—some friend was holding her up. I wasn't going to intrude on her—she was too distraught. But then she came over to me. Of course I went to her and hugged her.

"She was a fabulous child," I told her. "She was a star."

I've looked at that pageant video several times. They made JonBenét look like a clown. Someone else taught her those pseudo-adult movements, the provocative walk, the poses, all of it.

The pageants were Patsy's gig. JonBenét was her alter ego. Patsy had the money, she had the costumes, and she had the kid. She could relive her own pageant thing. You got the picture right there. Patsy didn't have a sense of proportion about how this should fit into her child's life. What I saw on the pageant video . . . you don't do that to a six-year-old.

—Kit Andre

On Thursday afternoon, January 2, Denver police chief David Michaud attended a meeting of the Colorado Consortium for Community Policing, of which he and Boulder police chief Tom Koby were board members. Michaud was surprised when Koby walked in. If the Ramsey case had been his, he would have skipped this meeting. Michaud understood that Koby was facing the biggest case of his career. His own department had three hundred detectives on call and over eighty homicides a year. Koby probably had sixteen detectives in Boulder, and if he had two homicides a year, that was a lot.

Michaud also knew that expertise came with volume. When Koby left the meeting early, Michaud followed him out the door.

"If there's anything we have that you need," he told Koby, "feel free to ask. We'll give you anything we've got."

"Thanks," Koby replied, and continued down the hall.

On Friday, January 3, Bill Wise learned about the list of questions Detective Arndt had faxed to Bryan Morgan before the Ramseys left for Atlanta. Arndt's questions had put both the police and the DA's office in an embarrassing position. If the press ever got hold of the list, it would look as if the police were counting on the Ramseys' attorneys to help them interrogate the prime suspects. Also, Arndt may have asked one question too many: "What had JonBenét eaten before she went to bed?" That was enough to tip off the Ramseys' lawyers that the autopsy findings may have contradicted information the couple gave Detective Arndt on December 26.

Pete Hofstrom and the police considered the Ramseys prime suspects. There was no evidence of an outsider in the house when Jon-Benét was murdered. No one in the neighborhood had seen or heard anything suspicious—other than the reported scream that had come from the direction of the Ramseys' home. More important, the police had told Hofstrom that the autopsy showed semen on the corpse. To the police this suggested John Ramsey's involvement. The ransom note had been written on the Ramseys' own pad of paper, and since there was no evidence of an intruder, who besides one of the Ramseys could have written it? Even so, Hofstrom knew it was still too early to focus *only* on the Ramseys.

It bothered Hofstrom that Eller had pushed the FBI out of the case and that Koby had rebuffed Sheriff Epp. Hofstrom knew the Boulder police needed all the help they could get. He didn't yet know that Koby had also rejected an offer of help from the Denver police.

In Hawaii, DA Alex Hunter was briefed on the autopsy, though John Meyer wouldn't be submitting a written report for weeks. Hunter was told that his staff members DeMuth and Pickering had very different impressions of the autopsy findings than Detectives Linda Arndt and

Tom Trujillo, who had observed the procedure for the police. The detectives apparently thought they had a clear-cut "Gotcha!" DeMuth and Pickering said the results of the forensic tests might be weeks away. Until then, it was less than certain that the case would come together.

Hunter was surprised to learn that John Ramsey was being represented by Morgan and Haddon and that Patsy had retained a separate attorney, Patrick Burke, a sole practitioner with offices in both Boulder and Denver. Hunter wouldn't have expected a legal team of this caliber to be assembled so soon. Also, Haddon, one of the most powerful lawyers in the state, had hired Pat Korten, a former spokesman for the Department of Justice, as a press representative for the Ramseys. It was clear to the DA that the Ramseys' attorneys were looking not just to protect their clients' rights but also to influence public opinion.

A few days earlier, the police had asked Hofstrom to help them persuade Patsy Ramsey to give them a second handwriting sample. The value of her first sample was questionable because she had been heavily sedated when it was taken. In his role as go-between, Hofstrom called Bryan Morgan on behalf of the police, and the two met for breakfast. The meeting was cordial, but Morgan said he'd have to talk to Patsy. By Saturday, January 4, the Ramseys had returned to Boulder from Atlanta, and Morgan called Hofstrom to say that Patsy had agreed to give another handwriting sample as long as it was not taken at any law enforcement facility. Morgan said that Patsy would be available in an hour and suggested Hofstrom's home in Boulder. The Ramseys, Morgan said, didn't want to be seen by the media as suspects buckling under to the police. When Hofstrom hung up, he called Eller, who agreed to Morgan's conditions. Within the hour, several detectives met Patsy and John Ramsey at Hofstrom's home.

In the dining room of Hofstrom's 1950s-vintage ranch-style house, the police asked Patsy to write out the text of the entire ransom note, including the passage about JonBenét being beheaded. When she got to that passage Patsy broke down. She couldn't finish, and John Ramsey became testy—not because his wife was being ill-treated but because she had to write the same thing again and again. Under the circumstances, the police agreed that he could give his third handwriting sample the next day, Sunday, January 5.

That same evening, Priscilla and Fleet White, who had returned to Boulder the previous day, were interviewed again by Detective Arndt. Priscilla told her that Patsy was affectionate with her children and was always with them. She also said that John and Patsy weren't big drinkers but may have had one or two glasses of wine at their Christmas dinner. White told the police he now remembered that when John pulled open the door to the wine cellar, he might have shouted out "Oh my God, oh my God" a split second or so before he turned on the lights. It was likely that his eye was caught by the white blanket on the floor, reflected in the ambient light. Yet, White told the detectives, when he had looked into the darkened room earlier that morning, he had not seen anything.

Arndt asked if she and Detective Harmer could interview the Whites' children, Daphne, six, and Fleet Jr., seven. The Whites agreed, and the interviews were held a few days later. Since the Whites had a key to the Ramseys' home and because of Fleet White's angry outburst at John Ramsey after the funeral, the Whites were asked to give blood, hair, saliva, and handwriting samples, which they willingly provided. The Whites would soon become the most cooperative witnesses. Some detectives believed they might unknowingly hold the answers to key questions. Over the next two months, the Whites would be interviewed eighteen times, often at their own request.

RANSOM NOTEPAD FOUND

Investigators found the notepad used to write a ransom note in JonBenét Ramsey's murder inside the Boulder family home, sources close to the investigation confirmed.

"It was made of the same kind of paper used in the ransom note, and it may have imprints from the pen used to write the note," said a Boulder friend of the Ramseys.

A small foreign group reportedly wrote the letter addressed to John Ramsey. "I don't think it said anything really bad about John, but it had a problem with some of the countries his (American) company was doing business with," said one friend. "They really . . . said how they would kill his daughter."

—Alli Krupski
Daily Camera, January 4, 1997

★ ★ ★

I spent four years as a spokesman for the Justice Department. I'm accustomed to working with lawyers and major criminal cases. I've handled a number of terrorism cases: an airline hijacking, the Achille Lauro case, the Cuban riots at the Atlanta federal penitentiary. In cases like this, you're always faced with strategic considerations.

There are things I would like to have done in the Ramsey case that, for legal reasons, were impossible. I had to bite my tongue.

Even before I arrived in Boulder, the Ramseys had decided that their friends should not become involved. The hope was that this might prevent the case from turning into the media circus it nonetheless became.

I flew to Boulder on January 2 from Washington, D.C., to meet John and Patsy Ramsey. The firm I was working for, Rowan and Blewitt, had been hired by Haddon, Morgan and Foreman, a criminal law firm that had been retained by the Ramseys' business attorney, Mike Bynum, the day after the body was discovered.

The next day, January 3, I met with the Ramseys at the home of one of their friends. I was struck by their grief. It was so enormous, so emotional. In that first meeting, John tended to accept the recommendations of his attorney on strategy. In the coming days and weeks, he became more assertive about making decisions that might not have been what his lawyers would have preferred.

By then I had seen their CNN interview on January 1. They were sincere, grieving parents who were terribly upset. That came through with crystal clarity. Within twenty-four hours, the networks and news organizations had purchased rights to the pageant video and still photos. They paid a hell of a lot of money, and there wasn't much we could do about it.

On January 4, I was at Peter Hofstrom's house with Patsy when she gave her second handwriting sample to the police. They had her sit down and write the precise wording of the note. "Speaking to anyone about your situation, such as the police, FBI, etc., will result in your daughter being beheaded." For all the anguish it caused, I don't think it helped the police one bit. They were taking a woman who had just lost one of the most precious things in her life and rubbing her nose in it, almost gratuitously. Patsy wasn't able to write it. The whole episode just sickened me.

Our strategy from the very first day of my involvement and for some weeks thereafter was to minimize the opportunities for the Ramseys to be photographed. Our highest priority was to keep a low profile—let them grieve privately and work their way through all of this. That's why we agreed they should stay with their friends.

John Ramsey had a strong desire to track down the killer, through newspaper ads, public appeals, or whatever was necessary. That has been his desire from the very first day.

He hired several investigators, along with John Douglas, an ex-FBI profiler. Douglas was very emphatic about putting some of the ransom-note handwriting out there to try to get people to pay attention and pass along tips that might lead to the killer.

Keep in mind that you reach a point where, without police powers, you can't go further. For legal reasons, a lot of what I'm talking about had to be put on the shelf.

—Pat Korten

On Saturday, January 4, Alex Hunter returned from his vacation in Hawaii. The DA knew he wasn't coming home to a case that would be solved in a few weeks. That same day, the police finished their search of the Ramsey house. For nine days they had fingerprinted, vacuumed, and gathered evidence. All of it would be analyzed and tested by the Colorado Bureau of Investigation and the FBI in the coming months. The initial search warrant had been extended three times, and over eight hundred items were taken into custody. Detective Byfield, for example, had found duct tape that looked similar to the tape found in the wine cellar on the back of two paintings, one of which hung in JonBenét's bedroom. The police would later learn that this tape had been placed on the frames by Better Light Photography Studio in 1993 and didn't match the tape Ramsey said he had ripped off JonBenét's mouth.

The Ramseys' home, which had a red brick Tudor façade, contained 6,866 square feet of living space, and nearly filled a half-acre lot. There was no fence surrounding the property. The front of the house was built in 1927, and the rear was added later and had been remodeled several times over the years. A back elevator had been replaced with a spiral staircase when the Ramseys renovated the house in 1992. The floor plan was a maze, and the decorating was unusual: flowered carpets, thick white moldings, vivid colors.

The living room furniture was reproduction French provincial, and the walls were hung with 19th-century French and English oil paintings. A floor-to-ceiling Christmas tree stood on a handmade rug. Just beyond the living room was the sun room, with leaded-glass windows, which looked out on the street. Its walls were covered with a forest landscape mural. A Chippendale dining table was 10 feet long. A wrought-iron sideboard had a marble top. Patsy told many of her guests that it had been purchased from Tiffany's in New York, though Tiffany's sells jewelry, table settings, and decorative pieces but no furniture. At the rear of the house was the family room, with a Chinese needlepoint rug, silk-covered club chairs, and wall units in which family memorabilia were displayed.

In the white-and-gray kitchen there was a large built-in refrigerator and an island counter. Copper pots hung from a ceiling fixture, and there was an eating area with three bar-height chairs. To the side was a butler's pantry. The garage held the usual assortment of drills, saws, and tool chests. Skis hung from a ceiling rack.

Behind the kitchen, just inside the patio door, a spiral staircase led to the second floor. On the second floor landing were a stacked washer and dryer in a closet, a sink, an ironing board, and a microwave on a countertop. From this landing there was direct access to three bedrooms and a playroom. A staircase led to the third-floor master bedroom.

JonBenét's second-floor bedroom, with a porch overlooking the south yard and patio, was closest to the spiral staircase. The room had a hand-painted hat motif, and the nursery rhyme "Hey, Diddle, Diddle" was painted on a carved corner cabinet. The police had removed a small piece of carpet in front of the night table between the matching English burl walnut single beds. To the left of the bed, the police had removed two additional pieces of carpet. At the foot of JonBenét's bed there was a hand-painted locker that matched the fabrics in the room. All of JonBenét's sheets, pillowcases, and bedcovers were taken into custody by the police. Fingerprint powder was everywhere except on the painted hooks of a trompe l'oeil hat rack stenciled on the closet doors.

JonBenét's closet was stuffed with clothes. A small TV set with a built-in VCR sat on a shelf inside her closet. Other shelves held dozens of cartoon and Shirley Temple videos. To the right of the closet stood a pageant trophy as tall as the light switch. Another trophy was even taller. There was a floor-to-ceiling Christmas tree in the room too. In her bathroom hung an original pastel, called *Tea for Two,* by a Boulder artist.

JonBenét's pageant costumes were stored in her half-sister Melinda's bedroom, a few feet away. There, skirts, hats, boots, and dresses filled the closets and shelves. The drapes, daybed, and walls were done in a matching pattern of red roses and vines. The book *The 7 Spiritual Causes of Ill Health* lay on a hand-painted table. John Andrew's room, color coordinated with vertically striped fabrics, was next door to Melinda's. There, the police removed two more pieces of carpet.

Burke's bedroom was also on this level but was separated from the landing by the children's playroom. The wallpaper depicted World War I fighter planes, and a large wooden propeller hung over the small windows, which afforded minimal daylight. Two TV sets and a VCR shared a bookcase with a fish tank. Learning programs such as *Practicing Landing* and *First Few Hours of Voyage* sat beside his computer on a shelf.

The third-floor master bedroom had a cathedral ceiling and a view of the Flatirons. A framed print of red flowers hung over the fireplace. The king-size bed had a 4-foot-high hand-carved headboard. A Rider workout machine sat beside an exercise bicycle. A corner desk held a computer. Displayed on the floor and shelves were twenty-three of JonBenét's pageant trophies. In a children's play area stood a 5-foot-tall pageant trophy next to one that measured 8-feet-1.

A bookshelf contained such titles as *Children at Risk, Children All Wide World Straight Talk,* Tom Clancy's *Red Storm Rising, It Ain't as Easy As It Looks,* and *The National Geographic Society Index.* On another shelf: *The Cancer Conqueror: Incredible Journey to Wellness, New Cures for Almost Every Major Disease,* and FBI profiler John Douglas's 1995 memoir, *Mind Hunter.* On a night table were *When Goodbye Is Forever: How to Deal with the Death of a Child* and *Learning to Live Again after the Loss of a Child,* by John Bramblet. Apparently John Ramsey had explored a good deal of popular literature on death and mourning since the loss of his oldest daughter, Beth.

In every room of the cluttered basement, the police found the cast-off possessions of six people: old lamps, toys, beach balls, Easter bunny outfits, pageant decorations, a painter's easel from Patsy's recent art classes at CU, a Halloween lantern. Nothing was put away neatly. In the basement hallway, a scarecrow was pinned to a wall.

The police removed the suitcase they had found beneath the three side-by-side windows at the rear of Burke's train room. They also removed the windows themselves and the exterior window grate. The suitcase had no dust on it, and a few pieces of broken glass lay on top of it. Inside, they found a blanket with what turned out to be John Andrew's semen on it.

A little carousel rocking horse and child-size blue-and-red chairs stood against one wall. The train set was mounted on a platform in the center of the room. On one wall were three framed movie posters: *Star Trek, Somewhere in Time*, and a third poster of Spencer Tracy and Frank Sinatra in *The Devil at 4 O'Clock*. Leaning against the wall was a poster of *Agatha Christie's Death on the Nile*. In the small storage closet where Fleet White and John Ramsey had looked just before JonBenét's body was found, the police found a plaque with the lettering SBTC on it.

Down a short hall was the boiler room, which had a utility sink and an exposed ventilation duct leading to the street. At the rear of that room, a door led to the wine cellar. The door and its painted jamb and frame were removed by the police. Just outside the room, they found two partial sets of golf clubs belonging to John Ramsey. Inside the room was a large corrugated box with six partly used cans of interior paint and seven more gallon-size interior paint cans. Built into the floor was a safe. A greenish-blue tarp lay over it. A bicycle missing its front wheel was propped up in one corner beside some lumber and other construction material. Throughout the house the police had ripped out every toilet, looking for evidence in the plumbing traps.

The evidence taken in the search was itemized on thirteen hand-written pages, which were signed by Detective Byfield. Every notepad and pen in the house was taken. Among the 132 items in the first inventory were the Avalanche sweatshirt and the blanket that had covered JonBenét's body. Detective Everett photographed a shoe imprint that was discovered in a powder-like substance next to where JonBenét's body had been lying. Inside the wine cellar, fibers, hair, and the pink *Barbie* nightgown were collected. Just outside the room, there were wooden shards near an artist's paint tray that also held part of a broken paintbrush; several paintings, one of which Patsy had done in Michigan, of flowers in a box on her porch; rope; string from a sled; and down the hall on a counter, a red pocket knife. Black sheet metal, wire, vacuumed hair and fibers from almost every room of the house, bedding, street clothes, underwear, prayer books, Christmas gifts, pieces of glass from the broken window, toilet tissue, toilet seats and lids, books, and newspapers were also collected. The list grew longer by the day. Patsy's and John's clothing, camera, computers, and 180 videotapes were hauled away in box after box.

Before the police left, they photographed every inch of the house and all its remaining contents. On January 30,1997, a judge signed another warrant allowing the police to search for pornography on the hard drives of the seized computers. During the last days of June 1997, there would be a third search of the Ramseys' house.

In Atlanta, the visiting Boulder detectives found they couldn't escape the media even in that city. If they so much as drank coffee in a restaurant, some reporter would appear beside them. When they called CNN producer Mike Phelan to request transcripts of the Ramseys' New Year's Day interviews, Art Harris, an investigative reporter for the network, called back. Harris told Larry Mason he'd be more than happy to deliver the transcripts. That evening, January 2, in the restaurant of the detectives' hotel, Harris sat down, opened his laptop, and started questioning Mason about the Ramsey case as Detectives Thomas and Trujillo looked on. Mason scolded Harris for misrepresenting his intentions, and Harris apologized. Then he handed Mason a transcript of the edited videotape, which the police could easily have downloaded from the Internet.

Steve Thomas, a former SWAT team officer and a by-the-book detective who was conducting his first murder investigation, was furious when he saw Mason and the CNN reporter together. That evening, in his phone report to Eller, Thomas mentioned Mason's meeting with the CNN reporter.

Thomas and Mason had already been quarreling. Soon after they arrived in Atlanta, Thomas needed some colored pens and paper and asked Mason to get them. Mason refused. "Look, I'm the supervisor," Mason said. "If you don't like it, I'm sorry, but that's just the way it is." The case was nearly a week old, and with the pace and pressure, tensions were getting to both officers. They had known happier times together. When Thomas was involved in a shooting as a member of the SWAT team, it was Mason who signed the recommendation for Thomas to receive a medal of valor.

During the three days that the Boulder detectives were in Atlanta, they interviewed John Andrew and Melinda Ramsey. Then they visited Lucinda Johnson, John Ramsey's first wife and Melinda and John Andrew's mother; Lloyd Sandy, a friend of Nedra's; Rod Westmoreland; and several former neighbors of John and Patsy Ramsey. Before they went back to Boulder, they also spoke with Nedra and Don Paugh and with Rev. Harrington at the Peachtree Presbyterian Church and visited the funeral home in Marietta and JonBenét's grave.

On Saturday, January 4, when the detectives' work was almost completed, Mason, with Eller's approval, gave an interview to a local reporter and issued a press release provided to him by the Boulder PD.

January 4, 1997

Press Release
[Boulder Police Department in Atlanta]

During our investigation the news media and local press have also researched the Ramsey family and their ties to the Atlanta area. If any of you have uncovered information that may be of value in this case, we would appreciate your forwarding the information to the investigators at the Boulder Police Department. We are asking that if any citizen has information that could be of assistance in this case, that they call 1-800-444-3776.

When Mason returned to his hotel room that night, he found a fax from Eller telling him to cancel the interview. Eller gave no explanation. Mason phoned his boss and said he'd already done the interview. He had received the fax after the fact, he said. Eller said he didn't believe him. Meanwhile, unknown to Mason, CNN, citing an unnamed source, had reported that the Ramseys had agreed to an interview with the Boulder police.

When the Boulder detectives returned home and reported to headquarters the next evening, Eller called Mason upstairs to Chief Tom Koby's office. As soon as Mason saw Sgt. Robert Thomas, Jr., of internal affairs, he knew he was in trouble. When Greg Perry, the police union president, walked in a few minutes later, his fears deepened.

Eller told Mason to sit down. "I'm fine standing up," Mason replied. Eller again ordered Mason to sit down. This time he did.

Eller accused Mason of leaking to CNN the fact that the Ramseys had agreed to an interview with the Boulder police. This was information Eller said he had personally given to Mason on the phone when Mason was at the Roswell, Georgia, police department the night before. It was, said Eller, information that nobody else knew. Mason denied the charge. He said he had not released any unauthorized information.

"You're lying," Eller said. "I know for a fact you did."

"I'm not lying," Mason shot back. "You're absolutely wrong."

At this point, Koby had to calm him down. And then the chief suspended Mason. A few weeks later, he would be reassigned to patrol.

"Don't sell your house," Mason said to Eller as he left. On the spot, he had decided he would sue both Eller and the department for false accusations and wrongful suspension.

As Mason drove home, he brooded on the Ramsey case. He wanted to interview JonBenét's brother, Burke. His own children often didn't remember awakening during the night and being put back to bed. Mason wanted to ask Burke about his dreams that night. Sometimes kids wake up to something and go back to sleep believing they've had a dream. That was the kind of question he wanted answered.

The next day, Monday, January 6, Bryan Morgan, one of John Ramsey's attorneys, told Eller that someone from "his [Morgan's] side of the table" had disclosed the information to CNN. Despite this information, and though Eller had information that could have caused him to believe he had wrongly accused Mason—and though news of Mason's suspension had not yet been released to the media—he did not change course. That afternoon Mason retained Marc Colin, an attorney who specialized in representing police officers. Two days later, Colin discovered that the Roswell police, unknown to Eller or Mason, routinely taped all incoming and outgoing phone calls. That information was relayed to Boulder internal affairs investigator Robert Thomas, who learned from the tapes that Eller had in fact told Mason nothing about the information that CNN aired.

Despite this evidence of Mason's innocence and Eller's duplicity, it would take a year before Larry Mason was completely exonerated. He had been relieved of his duties so early in the investigation that he hadn't yet transcribed his taped interviews or completed his report for the period after JonBenét's murder when he was on the case—December 26, 1996, to January 5, 1997. Not until December 1997 would Chief Koby publicly apologize for Mason's suspension. It would be another six months before Mason was asked to submit his report.

In contrast to what occurred with Mason, John Eller had bonded with most of the rank-and-file officers. Even though he had risen to become part of management, he had never forgotten his days as a street cop. Unlike many of the commanders, Eller still wore his gun. Every New Year's Eve he would hold a party and invite the entire department. None of the brass showed up, but his home was always wall to wall with officers. They'd eat, drink beer, and sing while Eller played the guitar. He took an interest in his officers outside of work and knew the names of their wives and kids. In the coming weeks and months he would use his own credit card for purchases that detectives needed on short notice. He opened an account at the Red Robin restaurant so they could eat around the clock. Eller would tell the detectives, "Forget about what you're seeing on TV or reading in the papers. Do your job." He would shield them not only from the press but from his growing problems with the DA's office.

On Saturday, January 4, Eller had met with the DA's staff to discuss a number of subjects, including the escalating media coverage. The press was stepping up its accusations of sloppy police work done during the first days of the case, allegations that Alex Hunter's staff felt were justified. Even though some of the reports were inaccurate, Eller told the DA's people that rather than correct them, Chief Koby wanted his department to provide as little information as possible to the press. Everyone on the law enforcement side—from the coroner to the DA's office to the police department—knew that the integrity of the case had to be protected. What they disagreed on was how to go about protecting it from the media.

By now, the press had reported that JonBenét's skull had been fractured, that she'd been garroted, that the ransom amount was an odd figure, and that the paper used for the note had come from inside the house. During the meeting, Eller said that these leaks would jeopardize the case.

He said flat-out that he suspected Hunter's office of the leaks. He didn't trust them. Bill Wise, who had dealt with the media for twenty-five years, told Eller that he and Chief Koby were overreacting. The DA's office, he admitted, had always been more open with the press than the Boulder PD. Hunter, who had just returned from his Hawaiian vacation that day and had not yet been completely briefed, suggested that his office could take some of the pressure off the police by using its open relationship with the media. Chief Koby called Hunter later in the day and agreed.

The most sensitive potential problem facing the police was the fax that Detective Arndt had sent to the Ramseys' attorney. It was sure to leak and to embarrass not only the police but Hunter's office as well. Bill Wise, who could hardly disguise his contempt for the Boulder PD, told Eller that Arndt's fax was an even dumber mistake than trying to withhold JonBenét's body. And by the way, Wise added, he understood that the press might already have wind of it.

"If you keep talking like that, we'll kick you guys out of the case," Eller replied furiously. Wise thought Eller was behaving like a kid threatening to take his bat and ball and go home.

Wise then suggested a way to cope with the "Arndt problem." He proposed telling selected members of the media that a list of "housekeeping" questions had been submitted to the Ramseys via their attorneys, as an interim measure until formal interviews could be conducted—such questions as "When is milk delivered to your house?" "How many times has Federal Express delivered a package?" "When was the handyman last at your home?" These were, of course, all fabrications, including the date when the police had submitted the questions. The press was sure to gobble it up, but Wise was troubled. He had never before deliberately misinformed the press.

That same afternoon, Pat Korten, the Ramseys' press representative, met with John and Patsy at the Fernies' home. Korten's job was to take the pressure off the lawyers so that they could concentrate on lawyering; he would deal with the media.

The Ramseys told Korten they wanted to release several non-pageant photos of JonBenét so the public could see her as she really had been—a sweet, normal kid, not much different from any other little girl her age. Korten told them that given a choice, all the media—newspapers, magazines, and TV—would use a pageant photograph. It was simply too late to manage JonBenét's image. Korten pointed out that all the TV networks and tabloid shows had representatives in town. He told the couple that their daughter's murder was sure to become the next media circus after the OJ business.

Korten then asked whether John and Patsy planned to attend church the next day. By now he knew that they were enthusiastic and regular attendees of St. John's. He also knew that their presence or absence would make news. His first suggestion was that Patsy and John stay home, but Patsy wanted to go to church to thank her friends for supporting her. Korten said he would see to it that their appearance didn't get out of control.

Later that afternoon, Korten called the major media outlets and asked what their intentions were for covering the services. Almost all of them said that if the Ramseys attended church, they would be there. Many journalists felt the call was an invitation.

Korten then visited Rev. Hoverstock and offered to help keep the press under control. He said he would do what he'd done hundreds if not thousands of times in his career: he would tell the press, "You're here to get a picture. I'm here to see that everything is done in a way that doesn't cause embarrassment or turn this into a zoo. Let's work together."

Korten arranged with Hoverstock to have the entire congregation leave the church by the front door, which opened onto the street, not the side door, which was usually used. That way the press would get their pictures and the integrity of the service would be preserved.

On Sunday, January 5, I attended church, and again I was late. I parked in the back and walked around the building. There, standing out by the side, was Jim Barbee, a parishioner. He gave me a hug—something he'd never done before. As we hugged, I looked over his shoulder and saw a sea of cameras. Behind them was another sea of satellite trucks.

I was taken aback. I'd never have imagined it. I was speechless.

In front of the church were more media. Some twenty of these people showed up every Sunday for the next few weeks. Later they stayed across the street, but that first time they were right on the sidewalk.

Jim stayed outside, and I went upstairs to the balcony. That Sunday, the bishop was there. Later I found out that Burt Womack, the bishop's right-hand priest, had been scheduled to visit and bless the new members, but he had a medical emergency. That's why the bishop was at St. John's that week.

The bishop said he was there to support Rol. He talked about the dignity of suffering, that God was with the family, and that God was also with the person who had committed this murder.

Rol's voice was husky that day, as if he had a cold. He said the only things holding him together were his cup of tea and his cross. Then he told the congregation that there had been a lot of unkind talk on the radio. He wanted us to know that the Ramseys had nothing to do with the death of their daughter. He asked the congregation to form a corridor along the path outside the front door of the church to show support for the Ramseys as they exited.

When the service was over, Barbara Fernie came out with Patsy on her arm. John and the rest of the Fernies were behind them. I left the balcony.

As I walked out the front door, I saw everyone lining up. A stranger was helping them form a line. I later learned that he was the Ramseys' press representative. I was startled. I stood aside, and without really thinking, I became part of the corridor and the gawkers.

The Ramseys stopped at the front door and talked to the bishop before they walked down this corridor formed by the congregation. They looked devastated. Patsy was limp, possibly because she was sedated. But what really broke my heart was seeing Burke. He came out first, with a little friend. These two little boys with all these crushing people around. That wasn't fair.

At coffee, I saw the Ramseys as people for the first time. They were surrounded by friends and well-wishers. I didn't speak to either Rol or the Ramseys. Somehow I felt there was something shameful about all of this. All of it—the case, the press, the church's place in it. Even if you had nothing to do with it directly, it wasn't good. Then John Fernie pulled his car around in the alley and they all left.

A few minutes later, everyone was talking about the media, calling them sharks. I remember that there was a universal disgust.

When I left by the back door, suddenly somebody with a camera jumped out at me from behind a bush. I look nothing whatsoever like Patsy.

As I drove home, I started to understand the terrible conflict of interest I felt. I thought church members would feel ill at ease talking to me. If you're devoted to the free access of information in this society—which you are if you work for a newspaper—and you also have confidential information from fellow church members, there's a direct conflict of interest.

That night I saw the TV coverage of the scenes at church. I was appalled. It looked so staged. I felt sorry for Rol. He seemed to be a fly caught in a web. I didn't know what to think of John and Patsy. Everyone looked horrible. What happened at St. John's that Sunday was clearly orchestrated. It was not spontaneous. The church had been used.

But the media became the thing the members focused on. And that's when my conflict became the most excruciating. I felt violated. By the press. By my own church. I felt like my church was just looking for somebody to hate. They really wanted to hate whoever had committed this crime, but they didn't know who that was, so the media was the next best target.

Later I asked a reporter friend of mine, "How did this happen?" He told me he'd gotten a call from Pat Korten, the Ramseys' press representative, telling him to arrive at St. John's at a certain time. He said everyone had been called.

The hypocrisy was clear: Korten had us form a cordon in order to shield the Ramsey family from the media circus that he himself had instigated. I felt the church had fallen into the hands of a master manipulator.

—Niki Hayden

★ ★ ★

I was standing out there that Sunday, taking pictures for my paper. I knew Pastor Rol. He looked at me the same way he was looking at all the media—with complete contempt.

When most of the press had left, he came over to me. "Why do you have to do this?" he asked. I told him that this was my job. I had to put food on my family's table.

He didn't respond. He seemed not to understand me. Then I added, "I'd much rather be photographing elk in the mountains. That's what I really like to do."

—A news photographer

7

On Sunday morning, January 5, John Ramsey was still angry about what Patsy had been put through the previous day when she gave her second handwriting sample at Pete Hofstrom's home. However, as he had promised, he gave four of his own samples to the police before going to church with his wife.

Now that the Colorado Bureau of Investigation had determined that the ransom note was written on a pad that came from the Ramseys' house, the police had to obtain unsupervised and casual handwriting samples from the family and their friends. Analysts would need a variety of specimens to compare with the ransom note. Just before the Boulder detectives left Georgia, they asked the Roswell police to search Don and Nedra Paugh's garbage for the family's handwriting samples and any other useful evidence that John and Patsy might have left behind.

Meanwhile, Detectives Gosage and Harmer had gone to Charlevoix, Michigan, to search the Ramseys' summer house, a two-story white Victorian overlooking Round Lake, where they moored a powerboat, the *Miss America*. They kept their sailboat, the *Grand Season*, at nearby Lake Charlevoix. The detectives were looking for evidence that someone had attempted to contact the Ramseys with the intent of harming them. The police hoped that the Ramseys' caller ID telephone devices, answering machine tapes, computers, or mail might hold some clue about who might have murdered JonBenét. Perhaps there might be other evidence related to the crime scene. Also, they would contact several people about the Charlevoix Little Miss pageant. The police were hoping to learn more about JonBenét's pageant activities. In all, the detectives stayed in town for three days. They discovered nothing useful.

When DA Alex Hunter returned from his vacation and was briefed about the case, he took an interest in the pageant aspect. He learned that Pam Griffin, who sewed JonBenét's pageant costumes, had been the first to shed light on the subject, when Mason interviewed her the day after the murder. Since then the police had discovered that a dozen or so families in Boulder County participated in pageants. Hunter asked to see the pageant video of JonBenét that was making headlines. He knew nothing about children's beauty pageants and had never seen such a display. The tape made him blush.

The police had found out that few of JonBenét's school friends or their parents had been invited to watch her compete. The pageants were a separate world from the rest of the Ramseys' life.

During the winter of 1995 and the first months of 1996, JonBenét had competed in her first pageant, at the Twin Peaks Mall, just twenty minutes from Boulder. The judges ignored her. Not long afterward, Patsy entered JonBenét in the Colorado State All Star pageant in Denver. John, Patsy, Nedra, and Burke were in the audience to cheer her on.

Pam Griffin told the police that when she first spotted JonBenét performing at the All Star pageant, she saw that Patsy didn't know how to apply pageant makeup or style her daughter's hair. When Jon-Benét presented herself in front of the judges, she mouthed oohs and aahs and rolled her eyes in a very amateurish way. Even so, Pam thought she showed promise. Pam, who was there to watch another six-year-old whose costumes she'd designed, introduced herself to Patsy, and they realized they lived only twenty minutes from each other. Pam suggested that she could make a few alterations to the party dress JonBenét was wearing. Patsy accepted the offer. "Do whatever you need to do to make it look better," she said.

Patsy enjoyed visiting Pam Griffin's simple home in Longmont. She would walk in, kick off her shoes, and watch several seamstresses assemble costumes in Pam's basement workshop. Sometimes Patsy would bring lunch for everyone. Other times she would sit out on the patio with Pam and talk about her battle with cancer or her worries over JonBenét's incontinence. Patsy told Pam that JonBenét often waited until an emergency was imminent and as a result was still having accidents. Pam said that when her own daughter, Kristine, was small, she also used to wait until the last possible second and sometimes miscalculated. Patsy complained that JonBenét had frequent infections that were hard to clear up because her underpants were always wet. JonBenét would often fall asleep in her bedroom in front of the TV set, she said, and Patsy would wake her up at around midnight to make sure she used the bathroom. Sometimes Patsy was just in the nick of time, but sometimes she was too late. Pam understood how aggravating that could be for a mother.

In all, Pam Griffin made half a dozen outfits for JonBenét, some of which cost as much as $600. Several of the outfits were not typical pageant attire but more like theatrical costumes. One day Patsy's mother, Nedra, who occasionally came to Pam's house with Patsy, showed her a photograph of an outfit with marabou and glitter. Nedra said it was just right for "Patsy's doll baby," as she like to call JonBenét. She thought it would be perfect for the "Anybody from Hollywood" category at the next pageant, where the children could dress as Shirley Temple or Charlie Chaplin or any other star—or, for example, a Las Vegas Ziegfeld Follies showgirl, which Nedra thought would be perfect for JonBenét.

When JonBenét was at Pam's house, she loved to look over Kristine's collection of pageant crowns. One was displayed in a cabinet by the Griffins' front door, and two others sat under a blue light in a waterless fish tank near the stairs to the basement workshop. Soon JonBenét knew all about the various types of crowns. Standard crowns, metal circlets with scalloped top borders, often elaborately decorated, were usually awarded to division winners. Kristine's pink "bucket crown," a standard crown with a fabric cap enclosing the center, was the prize of all prizes, presented only to the overall pageant winner.

Kristine, a high school senior, loved to coach JonBenét. She taught her the walk, the wave, and the pageant poses on a small mock runway in her basement. The girls giggled, surrounded by the hundreds of costumes Pam was working on for girls all over the country. Off to the side was one of Kristine's 8-foot-high trophies. When the girls got tired of pageant practice, they would plop down on the couch and play Nintendo, even though Patsy was paying Kristine $20 an hour for pageant lessons.

On June 1, 1996, JonBenét appeared in the Royal Miss state pageant in Denver and a month later in the Gingerbread Productions of America pageant, where she won her division title, Mini Supreme, Little Miss Colorado. JonBenét loved hanging out at pageants and playing with the other kids. When Nedra was there, she would give each of the children playing with JonBenét a dollar to buy cookies. Patsy gave presents of hand lotion to all the little girls.

Most pageants include a "Most Photogenic" or "Photo Portfolio" category, where the entrants are judged solely on their photographs. Pasty decided it was time for JonBenét to have a portfolio, and Pam Griffin recommended a photographer, Randy Simons, who could make a six-year-old look twenty. When a pageant favored the seductive look, Pam told Patsy, Simons was the best.

On the July Fourth weekend, Patsy entered JonBenét in the Royal Miss pageant in Denver's Sheraton Hotel. Patsy, her sister Pam, and Nedra all attended. During the three-day pageant, Patsy did a lot of socializing with the other mothers. There was a pizza party, a "Your Favorite Star" party, and a party where all the mothers and daughters dressed alike. Tammy Polson, one of the mothers, talked to Nedra, who chatted cheerfully about "her girls." That's how Polson learned that Patsy and her sister Pam had both competed in the Miss America pageant.

In the Denver event, JonBenét's song and dance routine and makeup were perfect. Everyone at the pageant considered her a strong competitor. Mark Fix, a photographer, could see that she wanted to win. He couldn't put his finger on how he knew it, but her desire to win was obvious, he said.

JonBenét won overall in her division but missed the best-in-pageant prize that she wanted. Though she was disappointed that she took home only a small trophy, she didn't cry.

The Gingerbread nationals were scheduled for August 1996. Pam offered to take JonBenét to the pageant, since it conflicted with the Ramseys' family reunion. Patsy said no thanks, Pam told the police. JonBenét had to be with her family, Patsy said. This would be true for any pageants that conflicted with family events. Moreover, when the Royal Miss nationals moved to Las Vegas, Patsy told Pam that John didn't want his six-year-old daughter exposed to Vegas.

The Ramseys spent the summer of 1996 in Charlevoix and Atlanta, where JonBenét entered the Sunburst pageant, which cost Patsy over a thousand dollars in entry fees. JonBenét was first runner-up in each of the nine categories in her division, but once again she missed out on the overall title. Her performance, Pam said, was still a big accomplishment. It was her first experience competing against top-of-the-line entrants—southern girls who already held numerous titles.

After Sunburst, both Patsy and Nedra called Mary Clark, the pageant director. They wanted to dissect every detail of JonBenét's costumes, music, and performance. Exactly what were the judges looking for? How could they hone a competitive edge for JonBenét? It was obvious to Clark that Patsy was ready to spend any amount of money, go to any length, to ensure a win for her daughter.

Kristine said that JonBenét often gave her prizes away to new-comers who hadn't received any. But unlike many regulars on the circuit, she didn't appear at pageants she'd previously won simply to present trophies to new winners. Instead, Patsy had JonBenét compete all over again at those pageants.

One day Patsy suggested to Pam Griffin that they make a few dresses to have on hand for kids who showed up in "civilian" clothes. Patsy said she didn't want some little girl to feel humiliated. Pam felt that Patsy was a genuinely kind person but also knew that Patsy always wanted to make the best possible impression on people.

On December 17, JonBenét entered the All Star Kids Christmas pageant at the Airport Holiday Inn outside Denver. Her parents watched her win several titles, including Little Miss Christmas. When it was all over, John carried all her trophies and costumes to the car. It would be her last pageant

For me it started when my daughter, Kristine, was barely two. Now she's nineteen. My daughter had big blue eyes, dimples—she's everybody's idea of a little doll. One day we were in Montgomery Ward looking for an Easter dress. A lady came up and said that if I would let my daughter model in the store's Easter fashion show on that coming Saturday, they'd give us the dress. I had no idea what would happen. That Saturday, Kristine just strutted. She showed off her bonnet and how to take off her gloves. She really enjoyed it.

I enrolled her in a little rinky-dink ballet school in Boulder. Then I saw an ad in the newspaper for the Our Little Miss pageant. Kristine entered

the pageant and did everything wrong, but it was fun. She won a T-shirt and a little trophy. A little girl winning a beauty pageant is like a little boy hitting the T-ball.

Within a few years, Kristine was winning state and national competitions—Miss Photogenic, Miss Talent. An agent found us, and my daughter started doing newspaper and magazine ads for stores like Foley's. She was soon making $75 an hour. Afterward, she did three movies and some national television commercials. She appeared in a John Denver movie, a Perry Mason movie, and Mary Higgins Clark's Stillwatch. *It wasn't long before she had a nice bank account for college and paid for her own car. The whole experience built a lot of self-esteem for her.*

I really enjoyed watching my daughter compete and act in television shows. The funny thing is that nobody except the people who go to the pageants even knows about them. There is Little Miss Colorado, All Star Kids, Cinderella, Royal Miss, Miss this, and Miss that—so many pageant systems. It's like franchising.

I've thought a lot about JonBenét's death. It's true that if a child is found dead in her own home, that alone makes the parents suspect. I don't understand why the police didn't immediately have officers come and examine John and Patsy's bodies for scratches or whatever. Why would you not do all that? I was a registered nurse; I know it's not wrong to suspect a family in a case like this.

—*Pam Griffin*

On Monday morning, January 6, photos of the Ramseys emerging from St. John's and meeting the bishop were on the front page of all the local papers. When Alex Hunter saw the newspapers and TV coverage, he said to himself, These people aren't getting good advice. His common sense told him that people don't behave this way in deep mourning. The scene at the church looked staged, and raised questions in his mind about the Ramseys' role in their daughter's death.

Trip DeMuth and Pete Hofstrom told Hunter that they too were puzzled by Sunday's events.

RAMSEYS RECEIVE POLICE QUESTIONS

Police on Sunday submitted a list of written questions to the parents of child murder victim JonBenét Ramsey, but authorities said a formal interview still must be conducted.

To do otherwise "would not be treating them as they (police) treat other suspects," said assistant district attorney Bill Wise.

On Sunday, Wise said, "A few questions were submitted by the police in writing that are housekeeping questions. They go to, "When is the milk delivered to your house? How many times has Federal Express delivered a package?"

—Charlie Brennan and John C. Ensslin
Rocky Mountain News, January 6, 1997

On January 6, the police department notified the local press that Chief Koby would discuss the Ramsey investigation on January 9. It would be a roundtable discussion. Koby selected reporters that he had worked with before—all of whom would still be working there after the sensation died down. "The rest of the press will be going on to their next firefight," Koby said. Boulder's city-owned TV Channel 8 would broadcast the event.

Koby wanted to speak directly to Boulder's residents and to respond to the questions *he* believed should be answered. He wasn't interested in Dan Rather or some other media star shouting questions at him, and he didn't want his words filtered through the press.

Rocky Mountain News reporter Kevin McCullen was named one of the roundtable invitees. Immediately he was bombarded with calls from all three TV networks for on-air interviews before and after Koby's telecast. That was when McCullen realized that JonBenét's murder was more than just a Boulder story. Joining McCullen would be Ron Baird of the *Colorado Daily*, Alli Krupski of the *Daily Camera, The Denver Post's* Mike McPhee, and Jim Burrus, managing editor of the *Boulder Planet*.

That same day, January 6, was the first day of school after the Christmas break. TV news trucks would be parked in front of JonBenét's school for days, and Charles Elbot, the principal, had hired security people to make sure that the reporters hung back and didn't frighten the children by shoving microphones into their faces.

That morning, before school opened, Elbot and several teachers checked the halls to make sure that none of JonBenét's artwork or poetry was displayed where a reporter could grab it.

Elbot held an assembly before classes began. He was straightforward with the children. "In life," he said, "difficult things happen, and part of the challenge we're left with is not only trying to find our own way through the difficulty but to help others."

During recess that day, Elbot walked around to see how the students were doing. A second grade girl came up to him and said, "If I died, no one would care."

"What do you mean?" Elbot asked.

"You know. If I die, there wouldn't be all these people around—there wouldn't be all this fuss."

"If something happened to you, I would care and your parents would care and your friends would care," Elbot replied.

"Yeah, but all the people . . . the world wouldn't care."

"That's not true."

"The reason people care about JonBenét is because she was rich, and pretty, and things like that."

It struck me, listening to this child, how much of her self-worth was affected by the media attention to this story. I suppose if you grow up with TV, then what's important is what the media says is important. And the question is how deeply self-worth is influenced by that. To that little girl, being noticed or ignored by the media was more powerful than the attention of significant people in her life.

The next day, a teacher ran into my office. A Japanese TV crew was on the playground and starting to interview the kids. A local crew had told them it wasn't right, but the producer ignored them.

I put a stop to it. I asked the two Japanese producers to come to my office, then I called the police. Two hours went by and the police didn't show up, so the producers left. The tabloids called. I was offered money to appear on talk shows. I found reporters walking around the halls of the school and had to escort them out.

When the media throws this spotlight on you, the appearance of things begins to change. Instead of giving you a clearer picture, the media transform the situation. This little girl's death became so much more complicated because of the impact of the media. It seems that respect for people's lives, a certain level of common decency, is sometimes lost in the struggle for the story.

These are a few of the things I learned from being involved in this tragic event. I've never had occasion to deal with the media to this extent before. And I wonder how my life has been altered by this.

As a result of this difficulty, there was a deeper sense of community within the school, among both the kids and the adults. We shared a real loss and some real sorrows and fears.

In May, before the school year ended, the Student Council held a tree planting ceremony. Patsy and John came. We wanted to honor the life and death of JonBenét. We needed to find a way to touch her and to let go.

—Charles Elbot

I started to worry that the media would be knocking on my door. The people from Time and Newsweek were reasonably polite. I told everyone I didn't have any comment. There were days I turned off the phone. Some of my friends had reporters camped outside their front doors. At school, they even photographed the children through windows. It was gross. It really felt as if we were under siege.

You know, when you pay reasonable taxes as we do here, you ought to have a reasonably professional police department. At first I thought they had this case under control. I felt there would be an arrest in the first four or five days. The police didn't say much, and I thought that was good. They were getting the job done.

I knew they were having long visits with lots of people. All the questions they asked concerned possible child abuse or sexual abuse.

Then the police left a message at school that they wanted to talk to Megan. No rush, they said.

When we did get together, they acted like they were doing us a favor. After school one day, Detective Linda Arndt came to our home with her partner. I didn't give Megan a lot of warning, didn't want her worrying about it. I just told her to answer the questions as best she could. We all sat down on the family room floor and introduced ourselves.

They showed her their badges and she held them. That was kind of nice. Then they got out their tape recorder. Which didn't work. They sat there and fussed with it for five minutes or so. Megan was getting nervous. It seemed stupid that they couldn't get it to work.

Finally they decided to go on without the recorder. They told Megan that they wanted to find out who did this to JonBenét and that it would help them to learn more about what JonBenét liked to do, what games she enjoyed playing.

Megan started describing different games. They weren't familiar with any of them. Pearl beads—they'd never heard of that until we showed them. Then they asked about make-believe games.

"We were going to play Kitty," Megan said.

"What's that?"

Kids have all sorts of different names for games, but these officers didn't seem to know any of them.

"Did you ever have any secrets?" they asked. "It's OK to have secrets. But now that JonBenét is dead, you don't have to have any secrets."

Then they wanted to know what the girls did in the bedroom, what they did in the bathroom. They even talked about bath salts and bath oil and shampoo.

Had they ever been down in the Ramseys' basement? Megan said they'd been down there once, but it wasn't a place they played in regularly.

What struck me was that these detectives obviously didn't have kids. They didn't seem to understand that a child's automatic first response to a lot of questions is "I don't know." Who broke the glass? I don't know. As a parent, you learn to ask follow-up questions if you really want to get information.

Then I sent Megan outside to play so I could talk to them privately.

By then, Bill McReynolds—Santa—had been on TV, and I remembered what JonBenét had told me about Santa visiting her. He just kept looking weirder and weirder to me on TV. I told them what JonBenét had said—that Santa was going to pay her a special visit after Christmas.

They said thanks. They would check into it, they said. Again, no follow-up questions. No probing for details that I might be forgetting.

I'm not a professional, but those officers didn't seem highly competent. I read a lot of mysteries, but I also know life isn't like a mystery novel.

Later I found out that they had never interviewed any of JonBenét's inner circle. Two other kids who were close to her seemed to have fallen between the cracks.

So I called some close friends of the Ramseys, and they had the Ramseys' investigator call me. I told him the whole story. He seemed much more interested. He had a lot more questions about JonBenét's demeanor than the police ever had.

—Barbara Kostanick

Bill McReynolds, who had been Santa at the Ramseys' Christmas party for three years, was placed on the list of suspects the day after the murder. Patsy and John told the police that he was close to their daughter.

The police learned that McReynolds had arrived at about 5:00 P.M. for the Christmas party the Ramseys gave on December 23. Christmas was a big production for the family. There were decorated artificial trees in every room on every floor, and the living room tree was covered with magnolias. The previous year, JonBenét had taken McReynolds on a tour of the house—to her bedroom and even down to the basement, to show him where the family kept their Christmas trees. She showed him her scrapbooks and called McReynolds "old Sam."

This year McReynolds, still frail from the open-heart surgery he'd had a few months earlier, brought his wife, Janet, along. He mixed with the guests, read little poems about each of the children, gave them their gifts, and spoke with most of the guests. An hour and a half later, he and his wife left the party.

On January 3, Detectives Pat Wyton and Nathan Vasquez interviewed McReynolds. He told the officers that on Christmas Day, his daughter Jo and her children had come to visit at their cabin near Nederland, in the mountains twenty miles west of Boulder. Later that day, Janet's daughter, Vicky, her husband, Al, and their daughter, Willow, arrived. A number of friends stopped by as the day went on, McReynolds said. Then he and his wife went to bed at about 10:00 P.M. They confirmed each other's story that neither of them had left the house that night. The next morning, December 26, they rose about 8:00 A.M., they said, and stayed home all day. Without some independent corroboration, Bill and Janet McReynolds remained suspects.

In the early evening of January 6, neighbors gathered at 789 15th Street, the home of Patrick and Mary Vann, who lived three houses away from the Ramseys. They were meeting to discuss the implications of JonBenét's murder for their neighborhood.

The Vanns had been away in Texas on a holiday visit when Jon-Benét was murdered and had returned on December 27. Mary Vann knew Patsy reasonably well. They had met through various charities in which they were both active, such as the University Women's Club. Over the years, the two couples had met at a few parties. The Vanns' yard was the furthest point on the block where JonBenét was allowed to play alone. Patrick Vann used to see JonBenét rollerblade up to their house and then circle back home.

Mayor Leslie Durgin, who worked with Mary Vann at Chautauqua Park, had suggested that police chief Tom Koby be invited to this gathering of neighbors.

"Do we have cause to be anxious?" they asked him.

"There is no murderer loose," Koby said. "I am fairly confident of that." He updated the twenty or so guests on the investigation but never said directly that the Ramseys might be involved. Before Koby left, he invited anyone who might have questions in the future to contact him directly.

Pat Vann felt the chief had calmed everyone. Nevertheless, the next day Vann called a Denver burglar alarm company and had a system installed in the house and on its perimeter.

——•••——

ROWAN & BLEWITT
INCORPRATED

Memorandum

To: The news media
Fr: Pat Korten

John and Patsy Ramsey have cooperated extensively with the police and other law enforcement authorities from the very beginning of their investigation, and this cooperation will continue. Written answers to all of the written questions submitted by the Boulder Police Department have been delivered to them this afternoon.

——•••——

ANOTHER GRIEVING DAD CRITICIZES RAMSEY' 'DEFENSE' CONDUCT

CALIFORNIA MAN RAPS HIRING OF PUBLICIST, CNN INTERVIEW

The grieving father in another high-profile murder case said Monday that he disagrees with how John and Patricia "Patsy" Ramsey have handled themselves in the wake of their daughter's death.

"I think the parents have made some terrible decisions thus far by hiring lawyers and a publicist and refusing to talk to police," Marc Klaas said in an interview aired Monday by *AM Live* on WPVI, the ABC affiliate in Philadelphia.

—Charlie Brennan
Rocky Mountain News, January 7, 1997

★ ★ ★

On Tuesday, January 7, Detectives Wyton and Vasquez went to the Ramseys' hangar and interviewed Michael Archuleta, John Ramsey's private pilot; Richard Bjelkovig, his copilot; and other personnel. The detectives learned that the Ramseys had planned to leave for their Christmas vacation at 7:00 A.M. on December 26. Archuleta mentioned that they had expected to leave their home for the Jefferson County Airport at about 6:30. On Christmas Day, at about noon, John Ramsey had come to the hangar and spent a long time checking the plane and talking to people who worked there. The next day, Archuleta said, he and his wife woke at about 4:30 A.M. He left for the airport at around 6:00.

About ten minutes after Patsy Ramsey called 911 and three minutes after Officer Rick French arrived at the Ramseys' house, John tried to call Archuleta at the airport. Instead he reached copilot Bjelkovig. Ramsey told Bjelkovig that JonBenét had been kidnapped. Archuleta was still en route to the airport. Bjelkovig reached Archuleta's wife at home to tell her the news.

By 6:05 the police, the Fernies, the Whites, and the Ramseys' pilots all knew about the kidnapping, though the ransom note had threatened that JonBenét would die if Ramsey informed anyone. The police were puzzled about why John Ramsey was in such a hurry to tell his pilot that his daughter had been kidnapped.

When Ramsey finally talked to Archuleta that morning, he instructed the pilot not to fly to Minneapolis. Instead, Archuleta was to notify the commercial airline on which Ramsey's children were arriving from Atlanta and leave word for them to call their father. At 1:30 P.M., just twenty-five minutes after JonBenét's body was found, John Ramsey called Archuleta again, at his home.

"She's gone," Ramsey said. "They've killed her." Then he told Archuleta to ready the plane for a flight to Atlanta that evening. Fleet White then called Archuleta at 3:00 P.M. to say that the trip to Atlanta was canceled. Ramsey's flight plans raised more questions for the police: Why had Ramsey called Archuleta so soon after JonBenét's body was found, and why did he want to leave Boulder?

Like so many other questions, these would remain unanswered until the Ramseys could be interviewed.

Also on Tuesday, January 7, Pete Hofstrom and Trip DeMuth were in the courtroom of Boulder County judge Diane MacDonald requesting that the search warrant and supporting affidavits, which included facts about the crime and a list of everything taken from the house by the police, be sealed from the public for ninety days.

Hofstrom argued that in the midst of an ongoing investigation, disclosing crime-scene details known only to the killer and to the police would hamper both the investigation and resolution of the case. Bruce Jones, a Denver lawyer experienced in First Amendment issues, responded on behalf of ABC KMGH—Channel 7 TV and other media outlets. He said that the public deserved to know how the case was being handled. They had been leaked only bits and pieces, and the public was seriously concerned. Tom Kelley, representing the *Daily Camera*, echoed that sentiment. He told the court that the public would only be confident in the investigation if they were given the facts.

Judge MacDonald decided to seal the documents for thirty days or until an arrest was made—whichever came first. A month later, on February 4, Trip DeMuth would ask for another thirty days. Judge MacDonald would grant fifteen.

By now the Ramseys had agreed that JonBenét's nine-year-old brother, Burke, could be interviewed about what he remembered from the night his sister had been murdered. At 9:00 A.M. on January 8, Detectives Harmer, Arndt, and Gosage arrived at the Child Advocacy Center in Niwot to observe the interview. The detectives stood behind a one-way glass window as Boulder child psychologist Dr. Suzanne Bernhard talked to the boy. Patsy Ramsey waited in another room, sobbing, her shoulders shaking. There was no attorney for the family in the room with Burke. Still traumatized from the events of the last thirteen days, the child seemed indifferent. His lack of affect was pronounced. He didn't want to talk about his sister's death. As they played games, Bernhard asked Burke about how they all got along in the family. Delicately she touched on the topics of sexual and child abuse. He didn't respond as a molested child might. When they talked about secrets, Burke said pointedly that if you told someone a secret it was no longer a secret. He didn't seem to be holding anything back, and he appeared to be dealing with the absence of his sister in the expected way. There were several breaks during the two-hour interview, and the detectives took the opportunity to suggest additional topics to the psychologist.

The results were inconclusive. Burke gave the police little information about the night of JonBenét's death that they did not already have. And when they screened the videotape, it was hard to tell if Burke might be hiding anything.

Also on January 8, Detectives Thomas and Gosage interviewed Laurie Wagner, a vice president at Access Graphics. She had been John Ramsey's employee for over ten years. The detectives wanted to find out more about the company and about the relationships among the various employees, including Wagner's relationship with the Ramsey family. They gave no hint that they considered Ramsey a suspect.

At the time, Wagner was not asked for a blood or handwriting sample. A year later, however, in January 1998, the police told her that there was an unidentified print on the ransom note. They asked her to provide palm prints and fingerprints, which she did.

I went to work for John Ramsey in Atlanta in 1986 and came to Boulder in 1990 with a dozen or so other employees. The simplest way to explain Access Graphics is that we are a wholesale distributor of high-end PC computers. We don't manufacture products—we sell the products made by other companies to resellers. We offer support services, consulting services, and teaching. We sell all over the world.

John started Advanced Products Group in Atlanta and merged with Eric Crod of CAD Sources Inc., in Piscataway, New Jersey, and Jim Hudson of CAD Distributors in Boulder to get a competitive edge in the marketplace. The three companies became Access Graphics, with corporate headquarters in Boulder.

CalComp, a subsidiary of Lockheed, acquired 20 percent equity in the new company. Access soon surpassed CalComp in both size and profits. When Access showed rapid sales and profit growth, Lockheed picked up its option to acquire the company.

In 1991 John became president. He recruited young employees and gave them a relaxed, exciting work environment—no dress code, an open-door policy, with everyone on a first-name basis. There were lots of opportunities for advancement. We had very little employee turnover. The average employee age is the mid-twenties.

Then Lockheed merged with Martin Marietta. Now Access Graphics has more than six hundred employees worldwide—over four hundred people working in 70,000 square feet of offices on the Pearl Street Mall. You can sit outside, relax, discuss creative ideas, and listen to the musicians on the Mall. Who wants to be in an industrial park? Boulder is a good place for entertaining clients.

When JonBenét was murdered, we, as a company, got attention that nobody anticipated.

At first the media was looking for some connection with the company. Could there be a disgruntled employee? The sophistication of the reporters differed considerably—the Today *show to Geraldo to you name it. Larry King never gave up.*

One day a tabloid contacted my ex-husband. That's when I knew they were looking at me. When the Star *showed up at my front door, I wasn't shocked. The reporter had this little camera he sort of flipped out from behind his back. They said I was in the Ramseys' home the night of the murder. They said John and I were involved. "We know it, the police know it. People have sworn to this."*

I said nothing. I wanted to hear where they were going with all this. "We know you traveled with John Ramsey."

Of course I did. He was my boss. Why lie? I just closed the door.

—Laurie Wagner

GRAND JURY IN RAMSEY CASE?

The death of JonBenét Ramsey may be one of those rare situations where a grand jury probe may be necessary, legal observers said yesterday.

Bob Miller, the former U.S. attorney for Colorado and a longtime district attorney in Greeley, yesterday called grand juries a strong instrument for breaking logjams caused by the refusal of people to talk or hand over evidence. Miller said it is not commonly understood that police don't have the power to subpoena witnesses or documents, while grand juries do.

"It would be a real tool, if they are road-blocked," said Miller. "It is true that nobody has to cooperate with the police—I mean, you don't even have to be a suspect. You can just tell them to go to hell."

Dave Thomas, district attorney in Jefferson County, assumes the Boulder D.A.'s office has "considered" or "pondered" the use of the grand jury in the Ramsey case.

—Howard Pankratz
The Denver Post, January 9, 1997

On January 9, a local radio station reported a rumor that John Ramsey had confessed. Access Graphics was flooded with calls. Karen

Howard, director of worldwide communications, was in her office trying to come to grips with the possibility that the report might be true. When a local station made the announcement, her boss, Laurie Wagner, went white. Still, Wagner waited, not wanting to compound the problem by acting too quickly. Nevertheless, Howard began to prepare an e-mail to employees, just in case the rumor was true. When it proved unfounded, Howard sent out an e-mail saying that this was an example of how the media should not be considered a reliable source of information.

Detectives Thomas and Gosage were at the Access Graphics office that day, conducting interviews. Among others, they talked to Patsy's father. Don Paugh, who had helped get the company off the ground in Atlanta, continued to work with his son-in-law when John made the move to Boulder in 1991. At the time of JonBenét's murder, Paugh owned a condominium in Boulder, where he spent most of his time, and a home in Roswell, Georgia, with his wife, Nedra, who would often come to Bolder to visit. Paugh's Boulder home was just down the street from a restaurant called Pasta Jay's in which John Ramsey happened to be an investor. When the detectives interviewed Paugh on January 9, he said that on December 18, Jeff Merrick and his wife, Kathy, Jason Perkins, Cameron Hindson, Tom Carson, and Mike Glynn had eaten together at Pasta Jay's. Paugh thought it strange that former Access Graphics employees were dining with a current employee like Carson.

The next day, Thomas and Gosage would follow up and interview Tom Carson at the Access Graphics office. They asked him where he'd been on Christmas night. Carson said that on December 24 he'd taken a United Airlines flight to Chicago and then gone on to Paris, where he spent Christmas Day. Later Thomas was able to confirm that Carson had indeed been on the transatlantic flight at the time Jon-Benét was murdered.

By the evening of January 9, the national press, as well as journalists from England and the Far East, were swarming on the front lawn of the Boulder Public Library, which also houses the studio of Channel 8. The parking lot along nearby Boulder Creek was packed with satellite trucks. That afternoon an arctic cold front had settled on Boulder, and the weather contributed to everyone's foul mood.

The media were indignant. In scheduling his roundtable, Chief Koby had not only snubbed all the national press, which had advised his office of their presence in Boulder, but also seemed to be avoiding local writers who were breaking important stories on the case. It was obvious that Koby had invited only reporters he thought would go easy on him.

When Kevin McCullen of the *Rocky Mountain News* walked into the library's foyer, he was astounded to see more than a hundred reporters who hadn't been invited. Though they weren't admitted, they had gathered in the lobby nevertheless, where rows of chairs were arranged in a semicircle in front of a large TV. Koby and his invited panel were 40 feet away, behind the TV studio door.

"This has to be a joke, right?" one reporter said. To get a shot of Koby, television cameramen and still photographers had to photograph the TV screen.

In the studio McCullen, seated next to Koby, noticed that the chief seemed nervous as he looked over his prepared speech.

Tom Koby was known for a couple of things in Boulder—his hard stand against underage drinking and his firm endorsement of community policing: His officers were expected to know the people in the neighborhoods, listen to their concerns, and educate them on how to prevent crime before it happens. He also took an unusual position for a police chief: he refused to work with the Boy Scouts' Explorer program on law enforcement because the national organization refused to allow gays to participate in scouting programs. Koby rarely wore his uniform, and people who didn't know him would never suspect that he was a cop.

"It is the best judgment of the Boulder Police Department that this is a one-time occurrence. . . . We do not believe we have a serial situation," Koby said at the outset of the roundtable in his Texas drawl. He drew most of his syllables out for an extra beat or two, which gave the impression of a man not in a big hurry. Even tonight he seemed laid-back.

"There have been many stories and much speculation about who killed JonBenét. Prejudging and media hype have never solved a crime. The reality of the situation is that often these types of investigations take time. Again, it is unfortunate those who have anointed themselves as experts have seized the opportunity to offer criticism which has no basis in fact. Over the last five years, from 1990 through 1995, we have had fifteen homicides in Boulder. We have solved thirteen of them. We will not lose the focus of this investigation to respond to meaningless and unfounded remarks." The reporters in the foyer exchanged smirks.

Once the questioning by the panel began, so did the second-guessing by the crowd in the lobby. Everyone seemed to want to shout out a question, but no one did, lest they miss something important. Still, why weren't the favored few asking *this?* Why weren't they pushing Koby on *that?*

According to Koby, a rumor had sprung up earlier in the day—even surfacing on a Denver radio station—that a Ramsey family member had confessed. It was totally false, he said, and it was an example of how the media were making his department's job harder.

"So I am just here to tell you that one of the most helpful things—if you and your colleagues would like to help—would be to back off a little bit, give us some room to do our jobs," Koby told his audience.

Koby confirmed that in their initial search of the Ramseys' house, it didn't "appear" that his officers had looked in the room where Jon-Benét's body was later found. He explained that "this house is a large mansion" and that the officers hadn't reached the so-called wine cellar that morning. Moments later, he insisted, "Most legal experts will tell you, police officials and legal experts will tell you, we've done it just right."

Most of the reporters felt that Koby knew mistakes had been made, but what struck Kevin McCullen was that Koby seemed to believe what he was saying. The chief really *was* convinced the police had done everything right.

"Three things can happen in any investigation like this one," Koby continued. "One, . . . you show up and the person responsible is waiting for you. Second, you never solve the case. Third, it takes a while to work things out. This case [is] an investigation that is complex and complicated and it will take some time to work out."

Mike McPhee of *The Denver Post* asked if the Ramseys had been interviewed.

"We were with the family for quite a period of time during the first day," Koby replied. "There is no way to interview parents at that point in time. It's impossible. So, were we communicating with John and Patsy? We were. Were we interviewing John and Patsy? No. That would have been totally unreasonable."

Then Alli Krupski, from the *Daily Camera*, asked why the police seemed to be responding with more intensity to the Ramsey case than they had to the death of a poor Latino a few weeks earlier.

"I think that is also a media question," Koby answered. "Why has the media given so much attention to this case and literally no attention to the case you just described? I have never, in the twenty-eight years I have been in this business, seen such media focus on an event. It is intrusive, and making it much more difficult to work through this situation."

Earlier in the week, Koby had told McCullen, "It's not OJ and it's not LA here in Boulder. Our guy won't walk." Now McCullen asked Koby to expand on that. "The reference," Koby answered, "is that we are not going to have this case tried in the media."

Someone asked Koby whether John Ramsey's picking up his daughter and bringing her upstairs had contaminated the crime scene.

"No, we didn't lose anything," Koby replied. "We feel pretty confident that we did it right." Again it didn't seem to McCullen that Koby was covering up. He seemed to mean exactly what he was saying.

Jim Burrus from the *Boulder Planet* asked, "How much experience do you, as chief, and does John Eller, as commander of the detective division, have in investigating homicides?"

"I have no experience running a homicide investigation," Koby replied, "but I have twenty-eight years in the business, with a lot of investigation experience. . . . I don't have John's résumé in front of me. [We do] have [people] who are involved in homicide investigations that we have [conducted] over the last several years."

Alli Krupski asked why Koby didn't believe in the public's right to know more about the status of the case. Koby pointed out that the evening's briefing was meant for the people of Boulder because the investigation meant "a great deal" to the local community. "But the reality is this situation is a curiosity to the rest of the country," Koby said. "And quite frankly, it is a sick curiosity in some ways."

To many of the reporters, the police seemed to be saying that there was something dirty about their profession and his office wasn't going to keep them informed.

The criticism from reporters in the foyer was immediate. The verdict was that nobody had really interviewed the chief. "If I had been there, I would have beaten him up," one TV reporter told a local journalist.

Stephen Singular, author of the book on the life and death of Alan Berg that became Oliver Stone's film *Talk Radio*, had been watching Koby on TV in the foyer. When the police chief commented, "The less you know, the easier it is to give advice," Singular wondered whether the case was really so complex that the police weren't going to solve it for a long time. Had they botched it so badly in those first hours that it would never be solved? What were the hidden facts that made the secrecy of the police so imperative?

To Singular, Koby's virtual silence was deeply disturbing. He knew that the information void would be filled with speculation, conjecture, guessing, projection, and fantasy. The talking heads—the so-called experts—wouldn't have read the police reports, wouldn't have talked to witnesses, wouldn't have seen any of the evidence. The wall of silence from law enforcement, Singular felt, would soon be battered by noise from the media. It was a dangerous trend.

8

In the late eighties I went to work for a tabloid newspaper, and now I'm a writer for another tabloid. Before that I was in marketing. Now that I work for a tabloid I get to travel, eat wherever I want to, and stay in the best hotels.

Most of the time I write about celebrities who get drunk and throw up in public—no economic summits or Nobel laureates. When some actor dies on location, you fly there. You're part of a "gang bang." Five or six reporters from your newspaper drop into town with fifteen grand in each of their pockets. You own the fucking place in twelve hours.

I covered O. J. Simpson's criminal trial. Almost everyone who worked for a tabloid covered OJ. One paper offered Kato Kaelin, OJ's houseguest, a quarter of a million dollars for his story. He passed, saying he didn't want to profit from Nicole Simpson's death. Of course at that very moment his agent was shopping a Movie of the Week deal for him. Nicole's parents were selling stuff to the tabs. We all had DA sources, cop sources, drug buddy sources, everybody who had ever fucked anyone. During the Simpson case, you had mothers selling out daughters, sisters selling out sisters. That's how you get cynical.

When The New York Times *wrote that the* National Enquirer *was the Bible of OJ coverage, all the reporters working eighteen hours a day producing those stories got offered better jobs.*

The day JonBenét's pageant video aired on TV, the tabs dumped eighteen reporters into Boulder. Then they hired freelancers and all the private investigators they could find who hadn't been grabbed by Time *or* Newsweek. *Everyone was working twenty hours a day. I was one of the first to arrive.*

*I've never seen the kind of hostility toward the media that I encoun-
tered in Boulder. The residents seemed personally insulted, as if they were
actually involved in the crime—like it somehow had something to do
with them, when it didn't.*

*In the Simpson case, everyone and anyone was lining up to sell their
souls. In Boulder, we all ran into a wall of silence from law enforcement,
from prosecutors, city officials, neighbors, the Ramseys' friends, the Ramseys' enemies, businesses in every area. Money had nothing to do with it.
It was all "Who the fuck are you?"*

*When you can't get the DA's office or the police to talk to you, you go
to friends of the police, to ex-cops and ex-cops who are private eyes. By
now I've spoken to maybe thirty PIs. You don't do anything illegal. You just
ask, "What do you know?"*

*I've always worked against the pressure to deliver a story a week. All I
do is hire more private eyes. Maybe I have four of them working at once.*

*Boulder became a long process, and far from an easy one. It was all
about building relationships. It took time. In some cases, to get to someone, you had to take them information that they didn't have.*

—A tabloid journalist

Tabloid headlines screamed that the Ramseys had murdered their daughter, while the mainstream national and local media restricted themselves
to saying that the Ramseys were not cooperating with the police.

When the Ramseys returned to Boulder from burying JonBenét,
Bryan Morgan, their attorney, wrote to John Eller, offering to make
his clients available for a joint interview on January 18, at 10:00 A.M.
Morgan stated conditions: the police could question Patsy for only
one hour, and a doctor had to be present, since she was still ill; the
location must be somewhere other than police headquarters; the per-
missible topics were to be determined by Morgan's office; and
Morgan himself would select which police officers would conduct
the interviews.

A few days later, Eller rejected the offer. In a letter to Morgan, he said
that an interview under the specified conditions would not be helpful.
"The time for interviewing John and Patsy as witnesses who could provide critical information that would be helpful in the initial stages of our
investigation has passed," Eller wrote. He offered a counterproposal: he
wanted to interview the Ramseys separately on Friday, January 24, at

6:00 P.M., and he would not consider any restrictions on the length or the place of the interviews. Eller waited for a reply.

On January 10, the day after Chief Koby's press conference, Alex Hunter and Bill Wise met to discuss how the DA's office should handle the media. They agreed that Koby's stonewalling had backfired.

"It's shoot yourself in the foot," Wise told Hunter, "then before you get it Band-Aided, you shoot yourself in the foot again." Wise wasn't about to let the police chief destroy his office's carefully cultivated twenty-five-year relationship with the press.

Hunter decided that he would make himself more available to reporters. His office would try to be helpful—not to pass on information about the case, but to stay in touch. The idea was to say to reporters when appropriate, "You're wasting time if you go down that road." That approach, Wise knew, wouldn't entirely satisfy the hungry media, but it might take some of the edge off reporters' antagonism.

Once they had their strategy in place, bookers for ABC's *20/20*, the *Today* show, *Larry King Live*, and *NBC Nightly News* all started to call Hunter. He chatted on the phone with the producers but declined invitations to appear on their shows. When he was ready to speak publicly, he said, he would hold a press conference.

My first memory of death was my father shooting a BB gun and killing a robin. He started crying, and so did I. To this day I don't know why he cried, because it was his choice to kill the robin. I was about ten at the time and I didn't know very much about death.

My father died of a stroke in 1983, when he was in his early seventies. It was hard for me. I loved him a lot, but we had grown apart and hadn't seen each other since I went to the University of Colorado in 1955. In those days I wasn't prepared for death.

My mother died in February of '97, and I was better prepared for that. I'd changed her diapers and had an opportunity to be with her in the last weeks of her life. I was surprised I didn't grieve more than I did. My sisters and I spread her ashes up by the Continental Divide.

My father had been active in local small-time politics in Briarcliff Manor, New York, where I grew up. He was a Republican. Never swore, was kind, and just a good guy. Indirectly, he prepared me for public service. My present wife's father, a former FBI agent, DA, and judge from California, later became a second father to me.

I remember driving west in September of 1955 and coming across the plains, watching the Rocky Mountains rise up before me. Then I reached a mesa just outside of Boulder and saw this little town sitting at the foot of the Front Range of the Rockies. I was looking at a very special place. It was completely different from New York, and I was just eighteen.

In the East, family means a lot, but I soon discovered there was no sense of that in Boulder.

—Alex Hunter

Alex Hunter and Bill Wise met at the University of Colorado School of Law in 1960. Hunter, two years ahead of Wise in school, was already winning top awards in national and international moot court competitions when he made Law Review. Hunter graduated near the top of his class; Wise, near the bottom of his. After graduating in 1963, Hunter became a clerk for Leonard Sutton, chief justice of the Colorado Supreme Court, and traveled around the state working on Sutton's reelection campaign, at a time when justices were elected by popular vote. This got Hunter thinking about public service. In the spring of 1965, he became a part-time deputy DA in Boulder under Rex Scott.

After his graduation, Bill Wise hung out his shingle as a sole practitioner, but in 1967 he traded in his "typewriter and card table" office for a law partnership with Hunter and Richard Hopkins, another friend. Around that time, Hunter and Wise began to buy property in Boulder County. Neither had much money, but both had little to lose. "One dollar down and a dollar forever" was their motto.

They bought a nine-acre parcel in an industrial park for $120,000. They borrowed the down payment and then borrowed the balance— at a time when they didn't have a thousand dollars between them. Soon they were able to buy a residential block zoned for business in downtown Boulder; they planned to put up an office building. Wise told one friend that while they were sleeping one night, the city council rezoned the land to residential and they never made the money they'd anticipated.

In 1972 Hunter started thinking about making a run for governor. Even though he had been more politically conservative than most of his Boulder contemporaries in the late sixties, he became chairman of the Democratic Party in Boulder County. He knew that a traditional first stop on the road to the capital was the DA's office in Boulder, so that's where he decided to begin, though he knew that his first election wouldn't be easy. Wise and Hunter gave up their law practice in June 1972 and sold half of the eleven hundred acres they owned in Lyons, Colorado, for $150,000. The citizens of Boulder contributed $500, and Wise and Hunter put $30,000 of their own money into the campaign. Wise became Hunter's campaign manager. His philosophy was "Bad ink is better than no ink."

Hunter ran against Stan Johnson, an ex-FBI agent and a good DA. Hunter's campaign ads said: "Stanley Johnson has never even tried a case in 3½ years." Wise and Hunter assumed that the voters didn't know that *most* DAs don't try cases.

In September 1972, Alex Hunter won the primary by fewer than 300 votes. With that victory under his belt, he and Wise targeted University of Colorado students, since this would be the first year that eighteen-year-olds were allowed to vote in Boulder County. Among other things, Hunter called for reclassifying marijuana possession as a misdemeanor, while Johnson took a law-and-order stance, saying that marijuana use leads to heroin addiction.

Although *The Denver Post* came out against Hunter, he profited from having positioned himself in an emerging liberal community. He was elected by 687 votes out of some 68,000.

CU students voted en masse, and Hunter's percentages from the campus precincts were enormous. That same year, liberals who advocated controlling the growth of Boulder and protecting the environment won a number of local races and formed a new establishment. Boulder had survived transient hippies and the antiwar movement and was coming into its own. The city elected a black mayor and issued its first same-sex marriage license. Soon some would call it the People's Republic of Boulder.

When Alex Hunter became DA, he named Bill Wise his first assistant. Wise had no desire to try cases, so instead he worked as press liaison and administrator, preparing budgets and signing payroll vouchers, while Hunter tried cases. Wise and Hunter soon learned that the DA's office couldn't fool the press. "If we made a mistake, we admitted it," Wise said.

Hunter had intended to stay in the DA job for four years, then move on, he hoped, to the Colorado attorney general's office, the rung just below governor on the political ladder. Busy with his job, Hunter's land investments failed and he found himself overleveraged. It wasn't long before he had to file for bankruptcy under Chapter 11.

But at the same time he was enjoying the DA's job. He started a

Consumer Unit and a Victim Witness Unit—community services that didn't exist elsewhere in Colorado at the time. At his request, the county commissioners budgeted $5,000 to compensate crime victims. Hunter began to build a relationship with local citizens. Before long he was attracting good people to his office, too, including Pete Hofstrom from the sheriff's department.

Whenever Wise and Hunter heard that someone was interested in running for DA, they would sit down and talk that person out of running, pointing out that with Hunter's record of community services and low crime, no one could unseat him. Hunter also created the impression that he had the money to run a tough campaign, though in fact he didn't.

By 1976 Hunter found himself enjoying being a big fish in a small pond. He ran—unopposed—and was reelected.

In subsequent years, he would put down roots. After the dissolution of his first marriage, which produced three children, Hunter married Margie, a gynecologist, and the couple had two children together. They moved into a ranch-style house with a sunroom that overlooked a small stream. Beyond was a view of the Flatirons and the Indian Peaks. Like most Boulderites, Hunter was physically active. He liked to work up a sweat on the squash court and on his Schwinn exercyle.

After Koby's press conference, Hunter asked his chief deputy, Bill Nagel, to contact out-of-town DAs who had handled two recent high-profile cases—Jeffery Dahmer and Polly Klaas—for any advice they could give. Michael Meese, of the Sonoma County DA's office in California, sent to Boulder a complete report of what they had learned from the Polly Klaas kidnap-homicide case. It included strategies for investigative teams, data processing, and press control. Hunter was particularly interested in the reports on media guidelines.

Bill Wise and his wife, Diane Balkin, a Denver chief trial deputy DA, suggested—independently—that Hunter retain Barry Scheck, a well-respected DNA specialist from New York, as a consultant.* Then Wise thought of hiring Dr. Henry Lee, a Connecticut criminologist who had gained national prominence in the Simpson trial.

* DNA is the abbreviation for deoxyribonucleic acid, the genetic material that is the "blueprint" for the development of every living thing. Except in the case of identical twins, every individual's DNA is unique and unchanging throughout life. It is found in cells from skin, blood, hair follicles (although not the shaft), saliva, and semen. In 1984 researchers at Leicester University in England invented a technique for recording segments of DNA in a pattern resembling a grocery bar code.

Because the media made no clear distinction between police work and the DA's job, Hunter knew that the presence of Lee and Scheck might help his friend Tom Koby present a better image of Boulder's investigative efforts. It might also change what Hunter feared was the small-town image Koby had given the case.

Scheck usually worked for the defense*. He had destroyed the credibility of a police criminalist, Dennis Fung, on the witness stand in the Simpson criminal case. So it might prove tricky to convince Koby to accept Scheck's role in the case. On the other hand, when law enforcement retained experts like Lee and Scheck, they became unavailable to the defense.

Bill Wise spoke to Henry Lee, who said he liked the idea of working with Barry Scheck again. He didn't know if his schedule would permit him to sign onto the case, though. The two men agreed they'd talk after Wise spoke to Scheck.

John Meyer understood that his written autopsy report would be the official record of his findings. As coroner, he was the collector of objective evidence. Though JonBenét's autopsy was only one of the 140 or so he did in a year, Meyer understood its importance and was in no rush to finish the report.

Under Colorado law, there is no provision for public access to autopsy findings until the reports are completed, so no one could legally obtain access until Meyer was ready to file his report. As he worked on it, the Boulder County District Attorney's office prepared for a battle with the media, and by the end of the month, deputy county attorney Madeline Mason, on behalf of Meyer, would argue against release of the report. Meanwhile, Meyer took his time, knowing that the moment it was released, forensic pathologists and the press alike would scrutinize it.

As he wrote, Meyer prepared for the questions that would be asked when he appeared as a witness. Both the prosecution and the defense would be relying on his report, not on his memory, so he knew he had to be extremely thorough in the details.

* Barry Scheck is codirector of the Innocence Project at the Benjamin N. Cardozo School of Law in New York, which uses DNA testing to exonerate inmates wrongfully convicted of crimes. Mr. Scheck is also commissioner of New York's Forensic Science Review Board, an agency charged with creating the states's DNA databank. "In 11 cases where DNA testing has exonerated a wrongly convicted person," Scheck wrote in *Newsweek* on November 16, 1998, "DNA has also led to finding the real perpetrator."

The report Meyer was preparing stated that on the right side of JonBenét's chin, he had spotted a superficial abrasion measuring about 3/16 by 1/8 inch. There was another abrasion on the back of her right shoulder and also several linear hemorrhages across her left shoulder. On the left side of her lower back were two very small dried abrasions, which Meyer planned to describe in his report as "rust-colored to slightly purple in color."

On the back of JonBenét's left leg, roughly 4 inches above her heel, Meyer had seen two more scratchlike abrasions, between 1/8 and 1/16 inch in size. For his report, Meyer wrote, "The examination of the extremities is otherwise unremarkable. On the middle finger of the right hand is a yellow metal band. Around the right wrist is a yellow metal identification bracelet with the name JonBenét on one side and the date 12/25/96 on the other side. A red ink line drawing in the form of a heart is located on the palm of the left hand."

The coroner noted that JonBenét's fingernails had been clipped and sealed in envelopes for further examination and that after examining JonBenét's genitals, he had swabbed her thighs and taken several swabs each from her vagina, anus, and mouth.

Meyer remembered what the police had done during the autopsy. Detective Arndt had stepped away to call Detective James Byfield, who was drafting an addendum to the original search warrant so that the police could obtain additional evidence from the Ramseys' home. Arndt told Byfield that fibers had been found on JonBenét's shirt and that similar material had been discovered in her pubic area. She also reported the green fibers in the child's hair.

At the same time, Detective Trujillo had called the Colorado Bureau of Investigation to ask about the feasibility of lifting fingerprints from JonBenét's skin. It was a long shot, Trujillo learned, because of the skin's comparatively rough texture. Meyer had suspended the autopsy while a CBI technician walked Trujillo through the process. The best approach would be to tent or otherwise encapsulate the body, then to "fume" the remains with Super Glue. The glue vapor would adhere to any prints on the skin and enhance them enough to make them visible under a fluorescent light source. Trujillo ended up using a different, simpler method and lifted one partial print.

Meyer decided not to make note of those events in his report. Afterward, he had continued with an internal examination of the body. He had seen no sternal or rib fractures. He noted that he had found some scattered petechial hemorrhages on the surface of each lung and on the front surface of the heart. These suggested death by suffocation. The bladder, he noted, had been contracted and held no urine. The esophagus was empty. The small intestine had contained fragments of a yellow to light-greenish-tan material, apparently remnants of a fruit or vegetable—possibly pineapple.

The next thing Meyer noted in his report was a fracture of the skull that had not been visible before he removed part of the skull. There was subdural hemorrhaging over the surface of the right cerebral hemisphere and a thin film of subarachnoid hemorrhaging over the whole right cerebral hemisphere. In the report, he wrote about an extensive purple bruise, about 8 by 1¾ inches in area, underlying the skull fracture, as well as a bruise at the tip of the right temporal lobe measuring about ¼ inch square. The tip of the left temporal lobe, Meyer noted, showed only very minimal bruising.

After writing about the brain, Meyer moved on to the upper body. Examining the thyroid cartilage, cricoid cartilage, and hyoid bone, he had found no signs of hemorrhages or fractures.

Meyer remembered that shortly before he completed the autopsy, Arndt had called Byfield again to tell him there was a skull fracture and hemorrhaging of the brain, which were consistent with a blow to the head. She had sounded surprised because when the body was lying near the Christmas tree, there had been no external indication that the child had sustained a head injury.

His report nearly finished, the coroner locked it away in his office safe, where it would await the outcome of the legal battle to keep it from the public.

On Friday afternoon, January 10, a few minutes after Meyer gave an interview to CNN to answer some technical questions about the case, a phone message caught his eye: it was from Tom Brokaw.

Brokaw's producer told Meyer that NBC had an advance copy of the *Globe* tabloid, which featured photographs from the autopsy and crime scene. Were they authentic?

"I can't tell you without seeing them," Meyer replied.

"I'll fax them to you," the producer said.

Meyer studied the faxed images and saw that the photographs were genuine. Some of them had been taken by his staff. Minutes later, Meyer was in Sheriff George Epp's office, one floor above his in the Justice Center. The coroner was shaking.

"George, I've got a problem. I need your help."

Wordlessly, Meyer showed Epp the fax he had just received and his set of original photographs. Then Meyer called Bryan Morgan and told him about the call from NBC and what to expect.

When Meyer left, the sheriff assembled three of his top investigators, Detective Steve Ainsworth, Sgt. George Dunphy, and Lt. Steve Prentup. Step one: interview Meyer and his staff and get them polygraphed. Step two: contact Photo Craft, the lab that had handled the photos, and interview everyone who might have touched either the film or the finished prints. It surprised Detective Ainsworth that the coroner had sent this highly sensitive material to the most ordinary little shop with no special security and no extra precautions. "We take our film to K-Mart to get the two-for-one deal," Ainsworth said half aloud. "I need to go to school on this one." That afternoon, one by one, Meyer's staff was questioned. Everyone agreed to be polygraphed.

It was 9:00 P.M. when Roy McCutcheon, the owner of Photo Craft, told the sheriff's detectives about Shawn Smith, who ran the minilab and personally handled all the coroner's work. *The Late Show with David Letterman* was still on when the officers showed up at Smith's home, a short way up Four Mile Canyon.

"You must know something about this," Lt. Prentup said to him.

Smith told the officers he had no idea how the pictures had been obtained by the tabloid. He agreed to take a polygraph the next day.

The next morning, January 11, the coroner's staff and Shawn Smith were taken to Amich & Jenks, a polygraph firm in Wheat Ridge, just west of Denver. Everyone on Meyer's staff passed except for Patricia Dunn, who had shot some of the photos. Her polygraph results were inconclusive.

Shawn Smith was next.

"Did you arrange with anyone to give or sell those JonBenét photographs to the media?"

"No."

Jeff Jenks, the examiner, had Smith hooked up to the polygraph in an 8-by-10-foot windowless room. Smith's respiration, sweat output, blood pressure, and heart rate readings were fed into a briefcase-size machine.

"Did you give or sell any of those JonBenét photos to anyone outside of Photo Craft?"

"No."

"Do you know for sure who distributed those JonBenét photographs to the media?"

"No."

Jenks excused himself and joined Prentup, who was watching the examination from the next room. "He's either involved or he knows someone who is," Jenks told the officer. He went back inside and sat down next to Smith.

"You really need to come clean on this," he told Smith. "Sometimes things happen in people's lives. They get in a bind."

Smith didn't answer. A few minutes later, Prentup and Smith left for Boulder. Smith still wouldn't talk.

The next stop for the detectives was the Hotel Boulderado, where many out-of-town reporters were staying. Registration records indicated that NBC, ABC, CBS, and all the cable channels were still in town. Prentup checked the list for tabloids. When he saw the *Star*, the *National Enquirer, Hard Copy*, and *American Journal*, Prentup felt as if he were looking into an abyss.

Late in the afternoon, back in his office, Prentup listened to a voice-mail message. "I'd like to give you a hypothetical," said Peter Schild, a respected defense attorney, who had once worked in the public defender's office. "If I had someone who has some knowledge about the JonBenét photos that the *Globe* is publishing, someone who should have known better . . ."

Schild was obviously speaking for someone. Probably Smith, who was under pressure, was starting to crack.

Prentup called Pete Hofstrom, who in turn called Schild.

As any good attorney would, Schild wanted immunity for his client in exchange for his client's full cooperation.

"Schild says it's someone you know," Hofstrom reported back to the detectives.

"No sale," Prentup told him. "We don't like bargaining with someone who's hiding behind his lawyer's skirt. Our terms are full accountability and a complete and honest statement in exchange for our not arguing for any particular sentence. We'll live with the judge's call."

The detectives could tell that Hofstrom wanted to get this incident out of the way. What mattered was solving JonBenét's murder.

On January 14, the day after the *Globe* appeared in supermarket racks, Hofstrom met Schild for breakfast at the Harvest restaurant on

Pearl Street. The detectives knew that Schild's mystery client would also be at the meeting. If the three of them couldn't work out a deal, the client's identity would remain a mystery to the officers.

Schild trusted Hofstrom, who was known to prefer precharging plea bargains, which Boulder's defense attorneys called negotiations. More important to the attorney, however, was Hofstrom's understanding of the human condition, particularly in criminals. They might have done terrible things, but he still cared about them as human beings.

Within an hour, Hofstrom called Prentup: Schild would deliver his client as soon as the plea agreement was typed.

Dunphy and Prentup waited on the second floor of the Justice Center for Schild and his client, Brett Sawyer, a former deputy sheriff, who was now a private investigator handling mostly divorce cases and insurance claims.

Sawyer said to Prentup, "Well, I guess this means I lose my concealed weapons permit." It was his only comment.

Ainsworth escorted Sawyer to what detectives call the hard room—nothing on the walls, no table, only one hard plastic chair coated with Armoral, so slippery that nobody could sit comfortably. The interview was videotaped through a one-way mirror.

Sawyer told them that it began with a phone call the morning of Friday, January 3, when Brian Williams, an editor for the *Globe*, told him, "We're looking for information the rest of the media doesn't have." Sawyer took the job. He would be paid $50 an hour. He claimed he had no idea the *Globe* was a tabloid.

Sawyer suspected that the police had their film developed at Photo Craft, and he went to see his friend Shawn Smith, who worked there.

"We don't work for the cops anymore," Smith told him, "but we do the coroner's processing."

Sawyer told Ainsworth that a moment later he found himself peering through a photographer's magnifying loupe at the internegatives of JonBenét's autopsy and the crime scene photos that had been taken by the coroner's investigator. The six-year-old child was just three weeks younger than his own son and one grade behind him at the same school.

Sawyer waited while Shawn Smith made the prints he'd requested. An hour later, he handed them to a courier.

Two days later, Sawyer told the officers, Brian Williams called and said the pictures were being shown to one of the *Globe*'s experts. Sawyer would be paid his fee of $500, plus a $5,000 bonus. On Saturday, Sawyer told Ainsworth, he woke up to the *Daily Camera*'s front page headline TABLOID OBTAINS MURDER-SCENE PHOTOS. The article said there would be a full investigation and potential felony charges against whoever had compromised the case.

Ainsworth asked Sawyer why he had turned himself in.

"My conscience got to me," Sawyer said. He worried about embarrassing his family.

When Sawyer's interview was over, he agreed to sign his statement. Half an hour later, Ainsworth called Shawn Smith, who continued to deny everything.

"You know Brett Sawyer, don't you?" Ainsworth asked. Then Smith admitted everything.

What struck the detectives was that if Sawyer hadn't turned himself in, Smith would never have talked. A court date of February 20 was set for Sawyer and Smith.

When the *Globe* published the photos on January 13, it promised its readers an exclusive glimpse into JonBenét's TERRIFYING LAST MOMENTS IN THE HOUSE OF HORROR. The tabloid claimed the photos held answers to what happened the night JonBenét died: CORONER: THIS WEAPON KILLED JONBENÉT, 6.

When the photos appeared, the DA's staff saw them for the first time. One prosecutor joked that "it was as tasteful as you can get with stolen property. The only part of the body shown was a hand hanging down." Hunter's office would not receive a complete set of photos until mid-April.

Within hours the other tabloids had called police headquarters and the DA's office for reactions to the *Globe*'s publication of the photos. Don Gentile of the *National Enquirer* was first. Two other tabloid reporters offered Bill Wise money to answer their questions. "They're naive," Wise said. "Boulder's a city that as public officials go is virtually bribery-free."

The tabloids used their money. Reporters like Marilyn Robinson of *The Denver Post*, and Mike Gudgell of ABC found themselves without a story most of the time. "I'm going to lose my job," Wise kept hearing from some reporters. At the time he felt sorry for them. Then he started getting calls from private investigators who claimed they were looking for work. In all, twenty-six PIs called. What they really wanted, Wise knew, was information for their clients—the tabloids and even some members of the mainstream media, who were employing the same methods.

No one could stop the tabloids from using money to get information. Sometimes it worked—even in Boulder. More often, however, it didn't, and by the end of April, there were three criminal investigations into the tabloids' business practices. After the *Globe* published the autopsy and crime scene photos, a police investigation and litigation by the county of Boulder stopped the publication of additional pictures. One tabloid offered a handwriting expert $30,000 for a copy of the ransom note, which resulted in an investigation by the Jefferson County DA's office, to which the offer had been made. When the *Globe* purchased photographs taken inside the Ramsey house by the Ramseys' own investigators and published six of them, another police investigation and an imminent court proceeding halted publication of the rest of the pictures.

THIS MURDER IS OURS, CHIEF

ON THE POLICE, THE MEDIA AND THE DEATH OF A BEAUTIFUL YOUNG GIRL

Thomas Koby made an unusual appearance on local television. There was still no suspect, he said, but he thought it would be "healing" to let people know they were doing all they could. (Very Boulder, I thought, in keeping with a place where snow is cleared from bicycle paths before roads.)

Let's get this straight. Chief Koby believes that this crime belongs to Boulder and that the rest of the country is just rubbernecking. Hello? Maybe I am new here, but when I think about JonBenét Ramsey, it is not a matter of prurient curiosity; I'm wondering what to believe in. Wanting to know who did it "is a natural response," the chief allowed (though only for Boulderites). "It is often an effort to assure ourselves that such a tragedy will never happen to us." Well, yes. Beyond that, there is the question of whether this is a work of the darkest evil imaginable or a more or less random act of malice and greed gone awry. Evil on this scale is impossible to comprehend. To know who murdered JonBenét Ramsey is to know what world we live in, where we are.

Not incidentally, the national press is in Boulder because despite its tabloid aspects and despite what the tabloid press will do to exploit the story, the murder of JonBenét Ramsey is important. Listen to her mother, who said on CNN: "You know, America has just been hurt so deeply. . . the young woman who drove her children into the water, and we don't know what happened with O.J. Simpson. America is suffering because we have lost faith in the American family."

Give the rest of the country a break, Chief. And don't kill the messengers. They work for you.

—James R. Gaines, former managing editor of *Time*
Time, January 13, 1997

Meanwhile, Bryan Morgan, who had just received Eller's response to his proposal for the Ramseys' interviews, wrote to the commander about requests he'd made of Pete Hofstrom. The police scheduled the testing of evidence, and Morgan wanted it on record that no physical evidence should be destroyed during the testing process. In addition, he reminded Eller that care should be taken in conducting DNA tests so that they didn't consume all the DNA and leave none for the defense to test independently. Morgan also objected to the use of RFLP DNA testing and wanted to know which PCR DNA systems were being used.*

More important, he made a formal request that representatives of the Ramseys be present when the swabs that contained the substances to be tested were split. The vials or other packaging should be preserved with the swabs themselves, Morgan wrote. In addition, he asked for the names of all the labs being used.

Hofstrom and Bob Keatley, the Boulder Police Department's legal adviser, could see a legal battle looming. The Ramseys' attorneys were raising many of the same points concerning the preservation and con-

---

* An RFLP (restriction fragment length polymorphism) test is a sophisticated DNA test measuring varying lengths of DNA strands produced by their reaction to a specific enzyme. The results can yield ratios demonstrating that the likelihood of two people having the same genetic patterns is hundreds of millions to one.

PCR (polymerase chain reaction) typing (also known as molecular Xeroxing) is a process in which tiny bits of DNA are replicated thousands of times to allow analysis and comparison. Once the DNA is amplified, it can be typed through genetic probes. While hundreds of genes can be examined, not all are suitable for forensic analysis. In the Ramsey case, the DQ-alpha and D1S80 genes were among those compared. The genes analyzed through PCR are not the same as those examined through RFLP testing, but PCR results can also yield ratios demonstrating that the likelihood of two people having the same combination of genetic markers is hundreds of millions to one.

tamination of DNA that had come up in the Simpson criminal case.★
The battle on the horizon was made even more obvious on January
15, when Patrick Burke, Patsy's attorney, advised Keatley that Jon-
Benét's death did not void her physician-patient privilege.

On January 13, the day Morgan wrote to Eller, Detectives Thomas
and Gosage continued their investigation of ex-employees of Access
Graphics. They interviewed Kathy and Jeff Merrick for a second time.
Merrick confirmed Don Paugh's story about his having dinner at
Pasta Jay's with current Access Grphics employee Tom Carson and his
anger toward John Ramsey. He said he'd remained friendly with several people from the company—what was so unusual about that? He
restated his alibi, and his wife corroborated his story. On Christmas
night he had been at home all evening, and she had been sick. When
the detectives asked him to take a polygraph test, Merrick refused.
The next day, Thomas and Detective Harmer interviewed Don Paugh
again. He confirmed that his son-in-law and Merrick were no longer
friends. Merrick remained a suspect.

Thomas and Gosage then interviewed Access Graphics employees
David Harrington, Susan Richart, and Jim Hudson and a former sales
representative, James Marino. Detective Thomas told Marino, "I know
you didn't have anything to do with this. I just need for you to answer
a few questions so we can cross your name off the list." The detectives
found nothing out of the ordinary about any of them. For the time
being they were cleared.

Several days later, Thomas and Gosage returned to Access Graphics and interviewed Gary Merriman again. A month later, Merriman
would be asked by police to write the figure *118,000* over and over
again, although he was never asked if he knew the amount of John
Ramsey's bonus for the year. He did. It was within pennies of
$118,000. After his seventh handwriting sample, Merriman felt he'd
written enough to fill the Library of Congress. "If you need more,
come back with handcuffs," Merriman told the detectives.

That was when they said they didn't think he'd killed JonBenét
but that he might have written the note.

Appalled, Merriman said, "I want you to repeat to me what you just said."

★The greatest risk of contamination of DNA comes from other DNA samples. Material
is collected with disposable tweezers by police officers and lab techicians, who are
required to change gloves each time they pick up a sample. At a complex crime scene, an
officer might use fifty or more pairs of gloves.

The detective repeated it.

"The next time you come into my office," Merriman said, "I'm having my attorney here."

In fact, his lawyer was present when the police returned for another handwriting sample. Gary Merriman understood that if his son had been killed, he'd want the cops to suspect everyone—his neighbors, the dog catcher, the milkman. Everybody. Nevertheless, he still felt he had to protect himself.

RAMSEYS HIRE FORMER FBI AGENT

Former FBI agent John Douglas, the inspiration for one of the central characters in the movie "Silence of the Lambs," has been hired by John and Patsy Ramsey to help investigate the murder of their daughter, JonBenét.

Douglas, former head of the FBI's behavioral science unit in Quantico, VA, worked on the Unabomber case, the Tylenol poisoning and other high-profile cases.

—Mike McPhee and Mary George
The Denver Post, January 14, 1997

6-YEAR-OLD BEAUTY QUEEN'S MURDER
HOW DADDY'S LITTLE GIRL REALLY DIED

UNTOLD STORY OF THE MURDER

Authorities are convinced JonBenét's death is a murder disguised as a kidnapping—and believe the little girl may have known her killer!

Sometime during the night after JonBenét's mom tucked her into bed, the killer crept into the girl's bedroom, not far from where her parents slept, and carried her silently to a little-used basement wine cellar.

The beauty queen was bundled in a blanket and her mouth covered with duct tape. Her skull was fractured by a blow . . . and she was sexually molested!

Then the killer wrapped a cord around her neck and used a wooden handle to twist the cord tighter and tighter around her neck until it choked the life out of her little body.

—David Wright and David Duffy
National Enquirer, January 14, 1997

Early in the afternoon of January 14, Joann Hanks, the office manager of McGuckin Hardware in Boulder, received a phone call from an anxious-sounding man who identified himself only as John. He said that looking over his American Express bill, he had discovered two charges made by his wife, Patsy Ramsey, on December 2 and December 9, for $46.31 and $99.88, and he wanted to know what they were for. Hanks recognized the name Ramsey. She told John that since the purchases were from more than thirty days ago, the records had been purged from her computer and she'd have to do a hand search. Ramsey said he'd call back on January 20. Hanks told McGuckin's head of security, John Christie, about the call, and he notified the Boulder police. Late that day, Hanks found the receipts.

Two days later, Detectives Ron Gosage and Steve Thomas, responding to Christie's call from the previous day, stopped in at McGuckin Hardware. They learned that Patsy Ramsey had used an American Express credit card on December 2 and December 9 for purchases of $46.31 and $99.88, respectively, and agreed that the person Joann Hanks had talked to was in fact John Ramsey, although the urgency in his voice that Hanks described seemed out of character from what the detectives knew of him. Hanks gave them the two credit card receipts, which they took to police headquarters and booked as evidence.

The detectives theorized that Ramsey had discovered his wife's December charges when he received his bill and might have suspected that she had purchased items used in the crime. The police contacted the FBI to help them set up a phone tap at McGuckin Hardware, awaiting Ramsey's call on January 20.

The next day, January 17, Thomas and Gosage continued an interview at Access Graphics with comptroller Susan Richart, who told them about Sandra Henderson, a former employee, who was in trouble with the law, and her husband, Bud, each of whom owed the firm $18,000. Add $100,000 to either of them and you had the ransom amount, which gave the detectives cause for suspicion. They put Bud and Sandra high on the list of those to be interviewed.

Richart told the detectives that John Ramsey's previous yearly net bonus, after taxes, was within a half dollar of $118,000. To her knowledge, the only other people who knew the exact amount were Lockheed Martin's evaluators; Ramsey's boss, Gary Mann; and Ramsey himself. She did not mention Gary Merriman. When asked if she had an alibi for the night of the murder, Richart said that she had been with her parents. Within four days of Richart's interview with the police, CNN reported a possible link between Ramsey's bonus and the amount of the ransom demanded.

The following day, Detective Thomas interviewed Mike Glynn, another former Access Graphics employee. He was cooperative. He told the detectives that he had been with his in-laws in Tucson, Arizona, the evening JonBenét died. Glynn had met Ramsey in 1991, while he was on the football coaching staff at the University of Colorado, and joined Access Graphics in 1992 as head of international business development, where his knowledge of several foreign languages would come in handy. Glynn and Tom Carson set up the company's overseas sales and distribution center. By 1996, however, Glynn didn't see room for advancement in the company and decided to leave. Ramsey offered him more money to stay, but on May 3, four days after Jeff Merrick left, Glynn went to work for CompuWare in Tucson, where his family preferred to live so that they could be closer to Glynn's ailing mother-in-law. Gary Merriman had told the police that Mike Glynn had a personal relationship with the Ramseys and was one of the few Access Graphics employees to have been invited to the Ramseys' home. In fact, the two families had often vacationed together.

Two weeks after his interview with the police, Glynn provided hair, blood, and handwriting samples.

John Ramsey seemed like an introvert. He was just nice and shy. He never wavered in what he was like, and you could tell he was a deep-thinking guy. I never saw him ruffled by any circumstances. Sometimes, internally, he must have been. One time we were negotiating with Sun Microsystems, our largest vendor, and the frustrations of dealing with the games played in the computer industry got to John. Yet he stayed level-headed. He steered away from confrontation.

Don Paugh was a real father figure around Access. He had the ear of everyone when he was human resources director. His job then wasn't to hire or recruit anyone, but he sure solved a lot of difficulties that arose in the company. Everyone enjoyed Don. He was always around. He lived by himself, and every once in a while, Don and I would sit on his porch, have a beer, and talk. When someone new was hired, he would take them to his porch and have a beer with them.

While John was low-key, Patsy was off the scale as an extrovert. Once John made a mildly sarcastic remark: "Patsy spent more money renovating the house than I did buying it." As I got to know John better, I saw the impact of his older daughter's death on him. Beth was her name. He was just eaten up inside. He read a lot to try to come to terms with it. It changed him.

Our families went on getaways together, sometimes into the mountains, where we stayed at our family's condo. We did the usual things families do—we skied, we cooked our own meals. Just hung out. In the summer we hiked. There was never any display of money on John's part. John enjoyed being outside. He loved Boulder. He loved his kids, and whenever I saw them, he always gave JonBenét and Burke equal time. He invited my family over for dinner several times. Patsy cooked.

The speculation that I ended on bad terms with John is just not true. In October, just before JonBenét died, I was trying to get John on our board of directors, but our bylaws limited the number of directors. At the same time, he was in discussions with Lockheed about possibly reacquiring Access Graphics and going public. So all this other stuff is just gossip, innuendo, and gross speculation. When I left, Jim Hudson was just coming back to run the European and Canadian operations.

I'd blow into town every couple of months and I'd call John or whoever was in town and we'd have dinner. I'd hoist a few.

—Mike Glynn

During the following week, Thomas and Gosage continued their interviews with Access Graphics employees. Michael Minard and Jason Perkins, who Don Paugh had noticed at the dinner at Pasta Jay's, were questioned. Curtis Fisher, a close friend of John Ramsey's and a consultant to Access Graphics, was also interviewed. The police had heard that Fisher and Ramsey had a disagreement, and they found it interesting that Fisher left Access Graphics just before Christmas. In their interviews with him, however, Fisher said he had left the firm on friendly terms. On the morning of December 26, he had been on his way to San Antonio.

When they reached the end of their interviews with company employees, the police had not yet uncovered any evidence to suggest a link to the murder of JonBenét.

9

Though the Ramseys were the unofficial target of the police investigation, less and less of the forensic evidence turned out to point to them. At the same time, none of it pointed to anyone else.

Since the autopsy, the police had thought there was semen on JonBenét's upper thighs. Then, on January 15, the CBI came back with the analysis. The substance thought to be semen was in fact smeared blood. There was no semen. JonBenét's body had been wiped clean, leaving a residue that was visible under the flourescent light at the autopsy.

This news changed everything, drastically.

The DA's staff knew the police now had to delete "slam dunk" from their vocabulary. Clearly, the CBI's findings disturbed Commander Eller even more than they did Pete Hofstrom. There was no evidence that John Ramsey or any other sexually mature male had ejaculated on the body. But the vaginal injuries the coroner had found, as the police detectives observed, certainly suggested sexual contact.

For his part, Hofstrom saw that the case seemed to be slipping away from the police, that there would be a very bumpy road ahead before the perpetrator could be identified, indicted, and convicted.

THE RAMSEY TEAM

PARENTS OF SLAIN GIRL HAVE AT LEAST
9 PROFESSIONALS WORKING ON THE CASE

Experts say John and Patsy Ramsey already have spent well over $100,000 on their investigation into the murder of their daughter.

[They have retained] nine professionals, including three high-powered lawyers, a Washington, D.C. publicist, a former FBI criminal profiler, two Denver private investigators, and two handwriting analysts.

—Charlie Brennan
Rocky Mountain News, January 19, 1997

* * *

On January 19, I was sitting on a bench by the church's side entrance with a friend of mine. The photographers were still camped outside.

My friend was talking about our lining up the day the bishop had come. "You would like to say that we did something wrong."

"I think we should have given quiet comfort," I replied, "but not public comfort." I knew the police were now looking at John Ramsey.

My friend started crying. "You know, that Pat Korten," she wept. "We were all taken aback . . . I think of what that child went through . . ." Then she really broke down and cried.

"You know," I said, "when all this is over, we will still be here." That is how our conversation ended.

I decided to write an editorial for my paper. It was entitled "Ramsey Case Shook a Boulder Church to Its Foundations."

I discussed how the church had been caught in the eye of a storm, the crush of the media. How we as a church would have liked to be observed. How, on the other hand, snowballs and eggs were thrown at journalists, while other reporters offered cash, and some posed as church newcomers to probe for information. How the media wanted to bend the bond between clergy and parishioner. I noted that good journalism can only happen when reporters listen quietly and with compassion for suffering. I pointed out that the media had to be sensitive to any community it serves by writing stories that are rich in fact, skimpy on speculation, and slow to judgment.

I said we cannot choose our tragedies, but we can approach them with dignity and grace. We can reexamine our faith. I said that if we learned nothing else from our ordeal, it is that faith accounts for little if it is never tested.

After I published my editorial in the Daily Camera, the comment got back to me that as a member of the church's inner circle, I had betrayed the congregation.

I called Rol and asked for a meeting—just the two of us. We sat at this little wrought-iron table just outside his office. We had coats and sweaters on.

He wasn't upset or angry. He was exasperated. He looked like a man who had been hunted down.

I told him that to the media, the church looked as if it was hiding something. He could defuse things perhaps, simply by saying that he was in a privileged position and couldn't talk.

"There might be an arrest soon," I added. "I just want to forewarn you."

He looked hard at me. "Do you think it is the person everybody is talking about?" He meant John Ramsey.

"It might be true," I said.

He looked out into space for a long, long time. He was stunned.

Then he said, "We just don't need to get our name in the newspaper all the time."

I had to smile. That was his whole response to my editorial.

—Niki Hayden

Though the media were still hounding him, in mid-January John Ramsey attempted to return to work. Gary Mann told Ramsey that the company was fine and could run without him for a while longer if he wanted to wait. Sales projections were up, a testament to the effort Ramsey had put in over the years. He could afford to take some time off—particularly now. But Ramsey wanted to try.

He was ashen the day he walked into the Pearl Street Mall offices. As he walked through the office thanking people for their support, his colleagues noticed that he seemed unsure of himself, distracted. Ramsey told one director that he didn't want anyone to be afraid to talk to him, and he certainly didn't want to be shut off from his employees. In the few meetings he attended, however, it was clear he had to work hard just to concentrate. To one executive, he looked like a man still in trouble.

Karen Howard, director of worldwide communications, thought that Ramsey needed someone to talk to—besides all his lawyers. Howard, who had known him for years, felt he knew something about JonBenét's death but couldn't talk about it. She thought it was something he didn't have anything to do with, but she also saw a man who didn't know how to help his wife deal with their daughter's death.

That week, Carl Whiteside, director of the Colorado Bureau of Investigation, called Alex Hunter and asked if the two of them could meet with police chief Tom Koby to discuss the request from the Ramseys' attorneys to have one of their representatives present during the CBI's testing of evidence. Whiteside told Hunter that since the day after the murder, Koby had not returned his calls, and he felt the chief had no interest in what he had to say. Whiteside also thought the Boulder police were using his staff inefficiently. It looked as if the right hand didn't know what the left hand was doing. Koby's officers were always dealing with different people at the CBI. By now the DA's staff had made their own inquiries, which should have been coming through the police department, and often Detectives Wickman and Trujillo, who were handling the evidence, didn't even know what information the DA's office had requested. It was a mess. Whiteside wanted someone on the CBI's staff to act as liaison and to handle all the evidence.

Whiteside also wanted Hunter made aware that the police had requested that none of CBI's findings be shared with the DA's staff for fear the information would be leaked or shared with the Ramseys' attorneys. It was standard procedure for Hunter's office to receive lab test results when the police did, even in cases where charges had not yet been filed. Whiteside was concerned that the police and Hunter's office were not on the same page.

Hunter arranged to hold the meeting in his office at the Justice Center, but when Whiteside arrived, Chief Koby excused himself. He said he had to be somewhere else. Whiteside was upset, but he agreed to stay and discuss some of the issues with Hunter and his staff. When Hunter learned that the CBI's analysis and test reports were being withheld, he was outraged. Whiteside agreed to provide Hunter's staff with copies of the reports at the same time they were given to the police.

Whiteside also told the DA that he didn't want the Ramseys' representatives in his labs—he wouldn't want to deal with *any* uncharged person's delegate.★ That was CBI policy, and that was how he read the law. Unless the Ramseys were charged, he saw no reason for defense attorneys to know the test results—or even what type of evidence they were testing. In his opinion, law enforcement's advantage was seriously diminished if the target of an investigation knew what the police had before formal charges were filed. It gave the defense extra time to plan an effective strategy.

Hunter replied that they were trying to be cooperative with the Ramseys' attorneys, and often honey worked better than vinegar.

★ A Colorado statute, C.R.S. 16-3-309, generally authorizes the use of laboratory testing procedures by the prosecution, so long as procedures are in place to preserve possible exculpatory evidence (evidence that points to the possible innocence of a person). The statute hints, however, that "when a suspect has been identified or apprehended," the suspect or his counsel may have a right to be present at destructive procedures that will not leave enough evidentiary material for later defense testing. The statute does not provide for a definition of "suspect" or explain what degree of suspicion is necessary before one is deemed to have been "identified." Whiteside apparently took the view that a person was not a suspect until he had been named by police as such, charged or arrested in connection with a crime.

Whiteside didn't like Hunter's approach but admitted that the evidence wasn't his. It was the Boulder PD's and Hunter's. They could test it somewhere else, if they wanted. They could go to Cellmark Diagnostics in Maryland. Then he'd be out of it. Hunter said his staff would discuss the matter with the Ramseys' attorneys.

That same day, Koby met with Eller to discuss the problems he was having with the DA's office and the media. Now that the search of the Ramsey home was complete, Koby wanted to know if Hunter's people were still dissatisfied with the job Eller was doing. Yes, Eller replied. In fact, now they were suggesting interview subjects for his detectives.

Koby, who had come close to replacing Eller after he tried to withhold JonBenét's body from her parents, now told the commander that he would back him against both Hunter and the press. These problems overshadowed whatever early mistakes Eller might have made, and this was *their* case. Eller agreed with Koby that it wouldn't be productive to talk to the media. Their job was to solve the case.

Koby then told Eller, mainly in jest, that with all the meticulous notes he was taking, they should write a book someday and tell their side of the story.

On January 20, Detectives Thomas and Gosage went to McGuckin Hardware to await the expected call from John Ramsey. The detectives planned to use the local phone company's *57 feature, which was available to the police, to trace the call.

The call came in at 10:45 A.M. "I called last week looking for some receipts," he said.

"I've got one, and I need the number verified," Hanks replied.

Today Ramsey seemed calm and composed. When he gave the account number, however, Hanks said it wasn't correct.

"But you were able to pull a purchase on an AmEx on December 2 for $46.31 and on December 9 for $99.88?"

Hanks said that she had receipts for those amounts but on a different American Express account. Patsy's name was on the card that was used, Hanks said, and it had a different account number. Hanks asked Ramsey to fax her a signed request for the receipts so that she could release them. After Ramsey hung up, the police traced the call to 303-573-5294, which was listed to Touch Tone, Inc., in Denver. Detective Thomas called the number immediately, but it was busy.

A few minutes later, Ramsey called Hanks to ask if she'd received his fax. She said that she had and agreed to fax the receipts to the telephone number he provided.

"Is there an itemized invoice available?" he asked.

"I do have the itemized [receipts]," Hanks replied. "I will get those off to you right now."

When the police used *57 on Ramsey's second call, the trace was unsuccessful. They called the U.S. West telephone company to trace the fax number Ramsey had given. It turned out to be an MCI 800 number, and it was traced to Georgia and back to Denver, Colorado, and then to Touch Tone, Inc. Eventually the police found out that Touch Tone was a "skip tracing" firm—a company that locates deadbeat debtors. The phone technology it uses is designed to hide a caller's location and identity.

The police were suspicious. Why would John Ramsey want to conceal where he was calling from? Or if the caller wasn't Ramsey, where did he learn about Ramsey's American Express bills? Thomas and Gosage decided to investigate Touch Tone. The police would also request from the Ramseys their credit card statements and purchase receipts.

Meanwhile, the detectives had made some progress. Thomas discovered that the store's computerized sales slips did not list the name or item number of what was purchased next to the price, only the section of the store the item came from. The items listed on Patsy's receipts included one for $2.29, which came from an area of the store that displayed rope. There was also an unspecified item that cost $1.99, which came from the department where duct tape was sold. But there was no way of proving from the store's purchase records that Patsy had bought the tape or cord on December 2 or 9.

The next step for the detectives was to see if McGuckin's in-store antishoplifting security cameras had recorded Patsy looking at or picking up duct tape or rope or placing the items on the checkout counter on either December 2 or December 9. When Thomas screened the videotapes, he discovered that McGuckin recycled the tapes after thirty days. The tape of December 2 had been recorded over on January 2, and the tape from December 9 had been reused on January 9. Unless she provided the police with the information, there was no way to find out what Patsy had purchased.

The detectives' list of questions for the Ramseys was growing daily.

★ ★ ★

BEAUTY QUEEN'S NIGHTMARE LIFE OF SEX ABUSE

LIE DETECTOR PROVES DAD HIDING TRUTH FROM COPS

Little beauty queen JonBenét Ramsey was brutally assaulted and abused the night of her horrifying murder—but it wasn't the first time she'd been sexually attacked!

And her killer savagely bludgeoned her with a golf club before she died. These shocking details, kept secret in the hush-hush investigation by police in Boulder, Colo., were uncovered by an ENQUIRER team probing the mysterious Christmas murder of the tragic 6-year-old.

John and Patsy Ramsey did NOT disclose everything they knew or suspected about the murder of their beauty queen daughter.

That's the shocking conclusion of a top lie detector expert after analyzing the parents' comments on CNN-TV.

Verimetrics—a super-sophisticated lie detector—is a computerized version of the Psychological Stress Evaluator (PSE) which is used by law enforcement officials and courts of law in California, Florida, Louisiana and several foreign countries including Israel and Canada.

Mr. Ramsey is deceptive when he claims he told ALL he knows to the cops. "When he says, 'We shared all of our thoughts with the police,' Mr. Ramsey is being less than truthful," said Jack Harwood, a state licensed civil and criminal investigator for nearly 40 years.

—Patricia Towle
National Enquirer, January 21, 1997

On January 21, Bryan Morgan hand-delivered his reply to John Eller's letter concerning the Ramseys' interviews. Morgan rejected the police department's request that the Ramseys be interviewed on Friday, January 24. In his letter, he characterized Eller's conditions as cruel and insensitive. To start an interview at 6:00 P.M. without a cutoff time meant that they could still be sitting there at 1:00 in the morning.

That same day, Patsy's attorney, Patrick Burke, met with Pete Hofstrom to discuss The CBI's insistence that only representatives of charged persons had the right to observe their physical evidence tests. Hofstrom, who may not have understood the law, suggested to Burke that he could designate the Ramseys as suspects for the purpose of permitting a representative to witness the testing. Burke said he would discuss the matter with his clients. Burke, solidly built at forty-seven, had once served as assistant attorney general for Colorado and, before that, had been a public defender. Hofstrom knew that beneath Burke's sweet-guy demeanor was a tough opponent.

The next day Burke hand-delivered a letter to Hofstrom, agreeing to Hofstrom's suggestion designating the Ramseys as suspects for the sole purpose of allowing their representatives to observe the testing procedures.

When Carl Whiteside was told about Burke's reply, he faxed a formal letter to Alex Hunter stating that he would not let any of the Ramsey representatives observe the CBI's testing unless the Ramseys were "charged defendants." That was the way *he* read the law. He would not accept Hofstrom's "designated suspects," and he had made his position clear in Hunter's office. The next day, Hofstrom told Burke the CBI's reading of the law, and Burke withdrew his approval for the Ramseys to be named "designated suspects." But Burke voiced no objection to the CBI's tests as long as they did not destroy or consume the evidence.

In the meantime, the Ramseys' attorneys had been looking for a prominent DNA expert to represent them. They contacted Barry Scheck, who at the time hadn't been called by Hunter's office but who later said on the Larry King show that he declined any association with the Ramseys.

During the same week, the CBI discovered that the stain found on JonBenét's panties contained the DNA of more than one individual. JonBenét's DNA was the major component, but there was a minor component consisting of DNA from another person—or possibly more than one. The CBI told the police that the Ramseys' neighbor Joe Barnhill could be tentatively excluded as a source for the minor component of DNA, if the minor component came from one source, but that he could not be eliminated if the minor component originated from two or more sources. Further testing would take several months, the lab said.

A week later, on January 30, the police asked the Barnhills' boarder, Glenn Meyer, for another handwriting sample, the first one having shown some similarities to the writing in the ransom note.

Meanwhile, Detectives Thomas and Gosage were still working on the list of Access Graphics ex-employees, and on January 21 and 22 they interviewed Bud and Sandra Henderson, who each owed Access Graphics $18,000.

Bud Henderson had come to Colorado in 1971 and married his fourth wife, Sandra Chiselbrook, in 1984. That year the couple started Henderson Technology, which sold telecommunications equipment. One of their suppliers was CAD Distributors of Boulder. Henderson purchased equipment from CAD Distributors, while Sandra went to work for Jim Hudson, who owned the company. Before long she became operations manager, supervising the employees who took the orders and shipped the merchandise. Then CAD merged with John Ramsey's Atlanta company and CAD Sources of Piscataway, New Jersey. This is the combination that became known as Access Graphics, with John Ramsey as president.

Henderson Technology ordered equipment from Access Graphics, which Henderson then sold. Sandra paid the bills and kept the books. In 1991, without prior notice, Access abruptly placed a credit hold on Henderson Technology's account and told Bud Henderson he owed the company $145,000 for invoices that his wife hadn't paid. He was shown a promissory note with his and his wife's signatures. Henderson had never seen it and said that his signature had been forged.

"Where in the hell did the money go?" an infuriated Bud asked Sandra.

"We spent it," she answered.

Henderson later said that his wife had agreed to pay off the debt over the next twelve months, made only one payment, and then defaulted. Within a week Access Graphics fired Sandra Henderson when it was discovered that she had altered Henderson Technology's account at Access. Henderson said that his wife tried to delete the balance that was owed.

The company that bonded Access Graphics employees paid the firm $100,000, leaving a balance of about $40,000 to be paid. The Hendersons made one payment of $4,000 before they divorced in 1995. In family court, their outstanding obligation of $36,000 was divided into two notes for $18,000 each. By then, Henderson believed that John Ramsey was furious at him and his ex-wife.

He told the police that on the night of JonBenét's murder, he had been alone but had no witnesses to provide an alibi. Sandra's alibi checked out. On the night JonBenét was murdered, she was at the Independence halfway house, having just been released from jail on an unrelated charge.

During the interview, Detective Thomas gave Henderson a sheet of paper containing some typed words, handed him a pen, and asked him to print the words in capital letters—sometimes two, three, and four times. Henderson had to write out the words so many times that he memorized them. The police also took strands of hair from his head but didn't ask for a blood sample. When they asked him to take a polygraph, he refused.

A month later, Henderson was asked for another handwriting sample. Now the police wanted both capital and lowercase letters. Detective Thomas tried hard to persuade him to take a lie detector test because the police needed to eliminate suspects. You're just one of several suspects that need to be eliminated, Thomas told him.

Later in the year, Detective Melissa Hickman called him. Come down and take a blood test, she said. Later Hickman was taken off the case and the calls stopped. Bud Henderson never gave a blood sample and never took a polygraph test.

Everything they asked me to write was from the ransom note. I wondered if the police had my telephone tapped. You have to wonder, what do you say over the phone? You start to think people are following you. Every time I walk into a restaurant, go into a bar, the first thing I do is ask myself, Who in the hell do you see in here that looks like a detective? I've been stopped twice for absolutely no reason. They say I was weaving. They check my ID. These are Boulder cops.

I hear a knock on my door, I open it, and a video camera is running. The interviewer sticks a microphone in my face. "Have the police talked to you?"

Hard Copy went and taped Sandra going to prison. The media knew we owed Access Graphics money. How they found out, I don't know. One writer told me Sandra orchestrated JonBenét's murder from prison to get back at John. I have one friend that calls me "Killer."

Finally I did a long interview for Hard Copy and American Journal. It wasn't a hell of a lot of money.

I still get calls. A call a week. From Hollywood, from New York, even from the Daily Camera.

—Bud Henderson

Meanwhile, producers for TV shows such as *Extra* and *Hard Copy* started calling the Ramseys' housekeeper, Linda Hoffmann-Pugh. She received so many calls that eventually she got an unlisted number.

Then reporters started knocking on her door. One day, after she had stopped answering the door, someone from the *National Enquirer* left a note under her door, offering her $20,000 and a trip to Florida. That was enough money to buy a new car, which the family needed, so she agreed to give the tabloid an interview.

The *Enquirer* picked up the Pughs in a limousine and flew them to Ft. Lauderdale. Linda answered all their questions. One thing they were curious about was Patsy's attitude toward sex. The police had asked Linda similar questions. They wanted to know if Linda had found any signs of sex on the Ramseys' sheets. In whose rooms? She told them she'd found such signs only on Patsy and John's linens. Linda, who had shared her own problems with Patsy over the years, told the detectives that in June 1996, Patsy mentioned that she didn't take pleasure in sex anymore. She asked Linda for advice on how to make it better. Linda suggested some adult movies or some magazines. Better yet, she might want to see a psychiatrist. She and Patsy never discussed the subject again, Linda told the police.

FAMILIAR DETAIL DOTS RANSOM NOTE

WRITER APPARENTLY KNEW THAT JOHN RAMSEY
SERVED AT A NAVY TRAINING BASE IN THE PHILIPPINES

The ransom note tied to the murder of JonBenét Ramsey contains a reference to the Navy air base in the Philippines where her father once served, sources said.

People asked by police to give handwriting samples—Ramsey family members, friends, and past and current employees of Access Graphics and their spouses—are told to write the acronym "SBTC."

Investigators believe the acronym is a reference to the now-defunct U.S. Naval training center at Subic Bay, just west of Manila in the Philippines.

Meanwhile, sources close to the case said the four misspellings in the note appear to be deliberate, possibly designed to throw investigators off the author's trail.

—Charlie Brennan
Rocky Mountain News, January 23, 1997

★ ★ ★

Finally, on January 25, Bill Wise reached Barry Scheck at his home in New York as he was leaving for his daughter's soccer game. Wise introduced himself, outlined the status of the Ramsey case, and told Scheck that the CBI would be conducting DNA tests, which the Ramseys' attorneys wanted witnessed. The tests, Wise said, might involve the destruction of minute sample quantities. Shortly afterward, Scheck spoke to Alex Hunter about advising the Boulder DA's staff as well as the police. He agreed to consult for both, depending on how much time was involved. He made it clear that he didn't want to be part of a prosecution team, however, since he was now involved with the defendant-oriented Innocence Project.

Before the month was out, Hunter also spoke to Henry Lee. A week after that, Lee's employer, the State of Connecticut, said that he could consult on the case.

POTENTIAL PAST ABUSE IS PROBED IN SLAYING

Authorities are investigating the possibility of past child abuse in the murder of JonBenét Ramsey, sources said.

Over the past several weeks, police have questioned friends and relatives of the Ramseys about the family's behavior.

"They asked me if the first divorce ended because of child abuse or if I had heard anything about child abuse ever mentioned," said Shirley Brady, the Ramsey nanny in Georgia from 1986 to 1989. "And they asked me how the children acted when they were around their daddy."

—Alli Krupski
Daily Camera, January 24, 1997

On January 24, after the scheduled monthly meeting of the Colorado District Attorneys' Council, Hunter asked to meet privately with Denver DA Bill Ritter; Jefferson County DA Dave Thomas; Arapahoe County DA Jim Peters; and Adams County DA Bob Grant. All of them worked in the metropolitan area and had experience with high-profile cases. They also all had much more experience with homicides than he did. When Hunter showed up, the others took pleasure in kidding him, since he'd never before been personally active in the organization and had sent Bill Wise instead.

★ ★ ★

I came to Boulder in 1972 and went to the University of Colorado law school. After graduating, I got a job in Brighton, Colorado, as a deputy district attorney. Fifteen years later I was elected district attorney of Adams County, and reelected in 1996.

Hunter's approach to the Ramsey case is vintage Alex Hunter. We have Hunter saying, "Homicides I understand intellectually, but I don't understand them experientially." He never says, "I can take care of this. I'm Superman." He looks for people who have experience, gets them together, and sees what they have to say. He's got a prosecutor's heart in a Boulder body. You could write volumes and volumes about that.

When we first met with Alex, he said, "I'm not abdicating my responsibility. I just hope you guys will help me.

"I don't want you to take my heat," he said. "If something goes wrong, I want you to understand that it's all on me. That's what I'm elected to do, and that's what I want to do. But I need you to be candid and tell me everything and anything you can. Please don't hold anything back. I'm just looking to suck things out of you." Frankly, I don't think I would have done what he did.

Hunter wanted our input about some specific evidentiary areas. He asked us what we thought about the direction he was thinking of pursuing. He wanted to know where we felt he was off base. "Is there something I'm not thinking about?" he asked. He took our experiences away with him. Now he's attempting to adjust his relationship with the police in a complex case.

—Bob Grant

By now the DA's office and Chief Koby had agreed that there was a case against the Ramseys based on probable cause.* But Hunter wanted to see evidence that proved their guilt beyond a reasonable doubt.** Some

---

*The presence of facts or circumstances strong enough to produce a reasonable belief that the person charged with a crime is guilty. It does not indicate proof beyond a reasonable doubt but is enough to force the accused to stand trial. Also, in cases of search and seizure, it indicates the presence of sufficient evidence that the property subject to seizure is at a specified place.

**The level of certainty a juror needs in order to make a legal finding of guilt for a criminal defendant. This phrase is employed in jury instructions during a criminal trial, indicating that the defendant's innocence is presumed unless the jury can see no reasonable doubt as to the guilt of the person charged. This standard does not require that proof be so convincing that no chance of error exists. It means that evidence must be conclusive enough that all reasonable doubt is removed from the mind of an ordinary person.

detectives believed that the department's time and energy should be used to obtain the evidence to support reasonable doubt. Pete Hofstrom, however, didn't see it that way. The officers, he said, should march out and investigate the *entire* case and not only the case against the Ramseys. Let the evidence fall where it fell naturally. If it filled the gap between probable cause and reasonable doubt, that would be OK, but he didn't want the detectives to exclude anything that supported the notion that someone other than John or Patsy Ramsey had committed the murder. It was hard, though, because there weren't enough detectives to do both jobs, and Eller wouldn't request help from outside the Boulder PD.

Now that Larry Mason had been taken off the case, the police had to reinterview everyone he had spoken to during the first days of the investigation. The interview subjects were told Mason's notes and tapes had been lost, which wasn't true. Boulder detectives were required to write their own reports and transcribe their interview tapes, but Mason hadn't yet done this when he was suspended on January 5, and nobody else in the department was likely to do his work for him.

On January 27, Detective Jane Harmer interviewed Suzanne Savage, one of JonBenét's baby-sitters, who had a key to the Ramseys' home. She told Harmer she had given a key to another helper, Linda Wilcox. The day after the murder, Mason had asked Savage if Burke and JonBenét got along. Yes, she said. Did the two kids do any roughhousing? Did they get very physical with each other? No, said Savage. Mason's conversation with the baby-sitter had focused on the possibility that the family might be involved in JonBenét's death. Harmer's focus was different. What did JonBenét like to wear? Was she potty-trained? Savage repeatedly told Harmer that she only knew the family well when JonBenét was three. Since 1993, Savage had sat for the Ramseys only twice. Harmer still wanted to know if JonBenét had wet the bed on the nights Savage was there. No, she said. Would JonBenét cry if she was woken up? She might have when she was three, said Savage, but she had no idea about now. Back then, JonBenét had been a sound sleeper, and so was Burke. Then Harmer asked Savage if she knew whether John or Patsy were having any affairs—then or now. She had no clue, said Savage.

At the time of her interview with Detective Harmer, Savage gave the police a writing sample. In September she would be asked to give them palm prints and fingerprints. She complied.

I first met the Ramseys in 1991, when Take a Break, a professional sitting service, called me. JonBenét was seven months old.

Two years later, in 1993, Patsy was diagnosed with ovarian cancer and I went to work full-time for the Ramseys. It was a really hard time for Patsy. Nedra came to help, because Patsy had to be isolated from the family. She couldn't risk catching a cold or flu while she was in treatment.

I traveled with the family to Atlanta to take care of JonBenét and Burke. Patsy was open with everyone. Even if you just worked for her, she treated you like a friend. She made you feel comfortable. Nedra was different. She was the boss and you were the servant. In Atlanta I saw Patsy's pageant crowns. They were displayed in her parents' house, with pictures of her and her trophies.

JonBenét was a happy child, never really grouchy. She never fretted like some kids do when they aren't getting constant attention. Burke was quiet and self-entertaining. He liked learning to fly airplanes with his computer games.

When Patsy's cancer had passed, she wanted to make up for all the time she'd lost with the children. They were a busy family, always on a schedule, but their children were on a different schedule from other kids. Patsy and John used to pick up and fly off to here and there. Not what the average Joe Blow did.

John was gone a lot. It's hard to be a style-A family when your dad is gone all the time. I think they were used to it. They accepted it. Patsy stayed home and read a lot, and she'd go to church every Sunday with the kids. The following year, JonBenét went to preschool. That's when I stopped working for them.

In 1996, Priscilla White called and asked me to watch the kids again. They were having a surprise birthday party for Patsy. I hid out in a car down the block until Patsy's friends picked her up. By then, JonBenét had changed a lot. She was taller and thinner and her hair was colored. I didn't know about her pageants until that night, when I saw all her trophies.

Then Patsy called me on December 1, the night of the Access Graphics Christmas party. She wanted me to sit with JonBenét and Burke. Patsy told me to make sure JonBenét kept her hair in rollers overnight. She had a pageant the next day. Now tell me—what kid wants to sleep in rollers?

While we were watching TV in her parents' room, JonBenét put one of her crowns on my head. Then she started doing my makeup. She thought it was funny.

When I came home from working at the mall on December 26, I turned on the evening news. They were talking about a child's body being found in Boulder, but they didn't mention any names. Then my friend called and said that on her station, they said the dead child was JonBenét Ramsey.

My scalp tingled and the hair stood up on the back of my neck. I got really upset. Cried. Then my parents told me that Priscilla White had called but didn't leave a message. When I called her back, she told me it was true. I couldn't think of any explanation for what had happened.

—Suzanne Savage

Charles Elbot, the principal of JonBenét's school, called Susan Stine and Roxy Walker, two close friends of Patsy's, whose children also attended High Peaks Elementary School. Elbot wanted them to get a message to Patsy and John: "Let's get Burke back to school as soon as possible so he can have a normal school experience."

Through their friends, the Ramseys expressed serious concern about the school's security, even though the police had assured the principal that the buildings were safe. The Ramseys had hired a security firm in Denver, which suggested that someone should be with Burke at all times. That wasn't appropriate during school hours, Elbot said, because it would send the wrong message to the other kids. A compromise would have to be found.

Toward the end of January, Patsy and John, their security advisers, and a number of lawyers met with Elbot at the Ramseys' attorneys' offices in Boulder. Patsy was in a panic about Burke's safety, and she was also afraid of what the media might do to get to Burke. She told everyone that whoever had committed the crime against her daughter was still at large and might be waiting for an unguarded moment to take action against her son. "I've lost one child, and I don't want to lose my other child," she said several times.

Elbot wanted Burke back in class, but he certainly didn't want the school turned upside down. He pointed out that Burke's classroom was self-contained and there were no doors opening to the streets. Elbot knew Burke would be safe, but he also knew he had to create an environment where Patsy would feel that Burke was safe.

By the end of the meeting, they had agreed that an electronic alarm system would be installed at the school. Parents who regularly volunteered their time to the school would each carry a small transmitter that could signal both the police and the school office. Burke's teacher only had to push a button in her classroom and someone would be there.

A volunteer parent would stand guard outside Burke's classroom door. At recess and lunch, when he was outdoors, another volunteer would be within a few feet of him at all times. These precautions would continue until the last day of school.

After Burke was interviewed on January 8, the police wondered if he had held back any information about JonBenét's death. Burke's return to school sent a strong message to the police and the FBI. They were certain that parents who knew their child had relevant but concealed information would not allow him to get involved in a situation where he could talk freely to others. If he had secrets, Burke could easily share them with classmates he trusted. Burke's return to school seemed to close the door on the possibility that he knew something he hadn't told investigators.

BEAUTY QUEEN'S NANNY TELLS ALL

SHOCKING SECRETS BEHIND THE DOOR OF MILLIONAIRE'S HOUSE OF HORROR

"My hand trembled and my blood ran cold as I wrote out the word 'BEHEAD' in a felt-tipped pen while the police hovered over me. I knew then that JonBenét's killer had threatened to cut off the head of the beautiful child in his chilling ransom note."

In a wide-ranging exclusive ENQUIRER interview, Linda [Hoffmann-Pugh] unveiled intimate details of life in the Ramsey house— and new disclosures about the investigation into the murder that's sickened America.

National Enquirer, January 28, 1997

On January 28, Jacqueline Dilson, who worked at the Dakota Ranch, a small New Age retreat and conference center near Lyons, Colorado, sat in the office of her attorney, Larry Mertes. She was telling Detectives Wickman, Gosage, and Thomas and Pete Hofstrom that her boyfriend, Chris Wolf, might be involved in the death of JonBenét.

Her description of Wolf's behavior seemed to fit the profile of someone who had recently committed a crime.

Wolf had moved in with Dilson in her trailer in July 1995. He had a master's degree in journalism and worked as a reporter for the *Colorado Daily* and *Boulder County Business Reports*. He'd once interviewed Cheryl McGraw, an administrative assistant at Access Graphics, for a business travel story. In December 1995, Dilson said, Wolf had moved out of the trailer, but they continued to see each other. On Christmas Day 1996, Wolf was back living with Dilson. They went to a party together, Dilson said, but later Wolf refused to have dinner with her and her family. At about 10:00 P.M., Dilson said, she went to bed alone. She woke the next morning, about 5:30 A.M., just as Wolf was getting out of the shower. She noticed that his jeans and sweater, which were lying on the floor, were very dirty.

That evening, December 26, Dilson and Wolf were watching the late news. When JonBenét's death was reported, Wolf said he hoped "the fucker dies. He was sexually abusing her." Dilson said he was referring to the girl's father. The next day, Dilson said, Wolf was extremely agitated. He paced her house all day long.

Two days after meeting with Dilson, Detective Thomas asked Dilson how he could get in touch with Wolf. That same day, at 11:00 A.M., Wolf was stopped for a traffic infraction by the Boulder police after he left Dilson's home and just as he entered the city limits. The officer took him to the Boulder police headquarters to be interviewed by Thomas and Gosage, and not the sheriff's department. By the time Wolf was in the small windowless room with the detectives, he was agitated and uncooperative.

I don't remember being out Christmas night. The first I remember of the Ramsey case was reading about it in the Daily Camera *on December 27. I never heard of JonBenét. I've written for the* Business Report *all these years and never heard of Access Graphics, and I had no connection to anyone connected with the murder.*

I learned about the sexual abuse of children through a family member who had experience dealing with the subject. That's why I followed the story. When the Ramseys said on CNN that they wanted to get on with their lives, I thought it was awfully soon for them to making that kind of statement. I didn't have much sympathy for them.

Then one morning, I was driving from Lyons to Boulder and I was stopped by the police just after I passed the intersection where Highway

36 goes left and Broadway goes right. The cop car was just waiting for me. When she came up to me, she already knew my license was suspended for a traffic ticket in June of '96. I sat there not saying much. She said I had to come down to the police department to get everything straightened out. It sounded a little fishy.

I got mad when she cuffed me. For a speeding ticket?

I told her she should be looking for the killer of JonBenét and not pulling me over for speeding. Next thing I knew, I was sitting in an interrogation room with two detectives.

Thomas and Gosage tried to calm me down, but I was mad. I just went on and on about my suspended license.

"You do this for us, we'll do this for you," was Thomas's pitch. Otherwise I'd be in jail. Thomas was the negotiator, Gosage the tough guy.

Thomas pulled out a couple of sheets of paper with typewritten words on them, a blank line underneath each word. The first one was Mr. Ramsey. Then it hit me. I knew exactly what was going on. I just said, "No."

I shoved the paper back at them.

Thomas left the room, and Gosage started playing thug with me. He threatened and tried to intimidate me. "If you don't have anything to do with this crime," Gosage said, "what are you afraid of?" It was like he was going to arrest me for murder.

Thomas came back with a Polaroid camera. That's when I turned to the wall, turned my back to him. He never photographed me. Someone cuffed me again, twisted my wrists, and I yelled at the top of my lungs. "We're going to book you for obstruction of a police investigation," one of the detectives said. Next thing, they were taking me to jail. My wrists hurt for a while.

I just pretty much went through the process. I was given a ticket for driving without a license, and an hour later I was out.

A few weeks later, I went to get a copy of my police report and Thomas invited me in. I sat across the table from him and John Eller. "We have no interest in you," Eller said. I could tell he felt it was his responsibility to say that.

"Did someone give you my name?" I asked.

"Yes, someone did."

I didn't want to know who. I just wanted to get the cops out of my face.

—Chris Wolf

Chris Wolf would remain a police suspect. Soon he would join the Ramseys' list of suspects.

Meanwhile, the Ramseys' attorneys went on the offensive to counter the public's growing perception that John and Patsy were involved in the death of their daughter.

John Douglas, a former FBI criminal profiler, who now worked for the Ramseys, appeared on NBC's *Dateline*. His 1995 book *Mind Hunter* recounted some of the more famous cases he had handled, and it brought him national attention as an authority on profiling. His appearance on *Dateline* was timed to coincide with the publication of his new book, *Journey into Darkness*.

Douglas told *Dateline*'s Chris Hansen that he had sat across the table from some of the country's, if not the world's, greatest liars and that when he had met with the Ramseys for four hours, he left with the opinion that they did not kill their daughter.

In his new book, he wrote that parents who kill their children usually report them missing and leave a staged scene. When asked by Hansen if this fit the Ramsey case, Douglas said he couldn't see any staging by the Ramseys. In his entire career, he had never seen a case where a parent put a ligature around a child's neck or duct tape over a child's mouth. Also, Douglas told Hansen, parents who kill their children take pains to avoid being the person to find the body.

"From what I've seen and experienced [in this case]," Douglas said, "I say they [the Ramseys] were not involved."

Asked about the unusual amount of the ransom demand—$118,000—Douglas said that Patsy didn't even know the amount of her husband's yearly bonus. It was deposited electronically into a 401-K pension plan account. "This begins to tell me more about the person who's responsible," Douglas said. "This person has a very unique, intimate knowledge about his [Ramsey's] financial workings. Therefore, the person would have to be somehow related to his employment." This left a strong intimation that the murderer was probably someone John Ramsey knew.

10

On January 30, deputy county attorney Madeline Mason petitioned the court to seal the contents of the autopsy report. The coroner was still working on it, she said, and could not make it public.

Mason also argued, in a three-page motion, that the police investigation would almost certainly still be in progress when the report was completed and that its immediate public disclosure would probably hurt the investigation. The report, Mason pointed out, would corroborate or debunk various witness statements. If the public—including, of course, the murderer—had all the information, it would be far less useful to the police.

John Meyer planned to complete his report by February 11, one day before the scheduled hearing on the motion to seal the document.

EXPERT: KILLER KNEW JONBENÉT

JonBenét Ramsey knew her killer, and the killer had ready access to the family home, a renowned criminologist told The Denver Post.

Robert Ressler, who for 16 years was a profiler for the FBI's Behavioral Science Unit and the first manager of the FBI's Violent Criminal Apprehension Program, told the Post that his study of the case—including a visit to Boulder this week—convinces him that the 6-year-old was not killed by a stranger.

—Howard Pankratz
The Denver Post, January 31, 1997

When the *Star* received a tip on February 5 that John Andrew Ramsey had tried to arrange the death of his half-sister, JonBenét, they passed the information to the Boulder police.

A sometime police informant had told the tabloid that on the weekend of either Memorial Day or July Fourth 1996, while the Ramsey family was vacationing in Michigan, John Andrew had offered him $10,000 to ram a power boat into a smaller boat that would be carrying him and JonBenét. Supposedly, John Andrew would jump overboard to safety just before impact and JonBenét, he hoped, would be killed. The informant told the *Star* that he had rejected the offer.

Detective Jane Harmer was assigned to follow up on the tip. The informant was interviewed by local police in Waterford, Michigan, where he repeated the story he'd told the tabloid. Two weeks later, the Boulder police discovered that the informant had a dubious history. A check of Michigan police agencies revealed that he had come under suspicion—first for possibly planting drugs in an alleged dope house and second for refusing to take a polygraph test to confirm information he had provided in a cocaine investigation. By the end of February, Boulder police had decided that the informant's accusations were unfounded, and yet another lead in the Ramsey case would go nowhere.

In Denver, on Wednesday, February 5, Michael Tigar, the lead attorney for accused Oklahoma City bomber Terry Nichols, and Jeralyn Merritt, attorney for Timothy McVeigh, were arguing the reliability of handwriting analysis before federal judge Richard Matsch.

Alex Hunter took great interest in the proceedings, since he considered the handwritten ransom note the single most important piece of evidence in the Ramsey case. Besides, Michael Tigar was associated with Ramsey attorneys Hal Haddon and Lee Foreman, so his motion in the Oklahoma City case might offer insight into the Ramsey team's thinking.

The two defense lawyers representing Nichols and McVeigh were attempting to exclude testimony from the government's expert witnesses, who would tell jurors that McVeigh's handwriting matched that of a "Robert Kling" who had signed a rental contract for the truck used in the Oklahoma City bombing. In his oral argument, Tigar told the court that handwriting analysis was "junk science."

During the hearing, Judge Matsch said, "The problem with handwriting is that there is no verification-type testing of these opinion results. In addition, there has never been within the discipline any agreement on how to express the results." The judge added, "There is no standardized nomenclature. Therefore, it seems to me that we should draw the distinction between somebody getting on the stand and saying 'Yeah, written by the same person, or no, not written by the same person' versus 'These are the similarities or these are the dissimilarities,' and the jury can decide."

Judge Matsch asked Merritt whether she would object if a government witness were instructed to note only similarities or discrepancies.

"I object to it because it is too subjective," the attorney replied. "When we question these handwriting experts on the stand, you will see that they cannot answer basic questions, such as How many differences does it take before you will say that this is an irreconcilable, significant difference?"

"That's the point I made earlier," Matsch replied, "that there are no standards. And because there are no standards, it's not verifiable."

Later in the proceedings, Merritt added, "It's not science; and it's not science because it cannot be empirically tested. It isn't subject to peer review or publication. There is no known error rate. There is really a dearth of studies."

Attorney Tigar added: "The problem is that handwriting analysis, like hair analysis, is one of those fields invented by a small group of people. These people did not have any outside folks criticizing their work. There is the danger of oversell."

In the end, the judge ruled that he would not bar the government from presenting a witness to testify about similarities between the signature of "Kling" and McVeigh. But he would not allow any testimony offering definitive conclusions.

Weeks later, the court issued an even more restrictive ruling, and federal prosecutors dropped their plans to call handwriting analysts.

In Boulder, Alex Hunter asked his staff to study the limitations they might encounter in presenting handwriting evidence in court.

On February 7, Detective Arndt reinterviewed Bill McReynolds and his wife, Janet, upon their return from a long-planned trip to Spain. Again they said they had been at home the night of JonBenét's death. When Arndt asked what McReynolds knew about JonBenét's statement to Barbara Kostanick—that Santa would pay her a secret visit the day after Christmas—McReynolds said that though he was Santa at the Ramseys' Christmas party, he had never spoken to the child about meeting her. McReynolds agreed to give the police handwriting, hair, and blood samples. Several days later, Detective Gosage began a series of interviews with the family members who, according to the McReynoldses, had visited them on Christmas Day.

That same week, Koby and Eller met with Alex Hunter in his office at the Justice Center. Hofstrom and Wise joined them. Chief Koby said that his department would no longer share critical information on the case with the DA, because Eller thought that they might pass it on to the Ramseys' attorneys. Hunter was about to defend his office when Eller cut him off. Staring at Pete Hofstrom, he said, "We have the power to kick your ass out of this case, and we may exercise it."

Hofstrom knew Eller had the law on his side.★

"When our job is done," the commander continued, "we'll bring it over and deposit it on your doorstep."

Hofstrom said nothing.

"What are you going to do," Wise asked, "bring us twenty thousand goddamn pages some Friday night and say, 'We're arresting somebody Monday morning'? That's not a good way to run an investigation."

Though Hunter remained calm, Wise could see that it took great effort on his part.

"I can't believe how you respond to those people," Eller continued, referring to Hofstrom's handling of the Ramseys' attorneys. "You're such a Goody Two-shoes."

The way Hofstrom remembered it, Eller had asked him to get a second handwriting sample from the Ramseys, who didn't want to cooperate with the police because of Eller's attempt to withhold their daughter's body. Hofstrom had met with Bryan Morgan, and on January 4 Patsy Ramsey had given the detectives her second handwriting sample at a neutral location, Pete Hofstrom's home. Now the commander was turning the incident against Hofstrom.

Wise could see that Hofstrom was furious. Meanwhile, Koby sat there Buddha-like, as if he were a disinterested party rather than the chief of police presiding over an increasingly notorious and baffling homicide, the same chief whose answering machine chirped, "Hi, this is Tom Koby. It's a beautiful day here in Boulder, and I hope it's beautiful where you are too. Leave a message, and I'll call you back."

"I can't believe you used written questions," Wise felt obliged to say, referring to Arndt's December fax to Bryan Morgan, even though by now Wise had learned that Hofstrom had approved Arndt's actions. Eller ignored him and said to Hofstrom, "You're so clubby. The handwriting samples should have been taken at police headquarters, not at your house."

Hofstrom barely said a word. Finally Hunter spoke up. He asked Eller to explain how exactly the police and the DA's office would move ahead with day-to-day business.

The police would do what *they* determined was right, Eller told him. If they had any questions or needed any legal advice, they'd call. But they would no longer share information.

★There is no Colorado law mandating that the police department cooperate with the district attorney.

Hunter knew he was facing a common problem. A colleague of his had once put it this way: "The cops are where the rubber meets the road, but the DA is where the Constitution meets the cops. The conflicts are endless." Endless, yes. But not usually so acrimonious.

On February 6, Alex Hunter's elderly mother, Virginia, died suddenly in the Boulder nursing home to which she'd just been moved. A diabetic, she had been given a glass of prune juice, which has a high sugar content. She had died almost immediately. Hunter's two sisters flew in from the East Coast to attend the memorial service, but he felt unable to grieve for his mother properly amid the almost hourly crises of the Ramsey case. After the family had spread their mother's ashes in the mountains along the Continental Divide, Hunter went back to work. It wasn't long before he was comparing his own situation with John Ramsey's.

When Ramsey had lost his daughter Beth, he wasn't under public pressure and, as Hunter understood the situation, had been able to grieve properly. Now, after JonBenét's death, he appeared composed in public, though more than likely he couldn't grieve properly either, thought Hunter. Patsy, on the other hand, expressed her pain openly—anytime, anywhere.

Sheriff's patrol deputy Kevin Parker was working traffic on February 10 when he responded to a possible felony–menacing call. As Parker pulled into the parking lot at 4939 North Broadway, just north of Boulder city limits, he found Jay Elowsky handcuffed and sitting in the backseat of a Boulder police car. A silver baseball bat and a 40 Caliber Sig Saur pistol had been found in a search of his BMW. Most cops knew Jay Elowsky, who owned Pasta Jay's restaurant on Pearl Street.

The Ramseys had been staying at their friend Jay's house since returning from JonBenét's burial, and the media had been relentless, constantly shooting photographs through the windows of his home from a dirt berm nearby.

Lee Frank, a soundman working that day for NBC News, and his cameraman had been standing on the berm that morning, waiting to see if the Ramseys would come out. When they saw Elowsky's BMW back out of the driveway, they returned to their van parked in a lot behind the berm. Just then Elowsky pulled into the lot, got out of his car, and started screaming and cursing. He was wielding a baseball bat. Frank took refuge in a nearby engineering firm and called 911. His cameraman ran in the opposite direction. A moment later, two men left the engineering firm and Elowsky mistook them for the men from NBC. One of the men, after seeing Elowsky with a bat, picked up a pipe and went after him. Elowsky ran back to his car and buckled on his fanny pack, which held a gun, just as the Boulder police responded to Frank's 911 call. Elowsky was immediately apprehended.

Now, sitting in the patrol car, he still didn't understand that he had gone after the wrong men. The man with the pipe said Elowsky had threatened him and his friend with a gun. He wanted Elowsky jailed.

Sheriff's procedure required Kevin Parker to talk to those inside Elowsky's house to find out what had preceded the incident. Since the Ramseys were involved, Parker's captain told him to call Pete Hofstrom in the DA's office.

The officers would have to speak to Patsy Ramsey, who, according to Elowsky, was at home in his house. Hofstrom reached Patrick Burke, Patsy's attorney, in his car. As it turned out, Burke had just left Elowsky's home with Patsy. Burke explained the situation to Patsy, and she said that she would talk. The Boulder police had wanted to talk to the Ramseys for weeks, and now Patsy was coming in to speak to the sheriff's department. Kevin Parker knew he had a hot potato on his hands.

Since January 3, John, Patsy, and Burke Ramsey and Don Paugh and his daughter Pam had all been living in Jay Elowsky's home. Nedra and her daughter Polly would also come and go. Elowsky didn't mind giving his life over to his friends. At a time when the Ramseys were unable even to set foot in a market to do their own grocery shopping, he offered them the full use of his large home and spent hours talking to John and Patsy.

John told Jay about selecting JonBenét's casket and about how he'd wept when his brother had asked him to choose the color. When they were alone, Jay held John in his arms. They talked about God and how He would provide for them and how God was caring for Jon-Benét even now. Jay would repeat again and again that the promise of her life had not been lost with her death.

Sometimes members of St. John's stopped by and brought food, and on most days Rev. Hoverstock visited. One day Patsy saw someone on a TV talk show say that she should be arrested. The studio audience cheered. Patsy cried.

Jay tried hard to cheer up his friends. Once in a while he would open the door and holler out to Patsy and John, "Honey, I'm home!"

Now, Patsy entered the Justice Center by the backdoor with her attorney. She was wearing sunglasses, a sweatshirt, and jeans and was obviously trying to avoid looking like the well-groomed Patsy Ramsey familiar to TV viewers. Jeff Hendry, a sheriff's sergeant working with Parker, thought that nobody would recognize her if she walked down the street in those clothes. To Hendry, she didn't look like a former beauty queen.

Hofstrom, Patsy, Hendry, Parker, and Patrick Burke were all squeezed into Hofstrom's modest office, which was neutral territory for this high-profile witness. Parker sat on one side of Hofstrom's desk, and Patsy took a guest chair on the other side. Her lawyer, Burke, sat on the edge of the credenza.

With her sunglasses off, Patsy looked drawn and medicated, Parker thought. He knew that Patsy had lived in Atlanta, but she didn't know that he was from Marietta. He began by telling her what had happened: Jay was in jail. Parker said he had to know what had happened before Jay left the house. He asked if she'd seen any media people outside the house.

Patsy said she didn't like the press and started to cry. She said that she hated being followed and photographed through the window blinds at Jay's house. She couldn't go to a store without being photographed. Enough is enough, she kept saying.

To Parker it was clear that Patsy couldn't deal with the interview, and he let her know that he was there to help with her problems.

Burke, her attorney, was silent and let Patsy talk.

Patsy told Parker that Jay had left the house to take a box of sandwiches to a homeless shelter. She didn't see him take a bat. Later when she heard police cars and saw Jay's car being towed away, she called her attorney.

Hendry could see that Parker was working Patsy well. She was talking freely.

Then she told Parker that someone had broken into her house and killed her daughter. "There is still a murderer loose in the city," she said. "You know, my little girl was murdered. All these people are hounding us instead of trying to find the murderer. Somebody broke into our house, you know, killed my little girl," she repeated.

Burke seemed nervous, but he let Patsy continue. Hendry noticed that she cried when she talked about the media but not when she talked about her child's killer. Patsy kept going back to JonBenét's death. "Somebody breaks into my house, kills my little girl." Then she said it again in a flat, matter-of-fact way, as if by rote, Hendry thought. If Patsy wanted to talk, Parker and Hendry certainly weren't going to stop her.

Suddenly, Burke got up and placed himself between Parker and Patsy. He didn't say a word, just looked hard at Patsy while she pulled herself together. That ended the interview.

Burke had been there to make sure that Patsy didn't say too much, and Hendry had been there to make sure that Parker couldn't be accused of overreaching. Patsy was being interviewed as a witness, not as a suspect. They accepted that whatever she had said about JonBenét that afternoon could not be used against her if she were put on trial.★

During the interview, Hendry felt that Patsy had knowledge of the crime and wanted to talk. He thought John and Patsy were responsible for their daughter's death somehow, but which one killed her and which one was covering for the other—that, he didn't know.

It would be Hofstrom's job to charge Elowsky. John Stavely, a Boulder attorney, represented him. During the precharging negotiations, Stavely laid out all the mitigating factors: he began with a story of the poor guy besieged by the media.

Hendry had heard this kind of thing before, and he knew that only rarely was someone in Boulder charged with what he had really done. As for how often a criminal was convicted for what he had really done . . . well, that was even more rare. Hendry was a cop. He believed that if you broke the law, you should be punished, and without that—well, according to Hendry, without that, you have Boulder.

Two months later, the *Daily Camera* published an editorial on Elowsky.

PASTA JAY AND THE LAW

Did Jay Elowsky receive special treatment when he ran afoul of the law in Boulder?

With all due allowance for the pressure Elowsky was under, there's no excuse for his actions as described by the police.

Under a proposed agreement with the Boulder D.A.'s office,

★ Pete Hofstrom, who was present during the conversation with Patsy, was familiar with the Michael Manning case discussed on page 215. In that case the child's mother, Elizabeth Manning, was told she would be treated "as a witness" rather than as a suspect. She then disclosed that her child was beaten to death by her companion. When she was prosecuted for murder, the Colorado courts held that because of what a deputy had promised, neither Manning's disclosure nor anything the police learned from following up on it could be used as evidence against her. It is likely that the sheriff's officers interviewing Patsy Ramsey assumed that what she told them on that occasion could never be used against her. That was probably wrong.

Elowsky would plead guilty to a misdemeanor charge of menacing.

The charge is hardly trivial—penalties can include time in jail—but it generated charges of favoritism and "justice for the rich." Seizing on the remark of an assistant D.A., who reportedly told one of the victims that a felony conviction could cost Elowsky his liquor license and jeopardize a business loan, some complained that this man was treated differently because of his wealth and connections.

But hold it. The only way to know whether Elowsky received special treatment is to ask a simple question: Compared to what? How are other cases treated in Boulder? If the critics had asked, they'd know that he wasn't treated differently at all.

The usual practice in Boulder is this: If you didn't commit the crime with a gun or a knife, and if you have no prior criminal record, you're likely to end up with a misdemeanor charge the first time around.

There's not a scrap of evidence that this agreement was reached because a liquor license was involved. They did for Elowsky what they have done for many other defendants, and what any competent, reasonable district attorney's office should do: They treated him as a human being.

In 1996, according to prosecutors' records, 65 of 151 menacing cases involved defendants who, like Elowsky, had no prior record and didn't use a gun or knife. All 65 resulted in misdemeanor menacing charges.

You can argue that the usual practice is a mistake. You can argue that it was a mistake in Elowsky's case even if it was the right call in 65 others. But the only way to back up the charge that Elowsky's case was tainted by favoritism is to ignore relevant facts.

Elowsky received a year's probation and was required to spend two weekends on a Boulder County Jail work crew performing community service.

Back in '90, I met CU's football coach, Bill McCartney. I knew he was a religious man. I'd read his book, and I went and heard him speak. He was talking about men who give up their souls for financial gain. That sounded like me. I had been raised a Lutheran, but I was still living an immoral life while trying to find something. What do they say? I was burning the candle at both ends. Then one day I dropped to my knees. My heart literally gave out. I'd had a heart attack.

Coach Mac was there when I needed him. He made a vow to me that he would see me once a week to guide me to Christian maturity. And he kept his promise. Nothing happens overnight. It took years for me to change. I always knew about God, but I never pursued a relationship with Him. Mac was somebody who could teach me how to do that. Mac was Moses to me. He sought God's heart and commands and taught those to me. He taught them to a lot of football teams. Now, through the Promise Keepers, he's teaching them to men all over the world.

Earlier in 1992, I met John Ramsey. He was moving his business to Boulder and came into the restaurant quite often. He became interested in my place. Said he'd like to open a restaurant like mine in Atlanta. Something that could be franchised. I said to myself, Boy, that is exactly what I want to do. I want to be the next McDonald's! I showed him the kitchen. Took him to my other place, in Breckenridge.

John is a gentle man, very soft-spoken. Very smart. He started an operation in his basement in Atlanta and built it into a billion-dollar business in less than ten years. I was, like, thirty when I met him. And someone like him was interested in what I was doing. Blew me away. I said, Holy cow, this is someone I can learn from. When I had my heart attack, after my surgery he flew me to Michigan so I could recover at the home of my parents.

John's a great family guy. And we talked about that. "The second time around," he said, "you know, it's great. It's really great." He enjoyed his kids. It was never rush here or rush there or the kids are taking too long to get ready, the kids are taking too long to eat. None of that. He was just enjoying the moment. He is a man with a lot of patience.

He was also, like, a business consultant to me. We'd discuss how to plan and structure growth. Ramsey gave me a lot of time, and he wasn't even a partner. Then John and Mike Bynum set up an advisory board for me, which included eight high-powered businesspeople. Our mission was to make Pasta Jay's grow.

I started to try to be like them. I knew I had a good product. The sauce was the key. You could put my sauce on dog food and people would eat it.

In 1996 my lease ended; I had to move. For a while, I scrambled. By then I'd opened four other places, and the Boulder place was carrying them, supplying all the expansion money. But I had to close Boulder, and I had to pay vendors and meet payroll. I had a sense of impending doom.

John and Mike stepped up and said, "We'll loan you the money. We'll invest in you for a portion of the business." And I was able to open a new place at the foot of the Pearl Street Mall.

That was a relief. I'm not alone now. I'd been making decisions alone for nine years, standing or falling by them. Now I have partners. We have a game plan. We're going to sink or swim together.

And by then I had my religion. That was one common bond between John Ramsey and myself.

After JonBenét died, the Ramseys stayed in my home for almost eight weeks. It was a difficult time for all of us.

—Jay Elowsky

INTERVIEW SITE AT ISSUE

Boulder police have declined to meet with the parents of JonBenét Ramsey unless they come to police headquarters, which they will not do, Ramsey family spokesman Pat Korten said.

"Are we willing to negotiate the terms of such an arrangement? Of course we are, and we always have been," he added. "While we're happy to talk, we're not going to come to police headquarters."

—Kerri S. Smith and Mary George
The Denver Post, February 11, 1997

When *The Denver Post* reported that negotiations were taking place for the Ramseys to be interviewed, John Eller immediately told Pete Hofstrom that he suspected leaks to the media were coming from the DA's staff. The cord tied loosely around JonBenét's right wrist, the near-perfect match of Ramsey's bonus to the ransom amount demanded, the inclusion of the acronym SBTC in the ransom note, and the fact that the killer seemed to have wiped JonBenét's body with a cloth—all this confidential information had ended up in print. The police, Eller insisted, hadn't leaked anything.

When the press heard about Eller's accusations, they weren't surprised. In mid-January, Charlie Brennan of the *Rocky Mountain News* had discovered from an Access Graphics employee that people close to Ramsey were being asked to give handwriting samples containing the acronym SBTC. It was significant because when Ramsey was in the military, he was stationed at Subic Bay in the Philippines. Some investigators thought that SBTC might be a reference to Subic Bay Training Center, although that was not the name the facility was known by.

Still, Brennan had a hunch that the ransom note might contain the acronym, and he asked Hunter's office for a confirmation before publishing the story. A member of the DA's staff confirmed the fact. By John Eller's standards, that was a leak.

COPS ASK RAMSEY 'SANTA' FOR HAIR SAMPLE

Bill McReynolds, a former University of Colorado professor who portrayed Santa Claus at a party in John and Patricia Ramsey's Boulder home December 23, said detectives visited him Friday and collected "non-testimonial evidence" for testing.

"I've told them from the beginning that I would cooperate with them in any way possible," McReynolds said. "I know they don't think I'm a serious suspect."

—Charlie Brennan
Rocky Mountain News, February 12, 1997

On February 12, Detectives Thomas and Gosage began an investigation into the death of John Ramsey's oldest daughter, Beth. She had died in a car accident near Chicago in 1992, and the death had changed Ramsey's life in many ways. Immediately afterward, he immersed himself in books on how to deal with the loss of a child. He turned introspective. To many of his friends and associates, the change in him was noticeable.

The police wanted to find out if there had been a history of child or sexual abuse involving Beth. They were convinced that what Beth had confided to her girlfriends would give them insight into John Ramsey's conduct with JonBenét. The detectives began by interviewing Natalie Geroli, who had been Beth's closest friend. Two days later they saw her former teacher Elizabeth Bouis before visiting two more of her friends, Laura Foster and Lanie Bartlett. By February 21, Thomas and Gosage had completed a four-state trip and had also interviewed Tim Farrell and Marty Desantis, who were acquaintances of Beth. In the end, the detectives found no indication of inappropriate conduct by Ramsey toward Beth.

The investigation into Beth Ramsey was not the first trip to Georgia that Steve Thomas had made. In early January, he and Tom Trujillo had visited John and Patsy's former home on Northridge Road in Dunwoody, Georgia, where the family had lived when JonBenét was a baby.

Late one afternoon, Thomas and Trujillo had knocked on the front door of the Northridge house. The detectives introduced themselves, and the current owners let them into the house to look around. They had just wanted to get a feel for the place. In the backyard, Thomas and Trujillo stopped short. There, embedded in the cement of the patio, were JonBenét's and Burke's infant footprints—tiny but perfect.

The next night, the detectives went back to the house. It was raining, and they didn't want to disturb the owner. They walked to the backyard and again looked down at the tiny imprints, which glistened in the chilly drizzle.

Thomas began to weep.

Trujillo remained silent, waiting for Thomas to regain his composure.

From there, the detectives went to visit JonBenét's grave site.

Steve Thomas knew that no matter what lay ahead, he had to do the right thing. That was the credo his father had instilled in him, and now his father, who had devoted much of his life to raising money for the March of Dimes, was sick. His mother had died back in Arkansas when he was just seven. Thomas had gone to college at CU, studied sociology and criminology, and become a cop in 1986. Four years later, he was hired by the Boulder police as a patrol officer. Shortly afterward he was involved in two shootings, the second one as a member of the SWAT team. Both cases were deemed justified by a police review board. During that period, Thomas and Commander Eller became friends. By 1996, Thomas was working as a detective in a specialized narcotics unit. Just six months before JonBenét was murdered, he married Karena Jesaitis, a certified public accountant.

Steve Berkowitz, who had worked narcotics with Thomas at the Wheat Ridge Police Department in 1988, knew that if anything were ever to happen to one of his children, he'd call Steve Thomas. "Find her" would be all he'd have to say.

By now, Thomas was totally consumed by the investigation. He'd seen death before, but he had never seen the senseless murder of a six-year-old. He spent weekends working at police headquarters. He tossed and turned at night, and when he couldn't sleep, he turned on his computer and worked on the case. As the weeks passed with no answers to all the open questions about JonBenét's murder, he became more and more tormented. Sometimes Steve Thomas felt completely alone in his hunt for her killer.

PART TWO

The Hatfields and the McCoys

1

John Eller was now sixty-one. He was born in Vallejo, California, but grew up in Key West, Florida. In 1968, after attending college and spending three years in the air force, Eller joined the Coral Gables, Florida, police force as a patrol officer. Like all rookies, he sat in a patrol car learning radio procedures, watching what his partner did, and trying not to get hurt. Eller's early progress reports rated him satisfactory in judgment and knowledge of procedures. In 1970, however, a police board reviewed two minor, preventable car accidents that Eller had been involved in while on duty in a seven-month period. The board recommended that Eller be terminated on August 3, 1970. Five days before that date, Eller resigned, noting that he planned to continue his career as a police officer. Two years later, at the Metro Dade County Department of Public Safety, Eller became an investigator in vice and narcotics and a crisis-intervention specialist. Those who worked with him saw him as quiet and serious about his career.

Eller was soon promoted to sergeant and became a detective. He worked in Dade County's safe streets program. John Stack, a colleague, said, "He was viewed as a guy climbing the ladder to the top. He wasn't a 'street cop' learning from experience. Once he got it in his head that his way was right, that was it. He was never one to trust a DA." After a decade of civil unrest in Florida, Eller decided he'd had enough, and in 1979 he was hired by Boulder police chief Jay Propst as an administrator to help reshape the department. To Eller, Boulder's law enforcement was more conservative than Dade County's. In Florida, he'd chase a burglary suspect into a house and drag him out. In Boulder, he soon learned, officers set up a perimeter, made sure suspects stayed inside, and waited until they had a warrant to search and arrest. They followed the rules.

In 1991, twelve years after Eller arrived in Boulder, police chief Tom Koby, who had replaced Propst, assigned him to develop, implement, train, and manage a twenty-four-member SWAT team, even though Eller had never worked SWAT. When at first Eller failed to pass the physical fitness test, the other officers joked that he might not be able to make it around the block. One Boulder officer said that it was like putting someone in charge of homicide who'd never been a homicide detective. Nevertheless, Eller enjoyed the challenge.

During one drug arrest, Eller ignored the lead officer's advice to go through surrounding cover while approaching a house and instead ordered his men to make a straightforward entry up a driveway, an order that put the team in harm's way. Then, when the suspects scattered, the officers were not only in danger, they had no perimeter coverage. On another occasion, Eller put himself in the line of fire of one of his own officers. Soon after, Jim Kolar, the team sergeant, took his concerns to Koby. He told the chief that Eller's deficiencies in tactical training and judgment were endangering the lives of SWAT personnel. When Koby did nothing about it, six of the team members, with seventy years of experience among them, quit.

During his SWAT team tenure, Eller supervised the conversion of a former phone company property into the police department's new $7 million facility, which also housed the fire department. When that project was completed in 1991, Eller was promoted to commander under Koby.

Many of Boulder's hard-line police officers were loyal to Eller, whom they saw as a dedicated cop. He stood up for them, and he always insisted that integrity came first. But, Eller also rubbed a lot of people the wrong way. His detractors found him inflexible and vindictive when his decisions were questioned. Diplomacy and tact were not his strong suits. People either loved or hated John Eller.

"We want to do it differently from the way we've done it before," Tom Koby told Alex Hunter politely but firmly as they sat together in Hunter's office at the Justice Center. Koby wanted his friend to know that he agreed with Eller: the Ramsey investigation should be run in a more traditional way, without the DA's office. It was *their* job to find the killer, Koby said, not the DA's. He didn't want second-guessing from the DA's office about the police investigation.

Hunter protested that Eller was not conducting interviews and developing evidence in an unbiased manner. He was possibly ignoring possibly exculpatory evidence.* Hunter knew that a defense attorney would eventually challenge and probably destroy the case Eller was making. Furthermore, in Hunter's view, Eller didn't seem to care about protecting the case from a prosecutor's perspective.

Hunter decided this was a good time to tell Koby that he had asked Dr. Henry Lee and Barry Scheck to join the DA's investigation. Koby immediately complained that Eller and the detectives might see it as a lack of confidence in their ability—exactly the kind of backseat driving he'd been referring to, Koby said. When Hunter explained to him that Lee and Scheck's expertise would be fully available to Koby's people and that their solid reputations would help turn around the public's negative perception of the police, however, Koby didn't disagree. A few days later, he sent Detective Trujillo to Connecticut to meet Dr. Lee and give him the case report, videotapes, and photographic slides.

Koby knew that someday the case would belong to the DA's office and that they should reach a compromise now, not later, on how to cooperate. In the end they agreed to set up a "war room" at the Justice Center. There the police and the DA's staff would meet on equal ground, but information would be stored in computers protected by passwords known only to the police. No information they shared or discussed would leave the war room. At Koby's request, Hunter agreed to stay out of the day-to-day investigation; otherwise, the chief said, there could be no cooperation. Hunter was optimistic that Eller and Hofstrom would eventually work things out as they always had.

Though there was little forensic evidence so far, Hunter privately thought the Ramseys were probably guilty—because he saw no other explanation for what had happened. In the early stages he had expected something conclusive to come through eventually, that there was a realistic hope of some resolution.

Meanwhile the battle over the public's right to know the contents of the coroner's report was about to begin. At the Justice Center on Wednesday, February 12, First Amendment attorneys Tom Kelley and Bruce Jones, who were representing several media clients, argued before Judge Carol Glowinsky that the motion by Madeline Mason

---

* Evidence that points to the possible innocence of a person.

on behalf of coroner Meyer to withhold the documents from the public should be denied. Two Boulder PD detectives had also filed sealed affidavits, Judge Glowinsky informed Kelley and Jones. They opposed the release of the autopsy report and detailed the probable harm to the case from a premature disclosure.

The judge told Kelley and Jones that they could review the affidavits and the report in her chambers as long as they didn't reveal the contents to their clients.

"To explain how I lost a case when everything happens in open court is hard enough," Kelley told Judge Glowinsky. "To explain how this case was lost without disclosing what I know isn't fair to my clients." Kelley declined to view the contents. Instead he proceeded with his argument against the secrecy confronting the media.

Two days later, Judge Glowinsky agreed with the county's assertion that the case was still in the "early" stages of investigation. She ruled that the release of the entire autopsy report would hurt the case and said that there was significant forensic evidence that should remain confidential. However, she ordered an edited version of the coroner's report released to the public.

Many of the coroner's findings concerning JonBenét's genitals were excised from the document, but the phrase "abrasion and vascular congestion of vaginal mucosa" was made public. The complete report, the judge said, would be released in ninety days or when an arrest was made, whichever came first.

Meanwhile, the CBI reported to the police that a pubic hair had been discovered on the white blanket found around JonBenét's body. When the hair was evaluated under a compound microscope, it showed a high degree of "buckling," or twisting, and a greater degree of curl than chest or scalp hairs.★

The hair might have gotten there in several ways: A member of the Ramsey family or a guest could have used the blanket previously, the hair could have come from inside the clothes dryer when the blanket was laundered—or it could have been left on the blanket during the commission of the crime. All the Ramseys were asked to provide pubic hair samples. On February 13, as reporters were preparing to cover a press conference given by Alex Hunter, Patsy slipped into Boulder Community Hospital to give Detectives Arndt and Harmer

★ Hair has thirty-five characteristics, some of which are pigmentation, medulla, scales on the outside of hair, and the channel that runs through the center of each strand.

her pubic hair sample. A week later, John went to the same hospital and gave his sample. By the end of the month, the police had obtained samples from Melinda and John Andrew and from John Andrew's friend Brad Millard.

MEDIA STALKING HER, RAMSEY COMPLAINS

Patricia Ramsey called the Boulder County sheriff's department to complain she was "being stalked by the media" shortly before a family friend confronted three [sic] men near his home.

Sheriff's detectives interviewed Ramsey on Monday at the Boulder District Attorney's office as they investigated a report that Boulder restaurant owner Jay Elowsky had threatened a television news reporter and two other men near his home.

Sheriff's investigators did not ask Patricia Ramsey questions about JonBenét's death. She had her attorney present and met with sheriff's detectives at their request.

—Kevin McCullen
Rocky Mountain News, February 13, 1997

The morning the article about Patsy's interview with the sheriff's department was published, Jeff Hendry, the sheriff's officer who had been present at Patsy's interview, found himself confronted by a stranger as he worked the treadmill at his Boulder gym. "Yeah?" Hendry yelled at the unknown face as he took off his headphones.

"I want to talk to you."

"Go ahead."

"I don't appreciate what you did to Patsy," said the stranger.

"Who the fuck are you?"

"I'm Patrick Burke," the man answered. Hendry hadn't paid much attention to Patsy Ramsey's attorney in Hofstrom's office, and now he didn't recognize him in a T-shirt and shorts.

Burke told Hendry that he didn't like the article in the newspaper and didn't like the insinuation that the sheriff's department was able to interview Patsy when the Boulder cops couldn't. More important, he didn't like the fact that someone had leaked the story to the media.

"That information is public," Hendry told Burke. "I didn't talk to the press, Parker didn't talk to the press. That's what they got off the press board.

"And stay the hell away from me," Hendry added.

Afterward, the two men never spoke when they saw each other at the gym.

Alex Hunter had never held a press conference like the one that was scheduled for the morning of February 13. Just before he left the Justice Center for the city council chambers, where the press was waiting, he joked with a deputy DA that he would be doing battle with Goliath.

On a windy, partly cloudy day, Hunter, who was as yet unknown to most national media representatives, stood on a stage before a hundred reporters and photographers. The podium in front of him was adorned with the city's seal, a jagged outline of the Flatirons. Seated next to him was Tom Koby, in uniform, looking at his notes and ready to make his first public statement on the case since his January 9 invitation-only press conference.

"As I watched the dawn arrive this morning, I was doing my workout—which you don't allow me to do anymore midday," Hunter began, not fully realizing that his words were reaching millions of viewers across the country.

Hunter spoke of the pressure that everyone, including members of the press, was experiencing and noted that the police and the DA's office were all on the same team. While Koby, at his January 9 press briefing, had called public interest in the case "sick," Hunter went out of his way to say that he wasn't about to quarrel with the press. He called JonBenét's murder "a case like we have never seen before, a case like I don't think any of you have ever seen before. I know enough of you to know that we are all zeroing in on the same thing, that we are looking for the truth, and we are looking to do justice in this case."

His mission, Hunter said, was "to seek out the best of the best to work on this case. Because this is not Tom Koby and Alex Hunter's case. No, this is a case of the people of Boulder, the people of Colorado, and certainly, without exaggeration, the people across this country whom this case has touched."

Hunter's tone became more deliberate and emphatic. "We know where we're headed. We're going to solve this case, but we're going to do it *our* way. . . . I'm not going to file [charges] until I feel I *have it.*"

Hunter stressed that the press "shared responsibility." The media could—and should—help the American public understand that a resolution of the case would involve exhaustive investigation, a double-dotting of *i*'s and double-crossing of *t*'s. The road to justice, he said, would not be paved in shortcuts.

Without mentioning Pete Hofstrom by name, Hunter spoke of his office's "homicide unit," which had been together for twenty-three years. Then Hunter announced that he'd enlisted the help of Dr. Henry Lee and attorney Barry Scheck. At that moment, many reporters felt Hunter moved the case definitively into the national consciousness. With Lee and Scheck—household names from the Simpson case—the investigation of JonBenét's murder acquired star power.

Referring to the media criticism of his office, Hunter said, "We know there's sort of a sense of a David and Goliath thing. . . . Let me tell you what we have put together. We're calling it an expert prosecution task force." In addition to Lee and Scheck, Hunter said, his four Denver-metro-area peers would be on the task force—DAs Bill Ritter, Dave Thomas, Jim Peters, and Bob Grant. Local reporters knew that Peters and Grant had personally handled the prosecutions of three out of the five men then on Colorado's death row.

"We feel that we can match the resources of *anyone*, in bringing to bear on this case, in our search for the truth, to do justice, the very best that is available."

Hunter then looked squarely into the TV cameras.

"Finally, I want to say to you, *through* you, I want to say something to the person or persons who committed this crime, the person or persons who took this baby from us."

He paused a moment before continuing: "The list of suspects narrows. Soon there will be no one on the list but you. When that time comes—and as I have said to you, that time *will* come—Chief Koby and I and our people of the expert prosecution task force and the other resources that we bring together are going to bear down on you. You have stripped us of any mercy that we might have had in the beginning of this investigation. We will see that justice is served in this case. And that you *pay* for what you did. And we have *no doubt* that *that* will *happen*.

"And I say to you that there will not be any failure in that regard. We will ensure that justice is served for this community, for this nation, and, most important, for JonBenét. Thank you."

This was a surprisingly fierce Alex Hunter, whom the press had not seen before. Then Tom Koby took his turn.

The chief began by discussing the evidence in general terms. Some DNA testing had already been completed by the Colorado Bureau of Investigation, he said.* But some of the evidence would soon be transferred for further examination to Cellmark, a well-respected private lab in Maryland. It would all take time—"several months," Koby said.**

He ended by saying, "This is not going to be quick, in the face of this most difficult situation, as Alex pointed out—there are none bigger than this, that have gotten this kind of scrutiny. But you [police officers] have stood the tests, and you have responded professionally. You are true professionals, in the genuine sense of that word.

"And I think you could hear in Alex's voice, and I think for those of you who know me, you know that when I say this, I mean this: I truly love the people in my organization, and what they have been able to produce and what they have been able to withstand." Koby had taken just four minutes—much less time than Hunter.

The first question was addressed to Hunter: If the pool of suspects was narrowing, who still remained?

"I'm not going to get into whether it's ten people or a hundred. It's narrowed. . . . *Significant progress* is being made."

Then, inevitably, Hunter was asked about his David-and-Goliath

* The steps in DNA testing are as follows: Blood, semen, saliva, skin, or hair is labeled and shipped to a forensics lab. Only minute amounts—a single hair root, for example—are required. Then the sample is mixed with detergent and enzymes, which break open the cells and let out their DNA. The cell fragments are removed, and the remaining mixture is spun in a centrifuge tube. Pure DNA settles at the bottom. The DNA is then amplified. Its double helix is separated into two strands. Technicians add twenty-six short pieces of DNA, called primers: sequences of the chemicals C, A, T, and G that link to the beginning and end of thirteen different places on a person's DNA. Then replication takes place. When a primer attaches to the beginnings of one of the thirteen sites, it acts like the start button on a photocopying machine, turning on cellular machinery that makes a million copies or more of each site. Copies of the thirteen sites, each about one hundred to six hundred chemical letters long, are separated by size through gel electrophoresis. In this process, a drop containing millions of DNA fragments is placed at one end of a sheet of gel. Electric current pulls the fragment across the gel; the larger the fragment, the more slowly it moves. The fragments, tagged with dye, show up as colored bands under ultraviolet light. The lab compares the length of the thirteen markers to the lengths of a suspect's thirteen markers. The more markers that match, the greater the odds are that it is a definitive match. If all thirteen strands in one person's DNA are identical to all the lengths in another person's, the odds are one in trillions that it isn't a match.

**Test results can take from several days to weeks using the PCR method of testing. RFLP typing takes months. In some cases it can take up to ten months to obtain test results because the lab is so backlogged.

analogy, his contention that his team wouldn't be overpowered. Who was Goliath in this case?

Hunter avoided naming an adversary. "Who is Goliath?" someone repeated. "Who is your opposition?"

Hunter wouldn't budge. "There is no formal opposition."

"What kind of opponent is anticipated? Someone with lots of money?"

Hunter hesitated, unsure of himself for the first time. "The question's loaded. . . . I don't care who, ultimately, I come down on, but I'm going to be ready to match the resources of anyone because I think the case deserves that. So let me just put it simply: This case . . . deserves that we do the very best we can, bring in the best people. And that's what we're going to do."

Koby was asked about the DNA evidence.

"Next question," he said.

"Is the police focus inside or outside the Ramsey family?"

Koby again replied, "Next question."

When he was asked if this case put his professional future on the line, the chief's aide terminated the press conference. But Koby decided to speak further: "I was raised as a chief under the tutelage of Lee P. Brown, who was the chief in Atlanta, the Houston commissioner, and the New York drug czar, and Lee taught me three things about media management. One of them was, Don't answer stupid questions. Professional media people should ask you good questions. You don't have an obligation to reach down to the level of a dumb question.

"The second thing is, Don't answer questions that lead to speculation. Many careers and lives have been ruined by media speculation. And you have an obligation, I have an obligation, not to contribute to that phenomenon.

"And thirdly, Lee taught me, Don't answer questions that compromise your objective, particularly in a criminal case. So when we have questions that we don't respond to, what I am using is those criteria that Lee Brown drove into me long and hard over the years that I worked with him."

There was laughter in the audience—some nervous, some exasperated. At the end of the conference the consensus was that Koby had not handled the press well.

Later that evening, a reporter called Bill Wise to chat informally about Alex Hunter's performance.

"Yeah, I just talked to Hunter a few minutes ago," Wise said. "I told him, 'Gee, you must know something I don't know to have sounded so confident.' Hunter then gives me one of these sheepish looks and says, 'Well, I might have gotten a little carried away.'"

The members of the press had seen some posturing, some play-acting from Hunter. Nevertheless, when the reporter who spoke to Wise talked with a friend later, he was caught up in Hunter's enthusiasm. "I think they're going to get this guy after all," he said, not sure whether "this guy" was John Ramsey or a mystery intruder. "They're going to get him." For the moment, at least, he had bought into Hunter's bravado.

The next morning, Patsy Ramsey called Hunter. She thanked him for what he'd said about getting the killer of her daughter. She only wished the police understood that she and John had nothing to do with JonBenét's death. There was still a killer on the loose, she said.

In his second-floor office at the Justice Center, Sheriff Epp caught the press conference on TV and found it hard to watch. He felt that he no longer knew his colleagues, that they had become puppets whose strings were being pulled by the media. Maybe they were more like protoplasm in a petri dish with an electrical charge going through them.

Epp had known Alex Hunter for twenty-five years, and for the first time he was embarrassed for him. Alex was falling all over himself apologizing for the cops—even covering up for them. Epp thought it was a mistake.

Afterward, Epp went downstairs to see Hunter and told him flat-out that he was placing his loyalty to Koby above his loyalty to the people who had elected him. Epp knew that Hunter got the point, but he had no reply. Epp could see how hard it was for his friend to hear the truth. Hunter thanked Epp for his honesty.

Then Epp tried to reach Koby, only to find that the chief and his wife had left for a long weekend in Santa Fe, New Mexico, with city manager Tim Honey and his wife.

While Koby and Hunter were holding their press conference, Bill Wise was at the old courthouse at Pearl and 13th Streets asking the county commissioners for more money for the Ramsey investigation.

Hofstrom had asked Hunter for an experienced homicide detective and a full-time deputy DA. In addition, they needed money for Lee and Scheck and for a forensic psychiatrist, plus funds to support the joint war room with its computer equipment and paper shredders.

Wise brought the commissioners up to date on the anticipated costs for his department. He was surprised when they asked him if Pete Hofstrom would be doing the investigative work.

That's part of the problem, Wise replied. He'd like to do a lot of that and the Boulder Police Department says, Get out of our business. They don't want lawyers sticking their noses into their investigation . . . so we've told Pete to back off a little bit.

Commissioner Jana Mendez asked, Doesn't Tom Koby realize that an investigation that isn't done for prosecution purposes . . . ? Her voice trailed off.

I'm not going to criticize the Boulder Police Department, but I'd sure like to, Wise told the commissioners. Under the law, we don't control these investigations. If not for Alex Hunter's close relationship with Tom Koby, we wouldn't be in the case at all.

As he spoke, Wise knew he'd put his foot in it. The police certainly deserved criticism, but denouncing them in public was not his job. So far neither the Boulder police nor the DA's office had publicly acknowledged any problems between them.

The commissioners approved an additional $124,000 for his department.

Later that afternoon, Kevin McCullen, a reporter for the *Rocky Mountain News* who had been at the press briefing, stopped in as usual at the council chambers to listen to the official tape recording of the budget session. Taking notes, he heard his next headline.

After McCullen left, Jana Petersen, the commissioners' press representative, called Wise and told him she was sure McCullen would publish what Wise had said about the police. Wise knew immediately that he was in trouble.

Back at the office, he told Hunter what he'd said to the commissioners. For a moment they joked about whether the tape could be destroyed. Then Wise said that all he could do now was mop up after himself.

Calling McCullen, Wise admitted that his comments had been careless and pointed out that a story on his views of the Boulder police wouldn't help solve the Ramsey case. McCullen refused to bury the remarks.

Having been turned down flat, Wise decided to appeal to McCullen's editor, Deborah Goeken. She heard him out and said she would consider deleting his comments about the police in her reporter's budget story. An hour later, however, Wise discovered that the local NBC affiliate, Channel 9, had learned about his remarks from a commissioner and was going to air them. Knowing that his request to Goeken would only compound his difficulties, Wise called her to withdraw the request, but the story had gone to press without his comments in Friday's edition of the paper. The following day, the paper published Wise's inflammatory remarks together with his apology for criticizing the police.

Koby returned from Santa Fe on Monday and asked Hunter to take Wise off the Ramsey case. Hunter knew that if he let Wise stay, Eller would use it as an excuse to push the DA's office further out of the investigation. There was nothing to do but comply with Koby's wishes.

"Pig's ass," was all that Bill Wise had to say until Koby asked Hunter if he was going to discipline Wise.

"They should take some of those cops and beat them within an inch of their lives for the way they bungled this case," Wise told Hunter. "That's where the disciplining should be."

If the purpose of the press conference was to reduce the number of calls from the media, it was a failure. During the briefing, unhappy TV viewers called the Boulder DA's office to complain that their local station had preempted their soap operas, but by midafternoon, Hunter and Koby had calls from the *Detroit News*, the *Connecticut Post*, the *Today* show, *Good Morning America*, CNN, *Time*, and *Newsweek*. Producers at one network said that they would stay in town until the case was solved. ABC was already spending $150,000 a month to keep five producers in Boulder. CNN had an entire studio, a library of hundreds of videotapes, and an editing room set up at the Residence Inn.

Before the week was out, Hunter had received 170 calls from the media. Before long, he and Bill Wise were spending five hours a day talking to reporters.

While the press was chasing Hunter and Koby for sound bites, at police headquarters Detectives Jane Harmer and Melissa Hickman were interviewing Linda Hoffmann-Pugh and her husband, Merv, for a third time. The detectives went over the housekeeper's story again and collected additional blood, hair, and saliva samples. They wanted to know when Linda had last changed JonBenét's sheets. The Monday before Christmas, she told them. When they told Linda that John Ramsey had said he'd broken the basement widow to enter his home, she found it odd. She said that Ramsey always came in through the garage door, which he opened with a remote-control device, then through a door to the house that was never locked except when Nedra was home alone at night with her grandchildren.

Hoffmann-Pugh was then asked to make a list of everyone she knew who frequented the house and a list of those who had keys. After two hours of intense questioning, she was so upset that for a moment she couldn't find her own key. Months later, the police asked her about scuff marks they found on the wall below the broken basement window and near John Andrew's suitcase. Maybe someone had climbed in that night and left the marks. Had she ever seen the marks? No, she told them.

The police theorized that if someone other than the Ramseys had killed JonBenét, he or she might have used a key to get in, since there was no clear sign of forced entry. On December 26 John Ramsey had told the police there weren't any keys "hidden under rocks" in the yard and that only John Andrew, Nedra, and Linda had extra keys. But three weeks later, on January 21, Patsy's attorney told the police that the Whites, the Fernies, and Joe Barnhill also had keys. In April 1997, Ellis Armistead, an investigator hired by the Ramseys, would tell the police that there were twenty more extra keys outstanding. In the end, however, the detectives could find only nine people who said they had keys. Six of the keys were returned. Three were missing.

The police soon learned that the front door locked automatically when it was closed. The police were told that Patsy, possibly without her husband's knowledge, had hidden a key outdoors near the front door because whenever she went out front for something, she got locked out. Now that key was also missing.

I was born in Lyons, Kansas, and my dad was a poor wheat farmer. I had three brothers and one sister. I'm the youngest, and one of my brothers is twenty years older than me. He's a welder, with his own construction business in Fort Morgan, Colorado.

When I was thirteen we moved to Fort Morgan because my dad wasn't doing well. He went to work for my brother as a ditch digger. My dad was an alcoholic. He died in 1986. My mother was forty-one when she had me. I have six living kids. Ten grandchildren. And a paper route.

I have my ladies, the women I work for. I have a doctor's wife in Greeley, and a lawyer. I was working for a bonded agency called Merry Maids when I met Patsy. I started with her one day a week. I was dumbfounded, the place was so huge. It was too much for one person. Soon we had four people, once a week.

Patsy was warm and kind. Just a sweet person. But she had a hard time keeping up with the laundry. She was doing lots of charity work and was involved with her children's schooling.

Then I went to work for her three days a week, $72 a day. Monday, Wednesday, Friday. I'd get there at 9:00 in the morning and be gone by 3:00. That's when my daughter Ariana gets out of school. Sometimes I worked for Patsy on Saturdays and holidays. She gave me a $300 bonus at the end of my first year. That was October 27, 1996.

Patsy was afraid she wasn't going to live, that her cancer would come back and she'd never live to see the children grow up. She read a lot about illness and healing. Every three months she had a checkup. She believed if she prayed, everything would be all right.

Patsy admired John. He accomplished a lot. She told me that when they started out they had nothing, and they worked themselves up to where they were now.

I first met JonBenét when she was in preschool. She was home, like, half a day. Patsy called her Jonnie B. I spent half my time picking up after her. She and her brother would just leave everything on the floor—their socks, their shoes, toys, books, just everything. They were never trained to put things away properly.

I always came in the side door, and I'd walk right into the kitchen and not know where to start. Dishes all over. If they had Ovaltine, the jar would still be open. I always had to wipe the peanut butter off the counter.

"I think we ought to get a hamper," I told Patsy.

"Yeah, that sounds good," she answered. But we never got one.

"Linda is not here to pick up," Patsy's mother would say. "She's here to clean. How do you expect her to do a good job if she's picking up?"

"OK, Mom, I'll work it out."

Patsy's clothes went into the laundry chute. I never had to pick up after John. Maybe once—a pair of shoes. Patsy changed purses once a week. She'd lay her purse on the spiral staircase, and I'd clean it out and put it in the closet. She had maybe forty of them, and even more pairs of shoes.

I think the problem with the children was they didn't have any responsibility. They were spoiled. Burke had this red Scout knife and always whittled. He'd never use a bag or paper to catch the shavings. He'd whittle all over the place. I asked Patsy to have a talk with him. She answered, "Well, I don't know what to do other than take the knife away from him." After Thanksgiving I took that knife away from him and hid it in the cupboard just outside JonBenét's room. That's how that problem was solved.

These weren't naughty children. They dressed themselves, and Patsy did JonBenét's hair. All her daughter's clothes were organized in drawers. Turtlenecks in one drawer, pants in another, nighties and panties in one, socks in another. Dates on all their underclothes.

"Just go away and leave me alone," JonBenét said when I tried to help her with her boots. Sometimes she acted like a spoiled brat.

"No, don't you answer the door," she'd say when someone went to open it at a luncheon Patsy gave. "I'm answering the door."

JonBenét spent a lot of her time sitting on her bed watching Shirley Temple movies on her VCR. She loved them all.

She also loved being in pageants. If she didn't want to go, Patsy didn't make her. Nedra used to bring lots of things for JonBenét to wear. Nedra did most of the pageant planning. JonBenét would have to practice singing and dancing. Nedra and Patsy's sister Pam would decorate JonBenét's shoes, her gloves, put sequins on her hats. Some dresses were made from scratch, but they had fun altering most things. They prepared differently for each pageant. Sometimes it would take a month. They were always reworking something.

JonBenét played a lot with Daphne, the Whites' little girl. They were real close. And Burke had his friends, the Walker and Stine children.

When the Ramseys traveled, I started taking the children's dog, Jacques, home with me. It would always yip, yip, yip, and I couldn't take it. Joe Barnhill, the elderly neighbor from across the street, started watching Jacques, and they got attached to each other. Before long the dog was always running across the street to the Barnhills' house. Jacques started staying there, and when JonBenét wanted to see her dog, she went over and played with him.

In the summer of '96, JonBenét started wearing those diaper-type underpants—Pull-Ups. She even wore them to bed. There was always a wet one in the trash. By the end of the summer, Patsy was trying to get her to do without them. Then JonBenét started wetting the bed again. Almost every day I was there, there was a wet bed. Patsy said she wasn't going to use Pull-Ups again. She just put a plastic cover on the bed. No big deal to her. By the time I'd come in the morning, Patsy would have all the sheets off the bed and in the laundry. JonBenét's white blanket would already be in the dryer. The Ramseys had two washer-dryers—one in the basement and a stackable unit in a closet just outside JonBenét's room.

Patsy started to take a painting class, and JonBenét drew a lot with crayons and markers. People and flowers. They had a big easel, but most of the time JonBenét painted on a card table in the butler's kitchen. Patsy had her paints and brushes in a white paint tote. Sometimes she asked me to take her paints down to the basement when she was having some kind of party. That's what she'd say about everything, any kind of clutter: "Just take it down to the basement. I don't want to see it." On the day of the Ramseys' Christmas party, I took the paint tote downstairs.

Evenings were for the family. They did homework and had dinner together. Patsy worked on school projects with the kids. She was always doing something for the children on her computer. She read to them at bedtime. Sometimes she asked me to baby-sit if she couldn't find a sitter.

Patsy spent a lot of time alone in the house while John was away on business. She never kept a baseball bat under the bed, or Mace. Never even set the alarm. She didn't like it, because it went off accidentally and it drove the police crazy.

The last month I was there, nothing was different. Patsy went to New York with her family and some friends. JonBenét even ice-skated at Rock-efeller Center. When they came back, they got ready for another pageant. Patsy was always putting things off until the last minute.

On December 23, JonBenét was playing with makeup. "JonBenét, you are not going anywhere with all that on," Patsy told her. "You take some of it off." JonBenét did. At one o'clock she went to play with some friends and was back by four o'clock. Late that afternoon, she didn't want to wear a dress for their Christmas party. Patsy got a little agitated. Finally, Jon-Benét put on a velvet one with short sleeves.

I stuck around with my daughter Ariana to see Santa. We hadn't planned to stay, so Ariana wasn't dressed up. Patsy gave my daughter a Christmas sweater and a vest. Even lent her a pair of her shoes. At the last minute, Patsy wrote a little verse about Ariana for Santa to read.

At 5:30 P.M. Santa showed up. By then the Barnhills, the Fernies, the Stines, Pinky Barber, and the Whites, who came with Priscilla's parents, had all arrived. Maybe eight couples and their children. Most of the men *gathered by the spiral staircase. John made drinks for everybody from the butler's kitchen. The kids played in the living room by the big Christmas tree. That's where Santa read his little verses about everyone. This year Mrs. Claus was there too. Santa looked kind of sick.*

I was supposed to come back the next day, December 24, and clean up. I called Patsy and said I couldn't. I told her I had a fight with my sister and needed some money to pay the rent. I asked Patsy for a $2,000 loan. I told her I would pay it back $50 each week.

She didn't hesitate. "Sure." Said she'd leave it for me on the kitchen counter for my next regular visit on December 27.

The more I think about it, JonBenét could not have been killed by a stranger. I didn't even know that room was there. How could a stranger know to go there? How in the world did this happen?

—Linda Hoffmann-Pugh

2

By mid–February the FBI and the CBI forensics technicians had concluded part of their fingerprint typing and fiber analysis. CBI told the Boulder police that no prints had been found on the black duct tape that John Ramsey said he removed from his daughter's mouth and none were found on the broken artist's paintbrush used to make the "garrote" found around JonBenét's neck. The CBI had been able to identify two fingerprints found on a white bowl on the dining room table that contained uneaten pineapple. One print belonged to Burke and the other to Patsy. Since partly digested pineapple had been found in JonBenét's small intestine at the autopsy, the police wondered if the Ramseys had been less than candid about JonBenét's bedtime activities and what time she fell asleep. Patsy and John had never mentioned with whom, where, or when their daughter had eaten pineapple.

A palm print on the wine cellar door was identified as belonging to Patsy, and another of Patsy's prints was found on the door to Burke's train room, the room with the broken window. A print on the west patio door on the main floor belonged to John. The location of the prints meant very little, since Patsy and John, living in the house, often visited these rooms and fingerprints are almost impossible to date. Another fingerprint on the west patio door was later identified as belonging to Barbara Fernie. Eventually the CBI told the police that they had been able to match almost all the fingerprints the detectives had collected to people from whom the police had collected physical evidence. Another palm print found on the wine cellar door still remained unidentified.

The CBI had already determined that the stain on JonBenét's underpants—which appeared to be blood and turned out indeed to be blood—was not solely hers. A D1S80 DNA test showed that the stain came from at least two different sources.* After receiving the report, the police contacted the parents of JonBenét's playmates to see if any of the children had ever exchanged clothes with her. Priscilla White said she could not remember her daughter, Daphne, trading clothes with JonBenét, but Daphne told Detectives Arndt and Harmer that she and JonBenét sometimes wore each other's clothes. During their interviews, the police were told that Fleet White had sometimes changed JonBenét's panties. Months later, Pam Paugh, Patsy's sister, told a TV reporter that she knew White had changed her niece's clothes.

The new information meant a lot of follow-up work for the police in the coming weeks.

Meanwhile the duct tape was sent to the FBI, which had a large database for matching purposes. Special Agent Douglas Deedrick, an FBI hair and fiber specialist who had testified in the O. J. Simpson criminal case, notified the Boulder PD that he had found what seemed to be red and black microscopic fiber traces on the duct tape. The four fibers would have to be analyzed further to determine what kind they were. Shortly afterward the FBI began a chemical analysis of the adhesive on the duct tape. Eventually they hoped to be able to locate the manufacturer and possibly even find out the approximate date of fabrication. They told the police they might even be able to trace the tape to where it had been bought.

AUTOPSY SHOWS SEX ASSAULT

JonBenét Ramsey was the apparent victim of a forceful sexual attack in the minutes before she was strangled to death—an attack

---

* A D1S80 test is a PCR-based test that measures the genetic marker known as D1S80 on the DNA strand.

that left her body scraped and bruised, according to a partial autopsy report released Friday by a Boulder County judge.

During his Dec. 27 autopsy on the 6-year-old, Boulder County Coroner John Meyer found scraping and swelling of the child's vaginal area, as well as a series of scrapes on the back of her right shoulder, left lower back and left lower leg.

—Howard Pankartz
The Denver Post, February 15, 1997

In February John Ramsey met with Robert Phillips, his Boulder estate attorney, to deal with the financial matters relating to Jon-Benét's estate, which included a trust in her name to which he and Patsy had contributed $10,000 yearly. During the meeting Ramsey mentioned that he and Patsy were now staying at the Stines' house, where they had moved at the beginning of February and planned to stay until Burke's school year ended. Ramsey suggested that Robert and his wife, Judith, whom Patsy knew, join them at a restaurant. When Phillips told his wife about the invitation, she was astonished that the Ramseys could think about eating out with the media following them everywhere.

A few weeks later, before the dinner was arranged, the Phillipses' daughter, Lindsey, said that she wanted to play with Burke, so Judith drove her over to the Stines' house, which was just around the corner from her own home. She rang the bell, and a moment later, two little eyes peered out through the blinds. When a housekeeper opened the door, Judith saw Patsy, fully dressed and made up, sitting on the living room sofa, and talking to a woman who was visiting from Atlanta. Lindsey went off to play with Burke and some other children, and Patsy greeted Judith, who could now see that despite her attempt to look composed, Patsy was in fact distraught under the thinnest veneer of normalcy. Judith thought she might be heavily medicated. Soon Patsy was crying on Judith's shoulder.

"If only I had woken up. If *only* I woke up," Patsy repeated. "Why didn't I wake up?"

Later Judith asked Patsy whether she had seen Priscilla White.

"Oh, no, I can't," Patsy said.

"Why not?"

"Those memories ... I just ... I can't even go into their home. I can't."

Judith knew that the Ramseys had been making derogatory comments about some of their friends—particularly Priscilla and Fleet White—and had also been told by their mutual friend Roxy Walker that the Whites were questioning whether the Ramseys were involved in JonBenét's death.

Judith was a friend of Priscilla White's and knew that the situation had been devastating for everyone. Susan Stine had called Judith and said, "Either you're on the Whites' side or you're on *our* side," as if this were a divorce. Susan Stine and Roxy Walker were "Patsy's pit bulls."

Like many Boulder mothers, Judith was infuriated when Patsy said in her CNN interview, "Hold your babies close to you because there's a killer out there." Judith's daughter, Lindsey, wouldn't sleep in her bedroom for six weeks after she heard Patsy say that on TV. Judith couldn't understand how Patsy could be so callous as to arouse everyone's worst fears.

She was certain that John and Patsy knew more about JonBenét's death than they were saying. She couldn't imagine Patsy murdering JonBenét, but she *could* imagine Patsy being involved in a cover-up.

Like JonBenét, most of the Ramseys' friends' children attended High Peaks Elementary. At High Peaks, kids were seen not as numbers but as individuals, each with his or her own special possibilities. To make this work, the school relied heavily on volunteers.

Patsy was generous with her time and commitment to High Peaks. During the 1995–96 school year, Patsy had been in charge of the science fair, in which 138 children in kindergarten through fourth grade had participated. She created an environment in which students could discuss their projects with professional scientists so that even the scientists felt their time was well spent. She found three judges to review each project. For a meteorology project, Patsy got a meteorologist, for biology, a biologist. Charles Elbot, the principal, said that Patsy's science fair had been arranged with "thoughtfulness, finesse, and generosity of spirit."

Many parents who worked with Patsy said that she dared to think big. She was audacious, bold, and a natural leader. A born manager. Her friend Roxy Walker, more of a detail person, rounded up a group of parents to implement Patsy's ideas.

Patsy would call and say, "I need paper plates that will hold wet spaghetti and cups that people can drink from. Forks and knives. For fifty people. Can you bring that? Yes? No? Tell me, because I'm going to depend on you." She was effective—or arrogant, depending on your point of view.

The Good Fairy project was one of Patsy's ideas.

Instead of asking people to raise money in the usual ways—sales drives, auctions, or donations—in Good Fairy, teachers were to make a list of things they needed for their classrooms, items ranging in price from $3 to $200. The teachers would specify the item, where it could be bought, the catalog number, and the total price. Patsy then put together spreadsheets and sent the parents copies of each teacher's list.

Good Fairies were designated for each class. They called families and merchants and encouraged them to look over the list with their own kids and pick something to donate. The entire school was decorated in the fairy theme, with pink streamers hanging everywhere. Patsy and Roxy made it an event, and the arrangements became very elaborate—too elaborate for some people. Many parents disliked all the folderol that accompanied Patsy's projects. They would have preferred to write a check and be done with it. There were also some parents who thought that Patsy had made too big a deal of an elementary school science fair. But most people involved with High Peaks Elementary were dumbstruck by Patsy Ramsey's ambitious and well-executed projects.

I was a schoolteacher in Chicago and got bored with teaching. Got divorced. Got into the computer business and moved to Dallas. Met my second husband, Robert Phillips, who was the author of a software program. He lived in Atlanta, and before long I joined him there. It was a fairy tale.

Ten years ago we moved to Boulder. My husband changed his profession at age forty-four. He went to law school and passed the bar. I tried painting, then some sculpting, and soon discovered I wanted to be a photographer. A black-and-white portrait photographer. I love to photograph women.

I met Patsy and John back in '84, in Atlanta. They were already married, but none of us had moved to Boulder. Patsy worked with my husband at Hayes Micro Computer in Millcrest, Georgia. She was in charge of marketing his product, a sophisticated management system. Patsy was definitely a career woman.

She was friendly, lots of fun, a happy person, and a workaholic. She had the ability to make people like her. Whenever she was introduced, it was always, "This is Patsy Ramsey—she's the former Miss West Virginia." She loved it.

We all became fairly close. One year all four of us were on different business trips in San Francisco. Then we ended up going to Napa Valley together afterward.

Patsy and John were a close couple, very much in love. You felt the closeness. John was very attentive to Patsy and she to him. Lots of hand-holding, hugging. They adored each other.

John dressed casually, and Patsy always wore fine clothes. "When you go outside your home," she always said, "you dress up. Full makeup." In fact, she was always a little overdressed.

In '87 Patsy got pregnant. She loved that too. It would be her parents' first grandchild. John was the type of guy who would say, "Patsy, whatever you want. If you want to be a businesswoman, fine. If you want to be a mom, fine. Do whatever turns you on."

Patsy quit her job and started working with John in his computer business. She ran all the marketing out of the basement of their home, where John worked with Patsy's parents, Nedra and Don Paugh. It was a family thing. Patsy's sisters and their husbands were also involved.

The stairs to the basement had these little strings of lights. It was like walking into a movie theater. You went down to a large television room, and Patsy worked in a back room.

When Burke was born, John built an addition to their house so Burke could have his own room, plus quarters for a nanny. The sky was the limit.

Then John merged his business with one in New Jersey and one in Boulder. The new firm, Access Graphics, located its operations out west. By then, I was already living in Boulder.

Whenever they had sales meetings, Patsy took over, organizing the catering and all the other details. Burke and my daughter, Lindsey, played together, and the four of us adults would often see each other for dinner. Then some big company invested in Access and John became president.

I never thought John could get Patsy to move out west. But she turned out to be open-minded, and that surprised me.

They first lived in a condo on Pearl Street at 19th until they found a house. Like all of us, they went through "sticker shock." It's hard coming from huge, magnificent homes in the East that cost very little compared to the prices here.

Patsy liked one home in a new development outside of town, in Rock Creek, because it had streets and sidewalks where kids could play and ride bicycles. JonBenét had just been born, and Patsy didn't want to go through remodeling an old house. She wanted something brand-new.

John leaned more toward an older property, on 15th Street. He wanted to be in the city because he needed to establish himself and his family in the heart of the community where he was locating his company. When they asked us for advice, we said 15th Street was a better investment. The value would increase there far faster than out in the Rock Creek development. When they bought the house on 15th Street, they knew it had to be renovated. It was almost three stories, with an elevator that had to go.

John was busy running the business, and all the reconstruction was left to Patsy—dealing with builders, painters, and decorators, all of it. She always looked tired.

Then John lost his oldest daughter in a car accident in Chicago. It was devastating, and suddenly he looked like he was always hunched over. He started reading a lot of metaphysical books, on life after death. All kinds of spiritual books. Patsy told me he was trying to find answers to why this could possibly happen, and she was concerned for him. Patsy wanted to help, but she felt powerless to do anything for this person she really cared about. It frustrated her.

About that time, Burke started school and Patsy started volunteering at his school. She volunteered for anything and everything—fund-raising, parties, room mother. She organized magnificent parties for the children. She met the Stines, and they became close. Then the Walkers. She started to develop good friendships in places where she wanted to be.

Patsy was put on a pedestal by her friends. Roxy Walker would always say Patsy this and Patsy that, as if there were no higher authority than Patsy's opinion. Once I had to tell her, "Patsy is just a person." A person, of course, carrying a heavy load. It was, like, fix up the house, take care of the children, pull all the loose ends together in a city where she didn't know anybody. But she never complained.

The social rules in Boulder were different from anything Patsy knew in Atlanta. In order to fit into society, you have to find your own niche in Boulder. Patsy just didn't fit into jeans. She ended up getting tight black pants with rhinestone cowboy boots.

After the house was finished, she opened it up to visitors for Boulder's annual Christmas Tour of Homes. They let anybody view any room, even the bedrooms and bathrooms. They showed people their closets. My husband, Robert, who was now their family and estate attorney, warned them, "Close off your private rooms. Keep your guests on the first floor." They didn't.

Patsy wanted to make a statement. There were extravagantly decorated Christmas trees in almost every room. Everything she does is

Texas-size. Patsy is most comfortable in opulence. She wants the best of the best. But that isn't a Boulder thing. Most people in the community were shocked.

While the house was being remodeled in the summer of '93, Patsy went back east to judge a pageant in her home state. Roxy Walker called and said that Patsy was in the hospital. Her stomach had blown up like a balloon and it was discovered she had cancer—stage-four ovarian cancer. It doesn't get more serious. She had surgery immediately, then started going to Bethesda, Maryland, for treatments with experimental drugs.

It was life-or-death for her. Her mother came to Boulder and took over with the children. Patsy would go to Bethesda and become very ill, even in the plane on the way back. Sometimes she'd travel all by herself. She was desperate. She didn't want to die and leave her children motherless.

I kept thinking, Where the hell is John? I once asked her about that.

"Well, John has to . . . you know . . ."

I know John was worried and concerned, but it didn't change his behavior. He's a man of few words. And very concerned with his business.

In April or May of the following year she got a clean bill of health. If there is anybody who could overcome an illness by sheer will, it would be Patsy. Sheer determination.

One day soon after the good news, I found Patsy crying in the sun room in the front of the house. That's where she had spent most of her time when she was recovering. She talked more about religion that day than we had ever done before. She said God wanted her to be an example. So I asked her, "What are you going to do with that?"

She'd spend more time with the children, she said.

No, no, look at the bigger picture, I told her. You can do things to help other women who are suffering the same way. You need to get out and tell your story, how you licked it.

So she offered support to other women. She called them and talked. She'd send people the book that inspired her.

Patsy took this step forward and then took two steps backward. She returned to all her social stuff and pretty much dropped her cancer stuff. She spent a lot of time building up their position in the community. And she worked at her children's school relentlessly.

One day, in '95 or '96, Nedra took me upstairs. "Judith, you've got to see this." She showed me Patsy's closet. Nearby there was a display— almost a shrine. Pictures of Miss West Virginia. Patsy in every phase of her pageant days. Lots of paraphernalia on the walls. It surprised me.

Then there was the time Nedra pulled this little cowboy outfit out of the closet.

"This is not JonBenét's," I said. "What's it for?"

"Well, Judith, we're just getting JonBenét into a few pageants."

"Why would you do something like that?"

"You know, she's not too young to get started."

"And what if JonBenét isn't willing?" I asked. "What if she says, 'I'm not going to do it!' How would you respond to that?"

"Oh, Judith, we would never consider her saying no. We would tell JonBenét, 'You must do it. You will be a Miss Pageant.'"

It was sort of eerie. A little scary. The inevitability of it—from grandmother to mother and now to daughter.

Another time, Nedra was so excited about this little antique chair that JonBenét had picked out in Denver. JonBenét and Nedra had been shopping, and JonBenét insisted on buying this chair. Nedra was so happy that the child had selected something, that her granddaughter was showing signs of exquisite taste.

It was obnoxiously expensive. Thousands. For a child's chair.

"Well, as long as Mr. Ramsey brings the money in," Nedra said, "we'll spend it."

John would have been happy living in a cabin with log furniture. He often said that in conversation.

Early last November, there was a surprise birthday party for Patsy. Her birthday is in late December, but the family was going to be back east, so the party was in November. Priscilla White organized the entire thing. John told her, "Wherever you want it to be—the sky's the limit."

We all met at the Safeway Shopping Center and were loaded into a large bus—all kinds of people. Nedra, Don, John, Patsy's sisters, the Whites, Walkers, Stines, Fernies, Reverend Rol Hoverstock, and Patsy's entire softball team. Then the bus drove to their home and parked while John went up to the door. Patsy was flabbergasted.

"Should I change?" were her first words.

"No, no, come along right now," he told her.

Lots of laughing. Patsy didn't have a clue where we were going. Patsy and John sat in the back. There was an open bar.

At the Brown Palace in Denver, we had a private room. Fifty people. A band called the 4-Nikators. Sit-down dinner, open bar, huge bottles of Dom Perigon, and even cigars on the tables for everyone. Patsy was striding around big as life, puffing on a cigar like she owned the place.

The MC was a guy in drag—tiara, fluffy fur around his collar. Talked in a southern accent and did a monologue on Patsy—the Patsy Paugh Experience, from birth to the present. The family must have coached him. Lots of in-jokes and innuendo that I didn't understand. Then at midnight we were back on the bus. Patsy opened her presents on the way back. Everyone else was dropped off along the way, and Patsy and John were left alone on the bus.

That was probably the last time I saw JonBenét alive. Early that evening, before we left Patsy and John's home, both kids got on the bus to say hello to their grandparents and their aunts and uncles.

—Judith Phillips

WRITER: I understand you were out of town when JonBenét was murdered.

JUDITH PHILLIPS: I was in Chicago over the holidays.

WRITER: What did you think when you heard she'd died?

JUDITH PHILLIPS: I wasn't surprised that it happened. We're all given chances to learn significant lessons in our lives, and if we don't complete that learning process, we will be given that same lesson again—in spades. The death of Beth and then Patsy's illness affected John and Patsy temporarily, brought them some growth, but they went back to their old routines. They haven't changed their behavior. If you don't learn the lesson the first time, it comes back worse the second time, and maybe the third time. It's always bigger.

JONBENÉT ALL OVER THE WEB

About 1,000 miles east of Boulder, a computer in Kenosha County, Wis., is linked to other computers around the country to bring breaking information to the JonBenét Ramsey Homicide Web Sites—perhaps the world's most inclusive page on the young beauty-queen's murder.

The World Wide Web site, created by Ken Polzin Jr., a sheriff's department detective and city alderman, brings a mass of information to one locale:

Users can peruse stories and timelines on the case.

Video and audio clips are available to those with appropriate software.

A photo gallery brings who's who images to the screen.

And a variety of news organizations are a click away from followers who prefer unmoderated views on the murder mystery.

—Kieran Nicholson
The Denver Post, February 17, 1997

On February 17, Alex Hunter's office filed a motion in Boulder County court to prevent the search warrants obtained by the police from being made public until the investigation was complete and charges were filed. Also filed was a fourteen-page brief supporting the motion. It stated, "The owners of the property subject to these searches have not been eliminated from suspicion."

This was the first time any law enforcement official had gone on record to say that the Ramseys were suspects in their daughter's death.

In their opposing briefs, attorneys for the media did not sway Judge MacDonald from supporting the DA's position. "There is a substantial likelihood that disclosure of investigatory information at this initial stage of the investigation would compromise the integrity of the people's investigation," MacDonald ruled six days later. The warrants, affidavits, and inventory would be sealed for another ninety days or until an arrest was made. Included in the protective order was the phrase "other documents." This referred to a list of the people who had traps and taps placed on their telephones by the police.

e-mail Mon, 17 Feb 1997 14:32:28 —0700 (MST)

From: Hal Bruff, Dean of the CU Law School

To: Criminal Law Faculty

Alex Hunter has suggested to me that a Ramsey trial might provide a unique opportunity for the Law School to study a trial in depth as it unfolds, draw conclusions about the criminal justice system, and produce an archive of teaching materials. He would cooperate fully; of course we cannot know now whether a defense team would do so. Whaddaya think?

On February 19, Boulder County's police chiefs and sheriff held their monthly meeting. After the gathering, Sheriff Epp spoke with Tom Koby privately. "You're appearing to be arrogant with the media," Epp told him, "so if you've made mistakes, they will get you." Koby said he appreciated the advice, but Epp had the distinct feeling that Koby hadn't really heard him. That was a shame, Epp thought. In his opinion, Koby was heading for a fall.

Meanwhile, despite Alex Hunter's continued optimism, time had done nothing to improve the relationship between Pete Hofstrom and John Eller. Hofstrom got the impression that Eller wanted all requests for copies of police reports in writing. In a letter on February 18, Hofstrom had to resort to formal language, notifying Eller that on two prior occasions his requests had gone unanswered. This level of antagonism suggested to one deputy DA that the flow of information from the police was about to stop.

The investigation continued, however. Detectives Thomas and Gosage were back in Roswell, Georgia, reinterviewing family members. They learned that during World War II James Ramsey, John's father, was a pilot and received the Distinguished Flying Cross. His mother, Mary Jane Bennet, was a housewife. After the war, Ramsey's father ran the airport at Michigan City, Michigan, and later became the state director of aeronautics. A strong-willed man, he was known as Czar Ramsey. The family spent their summers in Charlevoix, where they purchased the house that now belonged to John.

Ramsey met his first wife, Lucinda, at Michigan State University and they married before he went into the navy and was stationed at Subic Bay in the Philippines. Before long, they had three children. After John's mother died and Lucinda's father died, Ramsey's father married his wife's mother. The family remained close until the late 1960s, when Lucinda was prompted to ask for a divorce after John had an affair. Close contact soon resumed, however, and when Lucinda met Patsy, the women became friends.

During the trip the detectives re-interviewed Nedra Paugh and asked for a third handwriting sample.

By now the officers had learned from several baby-sitters that JonBenét had regressed in her toilet training during Patsy's battle with cancer. In this interview, Nedra confirmed to police that at age six, her granddaughter was still in the habit of asking adults to wipe her when she was on the toilet. It didn't matter where she was or who the adult was—anyone within shouting distance would do. Some adults, thinking she was old enough to do this herself, stopped answering her calls, and it resulted in soiled underpants. JonBenét's apparent lack of embarrassment about adults wiping her made the detectives wonder if it had somehow invited activity that led to vaginal penetration.

Did Nedra think JonBenét would have fought an intruder? the detectives asked. "I guarantee you," she replied.

I'm from Ellenboro, West Virginia. Maybe a thousand people. Two or three churches, a restaurant, and three stores. I lived there before television, and when we got one, all the people on our street would come to our house and watch it. We couldn't see much, sometimes just shadows.

Patsy was not brought up with a deep religious faith. Actually, the healing power of Jesus didn't come to us until Patsy moved to Boulder and she met Betty Barnhill, who lived across the street. She'd had a healing experience. It had to do with a dreadful allergy problem. She gave Patsy lots of literature to read, and then one day Patsy was cured of her cancer. She believes she had a divine healing. I'd always heard about divine healing, but we weren't taught that in the Methodist Church.

John has always believed that what you receive, you should give back to the Lord. He doesn't attend church without giving. He was raised an Episcopalian, and when they settled in Boulder, John gave St. John's lots of things they needed—like a new sound system. And when Beth died, he established a children's Sunday school atrium in her name. JonBenét got her training there from Barbara Fernie.

It was wonderful when we lived in Boulder. You could hear the college band playing from Patsy's upstairs room. I loved the atmosphere. Patsy and John were beginning to like Boulder. None of the traffic and concrete that there is in Atlanta. They could run out and do an errand in ten minutes. In Atlanta it takes half a day.

Patsy was growing anxious about High Peaks, the school JonBenét and Burke were going to. There were children in some classes who would never be self-sufficient, physically handicapped, but they were being mainstreamed into the classroom. They have a right to be educated, but there were these other intelligent little boys and girls who were growing up to make a living, pay taxes, and they were sitting and waiting. The teacher told me her first obligation was to those handicapped children. And you just wonder how much time in the course of a day is spent on the children who need to be learning so that they can take their place in society. I know the teacher wanted to do more, but there was only one of her and an aide.

JonBenét started to read when she was about three. At first she wanted to be a ballet dancer, then an ice-skater, and finally she told someone she might like to be a veterinarian. On her last trip to New York, in November '96, she saw Grease, and the MC invited her to dance on stage before the show started. Nobody would ever pass her up. She just had that gleam in her eye. She and her partner didn't win, but they were runner-ups.

I made several trips to Boulder that last month. One was for the Boulder Parade of Lights that JonBenét rode in. It was cold. I didn't go to John and Patsy's Christmas party, because I was in Roswell. Don, my husband, was there and flew back standby on the 24th so we could spend Christmas Eve together.

I spoke to JonBenét Christmas morning on the phone. She was excited.

"What do you like the most about Christmas?" I asked.

"Baking cookies."

Like her mother, JonBenét loved to bake and decorate cookies. That afternoon she was supposed to make some plastic jewelry with her friend Daphne. My daughter Polly got her that gift for Christmas. And she was excited about going on the big red Disney boat after a few days in Charlevoix. Everything was packed.

I can tell you one thing. Whoever killed that child knew JonBenét's dog wasn't going to be in the house that evening. Sometimes Jacques would stay at the Barnhills' for a few hours and then he'd come back. He was always going back and forth. The killer knew the dog had already been taken across the street to stay with the Barnhills since the family was leaving the next morning for their winter vacation.

There were so many beautiful and wonderful people in Boulder, like the Barnhills, but now I can't tolerate even thinking of that place. It just makes me ill to even think that someone killed JonBenét in that place.

Now Patsy can never be happy on this earth. But she has to live someplace. We all have to live someplace.

—Nedra Paugh

For seven weeks the police had been interviewing the Ramseys' family, friends, and business associates without turning up any real suspects. They had finished their background checks on John Andrew and Melinda and had verified commercial airline schedules and private plane flight plans and found no record that either of them had traveled the night of December 25. Their alibis were solid. Besides the Ramseys, the only people apparently still under investigation were "Santa" Bill McReynolds and his wife, Janet; housekeeper Linda Hoffmann-Pugh; part-time reporter Chris Wolf; Bud Henderson, who owed $18,000 to Access Graphics; company executive Gary Merriman; and the Ramseys' friends Fleet and Priscilla White.

Next would come interviews with pageant photographers Randy Simons and Mark Fix, who had taken pictures of JonBenét. The police wanted to check the two men's whereabouts the night of the murder; they were also interested in finding out more about Patsy's and JonBenét's involvement in the pageants.

On February 20, Detective Harmer interviewed Randy Simons. Simons told her that on June 5, 1996, he had spent an entire day photographing JonBenét. Since JonBenét's death, his shots and Mark Fix's runway snaps had been sold to over two hundred magazines and newspapers, and now Simons was being pressured by the media for photographs of JonBenét in more provocative poses. He had never taken such shots, he told the police.

The night of the murder, Simons said, he had been at home alone in Genoa, 120 miles from Boulder.

Simons, a native of Denver, had been a professional news photographer since 1970 and had once worked for the Associated Press as a stringer. Several times he'd almost been killed while covering fires. In 1979 Simons decided he could make a better living—without risking his life—in fashion and advertising photography. When he opened his studio in Denver, upscale retailers like AP&S, Joslins, Fashion Bar, and Miller Stockman became his clients. When she was three, Kristine Griffin became his second child client. By the time she was nine, Kristine's annual income from modeling probably exceeded his, Simons said.

In May 1996 Kristine's mom, Pam Griffin, referred Patsy Ramsey to Simons, and she booked her daughter for a June 5 shooting. Because JonBenét was only six, Randy set aside only half a day. He knew he'd be lucky to get an hour or two from a child that young.

★ ★ ★

Patsy brought more clothes than I had ever seen a parent bring. In the makeup chair, JonBenét appeared quiet and shy, not scared. She kept looking at her mother.

In the studio, I shot close-ups with a cowboy hat first, then shots with flowers in her hair, which eventually adorned covers all over the world. Before noon, Patsy went out and got pizza for everyone, and then all of us went on location. I photographed the dance outfit with the polka dots next, then the harlequin dance costume. By one o'clock, JonBenét was tired of wearing the tap shoes, but she never complained about the heat or the bright sun. At the residential subdivision Ken Caryl Ranch, I did the Little House on the Prairie *dress—that playful shot of JonBenét hiding behind the tree.*

The half-day booking become a full day, and I got tired faster than Jon-Benét. At the Wilson White Fence Farm in Lakewood, which has a gazebo and carousel horses, JonBenét played peek-a-boo. She giggled and laughed. The wind began to blow, so I made Patsy my assistant. She held a reflector when we did the Little Red Riding Hood photograph. By then, I'd photographed JonBenét in eleven different outfits. She was a neat kid.

It wasn't long before the tabloids were saying that Patsy had forced JonBenét into some excruciating shots. I never saw anything like that.

I was paid $590 for the day. Patsy gave me a tip of $45. A month later, she ordered $960 worth of hand-retouched prints.

—Randy Simons

Three weeks later, on March 12, Detective Jeff Kithcart interviewed Mark Fix, who had also photographed JonBenét at various pageants. Fix, who had been a forensic photographer and had gone through 240 hours of police-academy training, was also a "certified protection professional"—a bodyguard. Kithcart was interested in what Fix knew about Randy Simons. Could he be a suspect? He said no.

Fix told the detective that Simons was into high fashion and pageants and had clients from all over the country. His specialty was shooting five- and six-year-olds, and he was known for his creative flair with lighting and retouching. A Randy Simons photo, Fix said, automatically gave a pageant contestant a higher score in the Miss Photogenic competition.

Simons was something of an "odd critter," though, said Fix. Right now he claimed that people were chasing him and that the Ramseys were pointing the finger at him. Simons had even told Fix that some paramilitary group was trying to ambush him and steal his negatives. He'd shot someone in the leg with an arrow to protect himself, Fix said, shrugging.

Back in May 1996, Fix had been photographing pageant contestants on stage in Denver. One of them was JonBenét.

JonBenét came out in this shocking outfit, and a noticeable murmur went through the room. There were all these feathers, like an ostrich. Someone called it a Ziegfield costume—so much more expensive and elaborate than anyone else's. You could see it was custom-tailored for her.

It was like showing up in a tuxedo when everybody is wearing sandals and T-shirts. Patsy realized she'd overdone it. She was as shocked as everybody else. I don't think JonBenét ever wore that outfit again, not even in the national pageant that I photographed two months later.

In July, at the national finals, JonBenét's costumes were less frilly. They were still on the cutting edge, but they'd been changed to fit the pageant system. By then, her singing and dancing routine had improved. She was really cooking. I don't know exactly how to describe it . . . she wanted to win. She was *going to win. It showed all the way through.*

The photograph I shot of her wearing a crown was just a simple runway photograph, but it appeared on the cover of People *magazine. She just walked up, struck a pose, and that was it. End of story.*

—Mark Fix

TWO ORDERED TO WRITE APOLOGIES
FOR RAMSEY AUTOPSY PHOTO SALE

"It is to be straight from the heart," said Judge Lael Montgomery, adding the public will not have access to the letters.

Lawrence S. Smith, 36 . . . pleaded guilty to two misdemeanors. Authorities dropped two felonies against Smith. Brett A. Sawyer also pleaded guilty to obstructing government operations.

Montgomery sentenced both men to three days in jail and 64 hours of community service. In addition Montgomery required Sawyer to give the $5,000 he received from the Globe for the photos to the Boulder District Attorney's office. Sawyer will pay a $500 fine.

"This charge was agreed to between (Chief Trial Deputy) Pete Hofstrom and myself before he was ever arrested," [defense counsel]

Schild added. "Our agreement was that Pete Hofstrom would ask the judge to sentence Brett to what he personally felt was appropriate, and it's noteworthy that Mr. Hofstrom did not ask the judge to give Brett any jail time."

—Alli Krupski
Daily Camera, February 21, 1997

The Ramseys were virtually under siege. John Ramsey had to sneak into his office building because he was constantly followed and harassed by reporters, photographers, and people on the street. Guards were now posted at the Access Graphics offices twenty-four hours a day.

At first, Ramsey worked a couple of hours at a time, then a half day or an evening. By the third week in February, he was able to make it into the office two days a week or three days every two weeks. When Gary Mann, his boss at Lockheed Martin, spoke to Ramsey, he heard a man totally consumed by the loss of his daughter. Nobody thought of asking Ramsey to return to work full-time. Mann understood that the company's management team would have to operate without him for months.

In the office, Ramsey would pace back and forth or stare through the floor-to-ceiling windows at the snow-covered Flatirons. Then, from the corner of his eye, he would spot a reporter or a photographer staking out the offices or going through the company's trash, and the police would be called. An alarm was installed on his office door to prevent break-ins. Denise Wolf, his secretary, had to do the cleaning in his office because they could no longer trust the janitorial staff not to rifle through—or steal—the papers on his desk.

"How does it feel to work for a murderer?" employees were asked by strangers on the street. Some of them were stalked, followed home. Others were ostracized by their friends for their loyalty to John Ramsey. The firm received obscene phone calls and hate mail and even a bomb threat. One day a photographer was discovered on the back fire escape trying to break into the building. An employee was offered $50,000 to bug John Ramsey's office.

With the office and employees of Access Graphics besieged, Lockheed Martin could have used the occasion to get rid of Ramsey, but Mann knew that he had looked out for their interests over the years, and the company was willing to allow the situation to play itself out.

No matter what, Mann was going to maintain the billion-dollar business Ramsey had built.

To Gary Merriman, life at the company was now like something out of *Night of the Living Dead*, especially since Access Graphics had been such a wonderful place to work before the tragedy. The front door to the building was in the heart of downtown Boulder, on the tree-covered Pearl Street Mall. Over the last six years, the company had expanded from twenty-five to more than four hundred employees.

The staff at Access was energetic and fearless. The average age was in the late twenties. The corporate culture was entrepreneurial. Employees were encouraged to take risks, and the company prospered. As it grew, Merriman was hired to head the new human resources department and to structure the company.

Despite its growth, the company had the atmosphere of a small shop. John Ramsey was decent to his employees, more patriarch of a large family than president of a company. He elicited loyalty and dedication from his employees. Introverted by nature, he treated people with respect and concern for their welfare. He often referred to Access Graphics as "four hundred families." And his staff responded accordingly.

In the office, no one ever heard Ramsey raise his voice—in anger *or* in delight. Even when frustrated by a setback, he dealt calmly with the problems at hand. Ramsey seemed to know that problems were not solved by being emotional.

What was most noticeable to Ramsey's colleagues was his sense of ethics. When people made mistakes, he never attacked their integrity. He was, however, offended by failure of character. On this point, he was firm. Business matters came and went, problems would be resolved or not, but character was permanent. If someone fell short in Ramsey's estimation—even if only in manners—he would remember it.

There was one unwritten rule that everyone at Access Graphics understood: John Ramsey never mixed work with his personal life. No matter how close they were to him or how long they had been associated with him, he almost never invited his employees home. You could have a close relationship with John Ramsey at work and never see him outside the office.

Within three days of the murder of JonBenét, Jane Stobie, a former employee of Access Graphics, called the Boulder police to say that she had important information for them. Two months later they still hadn't returned her call, so Stobie, an acquaintance of Denver DA Bill Ritter, called him and told him what she knew. A few days later, the Boulder police called.

On February 21 Detectives Arndt and Hickman interviewed Stobie at police headquarters. She told them that she had gone to work for John Ramsey in July 1991 as a specialist in Hewlett-Packard products. For three years she carpooled every day from Denver to Boulder with some of her coworkers. At first, Stobie said, the company was so small—and there was such an overlap of responsibilities—that it was routine for many of the employees to read each others' faxes. Then rumor had it that Calcomp, which owned 20 percent of Access Graphics and was itself owned by Lockheed, wanted one of the company's three founders, Jim Hudson, out. Eventually Lockheed exercised an option to purchase Access Graphics. The word was that John Ramsey got $8 million from the buyout. Overnight, a mom-and-pop operation was reporting to a Fortune 500 corporation.

Stobie saw Don Paugh, Ramsey's father-in-law, as a nice old southern gentleman and a father figure for some of the young employees. He was called the Andy Griffith of Access. Sometimes he would party with them at Potter's, a bar on the Mall.

But after John Ramsey's daughter Beth died in January 1992, employees at Access Graphics started getting "knifed," Stobie told the police. If an employee happened to offend Sun Microsystems, one of the firm's large suppliers, the person would be fired without warning. This seemed to happen again and again. At least that's how it looked to her, Stobie said.

In April 1993, Stobie told the police, Access sent her to Atlanta to manage the office there. Nedra Paugh and her other daughters, Polly and Pam, were running the so-called Atlanta branch. They sold supplies for the most part and were showing minimal profit.

Stobie found the Atlanta office totally unprofessional. There was pageant literature everywhere. Polly spent a lot of the day screaming at her husband. Stobie overheard conversations about oral sex and discussions between Nedra and some employees about the size of Burke's penis when he was born. All in all, it gave the impression of a place where the family got together rather than a workplace. Stobie felt that the Atlanta "branch" had become a potential embarrassment to John Ramsey now that Access had to answer to Lockheed, and she resented having to straighten out his family. In July 1993, Stobie said, she was ordered by Tom Carson to tell Nedra that the Atlanta office would close and that she would be laid off. Patsy's mother screamed and then sobbed, saying that she needed the job to keep her arthritis at bay. She had to be active. Stobie felt sorry for her, but the business came first. In 1994, not long after Stobie returned to Boulder, she was let go.

A few months after Stobie's police interview, she began to tell her story to various reporters.

The snow was still on the ground on February 23 when Geraldo Rivera taped two daytime TV shows at the Alps Boulder Canyon Inn. It was advertised as a "town meeting" but consisted of an invitation-only audience of local journalists, lawyers, pathologists, friends of the Ramseys, and some hotel guests.

In the first hour there was a debate between Dr. Cyril Wecht, a noted forensic pathologist, and Larry Pozner, a Denver criminal defense attorney. Wecht said that JonBenét was a victim of prior sexual abuse. In light of the possibility that semen was found at the crime scene, he said, this was a sex crime, with John Ramsey as the logical "primary suspect." Pozner was outraged at Wecht's statement and insisted that the presumed facts on which he based his claim were hardly reliable.

"He [Wecht] talks about semen," Pozner said. "What semen? Nobody's released a report saying they had found semen."

The second hour, taped the same afternoon, focused on how the Ramsey case was affecting various Boulder residents. Bill McReynolds, now known publicly as a suspect, proclaimed his innocence to Rivera's audience. Pam Griffin and her daughter, Kristine, talked about their experiences with Patsy and JonBenét during the previous year.

One local resident told Rivera that when he used to travel out of state and mention that he was from Boulder, people would say, "Oh, that beautiful place in the Rocky Mountains, right next to the Flatirons!" Now, he said, people asked him, "Who did it?"

The next day, on February 24, Detective Arndt reinterviewed the Ramseys' gardener, Brian Scott. She had already spoken to him earlier in the month.

Scott, who had graduated from the University of Colorado the year before, told the detective that he'd started working for the Ramseys in

June 1995 as a landscaper. The last time he was at the house was December 10. The family used large wooden candy canes to decorate the yard during the holidays, and he noticed that they hadn't been arranged properly. They needed deeper holes, which he dug before pounding them into the ground. Detective Arndt asked him what he remembered about the window-well grate near the rear patio. Scott said he didn't remember that the window was broken. He'd only been in the basement to fix the sprinkler clock. He didn't know there *was* a wine cellar, much less *where* it was. He did recall a broken window at the front of the house, but it was for the electrical cord for the Christmas lights and certainly not big enough for someone to crawl through—something like 2 inches square.

While Scott adjusted the candy canes along the front walk, he saw a blue Chevy Suburban pull up to collect JonBenét. She was wearing a pair of blue overalls and was being bratty about something. "I think she might have been giving orders," Scott said, "like, 'You get in the back. You do this.' Something like that." A moment later the car was gone. That was the last time he saw JonBenét.

On December 25, Scott went to the apartment of his girlfriend, Ann Preston, at around 10:30 P.M. and stayed until just after midnight, then went home alone. There was nobody to confirm his alibi for the rest of the night. Arndt asked him for a handwriting sample, and two weeks later he gave the police blood, saliva, and hair samples as well. Only then did he feel he was a suspect.

The Ramseys' street, 15th Street, was the nicest street in the neighborhood, better than 14th, better than 16th or even 13th. But 7th, 8th, and 6th were pretty nice too.

But the Ramseys' home could have been anyplace. From the property you couldn't really see the mountains, not even the Flatirons. As far as I could tell, never being on the top floors of the house, it didn't seem to have any views. The house didn't even have a front porch.

Unlike so many homes on the street, it didn't have a driveway out front. The Ramseys approached their home through an alley that ran behind the house. I never saw them enter through the front door—always through that alley and the side door off the patio. The alley was just wide enough for one car. It was all beat up, lined with trash cans. There was pavement in some places, gravel in others. I don't think they realized what an eyesore it was when they moved in.

I took it upon myself to trim the other side of the passageway. It could never be an elegant approach. It was not what I thought the Ramseys would want to see every day.

—Brian Scott

Late on the afternoon of February 25, Bill Wise walked into Alex Hunter's office and told him that two journalists, Dan Glick of *Newsweek* and Charlie Brennan of the *Rocky Mountain News*, wanted to see him as soon as possible about something they had uncovered. The reporters told Hunter that on December 26, 1974, Bill McReynolds's nine-year-old daughter, Jill, had been kidnapped with a friend, who was then sexually assaulted. Jill was released unharmed. In addition, the reporters had discovered that McReynolds's wife, Janet, had written a play called *Hey, Rube*, which was about the murder of a young girl that took place in a basement. It was based on the 1965 torture killing of Sylvia Likens in Indiana. Hunter immediately called John Eller and told him these details.

The next day, at police headquarters, Detectives Thomas and Gosage interviewed Janet McReynolds about her play and her daughter's kidnapping, details she and her husband had failed to mention in their previous interviews. A few days later, the detectives interviewed the McReynoldses' son Tristan, who had first met Patsy when he delivered a gingerbread house to the Ramseys from his bakery. Once she'd come into the bakery to inquire about his father's health. Tristan had been in Detroit with his girlfriend between December 24 and 26. The alibi of Jessie, the McReynoldses' other son, was also verified.

3

It was becoming clear to Pete Hofstrom and the Ramseys' attorneys that the CBI was not going to allow an outsider to observe its work. Carl Whiteside interpreted the law his way and would not budge. Toward the end of February, as Whiteside had suggested, the police sent some of the DNA evidence to Cellmark Diagnostics. The Maryland lab was not governed by Colorado law, and officials there would allow the Ramseys' representatives to observe their testing procedures if Hunter's office approved. On February 25, deputy DA Trip DeMuth wrote a letter to the lab approving observation by a Ramsey representative. Once testing began, it would take a minimum of six weeks before the results would be available.

WHAT'S ALEX HUNTER SAYING?

Thursday's weekly update press conference in Boulder, featuring District Attorney Alex Hunter, could have been titled: "Mr. Plea Bargain Meets Mr. Evidence."

The solemn D.A., who looks like he hasn't heard a good joke since New Year's, Thursday proclaimed himself as Mr. Evidence.

The declaration must have come as a surprise to other prosecutors and to attorneys and judges throughout Colorado, where Hunter has a reputation as a prosecutor whose office is an easy touch for plea bargains.

In fact, the Boulder D.A.'s office even is known to have contacted defense attorneys before an arrest is made to begin the discussions—a rather unusual tactic.

And so it was noteworthy that Hunter said he will not make an arrest in the JonBenét Ramsey murder case until all the evidence is sitting squarely on his desk.

"I am Mr. Evidence," Hunter said with a straight face.

—Chuck Green, columnist,
The Denver Post, February 28, 1997

When Jeff Hendry of the Boulder Sheriff's Department read Chuck Green's column, he smiled. He had more than one story of his own to tell about Hunter's office. For instance, there was the time the sheriff's department busted a drug dealer in his house and found a kilo and a half of cocaine, $80,000 in cash, semiautomatic weapons, Mac 10s, Uzis, and various handguns. While Hendry and his fellow officers were searching the house, his pager went off. Bill Wise's phone number appeared on the screen. When Hendry called, Wise told him the money was being seized under civil statutes and had already been settled: $20,000 of the $80,000 would go to the drug dealer's attorney. According to the law, proceeds from drug sales were to be confiscated, not given to the charged person. The cash had been sitting on top of the cocaine. It was clear to Hendry that this money represented cash from drug sales and should be seized. It was not covered by civil statutes, Hendry argued, which allowed money to remain the property of the suspect. Wise remained firm: the DA had already decided how it would be handled. Hendry concluded that Bill Wise's first concern was that the defense attorney be paid. When Hendry asked himself why, the only answer he could come up with was that this was Boulder.

The *Denver Post's* acid column about Hunter was the first in a series of newspaper articles and TV broadcasts that would attack the Boulder DA for his office's laid-back approach to the law.

Plea bargaining had been a major part of Hunter's first campaign platform, and he addressed it in his second term too. In the late 1970s, the DA's office had to contend with fifteen hundred felonies a year, at a time when there was only one criminal judge on the bench. A judge could handle perhaps sixty cases a year, according to Hunter. By the late 1990s, Boulder County had two thousand felony cases a year and only two district court criminal judges. Like all DAs, Hunter had to handle the overflow within the financial means of the community. Even in Boulder, with its low crime rate, plea bargaining was unavoidable.

I would have difficulty being a DA in Boulder. My personal philosophy involves taking a hard stand, using jails, using prisons, standing up to those who argue that you can fight crime by being nice to folks and seeking rehabilitation over and above punishment. Retribution has its own rehabilitative component.

Hunter has an unusual way of resolving cases. He doesn't call it plea bargaining. He calls it precharging negotiations, and he does it before charges are filed. It is a unique way of looking at things. You can run a system that way, an effective system, a system that's in tune with the community. And it works very well in Boulder.

Pete Hofstrom, who heads Hunter's felony division, is perfect for the job. He takes everything in, is excellent analytically. He can spot an issue, understand a case, and resolve it. He's effective in his job. But he's not a dynamic trial lawyer.

Everyone likes Pete. And he can flourish in a system with the Boulder prosecution philosophy for a long time.

—Robert Grant

* * *

Back in '78, Alex had this no-plea-bargaining policy. It got him national attention, but I don't think it lasted a year. We all realized that plea bargaining serves a purpose. It's not an evil thing. It's something that works.

Today I'm a defense attorney in Boulder. Back then I was with the public defender's office. During that no-plea-bargaining time, we defense attorneys were encouraged to come and have a dialogue with the DA. We plea bargained through precharging negotiations. Alex had deputy DAs screen the cases first. We would go in and lay out our case, sometimes too prematurely. At that point, a misdemeanor charge might be agreed to instead of a felony.

Technically, you could say there were no pleas bargained, because the charges weren't filed yet.

Today the vestiges of that era are still in Boulder. I would say in 10 percent of my cases, maybe 15 percent, I can go to the DA and say, "We need to talk. Here's what's wrong with your case." Or if we know what is likely to happen, plea bargain it before charging.

As defense counsel, I'm always asking, Who is this defendant? And also, Who is this victim? I have to focus just as much on how much the victim has been hurt as on what has happened to my client. In other words, Pete Hofstrom and I are clones of each other. If I walk in there and just tell my client's side without any awareness of the impact on the victim, Pete will say, "You haven't done your homework. Come back with the other side of the story."

—Paul McCormick

After I spent four years as a deputy DA for Alex Hunter, I became a judge in Boulder County. Some of us district judges would just flat-out refuse to accept plea bargains from Hunter's office. These were cases where we could see that the defendant deserved a heavier hand. An example: Hunter's staff would bring me someone arrested for driving under the influence and want to plead it to careless driving when it was easy to prove a prima facie* case on the actual offense. I would review it and say no.

The only other negative reaction I ever saw to all this plea bargaining came from the police. The community never said a word.

—Virginia Chavez

★ ★ ★

* A *prima facie* case is one where there is sufficient evidence to shift the burden of proof to the other party. The amount of evidence needed to make a *prima facie* case varies with the context: in some settings, proof beyond a reasonable doubt is required, in others only proof by a preponderance, or probable cause.

Soon after Alex Hunter hired Pete Hofstrom in 1974, the DA's office examined the issue of rehabilitation versus retribution for criminals. Determined to make the most of Boulder's politically progressive attitudes, in the early 1980s Hunter initiated a series of discussions with a broad spectrum of residents. During a ten-year period, he invited more than twelve hundred groups to his office. He met mostly with women, always asking the same kinds of questions: "A seventeen-year-old kid is caught committing a robbery with a .357 magnum. Do you throw the book at him? Do you give him another chance?"

"You get tough with *anybody* who brings a loaded .357 to a robbery," more than one Boulderite told Hunter. "If you slap his wrist and give him another chance, what message does that send?"

To some Boulderites it seemed that the DA didn't like coming down hard on crime. To others, it seemed that Hunter wanted to be in step with Boulder's citizens, but it was also possible that Hunter simply wanted to see if his thinking was in line with public opinion. In any case, he came away with a clearer picture of what was expected of him.

Hofstrom and Hunter examined the concept of deferred sentences,* as well as deferred prosecution** for first-time nonviolent offenders. Hofstrom believed that if such offenders made restitution, attended appropriate rehabilitation programs, and stayed out of trouble for a minimum of two years, their cases should be dismissed and their records sealed; something short of a conviction.

The attitude was deeply ingrained in Hofstrom, who had paid his way through college and law school by working as a prison guard and had maintained a deep interest in the plight of society's outcasts. Alex Hunter agreed with Hofstrom's position. As a result, rehabilitation became the first consideration for the DA's office.

★ ★ ★

* When a defendant pleads guilty, the prosecution may consent to a deferred sentence; in such cases, the defendant is ordinarily placed on probation, with conditions to be negotiated between the prosecution and defense. The probation may last as long as four years. If the defendant completes the probationary period successfully, the guilty plea is withdrawn and the original charges dismissed. If he fails to complete the probation successfully, his earlier guilty pleas will allow the court to enter a judgment of conviction and sentence him to any sentence authorized by law.

** A deferred prosecution is a more generous arrangement in which the defendant is not required to plead guilty. As with a deferred sentence arrangement, a period of probation is agreed to, with certain conditions attached. If the probation is successful, the charges are dismissed. If the probation is unsuccessful, the defendant must then go to trial, but since he has not pleaded guilty, he still has an opportunity to win acquittal. (C.R.S. 16-7-401 and 16-7-403.)

In a small town like Boulder, an attorney doesn't succeed or fail by his prowess in the courtroom, because so few cases go to trial. If only eight felony cases out of two thousand go to trial each year in Boulder, you have to ask yourself who really decides all those remaining cases.

If you're a defense attorney with such ferocious power that the DA's office is afraid to face you in court, you're in a fine bargaining position. Maybe there are a few attorneys like that in Boulder. But for the most part, you make deals by being on good terms with the DA's office. That friendship is your livelihood.

It's not that Boulder is unique that way. What is different is this "Magic Kingdom" business. People who practice law here like to live here. For the most part, they confine their practice to Boulder. They don't even like to go to Denver. Boulder is small; the legal community is small.

That's where Pete Hofstrom comes in. There's no question he regards his job as deal-making. He's utterly honest. He's not greedy, not selfish. He's not looking to make a lot of money or run for governor. He says that it's his job to make judgments about who deserves a good deal and who doesn't.

He has told my law students that there are basically three kinds of people who will come to a prosecutor's attention: one is the chronic fuck-up—not really evil but unable to manage in today's complicated world and therefore sees crime as an easy out; then there's the hard-core criminal, a sociopath who's greedy, selfish, doesn't care about hurting people—someone with no conscience whatsoever; finally, there's the citizen, a basically solid person with the right values, the right attitude, the right skills, who has now made a bad mistake.

Pete says you have to treat these three types differently, even if they've all committed the same crime. And he has confidence that he can unerringly place people in one category or the other. He understands that in his job, he pretty much has the power to determine the outcome even though it's the judge who pronounces sentence. Pete is comfortable in that role and believes he's perfectly capable of making these judgments.

—Marianne Wesson

The DA's office was soon half a step ahead of Boulder, which often found itself several steps ahead of other cities. Hunter used his office to initiate community programs. Having set up a consumer protection unit and a victim assistance program, he established a crime-prevention education program for all public school children called Safe Guard, a safehouse for domestic violence prevention, and a restitution-collection program for victims of crimes.

Hunter worked closely with Chuck Stout of the Boulder Health Department on the AIDS threat and supported the department's controversial needle-exchange program for addicts. When a drug bust netted the county over half a million dollars, he agreed that the money should be used for the education of teen mothers who were at high risk for becoming child abusers. The resulting Genesis program won a Ford Foundation award in 1996.

Hunter was way ahead of the curve in inaugurating and supporting such programs. He said he wanted to be innovative because Boulder expected it of him.

Boulder is a unique city. And Alex Hunter's strength in staying in office for twenty-five years is his identifying with the community—not in shaping the forces of the community, but in following them and anticipating what Boulder wants from a prosecutor. That is quite different from what most communities in this state want from a prosecutor.

Boulder has been a kind of magnet for different philosophies, ideas, and academics. It's always changing. It's a kind of Disneyland, Colorado, where you don't have to be at all concerned about the mundane part of life. You kind of just let it flow and things are taken care of. In Boulder, you can live in a world of ideas.

Hunter listens well and surrounds himself with good people. He doesn't believe he's 90 percent and everyone else is only 10 percent. He's a consensus builder, both in his job and in his political life. And again, I say he's in tune with the dynamics of his community.

Boulder lacks poverty, it lacks a ghetto—at least as a geographic entity. But there are pockets of low-income folks in the Boulder community, and there's a hell of a lot of diversity. It's racial, ethnic. But even the low income is at a higher level than you would normally think of in terms of a ghetto.

Alex doesn't fancy himself as a trial lawyer, and his ego isn't fed in the courtroom. His ego is fed in the political arena.

—Robert Grant

★ ★ ★

The Boulder City Council is, in many ways, responsible for the city's overall success. In 1967 the city agreed to tax itself to buy up tens of thousands of acres of open space, which it declared off-limits to development.

My parents came to Denver in 1947, when I was ten, to start the Julius Hyman Company, which produced the nastiest, most dangerous insecticides. Eventually they sold the firm to Shell Oil, which continued producing the same pesticides for a long time. If I had a personal bumper sticker, it would read, "Here longer than most natives."

I remember that the moment we got off the train in Denver, I was disappointed—no cowboys and Indians. But I soon discovered there were lots of fields to play in, an airport where you could watch planes, and an irrigation ditch you could tube down. All that was wonderful.

In 1960 I applied to Stanford and didn't get in. So I ended up at CU, which had been my third choice. Actually it was a kid's dream. The university was a kind of magic place. It had either the largest or second-largest number of astronauts among its alumni. Robert Redford used to be a waiter at the Sink. I studied history as an undergraduate and science in graduate school, but I really majored in student activism. I have to point out that I opposed the Vietnam War back when public opinion polls showed that only 1 percent of the country favored withdrawal.

Boulder was much more isolated than Denver, although the Denver-Boulder turnpike had just opened. Boulder had the main hallmark of a boomtown, the feeling that all things are possible. In those days there were lots of transient hippies and drugs. One anti-Vietnam protest on U.S. 36 turned into a kind of bloodbath. There was lots of tear gas. The liberals didn't seize the government until 1971, when I was thirty-five, and the present establishment wasn't locked in until the 1976 elections. Back then, I was always in the minority, but it didn't bother me. I understood things were changing.

The Danish Plan was my big contribution to Boulder and was adopted by referendum in 1976. It determined the growth rate for the town by controlling the number of building permits issued every year, with just a few exceptions and grandfatherings. The number of permits allowed was based on certain criteria, like the birth rate. The city had already voted in a height limitation for new buildings. There was also the "blue line," a zoning law which said that a building above a certain elevation couldn't get town water. Now, of course, the city owns almost everything up in the foothills. It's a wonderful place to live. I live just six blocks from the Rocky Mountains.

—Paul Danish

★ ★ ★

The city of Boulder became an island with a moat of undeveloped land around it, isolated from the other communities in Boulder County and from Denver and its surrounding municipalities. One former county commissioner called Boulder "twenty-eight square miles encircled by reality." The restricted growth of Boulder's residential areas led to steadily rising real estate prices. In the late 1990s, an average home cost $337,994.

Adding to Boulder's good fortune is the presence of a federally funded scientific research institute at the University of Colorado, whose students and staff constitute almost a third of Boulder's population. Over 36 percent of the city's adults have a college degree, and 26 percent have five years or more of higher education. Seven of ten Boulderites own bicycles. The result is above-average prosperity and relatively few residents whose lives are desperate enough to turn them to crime.

I'm now the director of public information at the University of Colorado in Boulder. I used to be the city's flack. I ran the press office. I could see everything that was happening in city government; I attended every city council meeting. The first mayor I worked for was Ruth Correll, and during her tenure the character of the town changed. Paul Danish was pushing slow growth, which attracted attention that this town had never had before. And I saw it all from the inside.

I helped promote the green belt. We built this buffer zone around ourselves because we didn't want to be part of the metroplex. We paid for that protection with our own taxes. Of course, it's like building a cedar fence. When you go to the other side of that fence, it looks quite different from the outside. We always sat in here and looked at what we were building and just didn't realize that the people on the outside were watching us build the fence.

So Boulder became an isolated conclave.

We have always viewed the world outside with a certain detachment, but we never seemed able to see ourselves with the same objectivity. At heart we are still a small town. Now the media comes from a place where TV news trucks are as common as taxicabs. Here in Boulder, we don't have cabs. Or so few they're barely visible.

I used to walk out my front door every morning and get my newspaper, pick up my milk, and say hi to my neighbor and the kid mowing the lawn.

That was my window on the world. Then there was the Simpson thing, the Susan Smith thing—all far away. Except now there's the Ramsey thing.

Here in Boulder, we believe we are smaller than we really are. Then when the TV lights and telephoto lenses come in, we have to realize that we aren't as small as we thought.

—David Grimm

This privileged community, whose people have little reason to fear crime—this complacent community—was an ideal environment for innovators like Alex Hunter and Peter Hofstrom to calibrate law enforcement to the needs of the residents.

In 1984 Hunter announced the formation of "domestic violence teams" to make recommendations following arrests in domestic abuse cases. Shortly afterward, he initiated a program where police officers would no longer act as referees in domestic fights but would arrest on probable cause. Then Hunter's office would prosecute abusers, even when the victim refused to file charges.

When six deaths from domestic violence occurred in Boulder County, outside of the city of Boulder, in the first seven months of 1993, Hunter named Kathy Delgado to head a specialized prosecution unit. Faced with the fact that by the time of trial, most domestic violence victims are no longer on the prosecutor's side, Hunter urged making arrests mandatory in all cases when the police are called in a domestic violence dispute. The controversial bill, signed into state law on June 2, 1994, was designed to break the back of domestic violence.

Hunter established hard policies on sexual assault and domestic violence. Perpetrators were sent to jail overnight or over a weekend, with no possibility of posting bond, until there could be a hearing. Hunter relented when defense attorneys argued that reputations on domestic violence cases could be ruined and civil liberties could be violated. He made no such provisions for sexual assault cases, however, and the defense bar believes that the DA's "tuna net" has swept up many innocent people, jeopardizing their jobs and reputations. They fault Hunter for neglecting to build in fail-safes to ensure that only true criminals are targeted.

In the early 1990s, Boulder's "rape crisis team" studied 116 cases of incest and sexual assault on both children and adults. Hunter's office claimed a conviction rate of 84 percent. In cases involving children, sixty defendants pleaded guilty to some charge, but it was found that only one out of sixty convicted sexual offenders went to state prison. Moreover, Hunter's office was found to be counting deferred prosecutions and deferred sentences as convictions. Plea bargains that sent first-time rapists into therapy rather than prison enraged Hunter's opponents. Some speculate that Hunter's political skill may have served to mute critical voices.

Some judges agree with Alex Hunter's opponents that because of the way he runs his office, his deputy DAs don't have the necessary courtroom skills. With so few cases taken to trial and even fewer courtroom battles in Hunter's jurisdiction, there is little opportunity for the DA's staff to acquire courtroom experience. According to criminal court judge Murray Richtel, Hunter's office is "rehabilitation- and treatment-oriented on a conscious level. It's not a trial-oriented system. The skills aren't there. That's not in any sense a criticism; it's just a fact."

One of Hunter's lessons about the law came from an earlier case involving a child's murder. Elizabeth Manning's three-year-old son, Michael, had became what one newspaper called "a punching bag" for Manning's live-in boyfriend, Danny Arevalo. On December 19, 1982, Manning helped wrap her son's body in a green blanket and a shower curtain and hid it in an air-conditioning vent. The body was later carried to an irrigation ditch in the dead of winter.

Before Christmas, neighbors noticed that the child had disappeared and informed the police.

While the winter snow was still on the ground, Manning was brought before Judge Murray Richtel in a civil proceeding and ordered to tell the police where her child was. She said her son was with friends but refused to say where for fear that social services would take the child away, she said.

Richtel sentenced Manning to jail for contempt of court, but she still wouldn't talk. As she sat in jail and refused to disclose her child's whereabouts, the public was aghast.

Three months later, on April 8, Manning was released pending an appeal of her sentence. As she left the jail, the police officer in charge of the case, Detective Greg Bailey, told her, "Betsy, you can either be a witness in a murder case or you can be a suspect in a murder case. It's up to you."

The next day, Manning decided to talk.

"I am going to interview you as a witness in this thing," Bailey said to Manning. "Because I am not going to advise you of your rights, they [the DA] cannot prosecute you for this."

"I'll do whatever I have to do," she replied, "to make sure he [Arevalo] pays for what he did to Michael."

"Go ahead and tell me what you've got."

"Mikey's dead."

"Elizabeth," Bailey said, "you don't really mean that."

"Yes, Danny beat Michael to death." Manning told Bailey that she had played a major role in her son's death and had helped hide the body.

Hunter, knowing that Manning had not been given the Miranda warning and that her statement could not be used against her, took the position that his office "hadn't agreed to immunity for anyone."

The public outrage over the murder and the fact that this mother sat in jail when she knew her son's body lay exposed in the snow convinced Hunter to file murder and child abuse charges against Manning as well as Arevalo. He took the position that discovery of the body would inevitably have occurred when the snow melted and that the shower curtain would have linked Manning to the crime. She would have been charged, Hunter said, statement or no statement.

The court ruled against Hunter. Manning's statement was deemed inadmissible, and all evidence uncovered as a result of her statement, including her son's body, was excluded. Hunter spoke out publicly against the judge and the judiciary.

All Hunter could do now was charge the defendants with felony child abuse and assault. Manning, furious with Hunter for prosecuting her, pled guilty and was out in a year. At Arevalo's trial she refused to testify, and he received ten years for felony child abuse.

Politically, Hunter had lost.

For his part, Hunter said that after this and a few similar experiences, he no longer allowed himself to be swayed by public sentiment into trying an unwinnable case, because in the end no one wins. He also believed that to charge an innocent person with a serious crime—and virtually destroy his life—was worse than not filing charges at all.

Pete Hofstrom, conservative by nature, agreed, and when the DA's lawyers wanted to file a case that he thought would be lost in court, he usually convinced them not to.

Despite some horrifying local crimes, the position taken by Hunter and Hofstrom has remained unchanged. In 1990 Michael

Bell, an escapee from the state penitentiary, murdered four people indiscriminately. Hunter, who is not opposed to the death penalty, talked to the families of the victims. He explained how the death penalty works in reality—how few murderers are sentenced to death, how many appeals are filed, how many years the process takes. In the end he accomplished something unprecedented: he and Hofstrom persuaded Michael Bell to plea-bargain to life in prison without parole—and saved the victims' families years of agony during the interminable appeals process.

Such strategies and philosophies are not to everyone's liking, but the community has kept Hunter in office. Boulderites seem to agree that he is serving them well.

Speaking about JonBenét's murder, Alex Hunter told a friend, "This crime doesn't have a statute of limitation. We'll wait as long as it takes to develop a solid case."

"You won't need very much evidence in light of what *they've* done to make your case," his friend replied, referring to the Ramseys.

It was at this moment that Hunter understood how emotionally involved local residents had become in the case—and how strong their opinions were. But he also knew that those opinions were based on very little relevant information and no hard evidence, and this frightened him.

What also bothered the DA, in the final days of February, was that the case was getting harder to solve, not easier. John's and Patsy's lives provided no easy answers, no pathology, no pattern of abuse, no skeletons in the closets–in fact, no closets.

Hunter knew that the detectives were putting in long hours, working six days a week. Some were still in Atlanta, interviewing every member of the family and many of their friends and former business associates. In Boulder they were talking to employees of Stevens Aviation, which maintained John Ramsey's plane, and Merry Maids, the cleaning company that serviced the Ramseys' house. The investigation was moving along, but the lack of concrete physical evidence against the Ramseys still hadn't led Eller to look elsewhere for suspects—not seriously.

John Andrew Ramsey and his friend Brad Millard had given pubic hair samples, which did not match the hair found on the white blanket covering JonBenét's body. The investigation of John Andrew and Melinda Ramsey was nearly over. As far as Alex Hunter knew, the older children were no longer suspects, and the Ramseys' attorneys were demanding that they be publicly cleared so they could get on with their lives. Hunter agreed. It was unconscionable to ruin the lives of these young people because of baseless suspicion.

It was clear to Hunter that he had no choice but to get his own investigators, who would pursue the case as he and Pete Hofstrom saw fit.

4

PATSY RAMSEY HIRES SECOND ATTORNEY

JonBenét Ramsey's mother has hired a second attorney, sources close to the investigation said Friday.

Patrick Furman, a criminal law professor at the University of Colorado in Boulder, has joined attorney Patrick Burke to represent Patsy Ramsey, the sources said.

—Charlie Brennan
Rocky Mountain News, March 1, 1997

The Ramsey defense team now included Patrick Burke and Patrick Furman, who represented Patsy, while Bryan Morgan, Hal Haddon, and Lee Foreman represented John. Morgan was the lead attorney for John's team, and Burke headed Patsy's team. Among themselves, the attorneys joked that the media were incorrectly thrusting Haddon into the number one spot, but no one minded, because Haddon had the most experience with the press, having been a key advisor to Gary Hart's failed presidential campaign. Nevertheless, the team worried, because Haddon sometimes lost his temper with the press and held grudges. He looked like a man who could deliver a punch as well as take one.

The team decided to divide up the media chores. Haddon talked to *The Denver Post*, Morgan handled the *Daily Camera*, and Patrick Furman dealt with the *Rocky Mountain News*.

★ ★ ★

"What I need now is a good digger in Boulder," Tony Frost, the executive editor of the Globe, *said to me in my uncle's Boca Raton home. I was intrigued by the Ramsey case and asked him if I was the type of person he might hire.*

"Yes," he said immediately. "I take one look at you and I don't think anyone would think you're a reporter. At least, not one of our *reporters."*

Frost was in his jogging outfit. I wore my Washington uniform—suit and tie. He's sweating and I'm sweating. Nevertheless, Frost reminds me of Pierce Brosnan. In his own way, he's James Bond.

—Jeff Shapiro

Jeff Shapiro had told his uncle, Richard Sachs, that he wanted to be a reporter. When Sachs arranged for Jeff to meet Tony Frost, Shapiro rolled his eyes. He didn't think much of the *Globe*. He thought its publication of the Ramsey autopsy photos was unethical—sickening, in fact. A few days later, however, Shapiro, twenty-three, a graduate of Florida State University, was on the *Globe's* payroll and on his way to Boulder as an undercover investigator. His job was to infiltrate the Ramsey family by getting close to John Andrew, then a student at the University of Colorado.

On March 2, 1997, Shapiro arrived in Boulder with $2,000. His contact was Craig Lewis, a *Globe* writer who was already in town. Lewis, a laid-back guy who wore black jeans, black leather jackets, and sunglasses, found Shapiro a rental car and gave him some pointers about Boulder. Then Shapiro was on his own.

When Shapiro first drove by the Ramseys' house, he was surprised to see how close it was to the student hangouts on University Hill. Then he discovered that John Andrew's fraternity house, Chi Psi, was at 1080 14th Street, just five blocks from his father's home. Shapiro realized that he'd never read that simple fact in any of the press stories. By midday he'd found a room at a youth hostel for $27 a day: no bathroom, white tile floor, a little narrow bed, and a night table. Not very elaborately appointed, but it had a perfect view of John Andrew's fraternity house. Settling in, he developed a routine. Every evening he visited every bar on the Hill looking for Ramsey's son. His cover was that he had graduated with a political science degree, couldn't find a job, and had decided to go to law school at CU. Shapiro knew that an antigovernment stance and his belief that O. J. Simpson had been framed by the police would also prove useful to his cover.

Soon he learned that John Andrew was no longer living at the fraternity house, so he moved out of the hostel and into a place at the University Court Apartments that he shared with a couple of students. He liked the small-town campus atmosphere—it was like being in school again. Still, he wasn't making much progress in finding Ramsey's son. Then one day, leafing through John Andrew's high school yearbook, he came across the name Allison Russ. On a hunch, he looked her up and discovered her phone number in the CU directory.

On the phone Shapiro introduced himself to Russ as Matthew Hayworth, a law student at CU, and said he was interested in the Ramsey case. She was reserved and laughed a little nervously when Shapiro told her that he wanted to help because he thought the Ramseys were probably innocent. "You saw what the LAPD did to O. J. Simpson," he told her, implying that the Boulder cops might be setting the Ramseys up. Russ soon became a little more chatty. Shapiro gambled. He told her he'd heard from a friend that lubricant had been found on JonBenét's body, in the vaginal area, and that it was complicating the DNA testing process. He asked Russ to take this information to John Andrew, who could then pass it on to his father's investigators. Allison said she would.

Shapiro still had many places to visit in Boulder. Next on his list was Pasta Jay's. There, he applied for a job—again as Matt Hayworth. He was filling out his application when a college student wearing an Atlanta baseball cap walked in.

"Hi, I'm John Ramsey," the student said to the manager.

Shapiro was in luck. His prey was standing not 10 feet away asking to fill out a job application. Then John Andrew caught him staring.

"I'm sorry," Shapiro said. "You just look like someone."

"Who do you think I look like?"

"Are you John Ramsey's son?"

"That's right," John Andrew said, then asked if Shapiro was a journalist.

Shapiro said he wasn't and added, "I think the police are doing to your dad the same thing the LAPD did to OJ. The police can play a lot of games with you. But I'm sure you've already found that out."

"I know," John Andrew replied.

Shapiro completed the job application and left Pasta Jay's.

He was furious with himself. He was sure John Andrew would

figure out that he'd been the one who called Allison Russ. The next morning he called her and explained a bit more. He didn't tell her he worked for the *Globe*, only that his name wasn't Hayworth.

"Jeffrey Scott is my real name," Shapiro said. Then he told her that he'd run into John Andrew. "He's a nice kid."

RAMSEYS ENTER PLEA ON INTERNET

JonBenét Ramsey's family has gone online to urge Boulder police to clear her older half-brother as a suspect in the slaying of the 6-year-old beauty princess.

"It should be made perfectly clear by the Boulder Police Department that John Andrew is not a suspect in this horrible crime," the family urged in a statement posted Sunday on the Internet.

"To continue to refuse to do so is cruel to a fine young man and the rest of our family," said the statement, which was signed by the 20-year-old's father and stepmother, John and Patsy Ramsey, and his mother, Lucinda Ramsey Johnson.

—John C. Ensslin
Rocky Mountain News, March 3, 1997

As the nation became obsessed with the Ramsey case, some turned to the Internet to keep up with developments. Finding information online was easy because of JonBenét's unusual name. By early 1997, a user could type it into a search engine and receive between three hundred and a thousand matches.

Most of those who logged on were housewives between the ages of thirty and fifty. Many of them went on-line just after the Ramseys appeared on CNN on January 1, 1997. Some men participated as well. At first everyone simply searched for information from newspapers and other sources. Then people sought out—or created—Web sites and began participating in discussion forums and message boards devoted to the case. There were even parody Web sites, including Gone with the Spin—a look at how the Ramsey camp manipulated the media—and Patsy's Postcards from Prison—which had photos of Patsy's prison pageant. Soon there were three hundred Web sites devoted to the Ramsey case.

Most of those who followed the case on-line had children of their own and were haunted by JonBenét's death. The regulars became emotionally invested in the case and in their cybercommunity. They supported their on-line friends through events in their "real lives," but they also bickered about the case. By spring 1997, the regulars had split into groups—the Pro-Rams and the Anti-Rams. Everyone wanted to recruit those in the third group, the Fence Sitters.

The first discussions started on a bulletin board run by the *Daily Camera*, with a core group of about two hundred participants, though it often seemed like more. In cyberspace, it's easy to steal names and hide true identities, and everyone began to wonder if the killer was among the participants. As is typical in cyberspace, conspiracy theories emerged. Pro-Rams were accused of being on the Ramsey payroll and of trying to control the news spin on the Internet.

By the summer of 1997, there were about a thousand people following the Ramsey case on-line, and they were dedicated. They dug through both mainstream media reports and the tabloids for nuggets of information, and they theorized endlessly. When the Ramseys appeared on television on May 1, 1997, the Boulder News Forum conducted its first real-time transcription of a TV event. The first message transmitted was, "Patsy has a mustache."

At 10:00 A.M. on March 3, Bill McReynolds, who was still considered a suspect by the police, met with Detectives Thomas and Gosage at police headquarters for his fourth interview. This time the proceedings were tape-recorded. By now the detectives had finished their background checks on the McReynolds family and friends, and they wanted to see if they had missed something. When this interview was over, however, they hadn't discovered anything new. Still outstanding were results of McReynolds's blood and hair samples and an analysis of his handwriting.

There's this feeling in Boulder that we've got to be protective of our Eden. We can't have this violation of our community. It means we'll be cast out of the garden. Boulderites are always looking at their image first—what this story is doing to the image of their town.

Almost everyone has written stories about me—the Denver papers, the tabloids, and even CNN. I've been on lots of TV shows. It's too late. There's nothing I can do about it. Lots of people think that I killed Jon-Benét, that Santa killed an angel.

Back in '72, my wife and I led a publicity campaign for George McGovern, which was run by Common Cause. That's when I met Paul

Danish and Ruth Correll. They were among the group that started to clean up the city. Boulder became a place where you could have an aesthetic experience. But maybe it's been overdone.

Recently the Boulder Dinner Theater was performing Grand Hotel. Now the city has an ordinance against smoking in public places. They threatened to close down the play because there were one or two smoking scenes. Sometimes I think Boulder is overregulated. Everything is protected. Overprotected. Boulder has become just too precious.

I have a Ph.D. in American Studies and a master's in journalism. In the '70s, I was teaching journalism at CU. Chuck Green, The Denver Post columnist, was in my first class. I didn't especially like the academic world; it's too isolated and remote. When I retired in '92, Marilyn Haus, who's in charge of downtown Boulder, hired me as a strolling Santa on the mall. I'd go into restaurants and different shops, like the New York Deli, where Mork and Mindy was filmed—an alien from outer space coming to live in this community.

One day in 1993 I was doing my "Ho, ho, ho" in the deli, and this lady with two children jumped up and asked if I would be their Santa. That's how I met Patsy Ramsey. I did the family's Christmas parties in '94, '95, and '96. JonBenét always made sure that I gave Burke lots of attention, then she would take my hand and escort me around to meet everyone at the party. After it was over, she always wrote me a thank-you letter.

In August of 1996 I had heart surgery and had to retire from being a strolling Santa. Patsy's 1996 Christmas party was on December 23. The family had just returned from shopping in New York City. JonBenét told me they'd seen Cats, Les Misérables, and the Radio City Music Hall Christmas show.

That same year, Charles Kuralt chose me as a Santa for his TV show. The crew followed me from one party to another for three days. By December 23, they'd had enough, so they skipped the Ramsey party.

Patsy was disappointed they weren't coming. As always, she wrote little notes about each child on this lengthy scroll. That evening, I told these stories as I passed out presents. JonBenét gave me a vial of stardust for my beard. Patsy presented me with a beautiful scarf and said, "You're a member of the family." I was a member of their club, and I wasn't a wealthy person.

Looking back, I always thought that if anybody wanted to do major damage to this family, they could do it at Christmas, because they all adored Christmas.

—Bill McReynolds

223

Meanwhile, the CBI informed the Boulder police that some other hand-writing discovered on the pad used for the ransom note was apparently written with the same felt-tipped pen used for the note. This handwriting, found on pages immediately preceding the place where the ransom note pages had been torn out, consisted of the phrase *Mr. and Mrs. Ramsey* and later became known as the "practice note."

The CBI's Chet Ubowski reported to the Boulder PD that there were "indications" that John Ramsey didn't write the note. Other "indications" pointed to Patsy Ramsey as the author. The evaluations were based on the handwriting samples that the Ramseys had provided thus far.

The police had voluntary samples from Patsy and prior "historical" samples, which they had collected from JonBenét's physician and from a notebook found in the Ramseys' Boulder home. Ubowski concluded that "there is evidence which indicates the ransom note may have been written by Patricia Ramsey." To be more certain, however, Ubowski needed more samples produced before December 26, samples that wouldn't "contain any elements of distortion, attempts to disguise handwriting, or nervousness."

When Detective Harmer had searched the Ramseys' Charlevoix home in January, she had noticed several handwritten items. Now, with Ubowski's report in hand, the court granted a second search warrant. On March 5 Harmer left for Michigan. It took her only an hour and fifteen minutes to collect thirteen recipe cards, an address book, two small legal pads, three notes from a kitchen corkboard, and a photo album with printing. The next day she returned to Boulder and placed the "historical" writings into evidence.

At the time, the entire contents of the ransom note had not been released to the media and the public. The police were investigating all possible influences on whoever had written it. They found, for example, that the note contained several phrases similar to snippets of dialogue in recent movies. On November 29, a month before JonBenét's death, the movie *Dirty Harry* had aired on TBS in Boulder. In the movie, a kidnapper tells Clint Eastwood, "If you talk to anyone, I don't care if it's a Pekingese pissing against a lamppost, the girl dies." JonBenét's ransom note threatened, "If we catch you talking to a stray dog, she dies." In *Dirty Harry* the kidnapper says, "It sounds like you had a good rest. You'll need it." JonBenét's ransom note said, "The delivery will be exhausting so I advise you to be rested."

In the movie *Speed*, a terrorist played by Dennis Hopper says, "You know that I'm on top of you. Do not attempt to grow a brain." The ransom note contained the following: "You and your family are under constant scrutiny as well as the authorities. Don't try to grow a brain John."

On the night JonBenét was murdered, the movie *Nick of Time* aired at 7:30 P.M. on a Boulder cable channel. The story centers on an unnamed political faction that kidnaps a six-year-old girl. The victim is told, "Listen to me very carefully." Bill Cox, who was staying with Fleet and Priscilla White, told the police he remembered watching the movie that night. The ransom note begins, "Listen carefully!"

The ransom note would become public only in September 1997. Karen Howard, an employee of Access Graphics, said that she was struck by the words "you are not the only fat cat around." Howard remembered that Patsy's father, Don Paugh, used the word *cats* all the time; for example, "Those cats down in marketing."

Once the CBI's handwriting analysts no longer needed the ransom note, the lab turned its attention to lifting fingerprints from the paper. Technicians would have to immerse the pages in various chemical solutions, which would react with the amino acids, fats, and waxes that are transmitted to objects by human hands. The pages would then be dried so that the chemicals could react with and expose any latent fingerprints or palm prints. The CBI told the police and Pete Hofstrom that the process would make the paper fibers swell, forever altering the relationship between the ink and the paper surface. As a result, further examination and analysis of the indentations in the paper, a critical component in handwriting analysis, might become impossible. The ink might run. Some of the tests might even cause the document to turn black.

Hofstrom knew that if the Ramseys were eventually charged in the murder, they would want their own handwriting experts to testify, and any reputable analyst would have to examine the original note to make an assessment. Hofstrom felt the Ramseys should have the same chance to review the documents that the police had.

He told Patrick Burke about the situation, and in a letter the lawyer registered a formal objection to destructive testing of the ransom note. Burke presented Hofstrom with a set of conditions to be met before he would allow the CBI to test the note for the police. He wanted access to the ransom note for the Ramseys' own handwriting experts. In addition, he wanted a first-generation copy of the note and 4 x 5 inch negatives of each page. Later the Ramseys' attorneys set further conditions: they wanted to see the ligature and the "garrote" used to murder JonBenét. They soon discovered what the media did not know. The cord tied around JonBenét's neck was not a classical garrote in which both ends of the cord are attached to a turning device such as a stick. In this case, the cord had been placed around JonBenét's neck like a noose, the cord pulled through a knot, and a stick tied to the cord 17 inches from the knot. The coroner was unable to determine if JonBenét's killer had turned the stick in garrote fashion to cause the strangulation or had used the stick only to pull the noose tighter around the child's neck to suffocate her.

Hofstrom thought some of Burke's requests were fair, and he also saw a bargaining opportunity for his office. He proposed that in exchange for giving the Ramseys' experts access to the note, Hunter's staff wanted to hear their firsthand analysis. This way Hunter's office could assess the opposition—see how good their experts were.

Burke agreed, but then Hofstrom had to convince the police that the Ramseys should be allowed to see and assess the rope, the "garrote," and the ransom note. Hunter consulted Bob Grant, a member of the task force he had assembled, who reminded him to look at the exchange only in the context of *his* case, not from the investigative perspective of the police. Grant said that Hunter should compare what would be lost and what would be gained before making a decision. It took some time, but eventually they got Eller to agree to the conditions. All the items could be examined in protective covers. In mid-April, Detective Trujillo delivered to Patrick Burke the requested first-generation copy of the note and 4 x 5 inch negatives. On May 18, at Mike Bynum's law offices, the Ramseys' experts—Howard Rile, a former handwriting analyst for the CBI now based in California, and Lloyd Cunningham, a retired San Francisco police handwriting expert who had worked on the Zodiac serial murders—pored over the original note from 9:00 A.M. to 12:30 P.M. Detectives Thomas and Trujillo and evidence technician Pat Peck observed for the police. At the same time, the Ramseys' attorneys and their experts also examined the rope and the "garrote." Pete Hofstrom and Trip DeMuth, representing the DA's office, showed up in the afternoon with sheriff's detective Steve Ainsworth.

Just after 2:00 P.M. Rile and Cunningham made their presentation. They had noted resemblances to some of Patsy's lettering as well as some variances. Their verdict: Patsy didn't write the note. Hofstrom and DeMuth listened carefully. The experts' presentation seemed to have some merit. Hunter's staff concluded that at least one of these experts would make a fine witness for the Ramseys.

Several weeks after the meeting, attorney Lee Foreman informed Hunter's office that since they'd had an opportunity to review the original ransom note, the Ramseys had no further objection to the police proceeding at once with the potentially destructive fingerprint tests.

Alex Hunter told Sheriff Epp that he thought a more objective investigation was still needed. The police were not looking hard enough at the possibility that an intruder had murdered JonBenét, and they hadn't even interviewed Boulder's registered sex offenders. When Hunter approached Koby about Eller, the chief wouldn't discuss the issue. The attention of the media had intensified Koby's initial resolve. He wasn't going to add to the frenzy by replacing Eller and confirming what the press was saying about the investigation. Eller would get the job done. Hunter could see that Koby wouldn't budge.

For his part, Epp thought that many of the problems in the investigation had arisen as a result of police union policies and the structure of the Boulder PD. A deep polarization between management and the rank and file had developed in the late 1970s over salary increases, benefits, and holiday time, which had resulted in a strong police union. Then, when Tom Koby became police chief in 1991, he downsized and completely restructured the department. The rank-and-file officers believed that Koby had done this to impress his friend Tim Honey, the city manager, and the city council. The union still talked about Black Monday, the day Koby's changes took effect. No longer could an officer climb the ladder to lieutenant and then to division chief. The positions no longer existed. Koby had combined them into a single management level called commander, and this one person would make decisions that in the past had been made by three people.

In the process, Koby got rid of many of the law-and-order-oriented officers that his predecessor, Jay Propst, had hired over the years from other jurisdictions. Commanders like Jerry Hoover, Glen Kaminsky, and Bob Etzkorn left the department. In their place, Koby brought in more liberally educated officers, and added laypeople like Virginia Lucy and

Kris Gibson, who had no practical law enforcement experience, to the command structure. Almost all of Koby's recruits were more open to Boulder's unusual system of justice. Up through the ranks came people like Commander Mark Beckner, Tom Wickman, Linda Arndt, Tom Trujillo, and Carey Weinheimer—officers who had virtually no experience with big-city crime. There were deep divisions within the department about how to deal with Boulder's criminals.

Koby had also moved the department toward community policing, a concept the city council approved, in light of the low street-crime rate in Boulder. Community policing emphasizes officer interaction with the public. The union objected that such "socializing" disrupted real police business—intervention in assaults, rapes, and the like. The hard-line officers didn't like "sitting around at ice cream socials." That wasn't why they'd become cops.

The union contract stipulated that officers would be rotated rather than kept in core positions. This meant that the position of detective was not a permanent rank, not a promotion, but a rotating job. When an officer was rotated out, it wasn't a demotion. There was no stigma in being sent "back to patrol." As the union saw it, more officers gained detective experience this way, and it raised morale. Patrol officers rotated into the detective division got their turn at the benefits that went with the job. They worked five days a week and got Christmas, New Year's, and Thanksgiving off. With one or two murders a year, the city of Boulder didn't need seasoned homicide investigators, the police union said. As a result, these rotating detectives never developed expertise.

Sheriff Epp thought that the Boulder PD's mandate to enforce the law had taken second place to the union's agenda. He himself ran his detective division in a more traditional way. Having gained a wealth of expertise in his eight years as a detective before becoming sheriff, he kept the majority of his officers in core positions. Some of his officers had been detectives for twenty years.

Epp felt that the union requirements benefited the police more than the public. Still, it was not union-stipulated matters that had prevented the Boulder PD from doing a good job on the Ramsey investigation. John Eller had to assume a share of the blame. From what Epp knew of Eller, it seemed that the commander didn't work well with people. Union leaders admitted privately that Eller had acted rashly in suspending Larry Mason, for example. And he was impatient and abrupt. "I don't have time to talk about it," Eller would some-times snap. "Go out and do it now!"

Epp shared these views. He also believed that the commander was looking for confirmation of his preconceptions about the Ramsey case. That he wanted answers was understandable, but Epp objected to his refusal to look at other scenarios.

In the first days of the investigation, Epp had been told by his offi-cers that Eller couldn't get organized. Of course, failure to secure the crime scene and failure to separate and interview the witnesses—including the Ramseys—could not be blamed entirely on Eller. The first officers at the scene had ignored or bungled procedures that were taught the first day at the police academy.

Epp wrestled with himself about what his department should do. After all, the sheriff's department shared jurisdiction for the city of Boulder. It was supposed to serve the same citizens.

Sitting around the conference table in Epp's office in a closed door ses-sion, Captains Shomaker, Hopper, McCaa, and Pringle of the sheriff's department discussed their role in the Ramsey case with Epp. What should we *do*? What should *we* do? The obvious answer was to start their *own* inves-tigation into JonBenét's death, starting with the premise of an unknown killer, someone not living in the house. Following all the leads, they would allow the evidence to show them the path to JonBenét's murderer.

But Epp worried that a separate investigation might ruin relations with the Boulder PD. Worse, it might be seen by Boulderites as polit-ical maneuvering at the expense of the police. Epp and his captains let the idea drop, but they continued to stew.

Alex Hunter hoped that a citizen would come in, write a letter, or call the tip line with information that would break the Ramsey case. It had happened in other cases. Sometimes he actually sat alone in his office waiting for a call from the police saying they'd found a smoking gun, something to hang the case on the Ramseys.

The tabloids had become just as restless as they ran out of negative items to print about the Ramseys. The *National Enquirer* worked on "Daddy's Secret Porn Life," in which it would claim that Ramsey had been seen leaving a house of prostitution in the red-light district of Amsterdam, where Access Graphics had a satellite office. When such stories appeared, the Boulder police weren't far behind, following leads as they appeared in print.

One tabloid reporter had called over two hundred escort services in the Colorado area looking for anyone who might have had contact with John Ramsey. After a stripper who called herself Sharon contacted the Boulder police to inform them about the reporter's investigation, Detectives Thomas and Gosage spoke to the Arapahoe County DA's office and the Aurora Police Department and met anonymously with several prostitutes the tabloid reporter had called, following leads supplied by the reporter. They found no indication that John Ramsey had been involved with local prostitutes.

Soon after that search for prostitutes, Detective Harmer received a phone call from Christopher Doherty, a reporter for the *Globe*. A woman named Kimberly Ballard had told the *Globe* she'd had an affair with John Ramsey from August 1994 through the spring of 1995, while Patsy was battling cancer. The *Globe* was set to publish Ballard's story, Doherty said.

When Alex Hunter heard about this, he knew that even if the allegation were true, cheating on a desperately ill wife was still a long way from murdering your six-year-old daughter. Detective Harmer, however, thought that Ramsey might have told Ballard something material to the case—perhaps a passing reference to something that only the police and the killer knew. The Boulder PD followed up on the lead.

Detectives Harmer and Arndt went to Tucson, where Ballard now lived, to interview her face-to-face, but she declined to meet them. Nevertheless, they conducted some background checks on her and visited the Brown Palace, the Denver hotel where Ballard claimed to have met Ramsey on several occasions. The hotel had no record of these visits. In the end, the police found no evidence that Ramsey had ever met Kimberly Ballard. On April 22, the *Globe* reported that the Boulder PD had Ballard under investigation. The tabloid published her story based solely on their interview, with no independent confirmation.

Two and a half months after the Boulder police began investigating John Andrew and Melinda Ramsey, they received the final pieces of evidence that cleared Ramsey's older children of any involvement in JonBenét's murder. Bryan Morgan wrote to Detective Thomas on March 4 stating that John Andrew had made an ATM transaction at the QT Store on Roswell Road, in Marietta, Georgia, at 9:00 P.M. on December 25. His friend Brad Millard had been present. To support his claim, Morgan enclosed the ATM transaction slip. He also repeated that Melinda had awakened her brother in the early morning hours of December 26, in time for him to stop at a store and still make an 8:30 A.M. flight to Minneapolis. It was impossible for John Andrew to have flown from Atlanta to Boulder, whether by commercial or private aircraft, commit the murder, and return in time to be awakened by his sister in the presence of Brad Millard, who had stayed overnight in John Andrew's room.

Morgan also wrote that John Andrew hadn't been in Charlevoix, Michigan, on either the Memorial Day or the July Fourth 1996 weekend. The accusation of a onetime police informant that John Andrew had tried to stage an "accidental death" in order to kill Jon-Benét was clearly preposterous. Morgan again requested an official announcement that John Andrew was no longer a possible suspect.

By now the police had received the test results from John Andrew and Melinda's hair, blood, and handwriting. At the time, the only possible match to evidence found at the crime scene was the pubic hair found on the white blanket in the basement, which held some slight similarities to Melinda's. But her alibi was even tighter than her brother's, and it was not likely that she had used the same blanket when she stayed with the family. The next day the police informed the DA's office that they would make a public statement regarding Ramsey's older children within the week.

Pete Hofstrom was encouraged to hear that the Ramseys' attorney was corresponding directly with the police. He hoped he would no longer have to be a go-between. Then, Chief Koby received a letter from Bryan Morgan. Presumably, Morgan wanted to deal with Eller's boss because the Ramseys still hadn't gotten over the commander's attempt to withhold JonBenét's body. Morgan requested a meeting to discuss the pending issues, among them John's and Patsy's interviews and the possible waiver of attorney-client privilege in any meeting between the Ramseys, their lawyers, and the police. Koby passed the letter on to Hofstrom, placing him back in the middle. Hofstrom told Morgan that topics discussed in such a meeting would not be used against the Ramseys in court. However, any lead developed or evidence discovered as a result of any discussion *could* be used in a future prosecution. Hofstrom told Hunter he hoped that these exchanges would lead to the formal interviews the police wanted.

★ ★ ★

When Hunter returned home on the evening of March 4, he turned on his TV to see district attorney Bob Grant, a member of his task force, on *Larry King Live*, hosted by Wolf Blitzer. Appearing with Grant were Janet and Bill McReynolds, along with Charlie Brennan of the *Rocky Mountain News* and Dan Glick of *Newsweek*. The McReynoldses were responding to rumors that they were suspects in JonBenét's death. They addressed parallels between their own daughter's kidnapping, Janet McReynolds's play *Hey, Rube*, and the murder of JonBenét.

As the hour progressed, Janet McReynolds became increasingly preachy: "I feel that . . . the media is saying to this collective community . . . in some ways she [JonBenét] deserved to die. That, at least, is a message that I am getting: She deserved to die because she was too beautiful. She deserved to die because she was from an affluent family. She deserved to die because she lived in an upscale community. She deserved to die because her family taught her gestures which might be interpreted as sexually suggestive. She deserved to die because she was in beauty pageants.... And to me, that is a crucifixion of an innocent victim."

Janet McReynolds's fervent outburst led the police to take an even harder look at her family. They began to search for their old handwriting samples as they awaited the results from the McReynoldses' blood samples.

POLICE CLEAR ADULT KIDS

HALF BROTHER, HALF SISTER ELIMINATED AS SUSPECTS IN JONBENÉT'S MURDER

John Ramsey's adult children from a previous marriage officially have been cleared of suspicion in the murder of their half sister, 6-year-old JonBenét Ramsey, a city spokesperson said.

The announcement about the Ramsey children marked the first time in the 10-week investigation that police have removed any name from the list of suspects.

Pat Korten, the Ramsey media consultant, posted on his Web site: "The Ramsey family is grateful that police have announced that John Andrew and Melinda are not suspects in the case."

Other developments in the case . . . The former lead detective

[Larry Mason] in the case was cleared of allegations that he leaked information to the media.

—Elliott Zaret
Daily Camera, March 7, 1997

Although Eller had pushed the FBI out of the day-by-day investigation on the afternoon JonBenét's body was found, the Bureau's forensics labs had been analyzing the evidence for the police since January 19, and its Child Abduction and Serial Killer Unit (CASKU) was evaluating and profiling the crime scene.

On March 7, Special Agent Gregory Bishea of the FBI's Chemistry Unit completed his initial examination of the black duct tape, including the yarn/scrim count and the percentage of calcium filler in the adhesive. With this data, the FBI and the police hoped to discover where the tape had been manufactured and when it was distributed. Previously, microscopic fiber trace evidence had been lifted by the FBI from the duct tape, and the source of the fiber was also being investigated.

The efforts of CASKU were not scientifically precise, but its work was important nonetheless. Its profilers studied the physical evidence and all the known circumstances of homicides in order to provide a probable portrait of the perpetrator.

JonBenét was at home in bed on Christmas night in an affluent neighborhood while her parents were supposedly sleeping, which by the profilers' standards put her at extremely low risk of encountering a stranger who intended harm. Her risk for murder by a stranger was also low because she hardly ever interacted with strangers, her circle of playmates and friends was constant, and she hardly ever played on the street unsupervised. Several of her parents' friends told police that JonBenét was always with a known adult.

Appearing in child beauty pageants, however, increased JonBenét's potential risk for meeting death at the hands of a stranger. Pageants exposed her to more potential suspects, including known pedophiles. Even though JonBenét had been found dead at home, the pageant connection couldn't be ignored. Had some stranger been attracted to her?

Pedophiles are persuasive by nature; they use attention, affection, and gifts to seduce a child, usually over an extended period. Force and violence are rarely involved, and the molester is not usually a stranger to the victim.

But if a stranger had murdered JonBenét in her home, he took a big risk that family members might wake and discover him.

The FBI believed that JonBenét's vaginal trauma was not consistent with a history of sexual abuse, and they had turned up no evidence of any other type of abuse. The sexual violation of JonBenét, whether pre- or postmortem, did not appear to have been committed for the perpetrator's gratification. The penetration, which caused minor genital trauma, was more likely part of a staged crime scene, intended to mislead the police.

Kidnappings are almost always committed for money or sex. Rarely can another motive be found. The FBI concluded that if the duct tape over JonBenét's mouth had been used to silence her during an attempted abduction, the kidnapper would have taken her out of the house immediately. There would have been no reason to stay where the kidnapper could be discovered at any moment. Instead, they theorized, the duct tape too was probably used as part of a cover-up, along with the loosely tied cord found around JonBenét's right wrist. Whether the duct tape had been placed on JonBenét's mouth before or after her death could be determined by an examination of the body and tape. Skin trauma would be evident if she had been alive when the tape was applied. Applying the tape after her death would not produce noticeable skin markings. Coroner Meyer had not reported any trauma to the skin around JonBenét's mouth.

The probable behavior of the offender was an important factor. If the killer did not intend to kidnap JonBenét, he or she must have been there for a reason, perhaps to assault her. But if there had been no intent to kidnap, why did the killer write the ransom note?

The FBI profilers who scrutinized the overall crime scene, the autopsy findings, and the fingerprints, fibers, and blood evidence told the police that the ransom note was the most important piece of behavioral evidence in the case. Of all the elements of the crime, it probably took longest to complete.

The police believed that if the ransom note was written before JonBenét's murder, that left the door open to the possibility of an intruder, but if it was written after she was killed, it was unlikely an intruder would have stayed to write it. But the FBI and the police could not determine when the ransom note was written.

Once JonBenét had been murdered, the only reason to write the note or to leave it behind was to provide a false motive for the crime.

And, to give credibility to the ransom note and a bogus kidnapping, the offender had to make the police believe that JonBenét had been restrained and silenced. That was called staging within staging.

The moment JonBenét died and her body was left in a place where it would be found, the ransom money was lost forever to the kidnapper. If it was a real abduction gone sour, why leave the ransom note? After all, the handwriting might lead the police to the killer. The only reasonable conclusion was that the note had been left behind in an attempt to hide the killer's identity and the real reason for JonBenét's death.

If the killer was a stranger, why did he wrap JonBenét's body in a blanket? Why try to comfort someone who was no longer of use? The dominant sign of hostility toward JonBenét was the use of the noose. Its elevation at every point around the neck was equal in distance from the shoulders, indicating that it had not been tied during a struggle. The FBI had never before encountered this type of violence in a child homicide. No parent who killed a child had ever used a "garrote" for strangulation.

The note, the cord around the wrist, the tape over the mouth, the noose around the neck, and the possibility of penetration all suggested that the killer had no fear of discovery during the crime, though John, Patsy, and Burke Ramsey were asleep in the house. A further analysis of the crime elements led the FBI to conclude that the killer felt comfortable and secure inside the Ramsey home. Few crime elements suggested an intruder or a stranger. Some of the FBI experts thought that the hard blow to JonBenét's head had been intentional. The injury did not have the characteristics of an accident. Besides, when accidents happen, people usually call for medical assistance. Still, the FBI noted, the blow to the head had not produced any bleeding and might not have been noticed at first. The experts considered an alternate explanation: the offender might have intended to hit a third party, missed, and hit JonBenét by mistake.

The police knew that when all the factors were considered, one scenario would be more compelling than the others. Various pieces of evidence might suggest other theories, but all the facts together could allow for only one. The FBI told the police that whatever theory they settled on must be fact-driven: They could change the theory as new facts emerged, but they could not twist the facts to fit a preexisting theory.

Regardless of the conclusions reached by the FBI profilers, the police were constrained by Colorado law. Behavioral profile analysis was admissible as expert analysis of a crime scene, but nothing about the personality of the presumed offender was admissible in court.

SNOW AT RAMSEY HOUSE LACKED FOOTPRINTS

Police who went to JonBenét Ramsey's home the morning she was reported missing found no footprints in the snow surrounding the house, sources said Monday.

This is one of the earliest details that caused investigators to focus their attention on the slain girl's family, police sources said.

—Charlie Brennan
Rocky Mountain News, March 11, 1997

John Fernie was angry when he read Charlie Brennan's story about footprints. Like many media stories, this one came from an unnamed source and made the Ramseys look guilty. Fernie wondered if the source had provided the reporter with all the facts. He knew that his own footprints were there in the snow that morning. He had driven up the back alley to the Ramseys' house just after 6:00 A.M. in response to Patsy's frantic call that terrible morning. He remembered walking along the brick sidewalk to the patio door, looking through the glass panel, and reading a line or two of the ransom note, which was lying on the floor just inside the door. Then he had run through the snow-covered grass, around the south side of the house, to the front door. If the cops had been looking, they would have found his footprints. A year and a half after JonBenét's death, Fernie told a reporter that the police *still* had not checked the shoes he wore that day, though a shoe imprint had been discovered next to JonBenét's body.

Carol McKinley, a reporter for Denver's KOA-AM Radio, disliked the way some reporters used the word *source* without further identification. She also noted that nobody was questioning it. In fact, McKinley knew that it was the official silence and resulting information vacuum that had created these endless "sources." After reading Brennan's no-footprints-in-the-snow story, McKinley knew that she had to develop sources of her own. One of her friends who was close to a Boulder officer investigating the case agreed to introduce her to the detective.

"I don't want to know anything you don't want me to know," McKinley told him. "I just want to know what this case is doing to your life, what you're thinking. Let me do a profile on you."

The officer agreed to be interviewed, but only after McKinley turned off her tape recorder did the real story begin to emerge. She could see that the detective needed to talk about his frustrations. He told her about the problem between Eller and the DA's office, and how leaks to the press were hurting the investigation, how some of his colleagues had been maligned in the press for months, and how the Ramseys' attorneys seemed to know everything the police were doing. "You must never reveal my name to anyone," he told the reporter. McKinley agreed.

"Keep this all under your hat," the officer told her. Never once, however, did he say that John or Patsy had murdered their daughter.

Before long, McKinley, like other reporters, had found additional sources in the DA's office, among the Ramseys' attorneys, and at the CBI. The information she had as a result permitted her to maintain a balance in her reporting. She leveraged information from one source and confirmed it with another.

The day Brennan's no-footprints-in-the-snow article was published, the CBI gave the Boulder police Bill McReynolds's DNA test results: On the surface the report seemed to exclude him. His DNA did not match the DNA found on JonBenét's underpants. Nor did it match some DNA that the CBI had found under her fingernails, which coroner Meyer had clipped and preserved. However, the CBI pointed out that the material found under her fingernails showed signs of contamination and the markers on the DNA typing were weak. The origin of the contamination had yet to be determined. Since handwriting and hair analysis for McReynolds still hadn't been completed, and Janet McReynolds's DNA test results were still pending, the couple remained suspects.

While Detective Thomas was reviewing the McReynolds file, his phone rang. It was Allison Russ, John Andrew Ramsey's friend. She told the detective about the calls from Matthew Hayworth and Jeff Scott. She also mentioned the different phone numbers he had given her. Later in the afternoon, Detective Harmer couldn't find "Matthew

Hayworth" at the youth hostel where Shapiro had first stayed.

At 8:45 the next morning, Thomas tried the second phone number. "I'm Steve Thomas, a detective for the Boulder Police Department, and I'm looking for Jeffrey Scott," he said.

Only half awake, Shapiro replied that he'd hoped to hear from a Ramsey investigator, not the police.

"Well, Jeff, I'm sorry," Thomas said with a laugh. "I've heard you have some interesting information. I'd like you to come in so I can interview you, see if it's important information. And we're not going to shine any bright lights on you."

"Do you know about the DNA results?" Shapiro asked.

"I can't discuss that with you," Thomas replied.

"Are you aware that someone is saying that John Andrew once tried to hire someone to run a boat over JonBenét?"

"I've heard that," Thomas answered. "Those are the kinds of things I'd like to ask you about. And, Jeff, I need to make sure you're not any kind of journalist or reporter before I let you into this department."

Shapiro told Thomas that he knew some guys from the Simpson case, but he wasn't a journalist. He'd think about a visit to police headquarters.

When Shapiro hung up, he called Joe Mullins, his editor at the *Globe*, and said that he'd made contact with Allison Russ, John Andrew, and the police. He also said he'd used a false name in identifying himself.

"You lied to the cops?" Mullins asked.

"I'm undercover."

"You *can't* lie to the police. What's this cop's name?"

That same evening at Kutztown University in Allentown, Pennsylvania, John Douglas, the former FBI profiler who had been hired by the Ramseys, held a press conference before giving a scheduled lecture. In answer to reporters' questions, he said he had been hired to determine whether John Ramsey was capable of killing JonBenét, at a time when, according to Douglas, Ramsey's attorneys weren't sure if their client was innocent. Douglas said he had never been asked to focus his attention on Patsy and therefore hadn't profiled her. And the Ramseys' attorneys, Douglas said, hadn't asked him if Patsy fit any of his criteria for the murderer. Journalists following the case assumed that Douglas doubted Patsy's innocence and wanted to protect his reputation now that handwriting analysis had not excluded Patsy—and in fact suggested that she might have written the ransom note.

Douglas was not the only investigator the Ramseys had hired. Private investigators retained by the Ramseys were reviewing other unsolved crimes of a similar nature, interviewing witnesses the police had not looked at closely enough, and following leads provided to them by the Ramseys and the public.

Steve Thomas was at his desk at police headquarters looking at the March 12 issue of the *Globe*, which featured photos of the inside of the Ramseys' house. Eight pictures traced the "evil killer's footsteps inside death mansion . . . From JonBenét's pretty pink bedroom to the cold dark cellar where her broken body was found." It was another exclusive for the tabloid.

Thomas couldn't figure out who had supplied the photographs. They had been taken by the Ramseys' own investigators after the police finished their search of the house in early January. He was certain they wouldn't have leaked the pictures to a publication that was implicating the Ramseys in the death of their daughter. Thomas was angry because photos of the crime scene should have been restricted to the police.

When his phone rang, he was surprised to hear Joe Mullins of the *Globe* on the other end. Mullins told the detective that "Jeff Scott" was actually Jeff Shapiro, a *Globe* researcher. This annoyed Thomas more than the photos had. Thomas told Mullins that he would reveal Shapiro's true identity to both John Andrew and Allison Russ.

By now Steve Thomas had been involved in almost every aspect of the investigation and, within the department, was gaining the reputation of resident expert. If anyone in the Boulder PD had an overview, it was Thomas. For his part, he was sure that Bill McReynolds, though his handwriting was questionable, was too frail to have committed the crime. Someone stronger than Santa had to have killed the child, who must have struggled at some time during the crime. Her weight alone, if she had been carried down to the basement, seemed to rule McReynolds out. Thomas estimated that Joe Barnhill, the Ramseys' neighbor, was strong enough, but his palsy eliminated him as the writer of the ransom note. The Ramseys' ex-employees' alibis seemed to be checking out. Thomas knew of no credible evidence that someone other than Patsy or John Ramsey could be involved—if not in the death of JonBenét, then in a cover-up.

Later that morning, Thomas returned a call from Iris Woodall, who worked at Home Depot in Athens, Georgia. She told the detective that Patsy Ramsey had shopped for duct tape in December 1996 with a child who resembled JonBenét. Thomas called Detective Evans of the Roswell police for assistance in pursuing the lead. The next day Evans interviewed Woodall and learned that during the week of December 7, Patsy had been in the Athens store and had asked her for help in locating duct tape. Woodall was shown a picture of the Ramseys, and she said that Patsy may have been accompanied by her husband. The police eventually pinpointed the date to December 12, 1996, the day before the Ramseys returned to Boulder to host a dinner.

When Detectives Gosage and Thomas made their next trip to Atlanta, they met Woodall and reviewed the accounting records of Home Depot's Athens store. There were approximately twenty thousand register receipts to check, to find one that matched Patsy's credit card number or, if a check was used, her Colorado or Georgia driver's license. After three days they came up empty-handed. This left the possibility that the purchase had been paid for in cash.

Law enforcement sources have admitted to ABC News that the murder investigation may be in trouble. Handwriting experts have failed to find a link between JonBenét's father and the ransom note; and although Patsy Ramsey, the mother, has given three writing samples, police have been unable to determine if she wrote the note either. Neither parent is yet talking to police.

From the beginning officials have been convinced that a tiny spot of fluid, found on the girl's leg, is semen. But lab tests of the fluid produced no DNA . . . and were therefore inconclusive. Sources say the killer wiped the body clean of any other evidence.

"In the absence of semen evidence, [said forensic scientist Moses Schanfield] it will be extremely difficult to find evidence that could lead to not only an arrest . . . but a conviction."

ABC World News Tonight, March 13, 1997

Since early in the case, the Ramseys' investigators, headed by Ellis Armistead, had been looking into possible suspects who knew the

Ramseys or could have had access to their home. They were now focusing on people they believed the police had overlooked or had passed over too quickly. On March 13, Armistead met with case supervisor Detective Sgt. Tom Wickman and Detectives Trujillo and Thomas to discuss several possible suspects the Ramsey team had come up with. The list included a known sex offender, an Access Graphics employee, and Glenn Meyer, who lived in Joe Barnhill's basement across the street from the Ramseys. The detectives listened without acknowledging whether these people had been investigated.

Two days later, on March 15, Armistead gave the police a dossier on Meyer, which showed that he had debts amounting to $70,000. Several weeks later, Thomas questioned Meyer at police headquarters about whether he had a prior record of assault, about his debts, and about his whereabouts on December 25 and 26. Meyer identified handwriting samples he'd given to the police and agreed to give another blood sample. Returning to the Barnhills' home, he probably wondered how the police had discovered he was in debt and why the polygraph he'd taken hadn't cleared him.

RAMSEY DOCTORS: NO HISTORY OF ABUSE

JonBenét Ramsey's family has provided the district attorney a psychiatrist's videotaped interview with the girl's 10-year-old brother, a pediatrician's records, and other information that they contend indicates the family has no history of sexual abuse, a source says.

The family has . . . allowed pediatrician Dr. Francesco Beuf and his nurses to speak with investigators.

—Clay Evans
Daily Camera, March 16, 1997

JonBenét Ramsey Information Update

Date: March 19, 1997
To: Reporters covering the Ramsey case
Fr: Pat Korten

News leaks appearing to come from law enforcement sources over the past few days have suggested, that there are some similarities between Patsy Ramsey's handwriting and that found on the ransom note left in the Ramseys' house on December 26.

Handwriting experts retained by the Ramseys, among the most highly regarded in the field, have concluded that neither John nor Patsy Ramsey wrote the note. While they noted some similarity between a few of Patsy Ramsey's letters and those found on the note, there were dramatic differences between her handwriting and the note in many other areas.

Now that the *Globe* had blown Jeff Shapiro's cover, he knew he would have to use his real name, but part of his cover story—that he was a student—was still intact. Joe Mullins had suggested to him before he left Florida that he visit the Ramseys' church and say he was interested in converting to Christianity. Perhaps he could discuss the Jews for Jesus movement. It might help him gain credibility among the parishioners. Shapiro considered the ethics of using religion to get close to someone and eventually decided he didn't care.

"When you're working undercover," Shapiro often said, "whether you're an investigative reporter, a detective, or an FBI agent, you don't have ordinary morals. You do whatever you have to do to accomplish your mission. And you don't let anything get personal."

On Friday, March 20, Shapiro visited St. John's for the first time and asked to see Rev. Hoverstock. On the door of his office hung a sign: NO MEDIA. THANK YOU.

Shapiro told Hoverstock he wanted to become a Christian. He was truthful with Hoverstock about his upbringing and told him how frustrating it was to graduate from college and be unable to find the right job. He said his parents were wealthy and that a lot of his friends were Christians. He was undercover, Shapiro told himself, and his ultimate goal was more important than these trivial white lies. He was in Boulder to find the truth, and he began to feel that God wanted him to help.

He mentioned his interest in the Simpson case and told the minister that the LAPD had framed OJ.

Hoverstock replied, "You've come at an interesting time."

Jeff nodded.

"We'll get to know one another, have some conversations," Hoverstock told Shapiro. "I'll learn more about you." Hoverstock invited Shapiro to services and seminars, to become more informed about Christianity.

From then on, Shapiro attended services every Sunday, and prayer classes, which he enjoyed. In some ways he felt more of a bond with the people at St. John's than with his fellow Jews. He felt good about what he was doing. He felt that he belonged. He purchased a Book of Common Prayer and a Bible.

Later Shapiro would tell his editor that he was getting two for the price of one—he was doing his job and acquiring spirituality.

My father always reminded me of Hal Holbrook in the movie Wall Street. *He's rational and likes to disarm people, doesn't like to provoke them. I'm sure he worked for the CIA when I was a kid. He'd leave in the middle of the night for places like Iran, the Middle East, and Europe. I think he helped build a power plant for the CIA out there and had some run-ins with terrorist organizations. Later he helped design the launchpad for the Saturn Five rocket.*

I was brought up in Boca Raton and attended Florida State University as a political science major. I wrote stories on Jim Garrison, the O. J. Simpson case, and John DeLorean for local publications.

When I was fifteen I started to go out alone. I saw homeless people in places my parents had never taken me. The contrast of people in limousines and people lying on the street starving affected me. That's when I decided I wanted to talk to President Reagan and find out why there are homeless people in such a wonderful country.

I snuck into the Boca Raton Resort & Club Hotel to see the president when he was in Florida. I knew that hotel like the back of my hand because I'd spent days there as a kid. I got past the Secret Service and all the way up a stairwell to the twenty-fourth floor, one floor below Reagan. That's when I was taken into federal custody.

I was wearing a shirt with an American flag and FREEDOM FOREVER printed on it, and I'd wrapped another little flag around my wrist. I looked like a comic book character.

When I was caught, I thanked God that I hadn't brought my Swiss Army knife. It might have looked like an assassination attempt. They interviewed me for hours. I told them I was interested in politics. I showed them how I'd driven my bike past the police at the golf course entrance. One of their cars followed me when they let me ride my bike home.

At twenty-two, I got an internship at the White House Office of Media Affairs, in the Clinton administration. Washington was like a futuristic Roman empire. There was a lot of beauty, a lot of corruption, and a lot of people compromising their values. I have a history of getting into confrontations—because I question the way things operate. That happened in Washington, so I went back to Florida and freelanced for the Miami Herald *until the* Globe *hired me.*

—Jeff Shapiro

The Boulder PD was now being criticized almost nightly on TV programs such as *Larry King Live* and *Geraldo*. Though detectives weren't being identified by name, it was hard for Steve Thomas and his fellow officers to take the constant ridicule. It wasn't only the national media that attacked them; the *Rocky Mountain News* and *The Denver Post* also chastised them. The attacks were excruciating. What made them worse was the continued silence of Chief Koby. With no one speaking up for them—and strict instructions that they were not to speak to the media—the officers were frustrated and angry. Officers who wanted the Ramsey case prosecuted without delay and were willing to ignore the presumption of innocence realized that the media could be an effective tool, indeed a weapon.

It was under these circumstances that one detective called Carol McKinley. He insisted on anonymity but wanted the public to know that the Boulder PD was doing its best and that they knew who the murderer was. The officer told McKinley that suspects were not always arrested immediately. Good police work took time. No matter what was being said, he and his colleagues weren't the Keystone Kops. His primary concern was the department's reputation, he said.

Meanwhile another source of McKinley's, an attorney for the Ramseys, told her that his clients were the victims of poor police work and media speculation. He believed the Boulder PD was using the tabloids and the mainstream media to convict his clients.

There was evidence that an intruder had killed JonBenét, he said, but to protect the investigation, he couldn't reveal the nature of the evidence. His clients were being framed, he claimed, and the public was being misled.

Though Alex Hunter didn't know who had killed JonBenét, he was certain that John Eller had been unable to see the big picture since that day in mid-January when the test on what was alleged to be semen came back negative. The commander was too focused on the Ramseys as the only suspects, a position that was unacceptable even to those in the DA's office who thought that Patsy and John Ramsey had killed their daughter. Hunter, who planned to hire his own investigators, first had to get the files from Eller for an objective review. That would be step one. Hunter told Wise, "How do you know you've got it unless you've read the whole case?" The second step would be to prepare the files for eventual transfer to a prosecutorial team.

Hunter told Koby his plan, and the chief agreed, as long as the DA's personnel did not interfere, second-guess, or reinvestigate. Hunter agreed. Eller also responded positively when Koby told him. Now the case file would be cataloged and indexed by Hunter's office.

Hunter would need two experienced detectives—officers who could be objective. He wanted at least one of them to look at the case from the point of view of the defense.

Tom Haney, recently retired from the patrol division of the Denver PD, was an obvious candidate. In his twenty-eight years on the force, he had investigated many of the city's most notorious murders. Haney met with Hunter and Hofstrom and then with Eller and Koby. They told him they were looking for someone with investigative experience who could handle the transition from investigation to prosecution. Haney said he could. Eller asked Haney his opinion of Lou Smit. "He's a hell of a guy and a great investigator," Haney said. "And he's solved some tough cases."

Smit was a legend among law enforcement personnel. Formerly captain of detectives in the El Paso County sheriff's office, he'd worked 150 homicide cases in Colorado Springs. Smit had recently solved a three-and-a-half-year-old kidnapping by matching a lone fingerprint, which had been overlooked, to one in a regional fingerprint database. At sixty-one, Smit had kept up with cutting-edge technology while retaining some tried-and-true methods. Once, he had sifted through a hundred bags of garbage to look for evidence that tied a murderer to his victim. Maggots crawled up his sleeves, but he found the critical evidence. Like a lot of dedicated officers, he'd been seen praying at victims' graves. He said that God was his partner.

Hunter discussed Haney and Smit with Koby and with Trip DeMuth, who felt that Smit was less pushy than Haney. Detective Tom Trujillo told Chief Koby that Lou Smit was their kind of cop.

Koby decided that Smit would do, and Hunter agreed.

Coincidentally, Hal Haddon, one of John Ramsey's lawyers, asked Haney to join *their* team. Haney had never worked on the defense side, and he had some concerns, but he met with Patrick Burke nonetheless. Patsy's attorney said he believed that John and Patsy were innocent. Moreover, he said, their investigation had uncovered possible suspects.

"I'm not sure I could rule the Ramseys out," Haney told him.

"They'll sit down with you," Burke replied. "They'll answer all your questions."

Haney wanted to ask if the Ramseys had taken a polygraph, but he decided it would be rude. The next day, Haney called Burke and declined the job. He just had that feeling in his gut.

On March 13, Smit agreed to work for Hunter. That same day the DA walked upstairs to the sheriff's office and asked Epp to lend him Steve Ainsworth for his investigation. The detective and deputy DA Trip DeMuth had a good working relationship. They had solved a murder case together in nearby Louisville. Ainsworth had worked on the Ramsey case the first weekend after the murder, and he was eager to rejoin the investigation. Epp was disturbed that Steve wouldn't be doing any interviewing, however. That privilege had been reserved for Eller's detectives. Instead, Ainsworth would remain in the office, where he would review material from the point of view of the defense, as Hunter's devil's advocate.

Lou Smit and Steve Ainsworth formally joined Hunter's team on March 17 and immediately reviewed the files. They began by examining a list of suspects the police might not have investigated fully. One caught their eyes—Kevin Raburn.

A Colorado Department of Corrections investigator, Steve McLaury, had called the Boulder PD on February 19 about a former inmate, Kevin Raburn, who was discharged from a Colorado prison just 200 miles from Boulder a week before the murder of JonBenét. Joan Wise, the counselor who had handled Raburn's discharge interview, noticed the ransom amount in newspaper stories and remembered Raburn saying that he had sufficient funds to live on. He mentioned $118,000.

Ainsworth soon discovered that Raburn had been jailed in Boulder during the previous month. He had stolen some batteries and spent several weeks in the Boulder County Jail. Ainsworth immediately found his fingerprint cards and a list of local contacts. Next stop was the Marine Park Apartments in Boulder, Raburn's last known address. That night Ainsworth visited Raburn's mother, Caroline, at her home in nearby Broomfield. He had also contacted the Boulder halfway house where Raburn had stayed; Kristen Weiss and Lynn Essig, employees at a bar where Raburn hung out; and Kevin Johnson, the manager of Rafferty's Restaurant, where Raburn had worked as a short-order cook in 1995 before going to prison. Meanwhile, Smit hit the bars, clubs, and restaurants where Raburn was a customer or had sought work. Within a few days, Smit received samples of Raburn's handwriting from the Department of Corrections. A week later, Ainsworth discovered that a friend of Raburn's lived on 17th Street, only a few blocks from the Ramseys' house.

The detectives, who were unable to find Raburn, pieced together a picture of his movements. His mother told the police that after her son returned to Boulder on December 20, he got his job back at Rafferty's.

Raburn was off from work on December 24, and Rafferty's was closed Christmas Day. According to his mother, with whom he was living, he spent Christmas night watching TV with her and his brother. Mrs. Raburn didn't remember if she turned on the house alarm, which she normally did before going to sleep. But she said that Kevin didn't have the access code. The police learned that a week after JonBenét's murder, Raburn lost his job at Rafferty's. He began working nights at Juanita's, another restaurant.

Raburn was suspect not only because of the $118,000 coincidence but because, from the night of the murder through the first week in January, his whereabouts could not be confirmed. And now he seemed to have vanished.

FAMILY GETS OWN DNA EXPERT

Forensic scientist Moses Schanfield has been tapped by attorneys for the parents of JonBenét Ramsey to possibly monitor additional DNA testing in the investigation of the 6-year-old's murder.

The legal teams hired by John and Patsy Ramsey haven't decided whether to take up an offer from prosecutors allowing them to monitor the testing. But if they do, Schanfield would be on hand to observe.

—Marilyn Robinson and Mary George
The Denver Post, March 21, 1997

Mary Lou Jedamus and Grace Morlock had been called to the Ramsey home by the police as victim advocates when the kidnapping of JonBenét was first reported. They tried to comfort the parents, and they listened to what the couple said. The detectives thought the advocates might know something that would aid the investigation. On March 21 and 25, Detectives Harmer and Hickman interviewed Jedamus and Morlock at police headquarters.

The Ramseys probably didn't know that their conversations with the advocates were not confidential or privileged by law.* Jedamus and Morlock were obligated to tell the detectives everything they could remember, since they worked for—and were partly compensated by— the police department.

Although victim advocates are not investigators, the police needed to know what the advocates remembered. They recalled that Detective Arndt had been businesslike and sympathetic. Compassionate might be too strong a word. She seemed to consider every possibility, and she was not adversarial. None of the officers had been antagonistic. No one had said, "Why did you do this?"

Morlock remembered that John Ramsey had cried but had tried to control his emotions even when he was so distraught that he could barely speak. He may have said, "If only the dog had been in the house." The advocates had also heard Patsy say, "Whoever left the note knew that I always come down those stairs in the morning." Morlock told the detectives she had seen John and Patsy sitting together in the dining room, holding each other and talking.

Both advocates remembered Patsy's hysteria as she sobbed and carried on. One of them had heard Patsy say, "If only it were me, I'd trade places with Jonnie B. Oh, please let her be safe, please let her be safe." Other than that, they had nothing more to contribute.

* Colorado law recognizes a privilege that can shield from disclosure the things that some crime victims say to a "victim's advocate," such as a community-based rape crisis or domestic violence counselor, but that term is expressly defined not to include a person employed by a law enforcement agency. C.R.S 13-90-107(I)(k).

About 40 percent of the cases I deal with involve death, either by acci-
dent or by foul play. Grief, loss of a loved one, and guilt are always pres-
ent in the survivors. No training can prepare anyone for the intensity that
surrounds the loss of a loved one, especially the death of a child.

In the immediate aftermath, the victims don't need therapy. They don't
need counseling. They need someone to recognize and meet their needs.
Sometimes they need to be encouraged to tell their story. The sooner they
can express themselves, the less likely they are to shut down. During
good crisis intervention, you create a safe space for someone to vent.

When a victim becomes a suspect, it can be difficult for an advocate. A
few can adjust, accept it as part of the nature of the work. Many can't see it
that way. They feel used. They hate the idea that they helped a criminal.

—Anonymous victim advocate

5

Jeff Shapiro started to hang out at Pasta Jay's. He drank a few beers and
watched John Ramsey's son bus tables. He was at a loss about how to gain
John Andrew's confidence now that his cover had been blown.

One night Shapiro wrote John Andrew a letter and left it with a
waitress at the restaurant. As he walked out to his car, Shapiro looked
back and saw Ramsey's son open it.

> *Unlike every other reporter working on this case, I have*
> *a different perspective. I have an interest in challenging the*
> *mainstream media, and exonerating anyone who is getting*
> *unfairly attacked by the media. I have a particular interest*
> *in helping you. I am a protector. This is not just about ambi-*
> *tion for me. There are still people who care about the truth:*
> *not everyone is deceiving and evil. All I ever wanted was*
> *the opportunity to become your friend. I wanted to leave*

here knowing I made a difference; knowing I had protected an innocent person from the onslaught of the judgmental media. I follow the advice Michael Dukakis offered me: 'Always tell the truth.' Only a reporter, one with great passion and ethics, can undo what the media has already done.

When a week passed and Shapiro hadn't heard back, he called John Andrew's mother, Lucinda, in Atlanta. Shapiro wanted to know whether an unsubstantiated rumor that Melinda had checked into a Georgia health clinic for depression was true. This time, he introduced himself as a freelance college journalist living in Boulder.

"Some people are saying these awful things about Melinda," Shapiro said.

"She's wonderful," Lucinda replied. "Just fine. The rumor you've heard is ridiculous."

Lucinda asked Shapiro if he knew her son. He said that he'd met John Andrew. Then he told Lucinda that his name was Jeff Scott.

"Are you the one who wrote him a letter?"

"Yes," Shapiro replied.

"I don't want to talk to you. Don't ever call this house." She hung up.

Shapiro was still determined to impress his editors, however. He took to driving around town in the hope of spotting someone involved in the investigation. One day he saw Alex Hunter walking alone toward the Justice Center. After taking a quick shot of Hunter with his disposable camera, Shapiro pulled up next to the DA.

"Are you Alex?"

"Yes, I am," Hunter said with a smile.

Shapiro told Hunter that he was an investigative reporter working on the Ramsey case but didn't mention the *Globe*. He told the DA that he'd worked on the Simpson case with Stephen Singular, a Denver author.

"Oh really?" Hunter said, and asked Shapiro to park his car so they could talk.

They stood out in front of the Justice Center despite the March chill. They discussed, among other subjects, pedophilia, Barry Scheck, and Henry Lee. Shapiro told Hunter he'd heard that the "semen" found on JonBenét's body was really some kind of liquid soap, like Phisoderm. Hunter smiled. Then Shapiro asked if the DA's office was getting closer to an arrest.

"No, no, no, no," Hunter replied.

Shapiro searched in his backpack and gave the DA a copy of "Code of Silence," a paper he'd written about the Simpson case.

"I'd like to talk to you again," Hunter told him as he walked into the Justice Center.

Shapiro rushed to a student computer lab and wrote his report, which he faxed to the *Globe*. Then he called Mullins, his editor.

"We need to know what Hunter meant by 'looking into the area of pedophilia,'" Mullins said. "Go back and see what he says about that."

En route to Hunter's office, Shapiro was apprehensive. To his surprise, Hunter invited him in. Before the DA could say a word, Shapiro blurted out: "I wasn't straight with you outside. The truth is, I work for the *Globe*."

"Mullins called me after he received your phone call," Hunter said grinning.

"He did?"

"He told me you're young and you're a bit overenthusiastic," Hunter continued. "He wanted to make sure you weren't getting too excited about your job. Something like that." The DA smiled.

The situation was bizarre, Shapiro thought. Here was the DA talking to his editor after he had publicly expressed outrage at the *Globe* for publishing the autopsy and crime-scene photos. Before long, though, they were joking about the Simpson case. It struck Shapiro that Hunter was asking most of the questions. He wasn't the interviewer; he was the interviewee.

Hunter suggested that they keep in touch, and Shapiro gave the DA his pager number.

A couple of days later, Shapiro's pager buzzed. Though he didn't recognize the number, he returned the call.

"Hey, buddy," someone said.

"Alex." It was Hunter.

"I'm thinking of meeting Stephen Singular," Hunter said. "I want to know what you think of him."

Singular had some good ideas, Shapiro told him. Then he requested a meeting. In the intervening days, Mullins had told him that the *Globe* was looking at a wild rumor. They'd heard that the Ramseys were hinting that Fleet White was somehow connected to the murder of their daughter—a rumor that was never substantiated. Surely Alex Hunter would know something about it.

"Did Mullins ask you to come back?" was how Hunter greeted me.

I laughed. "Yeah."

First I asked him if the rumors were true that the Whites were distancing themselves from the Ramseys.

"No," he said. "It's the Ramseys who are distancing themselves from the Whites."

"Who else knows about this?" I asked.

"I would think the Enquirer is already on that story." I realized that Hunter was talking to several of the tabloids.

As we kicked around different theories of the case, Hunter became my commander-in-chief. I started to think of stories in terms of what Hunter said rather than in terms of what my editors wanted. If Hunter had a theory, I figured it was worth pursuing.

Around the same time, in late March, I called Pam Griffin, JonBenét's pageant seamstress. She was very talkative. Of course I didn't tell her right off that I worked for the Globe. I knew she'd find out the truth eventually.

She was a close friend of Patsy's, and I figured she might know what was in the ransom note. I asked her if the words foreign faction were used. She said she believed they might have been. Alli Krupski, a reporter for the Daily Camera, had told me she'd heard from a cop that the word Iran was also in the note. So I called the director of the International Institute for the Study of Terrorism at George Washington University for information on Iranian terrorist groups thought to be active in the U.S. He gave me the name of one death squad—Missionaries of Iran. They strangle people and sometimes behead them. That connected to rumors I'd heard that the ransom note threatened JonBenét would be beheaded. So I concocted this crazy but fascinating conspiracy theory, called Guardians of the Revolution.

I decided to write up my theory and give it to a few people. I hoped the Ramseys would hear about it and that I might get closer to them. The story was never intended for publication.

I decided to take my article to Fleet White. I went to his house and found him working in his garden. He had an impressive view of the foothills.

"Who are you?" he asked.

"I'm just a kid who's interested in the case. I wrote something that I want to leave with you."

"I'm not doing interviews. Don't come any further."

I left it on a wooden post.

Then I faxed a copy to Pam Griffin. She faxed it to Denise Wolf, Ramsey's secretary, who gave it to John. Pam later told me that Ramsey called and said, "Interesting, but unlikely." Pam then faxed it to Nedra, Patsy's mother, who believed it entirely. What I didn't realize then was that John Ramsey would have known the word Iran didn't appear in the ransom note.

I also gave a copy of the article to Alex and told him that I'd seen Fleet White.

"Don't you find it strange that this guy is so fuckin' angry?" Hunter asked. Then he started explaining how John and Fleet got into this big argument in Atlanta—"Lots of words spoken, and they really haven't talked much since," Hunter said. None of that information was public at the time.

"As a prosecutor, it would be irresponsible for me not to look in other places, wouldn't it?" Hunter seemed to be thinking aloud. "I want to know who this guy Fleet White is. I want to know about his life in Newport Beach, California, before he moved here. I'm just interested—that's all I'm saying."

I felt like some young Washington aide getting orders from his senator. The biggest case in the country, and Hunter is asking me for help. It boosted my ego.

The next Sunday I attended church, and as I sat down, to my left, in the row right in front of me, were Patsy and John. Burke was sitting with the Stines, near me. I had to look away fast, not wanting to draw attention to myself. Patsy looked like she was in tears and scared. John was just calm. Burke was happy as a clam, hopping around with a friend.

As the Ramseys prayed, I couldn't take my eyes off them.

As always, about midway through the service, Hoverstock directed the congregation to private prayer. I'd always prayed for JonBenét.

Patsy looked as if she was groomed for prayer. Her posture was solid as a rock. Yet she trembled, and tears were coming from her eyes. Under her breath, I could see her mouthing the words, "Please, please." It seemed to me she was asking for forgiveness. I had never seen anyone pray for his own soul the way Patsy was praying for hers. She seemed obsessed, fixated on her prayer.

John covered his eyes with both hands and would occasionally lift his hands as if he wanted to block the sun from his eyes. Then he'd go back to covering them with both hands.

When I returned from taking communion, I passed the Ramseys and looked into Patsy's eyes. She was still saying, "Please, please." That was when I felt in my heart that she had murdered JonBenét. At that moment, I decided she was the killer.

Hoverstock then asked the congregation to take the Peace: "Everyone rejoice and greet one another." He walked down the aisles, hugging and kissing everyone. Row by row, he was greeting people, shaking hands and talking to them. When he got to Patsy he walked right by her, not saying a word.

My jaw dropped. I realized that Hoverstock had to believe Patsy was involved. As a priest, he might be able to forgive her, but as a man, I assumed, he could not bear to look at her.

A month later, I asked him about that moment. He insisted he hadn't seen her. Bullshit! He saw her.

After the service, in the reception hall, John stood apart from Patsy, off in a corner by himself. Her gal pals surrounded her and smiled or cried from time to time. Some of her friends gave her flowers. John just stood alone with his hands in his pockets. I wanted to say to him, "You didn't do this, did you? I understand."

A few moments later, Patsy walked over to a window that looked down into the basement where the playroom is, where JonBenét used to play. She broke down in tears, hysterically.

I knew she must have done it.

By then John had a dead look in his eyes. He had gone downstairs to the playroom and he was walking around, like he was collecting memories. A moment later, a little girl joined him and tried to hold his hand. He just looked at her and smiled. I got the feeling that he wanted to cry.

Just then a lady came up to me. "Who are you? Who are you?" she repeated pointedly.

"Jeffrey. I'm new in the church," I answered. I could tell she sensed something was up.

"I'm looking for a last name," she insisted.

"Shapiro."

"Shapiro?"

"You know, like the lawyer," I replied.

"The lawyer?"

"Like Robert Shapiro. He represented O. J. Simpson," I answered.

"Jeffrey, are you a member of this church?"

"I'm actually Jewish, but I've told Father Hoverstock that I want to *learn about Christianity."* I had to walk away from her. She continued to stare at me until I left the church.

I wrote a story about that Sunday—"The Ramseys' Private Hell"—but it was never published.

—Jeff Shapiro

JonBenét's medical records were important to the investigation since there might be evidence of child molestation or physical abuse in the files of her pediatrician, Dr. Francesco Beuf. During the first days of January, the Ramseys and their attorneys met with the doctor. Having reviewed his records, he guaranteed them that there was no indication of sexual abuse.

Three weeks after JonBenét was murdered, William Gray, a Ramsey family attorney, released a letter to the press saying that "pediatric consultations showed no history of child abuse." On February 14, the same day that a partial autopsy report was released, Dr. Beuf was interviewed by Paula Woodward on KUSA, Channel 9. He said, "There was never any hint whatsoever of sexual abuse" and "I didn't see any hint of emotional abuse or physical abuse."

Without the Ramseys' consent, the physician could not release JonBenét's medical history, which was protected by Colorado law. On February 10, Detective Harmer obtained a signed release from Patsy and John allowing her to speak to Dr. Beuf's nursing staff. The next day Harmer talked to Barbara Frey and later interviewed Judy Klingensmith, a nurse who had last seen JonBenét in mid-November 1996.

On March 25 Detective Harmer was allowed to interview Dr. Beuf and summarized the dead child's medical history:

JonBenét was born on August 6, 1990, in Atlanta. Beuf become her doctor when the Ramseys moved to Boulder in late 1991. On December 6, 1991, he treated JonBenét for a fever, cough, and wheezing. Over the next ten months, she had the usual colds and coughs of a toddler. In January 1993, JonBenét was diagnosed with her first ear infection, and Dr. Beuf prescribed amoxicillin. By the time JonBenét was two and a half years old, she had a history of coughs accompanied by low-grade fever.

In March 1993 JonBenét had her first serious illness. Her temperature rose to 102, and she had difficulty breathing. She coughed up yellow mucus and looked droopy. She soon recovered.

Three months later, just after July 4, Patsy Ramsey was diagnosed with ovarian cancer. It was just one month short of JonBenét's third birthday. The child, who went to stay with her grandmother Nedra, regressed in her toilet training and eating habits. Suzanne Savage, a baby-sitter, began to help Nedra care for JonBenét.

On August 31, 1993, Patsy, responding to Dr. Beuf's questions, said that her daughter didn't have any fears or phobias and that no aspect of JonBenét's sexual education needed to be discussed.

At three years and one month, JonBenét was brought to see the doctor. Her buttocks were chafed red from diarrhea, as was her vaginal area.

Two months later, JonBenét was back in the doctor's office with a cough and a stuffed nose. She was sleeping poorly, was grouchy from fatigue, and had bad breath. She appeared to have chronic sinusitis. At the end of 1993, JonBenét, at age three, was still drinking from a bottle, and Patsy and John were having problems weaning her.

In January 1994, JonBenét's bad breath had returned; she had a cough and was congested. On February 4, Nedra suggested to Dr. Beuf that her granddaughter might have Fifth disease.★ Dr. Beuf told her that no medication was necessary. By April, JonBenét's breath was still bad; she also had a runny nose and little appetite, slept poorly, and had a bladder infection and vaginal discharge. She was diagnosed with vaginitis. Dr. Beuf advised the Ramseys against bubble baths and prescribed amoxicillin.

Three weeks later, on May 18, JonBenét was still coughing. She had a stuffy nose and was congested. Her ear hurt, and she was cranky. The diagnosis was allergic rhinitis, and Benadryl was prescribed. A week later JonBenét was still coughing. Dr. Beuf prescribed Suprax.

On October 5, 1994, when JonBenét showed up at the doctor's office for a checkup, she had a scar on her left cheek. She'd been hit accidentally by a golf club when the family was in Charlevoix. A week later a plastic surgeon in Denver was consulted. There was no injury to her cheekbone, nothing to worry about. Beuf was told that she was getting along with her brothers and older sister. But she was wearing Pull-Ups at night because she sometimes wet the bed. That same day Patsy filled out a developmental questionnaire. She said there were no aspects of JonBenét's behavior or sex education she

---

★ Fifth disease (erythema infectiosum) is a childhood viral illness, often accompanied by a rash. Having been the fifth such childhood viral illness to be isolated and identified, following others such as chickenpox and measles, it was called Fifth disease.

needed to discuss. Again she noted that her daughter had no fears or phobias. JonBenét was four years and three months old.

On November 1, Patsy brought JonBenet into the office because she'd had diarrhea five times and was lethargic. One bowel movement appeared to be bloody. Three days later, JonBenét was badly congested and had a deep cough. Her breath was bad, but her diarrhea was gone. Within a few days she was fully recovered.

On New Year's Day, 1995, JonBenét was down with chickenpox. The characteristic rash even appeared in her vaginal area. Avino, Benadryl, and Lanocaine were recommended. By the end of the month, she still had a bad cough and was not sleeping well. Robitussin was no help. In mid-February, JonBenét was back at Dr. Beuf's office, with a cough and a temperature of 99.3. A month later, she complained of a stomachache but was sleeping well. In April she had another cough, but John Ramsey told Dr. Beuf's office that he didn't think his daughter needed to be examined.

At Alfalfa's food market on May 8, JonBenét fell and landed on her nose. It was not broken. Seven and a half months later, she tripped and hit her head above her left eye. At the time, she had a stuffy nose and bad breath and was coughing.

Almost a year later, in March 1996, JonBenét was coughing a lot, and two months later she bent the nail back on the fourth finger of her left hand in another fall. Though it was swollen and painful, there was no bruising. Beuf recommended ibuprofen.

Three months before JonBenét's death, on August 27, Patsy told Beuf that JonBenét was a good sleeper, wasn't hard to get to bed, and was easily awakened in the morning. She wasn't interested in the opposite sex, behaved modestly in public, and didn't engage in sex play with her friends. She was, however, asking about sex roles and reproduction. She was not rude or afraid of either parent. She didn't seem to be bossy with her brother, Burke, didn't react with tantrums, and was active. She loved fruit and some vegetables. Patsy said she was delightful and doing very well. Burke had his annual checkup the same day.

The next week, JonBenét's cough was back and Beuf suggested she take Robitussin. In October, two months before her murder, she had a stuffy nose and bad breath. She was diagnosed with allergic rhinitis. On November 12, JonBenét was checked for the last time by Beuf. She had a runny nose and a cold sore and was sneezing. Three weeks later her eyesight was checked by Dr. Marilyn Dougherty. In early December, JonBenét missed a pageant appearance because she was sick, but she didn't see Dr. Beuf.

Dr. Beuf told a reporter covering the story that JonBenét had had an average number of physician visits for a child her age.

The police now had to collate the medical data with other information before any conclusions could be drawn.

I got to know Suzanne Savage from church. When she was totally overwhelmed by her workload at the Ramseys', I helped out. Ended up staying for almost three years. After I left the Ramseys' on Labor Day of 1995, Linda Hoffmann-Pugh started to work for them. The Ramseys weren't warm and affectionate people. They were very professional, very down to business. They communicated with each other like two people who are amicably divorced.

I was working for them when Patsy got sick with cancer and after she recovered. During that time, Nedra moved in and was caring for the children. Then Patsy had what she called her divine intervention and was cured of her cancer. After Patsy finished decorating the house, Burke became her favorite child. She spent all of her time at his school. He was her first project.

At that time JonBenét was too young to do anything spectacular. She hardly got Patsy's attention. Suzanne Savage was in charge of her. JonBenét wasn't in school yet, and her world revolved around adults, whereas Burke's life revolved around his friends.

Then, when JonBenét started school, she became Patsy's second project. The children really were like projects to her. I'm afraid that after JonBenét became Patsy's focus, she also became her obsession.

I think that to Patsy, nothing and no one had the right to be imperfect. Everything had to fit Patsy's image of what it should be. So JonBenét was under immense pressure to fit the image Patsy had of her new project.

When the police interviewed me, they asked if the kids wet the bed a lot. I said yes. Detective Harmer asked if I thought that was unusual, and I had to say, "Not really. Not at that age." Burke wore Pull-Ups until he was six, and JonBenét always wore them. But I also told the police it was curious to me that Burke stopped wetting the bed when he stopped being the focus of Patsy's attention. And that was when JonBenét became a chronic bed wetter. But you know if you have little kids around that age, they are bed wetters. When I left in September of 1995, they were both still wetting their beds.

Then the detectives asked me about the Bible on John's desk in the bedroom. The cover was embossed JOHN AND PATSY RAMSEY. *Sometimes it was by the bed. It was always being read. I know, because I never had to dust it. I told the police that I never saw it open; it always had a bookmark in it.*

I don't remember if I told them about the large photograph John had of an aircraft carrier. On the bottom of the picture in fancy writing were the words Subic Bay Training Center. *The script was faint because it blended in with the water, so the words were hard to read. It used to hang behind his desk in the bedroom.*

—Linda Wilcox

Every media outlet was eager to interview the Ramseys, but the only time John and Patsy had talked to the press was on New Year's Day. Like most of the networks, CNN was still camped out in Boulder. Mike Phelan, a CNN producer who had been in Boulder for two months, called Pat Korten daily asking for an interview. It was a small ritual. Every day Korten would say no.

Phelan's network had set up an office with a full workstation and a library of 186 related videotapes, including the unedited version of the Ramseys' New Year's Day interview, which the Boulder police had wanted since January 1.

On March 12, John Eller learned from CNN editor Tom Watkins that two copies of the unedited tape were in Boulder. He consulted the police department's legal advisers, who told him that the tape was in their jurisdiction. On March 26 Detective Thomas obtained a search warrant to enter CNN's hotel room at Marriott's Residence Inn Hotel and take possession of the tape. When Thomas showed up at the door, Michael Phelan called CNN's attorneys in Atlanta.

The network was prepared for this move from the police, and a deal was struck. In return for CNN's turning over the tape, the police department agreed that it would make it available only to law enforcement personnel working on the case. Bob Keatley, the police department's legal adviser, signed the formal agreement with CNN, which protected CNN's copyright. Two days later, CNN turned over the videotape to Thomas, who made copies for the department.

Now, for the first time, the Boulder detectives could look not only for inconsistencies with the Ramseys' previous statements to police but for behavioral patterns. A copy of the tape was sent to the FBI for analysis by CASKU.

When word reached the Ramseys' attorneys that the police had the videotape, they asked Hunter's office for access to it, too. It would be almost a month before Tom Kelley, representing CNN, authorized the DA to provide a copy to Haddon, Morgan and Foreman.

The Ramseys' attorneys had made some changes in their approach to the press. Pat Korten was let go. It was an effort to simplify logistics and reduce costs, they said. Later one Ramsey attorney would say that the hiring of Pat Korten was the single biggest mistake they had made in the first months of the case. Rachelle Zimmer, an attorney in Haddon's office, would now handle the media's questions.

Meanwhile, Alex Hunter was thinking of designating a press representative to deal with the eighty-two individuals from national TV networks and papers throughout the country who called his office regularly.

Journalists, of course, were being pressured by their editors and producers. Reporters from the Denver papers were told to look for a story every day because public interest was growing. Some writers without many sources fed what information they had to Hunter's office, hoping to get something in return.

To Hunter's staff it sounded as if the information they were getting had come from the police, but when they checked their set of police files they came up short. Hunter surmised that Eller and his detectives were withholding information—specifically, test results. Hunter speculated that the police wanted the press to hear directly from them and were sending a clear message: they didn't trust Hunter.

The tabloids were offering money to people close to Hunter's staff in exchange for information, and Hunter wondered if the police were getting similar offers. When the tabs called Bill Wise, he always treated them cordially but said little. To get him to talk, they started feeding him information, which proved reliable. Again it looked as if it came from the police department. Again, some of it was unknown to Hunter's staff.

During a conversation with a local reporter, Wise learned that Chuck Green, a featured columnist for *The Denver Post*, was about to publish a story about Pete Hofstrom's breakfast meetings with Bryan Morgan. Whoever leaked this information to Green had suggested that Morgan and Hofstrom had a social relationship, that they were "chummy."

Wise asked Hofstrom to review his appointment calendar since the beginning of the case. It showed that Hofstrom had four breakfast meetings with Morgan—all in restaurants. Then Wise called Green to offer him the facts. He provided the columnist with the dates and locations of the meetings and added that the police had *asked* Hofstrom to negotiate with the Ramseys' attorneys on their behalf for additional handwriting samples and interviews. Green decided not to run the story.

In reality, Pete Hofstrom was speaking to the Ramseys' attorneys whenever the police needed his assistance, mostly with Bryan Morgan. They had a cordial and respectful understanding: you be honest with me, and I'll be honest with you. Hofstrom had a much more difficult time dealing with Eller. It became particularly frustrating when he began to suspect that the police weren't giving his office all the facts. He'd resigned himself to the reality that Eller was part of his life, but he probably would have agreed with the deputy DA who characterized the commander as one more cop who liked to beat up on prosecutors. Hofstrom wanted the police to let the evidence lead the investigation wherever the hell it was going to lead them, without obstruction and subterfuge, so that the DA's office could eventually prosecute the charged suspects confidently.

Hunter could see that Hofstrom was under stress. Pete had chronic blood pressure problems, and they appeared to be worsening. He had begun jogging to work off some tension, but it didn't seem to help. Bill Wise noticed that his door was now always closed. This was not the Pete Hofstrom they had known for twenty-three years.

Hofstrom's first full-time job, at age twenty-six, was at San Quentin. He was just over 5-feet-4, and going to school at San Francisco State while working the four-to-midnight shift at the prison. Hofstrom wanted to become a lawyer. Eugene Ziemer, his lieutenant at San

Quentin and a Colorado native, told him there was a great law school in Boulder that he should aim for.

San Quentin, the prison that once housed Charles Manson and Sirhan Sirhan, had its problems in the 1970s. The general population included the Mexican mafia, the Aryan Brothers, and the Black Guerilla Family. On one occasion the inmates killed six people.

Hofstrom's first assignment at San Quentin was to lock up the cellblocks. Because he'd had polio and walked with a distinct limp, his nickname was "March of Dimes." But nobody dared call him that to his face: he was gutsy and bold. Another one of his jobs was to keep the inmates in line—literally. He was in charge of the chow line and the line to and from the cells. "You're just like a cop on the street," Ziemer told him. "The inmates pick up on your confidence—or lack of it—right away." Pete Hofstrom was known for not backing down.

But he was thoughtful and self-motivated. When he had difficulty with an inmate, he would read the guy's file and then go and talk to him. Before long, this unusual approach got him noticed, and he was promoted to correctional counselor. Hofstrom actually loved to talk with the inmates and to make his own evaluation of their behavior. He often picked up on changes in behavior that warranted his lieutenant's attention.

Following Ziemer's advice, Hofstrom moved to Boulder to attend law school at CU. It was 1971. Alex Hunter would be elected DA the following year.

Boulder was undergoing a sea-change: young people were moving into public office, replacing the older law enforcement officers from the pre-*Miranda,* pre-*Escobedo* days.★ Hunter and Dave Torke, who would later become a judge, worked in both the sheriff's department and the police department introducing officers to post-*Miranda* law enforcement.

While he attended law school during the day, Hofstrom worked nights as a jail supervisor, where he met Sheriff Brad Leach. Hofstrom was always saying, "It's how you treat people, how you communicate, that matters." When the department wrote a new policy on inmate visitation, Hofstrom recommended extending visiting hours to three nights a week because it would have a calming effect on the inmate

★ In *Escobedo* v. *Illinois*, Danny Escobedo was questioned several times without the presence of his lawyer. The final time, he made a self-incriminating statement. His eventual conviction was overturned when the court ruled he'd been denied his Sixth Amendment right to counsel.

population. The department tried it out, and Pete was right. His reputation grew as someone who did not believe in a one-size-fits-all approach to people, not even to criminals.

I started as a secretary in the sheriff's office, detective division, in 1971—just two detectives and me. I'm from Lincoln, Nebraska, a very conservative state, and I was real straight. Back then, the sheriff's department didn't have a height requirement. My husband is 6-feet-4. Brad was, like, 5-feet-5. Pete Hofstrom was a little shorter, and the fingerprint guy was maybe 5-feet-6. Hopper, who's still here, is, like, 5-feet-3. We had some terrific people.

To know Pete Hofstrom is almost to love him, even though he's the most eccentric person I've ever met in my life. Considering all the years I've lived in Boulder, that's a pretty profound statement.

Pete had his eye on being a DA.

As the department grew, Alex Hunter started hiring and Pete was a known commodity. If you have the opportunity to grab a known commodity, you grab it.

I'm you-do-the-crime-you-do-the-time. I have a real issue with extenuating circumstances—that everybody's behavior is excused in some way or another. We've created a society full of excuses. Three strikes and you're out. I don't care if it's a freaking doughnut that you stole on the third strike. Now Boulder people just look at me and shake their heads. I'm from the old school.

Hofstrom is even older. But he's liberal. Pete is very good at seeing the overall picture. Cops are always looking at the 95 percent that is OK in a case. He's going for the 5 percent that's a potential problem. It's one thing to look at a case from probable cause. Pete considers what's necessary to prosecute someone.

I'd always say to Pete, "This is not for us to decide. It's for a jury to decide. Or for a judge to decide."

—Sandy Long

6

Moses Schanfield, a DNA expert and forensic scientist, was now consulting with the Ramseys' attorneys, who notified Cellmark Diagnostics that they no longer required one of their experts to be present during the DNA testing procedures. Cellmark's work could proceed without them, as far as the Ramseys were concerned. Presumably, the lawyers had decided that if the test results implicated their clients while their own representative was present, it would be extremely difficult for them to challenge Cellmark's methods. Better to position themselves so that a legal challenge could be made against both the science and Cellmark's findings.

Kary Mullis, the primary developer of PCR typing and a Nobel laureate, had often said that this testing was never intended for police forensic work because it was too vulnerable to contamination. In the Simpson criminal case, Mullis had told Barry Scheck that the process was too delicate to be reliable when blood and other fluids were collected from crime scenes. But now Scheck was on the prosecution's side in the Ramsey case. He could play devil's advocate and, perhaps more important, advise the DA on how to combat a possible challenge to incriminating DNA test results.

At every opportunity, the Ramseys insisted that an intruder had entered their house, citing publicly the missing home keys, pry marks on the doors, and the broken window in the basement. The police felt strongly, however, that none of these points of access had been used. During their initial inspection of the exterior of the house on the day JonBenét's body was found, detectives had noticed an intact spiderweb on the grate covering the window well in front of the broken basement window. It extended from the edge of the grate to some nearby rocks, and this seemed to confirm that nobody had entered through that window recently.

If the police could prove that the spiderweb found on the grate had been present before nightfall on December 25 and had not been disturbed during the night, they could rule out the possibility that somebody had used the broken window to enter the house. They also had to know whether it was possible for a new web to be spun in the time between possible entry by an intruder on December 25 and discovery of the web by police on December 26, when they photographed it. If that was possible, they would have to consider that the window was a likely point of entry for an intruder.

On April 2, Detective Michael Everett of the Boulder PD called entomologist Dr. Brent Opell of the Virginia State University Department of Biology, who was known as Mr. Spider Man. Opell told the police that there are two general types of spiderwebs. The first, which are called cob or funnel webs, once established are constantly reworked and added to by the spider. The second, manufactured by orb-weaving spiders, is regularly replaced by the spiders and can be completed at any hour of the day, in less than twelve hours. The police also learned that if the grate covering the window well had simply been lifted and the web damaged, the type of web would be hard to identify, but if something the size of a man had passed through the web, it would have been destroyed. Everett sent Dr. Opell an enlarged photo of the web in question. The entomologist said it appeared to be of the funnel type.

Six months later, on October 25, Everett traveled to Vancouver Island and met with another expert, Dr. Robert Bennett of the British Columbia Ministry of Forests. The detective had with him a newly enlarged and enhanced photograph of the spiderweb that had covered part of the window grate. Bennett confirmed that it was a funnel web.

Photographs of spiderwebs and spiders have been used as evidence in court cases. Different types of spiders build different types of webs. The varieties of design and the behaviors associated with web-building are well understood.

Spiders hibernate in the winter in temperate zones. Boulder is definitely a temperate zone. Therefore, during winter, there is markedly less or no activity at all by the spiders normally found in Boulder.

If a spiderweb is destroyed in winter, a spider will emerge if it's warm enough. This often happens on a warm day, particularly if the spider is in a spot with southerly exposure. Indoors, spiders are active all winter. Heat or rising temperatures produce activity. Some species are active at very low temperatures, only slightly above freezing, while others need higher temperatures to become active.

In your situation—Boulder, winter snow falling, then melting away, then falling, the weather warm enough—the spider would definitely be out.

If a web is disturbed, a spider would drop out of the web on a silk dragline, wait, climb back up the dragline, and be back where he first started from.

Again in your case, a web was broken one night when someone came by. The temperature rose the next day, and that day or thereafter, a new web could have been spun. Let me tell you a true story about a spiderweb.

In the 1600s, Robert the Bruce, one of Scotland's national heroes, was injured and being pursued by the British. The Bruce crawled into a cave to hide. The next day the British came upon the cave, saw a spiderweb across its mouth, and figured that nobody was there. In fact, a spider had spun the web overnight. Robert the Bruce lived to fight another day.

—*Robert Bennett*

Dr. Bennett confirmed that if the temperature rises sufficiently, spiders can come out of hibernation. In Boulder, on Christmas night 1996, the temperature reached a low of 6 degrees, but it rose the next day to a high of 51. And the grate faced southwest—toward the sun. Perfect conditions for a hibernating spider to wake up and repair a damaged web. In October 1997 Detective Everett would learn from the National Oceanographic and Atmospheric Administration that it was impossible to determine the condition of the dew frost or snow cover on the ground around the Ramsey residence during the night of December 25 and into the morning of December 26.

In Boulder on April 2, Detective Steve Thomas spoke to Sergeant Tom Athey of the Charlotte-Mecklenburg (North Carolina) Police Department. Athey told Thomas that they had a suspect in custody who might have been involved in the murder of JonBenét. On March 21, John Brewer Eustace had allegedly kidnapped a two-year-old child from a ground-level apartment. The child had then been violently sexually molested and found dead with a cloth in her mouth. Entry to the apartment had been made through a small ground-level window that was covered with a screen while a baby-sitter was within earshot of the baby's crib.

The Charlotte-Mecklenburg police had found in Eustace's residence a kind of shrine full of JonBenét's photos carefully cut from newspapers and magazines. Eustace admitted to masturbating while viewing the photographs. Within two days Steve Thomas and Ron Gosage were on a plane to North Carolina to interview Eustace, now a suspect in the death of JonBenét.

At 2:20 P.M. on April 5, Thomas and Gosage arrived at the Charlotte-Mecklenburg Police Department and met with Detective Chris Fish. Gosage, who had a two-year-old, became ill when he saw the photographs of the murdered toddler. At 7:30 that evening, the detectives met John Eustace. After two hours of refusing to answer questions, he waived his rights and agreed to be interviewed by the Boulder detectives. Eustace said he wasn't in Colorado on Christmas night and had never killed anyone. He even pulled hairs from his head and gave them to Thomas and Gosage. He also gave them a handwriting sample. When asked for a pubic hair sample, however, he refused. Later, while Eustace and the detectives took a break to visit the prison toilet, Thomas again him asked for a pubic hair. Again Eustace refused. Gosage pointed out to Eustace that he'd agreed to cooperate. Finally, the prisoner lowered his pants—to show Thomas and Gosage that he *couldn't* give them the sample they wanted: he was clean-shaven not only around his penis but throughout his lower extremities. He said, "I know all about pubic hair and DNA. I'm too smart to leave anything behind."

The next day Thomas and Gosage discovered that at midnight on December 26, Eustace had been working at the Qualex Plant in Charlotte. Between midnight and six in the morning, a coworker remembered talking to him. At 9:37 Eustace clocked out and left for the day.

John Eustace, with his airtight alibi, was just another of the forty-three possible suspects the Boulder PD would interview within the first four months of the investigation. It would take almost a year to check on another fourteen.

MOM SAW MURDER

THE CHILLING STORY SHE'S TELLING FRIENDS

Police are investigating a horrifying new scenario in the JonBenét Ramsey murder case—that the beauty queen's own mother Patsy witnessed the death of her little girl!

In another bizarre twist, Patsy is telling friends she's losing her memory—and can't even recall what happened on the night the 6-year-old was brutally murdered!

National Enquirer, April 8, 1997

★ ★ ★

While Lou Smit and Steve Ainsworth were trying to locate Kevin Raburn, the released convict who seemed to have disappeared, they continued to search for new leads. Daily, Smit looked at the crime scene and autopsy photographs and read police reports, hoping to discover overlooked clues. He had solved several cases simply by reading and rereading old police files.

On Wednesday, April 9, as Smit was looking at the autopsy photographs yet again, he noticed something unusual about several marks on JonBenét's body. In one photograph, he noticed two dried rust-colored abrasions on her lower back; in a second photograph, just below her right ear and at a right angle to her cheek, he saw another set of rust-colored abrasions; and a third photograph showed two marks that looked like scratches on her lower leg. Smit asked Trip DeMuth and Ainsworth to look at the photos. They agreed with him that the three sets of abrasions appeared to be identical. In the final coroner's report, they would be described as "rust-colored to slightly purple" discolorations of unequal size. The investigators agreed that there was about the same distance between the symmetrical marks.

To Smit the marks looked as if they had been made by the two electrodes of a stun gun. Stun guns, about the size of a TV remote control, are used primarily by police and security officers to immobilize people with a charge of electricity. In 1991 the LAPD's officers had been caught on videotape trying to incapacitate Rodney King with a stun gun.

On Friday, April 11, Smit, DeMuth, and Ainsworth went to the coroner's office and laid out the photographs for John Meyer. "Are these abrasions consistent with a stun gun or taser?" they asked. Meyer wouldn't commit himself to a definite answer. DeMuth asked Meyer for a complete set of autopsy photographs and had some of them enlarged to life size.

Someone might have used a stun gun to subdue JonBenét during the crime. It was also possible, however, that Patsy or John or some third party had used such a device on their daughter for perverse reasons. Either way, the detectives now had to investigate the possibility that a stun gun had been used on the child.

Five days later, on April 16, Lou Smit drove to Lakewood, just outside Denver, to see CBI inspector Pete Mang, who had begun his career at the FBI. Mang suggested that Smit talk to Sue Kitchen, another CBI investigator, who had worked on a murder case in Steamboat Springs in which a stun gun was used. Two days later, Kitchen told the investigators that in her opinion, the small abrasions could have been made by a stun gun. She referred them to Arapahoe County coroner Mike Dobersen, who had solved a murder involving a stun gun in 1993. The device had been found in a suspect's car, and the body of the victim was exhumed eight months after burial. Tissue from the corpse was tested for evidence of electric shock, and it proved positive. The suspect and her boyfriend were later charged and convicted.

After viewing the photos, Dobersen told the investigators that the abrasions on JonBenét's body could have come from a stun-gun injury but that there was no way to know for sure without checking the skin tissue under a microscope. Before taking the extreme step of exhuming JonBenét's body, Dobersen advised them to find a stun gun or taser with prongs spaced the same distance apart as the marks on JonBenét's body and compare them to a life-size photograph.

By the end of the month, Smit had tracked down several Air Taser stun guns whose measurements and characteristics were consistent with the marks in the photos. He had even discovered a local distributor, Upper Edge, in Greeley, northeast of Boulder. There Ainsworth and DeMuth photographed different types of Air Tasers.

When the investigators had collected enough information on the subject, they decided to inform the police. Eller's detectives derided Smit's theory as "hogwash," perhaps because it presupposed an intruder. Hunter thought the police might have rejected the idea because it would be hard to convince a jury that the Ramseys had used such a device on their daughter.

Nevertheless, Smit wanted to ask the Ramseys and their family if any of them had ever owned, borrowed, or seen anyone with a stun gun.

By April 11, Hofstrom thought that his attempt to broker a deal for the Ramseys' formal interviews with the police had progressed far enough, and he suggested a meeting. Patsy and John Ramsey, their attorneys, and Tom Wickman of the Boulder police met to see if the deadlock could be broken. Wickman, representing Eller, was a far less adversarial presence than the commander. Hofstrom began by saying that they all had to work together to move the investigation onto a new track. Wickman agreed, telling the Ramseys they had been treated unfairly in the past and that the police needed their help to solve JonBenét's murder.

The attorneys suggested conditions under which their clients would grant interviews to the police: John and Patsy would be interviewed separately, each for no more than two hours. There would be a two-hour lunch break between their interviews, when the Ramseys could consult with their attorneys, advisers, and experts. Under the law, they could have their attorneys present, and the questioning would take place in the office of a neutral Boulder attorney. The most important condition was that the Ramseys' attorneys be given copies of all written police reports that contained statements made by their clients between December 26 and December 28.

After the meeting, Hofstrom and Hunter discussed the conditions. The DA told Eller and Wickman that he saw little point in withholding the documents that had been requested. If the Ramseys were charged, Hofstrom told the police, they would obtain the documents anyway, as part of the discovery process.*

But the Ramseys hadn't been charged, Wickman and Eller insisted—they were only suspects. The police were furious that they'd had to wait so long for interviews. Now, on top of the delay, the Ramseys wanted to see their prior statements to the police. Wickman and Eller thought it would compromise the interview process, if not the entire case. Reminded of what they had told the police earlier, the Ramseys could tailor their new answers accordingly.

But Hunter could understand why their attorneys wanted the Ramseys' earlier statements—it was likely they were already looking at their clients as charged defendants. "These people aren't right off the boat," was how the DA put it. "It was obvious they were prime suspects from the first days of the investigation." There was nothing out of the ordinary about the police having to wait to interview the Ramseys—any good defense lawyer would have tried to delay his clients' interrogation.

Hofstrom negotiated with the police, and Eller and Koby grudgingly agreed that the DA could release the statements the Ramseys had made to the police, though not the entire contents of the officers' reports. The police would hand over a total of twenty-six pages. The decision infuriated Steve Thomas, who had been selected to interview Patsy. It would be like having one hand tied behind his back.

*The law demands that a defendant receive the names and addresses of all likely witnesses, all written and recorded witness statements, all police and scientific reports, notes and test results, tangible evidence, incidentals like crime-scene logs and telephone records, fingerprint lifts, records of blood swatches or pictures thereof, and any other results of all law enforcement investigations. The process by which this is accumulated and passed on is called *discovery.*

The interview was set for Wednesday, April 23, at 9:30 A.M. From Hunter's point of view, the process was moving forward.

Within a day of the agreement, Patsy gave the police a fourth handwriting sample and agreed to identify her prior writings. The Ramseys also gave the police permission to search their home again. Then Smit gave Trip DeMuth copies of the requested statements from his set of police files, which DeMuth delivered to the Ramseys' attorneys.

That same week, Carol McKinley's source in the Boulder PD told her that he and his colleagues were outraged that the police had to bargain with the Ramseys. It was the last straw, he said.

John and Patsy's participation in a meeting with Hofstrom and Wickman suggested to Hunter's office that Ramsey was becoming more active in the day-to-day decision-making in the case. He was also back at Access Graphics full-time. Gary Mann, the parent company's vice president, had taken the position that John Ramsey was innocent until proven guilty, so Ramsey was still running the company for Lockheed Martin. Mann saw that although Ramsey was under enormous pressure, he didn't miss a beat when it came to work. Sales and profits at Access Graphics were increasing, and the company was ahead of last year's record. With those results, Lockheed decided that now was the time to sell the company. Management had first discussed that possibility with Ramsey during the summer of 1996. At the time, Ramsey had mentioned buying the company himself, but with JonBenét's death, he dropped the idea. Mann told Ramsey that he could stay with Lockheed Martin if he wanted to.

With the sale of Access Graphics imminent, Ramsey decided to move his family back to Atlanta. The family had imposed on Jay Elowsky and the Stines long enough. It was time for their friends' lives to return to normal. In Atlanta the Ramseys' day-to-day movements would be less noticeable, and the media would have other stories to cover. Also, Patsy would be close to her parents and sisters, who could help care for Burke when she and John traveled. There was no reason to stay in Boulder any longer.

Gary Mann considered John Ramsey a big asset for Lockheed, and he wanted to keep him in the corporation after Access Graphics was sold. Lockheed Martin was primarily in the airplane business, however, and it had no information division in the Atlanta area. It was unclear where Ramsey would work when his company was sold.

★ ★ ★

JONBENÉT KILLING ATTRACTS
FOLLOWING OF INTERNET USERS

The nation's obsession with computers and the JonBenét Ramsey slaying have converged on the Internet.

At least 30 Web pages have sprung up, offering information, speculation and photographs related to the 6-year-old Boulder girl's death.

One is sponsored by a Kenosha, Wis., alderman and police detective. Another is an informal poll on who committed the crime. A "scientific laboratory" has a page analyzing John and Patsy Ramsey's use of words during their interview on CNN.

—Burt Hubbard
Rocky Mountain News, April 13, 1997

Nine months before JonBenét was murdered, the company I worked for was absorbed by a conglomerate. I found myself retired at forty. I became a voracious reader of nonfiction, taught myself to bake excellent French bread, and wall-papered the master bath. And I discovered the Internet. I surfed the Net in earnest, but with no real goal—just for information. I was in the kitchen washing dishes when I heard about JonBenét's murder on the radio. The next morning I found Denver-area newspapers on-line and read about the case. One of those papers, the Daily Camera, *already had a bulletin board devoted to JonBenét's murder. I joined dozens of people on-line who followed the case on a daily basis. It was almost like joining other kids on a playground. Those of us who had been around longer would be irritated by "newbies," who would surf in, post something like "I think the older brother did it," and then have the gall to be offended when we verbally ripped them to shreds.*

I was amazed by the lack of curiosity. Many people on-line showed no motivation to seek out facts on the case. As an early riser, and with the added benefit of being on the East Coast, I took it upon myself to inform people. Each morning I would get up and go straight to the computer. I had a route that took me to each of the major dailies that could be counted on to have Ramsey stories. I looked at over thirty-five Web sites that I maintained as bookmarks on my hard drive. When there was interesting information, I posted the Web address, along with a one-sentence synopsis of the item, on the Boulder News Forum. Others needed only to look at my morning posting to find out what had happened in the last twenty-four hours. Then I began my route again in preparation for the next day's postings. My friends were counting on me. I had a goal.

It's not always easy on-line. In the summer of 1997 our community of bored housewives on the Boulder forum was invaded. The hackers harassed us and made it impossible for our discussions to continue. It was a difficult experience. But if that hadn't happened, I wouldn't have my Web page. Because the hackers made it tough for people to find my daily postings, a benefactor offered to set me up with my own Web page. Mrs. Brady's URLs, as the page is called, gets about 750 hits a day.

Several news articles about Internet interest in the case quoted psychiatrists saying we "had no life." But later articles were more accurate. One even noted how the Boulder County District Attorney's office and the Boulder Police Department used the Internet community as a resource.

We weren't just kooks with nothing else to do. We had a genuine interest in the case.

There is still bickering in our cybercommunity. Theories are still debated, and rumors abound. But the crusade continues, and newbies are still arriving. I just got an e-mail from a new computer owner, who says that one of the reasons he/she bought the computer was to stay abreast of the Ramsey investigation with other interested parties. "Let me know how I can have an ongoing chat with other interested sleuths regarding this case," the e-mail said.

—Mrs. Brady

After much agonizing, Alex Hunter and Bill Wise finally decided that too much of their time was being taken up by the press. They needed an experienced press representative who understood the criminal justice system and could get along with reporters, write press releases, and provide appropriate general information about past cases and the office. Jana Petersen, who worked for the county commissioner's office, was Hunter's first choice, but the county wouldn't release her. Soon résumés started pouring in.

Suzanne Laurion's letter caught everyone's eye. Laurion had a Ph.D. in mass communications from the University of Wisconsin, where she had specialized in exploring how news stories affected audiences. She had worked in broadcasting as a reporter. Now she was an adjunct professor at CU. She saw the job as an opportunity to expand her teaching abilities. Laurion told Hunter and Wise that she wanted to be involved in a historic media situation like the one in Boulder. By the end of April, Hunter announced that Suzanne Laurion had been hired to field all media inquiries.

RAMSEYS MAY MOVE TO ATLANTA

The parents of slain beauty queen JonBenét Ramsey plan to sell their Boulder home and may move to Atlanta, family friends said Monday.

"There is no way they ever want to live in that house again, so they're going to put it on the market," a family friend said. "Right now, people know about it through word of mouth, but (the Ramseys) should sign a listing contract soon. . . .

There are just too many bad memories in their house since (Jon-Benét) died."

—Alli Krupski
Daily Camera, April 15, 1997

COPS FIND MURDER WITNESS

...HE REVEALS DADDY'S SECRET

A secret witness has been found in the JonBenét murder investigation. And police believe this man could provide key evidence against her father John Ramsey, an ENQUIRER team has discovered.

He's John's best friend, Fleet White, who was at Ramsey's side when the 6-year-old's beaten, molested body was found. He alone knows Ramsey's actions in the moments surrounding that gruesome discovery.

National Enquirer, April 15, 1997

Since Fleet White and John Ramsey's loud argument in Atlanta on December 31, the day of JonBenét's funeral, the two men had been at war. It was rumored that White had accused Ramsey and that John had accused Fleet White. It was also rumored that White was a suspect in the murder of JonBenét.

In the first weeks after JonBenét's death, TV tabloids scanned the Whites' phones. Conversations they had with family members and close friends ended up in print. The media were a constant presence in their life, knocking on their door and camping outside their home.

To those who knew Fleet White, it was obvious he found this treatment unbearable. By the time the *National Enquirer* published the "Cops Find Murder Witness . . . He Reveals Daddy's Secret" cover story, White was at the breaking point.

At forty-seven, Fleet White was close in age to John Ramsey, who was fifty-three when JonBenét died. White's children were roughly the same age as JonBenét and Burke. Since moving to Boulder in 1994, White had been good friends with Ramsey. White's daughter, Daphne, often played with JonBenét. It was the Whites' home where Burke was taken on the morning of December 26.

The DA and the police knew that Fleet and Priscilla White had never accused the Ramseys of the murder. The couple had, however, provided valuable information to the police. White had been just a few steps behind John Ramsey in the basement when Ramsey first saw JonBenét's body, and he had followed Ramsey into the wine cellar and even touched her dead body. That entire day he was privy to Ramsey's actions, many of which had never been observed by the police. The police also thought that White had insight into the Ramseys' general behavior and possible motives.

During the first week of April, Fleet and Priscilla went to see police chief Tom Koby, outraged at what was happening to them. They asked for the chief's help in getting the media off their backs and clearing their name. The chief refused. There was still a question about why White hadn't seen JonBenét's body when he opened the door to the wine cellar early on the morning of December 26, although John Ramsey had seen it six hours later. Koby said that if he publicly cleared one suspect, everyone would be camping outside his door. Then the Whites walked into Alex Hunter's office unannounced. Bill Wise could see that White was close to the edge. After a short conversation, Hunter introduced Priscilla White to Lou Smit while he talked privately with Fleet.

On April 15, the *National Enquirer* wrote that White "told investigators . . . [that John Ramsey] tried to keep White from opening the door to the small basement room where JonBenét's body was found." The tabloid added that "White and Priscilla have made some awful allegations to Boulder police about John and Patsy and the Ramseys will never speak to them again." It was after reading this that Fleet

White stormed into Koby's and then Hunter's office and demanded to be publicly cleared as a suspect. Hunter said that he had never seen such anger. "We can clear the guy," Pete Hofstrom suggested to Hunter. "And then later on, if we decide he's not clear, we'll unclear him." Hunter talked to Koby about White. He told the chief that unless they did something to appease White, they might lose an important witness. Koby reluctantly agreed. He would talk to Eller, and hoped the commander would agree to clear the Whites.

When Hunter saw a draft of the Boulder PD's intended public statement, however, he objected to the wording. The Whites, he felt, should not be "cleared" of any suspicion, because Fleet White's demeanor after JonBenét's murder was still open to interpretation. It might be better to use the words "are not suspects" rather than "cleared." White would later learn about Hunter's involvement in the wording of the press release and hold it against him.

The next afternoon, April 16, the police department included the following statement from Chief Koby in the City of Boulder's Ramsey Update No. 40:

> *Mr. and Mrs. Fleet White, Jr., are not suspects in the Jon-Benét Ramsey murder investigation. They are considered key witnesses. The Boulder Police Department appreciates the full cooperation they have received from the Whites since the beginning of their investigation. I feel this response is necessary due to the inaccurate portrayal of Mr. and Mrs. White in certain media publications.*

Fleet and Priscilla were the first people to be named key witnesses, when the Ramseys themselves had not officially been named suspects. The media knew why the Whites were so important to the case.

Detective Steve Thomas, for one, thought that Fleet White was crucial. His experience as a narcotics detective told him that given White's highly emotional state, he would have to be nurtured a little to provide credible testimony. Melody Stanton, who lived across the street from the Ramseys and had said she heard a child's scream the night of the murder, was another witness Thomas wanted to keep in touch with. Because the public didn't yet know about what she had heard, Trip DeMuth wanted Thomas to stay away from Stanton. DeMuth was afraid that once Stanton understood how important a witness she was, she would get nervous. Though Thomas felt otherwise, he followed DeMuth's advice.

Ever since watching Tom Koby's January 9 press conference from the lobby of the Boulder Public Library, Stephen Singular had often thought about the peculiar nature of the Ramsey case. He had spent fifteen years writing true-crime books, and of course JonBenét's murder interested him. Soon he began to talk to some of the Ramseys' acquaintances. During one conversation Pam Griffin talked to him about Fleet White, whom she met while she was caring for Patsy on December 27 at the Fernies'. Pam understood how distraught Patsy and John must be, but it was White's behavior that caught her attention. She got the impression that White was trying to control and manage things that day, and he seemed not to want Pam to be alone with Patsy. Of course White didn't know who Pam was or how close she was to Patsy; nor did she know at the time how close the Whites were to the Ramseys. Still, she had an uneasy feeling about Fleet White. For his part, Stephen Singular couldn't stop thinking about White as he drove from Denver, where he lived, to Boulder for a meeting with Alex Hunter. He had read the *National Enquirer* that morning, but he was apprehensive about bringing up White's name at this first meeting with the DA.

Like most Americans who were following the case, Singular thought the Boulder police had little homicide experience. He surmised that so far the cops had dealt only with the surface, that they hadn't gone deep.

In his own investigations, Singular had learned that inevitably the perpetrator's prior behavior foreshadows the crime. Though there seemed to be no sign of aberrant behavior in either John's or Patsy's background, Singular understood that seemingly good people can sometimes do terrible things.

As he followed the story, he saw that during the first weeks, the media implied that John Ramsey was a child molester who had killed his own daughter. Then Patsy was put in the hot seat, portrayed as a religious fanatic who read the Bible compulsively. To Singular, it was obvious that the media were considering only two possibilities—that one or both parents had killed their child or that an intruder had entered the house and killed JonBenét. Singular believed there were numerous other possibilities, which was why he had contacted Hunter. On TV the DA seemed reasonable, bright, and sensitive—not like most prosecutors, who tend to swagger. Singular had sent Hunter a fax, saying that he was the author of a book about talk-show host Alan Berg, who had been murdered in Denver, and Hunter had asked him to come in and talk.

The meeting with Hunter and Bill Wise took place on April 15. Hunter was more open and friendly than Singular had expected him to be, and Singular told them what he had learned about people on the periphery of the Ramseys' life—acquaintances connected to the world of pageants.

"Have you looked at the Internet?" Singular asked. "What do you know about the pageant world?" Hunter admitted he knew very little. Singular gave Hunter the names of Pam Griffin, Randy Simons, Trish Danpier, a former Miss Colorado, and pageant director LaDonna Griego, among others. Hunter knew about Griffin and Simons from police reports.

Singular suggested that JonBenét's murder might have originated outside the family, in the pageant world, which was a mixture of children, sexuality, and business opportunities. The exploitation of children for economic gain was at the underbelly of America, Singular said, and JonBenét Ramsey could have been one of the victims.

As a pageant participant, JonBenét had been photographed many times in her life. Singular wondered if maybe the child had been taken from her home on Christmas night to be photographed again, without one parent's knowledge, and been brought home dead. He intimated that one of "Boulder's public officials" might possibly be involved in child pornography with one of John Ramsey's friends.

"It's a federal issue. I'll speak to the FBI," Hunter said. "I am not going to give this to the cops. I don't want them to screw it up. I know work needs to be done in that area." Singular got the impression that Hunter was giving him an assignment: look into the child pornography business and get back to me.

While he saw that Hunter was trying to keep an open mind about who had killed JonBenét, Singular also couldn't help but notice that the DA was overwhelmed. He was receiving an enormous amount of attention, and that could be very seductive.

On April 18, Hunter gave Jennifer Mears of the Associated Press an interview. It was the first time the DA had publicly acknowledged that the Ramseys were at the center of the investigation.

DA CONCEDES RAMSEYS
ARE "THE FOCUS" OF INVESTIGATION

The parents of JonBenét Ramsey are "obviously the focus" of the investigation into the child beauty queen's slaying, Boulder District Attorney Alex Hunter acknowledged Friday.

Hunter stressed that John and Patricia Ramsey have not been named suspects, but said: "Obviously the focus is on these people. You can call them what you want to."

—Jennifer Mears
Associated Press, April 19, 1997

The story became front-page news. Hunter, who so far had been careful not to go on the record about his interest in the Ramseys, called the AP within hours of the story's publication.

"I'm not upset with the story," he said. "It's the quotes. They make me sound stupid." It was the first time a public official had ever called Mears to discuss the way his quotes portrayed him.

INSIDE THE "WAR ROOM"

They call it the "war room." Behind the locked doors of a converted conference room, its windows masked with paper to insure privacy, prosecutors and investigators pursue paper trails and plan strategy in the hunt for the killer of JonBenét Ramsey.

Not even janitors can enter the 18-by-21-foot room in the district attorney's first-floor quarters in the Justice Center. Steps have been taken to safeguard security of the two computers in the room, both of them tied into the Boulder Police Department computers.

On a typical day, Lou Smit, a retired Colorado Springs detective hired by DA Alex Hunter. . . can be found poring over 13,000 pages of reports. The pages are gathered in 15 loose-leaf notebooks, each with a laminated picture of the 6-year-old beauty queen on its cover.

—Marilyn Robinson and Kieran Nicholson
The Denver Post, April 19, 1997

★ ★ ★

By mid-April, the war room on the first floor of the Justice Center had been outfitted with a large conference table, computers, and cubicles. There was a small adjacent room and lots of wall space for charts, and even a toaster oven where you could bake a small cake. No matter how well appointed it was, however, Steve Thomas knew that the war room wasn't going to work out. Lou Smit, the police, and the prosecutors each had different roles in the case, and each group saw the same data differently. There were ongoing personality clashes. It wasn't long before Smit was telling the detectives that he wasn't so sure the evidence against the Ramseys was strong. As he reviewed the officers' reports and compared their contents, he could see there was a strong possibility that an intruder could have entered the house and killed JonBenét.

The police detectives were particularly irritated at Ainsworth, who was acting as Hunter's devil's advocate, looking at the evidence from a defense perspective. He was supposed to be a cop—on *their* side.

To break the deadlock, Koby suggested to Hunter that they use a professional mediator to explain to his officers that the way lawyers operate doesn't damage the integrity of police work. Hunter, who had used mediators in the past to iron out policy conflicts, was all for it. Hofstrom felt it was a waste of time. Nevertheless, they turned to Richard Rianoshek, who had been a cop in Chicago and a detective and police chief in Aspen. He specialized in helping organizations work more effectively. Rianoshek knew that all DAs and police departments face essentially the same problem. It was endemic to law enforcement: prosecutors were often at odds, and the police were frustrated by legal hair-splitting. Throw some controversy into the mix, and the problems would be magnified. In the Ramsey case, given the enormous pressure from the media, Rianoshek knew it would be a miracle if anything worked.

The mediators first met with each side separately, in a small conference room on neutral ground at the University of Colorado. Then there were two meetings with both sides. Hunter, Hofstrom, DeMuth, and Smit attended these meetings, as did all the police detectives plus Wickman, Eller, and Koby. Each session lasted four hours.

Many grievances came to the surface. For example, the cops couldn't get past Hofstrom's four breakfasts with Bryan Morgan. Consorting with the enemy! It was like Hofstrom's notorious precharging negotiations, which were just one step away from plea bargaining. Hofstrom could have accomplished his job with simple phone calls, a detective said. Steve Thomas repeated that Hunter's staff was interested only in proving that an intruder had killed JonBenét. Hunter's staff, on the other hand, was convinced that the police were determined to build a case against the Ramseys and refused to look elsewhere.

Rianoshek painstakingly showed both sides that their perceptions were inaccurate. He clarified what the police had said: they might be leaning toward the Ramseys, but if evidence appeared pointing to someone other than the couple, the evidence would prevail. Rianoshek repeated the DA's position: they weren't fixated on an intruder. They also thought the Ramseys had committed the crime, but they wanted the police to investigate every possibility. Nevertheless, the meetings deteriorated into mutual accusations, and in the end nothing changed. The inhabitants of the war room were never going to be friends.

When Lou Smit reflected on what he'd been observing, he saw one of the roots of the problem. Over the years, the DA's office had never bonded with the police. Where he came from, and in most jurisdictions, the DA's investigators were ex-cops. The detectives on the police force were their buddies. They played softball, drank beer, and went to sports events together. By contrast, Alex Hunter hired a former police officer only once in a great while. These days, the closest was Tom Wickman's ex-wife, who was now one of Hunter's investigators.

It wasn't long before the daily status meeting, where each detective and deputy DA brought the group up-to-date, fell apart. Nobody wanted to reveal anything for fear of leaks by the other side. The daily reports became monotonous: "Haven't done anything. Nothing on tap for today." Some detectives were even afraid to use the phones in the war room for fear the DAs would hear who they were talking to—the pay phones in the halls of the Justice Center were in constant use.

The media made this not only a police case but the DA's case. Hunter was no longer in a peripheral position. The case was thrown into disarray by the fact that there were three cameras and four tape recorders operating every time anybody opened his mouth.

The war room became a liability when it acquired a media life. It had been designed as a setting for open communication, but suddenly the media depicted it as the setting for potential breakthroughs—a place from which truth would emanate. It became a liability.

—Bob Grant

On April 22 the FBI's Child Abduction and Serial Killer Unit heard about the terms for the Ramseys' scheduled interviews. They told the police that "the conditions would not likely lead to a productive investigative interview." The FBI proposed open-ended interviews for Patsy and John and no breaks between the sessions for the Ramseys to consult each other or their attorneys. The venue should be a bare room in a law enforcement establishment, not an attorney's office. Providing the Ramseys' attorneys with police reports was also a mistake, the FBI said, but it was too late to do anything about that because they had been delivered the day before. Convinced that the FBI was right, Eller canceled the interviews one day before the agreed-upon date. Patrick Burke was informed by phone. Both Hunter and Koby foresaw disaster—not only for the investigation but in terms of public relations.

The next day, April 23, attorneys Haddon and Burke wrote the following letter to Hunter on behalf of their clients and released it to the media with several pages of supporting documents.

VIA HAND DELIVERY

Alexander M. Hunter
Boulder County District Attorney
Boulder County Justice Center
1777 Sixth Street
Boulder, Colorado 80306

Re: John and Patsy Ramsey

Dear Mr. Hunter:

By this letter, we express our profound dismay at yesterday's actions by the leadership of the Boulder Police Department. After representatives of the Boulder Police Department and your office requested and agreed to a format for separate interviews of John and Patsy Ramsey beginning at 9:30 A.M. today, we were advised at approximately 4:00 P.M. yesterday afternoon that the interviews were canceled because Boulder Police Department leadership no longer agreed to the format of the interviews—despite previous statements to the contrary.

This action is incomprehensible in light of the previous history of this issue. The Police Department, directly and through a campaign of leaks and smears, has portrayed the Ramseys as unwilling to grant police interviews or assist the investigation. Although we know this innuendo to be false, we have avoided criticizing the police because we believed that it would only fuel a media war which would be counterproductive to the overarching goal—finding and prosecuting the killer of JonBenét Ramsey. Yesterday's actions make further silence untenable.

The letter went on to chastise the police, and then restated almost the entire lengthy history of Ramsey/police negotiations from the Ramseys' point of view. The lawyers revealed that the police had tried to withhold JonBenét's body in return for interviews with the Ramseys—the first of many insensitive and incomprehensible actions, the attorneys said. By addressing this letter to Hunter, the Ramseys drew a line in the sand. The last paragraph made it clear how they would proceed in the future.

It is apparent that the leadership of the Boulder Police Department lacks the objectivity and judgment necessary to find the killer of JonBenét Ramsey. Mr. Hofstrom told John and Patsy that he wanted their help to solve this crime. They remain willing to meet with Mr. Smit, Mr. Ainsworth or any other member of your office to that end.

Sincerely,

[signed]
Harold A. Haddon

[signed]
Patrick Burke

★ ★ ★

This letter become the number-one story in Colorado and was publicized nationally as well. For the next several days, even mainstream media headlines had a sensational tone:

INTERVIEW PLAN BLOWS UP

SNARLING STARTED BEFORE

FBI SAVES PROBE FROM DISASTER

RAMSEYS DENOUNCE POLICE

WAR OF WORDS ESCALATES RAMSEY STANDOFF

COPS, DA RESPOND TO RAMSEYS

BOULDER AUTHORITIES, RAMSEYS NEGOTIATING

Every TV outlet scrambled for any scrap it could get about the battle between the police and the Ramseys. Phil LeBeau, of Denver's KCNC, Channel 4 TV, snagged an interview with Patrick Burke and Hal Haddon at their respective law offices in Denver. He wanted to know: What kind of police department would withhold the body of a child and delay her burial?

When LeBeau concluded his live report at 4:15 P.M., the newsroom staff told him that Patsy Ramsey had called the station and asked to talk to him. They'd given her the news van's direct phone number.

A minute later, the phone rang.

"I'm glad that our side of the story is finally getting out," Patsy said. "We've been sitting here taking it for three months, keeping our mouths shut while the cops are basically portraying us to be a couple of killers—uncaring parents, uncooperative."

LeBeau asked to call back since he was about to do another broadcast.

"You call [a third party], and they'll get to me," Patsy replied.

LeBeau broadcast his 5:00 P.M. report, in which he didn't mention Patsy's call, and then called the person Patsy had named.

"Thank you again for your report," Patsy told him when she came to the phone. "John is here, and he appreciates the fact that you're being honest about what's happening." LeBeau made a pitch for an on-the-record interview the next morning.

Patsy called early the following day.

"Are the Boulder police framing you and your husband?" LeBeau asked her.

"I can't talk about that. I pray we can still work this out, that the killer of JonBenét be found."

"Why won't you cooperate with the police?"

"We'll sit and talk with them for twenty-four hours a day," Patsy replied, "if that's what they want." The police had just called off the interviews, she added. "You'd think if they think we're guilty, they'd want to talk to us."

Finally LeBeau told Patsy he was going to put together a report based on their on-the-record conversation. The station started promoting "A Conversation with Patsy Ramsey" the same day.

Meanwhile, Pete Hofstrom, Alex Hunter, John Eller, Tom Wickman and Tom Koby worked all night and into the next day to save what was left of their relationship with the Ramseys' lawyers. "We acknowledge the unfortunate miscommunication," Hunter and Koby said in an open letter to the attorneys, "and we're encouraged to hear you indicate a continued willingness to accomplish the critical interviews with Mr. and Mrs. Ramsey."

The police listed their requirements and released them to the media so as to preempt a charge of Hofstrom's so-called "chummy" negotiations with the Ramseys' attorneys. Eller, who had never liked Hofstrom's style, was now dealing directly with the Ramseys' attorneys by way of the media. It was Eller's way of reminding everyone that this was his case.

On Friday, April 25, *The Denver Post* published a list of police demands:

John and Patsy Ramsey will be interviewed separately.

Patsy Ramsey will be interviewed first.

There will be an open-ended time frame for the interview.

The interviews will be tape-recorded.

The interviews will be conducted by two Boulder police detectives selected in consultation with Hunter.

The interviews will be conducted at a neutral location, such as the Child and Family Advocacy Center in Niwot.

The conditions are "consistent with standard police interview techniques."

After this was published, Hunter told the press again that though the Ramseys were the focus of the investigation, they were not the only suspects. It was a deliberate attempt to appease the Ramseys so that negotiations could continue. By Saturday evening, the Ramseys had agreed to all but two of Eller's conditions. The interviews would take place at the DA's offices, which they considered more neutral, and Pete Hofstrom would be present during the questioning.

On Monday all parties were back on board with an agreement that the interviews would take place on April 30 beginning at 9:00 A.M. Charlie Russell, another of the Ramseys' media representatives, called handpicked members of the media to tell them that everything was back on track.

On April 23, Detective Melissa Hickman returned to Boulder from the Aerospace Corporation in El Segundo, California. In addition to its work for the government, the company did sound and photographic enhancement on a nonprofit basis for law enforcement agencies, using state-of-the-art technology. Hickman had taken the audio tape of Patsy Ramsey's 911 call to the Southern California firm. The tape included a few additional seconds of sound along with Patsy's frantic call for help, sounds that may have been recorded when she replaced the headset improperly. The police had been unable to decipher the additional sounds.

In February, Detective Trujillo had sent a copy of the tape to the U.S. Secret Service, but their attempt to enhance the recording had not succeeded. Aerospace used a different technology, and voices in the background could now be heard more clearly.

Hickman listened to the tape and wrote down what she heard.

"Help me Jesus, help me Jesus." That was clearly Patsy's voice. Then, in the distance, there was another voice, which sounded like JonBenét's brother.

"Please, what do I do?" Burke said.

"We're not speaking to you," Hickman heard John Ramsey say.

Patsy screamed again. "Help me Jesus, help me Jesus."

And then, more clearly, Burke said, "What *did* you find?"

This snippet of conversation was obviously important. Patsy and John had told the police, and CNN on January 1, that when they found JonBenét missing, they checked Burke's room for their daughter, who sometimes slept there. They had never said what they found in Burke's room. Later, Patsy said they did not awaken Burke until about 7:00 A.M., when her husband roused him to have him taken to the Whites' home.

In Boulder, Hickman and her colleagues debated the scenarios. They couldn't believe that John Ramsey would have forgotten to mention to the police that his son had gotten up and spoken to him and his wife that morning after Patsy checked on him and before the police arrived. Perhaps it was conceivable that *she* didn't remember because she was so distraught. But on the tape, John had directed a statement directly to Burke. How could he have forgotten talking to his son? The Ramseys' credibility was now seriously in question.

The police decided not to tell Hunter or anyone on his staff what they had learned. They feared leaks of this valuable evidence. The police also decided not to ask John or Patsy Ramsey about the 911 call in their scheduled interviews, for fear of tipping their attorneys to what they had discovered. More than a year would elapse before the police told Hunter's staff about the enhancement tape of the 911 call.

When Burke had been interviewed on January 8, he was not questioned about his whereabouts that morning. But even in that interview, the boy had not told the police that he was asleep when the 911 call was made. The police needed to know what he remembered about that morning and if his memory differed from Patsy's. The detectives would have to wait until June 10, 1998, when Burke was interviewed again, to ask him.

7

James Thompson, known to his friends as J. T. Colfax, worked for M&M Transport in Denver. His job was to pick up cadavers and deliver them to funeral homes. On April 28, he went to pick up a body from the morgue at Boulder Community Hospital. The cadaver was having its eyes removed for donation to an eye bank, and Colfax was told to come back later.

At around 1:00 A.M., Colfax went back to the morgue, just to hang out. On a whim, he leafed through the log book, came to the month of December, and tore out the pages with an entry about Jon-Benét. Later that morning, he photocopied the log pages, wrote "All in a Night's Work" on the copies, and mailed them to friends in New York and California.

That afternoon, low on cash, Colfax tried to shoplift a photo-finishing order he had placed at Safeway Photo Processing. He was arrested. The police looked at the evidence—twenty-seven photos—and discovered that the pictures were of cadavers. Colfax found himself in a police car en route to the Denver PD. Which one of those people had he murdered, the cops wanted to know. None, Colfax said, he just liked to photograph dead people. Did you murder Jon-Benét Ramsey? No, he said, he had been in Vancouver, Canada, on December 26, at the Royal Hotel on Granville Street. One officer shouted that he was a pervert.

Two days later Colfax made bail, was given a court date, and became an item in the Denver papers. Mike O'Keeffe, a reporter for the *Rocky Mountain News*, was told by a friend of Colfax's about the morgue log pages. O'Keeffe passed the information on to his colleague Charlie Brennan, who was covering the Ramsey case. Brennan in turn called the morgue to inquire about the log pages, not mentioning Colfax's name. That afternoon, when the pages were discovered missing, the sheriff was called. Until then, no one had noticed they were gone.

Meanwhile Colfax, who was becoming a minor media celebrity, confessed to the press that he'd stolen some morgue log pages containing JonBenét's entry—as a souvenir. When the Boulder police heard Colfax's tale, they assigned Detective Ron Gosage to pay him a visit.

It was raining when Gosage arrived at Colfax's Denver apartment. The log pages from the morgue were lying on the floor. Within minutes he was arrested. On the way to Boulder, Gosage chatted with Colfax. Out of the blue, Gosage asked, "What do you think—are people born gay or do they become gay?" The conversation was so casual, it was like talking to someone at a party. "I was born gay," Colfax replied. "Nobody wants to be gay." Suddenly it occurred to Colfax that homosexuality might have something to do with JonBenét's death. Gosage asked him if he knew JonBenét's brother, Burke. No, Colfax replied. What about John Andrew? He didn't know either of them, Colfax said.

Colfax understood he was a suspect. Later that afternoon he was formally interviewed. The police asked him to describe the morgue. It was orange, he said—no, it was governmental green or gray—shit, he couldn't remember the color. Then they got around to JonBenét's death. Did you know the Ramseys in Boulder? In Denver? Colfax said he'd lived Atlanta but that he didn't know Patsy Ramsey. Gosage grilled him for two hours. Then Colfax gave the detective the hair evidence he requested.

Gosage cut his hand pulling hair samples from Colfax's head. While Colfax completed his handwriting samples, the detective sat there wringing his hands while blood flowed from between his fingers. Next, Colfax's inner cheek was swabbed for a DNA sample. Then he was booked for criminal mischief and theft. Bond was set at $1,000.

Two months later, Colfax still had not been sentenced for stealing the morgue log pages. He was out on bail. One morning he visited Alli Krupski at the offices of the *Daily Camera* and told her she'd look good as a dead body. He'd been drinking. Then he walked 2 miles to the Ramseys' house. Along the way, two tourists stopped and asked him where Patsy Ramsey lived. "I think it's up here," he said, motioning them to follow him. When they arrived, the tourists took his picture in front of the house. Then he walked down to University Hill and tried to call Gosage through 911. Believing that the police were after him, he wanted to meet the detective. After he left the message, he walked back to the Ramseys' house. At around 11:30 P.M., he considered breaking in and spending the night but then decided against it. Better to write the Ramseys a note.

"If you hadn't killed your fucking baby," Colfax wrote, "this wouldn't have happened." He stuffed the note and some pages from a paperback book, *Interview with a Vampire*, into the front door mail slot, took a matchbook, printed Gosage's name on it, and set fire to the paper. He watched it scorch the inside wall from a nearby window, hoping that because it was made of brick, the house wouldn't burn down.

The next morning he called Gosage again. This time he confessed to trying to burn down the Ramseys' house, which the police knew nothing about. Within an hour he was arrested. Six months later, on January 16, 1998, Colfax was sentenced to twenty-four months' probation for first-degree arson, a class-three felony. For stealing the morgue log pages, he was sentenced to two years in the county jail, with no credit for the seven months he had sat in jail after turning himself in for the arson. By then, Lou Smit and Trip DeMuth had interviewed him several times. Colfax's alibi for December 26 checked out.

I grew up in Colorado. My father was a navy recruiter. I hated school, probably because I was gay. I felt pretty isolated. Then I finally met some artists, and we got to be friends. When I returned from the military in '87, I had my first sexual experience.

Some strangers say my art projects were off-the-wall. In '94, after my mother died, I wrote a letter a day for a year to four people in Clarksburg, West Virginia. I listed each person's name and phone number on the other person's letter so everyone would begin to talk to each other. In the letters I told about getting drunk, buying cocaine, and having sex with another guy. Then I did the same thing in Blytheville, Arkansas. I just picked the cities at random. They were all small towns. I'd lived in New York, San Antonio, Los Angeles, Denver. The Associated Press, the Washington Post, Newsday, *and the* Philadelphia Inquirer *wrote stories about my exploits.*

In Los Angeles I saw my first body. In MacArthur Park. That's when I got a job at a mortuary transportation service picking up bodies. In Denver I made $13 a body, seven days a week. It was a one-man job at hospitals and nursing homes. Two men when the coroner called.

Soon I started photographing bodies with funny signs attached to them. TIME'S UP. YEE-HA. GETTING FIRED ISN'T THE END OF THE WORLD. HAPPY HALLOWEEN. *I never moved a body in any particular way. Never sat them up. I just threw the signs on them as they were lying there. It was art. Good art. I included the photographs in my collages.*

The morning after JonBenét was killed I was crossing the Canadian border into the United States. A week later I read about her in a Portland paper. I was out of money, so I called my father in Aurora and came home. I found another job with a body transporting company near Boulder. My boss seemed upset that he'd missed being selected to pick up Jon-Benét's body.

—J. T. Colfax

On Tuesday, April 29, the day before the scheduled police interviews, all of the Ramseys' attorneys walked into the Access Graphics offices on the Pearl Street Mall and went directly to John Ramsey's fourth-floor office, with its view of the Rockies. They were soberly dressed in black and navy. Shortly afterward, Patsy and John arrived. They seemed nervous as they made their way upstairs.

Before long Patsy left her husband's office and walked aimlessly down the hall. Then she went back in. Forty-five minutes later she was pacing the halls again. Before noon, she left the building by a fourth-floor exit to the alley. When she returned, she found the door locked. She banged on it, but a security guard refused to admit her—she didn't have company ID. She had to walk around the building and enter through the front door, where the receptionist knew her.

By dinnertime, the meeting had disbanded.

Meanwhile, Steve Thomas and Tom Trujillo were at police headquarters consulting with the FBI's Child Abduction and Serial Killer Unit personnel, who had come to Boulder to assist the detectives. The Boulder PD had waited months for this opportunity to question the Ramseys.

Along the way, the detectives had been divided in their opinions about the parents' culpability. For example, Trujillo and Wickman had at one time speculated that John Ramsey and JonBenét had some type of sexual relationship, but Thomas and Gosage didn't believe it for one moment. By now, however, all the detectives felt that Patsy was involved in JonBenét's death and that although John Ramsey had nothing to do with the actual murder, he was likely to have contributed to its cover-up.

All the detectives agreed that one major mistake had been made in the first weeks, even before the CBI determined that there was no semen on JonBenét's body: Patsy had not been arrested. The detectives were sure that if only Hunter had agreed to jail Patsy—even for a short time—she would have caved in. Every time they themselves walked into a cell and heard the heavy steel doors clang shut behind them, a fear of never being able to return to the outside world hit them. If Patsy'd had to face that kind of dreadful uncertainty about her future, she would have broken down and the case would have been solved that very day, the detectives believed.

The detectives and Hofstrom had also long been divided on how to deal with the Ramseys—whether to push them or soften them up. Now that the interviews were imminent, they had to talk strategy. Thomas and Gosage met with Hofstrom. As expected, the police and the DA's office still had opposing views on how to handle the questioning. Hofstrom wanted to use the interviews to "build bridges" with the Ramseys. It would be wrong, he indicated, to challenge them during the interviews and let them see that they were the sole target of the investigation. Better to make them feel that the police were sincerely interested in finding the killer—as they were. Then sometime in the future, if they were the killers, they would let their guard down and be caught. The police had a different approach. They thought it was better to lock the Ramseys into their stories of what they remembered about Christmas night and the morning after. Then take them through every minute and make them prove that they were innocent. For example, on December 26 John Ramsey had told Rick French that he'd carried a sleeping JonBenét to her room and then read her a book. Patsy had told the same officer that JonBenét never woke up after being put to bed, even when Patsy changed her clothes. Which story was correct? Since this was the first—and maybe the only—interview that the police would conduct with the Ramseys, the detectives were in favor of using a tough approach: challenge everything the Ramseys had said and would say.

Everyone agreed it was imperative that the detectives not reveal to the Ramseys and their attorneys what had been uncovered in the police investigation. At the same time, they had to find out what the Ramseys knew and remembered—and, most important, see how it stacked up against what the police had learned. The detectives had to decide which questions to ask and which to avoid.

They agreed, for example, that they wouldn't directly mention the pineapple found in JonBenét's intestines. The police thought it was better to lock the Ramseys into the story they had told on December 26—that the sleeping child had been taken upstairs and put right to bed for the night—and confront them later with any possible conflicts. The audiotape of Patsy's 911 call would also be off-limits for the interview. Better to leave the Ramseys—and the DA's office—unaware of what the detectives now knew.

The detectives also wanted to hear once more from Patsy what she had done after she left her bedroom that morning. She'd told Officer French that after leaving her room, she first checked JonBenét's room and found it empty; then she went downstairs to see if her daughter was there and instead found the ransom note; then she returned to the second floor, cried out for her husband, and went to see if JonBenét was in Burke's room. Later that day, however, Patsy told Detective Arndt a different version of the story—that she'd first stopped just outside of JonBenét's bedroom to do some washing in the sink and had then gone downstairs and found the ransom note. Only then, she said, did she return to JonBenét's room and find it empty.

Which was the truth? That, among other questions, preoccupied the detectives as they prepared for the minefield of the interviews.

On April 30 at 9:05 A.M., Patsy Ramsey began her scheduled formal interview with the police. Detectives Steve Thomas and Tom Trujillo asked the questions. Pat Furman, Patsy's attorney, led her by the hand into the DA's conference room at the Justice Center. He seated her, then pulled up a chair next to her. Ramsey investigator John Foster sat with his back to the wall on Patsy's side of the room. Pete Hofstrom observed from a corner of the room.

John Ramsey would be interviewed later in the day, when the detectives were done with his wife. The other attorneys for the Ramseys waited in Hofstrom's office.

For six hours Thomas and Trujillo sat face-to-face with Patsy Ramsey and led her through the pertinent events of the days leading up to and following Christmas. More often than not, her answers were ambiguous and selective.

The detectives asked her about what had happened when the family returned from the Whites'. She said that JonBenét had been carried directly to her room and put to bed for the night. She hadn't awakened. What was the last thing JonBenét ate that night? Patsy didn't remember. Earlier in the year she had answered the same question posed to her in writing by Detective Arndt. She had replied in writing through her attorneys, "Cracked crab at the Whites'." Two hours later, after a break in the interview, Trujillo returned to the same question, and this time Patsy remembered that her daughter had eaten cracked crab at the Whites'. The detectives now had her locked into an answer in conflict with the findings of the autopsy. Asked whether anyone in the family had snacked after they returned home that night, Patsy said she knew nothing about any food eaten by anyone. The detectives did not reveal that fingerprints—hers and Burke's—had been found on the bowl containing pineapple on the dining room table. Later they speculated that the only explanation for the discrepancy was that the children—either alone or together—had eaten the pineapple without their mother's knowledge and that Patsy's fingerprint dated from an earlier time. It was also possible, however, that Patsy now knew about the pineapple—the information had been released in the edited autopsy report—and thought it was better that she stick with her earlier written statement.

The detectives asked Patsy what happened after she found the ransom note—whether she turned the light on in Burke's room when she went to look for JonBenét. She didn't remember. Did she awaken Burke to find out if he knew where his sister was, or did he awaken by himself? No, she was sure he stayed asleep until John got him up for the move to the Whites'. The detectives asked her the same question several times during the six hours, and each time she gave the same story, though it conflicted with what they had just discovered on the enhanced audio tape of Patsy's call to 911.

Since fibers had been found on the duct tape, JonBenét's body, the white blanket, and the floor of the wine cellar; Patsy was asked about her clothes. She said that she wore the same red sweater, black slacks, and jacket on Christmas night and the morning after. She said she had put them on that morning because they were lying where she had left them the night before. The police thought it was odd that a well-groomed woman like Patsy would wear the same clothes two days in a row—they had understood that she hardly ever left her bedroom without fresh makeup.

Patsy was asked about the ransom note. How did she feel about the fact that some handwriting experts believed she wrote it? She didn't know that to be the case, she said. What about the fact that her pen was used to write it? She replied: "It was?" Thomas asked why the handwriting looked like hers. "It looks that way because it may have been written by a woman," she answered.

"I did the best I could. I just put her to bed," Patsy said in answer to one question. "I *just* don't know that," she would say again and again.

There were several breaks before lunch, during which Hofstrom allowed Patsy and her attorneys to use his office. Thomas worried that they were telling John Ramsey what his wife was being asked, to make sure that his story would not be at odds with hers.

After the first break, she was asked if she would take a polygraph. "I'll take ten of them," Patsy replied. Later, when the detectives requested that a test be administered to her, Patsy's attorney and Pete Hofstrom were unable to agree on the terms.

In the afternoon, Thomas asked Patsy if she or any member of her family had purchased duct tape or cord prior to the murder. They knew she might have bought tape at Home Depot in Athens, Georgia, or at McGuckin Hardware in Boulder. Patsy couldn't remember buying such items. She'd have no need for them, she said. Her answer was no.

Patsy was shown a photo of the flashlight that had been found on the kitchen counter—which detectives surmised might have been used in the blow to JonBenét's head. Patsy said the family owned one like it but she couldn't tell from the photo if this was the one.

Patsy was not only vague, Thomas felt, but coy and charming, even flirtatious, her eyes wide and her head cocked to one side. Thomas, who had grown up in the South, was familiar with the demeanor. Thomas knew better than to be influenced by it. He was also trained to be circumspect. He was sure that Patsy was involved in her daughter's murder. He just didn't know *how*.

When Patsy's interview was over, it was John Ramsey's turn. Dressed casually, he sat down, crossed his legs, and put his hands in his lap. He was at ease. His attorney, Bryan Morgan, sat next to him.

The detectives took Ramsey through his previous statements. When they questioned him about putting JonBenét to bed and reading to her, he said that she had been asleep and that Rick French was mistaken—he hadn't said, "I put her to bed and read her a book." What he had said was, "I put her to bed and then I read a book." Ramsey also told the detectives that Burke had slept through the events of that morning until he was awakened for the short ride to the Whites'.

John Ramsey said that he had gone down to the basement at around 10:00 A.M. that morning. It was the first the police had heard about this.

None of Detective Arndt's reports indicated that Ramsey had visited the basement before the body was found. Ramsey now told the detectives for the first time about his finding the broken window open, which had surprised him. Taken aback by the revelation of Ramsey's visit to the basement, Thomas asked him why he didn't report what he found to Detective Arndt since someone could have entered through the window. Ramsey said he didn't know why. He just didn't know, he said a second time. When asked if he also went into the boiler room and checked the wine cellar. He didn't go into that area of the basement, he said.

Ramsey was asked to tell the detectives how he had found Jon-Benét's body. He said that after he opened the door and as he was still reaching for the light switch, he saw to his left the white blanket and his daughter's hands protruding. Then he screamed and went inside. He didn't remember exactly when the light was turned on. He wasn't sure he saw the blanket while the room was still dark.

"When you opened the door, did you see the blanket and Jon-Benét before or after you turned on the light?" Ramsey was asked again. He said he didn't remember. He didn't remember turning on the light. He just didn't remember. He didn't indicate whether he'd stepped into the room before seeing his daughter on the floor. It had all happened so quickly, he said.

Then Thomas told Ramsey that Fleet White had been in the basement early that morning and had opened the wine cellar door but seen nothing in the room. Ramsey was surprised. He said he had no knowledge about White being in the basement earlier that morning. How did he explain the fact that White opened the door to the wine cellar, looked in, and didn't see the blanket and the body, whereas he had seen them both almost immediately? I just don't know, Ramsey said. I can't explain it.

By now the police had asked Vahe Christianian, the co-owner of Mike's Camera in Boulder, to measure the ambient and reflected light inside the wine cellar with its door open and the lights out, to verify what could and could not be seen during a quick glance inside the room. The test showed that there was not enough light to see anything in the dark unless the viewer had spent time getting accustomed to the darkness or his eyes adapted quickly to the surroundings.

However, there was a possible explanation. JonBenét's body was inside the room and to the left. It might not have been visible to White standing just at the threshold and blocking reflected light from entering the room. Yet if someone stood 5 to 10 inches *inside* the threshold, more reflected light would have entered. Then, looking directly to the left, the person might have seen the white blanket in the dark room. Maybe there was enough reflected light from just outside the door.

The detectives asked Ramsey why, just minutes after finding Jon-Benét's body, he had called his pilot to have his private plane take him and his family out of state that afternoon. Ramsey said that he had wanted to get back to Atlanta—where he and his family would be safe. Reminded that he had made the phone call within twenty minutes of finding his daughter's body, Ramsey repeated that he had felt his family would be safer in Georgia.

Finally, he was asked what he thought of polygraph tests. He said, "If they are accurate, I'm for them."

"What if I asked you to take one?" Thomas said.

"I have never been so insulted in my life as by that question," Ramsey said angrily.

"Will you take one?" the detective asked.

"No," was Ramsey's answer.

John Ramsey's interview lasted just over two hours. The detectives felt no need to go into a second day.

After the tapes of the interviews were transcribed, the police evaluated the Ramseys' interviews. It became clear to them that Patsy didn't want to revisit the unpleasant events of December 25–26, 1996, and couldn't be shaken from her picture-perfect view of her life and family. John Ramsey seemed more realistic in his attitude toward the tragedy. The detectives felt confirmed in their belief that Ramsey was probably not involved in the actual murder of his daughter. But Patsy was—the officers were sure of it.

Like all investigators, Thomas and Trujillo would like to have found a motive—or at least a reason—for JonBenét's murder. Maybe the child's bed-wetting had gotten to her mother. Maybe the fact that the six-year-old still demanded help in the bathroom had somehow precipitated the events of that night. Nothing was evident, however. Of course the police knew that they weren't required to find a motive. Their job was to connect evidence to a suspect.

The following day, Alex Hunter was briefed on the interviews. There would be no arrest warrant issued at this time.

8

RAMSEYS FINALLY GIVE INTERVIEWS

"It was a full day," Sgt. Tom Wickman said as he left the Boulder Justice Center late in the afternoon.

"It's extremely important that you say this is an open-minded investigation," [Alex] Hunter said. "You can't have on blinders."

In March, while discussing possible DNA, Hunter also hinted that the investigation was focusing on John and Patsy Ramsey.

"I don't want a court down the road—be it a trial court or an appellate court—to make a ruling that disallows this evidence because they weren't given this opportunity," Hunter told the Post. "I'm not going to gamble with this evidence."

—Marilyn Robinson and Mary George
The Denver Post, May 1, 1997

Charlie Brennan of the *Rocky Mountain News* was one of the reporters who had staked out the Justice Center the day of the interviews, hoping to see the Ramseys and their attorneys. All he got was a quick glimpse of John Ramsey arriving after 3:00 P.M. He didn't see the Ramseys or their attorneys leave. When he checked his voice mail the next day, he heard, "Call me as soon as you get this. Give me a phone number where you can be paged or called Thursday morning." The message had been left the previous evening by Rachelle Zimmer, a spokeswoman for the Ramseys.

Like a few other reporters, Brennan had been told by Charlie Russell, another Ramsey spokesperson, that he shouldn't leave town. An hour after hearing the voice mail message, he was in Boulder with a photographer, waiting in front of Dot's Diner, at 8th and Pearl. When his cell phone rang, Rachelle Zimmer gave him a password— "subtract"—and designated a place where they should meet.

"You're not to ask them anything about the murder," Zimmer told him but did not say who "they" were. "There will be lawyers present. You can't photograph them. And you can't ask the attorneys any questions." The list of restrictions went on: Don't ask about yesterday's interview with the police. Don't disclose today's location, even afterward. The interview would last thirty minutes, Zimmer added before hanging up.

A private security guard met Brennan and six other reporters at the side door of the Marriott Hotel in Boulder. They had all been given the same password. They were shown to a small, tastefully appointed ground-floor lounge. A lavish bouquet on a low table separated the media from an empty couch.

As they waited, Paula Woodward, an investigative reporter for KUSA, NBC's Denver affiliate, asked Carol McKinley a question: "Who do you think killed JonBenét?"

"This isn't the place to talk about that," McKinley replied.

"You think they did it, don't you?" Woodward insisted.

"That's not something I want to talk about—not right now," McKinley said as she returned to her seat.

Rachelle Zimmer, who had been hovering about the room, made a final check before John and Patsy Ramsey entered with their lawyers and Patsy's father. John was neatly dressed in a tweed jacket and paisley tie; Patsy wore a blue suit, with a silver angel pin on her right lapel. Her eyes were clear; her smile, warm. She sat to John's left, exactly as she had during their January CNN interview.

Most of the reporters, who had never seen the Ramseys in person, found their quiet grace impossible to reconcile with the rumors building around them.

John Ramsey spoke first: "We've been anxious to do this for some time, and I can tell you why it's taken us so long." Ramsey explained that their first obligation had been to talk to the police. Now that they had, they wanted to "clear up some issues."

Ramsey discussed how and why his attorneys had been hired, explaining his close relationship to Michael Bynum. Then he raised the subject the reporters had been told to avoid: "Let me address it very directly: I did not kill my daughter JonBenét. There have also been innuendoes that she had been or was sexually molested. I can tell you that those were the most hurtful innuendoes to us as a family. They are totally false. JonBenét and I had a very close relationship"—Ramsey stumbled over his dead daughter's name. Then he added: "I will miss her dearly the rest of my life."

Then Patsy spoke: "I'm grateful that we are finally able to meet together face-to-face. I'm appalled that anyone would think that John or I would be involved in such a hideous, heinous crime. But let me assure you that I did not kill JonBenét and did not have anything to do with this." She added, "We feel like God has a master plan for our lives and that in the fullness of time, our family will be reunited again and we will see JonBenét."

John said, "I have corresponded several times with a little girl about our son Burke's age in southern Illinois. She was very distressed by this. I have received a card from an elderly lady. I think she said she was eighty-five. She said she had to wait until she got her Social Security check so she could buy stamps to send us a letter. It's just been wonderful."

Patsy continued. "I know you have been diligently covering this case," she said, "and we have appreciated some of what you've said—I'll be frank, not all of what you've said."

Some of the reporters chuckled as Patsy continued. "We need to work together as a team. And we need your help."

Then Patsy held up the newspaper advertisement that had appeared four days earlier, in the Sunday edition of the *Daily Camera*, offering a $100,000 reward for information.

"We feel like there are at least two people on the face of this earth that know who did this," Patsy continued. "That is the killer and someone that that person may have confided in. We need that one phone call. We need the one phone call to this number that may help the authorities come to a conclusion with this case."

As Patsy repeated "one phone call," the reporters exchanged glances among themselves.

With less than twenty minutes left, Patsy asked for the first question. Phil LeBeau, who weeks before had received an unsolicited call from her, was first. "This is the same plea, I think," LeBeau began, "that you and John made in your CNN interview four months ago." The reporter wanted to know why the public had seen little evidence of other efforts by the Ramseys to catch the killer.

John responded, even though the question had been directed to Patsy.

"We've been distressed that the [original] reward [offer] wasn't better publicized," he answered.

Reporter Bertha Lynn, whose husband was a Denver district judge, wanted to know why two grieving parents had dragged their feet in giving police an interview if they wanted to catch their child's killer.

"The impression that we haven't spoken with police is totally false," John Ramsey replied. He detailed the time he and Patsy had spent with police on December 26 and 27.

"What *has* been delayed has been this formal interrogation of us as suspects," he went on. "Frankly, we . . . were, as you might imagine, insulted that we would even be considered suspects in the death of our daughter. And felt that an interrogation of us was a waste of our time and a waste of police time."

"Mr. Ramsey, what do you want to say to the killer of your daughter?" Paula Woodward asked

"We'll find you," Ramsey said evenly. "We will find you. I have that as a sole mission for the rest of my life."

"Patsy?" Woodward asked.

"Likewise. The police and investigators have assured us that this is a case that can be solved. You may be eluding the authorities for a time"— Patsy jabbed her finger toward the cameras as she spoke directly to the killer—"but God knows who you are, and *we will find you.*"

Those words would comprise the front-page headline of the *Rocky Mountain News* the next day.

Charlie Brennan asked the next question: Did the Ramseys fear a life spent under a permanent cloud of suspicion?

John replied that they weren't concerned: their true friends knew what they were made of. Then he added, "An arrest is absolutely necessary in our lives for closure . . . an arrest must be made for us to go with some semblance of a life and hope for the future."

Both John and Patsy clasped and unclasped their hands as they spoke, and Patsy often had both palms pressed together as if in prayer. The two of them didn't touch each other as they sat side by side on the love seat.

Clay Evans of the *Daily Camera* wanted to know whether they were now second-guessing anything they had done or not done to date. They said no. LeBeau then asked, "John, would you recommend the death penalty for the person convicted of killing JonBenét?"

Meeting LeBeau's eyes directly, Ramsey said: "I would absolutely want the most severe penalty to be brought."

"Patsy?" LeBeau asked.

She nodded slightly, then looked down. Her eyes welled with tears and her lips trembled, but she did not make a sound.

Then Bertha Lynn, pointing to the contrast between the JonBenét pictured in the advertisement and the child cavorting onstage in a provocative costume, asked the Ramseys whether involving their daughter in pageants now seemed a mistake.

"Those were beautiful pictures," Patsy said. "I'm so happy that we have those pictures. They're all that we have now."

John added, "That was just one very small part of JonBenét's life."

"A few Sunday afternoons," Patsy said.

"If you could," Phil LeBeau asked Patsy, "what would you say to JonBenét right now?"

"I'd tell her that I love her and I will be seeing her real soon. It won't be long."

Abruptly, Rachelle Zimmer brought the session to a close. Within moments, the Ramseys and their lawyers were gone.

Out in the parking lot, the photographer for the *Rocky Mountain News* turned his key in the ignition and told Brennan, "If those people are guilty, then I don't know anything about people." Brennan agreed. Their gentleness allayed any suspicion that they had killed JonBenét. To Brennan, they seemed trustworthy.

As he drove back to Denver to write his story, he heard Carol McKinley and Mike Rosen talking on the radio. The host of a morning talk show on McKinley's station, Rosen was a moderate conservative. Now he questioned McKinley aggressively.

"There was nothing substantial," Rosen protested. "None of you pushed them. Now you know why they didn't invite people like me or Peter Boyles," he said, referring to another controversial Denver talk show personality.

Back in his office, Charlie Brennan turned on the TV mounted over the city desk. Switching from channel to channel, he watched key passages from the Ramseys' news conference appear again and again. Some critics were already calling it an infomercial for the Ramseys. With repeated viewings, Brennan noticed that John Ramsey's eyes were focused somewhere in the middle foreground, on the floral arrangement. That seemed normal, Brennan decided. But Patsy's demeanor troubled him. She would shut her eyes for several seconds while she spoke. It was an odd little tic, Brennan thought. It suggested that she might be lying.

"I'm appalled that anyone would think that John or I would be involved in such a hideous, heinous crime." Patsy said. Then she closed her eyes and added, "I loved that child with my whole of my heart and soul."

Maybe it meant nothing, but she did it again when she said, "We would like to think that we don't know anyone that we ever met in our lives that could do such a thing to a child."

She shut her eyes again when she said: "I feel like [the police] are doing a broad investigation, and that is all I need to hear."

As Brennan wrote his story for the next day's paper, the confidence he'd felt in the Ramseys while in their presence began to recede.

We've been able to convict the Ramseys because they were outsiders.

Usually a crime like this will bring the community together, but we really didn't adopt them as one of our own. They were just one of dozens of families who came here to escape other cities. That made things easier on us.

—Peter Adler
Professor of Sociology, University of Denver

Now that they had completed police and media interviews, the Ramseys began to cooperate to some degree with the DA's office. They had met Pete Hofstrom earlier in the year and trusted him. Introduced to Lou Smit when they gave their police interviews on April 30, they came to believe he wasn't looking to target them. He didn't seem to have an agenda. It was likely that they were impressed not only by Smit's religious faith but also by his telling them that he intended to let the evidence lead him to JonBenét's killer. Not long afterward, Smit made the same statement to a colleague, adding: "If the evidence led to Jesus Christ, I would follow it." Experience had taught Lou Smit that an investigator had to get to know his target, look him in the eye from time to time. It was important to build a positive relationship with the target, not alienate him. Smit believed that after a bridge was forged with the Ramseys, he would be able to rely on his gut to tell him what the evidence couldn't.

Two weeks later, Smit, Ainsworth, and Hofstrom met with the Ramseys and showed them a photo lineup. Included were Kevin Raburn, his mother and sister, and two sex offenders the investigators were checking out. The Ramseys couldn't identify any of them. Without blood and hair samples from Raburn, who still hadn't been located, Hunter's office began to process the few handwriting samples they had culled from his prison files.

While Smit and Ainsworth continued investigating Raburn, unknown to them, the Longmont police were also looking for him. Back in March, when Smit and Ainsworth had first tried to locate him, Raburn was forging checks. Longmont detective Lee Scott tracked him down, unaware that Hunter's office was looking for him. Raburn agreed to turn himself in for check forgery and, still unknown to Smit and Ainsworth, appeared on May 13 at the police department, where he was released pending a court date. After that he became a fugitive, and Smit and Ainsworth were still unaware of his run-in with the Longmont police.

STUDENTS RIOT ON HILL
BONFIRES BURN AS 1,500 FACE OFF
WITH POLICE OFFICERS

It began as a simple end-of-the-semester party.

But soon, more than 1,500 people—mostly students from the University of Colorado—were overturning Dumpsters, setting bonfires and pelting law enforcement officers with rocks, bricks and bottles.

Police called the five-hour standoff in the University Hill section of Boulder late Friday and early Saturday the worst riot in the city in 25 years. Participants said it was the result of a year of simmering tensions between police and students over alcohol consumption.

The riot ended with 11 people arrested on various charges of assault and rioting. Twelve officers were injured—two of them hurt seriously enough to go on temporary disability leave.

When officers from the Boulder Police Department Hill team arrived at the scene, a crowd charged their Suburban truck, smashing the windows and caving in the side of the truck, [Police Chief] Koby said.

"(The crowd) came right at them," said Koby. "The crowd surged to upwards of 1,500, so we called for additional help."

More than 100 officers from 10 agencies, including the Boulder police, the Boulder, Jefferson and Adams county sheriff's departments, the Colorado State Patrol and police from Golden, Broomfield, Lafayette, Longmont and Louisville police departments—most clad in full riot gear—gathered on the Hill.

—Elliot Zaret
Daily Camera, May 4, 1997

★ ★ ★

This was not the first time there had been a ruckus on the Hill, a few blocks from the Ramseys' house. The Hill was a lot like San Francisco's Haight-Ashbury district of the 1960s. Since that so-called psychedelic revolution, recognizable hippie types had been camping out on University Hill's sidewalks in front of coffee shops and clubs, while Boulderites and students from the CU campus, a few blocks away, hung out in the bars, record shops, and movie theater. The mixture of street people, students out for a good time, and alcohol was often combustible, and the Boulder police had opened a substation in the area.

Now Tom Koby, whose detectives were resentful that he hadn't spoken up for them against the media attack on their handling of the Ramsey investigation, faced outrage from the rank and file. His officers were furious that Koby refused to let them respond as *they* saw fit to the rioters on May 2. At first he ordered them to stay out of sight. Then they were pelted with rocks.

There had been confrontations between the police and students over their underage and public drinking throughout the winter of 1996–97 and into the spring. In July 1990 the drinking age had been raised from eighteen to twenty-one because the governor believed it could save ten to fifteen lives a year and because the federal government threatened to withhold $27 million in highway funds if the age limit was not raised. In 1992 five hundred people had been involved in an incident where bottles, rocks, and burning branches were tossed at firefighters. More near-riots broke out in 1994, when three hundred people threw furniture and street signs into a bonfire and tossed bottles and rocks at police.

A week after the May 2 riots, the *Boulder Planet*, a weekly newspaper, quoted Koby as saying, "My officers would have been justified killing some of these young people." Koby hailed the restraint of his officers during the riots and said that a lack of education about alcohol abuse was one cause of the disturbance. Two weeks later, the *Rocky Mountain News* took him to task in an editorial.

RIOTERS EARN EXPULSION

The University of Colorado has begun to expel and suspend some of the students arrested during the early May riots that endangered lives, injured dozens of people and cost the city and property owners hundreds of thousands of dollars.

The university is wise to move so fast in meting out punishment.

In this case, the most commonly cited cause—the city's strict attitude toward underage drinking—was trivial, if it really existed at all in the minds of some rioters. As Boulder Police Chief Tom Koby has pointed out on several occasions, the rioters put lives at genuine risk.

Having said that, however, we do take issue with another of Koby's remarks, whose melodramatic quotient was wild and irresponsible. The chief told the Boulder Planet that his officers would "have been justified in killing some of these young people. . . . Somebody attacks you with a lethal instrument, you have the right to use lethal force."

Get a grip on yourself, chief. If Boulder officers had mowed down protesters with live ammunition it would have been a national scandal that would have ended more than a few careers.

Koby suggested that his officers, primed emotionally "to get in there and mix it up" with protesters, exercised extraordinary restraint . . . and they should be commended, but no police chief should run around implying that any other outcome in such a confrontation even given extreme provocation might have been "justified."

At the end of May, the rank and file raised their grievances against Koby at a special union meeting. Regardless of his praising them in the newspaper, officers felt he had shown dismal leadership during the Hill riots. "Community policing" was the hot topic at the meeting. Officers claimed they were spending more time serving ice cream to kids than arresting criminals. It was an exaggeration, but they felt hampered in their ability to respond to the public's needs.

As Steve Thomas listened to the arguments, he remembered an incident that spoke to the cops' underlying resentment. In the hot summer of 1993, Boulder's undercover narcotics detectives worked in stakeout vans videotaping the drug deals at Boulder's San Juan Del Centro low-income housing units. At the same time, Koby was trying to clean up the city's drug problem through education and meetings with community leaders.

Todd Sears, the lead detective, had edited down tens of hours of video into a catalog of San Juan's dealers, which he planned to use in court. On a Friday, when the department was poised to arrest the some thirty dealers, none of them showed up. The street had cleaned itself up overnight. As Sears tried to figure out what had gone wrong, his supervising officer dropped on his desk the edited videotape he'd made.

Eventually Sears discovered that Koby had, without his knowledge, shown it to police liaison Ron Brambila, a member of the minority issues coalition. For Sears, Koby's action not only subverted the arrest of the drug dealers but violated police and union procedure, which stipulated that evidence cannot be made public during an ongoing investigation. According to Sears Koby may even have been involved in obstruction of justice. Sears filed charges against the chief with the department's internal affairs sergeant, Mark Beckner. After an investigation, Sears' allegations were sustained, and Koby's boss and friend, city manager Tim Honey, was required to discipline him. In typical Boulder style, Honey ordered Koby to attend counseling with Honey and to explain his actions to the department's officers. When the narcotics team eventually arrested the drug dealers, Ron Brambila, to whom Koby had originally shown the videotape, appeared in court to support one of the dealers.* Sears resigned from the Boulder PD shortly afterward.

The May 2 riots had brought long-simmering resentments to a boil. The rank and file were so fed up that no one attempted to defend the chief's policies. One union official later said that the Boulder officers had turned into a lynch mob.

Though they didn't want to ask for Koby's dismissal, the police did want to take a vote by secret ballot. Seventy-eight members voted no confidence, thirty-one opposed, and six abstained. The no-confidence vote had passed by two to one. Though union officials didn't understand how their vote would be interpreted, the Boulder City Council would see it as a sign that the rank and file wanted Koby removed.

Within days of the meeting, the press reported that city manager Tim Honey was on his way out. According to the *Rocky Mountain News*: "Honey's performance recently has been criticized by at least four of Boulder's nine council members. . . . Honey's critics on the council have voiced concern about personnel issues. Honey also had defended police chief Tom Koby, who this week lost a vote of confidence conducted by the Boulder Police Benefit Association."

For six years, Tim Honey, with a master's degree in political science from Georgetown University, had seemed to be the perfect city manager for politically progressive Boulder. Its leaders thought of

---

* Ron Brambila also came to court to give moral support to Danny Arevelo, who was convicted of felony child abuse in the death of Elizabeth Manning's son, Michael, and sentenced to ten years.

themselves as innovators, looking for solutions to the complex issues facing local governments. Honey was hired to bring stability, vision, and direction to what some local residents called Utopia.

When he arrived in February 1991, he found a priority list of 104 items. Most issues in Boulder centered around the city's growth: Should there be more or less? What would be the impact of growth? In a style endemic to Boulder, combatants argued and fought long after a vote was taken, the losers trying to find a way to save whatever they had lost.

Seven months after he took the job, Honey hired Tom Koby as chief of police. Honey felt that Koby's twenty-five years in law enforcement had given him a real understanding of the relationship between public safety and other community issues. Within a year, Koby told the city council that police resources were inadequate. With the approval of Honey and the city council, he restructured the department, removing several layers of bureaucracy and creating management teams in their place. Once that system was in effect, he started his push for community policing, where civilians would work with the police to fight crime.

A week after the *Rocky Mountain News* published its story about Tim Honey's problems, he resigned. The police union was moving against Tom Koby, and the media were criticizing every move the police made in the Ramsey case. At the same time, Mayor Leslie Durgin told the press that she would not seek reelection. For unrelated reasons, the city's planning director left his post, and so did Boulder's superintendent of schools.

The official face of paradise began to collapse. Boulder would soon find itself without the stable day-to-day leadership it had taken for granted for seven years.

I got elected to the Boulder City Council in November of 1987 and I stayed until 1996. I was even deputy mayor for a while. The council hires the city manager, and he hires the fire chief and police chief. The council can't direct either of them to do anything, but we can certainly make our feelings known to the city manager—and there is nothing wrong with that.

The whole region north of Denver has boomed. There is now traffic congestion. People are getting short-tempered. And wealthier. That's always a bad sign. Wealthy people are very impatient.

Boulder became a city for people whose lives are not dependent on where they live. They can afford to live anywhere. You have to keep in mind that this place isn't real life. This is dreamland.

Before long, almost everyone that worked for the city of Boulder was forced to live outside the city because it became so expensive to live here. Like the cops. They live outside the city they are protecting, and they don't like that. Tom Koby was unable to give the rank and file the type of police department they wanted, and that wasn't good, either.

When I read in the Daily Camera *that this little girl was killed, I would never have predicted that the world was going to descend on Boulder. What surprised me is that as a city, we never got together to protect ourselves. The police, the city council, the mayor, and the district attorney never sat down together and said, "Look, we've got something that is snowballing. And the snowball is running down the hill." We do that for every other problem we have to solve. I'm not talking about solving the case. I'm talking about how to deal with the snowball when it hits Boulder.*

—Matt Appelbaum

JOHN RAMSEY TARGET OF PRANK POSTER

The Pearl Street Mall area in downtown Boulder was visited before daylight Tuesday by pranksters who hung posters that label the father of JonBenét Ramsey a killer.

The poster reads: "$100,000 reward for information leading to the arrest and conviction of the murderer John Ramsey."

—Charlie Brennan
Rocky Mountain News, May 7, 1997

The police told Alex Hunter's office that a quick review by the FBI of the transcripts of the Ramseys' police interviews and videos of their May 1 press conference and January 1 CNN interview had produced significant insights about how each parent dealt with the death of their daughter but nothing that would break the case open. There were few inconsistent statements between Patsy's and John's stories but many discrepancies between their stories and the facts surrounding the events of December 26. The police believed the Ramseys had been coached to protect their rights rather than feeling free to cooperate in finding the killer of JonBenét.

★ ★ ★

WOMAN HELD IN SLAYING HUSBAND
IS SHOT IN HOME AS
OFFICER STANDS OUTSIDE

With a police officer standing outside the house, a Boulder man was shot to death Friday morning at 845 Inca Parkway.

Cynthia Jakob-Chien, 43, was arrested on charges of first-degree murder late Friday. "The woman came down with the gun and surrendered the gun and herself," said Boulder police detective commander John Eller.

About 8:45 A.M., a man believed to be Ruediger Jakob-Chien called Boulder police requesting a "civil standby"—officer assistance while he removed property from the house. Police scheduled a 10 A.M. appointment with the man. An officer arrived at the house shortly before 10 A.M. and Ruediger and a friend arrived soon after with a U-Haul truck.

"The officer got out there, and both people seemed to be fairly congenial," said Boulder Police Chief Tom Koby. "The officer stood at the front door while he was getting his stuff, and things didn't work out."

Shots were fired inside the house. The man was found dead, and the woman surrendered to police.

"If somebody's intent on killing somebody, it's hard to stop the situation," Koby said. "You can't go in there and handcuff the woman to the couch and say, 'You stay here.'"

—Elliot Zaret
Daily Camera, May 10, 1997

The Ramseys renewed their advertising campaign and again offered a $100,000 reward for the arrest and indictment of the killer of their daughter. Clearly implied in the move was that they would no longer wait for the police to solve the crime.

The advertisement, which appeared in the *Daily Camera* on Sunday, May 11, sought help in locating "an adult male approaching young children in Boulder in late 1996." On Friday, May 9, a reporter for the Associated Press heard that the advertisement would refer to a suspect and asked Hunter's office for a statement, since this was the first time a description—no matter how sketchy—had been published. Suzanne Laurion responded in what the AP journalist considered her professorial voice: "Why would we have a comment? It's not our ad." This led the reporter to believe that the lead had been uncovered by the Ramseys' investigators and that the DA's office had nothing to do with the ad. On May 10, the day before the ad was to be published, Alex Hunter bumped into Bryan Morgan at a children's soccer game. The attorney for the Ramseys told the DA that his deputy, Trip DeMuth, had approved the ad. This put the DA's office in a precarious position. Now not only was Hunter's staff consulting with the Ramseys, they were acknowledging leads the police were investigating and giving them more credibility than was warranted. When Hunter confronted him, DeMuth apologized to his furious boss, but it was too late. By Monday, the day after the ad appeared, the Ramseys were publicly thanking Alex Hunter for acknowledging the involvement of his office in the ad campaign. Now the public knew for sure that the Ramseys had developed a dialogue with DA's office while they kept the police at arm's length.

Within hours of the Ramseys' appearance before the media on May 1, several of the tabloids sent new reporters to Boulder hoping to get interviews with the couple or their friends. Ken Harrell, a *Globe* writer from Florida, was one of the first to arrive. On May 11, the same day the Ramseys' advertisement appeared in the *Daily Camera*, Ken Harrell and Jeff Shapiro went to services at St. John's. Ken, an Episcopalian, even took along his Bible.

   Unknown to Harrell, Steve Thomas was in church that day too, and seated next to him. Thomas, of course, didn't know Harrell. The two men shook hands when the congregation took the Peace.

   When the service was over, Rev. Hoverstock asked Shapiro to step into his office. Harrell waited outside.

When I went into Rol's office, he said, "People are saying things about you. I just want to know the truth. Don't bullshit me. They say you're undercover, that you're working on the case."

I lied through my teeth.

He said, "Jeff, don't say these things. It's not going to serve your purposes." If I wanted to clear my name, he said, all I had to do was let him take a copy of my driver's license and he'd show it to the police.

"Do you feel comfortable with that?" he asked.

I gave him my license and he copied it.

Then I left, and Hoverstock asked to see Harrell.

—Jeff Shapiro

After Jeff left Hoverstock's office, I met with Father Rol privately. I told him I worked for the Globe and that I believed the Ramseys were involved in the death of their child. Then I asked, "Have they asked you for confession?"

For a moment he didn't answer. Then he said, "I have no respect for what you do for a living. You lie about everything."

"No we don't, Father. We don't lie," I replied.

I could see this strong man biting his lower lip. For a moment I thought he might throw me out of his office.

"As a forgiver of sins, the church is a house for all sinners," I said. "So I should be one of the first welcomed into your congregation." He remained silent and I continued. "You should not turn your nose up at any of God's children." He still did not respond.

"Don't you feel that if the Ramseys are responsible you have to do something about it?" I asked.

Finally he replied, "This is a sanctuary. I have to treat everyone in my church in an appropriate way. They came here to seek God and that is what they will find."

I could see he was offended that I was asking him about matters he considered privileged.

"I am here to find the truth," I told him. "If there are two murderers loose in your congregation, I would have no qualms about stepping over the boundaries of the church protocol to put them where they belong." Then I said I hoped he would steer the Ramseys in the right direction. Hoverstock stood there quietly for a second or two. I seemed to have caught his interest.

"The greatest sin of all is taking another's life," I continued. "I would not want to have your job. Mine is much easier. I can catch the killers and turn them over without any struggles of conscience. I understand that you can't. You have to save their souls."

"That is my job," Hoverstock said.

"Have you saved their souls?" I asked him.

He didn't answer.

Then he asked me to leave, but in a nice way. "I do love you," he said. "Come here, my brother," and we hugged.

Then I left.

—Ken Harrell

★ ★ ★

The next Sunday, Ken Harrell didn't go to church with Jeff Shapiro. When Shapiro entered St. John's, he saw John Ramsey sitting alone, so he sat down right behind him, a couple of feet away. Shapiro even shook his hand when Rev. Hoverstock said everyone should take the Peace.

I took communion with him, drinking my wine as he drank his.

Rol came up to John and put his hand on his shoulder as if to say, "You're going to make it through this. You're going to survive. You didn't do this."

Then he came to me, looked into my eyes, and said, "May you accomplish everything the Lord has sent you here to accomplish."

After the service, I talked to Hoverstock.

"I work for the Globe," I told him.

"I've heard that."

"When I'm undercover as an investigative reporter, I don't tell anyone. I needed time to think out what I said to you last Sunday. I respect you, Father; you deserve to know the truth."

"I respect you for telling me," Hoverstock said, "but you lied to all of us."

"I didn't lie," I told him. "I'm undercover."

"What's the difference?"

"There's a big difference," I explained. "If I were an FBI agent, you'd understand. But reporters have a role in a democratic society to find out the truth. That's what I'm here to do."

"That may have some merit. But what it comes down to is that I feel deceived."

Then I showed Hoverstock a picture of JonBenét in makeup. She looked sad.

"That's not the little girl I knew," he said.

"But this is what this case is about. I'm here to avenge that girl."

"So you're telling me that you're some holy avenger? No. You're a predator. You're all predators."

"I'm here to make a difference. Someday you'll understand I'm a good person."

"You are a good person," Hoverstock said. "But I don't like the fact that you're on John's case all the time."

"I'm not. I'm on Patsy's case. We're not in heaven," I continued. "We're still on earth, and God has given us our own laws to follow here."

As I left his office I recited from the Bible a verse that Chris Darden quoted to the Simpson jury: "For the Lord doth hate these things: a proud

look, a lying tongue, and hands that shed innocent blood."
  Hoverstock looked hard at me.
  Then I added, "Let justice be done though thy heaven fall."

—Jeff Shapiro

After church, Jeff Shapiro called Frank Coffman, an occasional contributor to the *Colorado Daily*. Coffman, a friendly guy about to turn fifty, had first met Alex Hunter in 1982 during a citizens' meeting and was currently writing articles on the Ramsey case. Coffman agreed to meet Shapiro at the Trident bookstore and café on Pearl Street, next door to the Rue Morgue mystery bookstore.

Over coffee, they talked about the case and eventually reached the topic of the garrote stick. In the photo the *Globe* had published, the wood looked like a manufactured item, slightly glossy and tapered. Then they looked at the autopsy and crime scene photos, which Shapiro had been given by his editor. Coffman said he'd once seen some white cord at the Boulder army-navy store that looked similar to the cord around JonBenét's wrist.

That afternoon, Shapiro visited the store Coffman had mentioned, which was just a few blocks from the Access Graphics offices. Sifting through the boxes of white cord, he found some that matched what he'd seen in the autopsy photo. Shapiro asked the cashier if John or Patsy Ramsey had ever been in the store.

"Not that I can recall," the clerk said.

That evening, Shapiro wrote a letter to Alex Hunter. He mentioned what he'd found and said that according to the clerk, the police had never visited the store to inquire about cord.

"People like you are going to make a difference," Hunter told Shapiro on the phone after receiving his letter. "Other journalists come in to get information. You come in to give *me* information." The comment gave Shapiro a huge boost.

Meanwhile, his editor was pushing him to develop a police source. Call Steve Thomas, Mullins said. Shapiro thought he was joking, since Mullins had blown Shapiro's cover by calling Thomas earlier in the year.

Nevertheless, Shapiro called Thomas and left a message, saying he had information the cops might need. Surprisingly, Thomas called back.

"I still have a working file on you," the detective said. "I look forward to seeing whatever it is you have to tell me."

Shapiro dropped off a note for Thomas at police headquarters. In it, he mentioned the white cord he had found—and also that the movie *Speed* contained a line similar to one rumored to be in the ransom note: "Don't try to grow a brain John."

"Jeff, I'm not interested in your theories," Thomas told Shapiro the next day on the phone. "I'm not going to give you any information in exchange. This relationship is going to be a monologue. That's all it will ever be. You talk to us. I say nothing."

"I just want to help," Shapiro said.

That afternoon, he went to police headquarters to introduce himself to Thomas. Shapiro was impressed with Thomas's appearance—he was in his mid-thirties and looked a bit like Clark Kent, in jeans and a T-shirt. On his way home, Shapiro stopped at the army-navy store again. He learned that after he'd delivered his letter to Thomas the previous day, the detective had visited the store and purchased all their white cord, forty-five pieces in all. Shapiro felt as if he'd accomplished something.

On May 19 I met with Steve Thomas. This time he was more professional-looking, in a white shirt and tie.

He took me into this little ice-cube room—nothing but a desk, a tape recorder, and couple of chairs on both sides. I put my $750 Zero Halliburton briefcase on the table.

"Does that need to be up here?" Thomas asked. "Would you mind if I opened it?" He searched my case, then said, "Mind if I pat you down and do a search?"

"No problem," I answered.

"I trust you don't have hidden wires on you that I don't know about."

"No."

Then Thomas introduced me to his partner, Ron Gosage. Gosage didn't say a word. You know—good cop, bad cop. Then Gosage turned on the tape recorder.

"Jeff, this is going to be a formal interview," Thomas began.

They wanted to know how I'd noticed the line from Speed. *I watch a lot of movies and have a good memory, I said. All the while Gosage just sat there with his arms folded.*

I told them about the movie Rising Sun, *and autoerotic asphyxiation—enhancing sexual pleasure by cutting off the oxygen supply. I'd been convinced for some time that the ligature had been used on Jon-Benét for that purpose. That interested them.*

Finally they asked me about the tabloids. They wanted to know if I had sources in the DA's office or the police department. I said I didn't.

They smiled and thanked me for coming in. I could tell they were interested in me.

—Jeff Shapiro

9

By spring there was much talk in the press about the mistakes the police had made in the first hours of the case and even more speculation about who was to blame for them. Because of Chief Koby's protracted silence about virtually all aspects of the investigation, most of the detectives working the case weren't known to reporters. In April, however, Kevin McCullen and Charlie Brennan of the *Rocky Mountain News* read the search warrant the police had obtained for CNN's videotapes and learned that Detective Linda Arndt had been the first detective on the scene and that she had arrived two hours and eighteen minutes after Patsy called 911. It was the first proof obtained by Brennan's newspaper that she had worked on the case. Then on May 14, Alli Krupski of the *Daily Camera* reported that both Arndt and Detective Melissa Hickman had been dropped from the case.

On June 8, the *Rocky Mountain News* published a scathing attack on the Boulder Police Department's investigation of the Ramsey case, using phrases like "series of missteps," "omissions," and "not-so-simple twists of fate that could enable the police chief's 'guy' to walk after all." Before publishing his story, Charlie Brennan had attempted to get the reaction of police chief Tom Koby. The chief declined to be interviewed or to address the issues. Brennan had made no attempt to contact Linda Arndt, though police policy would have prevented her from responding anyway.

Brennan wrote that on the morning of December 26, the cops failed to consider the "wealthy parents as possible suspects," were not "skeptical enough about the kidnapping," and failed to follow basic police procedure in questioning the parents.

Researching the story, McCullen and Brennan, having learned about Arndt's compassionate nature, began to speculate that she might have influenced some of Eller's decisions that morning. Maybe she had been protective of the Ramseys—and particularly of Patsy, who Arndt had discovered was recovering from cancer.

Brennan mentioned some of this in print. He quoted attorney Craig Silverman, who had been a top Denver prosecutor for fifteen years: "If there is fault, you can blame her with the fault of compassion." Brennan's report also alluded to the fact that a detective had "rebuffed a patrol officer's suggestion [that the flashlight on the kitchen counter should be seized as evidence], telling him to keep his nose out of the detectives' affairs, sources say." In addition, Brennan wrote, "A female detective at the Ramseys' home that day allegedly ordered that a sheet be placed over JonBenét as she lay dead on the living-room floor, according to unattributed sources cited in a May 30 report on ABC's *Nightline*." Brennan went on to say that some investigators feared the sheet might have picked up important trace evidence from the body.

After Brennan's story was published, Arndt asked Eller to stand behind her and correct falsehoods that were being repeated publicly about her role in the investigation. Eller refused. Soon the media were reporting that Arndt had moved the body and that she had asked Rev. Hoverstock "to gather everyone into a circle around the child and lead them in prayer." One article charged that "in the first week of January, without permission from the department, Arndt gave Ramsey attorney Patrick Burke a copy of the ransom note." Despite these inaccuracies, Arndt remained silent in her own defense.

Although the DA had hired Suzanne Laurion to shield him from the media, he still talked to journalists who had strong opinions about the case. Stephen Singular and Hunter spoke regularly. After their first meeting on April 15, they met again on April 29. At that meeting, Singular mentioned some witnesses he thought the police had failed to interview properly. He had been told the police were focused only on the behavior of the Ramseys. Had anyone seen Patsy hit JonBenét? the detectives would always ask. The answer was always no. Singular told Hunter that the police had failed to inquire about possible inappropriate behavior by others who knew JonBenét, for example, Randy Simons, who had photographed her. Several mothers of child pageant contestants, who had known Simons for years, found it hard to reconcile his strange behavior after the murder with the man they had known before. Two mothers claimed that Simons called them late at night and talked about how JonBenét had been sexually abused.

Hunter called investigator Steve Ainsworth into the meeting with Singular so that the detective could hear directly what some of the mothers had said. Later the DA called Pam Griffin to ask about the photographer. She said that Simons had once asked for permission to take her daughter's face and transpose it to a sexy body in a photograph. It was out of character for Simons, Pam said.

Hunter told Singular that he was having trouble getting the police to pursue the line of inquiry Singular was suggesting, and he asked the writer to see what he could learn about the people JonBenét saw *outside* her immediate family. Hunter wanted to know how she acted when she was not in the company of friends and family. The DA also wanted handwriting samples from the people that Singular thought should be considered. Finally, Hunter asked for help in finding potential sources of the ligature. He didn't care if it pointed to the Ramseys or someone else, he said. He wanted the information. Hunter was so intent on finding something everybody else had missed that some of his deputies had begun to refer to him as Dick Tracy.

Lou Smit and Steve Ainsworth read over the reports of the police interviews with Randy Simons. It appeared that he'd never been questioned in depth. Yet who better than a photographer to familiarize them with the fringe world of beauty pageants? On May 14 they drove to Genoa, Colorado, where Simons was living. The next day Simons granted Ainsworth an interview but was unable to shed much light on the case.

Still, because he was a professional photographer who sometimes photographed nudes, they investigated him as well. Without the photographer's knowledge, Hunter's office obtained handwriting samples and a sample of his saliva from a cigarette butt. A month later, on June 17, Ainsworth also interviewed pageant photographer Mark Fix. Eventually Ainsworth concluded that neither photographer had been involved in the death of JonBenét. Whether someone else connected with pageants had been involved was still an open question.

Stephen Singular returned home late the night he saw Alex Hunter. He stepped into his daughter's bedroom and stood in the dark, just listening to her peaceful, even breathing. He'd done the same thing every night for a couple of months after JonBenét had been murdered. He would wake up at two or three in the morning, walk to her room, and stand there listening to her breathing for a few minutes. He knew that what had happened in Boulder could happen anywhere.

10

DNA TESTS DONE, OFFICIALS MUM

The much-anticipated results of additional DNA tests in the Jon-
Benét Ramsey murder case have been returned to Boulder authorities, sources told The Denver Post Wednesday.

Authorities reportedly met in closed-door session, and officials
could not be reached for comment on the purpose of the meeting or
the results of the tests.

—Marilyn Robinson
The Denver Post, May 15, 1997

In Denver, Carol McKinley sat in her living room listening to her frustrated police source, who was calling from a pay phone. Chief Koby was
still refusing to defend his detectives from press attacks, and both Hunter
and Hofstrom were a lost cause, he said. The DA's office seemed more
interested in protecting the rights of the Ramseys than in putting them
in jail. John Eller was the only law enforcement official strong enough to
stand up the Ramseys' lawyers. Eller, he said, would never give up.

What had really gotten to the detectives, the officer said, was that
they were coming up against witnesses who could help the investigation but wouldn't cooperate. Under Colorado law, the police had little leverage. They couldn't force anyone even to return a phone call.

In another conversation, McKinley's source told her that some
detectives believed the war room was simply a place from which
Hunter's people intended to steal information about the case. Though
the computers were protected by passwords, it was possible to get
around them. One detective wanted to store all the information on a
Zip drive and take it with him each time he left the war room.* The
officer said that Eller had decided not to share with Hunter's staff
some of the results of the DNA testing that were now coming back.

At times Carol McKinley felt as if she'd become a psychotherapist.
Her source needed to vent, and he needed someone who would listen.

---

*A removable computer disk, similar to a floppy disk, with the capacity to hold informa-
tion that would fill a hundred floppies.

Lou Smit was another problem, though the detective didn't reveal the reasons to McKinley. He wouldn't listen to them and had his own ideas—like his nutty stun-gun theory. Smit thought there was a strong possibility that an intruder had entered the house. He kept talking about the pieces of glass that had been found on top of the suitcase under the broken basement window, about the shoe imprint they'd found near JonBenét's body, and about the unidentified palm print on the wine cellar door. The police had learned that the imprint was from a Hi-Tec shoe. But whenever the police came up with a good idea—like the question of how a stranger could even find the light switch to the basement—Smit ignored it. In the detectives' eyes, he was old, out of touch. Smit kept saying to them, "I want you guys to prove it to me." It was irritating, and the detectives resented him.

On May 19, Suzanne Laurion, who had been on the job as Hunter's press representative for less than three weeks, wrote him a memo: "One of the roles of the media is to listen to, organize and direct the public's response to political actors (e.g., Koby and Hunter). Hence, we can view . . . commentaries from this weekend as important to our understanding of how the general public may be feeling. . . . This is the sort of thinking we could address in a piece on the prosecutor's ethical obligations to contain trial publicity, and our commitment to serve and preserve the criminal justice system."

She enclosed two articles as examples of what she meant:

ENOUGH IS ENOUGH

The new reward ad the Ramseys placed in Sunday's *Daily Camera* has exposed a level of incompetence in Alex Hunter's office that cannot, and should not, be tolerated by the people who elected him to protect our interests and, in this case, our children.

Sunday's ad requested that Boulderites call in any information they have about a well-dressed man who may have been seen talking to children around Christmas, the time of JonBenét's murder.

Now we're supposed to believe that, for all the D.A. knows, any well-dressed white guy talking to kids may be the actual murderer. If Hunter can't do better than that, then he needs to make the information he has public in hopes that someone else can solve the crime.

Or there is another scenario. The investigation is rolling along fine.

The cops are closely watching the prime suspects. And our kids are safe. If that's the case, Hunter's office should let the Ramseys, provided they're not the suspects, in on the news. That way John and Patsy could stop wasting money on ads.

If the Ramseys are the prime suspects, then Hunter's office should stop moonlighting as part of the Ramsey PR team. If Hunter believes that the Ramseys will one day be tried for JonBenét's death, then he should be smart enough to realize that giving them permission to inquire about mystery murderers in ads will greatly weaken his case at trial time.

Hunter has stated all along that he wants to remain "open minded" during this investigation. That's a good idea early on, but after five months of investigating it's absurd. At some point, presumably long before now, being open minded creates incredible opportunities for the defense team of whoever is eventually arrested.

—Editorial
Boulder Weekly, May 15, 1997

AT A STANDSTILL IN BOULDER

The JonBenét Ramsey murder investigation has been dragging on for almost five months, and beleaguered Boulder Police Chief Tom Koby says he doesn't expect an arrest for several more months—if then.

The DNA test results are back from a lab in Maryland, but Koby hinted they don't seem to offer a solution.

Meanwhile the victim's parents, whom the police concede are suspects, have bought a couple of ads in Boulder's *Daily Camera* soliciting the public's help in finding the killer. A $100,000 reward is offered for information leading to a conviction.

In the most recent ad, they asked for information regarding a man who is alleged to have approached young children in Boulder late last year. The implication is that JonBenét was the randomly selected victim of some pervert.

The suggestion of a specific alternative criminal at least muddies the water, and plants that crucial seed of doubt in the public mind.

It's not the first time that's happened in cases handled by Haddon, Morgan and Foreman, John Ramsey's law firm.

No wonder Koby and District Attorney Alex Hunter are proceeding cautiously. Among other reasons, they're up against the best and they know it.

—Editorial
Rocky Mountain News, May 19, 1997

★ ★ ★

Laurion told Hunter that "Koby's stock is plunging at the moment" and that his own image needed immediate rehabilitation. It would take about two weeks of hard work, but he'd be pleased with the results, she said. Laurion then listed for her boss the upcoming stories that the DA's office should be prepared to respond to:

Release of information in the autopsy

Fifth handwriting sample

Timetable for investigation of ransom note

Unsealing search warrants

Haddon wanting DNA evidence

Contents of DNA tests

Next meeting with Scheck and Lee

Next development on Elowsky

Laurion also told Hunter that his staff should give thought to how information should be released and the effect of releasing information. Her memo stated that the DA's office "needed to get comfortable with a system for information dissemination." The staff should consider whether information would harm the case if released, whether it would advance the case if released, and whether it was information the public had a right to know. She also pointed out that Hunter had to be concerned at all times with the effects of what he said on "police detectives working the case, Hunter's own office, an eventual jury pool, the general public, news reporters, leakers, the Ramsey camp, spectators-turned-actors, those who will judge the Hunter legacy and the Boulder County voters."

Until now, Hunter and his staff had merely been reacting to events, playing catch-up—and none too effectively—with the press. With Laurion on board, they finally had someone who not only saw their predicament clearly but could also plan ahead.

Meanwhile, Steve Thomas visited McGuckin Hardware, which John Ramsey—or someone impersonating him—had called in January. In the sporting goods department, Thomas found white nylon cord similar to the cord around JonBenét's neck. He bought four packages of

Coghlan's Cord, for $2.29 each. In addition, he found black duct tape with the brand name Suretape. Both items sold for the same price and came from the same department that appeared on Patsy Ramsey's December 1996 sales slips.

A week after Thomas made his purchases, Dave Williams, an investigator for the Ramseys, called Joanne Hanks at McGuckin and asked for itemized receipts of Patsy's December 2 and December 9 purchases, only to discover that the police had them. In Patsy's April 30 police interview, Thomas had asked her about the purchase of duct tape, and Williams was following up for his clients.

Now both the police and the Ramseys' investigators knew that the items could have been purchased by Patsy just weeks before JonBenét's murder.

The court's protection of the search warrants for the Ramsey house was due to expire Sunday, May 25. Hunter's office told Judge Diane MacDonald on May 22 that nothing had come to light to remove the Ramseys as suspects and that there was no "smoking gun," but his office still objected to the release of the warrants. "Damaging as any particular leaks may have been," Hunter's office argued, "it would be much more destructive to the investigation to release to the media, and through the media to the killer or killers, the sworn documents which present in such highly organized and formal form the information in the hands of the police and the thought processes underlying the investigation."

Hunter prevailed. "The court finds that there can be no more compelling governmental interest than the arrest and prosecution of her killer," Judge MacDonald said, and ordered the documents sealed for an additional 120 days, or until the time of an arrest.

On May 12, deputy county attorney Mason had asked Judge Glowinsky to extend her seal on the balance of the coroner's autopsy report. Mason argued that the case was active, still in the investigation stage, and that the report contained a lot the public didn't know—including the position of the body when found, how JonBenét was dressed, details about the wounds and injuries she'd suffered, and evidence that had been found at the crime scene. If the information was released, it would make it that much harder for the police to weigh the credibility of witnesses' statements. Detective Sgt. Wickman provided an affidavit to support the coroner's request.

Judge Glowinsky ruled on May 15 that all but six brief sections of the report would be released on May 21; the entire document, on August 20. On May 20 Mason appealed the ruling, and on June 2 the Colorado Court of Appeals rejected the appeal. However, the appeals court gave Mason time to file for another hearing of the issue. Eventually the court denied Mason the rehearing but allowed her to take her request to the Colorado Supreme Court, which ordered the seal on the balance of the coroner's report to remain in place, pending its decision on whether to hear her last-resort petition.

On May 28, Detectives Thomas and Gosage finished their investigation of who had called McGuckin in January to request copies of Patsy's bills. The detectives were told by an informant that the calls had been made by an employee of Touch Tone, Inc., who had impersonated John Ramsey. The police were told that the employee had photocopied Ramsey's signature for the faxed authorization he'd sent to the hardware store.

Touch Tone employed several "investigators." Some of them had obtained various records belonging to John, Patsy, and John Andrew Ramsey, including bank account signatures, bank statements, and credit card receipts. In addition, they had obtained telephone records and banking information regarding the Ramseys' housekeeper, Linda Hoffmann-Pugh. Touch Tone employees had also obtained the names, addresses, home phone numbers, and toll records of the Boulder detectives working the Ramsey case.

The informant was an investigator for Touch Tone. He told the police it was common practice at the company to assume the identity of the person being investigated, which made it easier to obtain copies of personal and confidential records.

On May 29, Judge Morris Sandstead signed Detective Thomas's request to search the offices of Touch Tone. There the police found personal records relating not only to the Ramseys but to Jay Elowsky; to John Ramsey's first wife, Lucinda; and even to the Ramseys' chief investigator, Ellis Armstead. No one was ever prosecuted, for fear that rights to discovery in a court trial would force the DA's office to turn over a large part of the police file in the Ramsey case.

What the police didn't know was that Touch Tone's services had been paid for by a private investigator in California, who in turn had been retained by a tabloid TV program.

★ ★ ★

Also on May 29, Ann Louise Bardach, known for her investigative reporting, called Suzanne Laurion to introduce herself. She was coming to town to do a ten-thousand-word article for *Vanity Fair* on "this dreadful story," she said. Laurion called back an hour later and said that Hunter would meet with Bardach for a few minutes on June 2.

During the last week of May, Hunter, DeMuth, Ainsworth, Smit, and Detectives Trujillo, Harmer, Thomas, and Gosage met with Dr. Henry Lee to review a list of items that would need additional attention if the Ramseys' house were ever searched again. Lee also thought it was important to gauge the timing of JonBenét's head injury and strangulation and the injury to her hymen, to learn whether it had occurred before or after the blow to her head. Lee said that forensic pathologists should be consulted and recommended several.

By now the police were receiving forensic test results almost daily but withholding some of them from Hunter's office for fear of leaks to the Ramseys or the media. Over four dozen people had given blood, hair, and handwriting samples, all of which were tested, but none of them matched the forensic evidence from the crime scene.

Several pieces of evidence matched John and Patsy's samples, but that was logical and to be expected, since they lived in the house and had constant, lengthy contact with their daughter. Without semen or some other hard evidence, the incest theory went nowhere. A careful review of Dr. Beuf's medical records had given no indication of prior abuse. Nor could the police find any indication of prior suspicious behavior on the part of JonBenét's parents.

The police had hung their hat on the Ramseys as culprits, but they were still unable to provide the DA's office with enough evidence to warrant an arrest. Neither Alex Hunter nor the police were ready to admit that the case was unsolvable, however. Knowing that the ransom note was the best piece of evidence they had, Hunter hoped that the CBI's handwriting experts would find something solid, but Chet Ubowski would not take the leap and say that Patsy had written the note. The CBI expert refused to tailor his conclusions to the needs of the police and the DA.

To say that Patsy hadn't been excluded as the author of the note was only "soft evidence," as Hunter called it, and it might not be enough to charge her as an accessory. In addition, the DA believed that under

Colorado law an accessory could be charged only when a principal was charged.* Harder evidence would be needed to charge a perpetrator.

Hunter called his old friend Bob Kupperman, formerly of the Institute for Strategic and International Studies, who recommended using a psychological linguist, Donald Foster, a professor of dramatic literature at Vassar. Foster studied grammar, syntax, punctuation, style, and vocabulary to track down the authors of texts. He had accurately identified for the FBI source material for parts of Theodore Kaczynski's Unabomber manifesto. He had also identified the writer Joe Klein as the anonymous author of the novel *Primary Colors* and had identified William Shakespeare as the author of a previously anonymous Elizabethan funeral eulogy.

Hunter thought that Foster might be helpful in the Ramsey case. Just before the July Fourth weekend, he called Foster, who told the DA that he had once written a letter to Patsy Ramsey and another to her son, John Andrew, while following the case on the Internet. He said he had wanted to lend them some support. Hunter saw no conflict of interest.

Foster agreed to analyze the ransom note for the DA's office. He would also be sent Janet McReynolds's play *Hey, Rube*, Christmas letters and articles written by both Janet and Bill McReynolds, some of Patsy Ramsey's writings, and transcripts of the Ramseys' January 1 and May 1 press conferences. Not long after hiring Foster, Hunter said that "this case will come down to linguistics."

U.S. district judge Richard Matsch, who was presiding over the first Oklahoma city bombing trial at the time, had noted that handwriting analysis was not a science and wasn't subject to peer review and was therefore not verifiable. But the Colorado state courts felt differently. In many cases, state judges had allowed handwriting experts to testify about comparisons and to draw conclusions from them.

For months the Boulder police had been collecting Patsy's handwriting samples: beauty-pageant entry forms, school documents, applications, and business letters. They had recently visited the offices of Hayes Micro Computer in Norcross, Georgia, where Patsy had worked before marrying John. There they found more handwriting samples. This material was relevant for handwriting analysis but was of

---

*This is not Colorado law. The successful prosecution of an accessory does not require the charging of a principal. *Howard* v. *People*, 51 P.2d 594 (1935); *Britto* v. *People*, 497 P 2d 325 (1972).

limited value to Donald Foster. He needed lengthy texts and examples of Patsy's prepared and extemporaneous speeches. These would take time to find and even longer to analyze.

If the CBI were to state definitively that Patsy had written the note and Foster were to confirm that finding, Hunter would have something. He worried, however, that even with such positive findings, his staff might be unable to arrest Patsy. Linguistic analysis had never been used by experts in Colorado courts, so there was a question about whether Foster's findings would be admissible. The professor had never before testified in a criminal trial.

Meanwhile, Eller and his detectives were slowly coming to the realization that without a break in the case, Hunter would not arrest the Ramseys. One detective was sure that if the DA had charged them earlier, Patsy would have broken down and confessed. When that didn't happen, he suggested to his superiors that a grand jury be used to compel the Ramseys to talk. Hunter rejected the idea, saying it was premature. When immunity was discussed, he said he didn't want to give someone protection in exchange for testifying. Most of Eller's detectives believed that the moment had been lost forever. They didn't much care if the Ramseys suffered the shame of public condemnation for the rest of their lives.

Bill Wise, like the detectives, had been sure earlier in the year that the Ramseys were guilty. But that was before the alleged semen turned out to be something else. By May 1997 he was far less sure that a case against them could be proved. Wise hadn't lost hope entirely, but as his certainty diminished, he continued to think that if the Ramseys had killed their daughter, they deserved to suffer.

PART THREE

Stories within Stories

1

Late in the morning of Monday, June 2, Suzanne Laurion greeted Ann Bardach of *Vanity Fair* and escorted her to Alex Hunter's private office, where the journalist and the DA were scheduled for a fifteen-minute interview. Sitting down in one of the four old leather chairs that encircled a wood table, Bardach noticed a pencil sketch of President Kennedy hanging above Hunter's antique rolltop desk. Sitting atop the desk was a black three-ring binder, on its cover a color photograph of JonBenét Ramsey.

Bardach's fifteen minutes of interview time became half an hour before Hunter said they'd have to take a break. Oklahoma City bombing suspect Timothy McVeigh's verdict was to be announced. At 1:15 P.M. Hunter turned on his TV. Phil Miller, Jim Atherton, Pete Hofstrom, Susan Ingraham, Trip DeMuth, Bill Nagel, and several other staff members came in to watch. After it was announced that McVeigh was found guilty of the bombing and the murder of eight federal agents, Bardach stayed in Hunter's office and soaked up the conversation.

In his interview, Hunter had told her his impressions of the Ramseys and their attorneys and referred to John Ramsey as "Ice Man." When the DA talked about his team of investigators, he called Lou Smit "the ace" and "the fox." By the time she left the Justice Center, Bardach had over two hours' worth of tape-recorded material. A few days later, she called the DA's office with follow-up questions. When Hunter heard them, he replied that the statements Bardach was referring to had been given "off the record" and therefore didn't require a response. Afterward, Suzanne Laurion tried to clarify with Bardach which parts of her conversation with Hunter were off the record.

Bardach argued that her tape recorder offered evidence of what was "on the record."

By then, Bardach had already spoken with several friends and neighbors of the Ramseys. She had shown up at John and Barbara Fernie's house uninvited. John Fernie would later tell a reporter covering the story that when he and his wife arrived home, Bardach was waiting for them. When they refused her an interview, she became pushy, said Fernie.

Not everyone reacted to the journalist the same way, however. In time, she would meet with two police detectives to hear the cops' side of the story. It's possible that after all those months of talking to local media and the tabloids, the police and Alex Hunter both talked freely to Bardach because they felt they had reached the epitome of celebrity when this national publication sought them out.

Meanwhile, Bardach kept in touch with Suzanne Laurion. "The Ramseys are in a full-court campaign; they're doing a spin on Alex too," the journalist told Hunter's press rep. The DA should know about it, she added. Another time, she asked Laurion, "What is wrong with this town? In any other city, the Ramseys would have been behind bars long ago." Bill Wise was concerned because he had heard that Bardach was looking for dirt on Hunter and his staff.

At the end of June, Bardach asked for another interview with Hunter. She told Laurion she had conducted over a hundred interviews. She said there was some "serious stuff" being leveled against Hofstrom and Hunter and that most of it was coming from Hunter's usual allies. Hunter said that any such accusations were ludicrous; he had full confidence in the way his staff was handling the case. Laurion tried to get Bardach to submit her follow-up questions in writing, since the DA refused another interview.

Laurion became concerned that Hunter and his staff didn't understand the distinction between "on the record" and "off the record." She could see disaster looming on the horizon with *Vanity Fair*, and hoping to avoid further catastrophes, she sent a memo to Hunter, Wise, and Phil Miller. She warned them that not all journalists play by the rules, that not all journalists clarify the rules of an interview in advance—because that sort of talk makes sources nervous—and that some journalists are also careless about protecting their sources, even in off-the-record situations. "When they use what source #1 says to get the information from source #2," Laurion noted in her memo, "they 'inadvertently' reveal the identity of source #1 to source #2." The bottom line, she said, was that the DA's name might not show up in print or on TV, but it almost certainly would show up on the notepad of some source #2. Her memo continued:

> When I was a reporter, I rarely went off the record because most of my sources loved to talk and they would eventually blab stuff to me anyway . . . ON THE RECORD.
>
> Now that I'm working this case, I never go off the record. No way! As author/journalist Jay Crouse says, "Off the record conferences are subterfuges which stifle the voice of the press and deprive the people of their right to know."

The warning was tactful but plain. Laurion also sent Hunter and his staff the published definitions of *on the record, off the record, not for attribution, background,* and *deep background.*

The same day Hunter met with Bardach, June 2, Frank Coffman, a local writer and new friend of Jeff Shapiro's, dropped by the DA's office to leave a note for Lou Smit. Coffman was surprised when Smit came out to the reception area and suggested they have a chat. Over coffee at the Canyon Café in the Justice Center, Coffman told Smit he'd heard a rumor that the acronym SBTC, which had been mentioned in the ransom note, might stand for "saved by the cross."

The detective said he had to admit that there were "lots of wild things in this case." He asked if Coffman knew what movies had been playing in Boulder right before JonBenét was murdered.

Ransom was one, Coffman said.

"Well, what do you think that means?" Smit asked.

"Could JonBenét's death have been premeditated?"

"You're the one who used the word premeditated," Smit answered—as if confirming that he too thought the murder had been planned.

"This guy's going to be caught," Smit added.

That was odd, Coffman thought. The police didn't have to catch John or Patsy Ramsey—all they had to do was arrest or indict them. Coffman surmised that Smit was exploring an intruder theory.

"I've studied the whole thing, I've read everything," Smit said in a matter-of-fact—and somewhat superior—way. "Other people have a piece of the picture. I have all the information right up here," he said, pointing to his head.

Some weeks later, Coffman met Steve Thomas for the first time at police headquarters. "Do you think the crime was premeditated?" he asked the detective.

Thomas assumed that Coffman was referring to an intruder theory.

"That's not the way we think. That sounds like Lou Smit," he replied. "They're going by a different theory over there."

Smit and Steve Ainsworth were still investigating the possible use of a stun gun. By now they had learned that Air Tasers were sold locally by Boulder Security, and that another stun gun, called the Muscle Man, had the same characteristics as the Air Taser.

When they had gathered sufficient information, Ainsworth, Pete Hofstrom, Trip DeMuth, and Detective Sgt. Wickman met with the coroner, John Meyer. After reviewing the photos and this new information, Meyer concluded that the injuries on JonBenét's face and back were, in fact, consistent with those produced by a stun gun.

Soon after, Ainsworth learned of a 1988 Larimer County murder in which a stun gun had been used on a thirteen-month-old girl, Michaela Hughes, who had been sexually assaulted and killed. Ainsworth met with Dr. Robert Deters, the pathologist on the case, and showed him the autopsy photos of JonBenét. Deters agreed that the marks were consistent with a stun-gun injury, but he didn't think the body had to be exhumed. Nothing more would be learned by examining the skin tissue. Ainsworth asked Deters if a child of six would be immobilized by a stun-gun's electrical shock. Not only would the child be paralyzed, the coroner said, but she would have been unable to scream. That raised the question of whether JonBenét had screamed before the stun gun was used on her—if one was used.

In her June 3 column, Cindy Adams of the *New York Post* wrote that Commander Eller had applied for the job of police chief in Cocoa Beach, Florida. The next day, Charlie Brennan of the *Rocky Mountain News* obtained a copy of Eller's résumé from Florida. Brennan told Bill Wise that he had Eller's curriculum vita, and Wise asked for a copy. Since Hunter's staff could also obtain the document, Brennan saw no reason not to fax him a copy.

A few days later, Hunter spoke to Brennan. "Charlie, you might want to do a little digging into the time Eller spent with the community policing consortium," Hunter said. Brennan could tell that the DA was choosing his words carefully. "Apparently things didn't go so well for him there," Hunter told the reporter. "There might have been a charge of sexual harassment, or something to that effect."

On page four of Eller's résumé, it said that he had been a "loaned executive" from January to August 1995, serving as director of the Colorado Consortium of Community Policing.

Brennan decided to look into the matter. The media were well aware of the tensions between the DA's office and the police, and Brennan knew that this story would serve Hunter's purpose of discrediting Eller. Brennan had no interest in helping Hunter, but a charge of harassment against Eller would be legitimate news.

Brennan soon learned that indeed Eller had been loaned out to the community policing consortium for a year and that he had returned to the Boulder PD earlier than expected. Those Brennan spoke to praised Eller for the most part. A few confided that there may have been "personality conflicts" resulting in Eller's early departure from the consortium. Brennan could find no evidence of the charge and dropped the story. John Eller didn't get the job in Cocoa Beach.

If Hunter wasn't happy with Eller, Pete Hofstrom wasn't any happier with Tom Wickman, who was running the investigation for the commander. Hofstrom suspected that the police were not sharing all their information with the DA's office. He felt that Wickman hadn't been candid with him about whether a particular DNA report had been received. Hunter confronted Koby about it, and the chief admitted that his detectives were withholding information. Koby seemed to be more upset that Wickman had not been forthcoming than that Hofstrom had been deceived.

Hofstrom was also angry that the police still hadn't given him a printout of all the physical evidence. Without such a list, Smit and Ainsworth couldn't complete the organization of the files they had been hired to do. The two detectives were reduced to rechecking the police reports and pursuing a few independent leads. Their time and skill were being wasted.

★ ★ ★

BOULDER PROSECUTOR OUT OF LOOP

Police detectives investigating the murder of JonBenét Ramsey refuse to share the results of DNA analysis with the district attorney's office....Test results from Cellmark Diagnostics Laboratory, received by Boulder detectives May 13, remain a secret to Boulder County District Attorney Alex Hunter and his staff.

The relationship between the two offices has been stormy at several points in the Ramsey case.

— Charlie Brennan and Kevin McCullen
Rocky Mountain News, June 7, 1997

After the *Rocky Mountain News* published "Boulder Prosecutor Out of Loop," Hunter called Jeff Shapiro from his car phone. The headline, not the facts of the story, seemed to have embarrassed the DA.

"God, I hate that fucker," Hunter said. He meant John Eller, who was probably responsible for holding back the DNA results.

"Should we look into him?" I asked.

"Yeah, I think so," Hunter answered. "I think it's his turn"—meaning that Eller should get ripped in the tabloids.

"I can get you Eller's résumé," Hunter told me, "and I can get you the letter Larry Mason's attorney just wrote to the Boulder PD. He's suing Eller."

Hunter suggested we meet in his office. Later in the day, he started the conversation by discussing different ways I could dig up dirt on Eller. He handed me Eller's résumé from his recent job application in Florida and pointed to something on the fourth page.

"I think if you look far enough, you may find a sexual harassment charge somewhere here."

"Really," I said.

"When do you think this could come out?" Hunter asked. "I hate that fucker!"

We both started to laugh.

In my mind, Eller was the bad guy. He's the asshole. Then it hit me. I was reacting to Hunter's perception of Eller. Hunter said the police detectives were the good guys and Eller was the problem.

I asked him about Eller's claims that Larry Mason had leaked information to the media.

"It was someone in Bryan Morgan's office who really leaked that, not Larry Mason," Hunter said.

"What was leaked?" I asked.

Alex picked up the phone and said he was calling Bryan Morgan to get the facts.

"Did you ever dig that up for me?" Hunter asked Morgan a moment later.

I couldn't believe what I was seeing. The DA was calling Ramsey's criminal defense lawyer right in front of me to get information I had asked for.

I mean, would Chris Darden call Johnnie Cochran and say, "Did you check on that date I need for this Enquirer *guy?"*

It was bizarre.

— Jeff Shapiro

During the second week in June, Jeff Shapiro visited the Boulder public library to research garrotes. He learned that the Spanish conquistadors who colonized the Philippines had executed native revolutionaries by strangling them with a garrote in the same manner the media believed JonBenét had been murdered. Shapiro discovered that the garrote became the symbol of the Philippine revolution of 1872 and that every Filipino schoolchild learned that the revolutionaries had been garroted to death in public. José Rizal, who inspired the revolution, was himself sentenced to death on December 26, the same day of the year that JonBenét Ramsey died.

I knew John Ramsey had been stationed at Subic Bay in the Philippines, and he must have known about the role garroting played in the history of the islands.

I started to freak out.

I called Steve Thomas. Soon after that, he and Detective Jane Harmer saw me. I read them the material about the Philippines.

"I really want to help," I told Thomas.

"It seems like you've got the right intentions," Thomas said. "You care about this little girl—you seem to want justice for JonBenét. I'm committed to that, and as long as you are too, I'll be more than happy to continue these conversations."

I looked into Thomas's eyes and knew I was doing something right. That was when I started to look up to him like a big brother.

Several days after I met with Thomas and Harmer, Pam Griffin told Frank Coffman that Patsy Ramsey wrote the words Mr. and Mrs. Ramsey on the same lined pad that the ransom note was written on. Pam said Patsy had told her that it was the beginning of an invitation she was writing: "Mr. and Mrs. Ramsey . . . invite you . . ." By then there was a rumor that the cops believed this writing was a false start on the ransom note. If what Pam said was true, it was important to the police.

Moments after I heard what Coffman had learned, I left a message for Thomas on his voice mail. He called me back from his car, and I told him what Coffman had learned. I literally heard Thomas hit the brakes.

"Jeff, that's no fuckin' invitation."

The next day, the police asked Coffman and me to come down to headquarters so that Coffman could get Griffin on the phone and have her restate what she'd said. The police would tape-record the conversation. At first all we got was Pam's answering machine.

While we were hanging around, Coffman told Thomas that I was having conversations with Alex Hunter and that he was confiding in me. I'd told that to Coffman, but I would never have wanted the police to know—as I would never want Hunter to know I was talking to Thomas.

A moment later, Thomas took me with him into a small interview room. Before he said a word, I started to talk.

"Can we talk off the record?" I asked.

"OK."

I figured that if I didn't make a deal with Thomas right then and there, he'd go straight to Eller, tell him what Coffman had said, and that it would be used against Hunter. For sure I would be fucked.

"Nothing we talk about leaves this room," I said to Thomas.

Again he said, "OK."

"I spend a great deal of time with Hunter," I said, "like four fuckin' hours a day—sometimes in his office and sometimes on the phone. I've learned a lot."

Thomas just listened for a while. Then he asked if I knew Trip DeMuth or Pete Hofstrom. I told him I didn't even know who else worked in the DA's office.

"You really know Hunter?" Thomas continued. "I can't even talk to him. How can you?"

"Steve, all I can tell you is he likes me a lot."

"Jeff, if you've got Hunter's ear," he said, "do us both a favor—get him off the intruder path."

"I'll try," I told Thomas.

"We've got more evidence in here to nail these people to the wall right now," Thomas said, "and Hunter's office is looking for intruders."

Finally we reached Pam Griffin. As the police listened in on her conversation with Coffman, she told him it was Alex Hunter who, in a phone conversation with her, had suggested that the words Mr. and Mrs. Ramsey might be the beginning of an invitation.

— Jeff Shapiro

CITY OF BOULDER   FOR IMMEDIATE RELEASE
NEWS   JUNE 12, 1997

BOULDER POLICE ASK FOR
INVESTIGATION OF POSSIBLE THEFT
OF COMPUTER DOCUMENTS

Boulder Police have asked for an investigation by the Colorado Bureau of Investigation into a possible theft of computer documents from the police department computer located in the combined offices of the Boulder County District Attorney and the Boulder Police Department. This is the "war room" used by investigators assigned to the Jon-Benét Ramsey murder.

The police department has confirmed that someone gained access to a computer containing Ramsey case information at approximately 1 A.M. on Saturday, June 7.

— Boulder Police Department Press Release

When Carol McKinley read the police department's press release, she paged her police source, who told her the break-in was proof that Hunter's office was after the material in the police files. Tom Trujillo had turned on the computer in the war room, and when the start-up program didn't ask for his six-character password, he knew the computer had been tampered with. The room was supposed to be secure, yet the system date in the computer suggested that a break-in had taken place at about 1:00 A.M. on June 7.

Later that afternoon, McKinley spoke to Hunter. He was furious because Eller had personally accused him of the crime. "I think you or Bill Wise broke into the war room," Eller had said to him. "And a Zip drive is also missing." According to Hunter, Eller had acted like a raving maniac when the two men met behind the Justice Center near Boulder Creek.

Carl Whiteside, the CBI director, was attending a meeting in Breckenridge when the Boulder PD's press release was issued. When Whiteside was told about Eller's statement, he asked to meet with the commander. Whiteside worried that his agency would be dragged into the ongoing battle between Hunter and Eller.

"I don't know who exactly did it," Eller told Whiteside the next day, "but just look into it." Whiteside could see that Eller wanted to implicate the DA's office.

The computer in question was taken to the CBI. Whiteside asked Chuck Davis, his computer expert, to handle the technical side of the investigation. Whiteside didn't know at the time that two days earlier, Detective Sgt. Wickman had asked Davis to help with a computer that the Boulder police thought someone had broken into. When he arrived, Davis discovered that the police hadn't fingerprinted the computer, which by then had been handled by a half-dozen people without the precaution of wearing gloves.

Mark Wilson, head of the CBI's criminal investigation unit, and five investigators were assigned to the case. Hofstrom, Smit, Ainsworth, DeMuth, Wickman, Thomas, Harmer, Trujillo, and Gosage, all of whom had access to the war room, were interviewed. So were Hunter and Wise, though neither of them had access cards. Everyone provided the CBI with an alibi for 1:00 A.M. on June 7. Then Trujillo found the missing Zip drive in the trunk of his car.

The CBI team fingerprinted the entire war room and checked the records of the computer-controlled locks: there had been no entry at or about 1:00 A.M. on June 7. They examined the ceiling, the floor, the walls, the dust patterns, and anything else that might give them a clue. They concluded that only a ghost could have entered the room without proper access.

Meanwhile, Davis's investigation of the Compaq computer revealed that it had no modem or network connection. Only one fingerprint was found inside the unit, in a region where only an assembly-line worker could have touched it during the manufacturing process. Davis knew it was possible for someone to take the unit apart and pull out the plastic jumper cable beneath the BIOS chip that stores the password and completes the start-up circuit, and that would have erased the password. But Davis assumed that if someone knew enough to pull the jumper cable, he'd also be smart enough to enter a fake password and cover his tracks. Of course, a professional could have done the job and tried to make it look as if an amateur had done it.

Davis discovered that the computer's internal clock and calendar didn't work properly. The clock was losing almost ten minutes every two and a half hours. The next time he checked, it lost fifteen minutes in three hours. There was no discernable pattern to the time loss, but he discovered that when the chip was cleared, it didn't always reset to 00:00 hours, January 1, 1980, as it was supposed to.

Since the clock was malfunctioning, the time of the alleged break-in—1:00 A.M. on Saturday—was meaningless and therefore useless in the investigation.

Davis believed that the computer was defective. He tested another computer of the same model, purchased and installed in Boulder at the same time, and it turned out to have the same clock and chip problems.

The CBI concluded that the alleged break-in never happened. There had simply been an equipment failure. When Eller, Hunter, and Koby met with Davis and Mark Wilson, Davis explained that there had been no breach of security.

The next day, Hunter extracted a promise from Koby that Hunter and Wise would receive a letter of apology from Eller for his false accusations. But when the detectives working the Ramsey case heard about Koby's promise, they were outraged about what they felt was another instance of their chief not backing them. Eller never sent the letter.

Bill Wise was astounded at the level of distrust that Eller and the detectives had developed. He considered the majority of them level-headed, but now if something went wrong, Hunter was the easy target.

Wise asked himself, What was happening to Boulder?

Steve Thomas called me one evening. I couldn't tell if he'd had a beer or two.

"Jeff, I'm ready to fuckin' throw down my badge. I'll go on national TV, I'll go back to mowing fuckin' lawns if I have to, to get justice for this little girl."

That's when I realized that Thomas, who to me represented someone strong, had the courage to express his deep emotions.

"God chooses a path for all of us," I answered. "I think mine has been chosen. That's why I'm here to help."

"We can do this together," Thomas replied. "You have a role in this. Your relationship with Hunter is important—you don't understand how important." Then he added, "We do God's work."

That night, I understood that Thomas and I would devote our lives to getting justice for JonBenét.

Later that night I was having dinner with Frank Coffman when I got a page from a number I didn't recognize.

"Jeff, I'm kind of nervous," Steve Thomas said when I returned his page. "Are you going to keep it all cool?" I assured him I would. Then he gave me his home number.

We started talking at night. He'd tell me stuff about when he was a narc cop. We discussed the Simpson case. We talked about our love of cars. I told him I drove around just looking for a used Camaro. He liked Camaros too.

— Jeff Shapiro

2

Ever since JonBenét's murder, Peter Boyles, a top morning radio talk-show host in Denver, had been critical of the investigation. Bill Wise paid close attention to Boyles each morning as he drove the 26 miles from his home in Denver to the Justice Center. Most of the time, Boyles took shots at the police and at the *Daily Camera*, comparing it to *Pravda*. He often suggested that the Ramseys had killed their daughter. Then, as Chuck Green's columns in *The Denver Post* became more strident against Hunter in March and April, Boyles, a friend of Green's, joined in the attack on the DA's office. Now, in June, Boyles commented on the police withholding evidence from Hunter's office and on the computer break-in.

Listening in, Wise thought that much of Boyles's commentary was speculative—probably based on sources not connected with the investigation. Hunter and Wise felt that Boyles was farther off base than most reporters. He made it sound as if Hofstrom had chatted over coffee with Patsy Ramsey in his kitchen when she gave her second handwriting sample at his house—which at the time was neutral territory. Chuck Green was almost as bad. In one of his columns, Wise found what he considered to be seven major inaccuracies.

Wise talked to Hunter, who decided he wanted to put a stop to the flow of inaccurate information about his office. Hunter decided Green should be contacted first, then Boyles. Wise was apprehensive, afraid that Green would compound the problem by writing a column about Hunter's complaints. Nevertheless, he left a voice mail message for Green, saying he'd like to sit down with him—not to give new information, but to correct some misinformation.

Green not only returned his call, he listened intently. Green had reported that the Ramseys were "allowed" to leave Boulder after Jon-Benét's body was found. Wise said that was wrong. They had not been charged with any crime, so they were free to travel at will. Green had also written that the "police and prosecutors" had given the Ramseys written questions prior to their face-to-face interviews on April 30. Wrong again, Wise said. Hunter's office had not directed the police to submit the questions in January, and no questions had been submitted by anyone in April. Only the Ramseys' statements from police reports, written just before and just after the body was found, had been given to the Ramseys' attorneys. Green had also published that the DA's office provided the Ramseys with a copy of the ransom note. Wrong again. The cops had done that, not Hunter's office. Green's claim that the police had briefed the Ramseys on the details of the autopsy was also wrong. In fact, the coroner's office had given them an oral report, which is what any parent of a dead child would get. Wise's list went on and on.

Shortly afterward, Green visited Hunter in his office. The meeting went well, and as the months passed, they talked more and more. Their occasional meetings would last for an hour or so. Green gave his direct phone numbers to both Wise and Hunter and agreed to contact them more often when checking the accuracy of his columns.

The following month, Wise and his wife, Diane, bumped into Boyles and his wife, Kathleen, at the July Fourth Cherry Creek Arts Festival. Wise made Boyles the same offer he'd made to Green. Boyles agreed to listen to what Wise had to say. In the coming months, the two couples met for dinner and became friends. Afterward, Boyles's coverage of Hunter's office became far less aggressive. Wise told a reporter covering the story that he hadn't tried to put Boyles and Green in his pocket. All he'd wanted to do was curtail the unwarranted criticism of the DA's office. One writer who met with Hunter felt that the DA wanted to be portrayed as a guy on a white horse defending justice.

CITY OF BOULDER   FOR IMMEDIATE RELEASE
NEWS   JUNE 17, 1997

Members of the Boulder Police Benefit Association executive board met on Monday, June 16, with Boulder Police Chief Tom Koby to discuss issues raised during the membership's recent vote of no confidence. A list of four general concerns were presented to Chief Koby.

Leadership/management issues

Direction and philosophy of the Boulder Police Department

Boulder Regional Communication Center issues

Hiring/promotion policies

The BPBA executive board and Chief Koby agreed to additional meetings to be held throughout July.

— Boulder Police Benefit Association Press Release

Sheriff Epp didn't like the union's press release, especially because it was issued on city letterhead. That same week, Epp asked Steve Ainsworth, who had been working with Hunter's people for just over three months, to brief him on the status of the Ramsey case. Ainsworth told his boss that Koby continued to insist Eller was the right man for the job. Yet Eller hadn't assigned anyone in the police department to read the entire investigation file, Ainsworth said. How do you run a case you haven't read? he wanted to know. At least Hunter had instructed Trip DeMuth, Lou Smit, and himself to read everything they'd been given by the police. Also, the police refused to seriously consider any suspects besides the Ramseys. All he and Smit could do was run down possible suspects the police had missed or discarded, because Hunter had guaranteed

Koby that he and Smit wouldn't backseat-drive the police investigation. The only real lead they'd uncovered so far was the stun gun.

Epp became more and more frustrated as he listened to Ainsworth, and he assumed he was no different from the majority of Boulder's taxpayers on that score. Eventually, Epp knew, the union would force Koby out of his job, especially now that city manager Tim Honey had left. Epp began to hear from his officers that Koby was being called Dead Man Walking. It was a cruel but accurate description.

Epp didn't know what to do.

No matter which direction the police went in the Ramsey case, Alex Hunter and Pete Hofstrom told their staff that they themselves had to consider every possibility in the case. It wasn't likely that John and Patsy weren't involved, but it was still possible.

Lou Smit always found it useful to reread the police files. He was getting an overview of the case that no one else had. His partner in that was Trip DeMuth, who, like Smit, read every document as they cross-indexed the files with the help of a new computer program. Working side by side, the two men bonded. Smit admired DeMuth for his objectivity and fairness, and DeMuth looked upon Smit's experience as an invaluable tool.

Meanwhile, Steve Ainsworth met with Detective Jane Harmer to discuss several possible suspects the police might want to look at again. The Ramseys' gardener, Brian Scott, came up. Detective Arndt had interviewed him in February, but she was no longer working on the case. Ainsworth thought Scott's alibi should be rechecked and that he might be able to describe the condition of the grate covering the broken basement window. Harmer reinterviewed Scott, showing him two photographs taken just after the murder. One was of a bushel basket with some weeds in it, and the other was of the window grate. To the police, the ground cover around the grate looked as if it had been disturbed—perhaps because the grate was lifted up. Looking at the photographs, Scott said it looked as if the ground cover had grown underneath the grate, which indicated that it had been lifted, but he couldn't tell when. It could have been in September-October, when Ramsey said he entered the house by that broken window, or as late as December, when JonBenét was murdered.

After Harmer left, Scott remembered an encounter with Patsy that he hadn't mentioned.

★ ★ ★

I remember Patsy running out of the house, outraged at what had happened. It was October 3, 1995. O. J. Simpson had been acquitted. And I just happened to be there. You could see she was upset over it.

"He's getting away with murder."

I thought to myself, He could be innocent. He's been acquitted.

"It's a bad system, full of flaws," was what she was saying. It seemed to her he was getting away with it because he had money.

— Brian Scott

Two weeks later, Harmer spoke to Scott's girlfriend, Ann Preston, to reconfirm when Scott had left her place on Christmas night. She said it was around 12:30 A.M. Scott's saliva, hair, and handwriting samples would have to be analyzed before he was cleared.

On June 24, the *Globe* quoted sources who said that the garrote used to kill JonBenét was fashioned with a "makeshift paint stirrer left over from decorating" the house and that specks of color on the stick matched paint cans found in the basement. MURDER WEAPON LINKED TO MOM AND DAD, the tabloid's headline blared.

That same day, Paula Woodward, an investigative reporter for KUSA, NBC's Denver affiliate, was standing in line at a Boulder grocery store when she overheard a casual conversation between a customer and the checkout clerk. Fearing she might be recognized, Woodward turned her face away.

The customer told her friend that the Boulder police had visited Rev. Hoverstock to clarify the meaning of several passages in Psalm 118.

That evening Woodward called two sources she had cultivated during the investigation. One of them, an attorney for the Ramseys, told her that they had already considered Psalm 118 because of the $118,000 ransom demand. They had also discovered a passage in verse 27: "God is the Lord, which hath shewed us light: bind the sacrifice with cords, even unto the horns of the altar." Then Woodward's police source confirmed that the detectives had visited Hoverstock. What the source did not reveal was that they had found John Ramsey's Bible open to Psalm 118 during their initial search of the house beginning December 26.

The next day, Woodward aired her scoop that the police were investigating a link between the passage in Psalm 118 and the murder of JonBenét. The morning after Jeff Shapiro heard the news broadcast, he went down to the TV studio and paid for a videotape copy of Woodward's report. Then he called Frank Coffman.

"Turn to Psalm 118 in your Bible," Shapiro said.

Coffman read verse 27 in his King James version: "Bind the sacrifice with cords, even unto the horns of the altar."

"That's interesting," Coffman said, "but you need to find something that Patsy once said or some book she read in order for this to mean anything."

That afternoon, Shapiro was struck by something he had heard from the Ramseys' friend Judith Phillips. Several years earlier, in an interview in *Colorado Woman News*, Patsy had mentioned reading and relying on a book called *Healed of Cancer*. In that book, the author, Dodie Osteen, refers to Psalm 118, but to verse 17, not 27: "I shall not die, but live, and declare the works of the Lord."

Shapiro wrote a story for the following week's edition of the *Globe*.

One week later, Charlie Brennan heard from a colleague about the *Globe* story linking the ransom note to Psalm 118. In Brennan's *Rocky Mountain News* story, published on July 8, the day after Shapiro's *Globe* story hit the supermarket stands, he reported that "a confidante of Pasty Ramsey reportedly told the *Globe* that 'Patsy didn't let a day go by without reading (Osteen's) book, and she took Psalm 118 to heart, using it as a force to help her beat the cancer.'" The next day, Brennan reported the missing link that Paula Woodward's source had not revealed to her: in the Ramsey's house the police had found a Bible opened to Psalm 118. What Brennan didn't know was that it was on John Ramsey's desk.

DR. HENRY LEE: Well, to solve a case like building a table. A table has four legs. You need good investigation—good investigation team. You need good forensic evidence. In addition, you need witnesses and public support. Right this moment you don't have the four legs yet.

LARRY KING: How many legs of the table do we have?

DR. HENRY LEE: So far, I would say I have only one and a half, maybe.

—*Larry King Live*, June 26, 1997

★ ★ ★

On Monday morning, June 30, the police searched the Ramseys' fifteen-room house yet again. The couple had signed their consent on June 13. Jeff Shapiro was one of the few members of the press who showed up.

Pete Hofstrom, Trip DeMuth, Lou Smit, and Rob Pudim, an architectural draftsman, were the first to arrive from the DA's office. Joe Clayton, a criminologist from the CBI, arrived soon afterward. Steve Thomas pulled up in a Blue GT Mustang, wearing overalls and a dust mask. Gosage and several other officers soon followed. Before long, plumbers arrived to remove the boiler from the basement. The police used fiber-optic technology to look behind walls and inside the crawl spaces. They were looking for the roll of duct tape and the remainder of the cord, but found nothing. Reporters saw Detective Tom Trujillo attempt to climb through the broken basement window. Steve Ainsworth arrived to collect more fibers to compare with those found on JonBenét's body. If fibers had been transferred from any upstairs room to the wine cellar, the police would know where JonBenét might have been before her death or where the killer had been before the murder.

Jeff Shapiro was soon bored and left to visit Hunter at the Justice Center. The DA told Shapiro that the cops were planning to knock down a basement wall. "They're looking for the roll of duct tape," he said. "I don't think they're going to find it."

"You don't?"

"No."

Then Hunter told Shapiro that as far as they could tell from one police report, John Ramsey could have left the house for as long as fifty minutes the morning JonBenét's body was found (information that later proved untrue). "I think John may have taken all that stuff out of the house," Hunter said. "Someone got rid of it."

I asked Hunter what time the ransom note said the ransom was supposed to be picked up.

"Hmm. Let me check. Where's my copy of the note?" Hunter said, teasing me.

Hunter told me there was to be a call between 8:00 and 10:00 A.M. No one outside the investigation had been told that at the time.

"Can I just see what the handwriting looks like?" I asked.

He opened a spiral binder, took out some loose pages, and held them up real close to my eyes—so close that I couldn't read anything. Then he quickly pulled the pages back, put them away, and went, "Ha, ha, ha."

"Don't tell anyone I did that," Hunter said.

"OK."

That's when I got the feeling Hunter must know deep down that the Ramseys did it. All this other stuff was just talk.

That night I left Thomas a message on his voice mail: "I knew you had to drive a cool car. I'm proud of you, man."

— Jeff Shapiro

Stephen Singular knew that Hunter was talking to the tabloids—Jeff Shapiro had told him. Hunter had to know that the tabs were a driving force in shaping public opinion and that they were committed to the idea that the Ramseys had killed their daughter.

Earlier in the month, Hunter had told Singular it was difficult for the DA's office to do certain things that needed to be done in the investigation. When Singular gave him the idea of delving into the world of pageants, Hunter suggested, Why don't you go to the tabloids? They have money, they have freedom, they don't play by the rules. Then he suggested tracing what people were downloading from the Internet, although it might be an invasion of privacy.

Singular was taken aback. The DA was suggesting doing things that Singular himself considered legally tenuous.

"There are highly qualified people that you could involve who wouldn't have to worry about breaking the law," Singular told him.

Hunter didn't answer.

Singular understood that the DA was talking to many journalists and possibly enlisting their help too. He wondered if maybe Alex Hunter was dancing with the devil.

On July 2, Steve Thomas called Jeff Shapiro. "Some of the guys and I are going to sleep in the house tonight," he said. "We're trying to get a feel for the place."

"That's cool."

"I thought you might want to know," Thomas continued. "We're going to reenact some scenarios. If you want to come by—just by accident, like, walk by—feel free." Then Thomas added, "I'll try to help you out little by little. But be cool about it. Be careful."

"I will, and thanks a lot."

"Jeff, I know Patsy killed that girl."

It was the first time Shapiro felt that Thomas trusted him.

Later that evening, Shapiro went to the Ramseys' house. He climbed a tree on the next-door property at about 8:30 P.M. From there, he could watch the cops through binoculars.

Inside the house, the detectives spent hours running through different scenarios of what might have happened on December 26.* Sometimes with the lights on, sometimes with the lights off, they ran the scenarios, starting in JonBenét's bedroom, either just before or just after she went to sleep. In each scenario they took it for granted that either the killer or JonBenét, or perhaps both, knew the route from her bedroom to the wine cellar.

From JonBenét's second-floor bedroom, it was less than four full paces to the top of the carpeted spiral staircase that led down to the ground floor. The thirteen steps of the staircase could have been maneuvered in the dark by someone who knew them. A visitor—or an intruder—would need a light, the detectives reasoned, even if they did not have to control a struggling child. A parent or the child would not need a light. The flashlight found on the kitchen counter on December 26, which was normally kept near the kitchen, could have been used either as a light or as a weapon—in the kitchen or in another room. By now the CBI had determined that both the outside of the flashlight and the batteries inside held no fingerprints. Most likely they had been wiped clean. This was highly unusual. An intruder would probably have taken the flashlight with him when he left. A perpetrator who lived in the house might have removed his prints from the flashlight and the batteries in a moment of panic, though it would have been more natural to leave them.

Continuing with the scenario, the detectives saw that once they were down the staircase, there were several likely directions to the basement—none of them allowing for quickness or ease of movement.

A logical direction for the killer—or for a terrified JonBenét who was running away—would be down another short flight of stairs toward what the Ramseys called the butler's kitchen. There, a door to the left allowed a quick escape into the narrow side yard on the home's north side—but no access to the garage or basement.

Or, coming from the spiral staircase, someone might head straight

---

*The floor plans to the Ramsey house appear in Appendix A.

for the door that led directly to the brick patio at the southwest corner of the ground floor and then to freedom down the back alley.

However, to reach the basement from the spiral stairs, where the ransom note was discovered, a perpetrator or a fleeing JonBenét would be forced into a more circuitous route.

Once down the stairs to the butler's kitchen, the detectives realized, the perpetrator could only reach the basement stairs by crossing that room, climbing yet another short flight of stairs, then turning to the right to reach the door to the basement. The problem was that the door swung out into that narrow hallway. It became an obstacle that would force you to sidestep or squeeze around it to get to the staircase to the basement. This was a highly unlikely path for anyone who knew the house, and a stranger wouldn't have known the door was there.

The second route to the basement from the spiral staircase would first lead toward the patio doors, then veer left, right by where the flashlight was kept, through a 25-foot-long kitchen, where a fleeing JonBenét or an intruder would pass an island counter and three high chairs.

At the end of the kitchen was a short hallway, into which they would have to make a left turn, and there, immediately to the right, was the door to the basement. Opening that door, however, the detectives discovered that they were in total darkness. There was no light switch on either wall at the top of the stairs or immediately outside the basement door. Any stranger would grope in vain for a light. Eventually, he might discover it set high on the wall behind his back, inconveniently located opposite the door.

Once in the basement, a stranger would find no fewer than four closets, two storage rooms, and a hobby room. The wine cellar, where the Ramseys typically kept construction materials and their Christmas trees, was at the end of one basement corridor—past a utility sink, past the boiler room, and behind a door.

The investigators considered the possibility that JonBenét fled from her bedroom to this remote hideaway in the middle of the night to elude someone. If so, she would have run a straight path from the bottom of the basement stairs directly to the boiler room, winding up in front of the latched wine cellar door. Only someone who knew the house intimately could make this journey quickly. Or, as one officer suggested, a mischievous JonBenét may have been playing a game of catch-me-if-you-can and led her killer to the spot outside the wine cellar.

If JonBenét had been hit with the flashlight in or near the kitchen and was carried unconscious to the basement, the perpetrator would have followed the same route into the boiler room, winding up in front of the wine cellar door.

The detectives felt that in every scenario, JonBenét spent the final moments of her life just outside the wine cellar door, where the police had found wooden shards from the broken paintbrush that was tied to the cord at one end of the noose. That was also where they found Patsy's paint tote. The tote contained the unused portion of the paintbrush and additional brushes similar to the one used in the murder. After JonBenét was murdered, the police surmised, her body was taken inside the windowless room.

In an attempt to recreate the final acts of violence, the detectives screamed at different locations in the house, taking an intruder into account. At one point, Thomas ran from the house and slammed the door behind him. He wanted to know how long it would take someone to leave the house by the shortest route.

Just before midnight, Frank Coffman joined Shapiro. They stood on a wooden fence in the backyard and watched as lights in the house were turned on and off. They saw Detective Gosage, with a flashlight in his hand, performing a pantomime in which someone found John or Patsy and JonBenét, attacked one or the other, but ended up fracturing JonBenét's skull instead. With the flashlight still in hand, Gosage recreated a slightly different scenario in the kitchen. It looked as if the detectives thought the flashlight was the murder weapon.

After midnight, Shapiro saw the garage door open. Gosage pulled out in his Blazer. Steve Thomas and Lou Smit stayed until the early hours of the morning.

The next day, Trip DeMuth and Tom Trujillo maneuvered the basement window-well grate while Gosage inspected some spiderwebs to see if the grate could be moved without breaking the webs completely.

Watching the police that night, I thought about that movie Manhunter *where William Peterson talks to an unknown killer while hunting him down. One night I went back to the Ramsey house, looked up at Jon-Benét's window, and spoke to Patsy: "I know you walked in. I know you did it. Didn't you? Didn't you?"*

I found myself driving past the Ramsey house five to ten times a day. Sometimes I'd go into the backyard and eat lunch on the patio or in the playground. I would just hang out to get a feel for it, the way Thomas did.

"Home Sweet Home" is what I started calling the Ramsey house—my home away from home.

A few days later, Thomas called me and asked me to come in and meet Sgt. Wickman.

"Jeff, is your loyalty to the DA's office, the police, or the Globe?" Thomas asked.

I looked at him seriously. "My loyalty is to JonBenét. I will work with whoever I have to work with to do whatever it takes to avenge that girl."

At that moment I saw a look in Thomas's eye that I'd never seen before in my life. It was a look of total respect and admiration.

Thomas had told me they couldn't get to Hunter through the normal chain of command. They needed my help. That was when I decided to tell them some of the things that were going on in Hunter's office. I related to them some of my conversations with Hunter.

As Thomas questioned me about the things that were going on in the DA's office, I sensed he was trying to get negative information. They wanted to know all about Lou Smit. I called him "the fox," "the ace detective"—something I'd picked up from Hunter—and told them about his intruder theory.

Finally Wickman stood up and thanked me for coming in. Steve Thomas left with him. A moment later, he returned alone.

"That was good," he said. "Wick was totally impressed—especially the stuff about Smit." Then Steve continued, "I fuckin' can't stand Smit. Sometimes I'm in the DA's office talking to Smit and DeMuth. They're telling me about the intruder theory, and it's like—I just look down at my piece and I think to myself—well, I've got one in the chamber and seven in the clip."

We started laughing.

Thomas told me that he believed John and Patsy killed JonBenét. I said I thought it was Patsy who actually did it. Thomas just smiled. "You're on the right track," he said. Then we started talking more about Lou Smit.

"Jeff, this guy is convinced the Ramseys are innocent. He is obsessed with his Christian values. We're ready to arrest the Ramseys—and he's looking for intruders."

Then I tried to tell Thomas that Hunter is a good guy and that Hunter thinks Eller is the problem. I told him what he had said about Eller.

"That's because Eller is the only guy over here who challenges him," Thomas said.

"Isn't Eller kind of an asshole?"

"Jeff, Eller is a fuckin' good guy," Thomas shouted. "I wish I could just take you in the back and show you our files."

I could feel we were bonding.

"Just keep it between us, and we'll keep talking," he said. "We have to get Hunter off the intruder path."

I understood that I was the messenger from the cops to Hunter, and from Hunter to the cops. Soon I would become the messenger from God reminding Thomas and the cops that they were needed.

That was how we left it: my job was to get Hunter off that path.

— *Jeff Shapiro*

While the detectives seemed to be having doubts about Lou Smit, the veteran investigator was gaining admiration for them. Most of them were top-notch, Smit thought—honest to a fault. Their major problem was their lack of experience. How many murder cases did they have to solve in the last five years? Also, there was no devil's advocate in their ranks to keep them objective, a situation aggravated early in the case when the DA's office took the position that the cops weren't doing their jobs right.

One detective stood out in Smit's mind. Steve Thomas was a professional. He was dedicated and, like Smit, only wanted justice for the victim. Thomas knew the case from every angle, and he was in the field, where detectives should be. The only fault Smit could find in Thomas's thinking was that he'd started, like Eller, from the position that the Ramseys must have been involved in JonBenét's murder. Like most narcotics officers once he found his target he never let go. Thomas's lack of experience as a homocide detective seemed to prevent him from stepping back and looking at all the evidence from a different perspective. It was a shame, Smit thought, because under different circumstances, they might have made a team.

3

PORN EXPERT CALLED IN TO RAMSEY CASE

Authorities have asked an Arvada Police Department detective to investigate child pornography computer databases in connection with the JonBenét Ramsey homicide, sources said Wednesday.

Investigators searched for pornography in the Ramseys' home after obtaining search warrants.

"They were out (at the Ramseys' house) looking for every type of pornography you can imagine," a source said. "They were looking for things like pornographic movies, books, magazines and photographs."

The girl's autopsy report verified she suffered head injuries and that sections of her vagina showed chronic inflammation and epithelial erosion, or tissue damage.

The Ramseys have denied a history of sexual abuse in the family involving JonBenét or others.

— Alli Krupski
Daily Camera, July 3, 1997

RAMSEY PRESS ADVISORY

To: Media covering the Ramsey case
Contact: Rachelle Zimmer
Date: July 3, 1997

An article in today's Boulder Daily Camera reflects a despicable new low by some member or members of the Boulder Police Department who are engaged in a concerted and vicious smearing of character of John and Patsy Ramsey. Any suggestion or hint by such persons that John and Patsy Ramsey may somehow be connected with child pornography, and thereby implicated in the death of their daughter is totally outrageous.

The results of such searches were not revealed to the reporter for the most obvious reason: no pornography was found, nor has any evidence of any sort been found which in any way would link the Ramseys to pornography.

When the police had finished the four-day search of the Ramsey home, the couple wanted some independent reporters to determine how easy it would have been for an intruder to enter their house. Just before the Ramseys went to Atlanta, a Ramsey attorney contacted Dan Glick of *Newsweek* and offered him a tour of the house. That same week, Clay Evans of the *Daily Camera* was asked if he'd like a tour. Both reporters were told that they could not publish what they had seen or what their conclusions might be until the Ramseys gave them permission—if ever. Both reporters agreed to the conditions.

Evans found many of the family's personal effects—furniture, books, wall hangings, and even some food—still in the house. What interested him most was the basement. In his notes, he described it as "unfinished," with walls that had been repainted just before the murder. It had a claustrophobic feel, with low ceilings and small rooms. There were no lighting fixtures—just bare bulbs everywhere. Toilets and sinks were still disassembled from the various police searches. At the back of Burke's train room, Evans saw the place where the police had found the broken window. He saw that a full-grown person could have crawled through an opening of that size. Just past the boiler room was the unfinished, windowless room where JonBenét had been found. It didn't look like a wine cellar. The room was "dark and bunker-like, with waterstained cement walls and floor." The door and its frame had both been removed by the police.

After his tour, Dan Glick considered the relationship of JonBenét's bedroom to her parents' and Burke's rooms. To him, the path from the second floor down the spiral staircase to the basement didn't seem difficult, and though a stranger to the house, he easily found the wine cellar. He agreed that a grown man could have climbed through the basement window and escaped through any of several doors. An intruder with a key could have entered the house easily, and someone without a key could have entered through any of the doors that had pry marks. Of course, at the time, neither reporter knew that the doors with pry marks had been found latched from the inside and that a spiderweb extended across the grate at the broken basement window.

Just weeks before Glick's visit to the house, *Newsweek* had published an article by him and Sherry Keene-Osborn titled "Complications in the Case." The writers insisted that previously published information— that there was no sign of forced entry at the house and that semen had been found on JonBenét's body—was completely false. The article attempted to set the record straight on behalf of the Ramseys and their attorneys, since the police had made no attempt to do so.

Glick had turned a corner in his thinking. Balancing what little he knew of the evidence with his own investigation into the family's background, the fact that JonBenét told her friend's mother that Santa would visit her the day after Christmas, and now the house itself, Glick concluded that Patsy and John Ramsey were unlikely to have been involved in JonBenét's death. A few days after he saw the inside of the Ramseys' home, Glick told his friend Charlie Brennan that an intruder could well be the answer. He now thought the Ramseys were probably blameless. From then on, Glick's articles gave far more space to exculpatory evidence than to evidence pointing to the Ramseys' guilt.

On July 8 and 9, a moving crew packed the remainder of the Ramseys' belongings from the house on 15th Street for transport to Atlanta. Their new suburban home, which cost $700,000, was located near the cemetery where JonBenét was buried. The house where JonBenét died was put on the market for $1 million.

HANDWRITING TEST FAILS TO
CLEAR PATSY RAMSEY

Handwriting analysts can't rule out Patsy Ramsey as the author of the ransom note in her daughter's murder case, the *Rocky Mountain News* has learned. They can't say for sure that she wrote it either, sources said.

Results from the Colorado Bureau of Investigation analysis of Patsy Ramsey's handwriting have been in the hands of Boulder police since last June, but hadn't been disclosed publicly until now.

Earlier handwriting analysis eliminated John Ramsey, 54, as a possible author of the note.

— Charlie Brennan
Rocky Mountain News, July 9, 1997

Lou Smit had a hard time reconciling the grief-stricken Patsy, who reportedly was unable even to comb her own hair in the days after her daughter's death, with the person who was able to compose and write a two-and-a-half-page ransom note while her daughter lay dead in the basement. Smit was now ready to believe that John and Patsy could not have killed their daughter.

During the first days of June, the investigator received a phone call from Patsy Ramsey. She told him that the family was leaving for Charlevoix on June 6 now that Burke was done with school for the year. Patsy asked Smit to drive by their house each morning at 7:00 A.M., to check up on it. Seeing an opportunity to develop a relationship with the Ramseys, Smit agreed. On June 6, he made his first visit, and as he drove up, he saw the Ramseys themselves. They greeted him and then got into his van for a chat. Just before they parted, Patsy told Smit that she and her husband had nothing to do with the death of JonBenét. They wanted the killer to be caught, she repeated. The Ramseys and Smit then prayed together that he would find Jon-Benét's killer. From that day on, Smit would stop each day at the scene of the crime on his way to work and pray for JonBenét.

It wasn't long after that Smit received a letter from John Ramsey. The worst thing that I have ever done in my life, Ramsey wrote, is that I once committed adultery when I was married to my first wife. I wanted you to hear it from me, Ramsey continued, before you read it in some tabloid.

As he had always done in the past, Smit was letting the evidence lead him to the murderer. At this point, he saw no hard evidence against Patsy or John, but there were several strong indications that pointed to an intruder. One was the print of a Hi-Tec shoe that the police had found in the dusting on the cement floor near JonBenét's body.* Another indicator was a partial, smeared palm print that was found on the ransom note. Third was another unidentified palm print, this one found on the wine cellar door. Fourth were some pieces of glass found on top of the suitcase under the broken basement window that was found open and the scuff mark on the wall below the window. Fifth was the possibility that a stun gun had been used on JonBenét.

Smit also took into account the many outstanding copies of the house key. Then there was the strange fact that every object used in the crime—except the roll of duct tape and the remainder of the cord—was found in the house. Did it mean that the tape and cord

* Cement floors unprotected from an underlying earthen foundation will "dust"—that is, the unsealed concrete will start to disintegrate, and a powdery substance will appear on the surface. Cement floors in a low-traffic or poorly ventilated location are particularly prone to this phenomenon.

were brought into the house for the purpose of kidnapping Jon-Benét? If so, then it was logical that the intruder had taken them with him so that they couldn't be traced back to him. And if the roll of tape and the cord had belonged to the Ramseys, why weren't they left in the house with the other crime elements? This seemed to indicate that the intruder had come to kidnap JonBenét and that the murder somehow grew out of the planned abduction.

Since visiting the basement with the police on June 30, Smit had also been bothered by something he'd seen in the boiler room just to the left of the wine cellar door. There he had observed an exposed ventilation duct several paces from where the shards of wood, the paint tote, and the remnant of the broken paintbrush had been found. The duct vented through an opening at the front of the house where there had once been a window. If JonBenét had screamed near the duct, the sound could have traveled outside and been heard by the Ramseys' neighbor, Melody Stanton, although possibly not by Patsy and John, asleep on the third floor inside the house. In July, sound tests conducted by the police confirmed that sound traveled more easily from the basement to the street than it did up through the three floors of the house. If JonBenét had screamed in the basement, it was likely that she was down there when she was hit on the head, either with the flashlight or with, say, a golf club—John Ramsey's golf bags had been found nearby with their partial set of clubs. An intruder might have used a flashlight to find a hiding child if he hadn't discovered the light switch for the basement stairs. Since no fingerprints were found on the flashlight or its batteries, it seemed to Smit that it might have been brought into the house by an intruder, though the Ramseys had never denied that they owned a flashlight like it.

The basement was so cluttered, such a mess—if JonBenét's parents had killed her, they would not have taken her to this dark, damp pig sty to do it, Smit theorized.

All of his conjectures were very tenuous, Smit knew, and nothing that he wanted to mention to anyone just yet. Months later, however, he discussed his ideas with Steve Thomas. Thomas asked Smit the following question: after the scream—which the intruder had to assume was heard by the parents—would the intruder have hung around, taking the time to strangle JonBenét with the noose and then move the body into the wine cellar? After all, someone, having heard the scream, might be coming down the basement stairs, thereby cutting off the most accessible exit. Why move the child from one hidden place, the boiler room, to the equally hidden wine cellar? And, of course, there wasn't any evidence that JonBenét had ever even been in the boiler room. When Smit mentioned this theory to another detective, the detective asked, What if the scream wasn't JonBenét's? Maybe it was her mother's. Male, female, young, old—could anyone being wakened out of a sleep really tell who had emitted the scream? These questions, among others, made the detectives skeptical of Smit's scenario.

Nevertheless, Smit knew he had to ask the Ramseys if they had ever owned or possessed a stun gun and whether they owned or had ever worn Hi-Tec shoes.

On Saturday morning, July 12, Smit, Hofstrom, the Ramseys, and one of their attorneys met at the Justice Center for an informal tape-recorded interview. By now the Ramseys had come to believe that Hofstrom and Smit would be straight in their dealings. The absence of the police from the meeting may have led the Ramseys to conclude that Smit believed them possibly innocent of their daughter's murder.

The Ramseys said they had never owned a stun gun. John Ramsey thought he remembered being given a videotape on self-defense by Spy World, a high-tech security outlet in southern Florida, which might have included a segment on the use of stun guns. The family didn't wear or own Hi-Tec shoes, he said.

Five days later, Smit asked John Andrew about the same items. Like his father, he said he knew nothing about stun guns and didn't own Hi-Tec shoes.

Hoping that someone with information might come forward, Smit believed that the police or the DA should go public with what they'd discovered about a stun gun and asked permission to release the information. But Hunter considered the stun gun theory "iffy." He talked to the police about exhuming JonBenét's body, but they were against it. The media were sure to find out, they said, and exhuming the body would lend credibility to what the detectives called Smit's "wacko" stun-gun theory. Hunter knew they had another reason: no jury would believe that the Ramseys could have used such a device on their daughter.

Lou Smit's request was turned down. The police said they would inquire about a stun gun when they recanvassed the Ramseys' neighborhood. It would take another six months.

Meanwhile, on July 14, the Colorado Supreme Court denied the coroner's request to withhold his autopsy report from the public. Deputy county attorney Mason told the press that since John Meyer anticipated being called as a material and expert witness "at any future trial in this case," he would not comment on the supreme court's decision or offer an interpretation of the still-censored autopsy report.

The report, which detailed the long fracture to JonBenét's skull, the blood around her vagina, the abrasions to her hymen, and the severity of the furrow around her neck from the ligature, was in the hands of the press by midafternoon.

Dr. Richard Krugman—dean of the CU Health Sciences Center and a nationally known child abuse expert who had consulted with the police and the DA since March—told the media that on the basis of what he'd read in the report, JonBenét was not a sexually abused child. Then he added, "I don't believe it's possible to tell whether any child is sexually abused based on physical findings alone." The presence of semen, evidence of a sexually transmitted disease, or the child's medical history combined with the child's own testimony were the only sure ways to be confident about a finding of sexual abuse, Krugman told reporters.

Physical abuse was another matter. Krugman had occasionally seen injuries to little girls' genitals that were related to toilet training and had nothing to do with sexual abuse. In children, one had to separate sexual from physical abuse. By now the detectives had learned that at age six, JonBenét was still wetting the bed, and was asking adults to wipe her after she was done on the toilet. It was possible that the injury to her vagina was a result of punishment.

Cyril Wecht, a forensic pathologist who was appearing regularly on talk shows about the case, scoffed at Krugman's remarks. "How can anybody say, with the blood and the abrasions, that this was not sexual assault? What is he [Krugman] talking about?" Wecht theorized that JonBenét had died during sex play that had gone astray.

"My guess is the child had her head whacked against something and then was still alive and strangled," said Dr. Robert Kirschner, a retired deputy chief medical examiner for Cook County, Illinois.

Dr. Ronald Wright, formerly the medical examiner for the Fort Lauderdale area, stated flatly that it was clear the girl's vagina had been penetrated. He also believed that she'd probably been struck by a blunt object, such as a baseball bat or heavy flashlight. He too took issue with

Krugman's interpretation. "Somebody's injured her vagina. And she's tied up. Doesn't that make it involuntary sexual battery?" Wright asked.

The Ramseys' attorneys released a statement on behalf of John and Patsy Ramsey: "We have not had the opportunity to review the autopsy report, but credible experts who have, confirm what we have been saying all along—that there is no evidence of abuse or molestation prior to the night of her murder."

Two days after the release of the autopsy report, Tom Kelley, representing the *Daily Camera*, was in court seeking the police search warrants. On July 16, district court judge Daniel Hale heard arguments.

Kelley told the court that it was clear the investigation had stalled and the release of some information might encourage a witness to come forward. He pointed out that some of the material he wanted had already been provided to the Ramseys by the police, such as a copy of the ransom note and certain early police reports.

Two days later, Judge Hale upheld Judge MacDonald's previous ruling. The search warrants, affidavits, and inventories would remain sealed.

When Stephen Singular heard about the autopsy report, he decided to see how the police would respond to his theory that JonBenét had been taken from her home on Christmas night to be photographed and brought back dead.

Detective Sgt. Wickman agreed to hear him out but made it clear that he himself wouldn't say a thing about the case. He was true to his word. After the meeting, Singular had the feeling that the detective hadn't taken him seriously.

Hunter had run with Singular's ideas for a while but now seemed uninterested. Singular was tired of waiting for the principals in the case to wake up. He had shared his theory with anyone who would listen. Now it was time to write about it. He was sure it would attract interest. Maybe it would even produce some investigative activity.

Having hired his own investigation team before the police were ready to present the case to him, Alex Hunter had put himself squarely in the action. At first Koby didn't mind Hunter's attempt to involve himself in the case, because it took some of the heat off the police. To some of Hunter's colleagues, however, the DA's frequent public appearances seemed forced. It was obvious that Hunter had nothing concrete to offer, and some reporters were saying that he'd let himself be swept up into the circus. Metro DA Bob Grant, a member of Hunter's prosecution task force, knew it would take time for Hunter to gain some perspective and get down to planning a potential prosecution.

By mid-July that process had begun. Hunter started to dissect the police investigation—not to criticize it, but rather to consider what he would face in court.

Hunter could not ignore the possibility that someone other than John and Patsy would be charged, and in that case he would have to rehabilitate the Ramseys—show the jury beyond a reasonable doubt that they hadn't murdered their daughter.

Bob Grant said that the Ramseys would be the focus of any trial, whether or not they were charged. Anyone defending a third party would point an accusatory finger at JonBenét's parents. The police detectives might even be called as hostile defense witnesses. But if the Ramseys *were* charged, evidence pointing to a third party would be the core of the defense case.

In a shooting by police in Longmont in 1989, Hunter had unsealed police reports and displayed them in the public library. "Tell me what you think," he had asked the public. Their comments had helped him decide to take the case to a grand jury, and ultimately the police officers were exonerated. According to Grant, Hunter thrived on public input and community approval.

But the Ramsey case was different, Grant told Hunter. The DA couldn't walk down the Pearl Street Mall and ask Boulderites what they thought. He had to set his own agenda and adhere to it.

On July 23, the Ramseys' attorneys faxed the media the text of some full-page ads they planned to publish in the *Daily Camera*. "An Open Letter from John and Patsy Ramsey" addressed anyone who could help identify the killer. The text of the ad outlined a general profile of the killer—someone, the Ramseys said, who was no stranger to their family or home. The killer, they noted, would have displayed certain characteristics both before and after the murder. Likely precrime behavior was conflict with a female, conflict with family, financial stress, marital problems, legal problems, and employment problems. Typical postcrime behavior would include establishment of an obvious alibi; appearing to cooperate with the authorities; closely monitoring media accounts of the crime; appearing extremely rigid, nervous, and preoccupied during casual conversations; suddenly becoming religious; experiencing depression; and suffering from insomnia.

The next day, even before the first ad was published, the media were criticizing the Ramseys' effort as amateurish.

RAMSEY LASHES OUT AT POLICE

In a blistering statement Wednesday, John Ramsey denounced the Boulder Police Department's investigation into the murder of his daughter JonBenét and announced the family's plan to hunt down the killer.

The family will run a series of local newspaper ads seeking the murderer. The family also will distribute fliers in some neighborhoods with their profile of the perpetrator.

Gregg McCrary, a former FBI criminal profiler, called the profile superficial.

"What's missing here that's very important is there's no description of the characteristics and traits of the offender, crime and the crime scene analysis, an analysis of the content of the note, the medical examiner's report and what those injuries may or may not mean," McCrary said.

"I don't think the offender has any remorse for this crime because of the way the crime was committed. Right in the aftermath of this murder, the killer sat down and wrote a ransom note—he's not sorry he did it, he's just trying not to get caught."

— Alli Krupski
Daily Camera, July 24, 1997

MATT LAUER: Over the weekend the parents [the Ramseys] went on the offensive, placing a newspaper ad, and distributing fliers profiling the man who they believe killed their daughter. Former FBI profiler John Douglas helped write the profile, and he has been working with the Ramseys to help them find JonBenét's killer. . . . Mr. Douglas, did you do it with the understanding that the Ramseys might make it public?

JOHN DOUGLAS: I wasn't aware that they were going to make it public this soon. I think what's happened now is a feeling of frustration, desperation and anger on the part of the families. That information should have been put out by the police the first week after the homicide, not really now. So it's act of, really, desperation and frustration on their part.

MATT LAUER: Do you think this case will be solved?

JOHN DOUGLAS: I think, unfortunately, this may end up like many homicides in this country where we only solve 65 percent of our homicides, and this may be one of that 35 that does remain unsolved.

Today, NBC, July 28, 1997

While Hunter withheld comment on the ads, he considered which of his staff members would prosecute the case. At the same time, he fretted over the police department's lack of interest in working with criminalist Dr. Henry Lee and DNA expert Barry Scheck, whose services he'd enlisted in February. Few of the suggestions Lee had made during his March presentation to the police had been acted upon, and Eller's attitude toward Scheck was that he got people released from jail and won acquittals for defendants like O. J. Simpson. Nor had the police followed up on suggestions made by Lou Smit and Steve Ainsworth to check out all known sex offenders, track down all the missing keys to the Ramsey house, and recanvas the neighborhood for possible overlooked leads.

Apparently, the police thought all that could wait. Instead, they decided to consult with the FBI to get an overview of the case rather than put it together piecemeal as they had been doing so far. The FBI agreed to meet with the Boulder PD and members of the DA's office at the Bureau's headquarters in Quantico, Virginia, the first week of September. They said they would review all the evidence and give their expert opinion. Eight hundred pieces of physical evidence—including thirty-eight fingerprint cards—would be viewed by fresh eyes. The police wanted to know the FBI's opinion about what physical evidence pointed to the Ramseys and whether the Bureau's experts could map out the sequence of events surrounding the murder. Both the Boulder PD and the DA's office wanted to hear the conclusions of the experts firsthand.

Hunter's staff, which had never worked with the FBI like this before, was particularly interested in finding out from the behavioral specialists how often prosecutors had succeeded in getting FBI profile material admitted as evidence in court.

The trip to Quantico was sure to put more public pressure on everyone, however. Even now the DA's office was being deluged with letters of complaint: "Why is this taking so long?" "Obviously you've been paid off." "How come the rich always get away with it?" Hunter didn't delude himself that the public would get more patient over time.

IS THE CASE PROGRESSING?

Just as JonBenét's father was revealing a preposterously useless profile of her merciless killer, Boulder investigators were plodding along on their own determined path—a path now leading directly to the FBI in Quantico, VA.

Respected profilers say that unless a profile is meticulously defined by actual clues at the scene of a crime, it is little more than a wild guess.

For frustrated observers, [Hunter's] decision to send the lead prosecutor [Hofstrom] to Quantico is a major step in developing a potential case for presentation in court.

The methodical, determined course now being pursued by police and prosecutors is in sharp contrast to their earlier conduct—a bickering, mistrusting relationship best symbolized by police withholding critical evidence from the D.A.'s office.

— Chuck Green
The Denver Post, July 25, 1997

On July 28 the *Globe* published a cover story under the headline ARREST THEM NOW, COPS TELL DA. It emphasized the frustration of the police and asserted their view that Lou Smit, with his Christian beliefs, had somehow bonded with Patsy over their mutual religious convictions and that it was hindering the case.

When Steve Thomas read the story, he immediately asked Jeff Shapiro to come to police headquarters. The detective lost no time in escorting him into the witness room.

"Jeff, you fuckin' burned me," Thomas said.

"I told my editors our conversations were off the record," Shapiro protested. "I'm sorry—I know I screwed up. I didn't mean to."

"Fuckin' Koby says to us, 'We've got a fuckin' leak and I'm going to find out who it is!'" Thomas told Shapiro.

Shapiro didn't know what to say.

"If anyone thinks I'm leaking this . . ." Thomas continued. "Can you imagine what's going to happen if [Ramsey attorney] Hal Haddon puts me on the stand?"

Shapiro was embarrassed.

"I can't fuckin' lose my badge over you," Thomas said. "I'm the fuckin' thorn in the Ramseys' side. If I'm kicked out of here, or if us five detectives get kicked out, no one is going to be getting justice for this little girl."

Mumbling apologies, Shapiro left.

After that, Thomas ignored Shapiro's calls.

Indeed, in the span of seven months, Thomas had conducted 164 interviews and had traveled to Georgia, Arizona, North Carolina, and West Virginia. Thomas and a partner had interviewed every member of the Ramsey family, their friends, neighbors, ministers, and business associates, possible suspects, and prostitutes. Thomas had tracked down the sources of evidence, followed people and information on the Internet, looked into the world of beauty pageants, dealt directly with the Ramseys' investigators, and verified the alibis of over four dozen people. Eller had given him a free hand. There were few police officers who could match Thomas's encyclopedic knowledge of the case. He was determined to bring JonBenét's killer to justice.

Meanwhile, Carol McKinley's police source contacted her.

"We've decided to hire our own lawyers to look at the case," the detective told McKinley. "How do you think it will play out?"

"It's not going to make you look bad," McKinley reassured him, but she could sense how nervous the officers were about the step they were taking.

McKinley sat on the story for three days, not knowing if her source wanted it made public. Then she called the detective and told him that if she broke the story, it would reflect favorably on the police. The public would see there was forward momentum in the case. He agreed.

At 5:00 P.M. on July 31, McKinley called Eller. "I know about the lawyers," she said. "Do you have a comment?"

"I knew you guys would get this sooner or later," Eller replied. "Did the DAs tell you?"

When she said no, Eller didn't push her any further. He said he had no comment.

Next she called Dan Caplis, a talk-show host at her radio station, who was also an attorney. Caplis said he would call someone he knew in the Boulder DA's office to find out whatever he could. Caplis called Bill Wise to warn him about McKinley's story but just as important, to tell Wise something else—that he was the one who had brokered the deal between the police and their new lawyers, a fact Caplis hadn't told McKinley. When Wise found out, he was shocked.

In mid-July, knowing that the Boulder police had lost confidence in Hunter's office, Caplis had approached Richard Baer, a former New York homicide detective and prosecutor who was now an attorney in Denver, and asked if Baer would volunteer his services to the police. Caplis knew that powerful lawyers were representing the Ramseys, and he felt that equally high-powered attorneys should be advising the police. When Baer agreed, Caplis called several people at the Boulder PD, one of whom was Steve Thomas. The detectives liked the idea. Baer then recruited Robert Miller, a former U.S. attorney from Colorado, and Dan Hoffman, former dean of the University of Denver Law School. On July 24, the three attorneys met with Eller and the detectives working the Ramsey case. They discussed an arrangement in which the lawyers would work pro bono.*

It was a relief to the police to have their own attorneys. Like Caplis, these attorneys had no agenda of their own. The police could now get an objective opinion about whether they had a case against the Ramseys or should move on. The FBI had told the detectives that they had enough evidence for probable cause, but now Eller, like Hunter, wanted to know if they had enough to convict beyond a reasonable doubt. He and his detectives didn't trust Hunter and Hofstrom to tell them the truth. If they didn't have a case, they wanted to hear it from a neutral source. They were prepared for bad news.

Hearing all this from Dan Caplis, Bill Wise worried about how it would reflect on the DA's office. He called Hunter, who knew nothing about it. Within minutes, Hunter had Koby on the phone. The chief was more upset that Eller hadn't told Hunter, than that the news had leaked. The DA told Koby that he didn't want the story to air until an official announcement was made, because it would look as if the police were blindsiding the DA.

Carol McKinley called Hunter at home, and he agreed to go on the

---

* An attorney who accepts a case without payment, to fill a perceived social need to offer legal representation to the poor, is said to be working *pro bono publico* (literally, "for the public good"), or more commonly, pro bono.

air live the next morning at 5:00 A.M., August 1. It was a face-saving maneuver. He couldn't afford to let his office look incompetent. On the radio, he said he endorsed the police department's hiring of attorneys.

In fact, Hunter knew the reputation of the three attorneys, and he hoped their input would work to his advantage. Baer and Miller had a great deal of experience with juries and the rules of evidence. Let the police department hear from its own handpicked consultants that the investigation was flawed. It would take some of the pressure off him.

That afternoon, Hunter issued a press release: "There is no question that outside lawyers providing assistance to a police department is unusual in a criminal investigation. But almost everything about this case is unusual."

4

When Steve Thomas interviewed Patsy's sister Pam in Atlanta, she told him that one summer in Charlevoix, JonBenét was standing on the dock barefoot. Worried that she might get a splinter, Pam ran after her.

"You need to put shoes on," she told JonBenét.

"I don't want to," the child answered. "I want to feel the earth's life under my feet. I want to know what it's like to walk on something that is alive."

When the kids are in kindergarten, they only go to school for a half day. So we moms would pick the kids up, and while we waited, we would just chat. My youngest child, a boy, was a year older than JonBenét. My middle one, a daughter, was Burke's age. And my oldest, who was fourteen, would sometimes baby-sit JonBenét when Patsy had some activity at St. John's.

That's how I really met Patsy—through church.

When I first met JonBenét, she was two years old and had a discernible personality. She could walk into a room and everybody would stop and look—not just at her face. She was beautiful, but it was something else. She had confidence, and you had to take a second look. You'd ask yourself, Who is this kid?

On some Sundays after church, Patsy would take off with JonBenét and go to some pageant. The family was prepping all the time during the week. With that amount of participation, it wasn't just a couple of Sun-

days. And when she'd say, "I've got to go now," and "We're doing such and such," my eyebrows went up just a little, like everybody else's.

I mean, when Patsy said on TV that the pageants were just a couple of Sundays—give me a break.

— Patty Novack

During the first week of August, Jeff Shapiro called Patty Novack, who had cared for Patsy in the first days after the murder. He wanted to interview her about "anything," he said. Novack told him she had no comment. Shapiro continued to talk—about himself. He said he was young and looking for a story.

He thought he was playing to some bored housewife. That, I am not. I wasn't going to fall for his line. Again I said, "I have no comment," and hung up.

A second later the phone rang again. "Patty, Patty, you hung up on me," he said. "That wasn't nice."

Once again I said I had no comment.

"Surely you must think about what's going on," he continued.

"Of course I think about it. I've had discussions with my husband. But I don't have discussions with strangers."

"We could meet and have coffee, and then we wouldn't be strangers anymore."

"I don't think so," I said, and hung up.

A couple of weeks later, about six o'clock in the evening, Shapiro showed up on my doorstep with some flowers. He wasn't the first reporter to use that trick. Someone had tried that on Valentine's Day.

He just kept ringing my bell. I didn't answer. Then he walked over to the window. I could see him using his cell phone. Then our phone rang. I had to tell the children not to answer. They got scared.

Shapiro started calling through the window, trying to get my children to answer the door. That scared them more. Finally he put the flowers down and left. There was a note: "Dear Patty," it said. There was a peace sign and the word offering. He signed his name.

I called the police and asked what our rights were. They said they would issue a trespass ticket and charge Shapiro with harassment, since I had previously told him I had no comment.

I know he's trying to earn a living and pay his bills, but he can't do that at my expense.

— Patty Novack

★ ★ ★

When Carol McKinley first met Jeff Shapiro, she was working for KOA AM Radio in Denver. He simply walked up to her one day at the Justice Center and said he worked for the *Globe*. The next day she met him for breakfast, thinking they might compare notes.

Then he started calling her regularly, trying to get her to reveal her sources.

"I think we're talking to the same person," Shapiro said.

McKinley told him she wouldn't discuss her sources.

When he saw he was getting nowhere, Shapiro talked to her about his family. He said his mother had always been mean to him, didn't really think he was good enough. Shapiro told McKinley he needed somebody to be his big brother, like *his* source.

McKinley never revealed to Shapiro or anyone who her police source was. But when she compared notes with other reporters, it was obvious to her that there were only one or two detectives at the most who were talking to the media.

Julie Hayden, a veteran reporter for ABC's local affiliate, KMGH TV, Channel 7, had never seen the tabloids descend upon a town as they did on Boulder. One day Hayden arrived at a scheduled interview and her subject said, "Oh, I can't talk to you. I just sold my story exclusively to the tabloids."

What Hayden couldn't figure out was why the police and the DA's office were talking to someone like Jeff Shapiro and not even returning her calls.

Jeff would say, "Alex told me this. Alex thinks this and that." Then Jeff would say, "The police were talking to me." At first I thought he was lying. Then someone I trusted told me that they'd actually seen Jeff in Alex's office. Eventually I asked Shapiro to tell Hunter that I wasn't a bad person.

Shapiro would call me at home late at night or on my car phone. He'd page me. He'll never hang up until you say, "I have to go." I have to admit he's got a good technique. He works the phone well. He'll talk about personal things—how distressed he is: he plays for sympathy. He'd say he was feeling guilty about what he was doing, that he needed your guidance. He'd try to stir your maternal instincts. But you can't get too close to him. There might be a tape recorder in his pocket the whole time.

— Julie Hayden

On Sunday, August 3, the Ramseys ran their second full-page advertisement in the *Daily Camera*. They had previously asked the police to release the entire ransom note to the public but had been refused. The ad now sought the public's help in locating the writer of the note. In late April, before the Ramseys' experts were allowed to review the original note, their attorneys had made an agreement with the police not to release it as a condition of being allowed to keep photocopies of it. Now the ad reproduced the capital letters *D* along with *Do*, *M*, and *W* and the lower-case letters *k*, *r*, *u*, *th*, *of*, and *f* from the note, along with the same general profile of the killer that had been published the week before.

Also listed in the ad was a phone number for caller responses, which belonged to the Ramseys' private investigators. Television viewers were told by one ex–FBI profiler to call the police with information, since they were the ones gathering the evidence and running the case.

That same day, Denver morning talk-show host Peter Boyles, whose ratings were climbing as a result of his coverage of the case, took out his own full-page ad in the *Daily Camera*. It was addressed to Patsy and John Ramsey. He called their plea laughable and said they were not behaving like the parents of similar victims. He commented, "Fred Goldman's behavior exemplifies the true victim parent of a child who has been murdered.* You, on the other hand, have led Colorado and the nation on a seven month, low speed, white Bronco chase." Boyles stopped short of saying the Ramseys had killed their daughter.

Alex Hunter hoped that the information the Ramseys were publishing in their advertisements—a third and fourth ad displayed some phrases from the ransom note—combined with the $500,000 reward the *Globe* had offered in June might just produce something. Hunter's official position was that the Ramseys' ads weren't helpful, that it was unprofessional to release information that only the killer was likely to know—especially in a case like this, when all you had was a ransom note. Privately, however, Hunter understood the counterargument: that if you do release some information, someone might come forward and identify a suspect. Hunter was thinking of how the Unabomber had been caught when his brother saw some phrases

---

*Fred Goldman is the father of Ronald Goldman, the second victim in the O. J. Simpson double-murder case.

in the manifesto published in *The Washington Post* and *The New York Times* and recognized them from Ted Kaczynski's letters to his family. Hunter would have wanted the entire ransom note published, but it wasn't his case yet, and he couldn't go up against the Boulder police in public.

Lou Smit and Steve Ainsworth's list of people who had to be reinterviewed grew ever longer. By now Smit was all but certain that someone other than the Ramseys had murdered JonBenét. Nobody had been able to find any motive for them to kill their daughter. Nor had the police uncovered any indications of previous cruelty or perversity in either parent. Smit had to admit that the writing pad—and possibly the ransom note—was damaging evidence. But it was mitigated by the evidence that he thought pointed to an intruder.

In mid-July, on the same day that Smit asked the Ramseys about the stun gun and the Hi-Tec shoes, he spoke on the telephone to Sue Bennett, more widely known as Jameson. Under that name, she maintained a Web site that provided a detailed timeline of events connected with JonBenét's death, culled from various unofficial sources and public documents. She had contacted Smit at the suggestion of a journalist and provided him with information she thought he might not know.

Since February the police had been interested in Jameson, who lived in Hickory, North Carolina. They wanted to know how she got some of the information posted on her Web page—some information that had never been released to the public, including facts that even the police were originally unaware of. When the police learned that Jameson's real name was Bennett—which was John Ramsey's mother's maiden name—they became even more suspicious of her.

I used to go on-line to chat about home schooling. That's how I teach my kids.

After the murder of JonBenét, I spent more time on-line. I followed the case. I was curious. My first instinct was that the parents were going to be blamed for this, and I didn't think they were guilty. It didn't sound like something a parent would do. Then I read that JonBenét had an older half-brother. I went into one of the chat rooms to see if people were talking about him.

After I chatted a short time, someone called me a name. I was attacked. At the time, I was talking about what happened to JonBenét physically—in a blunt way. And of course that was why I was harassed. Someone even called me a pervert.

Then someone said that I was John Andrew—and that I was also the killer. I received one letter from a college professor suggesting I confess. I was even turned in to the police. I thought, This is ridiculous. I'm a middle-aged housewife with a bunch of kids. Later I learned I was actually considered a suspect.

I knew the authorities had to look at everyone. But it shocked me when I discovered the police were even reading conversations on the Internet.

—Jameson

Jameson told Lou Smit her theory of the murder: While the Ramseys were at the Whites' house on Christmas night, an intruder had entered their house and hid in the basement. The intruder was young and a friend of John Andrew's and might have had a history of pedophilia. Jameson said that after the intruder entered the house, he fantasized about kidnapping JonBenét for sex. While waiting for the family to get home, he wrote the ransom note. When they returned and JonBenét was put to bed, the intruder took her from her room and inadvertently killed her.

For his part, Lou Smit listened to Jameson and tried to reconcile what she said with what he knew. He encouraged her to deal directly with the Boulder police and gave her no investigative details about the case, but he couldn't dismiss her out of hand.

It was hard for Steve Ainsworth to wait in the wings. He and Smit hadn't been authorized to do too much. On August 7, he drove out to the Dakota Spa, the New Age retreat and meeting center in Lyons where Jacqueline Dilson worked. It was Dilson who had suggested to the police and the DA in January that her ex-boyfriend, part-time reporter Chris Wolf, had behaved oddly after JonBenét's death. Ainsworth had read the police reports about both Dilson and Wolf and felt that further follow-up was needed. Dilson told Ainsworth that on February 13, the day Koby and Hunter had first appeared on TV for a press conference, Chris Wolf "freaked out." She and her daughter, Mara, had both seen Wolf biting his nails when Hunter, looking into the camera, said, "We will get you." After the broadcast,

Wolf left, Dilson said. She added that Wolf had threatened to kill her in April. "I should just strangle you" were his words.

A month later, the Ramseys' investigators suggested that the DA should look at Wolf, not knowing that Ainsworth had already opened a file on him. Ellis Armistead, John Ramsey's chief investigator, faxed Ainsworth additional background information about Wolf. By the end of September, Smit and Ainsworth had received two more communiqués from the Ramseys' investigators suggesting that they continue to look at Wolf. It wasn't until February 1998 that Wolf was again contacted by the Boulder police. He was then working for the *Louisville Times* as a reporter. He agreed to give the police a sample of his saliva. Then he provided them with his palm prints and fingerprints and spent an hour supplying a handwriting sample. Wolf wondered if he would ever be cleared, since he believed the murder would never be solved.

The same day that Ainsworth interviewed Dilson, Bill Hagmaier of the FBI called Alex Hunter. Now that the trip to FBI headquarters in Quantico had been firmed up by the police, Hagmaier didn't want the DA and his staff to come east and be disappointed. The Bureau, he said, was not going to say that the Ramseys had killed their daughter. They were prepared to say that there was probable cause, but as of this date, the threshold of reasonable doubt had not been crossed.

Even though he now knew that there wasn't enough evidence for an arrest, Hunter told Hagmaier that he would still make the trip. He wanted to hear firsthand what the FBI experts had to say.

On August 13, the full, uncensored autopsy report, including six brief sections that had been held back from the public since May 15, was released.

The details previously not disclosed to the public were that a Colorado Avalanche sweatshirt had been draped over JonBenét's body after she was brought upstairs; that a red heart was found drawn on her left palm; that there was a sequined star on the front of her knit nightshirt; that she wore a gold cross necklace; that blue ties held her hair in ponytails; that the word *Wednesday* was sewn on her panties; and that a gold bracelet hung on her right wrist, bearing the inscriptions "JonBenét" and "12/25/96."

The public also learned that the possible murder weapon was something like a garrote made from a stick "irregularly broken at both ends and there are several colors of paint and apparent glistening varnish on the surface . . . Printed in gold letters on one end of the wooden stick is the word 'Korea.'"

Hal Haddon, one of John Ramsey's attorneys, told the *Daily Camera*, "The autopsy details released [Wednesday] confirm what we have known for some time—that this vicious murder was well-planned. The person who prepared the ligature and the garrote obviously put a lot of thought into this murder."

Months later, Bryan Morgan, another of John Ramsey's attorneys, told a British documentary filmmaker that after the release of the autopsy report he sat down with Ramsey to explain its contents. Throughout his professional life, Morgan had done this with many of his clients, most of them guilty of the crimes they were charged with. The attorney went through every detail of the coroner's findings with Ramsey, who became despondent and broke down. Morgan, who was likely to have had his doubts about Ramsey's innocence, watched his client closely. That was when the attorney discovered that Ramsey did not even know how JonBenét had died. What Morgan observed told him that John Ramsey had not killed his daughter.

In fact, the Ramseys' attorneys had, from the beginning, treated their clients as if they were guilty. It wasn't until one journalist confronted Hal Haddon and told him so that the attorneys started to think differently. Keeping the Ramseys isolated did not help, the reporter told Haddon. Also, adding Lee Foreman to the team—an attorney who more often than not defended guilty clients—sent the wrong message to the police and Alex Hunter.

Lisa Levitt Ryckman, a journalist who had left the Associated Press after seventeen years, had been working for the *Rocky Mountain News* for only two months when JonBenét was killed. Then, in April 1997, she was assigned to write a definitive profile on the Ramseys while her colleague Charlie Brennan continued to report daily events in the case. Ryckman's story would cover the three major tragedies in the Ramseys' lives—the death of John's daughter Beth; Patsy's cancer; and the aftermath of the death of JonBenét—but not the child's murder.

Ryckman went to Atlanta to conduct interviews with John's brother, Jeff, his daughter Melinda, and her mother, Lucinda, and would later talk to John Andrew in Boulder. She traveled to West Virginia to talk to Patsy's old school friends. She told all her interview subjects that she had no preconceived notions. "I'm going to let you tell the story," Ryckman said. "I'm not going to tell it." She emphasized that the Ramseys would be treated fairly. Word soon got around that Ryckman could be trusted.

The reporter met people who had unkind things to say about John Ramsey, but they wouldn't say them on the record, and the *Rocky Mountain News* refused to print negative comments without attribution. It was the paper's policy across the board.

On Sunday, August 17, ARE THEY INNOCENT? headlined the paper. The subhead added FRIENDS SAY THE RAMSEYS COULDN'T HAVE KILLED JONBENÉT. Accompanying the story on the front page was a large color portrait of the couple. Patsy had her arms draped around John's shoulders; her eyes were closed, and her smile spoke of satisfaction and contentment. John's face registered something closer to determination; his eyes were leveled directly at the camera.

Spread over ten pages was Ryckman's story—more space than the paper had given to any other article about the Ramseys to date. The interview subjects made the case that John and Patsy Ramsey could not be guilty. Old friends and relatives spoke fervently of how unfairly the Ramseys had been treated.

One photo showed Patsy sitting alone in JonBenét's bedroom at the family's Charlevoix vacation home, unaltered since the child's death. Patsy's fingertips touched a heart-shaped throw pillow embroidered with her slain child's name. Previously unpublished photos from the Ramsey family collection were also included in the spread.

Public reaction was quick and negative. Some phone calls were so abusive that Ryckman was frightened. She heard that even her colleagues saw her as "pro-Ramsey," a charge that frustrated her.

Meanwhile, Ann Bardach of *Vanity Fair* continued to call Alex Hunter, who was still refusing to grant her a second interview. Bill Wise didn't even return her calls. Bardach told Suzanne Laurion that according to her sources, the DA's office had stepped across the prosecutorial line and damaged the case irreparably. The word *malfeasance* had been used, she added.

Laurion once again tried to get Bardach to submit her questions in writing but to no avail. On August 16, the fact checkers for *Vanity Fair* called Laurion, which meant that Bardach had turned in her article. While Alex Hunter and his staff waited for the worst, Laurion sent Bardach a fax.

Annie...

Alex was very appreciative of this opportunity to comment on the Olbright and Sid Wells cases. . . .

In both these cases it was the District Attorney's decision, after careful consideration, that there was insufficient evidence to prove to a jury beyond a reasonable doubt that a named defendant(s) committed the crime. Under Colorado law, any citizen can challenge the decision of the District Attorney in a particular case by filing with a court a motion to compel prosecution. In both these cases, no such motion was filed.

Thanks, Annie for working so hard to let us have our say, even though we declined that follow-up interview. I thought it was really cool that you even called me from the plane Friday night just to respond to my question. I will miss you when this is all over.

Suzanne

That same day, Dick Woodbury of *Time* magazine put some questions to Hunter in writing. Laurion suggested how he might respond.

Q. What is Hunter's reaction to the escalation of the Ramseys' own investigation?
A. Whether the Ramseys' motivation is to uncover evidence or to enhance their public image, or a combination of both, it is their prerogative to take the actions they are taking.

Q. Haddon says he wants to publish the ransom note but Hunter's office doesn't want it released.
A. It's true that my investigators do not want the ransom note published.

Q. Haddon says he warned Hunter of impending escalation of the family's own investigation and Hunter grudgingly went along.
A. Yes, Haddon alerted me to the family's plans to print more ads and distribute fliers. It was not my place to either go along or not go along. The decision had already been made by the Ramsey attorneys.

Q. Exactly what is the purpose of the D.A.'s trip to Quantico?
A. Our purpose in visiting Quantico is primarily to get the FBI's perspective on the breadth and depth of the evidence collected by the Boulder Police Department.

On August 18, just after midnight, Sherry Keene-Osborn of *Newsweek*, who had developed a telephone relationship with Hunter, left a message for him, advising him to be careful in upcoming interviews:

> *Here are some of the things good reporters learn to do over the years: A reporter finds out something about the person they're interviewing, some personal thing, and pretends that has happened to them, too, to gain a simpatico relationship. Or the reporter gets into an intellectual discussion and the person lets down his guard and says things he doesn't mean to say. Getting the person mad is another way to do it if the other methods don't work. Confessing something to the person being interviewed makes the subject sympathetic to the reporter and more talkative. Reporters can be really nasty. Watch your ass!*

ARE POTENTIAL JURORS AFFECTED BY ADS?

The steady barrage of newspaper advertisements and fliers looking for help in apprehending JonBenét Ramsey's killer could be influencing potential Boulder jurors.

Jury consultants, former prosecutors and media watchers all say John and Patsy Ramsey have gone to great lengths to show both that they are trying to find the killer of their 6-year-old daughter and that they, themselves, are incapable of such a crime. Experts warn that potential jurors, who some day may even be asked to decide the couple's guilt or innocence, are being affected.

Michael Tracey, a professor at the University of Colorado, doesn't think the campaign will work. "Once public opinion is formed, it's very difficult to break it. For whatever reasons—some appalling reasons—the public opinion that the Ramseys are guilty was established early on," said Tracey.

— Marilyn Robinson
The Denver Post, August 24, 1997

★ ★ ★

379

Since the alleged break-in at the war room, none of the detectives wanted to work with Hunter's staff. They were even more disheartened because Koby hadn't supported them or Eller in this dispute with the DA's office. By now even the detectives were also calling the chief Dead Man Walking.

Carol McKinley reported how the detectives felt about Koby without mentioning the chief by name—she used the word *management*. After the broadcast, her police source called. "You should have said more," he said. She told him it would have been impossible to tell the full story without exposing him. He understood—he wouldn't want to be discovered as the source of a leak and lose his badge.

That same week, Fox TV offered McKinley a job covering the West Coast. She asked her police source if she should take it. Taking the job would be selling out, she said, and she knew he would never compromise himself that way, but she was a single mother and could use the money.

"Do it," he said. "Take the money and run."

She stayed put, partly because she felt she'd be abandoning him. She also didn't want him to think she'd simply been using him as a stepping-stone in her career. When she told him she'd declined the job, he said, "Good for you."

MOM DRESSED
JonBenét AFTER MURDER

SHOCKING NEW DETAILS FROM SECRET POLICE FILES

In a final grotesque act of love JonBenét Ramsey's mom Patsy redressed the little beauty queen in her Christmas finery after she died!

"JonBenét was wetting her bed almost every other day toward the end," Linda Hoffmann-Pugh, the former housekeeper/nanny at the Ramsey home, told the ENQUIRER.

"Sometimes she would be put in the other twin bed in her room if she had urinated in the first bed the previous night, or if Patsy checked on her and found her already soaked the same night—which she often did."

National Enquirer, August 26, 1997

★ ★ ★

On Friday, August 29, Tom Wickman told Hunter that not all of the physical evidence would be sent to the FBI for review. Some of the items had not been fully tested and evaluated by the CBI.

In fact, the police department had never told the DA that all the evidence would be given to the FBI. Hunter had just assumed that to be the case. He had arranged to make a swing of the East Coast after the Quantico meeting to see Donald Foster at Vassar and Henry Lee and Barry Scheck. But without an evaluation of all the evidence by the Bureau, the meetings with Lee and Scheck would be a waste of time, he thought. He would now have to backtrack and tell the public that this was just another step in a process and that there was still more to be done.

On Saturday morning, August 30, just days before his scheduled departure for the widely publicized conference, Hunter told Carol McKinley that he wouldn't be going to Quantico.

"They have half a loaf," Hunter told the reporter. "It's not enough for me to go." Knowing she was the first to hear of the DA's decision, McKinley called her police source to tip him off before airing her scoop. That afternoon, Hunter issued a press release noting that he wasn't going but that Hofstrom, DeMuth, and Lou Smit would meet with the FBI.

The next day, McKinley's police source told her that the department was frustrated by Hunter's decision. They had told the FBI that the DA was coming. Now they were going to look unprofessional.

"We're having a party," McKinley's source told her, "and the guest of honor decided it wasn't worth it."

5

On Saturday evening, August 30, Boulder, like the rest of the world, learned that England's Princess Diana had been seriously injured in an auto accident in Paris. Four hours later, in the early hours of Sunday morning, August 31, her death was announced. The media put Jon-Benét Ramsey on the back burner.

Vanity Fair, which was about to publish Ann Bardach's story on the investigation, considered postponing distribution of the magazine until after the funeral of the princess. For the moment, the cause of her accident was the mystery everyone wanted solved. The role of the paparazzi—who had been following the princess's car in the hope of photographing her—was the subject of almost every news broadcast. The involvement of the European and American tabloids in the tragedy was the subject of intense media scrutiny, since they paid the paparazzi handsomely for exclusive photos.

On September 2, the topic on *Larry King Live* was the paparazzi, tabloid coverage of celebrities, and the death of Princess Diana. On the show, the *Globe*'s editor, Tony Frost, who had once paid an exorbitant sum for photographs of the princess and her boyfriend, Dodi Fayed, on a yacht, vowed that he would never publish Diana's death-scene pictures. During the show's final commercial break, Larry King's staff told him that he had an important call.

King had been after John and Patsy Ramsey to be on his show ever since their January 1 CNN interview. Pam Stevens, one of King's producers, had even flown to Boulder on August 25, hoping to land the Ramseys, but so far they had remained elusive.

After the commercial break, King told his audience: "With us on the phone—she has called in—is Patsy Ramsey, the mother of the late JonBenét Ramsey, who obviously has something to say. Patsy, can you hear us?"

"Yes, I can."

"What prompted the call?"

"I am watching your show this evening," Patsy said. "I am just appalled and heartsick that you have stooped to the level of having Tony Frost on your program. He sits there so piously and says he will never print photographs of the late Princess Diana. Well, I'll have you know that he purchased illegally photographs of my sweet JonBenét, the autopsy photographs."

She and her family, Patsy said, were just normal everyday Americans, not famous like Princess Diana.

"These tabloid photographers have ruined our lives," she said. "They are printing false information. They stalk us. They stalk my child. It is just unbearable!"

"I guess no one can understand the pain of having a death," King said. "What's the latest? Is anything happening in the investigation that can clear you and get this over with for you?"

"I am not at liberty to talk about that," Patsy said. "I didn't call you to talk about that."

"But that's the only way this is going to stop—with you," King replied.

"The only way this is going to change is if a law is passed," Patsy said. She went on to credit her husband with a "wonderful" idea—a law requiring photographers to obtain a signed release before taking pictures of public figures.

"I took my son to a local department store to buy school supplies," she said. "As we were checking out, he looked to his left at his eye level. There was a photograph of his murdered little sister with the most horrible headline accusing his parents. I mean, I wanted to just—I didn't know whether to cry, be angry—you know, this is hurtful. . . . He looked at me like, you know, he tried to pretend he didn't see it. But how can you not see it when it is at a child's eye level?"

Soon time had run out, and King went off the air.

Charlie Russell, one of the Ramseys' attorneys' press representatives, happened to be watching the King show when Patsy called in. Later he told one reporter that Patsy was like Jell-O—the tighter you tried to hold on to it, the more likely it was to slip between your fingers.

That same day, September 2, *Globe* writer Craig Lewis received a faxed copy of Ann Bardach's as yet unpublished *Vanity Fair* article, "Missing Innocence," from a source in the magazine's distribution chain. Though it was only partly legible, Lewis called Alex Hunter and told him he had a copy. Lewis then went to the Justice Center, where Hunter and Wise waited nervously.

As Hunter read the story, he could see at once the impact it would have on the case. Bardach had launched a direct attack on both the Ramseys' innocence and on the DA's dealings with their attorneys and the Boulder PD. She revealed information from secret police reports and printed the full text of the ransom note—the first time it had been published in its entirety. Bardach cited as one of her sources a "deep throat" police officer.

Bill Wise was surprised that the full ransom note hadn't leaked before. The Ramseys, their lawyers, their investigators, their close friends, every detective on the case, the coroner, the city attorney, six people in Hunter's office, even Sherry Keene-Osborn of *Newsweek*—all had seen it, and some had copies. With all the money the tabloids threw around, it was ironic that it turned up in a publication that hadn't paid for it. Wise gave copies of the article to Hofstrom, DeMuth, and Smit. Bardach had attacked Hofstrom's integrity, made him look foolish and unprofessional, and implied that he was in awe of the Ramseys' attorneys. She also reported that Lou Smit had been called "a delusional old man" by an unnamed police source.

Wise made the article available to several Denver reporters. He saw no harm in giving them a good scoop.

That evening, Carol McKinley called her police source and told him to turn on his TV—Paula Woodward of Channel 9 was reading the ransom note on the air. McKinley's source, who had been watching coverage of Princess Diana, was puzzled and angry about its publication. He assumed the Ramseys' attorneys had leaked it—after all, they had been after the police to make the document public.

The next day, September 3, the *Rocky Mountain News* and all of Denver's radio and TV stations carried the full text of the ransom note, crediting *Vanity Fair*'s as yet unreleased story. But the story was buried under the obsessive coverage of Princess Diana's impending funeral.

The following day, Charlie Brennan reported some additional facts from Bardach's story.

PATSY RAMSEY INCONSISTENT ON DETAILS

Patsy Ramsey gave conflicting reports to police about whether she found the ransom note before or after she discovered that her daughter was missing, according to a story in Vanity Fair magazine.

And family friend Fleet White told investigators he didn't see JonBenét's body in a basement room when he checked it early the morning of Dec. 26, the magazine says.

Hal Haddon, an attorney representing the Ramseys, issued a statement: "The Vanity Fair article is glossy tabloid trash, filled with false and misleading defamation. What is most apparent from it is that certain unidentified police officers traded confidential information and police reports in exchange for an article that flattered them and smeared the Ramseys."

Boulder policeman Richard French, the first officer at the Ramseys' home, was troubled by how John and Patsy acted, according to the story.

A weeping Patsy Ramsey kept her eyes riveted on him, seeming to peer at him through fingers covering her eyes, French wrote in his report.

— Charlie Brennan
Rocky Mountain News, September 4, 1997

Jeff Shapiro, who had also obtained a copy of the *Vanity Fair* article, worried that Steve Thomas might be implicated as the police source Bardach mentioned. On Friday, September 5, he called the detective.

That evening, Thomas called Shapiro back from Quantico, where he had just arrived to consult with the FBI.

"Who is fuckin' doing this to me?" Thomas said. He was crying.

"All I know is that Bill Wise told one of our guys that he thought you did it."

"Those fuckers! Those fuckers!" Thomas yelled. "Do you know what will happen if it's on national TV that I'm the source?" He kept crying. "I don't know if I can do this anymore."

"You have to," I told him.

"I've been talking to my wife. I didn't sign up for this," he went on. "I'm just a blue-collar working detective trying to get justice for this little girl. I don't understand all this politics and stuff."

"You have to do your job. You can be cool," I said.

He kept crying. "I can't do it."

"This little girl needs you. God chose you to be her avenging angel and put you here for a reason," I told him. "You cannot walk away from it."

The roles had changed. I was now his big brother.

Then I started to cry.

"If I ever come forward to tell the world the truth, will you stand by me?" he asked. "Will you tell what you know about Hunter and the DA's office?"

"Yes," I answered. Then he said thanks and good-bye.

— Jeff Shapiro

Carol McKinley, who was attending a conference in Florida, called her police source while he was in Quantico to give him the public's reaction to the *Vanity Fair* article. When she reached him, he was scared—scared that he would be accused of leaking the information to Bardach. Still, he told her, Bardach's source shouldn't be blamed. "We've never had a voice," he said. McKinley agreed. Who could criticize any of them for wanting to vent their frustration?

Having read the entire *Vanity Fair* article several times, Alex Hunter saw that it was now almost impossible for the Ramseys ever to win in the court of public opinion. The mainstream media had now taken the same position that the tabloids had staked out from the beginning: who but the Ramseys could have killed JonBenét? Hunter wondered how he could obtain an impartial jury if the Ramseys were charged.

Then there was the attack on his office—particularly on Hofstrom and himself. Words Hunter had heard so often from Eller—*chumminess* and *web of influence*—were all over Bardach's story. The article accused the DA of incompetence and of favoritism toward the Ramseys' well-connected attorneys. Though Mike Bynum, John Ramsey's personal attorney, was a neighbor of Hunter's and had once worked for him as a deputy DA, the two of them had never talked about the case. Not only had Bynum not lobbied for special treatment, he had never even been invited into Hunter's home. For the first time in Alex Hunter's career, he was facing suggestions of professional impropriety.

"In all my political life," Hunter said, "these kinds of allegations have never been raised. I've been accused of excessive plea bargaining, and I've learned to deal with that in a healthy way. But this challenge to my integrity, I confess, has gotten my attention. No question, there is now a shadow hanging over me, and I don't know how dark it is. I wake up at night to the problem, stew about it, and then go back to sleep."

On September 6, Pete Hofstrom, Lou Smit, and Trip DeMuth left for Quantico. Hofstrom, sporting a University of Colorado sweatshirt, was more relaxed than usual with the local reporters who were on the same flight. He joked about the *Vanity Fair* story, introducing DeMuth as Boy Toy and Smit as Delusional Old Man, descriptions lifted from Bardach's article.

In Quantico, Detectives Thomas, Gosage, Harmer, Trujillo, and Wickman; their pro bono lawyers, who had accompanied them; and Hunter's team were driven to FBI headquarters in blue vans with tinted windows.

By now the Bureau's Child Abduction and Serial Killer Unit was quite certain that JonBenét's killer had never committed a murder before. The experts thought that the ransom note was written by someone intelligent but not criminally sophisticated. Someone who had planned a kidnapping in advance would have tried to impress the parents with how great a threat he or she posed. Words like *we* and *us*, *my group*, *we're large*, and *we're big* were absent. In the note, the kidnappers called themselves a "small foreign faction." That raised the question, foreign to whom? From whose point of view were they writing? Real foreigners would not refer to themselves as foreign. Here the author of the note had made a mistake, showing some weakness. There were also some inconsistencies: the note began formally, addressing "Mr. Ramsey," but toward the end addressed "John."

The FBI experts pointed out that every item involved in the crime seemed to have come from inside the house, including the pad, the pen, and the broken paintbrush. The duct tape and the rope for the ligature had most likely been purchased by Patsy Ramsey sometime in December. Nothing seemed to have come from outside the house. There was no evidence that anyone had turned on the lights during the crime, trying to find their way around an unfamiliar house. One agent told the assembled group: Is this an offender who came to the scene totally unprepared to do anything? If you were to believe that a stranger killed JonBenét, it would have to be someone very comfortable at the scene—which is very atypical. Kidnappers are usually in and out in a heartbeat. Just look at the Polly Klaas case. They don't kill and then hang around to write a two-and-a-half-page bogus note. And why choose, of all nights, Christmas, when someone else, maybe a guest staying with the family, could wander in? If the perpetrator had enough time to write the note at the Ramseys' home, he had enough time to take the victim alive or to take the dead body somewhere else. Then there was the scream. If it was loud enough for a neighbor to hear, a stranger wouldn't have hung around. After all, the parents might hear it and respond to their child's cry for help. Maybe the family dog would wake the sleeping parents? After all who knew besides those living inside the house that that night the dog would be staying with the Barnhills?

To the FBI profilers, the time spent staging the crime scene and hiding the body pointed to a killer who had asked, "How do I explain this?" and had answered the question: "A stranger did it." The staging suggested a killer desperate to divert attention.

Moreover, there was staging *within* staging: The loop of cord around one wrist was not a real indication that JonBenét had been restrained. The ligature that suffocated JonBenét—though she would eventually have died from the head injury—was in their opinion an unusual cover-up attempt, if that was what it was. The way the cord had been made into a noose—with the stick tied 17 inches from the knot—suggested staging rather than a bona fide attempt to strangle JonBenét. It suggested that the killer was a manipulative person, with the courage to believe that he or she could control the subsequent investigation. In short, everything about the crime indicated an attempt at self-preservation on the part of the killer.

On the other hand, the killer cared about the victim and wanted her found. He or she didn't want JonBenét outside in the dead of winter in the middle of the night. The child had been wrapped in a white blanket, her Barbie nightgown found lying next to her. Such caring and solicitude were not usually associated with a malevolent criminal.

Neither the behavioral nor the technical experts had ever seen a parental killing of a child that involved both a fatal injury and garroting, but that was a statistical detail, not evidence, they pointed out. And after reviewing what was known about the points of entry to the house, the shoe imprint, the palm print on the wine cellar door and the partial palm print on the ransom note—neither of which could be dated with certainty—the FBI told the visitors from Boulder that there was no hard evidence to indicate that an intruder had entered the house that night.

This was their best assessment of the crime scene, the FBI said. Where the Ramseys might or might not fit into it was up to the Boulder PD to determine. The circumstances seemed to rule out the involvement of a stranger. Nevertheless, it was a possibility, however remote.

The police then mentioned the Ramseys' behavior immediately after the body was found: the fact that John Ramsey was ready to fly to Atlanta with his wife annd son and leave his daughter's body—and the investigation into her murder—behind; the refusal to cooperate with the police; and the hiring of criminal attorneys. In reply, the FBI experts pointed out that no two people respond to trauma and grief the same way, and that the police should not overanalyze what they had observed. Most of the time, the parents of a victim are all over the police. "Why the hell haven't you caught my child's killer?" "What's going on? I want to know everything." In this case, the police had to acknowledge that it was their own commander's actions that had led to the long postponement of the parents' interviews.

The police also mentioned that the Ramseys had separate attorneys. Did this imply separate liabilities? They wondered aloud if one parent had knowledge of the crime before the fact, and the other had knowledge after the fact. The FBI had no answers to these speculations.

After the Quantico meetings, Detectives Thomas and Gosage visited Shurford Mills in Hickory, North Carolina, the country's largest manufacture of adhesives. The FBI had determined that the tape allegedly removed from JonBenét's mouth had first been manufactured in November 1996 under the brand name Suretape. The tape had a 40 percent calcium filler in the adhesive, and its yarn/scrim count of 20/10 helped pinpoint that Bron was the tape's distributor. The black duct tape Thomas purchased from McGuckin in May for the same price that appeared on Patsy Ramsey's sales slip carried the names Suretape and Bron.

6

Meanwhile, back in Boulder, Eller and Koby met to discuss how to deal with the *Vanity Fair* article. They knew that Bardach would never reveal her police source, and they doubted that he would come forward on his own. They discussed using polygraph tests to flush out the culprit, but Koby knew that without a hard lead, he didn't have the legal right to polygraph his officers. Eller and Koby knew they had to do something, but decided against a formal investigation. The department had already initiated two investigations relating to the case: an internal affairs inquiry into Larry Mason's charges against Eller, and the inquiry into the war-room computer break-in. Nevertheless, Koby announced that he was going to polygraph his officers, hoping the source might give himself up. This also seemed to be the right move for the department to make from a PR perspective.

On September 7, Koby went to Boston to consult with several local departments on the issue of police integrity. He had been planning the trip for some time, but now he knew what the real topic would be: the *Vanity Fair* article. The story was terribly damaging, not only to his department but to the city of Boulder.

When Greg Perry, the president of the police union, heard that Koby would be ordering polygraphs, he reminded the chief about a rock-solid provision in the union contract: until a suspect was named, no officer had to take a polygraph. Furthermore, the department was not allowed to discipline anyone for refusing to cooperate with an investigation. The purpose of a polygraph was to pressure a suspect and get him to confess. No one expected the test to reveal the truth. Still, an inconclusive result might be damaging: Officer X "failed" a polygraph. The union would not allow something like that to happen to one of their members because of the media—and they didn't care if it was *Vanity Fair* or the *Globe*.

Upon his return from Boston, Koby told his officers, "If you talk to the press, you're fired."

In New York City, Ann Bardach got a call from one of her two police sources. He told her that people thought John Eller was her source. Hunter will use the rumor against the him, the officer said, and it might cost Eller his position in the investigation. Bardach knew her sources, and Eller wasn't one of them—she had never even met the commander. She asked her source what she could do for the commander. Nothing, the officer replied. He didn't mind that Eller was under suspicion: it would take the heat off the detectives, he said.

Bardach, troubled by the conversation, talked to her editor. She asked *Vanity Fair* to call Tom Koby and set the record straight. The magazine refused. Eller was Koby's problem, they said, not theirs.

When Steve Thomas returned from the East Coast, he left a message on Jeff Shapiro's voice mail. Shapiro could tell he was still upset about the *Vanity Fair* article.

"I'm still disappointed in the department's leadership," Thomas said. "All the detectives are going to be polygraphed, maybe even prosecuted for leaking evidence. The Ramseys never had to take a polygraph, so why should we?" Then he added that three of the five detectives working the case were already consulting attorneys.

Shapiro then called Bruce Hagan, a producer for NBC's *Dateline*, and told him about the pending polygraphs and the possible prosecution of *Vanity Fair*'s police source. "I know a detective who might want to talk. Just listen to his story," he said, not revealing Thomas's name or that he was calling without the detective's permission. Hagan replied that he could have plane tickets waiting at Denver International Airport whenever they were ready to fly to New York.

Shortly afterward, Thomas called Shapiro. "I just got a voice mail from someone asking me to confirm that a guy named Jeff Shapiro is talking to some big East Coast media about the cops taking polygraphs. Just tell me the truth and we'll get past it."

"Absolutely," Shapiro told Thomas. "I talked to *Dateline*. It was supposed to be between me and them." Then he added, "I have this all set up if one day you want to go on the air."

"OK, that's no problem," Thomas said. "I understand."

I called Hunter and asked him if he was going to prosecute the detectives.

"What are you talking about?" he asked.

"About the Vanity Fair *leaks."*

"No. You're talking about this as if I'm going to press charges, and I'm not," Hunter said. "Tell them Koby has canceled the polygraphs. There's nothing more important in my entire life than seeing this thing move forward."

Then I called Steve Thomas. "Hunter's not pressing charges."

"That's fuckin' bullshit," Steve responded.

I had the feeling Eller was telling the detectives some things about the DA's office that weren't true, saying whatever he had to, to get everyone all worked up.

Now Hunter knew I had to be talking to Thomas, Wickman, or Gosage.

— Jeff Shapiro

By now, despite the lip service paid to it, preserving the integrity of the investigation was a distant memory. The infighting between the DA's office and the police department was being played out in the press through leaks. Some of the detectives understood that the leaks from the police suggested that the Boulder PD was more interested in saving face than in solving the murder. Of course, the Ramseys had been playing the image game in the press for quite a while. To that end, they would continue to provide leaks.

In the weeks to come, they would give out stories that pointed to an intruder. For example, Carol McKinley's Ramsey source told her that something had been found in the snow outside the house near the basement window grate on December 26. McKinley called Charlie Russell, one of their press representatives.

"What's in the snow?" she asked.

"A knee print."

"What else?" she asked. "Is that all you have?"

McKinley followed up with her CBI source, the DA's office, and police sources, but she came up empty. She was told that without a hand or finger imprint, toe print, or shoe print, there was no way to positively identify a knee print. McKinley believed that Russell may have led her astray.

In the preceding months, the Ramseys had launched a public campaign through advertisements, fliers, and direct mail. Now they were ready to present their case on national TV and in *Newsweek* magazine. Michael Bynum spoke to Dan Glick of *Newsweek* in late August to tell the writer that he could now publish a story about his July visit to the Ramseys' house. In a September 7 *Newsweek* piece, Glick and Sherry Keene-Osborn challenged the thoroughness of the police investigation and claimed that many presumed "facts" about the case—allegedly leaked by the cops and incriminating to the Ramseys—were simply wrong. A photocopy of the ransom note that Keene-Osborn had had access to for over a month was included in the article—its first appearance in print. It was likely that one of the Ramseys' attorneys provided her with the photocopy.

In writing about his visit to the house, Glick said that an intruder could have climbed through the broken basement window—an accurate observation that challenged what Ann Bardach had reported in *Vanity Fair* just days before. The *Newsweek* writers also attempted to correct several other misleading observations in Bardach's article. For example, she had written that John Ramsey made no attempt to collect the $118,000 needed for the ransom. In *Newsweek*, the writers outlined some of the steps Ramsey had taken on December 26 to obtain the funds. Glick and Keene-Osborn were getting their information directly from the Ramsey camp, and to some the story read like a defense brief for the couple.

There were others lobbying more directly for the Ramseys. In August, Alex Hunter had declined to be interviewed by ABC's Diane Sawyer, and Koby's office didn't even return Sawyer's personal calls. But while working on the *Newsweek* article, Sherry Keene-Osborn told Hunter that Michael Bynum had granted Diane Sawyer an interview and a tour of the Ramseys' house.

On September 10, just three days after the *Newsweek* story was published, *Prime Time Live* devoted a full hour to the Ramsey case.

"This is Mike Bynum," Sawyer told her audience, "a former prosecutor and close friend of the Ramseys. Since the murder, he has been by their side, and is now speaking for the first time."

"The Ramseys, in my opinion, based on everything I know,"

Bynum said, "are absolutely incapable of murder and incapable of harming that child."

"You're saying there has never, for a moment, been a flicker of . . . even doubt in your mind?" Sawyer asked.

"In my mind, that is absolutely correct."

Bynum told Sawyer about the Ramseys' most familiar complaint—that the police had tried to withhold JonBenét's body in exchange for interviews. He didn't know whether or not it was illegal, Bynum said, but he was sure it was immoral and unethical. "Hell no, you're not getting an interview," he had personally told the police, said Bynum.

Sawyer asked why the Ramseys had acted the way they had—with a seemingly unnatural restraint and concern for how they appeared to the public. She implied that innocent parents would not only give police an interview but most likely camp out at police headquarters and refuse to leave until the case was solved.

"In the circumstances that John and Patsy Ramsey were in," Bynum said, "you go ahead and do that, and pick up the pieces later, because you're going to be shredded."

"Innocent or not?"

"Absolutely," Bynum replied. "Absolutely."

"Polygraphs," Sawyer asked. "Have they taken a lie detector?"

"Not to my knowledge."

"Should they? Will they?"

"Not if I ever have anything to say about it."

"Why?"

"Oh, that's Ouija board science, number one," Bynum responded. "And I will also tell you, to my knowledge, that that request has not been made of John and Patsy."

Later Sawyer asked, "Who do the Ramseys think killed their daughter?"

"They don't know," Bynum replied. Then he said that the Ramseys had passed on leads to the police.

Sawyer asked if they were "real leads" or "serious leads."

"Very much so," Bynum told Sawyer. "We know absolutely that there is evidence of an intruder. But that information, interestingly enough, hasn't leaked out."

Together, Sawyer and Bynum walked through the now-vacant Ramsey home. Standing in the basement at the train-room window, Bynum demonstrated how the entire frame of the three-section, multipaned window could swing open, enabling a man of his size—"5-10 and 175"—to get through. He showed how a perpetrator could have reached the window merely by hoisting himself up, using an object such as the suitcase that police found beneath the window.

For the first time, the entrance to the wine cellar was shown on TV. Sawyer's voice-over described a windowless concrete room that was not as hidden as some press reports had suggested.

"Doesn't it almost have to be someone who at least knew where the wine cellar was," Sawyer asked Bynum, "or had a kind of map in their head of the house?"

"Well, I don't know that for sure, but that's certainly a possibility," Bynum replied. "I don't think that that house is one that is too difficult to describe, at least in terms of getting in and around the house."

Sawyer pressed Bynum about the evidence of the intruder that he'd alluded to earlier. "There's no fiber sample, there's no DNA," she said. "There's no sign of forced entry."

"Well, you know a lot more about the evidence, apparently, than I do," Bynum replied. "I don't think it's known what there is or is not. I think that there are things in terms of the actions of this individual in that house, the note that was left, that really have been kept very, very secret from the public." Bynum refused to elaborate about the details, however, to support his position that there was an intruder. Sawyer told her audience that over two thousand people had visited the Ramseys' house the previous Christmas for Boulder's holiday season tour of homes.

Another question raised by the case, said Sawyer, was whether JonBenét had been sexually abused. She presented Dr. Francesco Beuf, JonBenét's pediatrician, on the telephone. He had reviewed his medical records, the doctor said, and told the ABC audience that there was no history of sexual abuse.

Sawyer's broadcast marked the first time a network TV show had mentioned the possibility of an intruder.

Alex Hunter and Suzanne Laurion had different opinions about how the DA's office should respond in the wake of the *Vanity Fair* article. Laurion wanted the DA to stop talking to the press, including *The New Yorker* and Chuck Green of *The Denver Post*. She told Hunter that his involvement with the media would backfire. All he could think about, however, was how to restore his credibility. For the time being, he told Laurion, he'd follow his instincts. He approached Sherry Keene-Osborn to do a profile of him for *Newsweek*. The magazine declined her suggestion, so she prepared a profile of the DA for the *Colorado Statesman* instead.

By now the media frenzy surrounding Princess Diana's death was subsiding, and Ann Bardach was making the rounds of the talk shows to promote her article. One afternoon, Hunter assembled all fifty-five members of his staff and ordered pizza and soda for them. Everyone had felt the impact of Bardach's story, with its strong criticism of the DA's office. They should not take the broadsides personally, Hunter told them. Don't feel beleaguered, he said, and urged everyone to get on with the important work they were doing and to be proud of their efforts.

Hunter asked for questions, and for the first time, Pete Hofstrom talked about the case. Clearly, he was hurt. Bardach's accusations against him had been particularly unfair, considering Hofstrom's dedication and commitment to his work. Hunter's pep talk had come not a moment too soon. Nothing was more symbolic of his staff's feelings of persecution than Pete Hofstrom's having taken a day off from work—the first in twenty-three years.

To: Alex Hunter
Fr: Suzanne Laurion

Let's use the *Vanity Fair* article as a model: Would we have been better off granting a second interview to Annie Bardach refuting some of the ludicrous crap she cooked up? If so… and if we truly have nothing to hide… then maybe we adjust our interview policy. In addition to okaying interviews to those reporters who call us with scoops, we also okay interviews to those reporters who provide convincing evidence that they're about to challenge our office's credibility.

In Quantico, the police had been told that they still had a lot more work to do. It wasn't that they had done a bad job, but there were many tasks still to be completed before the case could be considered ready for presentation to the DA's office.

The detectives accepted the fact that they would have to get back to work: More than 180 videotapes from the Ramseys' home had to be viewed. Books from the Ramseys' shelves had to be examined and, in some cases, read. Pathologists had to be consulted to determine if

JonBenét's vaginal injury had taken place before or after her death and, if it was prior, to see if penetration had come from the child herself or from another person. The police would have to track down the origin of a small amount of cellulose that had been found in JonBenét's vagina.* The possibility existed that it could have come from the broken paint-brush used for the ligature. The knot on the ligature that acted like a slip-knot also required more investigation. Burke's friends and their parents had yet to be interviewed. More DNA testing had to be done—in the hope of finding a match for the foreign DNA found under JonBenét's fingernails and in her underpants, since it didn't look as if John's and Patsy's DNA matched it. The list went on and on.

Carol McKinley's source told her it would be hard work. He admitted that much of it should have been done earlier.

After the meeting with the FBI, Hunter's staff told him that the police detectives were more certain than ever that the Ramseys had murdered their daughter—that's what the cops were telling Koby. Hunter's rep-resentatives said that they hadn't reached the same conclusions.

The perceptions of the various participants at the FBI meetings were so different that to clarify matters for himself, Hunter asked to meet with Koby. They scheduled a meeting to discuss the FBI's evalu-ation, but first they decided they had to talk about the media in gen-eral and the *Vanity Fair* article in particular.

On September 15, Hunter met with Koby and the detectives' three pro bono attorneys. Everyone agreed that leaks tended to backfire on them. Bill Wise, for example, remembered the time when he confirmed for the *Rocky Mountain News* that the police weren't providing the DA's office with results of the DNA tests. He had expected the next morn-ing's headline to read COPS AREN'T COOPERATING WITH DA. Instead, the spin on the story was the reverse: BOULDER PROSECUTOR OUT OF LOOP, implying that Hunter was ill-informed about the investigation.

Koby and Hunter decided they should limit their press statements to joint releases, though they realized it wouldn't stop all the leaks, especially from the Ramsey camp. It was remarkable that this strategy meeting took place, given the wide rift between the Boulder PD and the DA's office. However, the previous Saturday, Hunter had met with

---

* Cellulose is a carbohydrate of high molecular weight that is the chief constituent of the cell walls of plants. Raw cotton is 91 percent cellulose. Other important natural sources are flax, hemp, jute, straw, and wood.

Koby and a mediator to plan some damage control in the wake of Ann Bardach's article.

The facilitator told them that their problem was even more intractable than some NATO situations he had handled. Koby agreed to write a letter of apology to Hunter's staff on behalf of the police, stating that the information leaked by his department to *Vanity Fair* was false and misleading.

As planned, on September 22 Hunter met again with Koby and pro bono attorneys Miller, Baer, and Hoffman, this time to discuss the FBI's evaluation of the Ramsey case. The attorneys said that the case was on track. The detectives were doing high-caliber work and good interviews. Despite what the detectives believed, however, it wasn't an 80 percent certainty that Patsy Ramsey had killed her daughter. It was clear that charges could not be filed against the Ramseys—or against anybody else—at this point.

Bob Miller had developed a long "to-do" list—people to reinterview and loose ends to be tied up. Among those to be questioned were friends of the Ramseys, children who had played with JonBenét, and a long list of peripheral people who had yet to be excluded as suspects. Richard Baer, who was familiar with the physical evidence, said he was working closely with Detective Trujillo and that he had his own to-do list. Optimistically, he said that he thought the case could still be solved.

Toward the end of the meeting, Koby suggested that Hunter convene a grand jury—to decide whether charges should be filed against the Ramseys or anyone else. The FBI had also mentioned this possibility. Hunter said he would discuss it with his staff but that to him it looked more like a political solution than a way of solving the case.

That afternoon, when Hunter told Hofstrom what Koby had suggested, Hofstrom, who had been at Quantico, said he simply didn't see enough evidence for a grand jury. He thought the move was premature and that the cops were looking for a way to relinquish their responsibility, which was to gather the evidence needed for prosecution. Then Hunter called Bob Grant, one of the metro DAs advising him on the case. "It's still too early," Grant told him, echoing Pete Hofstrom. "Before you take that step, get more of your investigation completed."

Constantly having to answer conflict-of-interest charges was getting to Alex Hunter. A shadow had been cast on the image of his office, and he wondered if it would recede in time for him to be of use in the Ramsey case.

A reporter for the *Star* tabloid had discovered on file in a local recorder's office a real estate partnership affidavit between Bill Gray, a civil attorney for the Ramseys, and Hunter. On September 22, Channel 7, the local ABC affiliate, began broadcasting a series about various legal entanglements among players in the Ramsey case, implying conflicts of interest and a so-called web of influence. Hunter's explanation that Gray had been his attorney only once, back in 1969, fell on deaf ears.

More problems loomed ahead. In the pipeline, as he put it, was a case in which it had taken his office nearly two years to file murder charges. The Boulder PD was furious about the delay, but Hunter's staff had thought there were mitigating circumstances and had looked deeply into the reasons why Michael Grainger had killed his 300-pound bedridden wife, Sonia. Hunter knew that given the current climate in Boulder, he was sure to be attacked for being soft on Grainger.

It wasn't only Boulderites who were doubting his methods, however. The eyes of the entire country were on him.

To: Alex [Hunter] and Bill [Wise]
Fr: Suzanne [Laurion]

I continue to be amazed at HOW MUCH reporters KNOW but are keeping out of their stories. If they're to be believed, they have so many police sources they know more than we know.

On September 23, Hunter told Koby that the time was not right for a grand jury. Knowing that work on the investigation still had to be completed, the police chief withdrew his request.

Two days later, Geraldo Rivera, who had been pursuing the thesis that JonBenét's killer must be a member of the Ramsey family, hosted "The Ramseys Fight Back" on his daytime TV show.

Jennifer Kay, a producer for Rivera's show, had persuaded Nedra Paugh, Patsy's mother, to give an impromptu interview from her home in Roswell, Georgia.

"Well, every day was Christmas to JonBenét," Nedra said. She sat slumped in a chair, a defeated woman, her heartbreak palpable. "She [JonBenét] had a wonderful life. I often looked at her and Burke as well and thought how wonderful life had been to them. She was beautiful. She was gracious, intelligent, loved life, loved her friends, loved animals. She loved everything. And that was taken away by a thief in the night as she slept. Now she is in heaven, and I'm sure she's a very good angel."

When Nedra mentioned the crime, it was in a string of half-completed thoughts and seeming nonsequiturs: "I didn't know that she had been mole . . . molested to some extent and hit on the head. I didn't know that. And somehow I hoped that she had died very quickly, and I think that she did. I . . . I really do believe that whoever has done this strangled her, because I'm sure that she put up a tremendous fight. Although she had tape on her mouth, she couldn't scream. But I knew she had fought.

"To think that a perfectly healthy, happy child, sleeping in her bed on Christmas Day, dreaming, as the story says, of sugar plum buds—and for someone to kill and murder, molest, and then, if that isn't enough, strike her on the head, is something—it's just more, because if that hadn't happened, she would be well and alive, making a contribution to the world."

After the segment with Nedra, Rivera chatted briefly with producer Kay, who shared her observations of Patsy, with whom she'd spoken the previous week in Atlanta without a camera crew.

"She told me, you know, she wishes that the police would not focus on her anymore but find who the real killer is," Kay said. "And she also told me she didn't care what the public felt about her being guilty or innocent. She knew in her heart she didn't do it."

After a panel discussion featuring various Ramsey friends and defenders, Rivera put the spotlight on the Ramseys themselves.

"Imagine this: Your beloved six-year-old, the child at the very soul and center of your existence, is snatched from her bed as you sleep. The child is then tortured, sexually assaulted, and brutally murdered in the basement of your dream house. Grief-stricken, your nightmare has only just begun, because almost everyone on the planet thinks that you did it. Now imagine—just imagine for a moment that you're innocent.

"We invite the Ramseys"—he paused for effect, then said, "come on down."

7

It was now clear to everyone in the DA's office that Hunter no longer wanted simply to prosecute the Ramsey case—he wanted to solve it. His staff had never seen him behave this way before. He wanted access to all the police evidence so that he could cut Lou Smit and Steve Ainsworth loose to investigate the case as they saw fit. He wanted Vassar professor Donald Foster to look into the writings of Janet McReynolds and other possible suspects as well as Patsy's. He was prepared to call upon both the CBI and Sheriff Epp for help.

Alex Hunter has a little girl and a little boy as well as older children. One child is about JonBenét's age. As a father, he understands that there could be nothing more horrible than having your daughter die, especially if it's by your own hand. I mean, if I were to accidentally kill my child, the horror I would be struck with for the rest of my life would be immeasurable. I can't even conceive of it.

So as a human being, Alex feels it immensely. And as a prosecutor, he has to do it right. He must do it in a way that he can accept because he's ultimately answerable to himself. He's going to make sure he does the right thing for number one before he satisfies the community. If the right thing ultimately disappoints the community or the police, he'll still do it. How can he live with that politically? I don't know.

I hope Alex has reached that point where he can decide which is more important—to live with himself as a human being or to pony up to someone else. But keep in mind that this is Alex's last term in office. You never want to leave a job on a down note. You want to have a swan song.

—former judge Virginia Chavez

As far as the DA's office knew, there was no DNA evidence to link JonBenét's murder to her parents or any other member of the family. No murder weapon had been identified by forensic evidence. The flashlight found on the kitchen counter, a possible weapon, would have been accessible to anyone. The Ramsey family background did not indicate any of the pathologies generally associated with this kind of murder or with child abuse. No one had seen either parent so much as scold their children in public.

The police were unable to find a motive for the crime. Hunter remembered what Dr. Lee had said to him early in the case—that JonBenét's death may have been the result of an accident, that what may have begun as an accident was then covered up to look like a murder. Lee had suggested that the investigators look at the evidence from that point of view.

Hunter understood that JonBenét's participation in beauty pageants caused people to think that Patsy was somehow suspect as a mother. But it was wrong to focus suspicion of murder on the Ramseys simply because of some choices they made for their daughter were wrong. As an officer of the court, Hunter was troubled that the public had reached a conclusion about the Ramseys' guilt.

"We don't have a filable case," John Eller told Alex Hunter in late September, referring to the Ramseys—not because there was evidence of an intruder, the commander pointed out, but because there wasn't enough admissible evidence against the Ramseys. There was no smoking gun.

Clearly, Eller had listened to the pro bono attorneys, who had become an asset to the investigation—and thereby to Hunter. They had accomplished what his office had been unable to do, and in a nonadversarial way. Even with Eller's new attitude, however, Hunter was unhappy with him and wanted the commander replaced. In the DA's eyes, Eller had a paramilitary approach. He stifled the instincts and abilities of some of his detectives, which in turn stymied and stalled the investigation. If they wanted to solve this crime, they needed creativity and ingenuity, not rigid, inflexible, linear thinking. Eller had to go.

Hunter knew that Koby had been avoiding the inevitable—removing Eller—since the beginning. The DA had never tried to pressure Koby about it, because he wanted to preserve his relationship with the police. Between them, they had to deal with more than four hundred felonies a year. Hunter hadn't listened to Koby when the chief wanted Wise disciplined in February. Why should Koby listen to Hunter's suggestions to remove Eller?

Nevertheless, Hunter knew that he and Koby had to come to terms about Eller. Frustrated, he called the chief. A few days later the two men met.

Koby began by telling Hunter that he was in the midst of restructuring the department. He wouldn't give any details other than to say that Tom Wickman now had full authority on the Ramsey case. Hunter thought Wickman was a good man, but he told Koby that some of the cops working the case were a hindrance. They were self-righteous, conspiratorial, judgmental, and unforgiving. Before Koby left, he told Hunter that the items on the to-do lists would be completed by December 1.

Thinking that Koby might listen to Epp, Hunter called the sheriff and asked him to try once more to influence the chief to remove Eller. Epp said he would.

Koby agreed to meet with Epp, and this time the chief indeed seemed to listen. Several days later, Koby called Pete Hofstrom to talk about Mark Beckner, a twenty-year veteran of the Boulder PD and now a commander, who had stood in for Koby on several occasions and was known for his organizational skills. What did Hofstrom think of Beckner? Eller's name was never mentioned. The DA's office had never had a problem with Beckner, Hofstrom said.

MORE DETECTIVES
MAY TAKE ON RAMSEY CASE

Police Chief Tom Koby said Friday that he's considering adding more detectives to the JonBenét Ramsey murder investigation.

"One of the things we are still assessing is all the information we got from Quantico," Koby said. "We have to look at our work plan and see if we need additional resources or not."

— Charlie Brennan and Kevin McCullen
Rocky Mountain News, September 27, 1997

When Alex Hunter read the "More Detectives" story in the *Rocky Mountain News*, he must have wondered how the other media would react. The to-do list was lengthy. The Ramseys' neighborhood had to be canvassed again. Cars that had been parked in the vicinity had never been checked. Investigators had to take saliva swabs from many people in order to eliminate them as suspects through DNA testing. The question of the foreign DNA found in the mixed stain on JonBenét's underpants might innocently be accounted for by finding a playmate she had exchanged clothes with. Interviews from as far back as January, February, and March still had to be transcribed. The possible use of a stun gun, the palm print on the wine cellar door, and the shoe imprint were still issues. Hunter hoped all of it would be accomplished before the press got wind of what was still under investigation.

On Saturday night, September 27, Steve Thomas called Jeff Shapiro. "Jeff, let's get together for a few beers," Thomas said.

The next day at 9:00 P.M., in Chautauqua Park, Gosage, Thomas, and Shapiro sat crammed into the detective's little Mustang.

The detectives were in gym clothes. Gosage had a baseball cap on backward. Shapiro was in a black James Bond blazer. It was raining outside, just like in some detective movie.

Thomas said he wanted to go over a few things. Before long Shapiro was talking about Hunter and how the DA had suggested that he get some dirt on Eller. Then Thomas asked him to describe Hunter's office. Shapiro now felt he was being interviewed.

"There's a picture of J. F. Kennedy over his desk," I said. "There's a table at the back." They start to laugh. "OK, OK, we believe you."

"Could you give Hunter a call and just talk to him for a minute," Gosage asked, "so we know you're telling us the truth?"

I said, "No."

Thomas looked at me like, Don't fuck with me.

I just looked back at Thomas. Finally I said, "Fuck."

Thomas activated his cell phone, and I gave him Hunter's home number. Hunter's answering machine picked up.

"What does Hunter see in you?" Gosage asked.

"I guess he likes me. I brought him information, like I brought you information," I told him. "When I talk to Hunter, it's different from the way I talk to you. He's more political. He's not military the way you are."

"Are you a double agent for Hunter?" Gosage asked.

"No. I'm a twenty-four-year-old kid caught in the middle of something."

"Junior detective," Thomas called me. Then Gosage repeated, "Junior detective." It was their joke.

"If I'm a junior detective," I interjected, "I should have a gun."

"You could be a private investigator if you want," Thomas said. "You don't need to be licensed in Colorado." I told them I'd start looking for a

badge. Steve said he'd introduce me to this guy who sold guns below cost, a Glock or a Beretta.

After that Sunday night, at Chautauqua Park, I felt like one of the boys.

— Jeff Shapiro

What Jeff Shapiro didn't know was that the detectives were wearing a hidden microphone and that the conversation was being recorded and transmitted by radio to a van parked just a hundred yards away.

The following Thursday, October 1, Gosage took the tape to Eller, who listened to Shapiro recount how Hunter wanted to smear him with the supposed sexual harassment allegation. Eller remained calm. The next day, he and Gosage met with Koby and played him the tape.

Koby was thunderstruck: Thomas and Gosage were not only trying to find the murderer of JonBenét, they were also investigating the conduct of Hunter's office. He was angrier at the detectives than at Hunter. On the one hand, the tape confirmed what Eller had been telling him all along about the DA's office; on the other hand, it gave the police enormous power over Hunter—power that Koby wouldn't allow them to use. Koby knew that Eller's rage at Hunter would destroy whatever was left of their professional relationship. The department's work would suffer. Eller would have to be replaced. Koby kept the original tape and ordered Gosage to destroy the copies in his presence. To Gosage, it was clear that Koby was "handing up" Eller to protect Hunter.* When Gosage told Thomas what had happened, Thomas believed it was more important to Koby to maintain his relationship with Hunter than to expose the DA's subterfuge.

Two days earlier, September 29, the Boulder County clerk's office provided copies of the previously sealed search warrants to the media and the public. Representatives of every newspaper, radio station, local television affiliate, and national network stood in line to obtain a copy of the sixty-five-page package, which cost $48.75. This represented the largest batch of released investigative material from among the eight thousand pages the DA's office had received from the police department to date. A total of 179 sets were purchased.

* Narcotics officers' lingo: to sacrifice one person for another.

By now Hunter had decided to give up his fight to keep the search warrants sealed. Both the text of the ransom note and a photocopy of the original had been published, and nine months of aggressive reporting by the media had led to the disclosure of many other details of the crime.

In a cover page to the search warrants, the DA's office wrote that no evidence of child pornography had been found to date, and for the first time it was confirmed that nothing "consistent with semen or seminal fluid" had been found at the crime scene. Two brief passages had been blacked out by Judge MacDonald, at the request of the DA's office. After the line "In the area where Det. Arndt had told Det. Everett that the decedent had been found by her father he observed two blankets on the floor in the center of the room," a line and a half were deleted. On the next page, which was a list of items removed from the Ramsey home, a line was censored by the judge. The second deletion was preceded by "any writing pads, lined and white in color, any examples of handwriting, any felt-type writing utensil with black ink." The media speculated that the deleted lines referred to the piece of duct tape found in the wine cellar. Only the police and the killer would know its color and width.

The newly released documents supported early press reports, which had stated that though there were urine and possibly blood stains on JonBenét's underpants and long johns, there was no corresponding fluid on her pubic area. Apparently the child's body had been wiped clean, leaving some smeared blood. The substance used to wipe JonBenét clean still had not been identified.

The warrants confirmed that fragments of a green substance, consistent with the decorative Christmas garland found on the spiral staircase, were found entwined in JonBenét's hair, which suggested that she might not have been awake but asleep, wounded, or already unconscious when she was carried down the stairs. The second addendum to the search warrant noted that when Sgt. Whitson first arrived at the Ramsey house, he noticed what seemed to be a pry mark on the door jamb. The damaged area "appeared to have been less weathered than the surrounding surfaces on the door and door jamb," the document said.

The Ramseys' attorneys were quick to point out in a press statement that the documents contained nothing to incriminate their clients. Hal Haddon said it was "significant" that people close to the investigation had not leaked information that was exculpatory to the Ramsey family, such as the pry mark. He also provided the media with a photograph of the door jamb, which the police had seen on December 26, and said, "The material released today demonstrates substantial evidence of an intruder."

The next day, the *Rocky Mountain News* published the 5 x 8 inch photograph alongside a story that quoted Haddon as saying that important evidence of an intruder had been withheld from the public.

The Ramseys' former housekeeper, Linda Hoffmann-Pugh, was surprised to see both the picture and Haddon's statement. The photograph showed the spot where a protective metal plate on the door jamb had fallen off months before the murder. She had seen the plate become looser until one day it fell off, revealing the same marks that she now saw in the photograph. Hoffmann-Pugh had taken the plate to Patsy, who wasn't concerned enough to have it replaced. The detached plate had sat on a shelf in the hallway near the kitchen. Now Hoffmann-Pugh wondered if the police had discovered it and made the connection.

SUSPECTED SEXUAL ABUSE REVEALED IN UNSEALED JonBenét DOCUMENTS

. . . 65 pages of search warrants and affidavits were released [yesterday]. Most of the brief segments excised at Alex Hunter's request appear to be references to the duct tape covering JonBenét's mouth, blacked out in the hope that only the killer would know its color.

— Charlie Brennan
Rocky Mountain News, September 30, 1997

After the Quantico meetings, Sheriff Epp felt that Hunter no longer needed Steve Ainsworth. The DA had never been allowed to give him free rein and assign him to interview a string of witnesses. He had done a good job for Hunter, but now Epp wanted his detective back.

The six months he'd spent on loan to the DA's office had been both fascinating and frustrating to Ainsworth. Some of his fellow sheriff's deputies had told him he was wasting his time looking for an alternate suspect. Ainsworth would reply, "Maybe so, but that's a door you're going to have to close sooner or later, so you might as well get it done now." Like Hunter, he believed that every possibility had to be investigated.

The Boulder police had a different attitude. In the first forty-eight hours after JonBenét's death, only about 25 percent of the neighbors had been home. Now the other 75 percent would have to be interviewed. "We don't need to do that," one detective told Ainsworth. "We know what happened. The Ramseys did it." That was the typical response of Eller's detectives when it was suggested that they investigate a new lead.

Ainsworth felt the only real piece of evidence against the Ramseys was that they were home when their daughter died. But there was evidence that pointed away from the Ramseys—for example, the broken glass on the suitcase under the basement window, the scuff mark on the wall—although nothing indicated a specific person.

Ainsworth thought the crime scene exhibited an "organized disorganization." In his opinion, the cord and duct tape had been brought to the house. "Using the pad and pen from the house," Ainsworth told one deputy DA, "was a stroke of genius," a ruse within a ruse. The intruder had made it look as if the Ramseys had committed the murder and had then covered it up in such a way as to make it appear that an intruder had killed JonBenét.

During the last days of September, a reporter told Alex Hunter, "If you don't have this solved by Christmas, you're out of here." To Hunter the statement seemed an exaggeration, just like the stories the reporter's newspaper published. But it was a clear indication of the public's frustration. Still, the public was no more frustrated than the police and the DA, who knew that the available evidence so far proved nothing.

In this climate, Hunter had been talking to Bill Wise and Suzanne Laurion about how to repair the reputation of his office. The *Vanity Fair* article had left a stain on just about everyone involved in the case and was still a topic of conversation. When Hunter talked to several journalists he felt comfortable with and asked how his office was perceived, they answered as he had expected: his credibility would remain an issue as long as he was DA.

While he mulled over whether or not to change tack, Hunter continued to give a series of interviews to *The New Yorker*, hoping to provide a more accurate picture of what he perceived to be his search for justice in the Ramsey case.

Meanwhile, Suzanne Laurion reminded him that he had many options, and on October 2, she presented him with an analysis.

10/2/97

To: Alex [Hunter] and Bill [Wise]
Fr: Suzanne [Laurion]
Re: Suspected problem and proposed solution

We've been beaten up by the press lately and we need to do some things to rehabilitate the office's credibility, assuming we determine for certain that our credibility has been damaged. "If there's gonna be a day that comes when we have a case," Hunter said, "I would like to be making these moves with as much credibility as we can."

Alex believes the solution lies in a two-pronged media campaign. (1) Open with a formal statement to the media, take no questions, but do work the media crowd for about a half hour before the statement. (2) Follow this with a series of media appearances with only one condition: Alex gets uninterrupted opportunity to speak his piece.

DAY 1: Meet on-the-record with two local daily papers.
DAY 2: Meet on-the-record with two daily Denver papers.
DAY 3: Hold news conference with local and Denver radio.
DAY 4: Hold news conference with four Denver TV stations.
DAY 5: Flip coin to choose among *Geraldo*, *Internight* MSNBC, *King*.
DAY 6: CBS.. network chooses program (*48 Hrs.*, Rather, *60 Min*).
DAY 7: ABC.. network chooses program (*PrmeTmeLve*, Jennings, *Nightline*, *20/20*, *GMA*)
Day 8: NBC.. network chooses program (*Dateline*, *Today*, Brokaw).
Day 9: PBS *Charlie Rose*
Day 10: Local weeklies (*CO Daily*, *Planet*)
Day 11: National weeklies (*Newsweek*, *Time*)
Day 12: *American Journal*, *Extra*, *America's Most Wanted*, *Inside Edition*

Alex says there are two potential "pegs" to hang this campaign on: (1) Koby's announcement that he's reorganizing his Ramsey team, (2) just before the [one] year anniversary.

After discussions with Alex, I concluded that THE MESSAGE needs to cover 3 R's: rift, role, resolution. We must be prepared to tell the truth about the rift between the cops and DA. We must have image-, example-laden statements about our role vs. that of the cops. We must give concrete reasons why we KNOW this is a more complicated case than people imagine.

RIFT

—Yes, it's bad. The FBI and CBI will attest that our guys are set to evaluate and analyze yet the cops are denying us access to the evidence.

—Yes, it's bad. When we tell the cops what further investigation we (including Henry Lee and Barry Scheck and our DA team) need to feel the cops have a complete case, they don't do the work and they don't explain their stubborn inaction.

—Yes, it's bad. The cops are in the war room no more than one day a week.

—Yes, it's bad. The cops are behaving so unprofessionally that their Chief has had to write letters of apology to us.

—Yes, it's so bad that the progress of the case has been hampered. For months we've felt the rift was nothing out of the ordinary, but now that we've hit 9 mos. mark and we see that the patient isn't getting any better and at times is taking a turn for the worse, we need to conclude that the rift may well be extraordinary.

—The cops will tell you that they can't trust us not to leak information to the Ramseys (as reported by *Vanity Fair* & Channel 7) or the news media (as reported by *Vanity Fair* & Channel 7). Well, I'd like to address each and every one of their suspicions head on and let you be the judge as to whether any of these charges of conflict of interest and malfeasance hold water. I assure you they don't and so-and-so and so-and-so will back me up on this. All of these folks stand ready to come on this very news program and back me up on what I'm saying tonight. You say you want character references on me and my office… well… here they are.

—Also understand that it's not unusual for a murderer who's yet to be caught to try to drive a wedge between the police and the DA over a high-stakes case. It is naïve to think

409

that whoever did this crime is ambivalent about the progress of the case. Whoever did this crime may very well be taking an active role in undermining the progress of the case.

((The toughest and most risky message (yet the most important charge to answer) is explaining the rift. Toughest because truth doesn't match the cops' truth. Most risky because it'll goad the cops into resurrecting *Vanity Fair*. And it'll give the Ramsey camp more fodder for declaring that "Boulder authorities" are unethical and incompetent and then they'll rush again to exclude us from their tirade… "accidentally" causing us more damage.))

ROLE
—Who our guys are and what they're doing.
—A computer database prepared for trial.
—But all this is on hold until we get a case from the cops.

RESOLUTION
—Mistakes WERE made.
—Nationally renowned forensic pathologists tell us flat-out that the evidence is even more difficult to decipher than they've imagined.
—We are open-minded, we are open to outside experts (list 'em all) and we are NOT doing anything to impede the cops' progress.

((I believe there are three camps out there who benefit from tearing down the DA's credibility: BPD wants to be able to lay blame at our doorstep when they can't make a case. Ramseys want us crippled in the court of public opinion before they face us in the court of law. Media gets new angle to keep story alive. I believe that all three of these camps have been equal players in negative press we've gotten the past three weeks. And all three will be in there swinging in the aftermath of our proposed media campaign. No matter how convincing our message, how impeccable the delivery, the aftermath will be ferocious. And the whole thing is liable to leave the public thinking that they wish everyone would **just shut up and solve the case.**))

A few days later, Hunter got a call from Koby, who wanted to see him as soon as possible. The chief said he had been thinking about the progress of the investigation and was considering some changes. Hunter had heard from Epp that Koby was moving toward replacing Eller, so he went into the meeting thinking the chief had actually made the decision.

When he arrived at Koby's office, however, there was a tape recorder on the table. Koby wanted him to hear something his detectives had brought in. Listening to the recording, Hunter realized that Thomas and Gosage had worn a wire during a recent meeting with Jeff Shapiro and secretly tape-recorded a conversation in which Shapiro revealed the content of his private talks with Hunter, including the DA's leaks to the *Globe*; Hunter's meeting with *Globe* editor Tony Frost; his attempt to smear Eller, and other indiscreet disclosures to Shapiro, whom he knew to be a tabloid reporter. Hunter understood that what he was hearing could cost him his job. Bardach's article had been based on unnamed sources, but this tape was hard evidence.

Hunter was speechless. The question of what Thomas, Gosage, or Eller might do with this information would trouble him for months. Only his close relationship with Koby protected him from exposure.

Koby made no comment about the tape, and quickly changed the subject. He told Hunter he thought that Mark Beckner was the right man to take over the Ramsey investigation. Beckner, the father of two, had come up through the ranks of the Boulder PD and had once headed the internal affairs division. He had graduated from college with a degree in criminal justice and joined the department as a patrol officer. He was organizationally sound—made assignments, followed up, met deadlines, and maintained quality control. More important, under Beckner's supervision, the detectives would no longer decide on their own assignments as they often had done under Eller. Koby said he planned to permit Eller to stay on as head of the detective division, a position he'd held throughout the JonBenét investigation.

Koby told Hunter that his decision had not been influenced by the internal investigation into Larry Mason's legal claims against the commander and the department. Nevertheless, the DA understood that Koby did not want Eller's reassignment to be perceived as having been motivated from outside the Boulder police department.

One detective who didn't know about Shapiro told a reporter covering the story that John Eller had taken the fall for the leaks in *Vanity Fair*. As always, he had protected his officers. They had always respected their commander, and this only increased their admiration.

When Tom Wickman told the detectives that Eller was being replaced, they were outraged, though Gosage had warned them it was coming. When they learned that Beckner would be heading up the investigation, they were stunned. It was all wrong to put a "grazer" in charge of the Ramsey case, they said, Dave Hayes, an old-time "meat eater," was their kind of man.★

In the coming months, John Eller would arrive at work, walk into his office, and close the door—something he'd never done before. At five in the afternoon he would open his door and walk through the detective division on his way out of police headquarters. As he passed by, some detectives would mutter under their breath, "Fucking Koby." One day a calendar indicating February 28, 1998, as the commander's last day with the Boulder PD appeared on the wall near Eller's door. Eller would mark off each day on the calendar. On New Year's Eve, he held his annual party. All his detectives attended with their families.

Around October 8, my editor, Brian Williams, called me.

"Alex Hunter feels that some of the things he said to you have gotten out. He wants your access terminated." Williams said it was completely over between me and Hunter.

I was floored, insulted. I had been fucked. I wondered if Hunter had found out all the stuff I was doing with the police.

Then Thomas called me.

"Jeff, you've got to decide if you're a journalist, a private investigator, a mercenary, or whatever the hell it is you're doing. I felt I owed you this phone call."

I told Thomas that Hunter had terminated me. He didn't sound surprised. He said things were hot, some confidentiality had been compromised. The detectives had all been told that if they were ever caught talking to one reporter, no matter how trivial the incident—a beer, a hello, a comment on the weather—their badge would be revoked. He said Koby had personally told him that if he ever talked to me again, his career was over.

"Who knows about things like Eller?" I asked Thomas.

★ Terms used by police officers: A *grazer* is someone who has come up through the ranks in the Boulder system. A *meat eater* is an officer who came from outside Boulder and had learned a tougher approach to crime.

"Me, Gosage, Wick. Koby. Whatever."
"Fuck! You shouldn't have told anyone about that."
I called Koby.
"I think we've had all the conversations we're going to have," he said
before I could open my mouth. Then he hung up.

— *Jeff Shapiro*

It wasn't long afterward that Shapiro found Melody Stanton, the Ramseys' neighbor who had heard the scream the night JonBenét was killed. Unaware of how important her memory of that night was to the police, she told Shapiro what she'd told the police on December 26. Also buried in his *Globe* story was the fact that Stanton's husband had heard a crashing sound—the sound of metal on concrete—sometime after the scream. This suggested that someone—possibly an intruder—had left the house. The story, which made headlines, was a scoop for Shapiro. His editor brought him back from banishment after the Hunter fiasco. Stanton was inundated by the media, however. Like Fleet White, she abhorred the intrusion and eventually moved. She would become a reluctant witness for the police.

Several months later, Steve Thomas talked to Shapiro again, despite Koby's warning. Thomas told him that Dr. Henry Lee thought the blow to JonBenét's head had been an accident. For Shapiro, that was a letdown. If the girl's death turned out to be an accident, how could anyone ever explain all the pain it had caused the families, the authorities, the people of Boulder, and the nation at large? "At least when this is over, you'll go on to the next big story," Thomas told him. "Once this is over, I'm back to some local robbery case."

On October 8, Hunter and Koby met again. This time the chief told the DA that the next day he would announce not just Mark Beckner's replacement of John Eller but also the withdrawal of his officers from the war room. This didn't surprise Hunter. He hadn't seen the police detectives in their joint room for months. Koby said he would tell the media that the relationship between their departments would continue along more traditional lines. Hunter asked the chief not to make both announcements at the same time, because it would appear as if they were no longer working together in the search for JonBenét's killer. Koby heard him out but rejected his suggestion.

It was evident to Hunter from the way the chief referred to Eller that he was devastated by his decision to replace the commander. Hunter, who had always blamed Eller for the failure in communication with Hofstrom, said he hoped that his deputy and Mark Beckner would find a way to cooperate. Koby said he'd spoken to some of his detectives and was sure the animosity would be put aside. Hunter thought this was naive, but he understood that it was what Koby wanted to believe.

Notwithstanding Koby's hopes, Eller's removal would be generally perceived as a victory for Hunter. Still, Hunter hoped it would become clear eventually that what had prevailed was the broader approach to the investigation that his office had advocated from the start.

SUPERVISOR OF JonBenét INQUIRY IS REMOVED FROM CASE

The head of the Boulder Police detective bureau [John Eller] was removed from his role as supervisor of the murder investigation.

An internal affairs investigation into Eller was triggered by what department officials characterized as a "serious allegation of misconduct" leveled by Sgt. Larry Mason. In June, Mason filed a notice of intent to sue Eller.

Marc Colin, a lawyer representing Mason . . . declined to say whether Eller's removal from the case . . . and Mason's lawsuit threat might all be linked.

— Charlie Brennan and Kevin McCullen
Rocky Mountain News, October 10, 1997

On Friday morning, October 10, Koby appeared before the press for the first time since his joint conference with Hunter on February 13, eight months earlier. Koby announced that Eller was out and Beckner was in and that he was adding three detectives to the case—Kim Stewart, Carey Weinheimer, and Michael Everett, who had been involved in the investigation earlier.

"I am relocating the investigation back to the Public Safety Building," Koby announced, "...where the staff of the district attorney are available to advise us but are not involved in the day-to-day investigation of the case."

Then the chief addressed his department's relationship with the DA's office. "Our relationship is strained," Koby said. "One side of the investigation [the police] has favored a hard line on pursuing this matter. The other [the DA] has been supportive of a less antagonistic approach." On media management, Koby noted, "My position . . . has been to be very closed with information. The district attorney has felt a need to be more communicative. Our difference of opinion on this matter has added to the strain."

After reading his prepared statement, Koby took questions.

Would the investigators look into local pedophiles or sex offenders, as reported in that morning's newspaper? "That's the problem with reading the papers," the chief replied. "Next question."

Could you tell us specifically what work needs to be done before the case is ready for prosecution? "I don't choose to," Koby said. "I could, but I don't choose to."

Could you give more details about why you decided to pull your team from the war room? "One of the things that has happened to us is you guys," Koby responded. He and Hunter would continue to do whatever was necessary to complete the investigation, he said, "in spite of what you are doing to us."

"Why is the media being blamed for your not completing this case?" a CBS reporter asked. "I mean, you keep throwing barbs at us, but does that change the evidence that you've gathered and the investigation that you're doing?"

"Have you read this?" Koby said, pulling out a pamphlet and holding it up. "It's the Constitution. How many of you in here have read the Constitution? Let me see a show of hands." He told the press their role was protected and their rights preserved by the First Amendment.

"With that awesome freedom comes an awesome responsibility," Koby lectured. "I think the responsibility is lacking in this case. I see a significant lack of leadership. I think that what's missing is the recognition that the reason you have so much freedom is [the duty] to uphold the rest of the parts of that Constitution."

"I heard you didn't like it," Koby said later to Kevin McCullen of the *Rocky Mountain News*, referring to his mentioning the Constitution.

"This wasn't the forum for those feelings," the reporter replied. Koby laughed.

Mark Beckner would no longer allow the detectives to be in limbo as they had been under Eller. For too long they had been unfocused, changing tack in the middle of something and never following up. Overnight, it seemed, Beckner gave them a sense of direction and forward momentum. He quickly instilled in the detectives a feeling that neither the media nor the DA would destroy them. With Beckner in the lead, they saw the opportunity to complete their investigation. One detective told Carol McKinley that it was as if Beckner had grabbed an unraveling ball of yarn and started to wind it back up.

On October 13, Beckner called Hofstrom and requested a meeting. During their conversation, Beckner casually asked whether it would help sway jurors if they knew that the Ramseys had "lawyered up" within days of the murder and had given official statements only after a long delay. Hofstrom was alarmed by the question, which was exactly the kind of prejudicial information that would not be admissible in court, he thought. He hoped it was not an indication of Beckner's understanding of fundamental legal procedure, because if it was, Hofstrom saw a rough road ahead for them.★ But he decided to give the new commander some time. Beckner also told Hofstrom that the police needed some of the Ramseys' records. And there was the issue of reinterviewing them. Since April, a lot of information had been developed, and the police wanted John and Patsy to answer some new questions. Hofstrom suggested that Beckner call Bryan Morgan directly, which the commander did. The lawyer sent him some of the documentation he had requested. Morgan also told Beckner he'd get back to him about another interview with the Ramseys. Hofstrom was encouraged that Beckner had taken matters into his own hands. He told Hunter that his relationship with Beckner looked promising.

Hofstrom may have been happy with Beckner, but the CBI wasn't pleased with how he was handling things. Chet Ubowski, the CBI's handwriting expert, learned from Detective Trujillo that Beckner had requested—and the DA's office had authorized—another handwriting analysis of the ransom note. Hofstrom and the police had looked for an expert who would testify that Patsy had written the note. They turned

★ At this point, the Ramseys had not been explicitly advised by the police of their right to silence. In such a case, if they were later to offer some explanation of events that seemed to be the sort of thing one would naturally bring up early on (for example, that one of them had heard noises in the night indicating an intruder), the prosecution could prove that they had not offered the explanation during their long months of "lawyered-up" silence. This proof would be entirely proper and possibly persuasive. The question is a subtle one, and Beckner's inquiry might have prompted a more nuanced reaction in a less gun-shy prosecutor.

to the U.S. Secret Service and got an opinion less conclusive than Ubowski's. The upshot was that the CBI's conclusions were now compromised. Under the process of discovery, the Ramseys would have the right to use the second analysis in the defense. The police had never bothered to ask Ubowski if he had put his entire analysis of the ransom note into his report and whether it was his final report. Either way, Ubowski was prepared to say, "Patsy wrote the note." The CBI saw this as one more example of the missed opportunities in the investigation.

District attorney Bob Grant, a member of Alex Hunter's task force, had now became the unofficial spokesperson for the Boulder DA. Grant had earned a Purple Heart for saving a man's life in Vietnam; Hunter had always admired him.

Bob Grant had a gift for speaking intelligently about the Ramsey case without mentioning specific evidentiary issues. He could explain the different roles and responsibilities of the police and the DA's office and clarify what was feasible as opposed to what the public thought should be happening. He wasn't afraid to take a poke at the media. He gave great sound bites and was a natural on TV, much more at ease than Alex Hunter could be. He was just the man to help restore Hunter's credibility.

Behind the scenes, Hunter had begun a series of getting-to-know-you off-the-record meetings with producers for network news anchors Dan Rather and Tom Brokaw and for Larry King. He'd even met with Tony Frost, the editor-in-chief of the *Globe*. Determined to put the *Vanity Fair* article behind him, Hunter was laying the groundwork for making his own TV appearances. He wanted to show that he could win in court, no matter what people might have heard about "his bunglegate and conflict of interest baggage," as he called it. He talked about his twenty-three-year relationship with Pete Hofstrom, his "felony man," who personally handled over four hundred cases a year. He said that his "tell-the-truth" dealings with public defenders had paid off, proving that advocates and adversaries can be truthful and still advance their agendas. It was one reason why the justice system in Boulder worked so well, he said.

While acknowledging the shadow hanging over him, Hunter stressed that he was a lawyer as much as a politician. He stated that there was no favoritism or selective enforcement in his office, there were only truth-seekers. The goal of his staff was to get "as close to justice as you can."

★ ★ ★

While Hunter may have been winning some of his battles in the war over public opinion, he was candid when dealing with DAs Bob Grant and Bill Ritter of his task force. He admitted that his staff was inexperienced. What does this type of evidence really mean? he would ask. When and why should a grand jury be convened? How do you stop the investigation from going in too many directions at the same time? What's the downside of this? What's the upside of that? They had many conversations about police-prosecutor relations and, of course, about how the DA's office should communicate with the Ramseys' attorneys. The task force DAs had supported Hunter, but now they told him what he was unable to admit to himself.

"You don't have the horsepower in your office to take this case to trial," Bob Grant said. To Grant, horsepower was attorneys who had been through a case like this before. "You don't even have someone who has done twenty homicides," Grant said, "let alone an attorney who has tried two or three child-victim homicides."

Alex Hunter got the message: it was time to think about bringing in some help. If the case went to a grand jury, he would need experienced prosecutors.

8

Earlier in October, Detectives Stewart and Gosage began reviewing the 180 videotapes that had been removed from the Ramsey home and booked into evidence during their first search, between December 26 and January 4. It would take them until October 23 to finish this task. Detective Gosage reviewed eighteen videos that had been shot at JonBenét's beauty pageants. Another had been filmed at her sixth birthday party. There was also a tape of a family Easter egg hunt, part of which had been shot in the wine cellar. The detectives also screened the Spy World self-defense video that John Ramsey had referred to during his July 12 interview with Lou Smit.

During this period, the detectives interviewed Burke Ramsey's teachers and followed up the information they'd been given about JonBenét's habit of asking adults to wipe her when she was on the toilet. Several experts told them that the age of modesty in girls was about seven or eight. Until that age, it wasn't uncommon for a child to ask for help from anyone around—a dad, a mom, a baby-sitter or a grandparent. It was just as common for a child not to ask for help and simply pull up her pants, producing a different problem for the parents. There were no statistics to indicate whether a child who asked for help on the toilet might also somehow invite sexual contact. To their surprise, the detectives also learned that bed-wetting was not unusual in children up to that same age. Some of the officers had their own child-rearing experiences but still consulted casually with friends. The opinion of those parents was that the age of modesty was much lower, maybe five.

During this time, the detectives also contacted the first of more than twenty locally registered sex offenders and checked the alibis of all of them.

Slowly, the police chipped away at the to-do list.

Meanwhile, Lou Smit met with Ramsey investigators Jennifer Gedde and John Foster to discuss several suspects who had turned up as a result of the newspaper ads. Smit now worked only with Trip DeMuth. The police detectives quoted in the *Vanity Fair* article had made such unkind remarks about him that he didn't feel like involving them in his work. Smit still thought about Kevin Raburn as a suspect.

My name is Kevin Raburn. I was raised in Boulder County, grew up in Louisville. High school in Lafayette. That's when I broke a window, in something like a milk truck. The judge gave me forty-five days in the Boulder County jail. That ruined my school totally. My mom worked to support my sister and me. She was a single parent.

In '87 Boulder was laid-back. I lived there when I was nineteen. Worked in Burger King, rode my ten-speed bike. Then I got a job cooking at Bennigans, 26th and Canyon. The rent was always high, especially for people who had to work. Everyone has a job and a half, two jobs, unless they have parents helping with the rent, which I didn't. Everything I needed I could walk to, even the foothills. The mountains are nice.

Then I started stealing bikes. That's something they don't like in Boulder. Bike theft is taken seriously. By 1990 I was sentenced to a halfway house, and I started violating their rules—walking away—and they put me back in jail. In '93 I did another bike theft. I like to ride bikes. Another theft, another felony, prison at Arrowhead, another halfway house. In '94 the mandatory parole kicked in, and I got a four-year sentence. While I was working full-time at Rafferty's, cooking, in '96, I failed my Breatha-lyzers and they sent me back to prison.

On December 26, the day JonBenét was murdered, I went to Juanita's near the mall in Boulder, looking for a second job. Got a job. Worked days at Rafferty's, nights at Juanita's. That's when the TV crews would come in and talk about the killing of JonBenét. It was on TV a lot, but I didn't think much about it. Lots of police around—Channel 7, Channel 4.

Then one night in February I stole some AA batteries for my Walkman. I don't even know why. I already had some. Next thing, I'm in jail again on a misdemeanor charge. Being jailed for battery theft when I should have been given a ticket. I just freaked out. My bond was $1,500. That night I lost both my jobs. Went to court and got one year of unsupervised probation. Had to pay off the batteries, court costs, do some community service. I was out of a job and penniless. While I was in jail, I found out that these guys Ainsworth and Smit were asking my mom and sister about me. Didn't say anything about JonBenét Ramsey. Didn't say what case they were working on.

Then I passed some bad checks, was given a felony summons, and given a court date. I'd found the checks in a jacket, walked into a bank at Broadway and Canyon, and got some cash.

Then I asked my lawyer why the cops were looking for me. He found out my file was in Hunter's office with the guys working on the Ramsey case. I was in shock. My lawyer looked at me kind of weird. I'm a con-victed felon, you know?

I got tired waiting for my court date, so in July I just got on a bus for Knoxville to see my friend Eric. I'm a football fan, and I like the university's football team. It wasn't hard to get a job, right off Cumberland and Kingston Pike. Right down from the campus.

Then on September 1, I was reading a newspaper and a cop drives by, looks at me strange, and I start walking. He pulled over and said I looked suspicious. I gave him my name, he checks on his car computer, and my warrant came up. They arrested me on a felony warrant for my check forgery and missed court date. The next day they said someone was com-ing from Boulder to pick me up.

That's when I realized they weren't coming all the way to get me on a check charge. On September 11, they came up for me in a sheriff's plane. Something was wrong. I'd known Gerry Leverentz in Boulder, and he had this guy Lou Smit with him. Smit told me he was working on the Ramsey case. Smit said he was just doing a background check on me. I told them I had a paid attorney and couldn't talk to them without him. Smit just said fine, OK.

On the way back, Smit helped turn the sports pages of the newspaper I was reading, since I was in handcuffs.

When I was booked in Boulder, I got a public defender, Cary Lacklen. He said to me, "You know something or you know somebody."

"I know nothing," I told him. "They ain't got nothing on me. I got my felony and my bike theft."

On October 20, Harmer and Weinheimer came to see me in jail. Then on the twenty-second Lou Smit and Harmer came back. There was a court reporter and my attorney. Smit wanted to know everything about Christmas night. They knew about Juanita's, the day I was there, December 26. But they wanted to know about the night before. I told them I was at my mom's house.

"I'm a thief," I said. "I'm not a killer."

Harmer wanted to know if I could have left the house that night. I told them if you open a window, the alarm goes off. If you open the front door, it beeps for a few seconds, so you can turn the alarm off if you know the code. If you don't know the code, which I didn't, the alarm goes off.

Smit asked if I'd been convicted of any sexual offenses. I said no. Asked if I'd gone into an adult bookstore in Boulder. I said yeah. After twenty minutes they were done. I just asked them to leave my family alone.

Then they took blood, hair, and handwriting samples.

Never heard from them again. Guess they figured out I didn't do it.

— Kevin Raburn

Charlie Russell, a Ramsey press representative, began telling some reporters that the police were at least seriously pursuing the possibility of other suspects in the case. He told one journalist that solid leads had come from the Ramseys' July and August advertising campaign. One of them pertained to a member of St. John's church, he said. He also noted that Janet and Bill McReynolds were still suspects. Some new facts about the McReynoldses had just come to light, and the Ramseys had hired investigators to stake out the couple's home in the mountains, waiting for the couple to return home from a trip East. They believed the police were wrong to discount McReynolds because of his infirmity at the time of the murder. The Ramseys were also still interested in Randy Simons and Chris Wolf as possible suspects, Russell said.

Several of their attorneys believed that Simons had the opportunity to commit the crime and had access to JonBenét. He also had no real alibi for that night. The police, they felt, hadn't investigated him thoroughly. If the case ever went to trial, the attorneys thought, Simons' background and bizarre behavior after the crime might be enough to sway a jury to reasonable doubt about the Ramseys' guilt.

Then there was Fleet White. The Ramseys' team hadn't spent a lot of time investigating him as a possible suspect, but they thought the police had manipulated White by telling him that Ramsey had named him as a possible suspect. The police had used this strategy with several witnesses—told them that the Ramseys were accusing them, which caused the witnesses to turn on the Ramseys.

Around this time, Trip DeMuth discovered that many of the police interviews with possible suspects had never been transcribed because detectives hadn't considered them important enough. Hofstrom wanted all of them transcribed. Who knew if some bit of information that had seemed inconsequential ten months ago wouldn't now provide an answer to important questions. Beckner agreed. He ordered all the tapes transcribed.

Now that Eller was no longer leading the Ramsey investigation, the police union took sides on Larry Mason's claims against Eller and the department. Earlier in the year, Mason had asked for financial assistance in his lawsuit, in which he claimed he had been wrongly discharged from the Ramsey case. Since Eller's allegation of Mason's misconduct was without any merit, the union had voted in January to give Mason the money. Now Marc Colin, Mason's attorney, said that he wouldn't settle until Eller had resigned from the Boulder PD.

Since the vote of no confidence against Koby earlier in the year, the chief had met with union leaders on five occasions to discuss their grievances. He conceded that the department "was maxed-out and worn-out." He admitted he never should have gone into the crowd of students during the Hill riots and begged them to go home. "I was wrong," Koby said. "I have learned from it. I'm ready to move on." However, those were not the only problems between management and the rank and file. There were also promotion and hiring issues that couldn't be resolved overnight. Union leaders gave Koby notice that another vote would be taken within a month. With the November elections less than a month away, candidates for the city council were calling for Koby to account to the citizens of Boulder.

When the union vote was taken in November, the results were as predicted—no confidence. But before the union could even digest the vote, Koby announced his resignation. I'm out of here by next year, he said. Start looking for someone else.

As if Eller's dismissal and Koby's problems with the union weren't enough, on October 20, Brooke Jackson, Detective Linda Arndt's attorney, wrote a letter to the police chief. News stories in the *Globe* and *Vanity Fair*, among others, had falsely defamed his client, he said. She had maintained her silence as ordered, but the Boulder PD had made no effort to defend her. "She has been allowed to become a scapegoat," Jackson wrote, "if not the primary scapegoat, by a continuous series of statements about one thing or another that she supposedly did that are simply false." Three days later, Koby called Jackson and indicated that indeed the statements circulated about Arndt were false and unjust. But according to Jackson, Koby said that neither he nor the police department would take any action to correct them. Jackson said that the Boulder PD had a responsibility to correct the public record on Arndt's behalf.

By February 2, 1998, the police had cleared only Detective Larry Mason. Linda Arndt filed a claim on May 19, 1998, demanding a jury trial, against Koby personally and professionally and against the city of Boulder. It alleged that Koby, knowing that information published about Arndt was false, had caused "acute embarrassment to Detective Arndt and irreparable harm to her reputation." Arndt sought $150,000 in damages.

Though by the end of October 1997 most Boulderites were trying to forget the Ramsey case, the national media were still laying siege to the city. Alex Hunter wondered if the Ramsey case was a sideshow to America or if the media had become a sideshow to the investigation. Either way, the DA knew that once the police presented the case to his office, he would have to decide what the evidence said. If there was evidence exculpatory to the Ramseys, he would have to make it known and take the beating from his critics—or he could let a grand jury deal with the evidence and the critics, as Koby had once suggested. But if there wasn't sufficient evidence to charge someone, he knew that Pete Hofstrom would be dead-set against convening a grand jury.

Hunter was reminded of the Manning case, in which a dead child's mother had confessed and implicated her live-in boyfriend,

Danny Arevalo, in the crime. A writer covering the Ramsey case was told by a jurist that in the Arevalo trial, Hunter had urged Hofstrom to put a key witness on the stand though Hofstrom didn't believe the person's information. Hofstrom, never one to cast ethics aside, was so troubled by what he'd done that in open court he asked the judge to strike the testimony of the witness as not credible.

Hunter didn't want another "Manning problem" with his chief trial deputy. If Hofstrom couldn't file charges in the Ramsey case as a matter of conscience, the DA knew he could not order Pete to act against his beliefs.

9

On October 24, John Ramsey's attorneys hosted their annual Halloween party. Hal Haddon and Lee Foreman showed up in drag. At another party, held at the Boulder Elks Club, Patsy's attorney Pat Furman showed up as Gary Davis, a convicted killer who had been executed on October 13—the first execution in Colorado since 1967. Taped to each of Furman's forearms, as part of his costume, was a large syringe. Furman had briefly represented Davis. James Aber, a public defender in Jefferson County, came dressed in a cowgirl outfit similar to one JonBenét had worn in a pageant; duct tape covered his mouth.

That evening, Aber discussed holding a murder mystery party with JonBenét's death to be solved by the guests. One of the Ramsey attorneys joked that the perpetrator would be Koby.

RAMSEY EXIT TO
FOLLOW TRADE OF BOULDER FIRM

Lockheed Martin Corp. said Monday that it has reached an agreement to trade Boulder-based Access Graphics Inc. and certain other assets to General Electric Co. for $2.8 billion in stock and that Access President John Ramsey will leave the computer distribution firm.

Daily Camera, November 4, 1997

★ ★ ★

A couple of days before the *Daily Camera* reported the sale of Access Graphics to General Electric, John Ramsey's attorneys visited Alex Hunter. They complained that Ramsey was going to take a financial hit in the stock trade between Lockheed Martin and GE. Not only had Ramsey's contract not been picked up by GE; he had been terminated before the sale was made. Laurie Wagner was the only Access Graphics employee from the Ramsey camp who was moving over to GE.

Hunter understood what the attorneys were suggesting: that John Ramsey might choose to seek financial restitution from the city of Boulder because the police had leaked information to the media that he was responsible for his daughter's death. They would claim that this had damaged his reputation and credibility, which in turn had curtailed his advancement as an executive. Hunter told Ramsey's lawyers to save their breath.

Shortly afterward, Sherry Keene-Osborn, *Newsweek*'s Denver correspondent, called Hunter and told him what she had heard—that Ramsey couldn't get a job and that he may be taking medication; she mentioned something about Ramsey having lost his stock. Hunter wasn't inclined to feel pity for him. There was so much conflicting information about the Ramseys that he had given up trying to figure out what was true.

A week earlier, Hunter's father–in–law had died in California. A former prosecutor and judge, he had been like a second father to Hunter, who had respected the way he lived his life and raised his children. Almost in tribute to the man, Hunter started to take a more conservative, tougher approach to the Ramsey case.

In the first week of November, Hunter met with Boulder County commissioner Paul Danish, who had recently lost his mother.

Danish told Hunter that he had cleared out his mother's apartment and found her diary of the period when she divorced his father. Danish was having a hard time mourning his mother's death, and it made Hunter think about how everyone grieves differently. He remembered that when his own mother had died, less than two months after JonBenét was murdered, he hadn't been able to lament properly.

Hunter had recently heard something Patsy Ramsey told a friend—that John often put himself in situations that didn't allow for venting of emotion. But he woke up in the middle of the night sobbing and crying, she said. That was his time to grieve; then in the morning, he would be ready to meet the challenges of the new day. It was ironic, because Ramsey's apparent stoicism in the face of Jon-Benét's death was exactly what made some people believe that he had murdered his daughter.

In the second week of November, Cordwainer Bird, a reporter for the *Daily Camera*, got a call from one of John Ramsey's lawyers. Ramsey wanted an off-the-record conversation with Bird; one attorney would be present.

Bird was not to tell anyone about the meeting—not even his editor. He wasn't allowed to use a tape recorder, and he could not take notes. He could not ask any specific questions about the forty-eight hours before and after JonBenét's death. Bird asked how many other reporters had been given the same opportunity. A handful, he was told, and everyone had been given the same conditions. He didn't know that Lisa Ryckman of the *Rocky Mountain News* and her editors had turned down the same offer.

Bird believed that a reporter should never shut the door on information. Here, he knew he'd be dealing with someone who was less than forthcoming and who had an agenda. Nevertheless, it would be interesting to hear Ramsey out, he thought. And maybe he could get something useful out of him.

Late in the afternoon of November 20, in crisp weather, Bird arrived at a house in Boulder where Ramsey greeted him at the door. The two men shook hands and made some small talk, then sat down a few feet apart. Bird's first impression of the fifty-four-year-old John Ramsey was of a poised, mild-mannered man—not gregarious and not a performer. Bird saw JonBenét's father as an ordinary man caught in far-out-of-the-ordinary circumstances.

Bird asked Ramsey what he had been like as a young man. Was he a drinker? Did he go out and screw girls? Did he think he was well endowed? Ramsey blushed, obviously embarrassed by the question. He thought he was fine, he said, but he was not King Kong. He had been kind of a boring kid, he said. He didn't take drugs. Didn't even like sports.

Sensing Ramsey's discomfort, Bird said he'd been told he could ask anything, so he plowed on: What about your sex life? Any kinks? With an embarrassed smile, Ramsey said he wasn't creative enough to be very wild sexually. Bird believed him. Ramsey came off as an all-

American guy who did what all-American guys do—bed their wives a couple of times a week or, if they're really unlucky, once a month. Asking questions, Bird was more interested in Ramsey's reactions to his questions than in his answers.

Their conversation turned to other topics—politics, money, children. Had JonBenét ever pissed him off? Bird asked. How did he react? What had she done to irritate him? Of course she'd made him angry, Ramsey said. She was a little girl and sometimes bratty. He had scolded her the way any father would. Ramsey's love for his daughter was audible in his voice. As they talked, Ramsey's attorney, who had been silent throughout the interview, shifted in his seat; Bird saw he had tears in his eyes.

Bird got the impression that the marriage of John and Patsy was loving but not passionate or exciting. Ramsey was settled into the marriage and comfortable in it.

Politically, he was a conservative, Ramsey said, but over the years he had learned to be both more tolerant and more compassionate. For example, he was uncomfortable with homosexuality but would not endorse antihomosexual legal or social measures. The strident public debate on abortion made him uncomfortable. Ramsey believed in God, he said. God would know if someone had done something that he hadn't admitted to, Ramsey said. Yes, God would know.

When the interview was over, Bird felt he'd learned nothing. Ramsey seemed earnest and sincere, but was bland and seemed never to allow his emotions to get the better of him. Only one thing stood out about him: John Ramsey hadn't dodged any of the questions. Bird hoped he wouldn't have to write up his interview. There wouldn't be much to say about JonBenét's father.

A few days later, Access Graphics held its quarterly "What's Happening Meeting," at the Boulder Theater on 14th Street. John Ramsey was to introduce Perry Monych, the new president of Access Graphics. In a short statement, Ramsey said that the sale of the company had been a strategic decision between two of the largest companies in the world and had nothing to do with the death of his daughter. Ramsey was restrained and unemotional, but Laurie Wagner could see that he was hurting.

Although GE didn't pick up his contract, Ramsey would stay with Lockheed Martin for six months after the sale to GE. Gary Mann, his boss at Lockheed, had wanted to keep Ramsey, but he wanted to keep his family in Atlanta, and the company didn't have a management opening in the area.

While John Ramsey was talking off the record to journalists, Michael Tracey, a professor in the school of General Mass Communications at the University of Colorado in Boulder, was talking to Bryan Morgan about making a documentary for British television about the media coverage of the Ramsey case.

Earlier in the year, Tracey, who had never met the Ramseys, had heard Chuck Green of *The Denver Post* say that "the Ramsey case was entertainment and that was why it was such a big story." That started the educator thinking, and by August, Tracey was expressing his own views on national TV: that the American public "knew" the Ramseys had killed their daughter just as every white jury in Mississippi of the 1950s "knew" that a given black boy standing before them was guilty. Having read Dan Glick and Sherry Keene-Osborn's coverage of the case in *Newsweek*, Tracey realized that many media outlets were reporting the story incorrectly, or only partially, and thereby depriving the Ramseys of the presumption of innocence. Several weeks before the death of Princess Diana, the professor started to write an article on the subject for the *Daily Camera*. It was published a few days after the Princess of Wales's funeral: "Media-Saturated Culture Quick to Judge Ramseys." Tracey drew parallels to the 1983 McMartin day care center case in California, in which, he said, a family had been wrongfully tried and ultimately exonerated, and to the climate in Great Britain in the wake of a series of IRA bombings in the 1970s. Tracey wrote about the corruption of journalistic values and the now-hazy line between the tabloid press and the mainstream media. He raised a question: Why did the public want the Ramseys to be guilty?

After Tracey's op-ed piece ran on September 7, Bryan Morgan paid him a visit at his university office. Sitting in the tiny room stuffed with more than a thousand books, Morgan told Tracey that Patsy Ramsey wanted to talk to one of his journalism classes about her experience with the press. Tracey thought the idea wasn't practicable: he was sure the media would storm his classroom when it was discovered that she would be talking to some college students. Nevertheless, Tracey told Morgan he would think about it, and the two men agreed to have lunch the following day. After the attorney left, Tracey glanced out the window at his unobstructed view of the Front Range and laughed. Patsy Ramsey's idea was astonishingly naïve.

Tracey speculated that the Ramseys, ready for a fight, were slowly coming out of their shell. Then he asked himself if their story wasn't a way of critiquing the media, which led him to the idea of making a documentary.

The next day, Morgan brought Pat Burke, Patsy's attorney, to their lunch. The two lawyers pitched their clients' desire to address Tracey's students. "Patsy has a degree in journalism," Burke said. Instead, Tracey broached his suggestion of making a documentary. Looking at the attorneys' facial expressions, he was sure his idea would be nixed. Two days later, however, Tracey heard from Morgan that the Ramseys were interested in meeting him. They liked his idea. That evening, Tracey called his friend David Mills, an established British documentary filmmaker.

Mills had, of course, heard of the Ramseys. Like most people, he had drawn conclusions about the case based solely on what he'd read in the newspapers. He believed the couple was guilty of killing their daughter. He told Tracey he wasn't interested in some child murderers in Colorado. Before the two friends hung up, however, Tracey persuaded Mills to consider making a documentary about the case. His arguments about the one-sided view of the media had convinced Mills. The two men agreed they would meet with Patsy and John Ramsey.

When Michael Tracey arrived in Atlanta on December 6, Bryan Morgan was already there. Ramsey came to the Hyatt Regency to pick them up. Shaking John Ramsey's hand in the hotel lobby, Tracey had the odd feeling that he might be face-to-face with a child killer. At the Ramseys' home, Tracey was introduced to Rachelle Zimmer, one of Bryan Morgan's associate attorneys, who was living with the Ramseys until they got settled in their new home. She was making cookies in the kitchen. Patsy was on the patio, talking on her cell phone.

"Well, they didn't have handsome professors when I was a student in journalism school," Patsy greeted Tracey. "Thank you" was the only reply the flustered professor could think of. Invited to sit down, Tracey told the Ramseys a little about himself. He'd received his doctorate in political science and American politics in Britain, and then moved to Boulder to teach in 1988, he said. His life's work, he said, was to think about the media.

"What do you want to do with us?" Patsy said. "What's your idea?"

It took Tracey a second or two to reply: "A story has been told about you and this murder. I want to see if another story *could* have been told."

He wasn't prepared to make a presentation, but he plunged ahead: he wanted to include material about the credibility of the tabloids and the inaccurate reporting by the mainstream press, he said. Patsy seemed to like what she was hearing. John was noncommittal.

Later in the afternoon, Ramsey took Tracey and Morgan back to the hotel so they could pick up David Mills, who had by then arrived from Hungary, where he was filming. Sitting in the car, Mills also had a strange feeling: Was he being driven by a murderer?

At dinner, Patsy was the perfect hostess. They dined in a wood-paneled restaurant that resembled an English gentlemen's club. Mills noticed the waiting staff's kindheartedness toward the Ramseys. He also watched the Ramseys themselves. John was very reserved, while Patsy was outgoing—exactly what he expected from a southern beauty queen. Theirs was an odd relationship, Mills thought. A small incident piqued his interest in the couple.

Ramsey had been telling Tracey about the media's incorrect reporting. For example, they had said that he flew his own jet to Jon-Benét's funeral. He didn't own a jet, much less know how to fly one, he said. Mills asked Patsy: "How have you coped over the past year?" Patsy started to talk about her faith in God and then suddenly broke down. Mills felt guilty. John Ramsey never moved or looked up as Patsy cried. It was Bryan Morgan who attended to her. The lawyer took Patsy by the hand and led her to the ladies' room so that she could compose herself. Mills wondered whether Ramsey was such a cold fish that he didn't care about his wife. Tracey asked himself, Why on earth doesn't this man get up and see if his wife is OK? Moments later, Patsy returned to the table. Without looking at her husband, she thanked her guests for being so kind.

Later that night, Tracey and Mills discussed the incident. Mills felt that the couple had developed an unusual codependency in which it was understood that one of them had to be rock-solid at all times, lest both of them lose control. Tracey saw it slightly differently. In his view, John held it together for both of them.

It was mysterious, however, and open to different interpretations. It was possible, for example, that John hated Patsy for showing weakness since he had mastered his own. When his daughter Beth had died, he had gone to pieces, but after reading many books about how to deal with a death in the family, he had found a way to control his grief. Perhaps he felt superior to his wife. When one writer was told about this incident, he said that Ramsey was surely a WASP of the stiff-upper-lip variety. Not only were they not given to histrionics; they were likely to ignore any unpleasantness, as if it had never happened. John Ramsey might have felt that his guests would be more comfortable if he didn't acknowledge his wife's little breakdown. His passing over it might also indicate that it wasn't worrisome. Then what had happened would be open to fewer interpretations.

On Sunday morning, December 7, Tracey, Mills, Bryan Morgan, and the Ramseys met again. Tracey emphasized that the proposed film would not exploit the murder of their daughter; its focus would be on journalism. If the filmmakers found no clear evidence of media distortion, they would say so in the documentary. Tracey told the Ramseys that the interviews would take several days. They would be given the opportunity to address allegations of sexual abuse and infidelity, which John Ramsey was very concerned about. Mills made it clear that he would have editorial control over the film, subject only to the broadcasters' rights. The Ramseys would not be allowed to screen the documentary before it aired on British TV. Bryan Morgan wanted a provision in the agreement that the film would not air in the United States as long as a grand jury was under active consideration. A handshake sealed the arrangement.

On the flight back to Hungary that afternoon, David Mills kept thinking that John Ramsey was too perfect. He couldn't find one flaw in the man. Eventually, he stumbled on one possibility: Ramsey didn't like confrontation. In both business and his personal life, he designed everything to avoid conflict. He tended to leave the dirty work to others.

Back in Boulder, there was a difference of opinion among the Ramseys' attorneys about whether the documentary would serve their clients' best interests. Hal Haddon advised the Ramseys not to proceed with it. Their interviews might become evidence, he said. They might say something open to interpretation that could eventually be used against them. Other attorneys felt that the couple had been burned in their previous attempts to communicate through the media, and that this film was sure to backfire. Bryan Morgan, on the other hand, saw the project as meeting the emotional needs of his clients. As their attorney and friend, he was concerned with their future, and he knew they needed to *do* something. Patsy decided they would proceed with the project. Mills and Tracey were told that they could begin filming after the first of the year.

10

The worst thing that can ever happen to you is to lose a child. It becomes a hole that can never be filled.

After Beth died, John didn't have a lot of pictures of Melinda and John Andrew around—just photos of Beth, even in his bathroom. He'd written a poem to her called "Daddy's Little Girl" that he kept on his dresser where he put his watch and loose change every night. Right where he could see it every day. Twice a day, really.

I remember some of that poem. It was a "Your First Steps" kind of thing. He wrote, "And the best thing of the day is to look after daddy's little girl . . ." and "You are growing older with woman looks that are now clear."

So John Ramsey had already lost one child. I cannot imagine anyone who has gone through that pain to intentionally inflict it on himself a second time. I cannot imagine it. Just cannot. His subconscious knew that pain. It is the worst pain ever. His subconscious would have stopped him. Whoever struck that blow, it wasn't John Ramsey.

—Linda Wilcox

The police were now working in earnest to complete the to-do list by December 1, as Tom Koby had promised. One open question was whether the penetration of JonBenét's vagina took place before or after her death. Also at issue was whether there had been any prior sexual abuse that her pediatrician might not have noticed.

On November 5, Detective Weinheimer arrived in St. Clair Shores, Michigan, to meet Dr. Werner Spitz, one of the world's foremost forensic pathologists. Weinheimer took with him a stack of black-and-white photographs of the cellulose that coroner John Meyer had found in JonBenét's vagina. Weinheimer wanted to discuss not only the cellulose but also the probable chronology of events leading up to JonBenét's murder. The detective told Spitz about the pineapple found in her small intestine, which might be an indicator of the time of death. Spitz said he would have to examine the slides of the cellulose before he could state anything definitively. He was willing to go to Boulder, he said. Ten days later, Weinheimer and Spitz met with Tom Faure, the coroner's chief medical investigator, at Boulder Community Hospital. By then Weinheimer had already consulted with another specialist, Dr. David Jones, a professor of preventive medicine and biometrics at the University of Colorado Health Sciences Center.

Spitz examined the four slides of tissue taken from JonBenét's vaginal area and discussed with Weinheimer and Faure what the coroner had observed about the head injury, strangulation, and vaginal cavity. After viewing the slides, Spitz repeated his opinion: the injury to JonBenét's vagina had happened either at or immediately prior to her death—not earlier.

The police had to piece together the findings of the various pathologists, who had explained to them that when food is swallowed, it goes first to the stomach, then passes to the duodenum, and from there to the lower small intestine. Eventually, the digested food passes into the large bowel, from which it exits. Food found in the stomach and intestines can sometimes be used to estimate the time of ingestion and to narrow the time of death.

In the Ramseys' dining room, just steps away from the kitchen, the police had found a bowl with fresh pineapple in it. Meyer noted in his report that the pineapple in JonBenét's small intestine was in near-perfect condition—it had sharp edges and looked as if it had been recently eaten and poorly chewed.

Based on the condition of the pineapple in her intestine, the experts estimated that JonBenét had eaten it an hour and a half or two hours before she died, most likely after the family returned home that night. If she had eaten the pineapple after 10:30 P.M., that made the approximate time of death not earlier than midnight.

Next, the investigators reviewed JonBenét's various injuries. A blow to the head can result in bleeding inside the skull, which can cause death immediately or sometime later. Microscopic examination of the area near the brain where the bleeding occurred can help determine how long before death the injury took place. But was it the garroting or the head injury that had caused JonBenét's death? The experts agreed that either would have been fatal.

According to the specialists, her head injury had likely come first. Since a six-year-old's skull is more resilient than an adult's, the blow must have been of tremendous force. The injury on her head was fully developed, which meant that her heart had beaten for some time after the blow. Also, the bruise to her brain did not immediately shut down all activity in JonBenét's body. However, the strangulation by the noose had created a deep furrow in her neck, which acted like a tourniquet and caused complete interruption of the blood flow to and from her brain. The specialists estimated that ten to forty-five minutes might have elapsed between the blow to her head and the cessation of JonBenét's vital functions, which was probably caused by the noose being pulled tight with the help of the stick attached to the cord.

The conjecture that the blow to JonBenét's head took place first fit the scenario that the police considered most likely: that JonBenét had been struck on the head with the heavy flashlight in or near the kitchen. The police had found it on a kitchen counter.

Finally, the detectives turned to the microscopic splinter of cellulose found in JonBenét's vagina, which looked like wood. The broken paintbrush that had been tied to the stick was splintered into shards. Logic suggested that a splinter of wood might have stuck to the perpetrator's finger before he or she penetrated JonBenét vaginally. It could also have broken off the end of the paintbrush if the stick, rather than a finger, was used to penetrate her.

If the cellulose did, in fact, come from the paintbrush, then most probably the "garrote" had been assembled before JonBenét was violated. Since there was some evidence of vaginal bleeding, it was also logical to assume that the child had already been strangled but was not yet dead when she was penetrated. Consistent with penetration of a female child of JonBenét's age, her hymen was torn. In such a case, the edges are pulled away and recede quickly, creating a visible difference between a torn and an intact hymen. Photographs of her injured hymen taken at the autopsy indicated to some experts a recent tear, fresh bleeding, and no healing. Logic suggested that JonBenét had been penetrated almost concurrently with her death.

There remained the question whether JonBenét had also been penetrated—that is, sexually abused—previously. Here the experts disagreed. Dr. David Jones said the child's vagina showed a history of abuse, since the cellulose dated from an old injury. Dr. Spitz, however, said there was no clear indication of prior penetration and that the cellulose dated from the injury that had taken place around her time of death.

I'd be driving someplace and I would ruminate over it. It's not like you can say, "I've done the autopsy. I've submitted my report. We've done our thing. It's not my problem anymore." It's an unsolved case I can't dismiss, because there is a possibility that I'm going to be involved in it again. I know I'm going to testify.

I try to theorize how things occurred. What are the triggers?

I'd come to the point that I was real clear on it and then, the next day or a week later, I'd think about it again and wouldn't be very clear on what happened. I probably have come up with a variety of different scenarios at different times. I don't think at this point, right now, I am that clear about what happened.

—*John Meyer*

Another item on the detectives' list was locating the missing keys to the Ramseys' house. Jay Pettipiece, a painter, told the police he couldn't find his key. Suzanne Savage, one of JonBenét's baby-sitters, found her key; she told Detective Harmer that she had never copied it or allowed anyone to have it, but remembered giving an extra one to Linda Wilcox.

During the second week in November, the police began recanvassing the Ramseys' neighborhood for unfamiliar cars that had been seen around the time of JonBenét's murder. Parking tickets had become known as a source of information after New York City serial killer David Berkowitz was placed at the scene of one of the Son of Sam murders by a ticket he had received.

In the Ramsey case, one of the previously unidentified cars was found to belong to Eric Keck, who often visited his girlfriend, Nicole Spurlock, on 15th Street. Even after the couple broke up, Keck continued to park his car in the area. Another unfamiliar automobile turned out to belong to Donna Norris, whose daughter, a student at CU, used her car and lived across the street from the Ramseys. In the end, though, none of the parking tickets or suspicious cars led to a connection to JonBenét.

Meanwhile, on November 10, Kathy Dressel, the CBI's DNA expert, and Melissa Weber, a DNA expert from Cellmark, met with the key members of the police department and the DA's staff to explain the function and the limits of DNA tests. Back in July, Dressel had reported to the police that John's and Patsy's DNA didn't match what was found under JonBenét's fingernails. Now she emphasized particularly the role of statistics and the margins for error.

435

The foreign DNA that had been found under JonBenét's fingernails was extremely weak and possibly contaminated. The contamination could have taken place at any time after the material was first lodged under the child's nails and until her body was placed on the floor near the Christmas tree. Although it was highly unlikely, the contamination could even have taken place during the autopsy. The clippers used to cut JonBenét's fingernails may not have been properly sterilized. It was also possible that the substance found was not correctly preserved before the DNA was extracted for testing. In any case, weak DNA would not provide a reliable sample to match another person's DNA.

Further confounding the experts was the stain found on JonBenét's panties, which was a mixture of DNA from two or more people. Here further testing was needed. The detectives were advised to take saliva swabs from possible suspects. The list of people to be tested in connection with the mixed DNA was long and included many of JonBenét's play-mates. If a match could be found, it might provide a simple explanation—for example, two children sharing the same underwear. In that case, an important door would be closed in the case: No defense attorney would be able to claim that the unidentified DNA found on the panties belonged to a unknown person—an intruder or stranger who might have killed JonBenét.

Meanwhile, both the CBI and the FBI were still examining and ana-lyzing the four red and black fibers found on the duct tape, and the fibers on and near the folds of JonBenét's labia, on her skin, and in the area around her vagina. The fibers on the duct tape were of a different origin than those found on the child's body.

Earlier in the case, the police had thought the fibers from the body came from John Ramsey's bathrobe or Patsy's black pants or from the blanket found near JonBenét or from the blanket that had been found inside the suitcase under the broken basement window. The fibers might also have come from JonBenét's own clothes or from one of her stuffed animals. By now, however, all of those possibilities had been excluded, and the only logical explanation was that the fibers came from whatever had been used to wipe JonBenét or possibly from someone who might have rubbed up against her when she was unclothed, which allowed the fibers to find their way along her skin and eventually into the folds of her labia. In any event, the clothes worn by Patsy and John on Christmas would have to be compared with the fibers.

The investigators also had to revisit the issue of the pubic hair found on the blanket that JonBenét's body was wrapped in. Early analysis had shown that it might be consistent with Melinda Ramsey, who had been cleared as a suspect in March. But that didn't mean the hair could not also be consistent with some other person. Alternately, the hair might have been transferred from the floor or some other object that the blanket had touched since it was last washed. The police wanted to use a newer method of comparison that was about to become available to make sure that the hair did not belong to John and Patsy Ramsey, who had previously been excluded.

Several detectives believed that JonBenét had suffered sexual abuse before the crime. Dr. David Jones, Dr. James Monteleone, professor of pediatrics at St. Louis University School of Medicine and director of child protection for Cardinal Glennon Children's Hospital; and Dr. John McCann, a clinical professor of medicine at the Department of Pediatrics at the University of California at Davis, thought that the damage to JonBenét's hymen dated from an old injury. Another expert, Dr. Richard Krugman, dean of the CU Health Sciences Center, suggested that the injury to the hymen might have been part of the staging that took place after her death. Dr. Werner Spitz said that JonBenét's vaginal injury dated to the time of her death. It was likely that the truth would never be known.

By now the detectives had a long list of open questions, and it was growing daily. It was clear that they had to interview the Ramseys again about new developments. For example, the police had learned from a confidential informant at the hospital in Charlevoix that Jon-Benét had once been hit by a golf club and had required stitches and that a plastic surgeon in Denver had been consulted. There was also secondhand information coming out of Charlevoix that JonBenét might have been the victim of child abuse. The police wanted access to these additional medical records in Denver and Michigan. Also, to further investigate the vaginal penetration, they wanted to know whether JonBenét had been prone to masturbate and whether she played doctor with her friends or brother.

The police hadn't yet discussed with the Ramseys their other suspects, such as Chris Wolf and Kevin Raburn. They wanted to ask about some of the books and videotapes they'd found in the house, and about the Bible, which was found open to Psalm 118.

Then there was the issue of where Burke's red pocket knife had been kept prior to the murder; it was found a few yards from

JonBenét's body. High on their list of questions was the family's movements early that morning, at the time of the 911 call, and the clothes the Ramseys wore that morning and the time and order in which they were put on, as well as when and where Patsy had gotten dressed and put on her makeup that morning.

The long list of questions demanded additional interviews with John, Patsy, and Burke Ramsey, but as of the end of November, the attorneys had not responded to the police department's request. Getting the Ramseys and their attorneys to agree to another round of questioning would be Mark Beckner's first real test since he had replaced Eller.

11

RAMSEY CASE COSTS CLIMB IN BOULDER

One of the Boulder police detectives investigating the JonBenét Ramsey murder case has received $22,726.09 in overtime pay since the child was found dead in her parent's home December 26.

As of October 19, Detective Steve Thomas recorded the most overtime of five detectives who have worked the murder case full time since the start of the year.

After Thomas, Detective Thomas Trujillo earned the most overtime, with $18,373.96, police records show.

—Kevin McCullen
Rocky Mountain News, November 10, 1997

On November 12, Sheriff Epp met with Koby. The week before, the chief had told the mayor, acting city manager Dave Rhodes, and his command staff that he would be leaving his post in 1998 and would soon make it public. Koby told Epp that he felt good about himself, because the week before, voters had agreed to a tax increase that would permit the implementation of his plan for more police officers and satellite substations. He was happy to be retiring, he told Epp.

But Epp wasn't happy. "I'm angry because of the way you guys have handled the Ramsey case," he told Koby. "It makes us all look bad." The sheriff complained that Koby had placed his loyalty to Eller above solving the case. Koby, he said, was still, at this late stage, blind to what had gone on in his department.

Epp felt that Koby had simply distanced himself from the problems of the investigation. Each time Epp had suggested that Eller be removed from the case, Koby had answered, "We've got them where we want them," referring to the Ramseys. The police simply didn't care that the Ramseys were being prejudged by the public and that they had lost their presumption of innocence. "Just let them sweat" was their attitude. Epp knew it was hard for law enforcement officers to see both sides of an issue and still do their job. But Epp had learned to walk a tightrope. You have to be honest and choose your words carefully. You may say that the evidence points in a particular direction, but you should explain that it is not conclusive. Epp had never once heard words to that effect from the chief of police.

KOBY ANNOUNCES HIS INTENTION TO RESIGN

Boulder Police Chief Tom Koby announced Tuesday he will resign at the end of 1998.

The announcement put an official lock on earlier indications by Koby that he would leave within two years.

"I think that what probably impacted me the most was losing my good friend and mentor (former City Manager) Tim Honey, and then having the mayor (Leslie Durgin) step down, who is one of my heroes," Koby said Tuesday night. "I'm pretty spiritually and emotionally drained. I know that I will continue to stay devoted to this community for the next year, and then I need to have some time to do some work on myself."

In May, the Boulder Police Benefit Association voted "no confidence" in Koby by a ratio of more than 2-to-1. Tonight the BPBA is scheduled to discuss progress made on concerns surrounding Koby's leadership.

—*Daily Camera,* November 19, 1997

The same day that Tom Koby made it official, John Eller put a FOR SALE sign on his front lawn and told the detectives that his resignation would be effective February 28, 1998. In Eller's living room hung an oil painting of the famed mission in Taos Pueblo, New Mexico, which he had painted in happier times. Now there was such an emptiness in his life that he couldn't even imagine picking up a paintbrush. He had resolved to remain silent about the Ramsey case until it reached some conclusion, but he also feared that it would never reach a courtroom. If it didn't, he said, he would write a book. Then he remembered the book *Guilty*, by Judge Harold J. Rothwax, of New York City, which Steve Thomas had given him. Rothwax believed that while the rights of defendants are important, they should not be protected at the expense of justice for the victims. He wrote, "Our system is a carefully crafted maze, constructed of impenetrable barriers to the truth. Even when the evidence against the accused is as clear as a ringing bell, lawyers will grasp at anything to fog the issues and mask the terrible facts."

Eller remembered that Thomas had told him about his first confrontation with Pete Hofstrom, while the police substation on University Hill was being set up in the early 1990s. Thomas was part of a team chosen to help clean up the Hill under Koby's community policing policy. Young people were out of control, throwing Molotov cocktails and cinder blocks at the police. Some nights the police would make fifty arrests, but only a few kids would go to jail. The rest would be processed and released with a summons. One night a girl, maybe five feet tall and eighty pounds, was arrested. Thomas was six-foot-one and 215 pounds, but she punched him with a closed fist and drew blood. Only after Thomas handcuffed the girl and took her to jail did he realize that his nose was broken.

Two weeks later, Thomas, who had charged the girl with a second-degree felony, received a letter from her mother asking that he not "ruin" her daughter's life. She didn't seem to understand that her daughter had punched him deliberately. He ignored the letter.

Shortly afterward, Pete Hofstrom walked into the Hill annex to see Thomas. "I noticed you charged this girl with a felony," he said.

"She broke my nose."

"I want to drop this to a misdemeanor."

"I'm not looking to ruin anybody's life, but she tagged me," Thomas said. "There has to be some consequence for her actions. I don't agree to a misdemeanor plea bargain."

"Look, I worked San Quentin," Hofstrom said. "I know what a felon is. And goddamnit, I respect those guys on death row. I had to feed some of them their last meals. You don't know what a goddamn felon is."

"Maybe not, but from where I come from, you don't punch a cop," Thomas replied. "She should consider herself lucky she didn't get her ass kicked." Hofstrom left without saying another word.

A month later, the DA's office pled the charges to a nonviolent misdemeanor. Thomas saw it as part of the culture of Boulder. Eller agreed. But he was damned if he would go along with it.

Commander Mark Beckner told Alex Hunter that he had scheduled a press conference for December 5. A lot of thought had gone into how Beckner would deal with the Ramseys and the media, much of it from forensic psychiatrist Steve Pitt, who had begun to work with the Boulder police in February. Pitt was an expert in behavioral profiling and he had advised the police on interview techniques to be used with the Ramseys.

In early November, Pitt was asked how the Boulder PD might use the media to its advantage when dealing with the Ramseys. A couple of weeks later, Pitt met with Tom Wickman, Alex Hunter and metro DA Dave Thomas, from Hunter's task force.

Though there was a liability in Beckner's holding a press conference when the police had nothing new to tell the public, Pitt emphasized that the goal of the press conference was to put pressure on the Ramseys to grant the police a new round of interviews. Pitt said the upcoming holidays, which coincided with the first anniversary of JonBenét's death, would be an excellent time for the police to update the media on the status of the investigation.

When he was told about the strategy, Koby balked. Pitt then requested a meeting with him and Mark Beckner. Over coffee at the Foundry coffee house, Pitt told them that a public request for the Ramseys to grant new interviews was essential: the Ramseys would not be inclined to refuse, because that would make them appear uncooperative. Pitt suggested that Beckner include the threat of a grand jury in his opening statement. And, the Ramseys were to be mentioned continually in every answer given to the media. A message was to be delivered to the couple: if you don't cooperate, somebody is going to push for a grand jury.

Koby finally agreed, on the condition that Hunter's office would not be involved in the press conference. Hunter accepted the condition but asked to be consulted on the wording of Beckner's opening statement. Within a day of their agreement, the threat of a grand jury had been leaked to the press. The Ramseys would feel the pressure sooner than Steve Pitt had planned.

REPORTS OF RAMSEY GRAND JURY 'PREMATURE'

Boulder Country District Attorney Alex Hunter yesterday denied reports he will soon ask a grand jury to investigate the murder of Jon-Benét Ramsey and consider indictments in the nearly year-old case.

Hunter's spokesperson, Suzanne Laurion, said, "Absolutely no decision has been made. It's premature to talk grand jury." She added, "This whole thing is certainly more media-driven than it is reality-driven." Laurion said the reports were nothing new, and that the D.A.'s team has been considering a grand jury for months, in addition to other options.

In Boulder County, a grand jury was seated in the fall of 1996 and has yet to hear a case, said Hunter.

—*Daily Camera*, December 1, 1997

In the early afternoon of December 1, Bryan Morgan called Alex Hunter and asked if he, Hal Haddon, and Patrick Burke could meet with the DA and Pete Hofstrom. In Hunter's office on December 3, Haddon asked Hunter point-blank where the case stood. Would Mark Beckner announce the convening of a grand jury when he held his press conference on December 5?

Hunter told the lawyers that as far as he knew, the police were not ready to present the case to his office, so he didn't see a grand jury as imminent. Haddon then asked whether there was a possibility of arranging another set of interviews with the Ramseys through some civil process. For example, they would consent to be interviewed under oath in a civil discovery deposition setting, with a court reporter present. Hunter said this would not be the same as twelve citizens sitting in judgment.

Next Patrick Burke spoke up. He said he didn't like the false information being circulated in the press about Burke Ramsey. The media repeatedly said that the boy hadn't been interviewed by the police. The lawyer reminded Hunter that Burke had been interviewed twice, once on December 26 by Detective Patterson and a second time on January 8 by child psychologist Dr. Suzanne Bernhard, yet the Boulder police kept giving the public the impression that no interviews of the boy had taken place. The lawyer wanted Hunter to "stand up and be courageous" and set the record straight.

Hunter reacted with irritation at the suggestion that the actions of the DA's office were—or could be—dictated by the police or anybody else. Then he confronted the real issue facing them. He told the Ramseys' attorneys what he was sure they knew—that there would soon be tremendous pressure from the police and the public to convene a grand jury. Hunter added that the Ramseys' image would be further tarnished if they didn't agree to nonconditional interviews with the police. They had to know that in such a complicated case, as the investigation proceeded and more information became known, specific questions were raised and these questions needed answers.

Patrick Burke argued that if their clients cooperated, it would give credence to the idea that they were involved in the death of their daughter. However, Haddon admitted that if the Ramseys didn't consent to the new interviews, they would be damned again in the press. Of course they were used to that by now, but it was an unpleasant prospect nonetheless. The DA implied that the real holdup for the Ramseys' attorneys was that Burke wasn't old enough to be coached for an interview or an appearance in front of a grand jury.

With nothing resolved and the atmosphere tense, the Ramseys' attorneys left. Hunter said that he felt Hal Haddon watched him as closely as anybody had ever looked at him in his life. It was as if Haddon was trying to assess by Hunter's every movement and gesture whether Hunter was being candid with him.

That afternoon Bill Wise spoke to Bob Miller, one of the three pro bono attorneys advising the police detectives. They agreed that any future action or decision the police took in this case would have to be clearly thought out. For example, if they asked to convene a grand jury, they had to be clear about its true purpose. Would it be to preserve testimony under oath, to get a reluctant witness to talk, to develop new evidence, or to seek an indictment?* Each one of those aims

---

*The common term *indictment* is an abbreviation of the document's formal name, a bill of indictment. Ordinarily, a bill of indictment is prepared for the signature of the foreperson by the prosecutor working with the grand jury. If the grand jury votes to indict, the foreperson and the prosecutor must both sign what is called a true bill of indictment.

would require developing a different strategy. Nevertheless, there was an advantage to using a grand jury, said Miller. Under a new state law, if a grand jury failed to indict, it could, if it wanted, issue a report giving reasons for its decision. Hunter's only fear, Wise said, was of a "runaway jury," predisposed to indicting the Ramseys. He was pretty sure that his boss was prepared for any other eventuality, he said.

On December 5, Mark Beckner stepped in front of a single microphone at Boulder's city council chambers. He was flanked by the eight police detectives who were now working the case. Seated before them were over a hundred members of the media. This was the first time that most of the press had seen Beckner—as well as the detectives. For the occasion, the police wore suits.

Beckman introduced his team—Detective Sgt. Tom Wickman, the case supervisor, Detectives Tom Trujillo, thrity-six, Steve Thomas, thirty-five, Jane Harmer, thirty-five, Ron Gosage, thirty-one, Kim Stewart, thirty-seven, Carey Weinheimer, thirty-three, and Michael Everett, thirty-three.

The commander began with some prepared remarks. Seventy-two separate tasks had been on his list when he assumed command, he said, and twenty-eight of those had been completed. Another dozen were in progress. The most important remaining task he added, was reinterviewing John, Patsy, and Burke Ramsey. "We have made a formal request for these interviews, and do expect this to be completed in the near future.

"When those and other jobs are finished," he continued, "we will be in a position to make a decision as to the next step in this case." Beckner went on to outline his options.

"One, we could seek an arrest warrant and prosecution. We could ask for a grand jury investigation. Or we could inactivate the case until such time as additional information becomes available." He had nothing more to say.

The first question directed to Beckner was, "Are the Ramseys still a focus of this investigation or have they been elevated to the status of suspects?"

"Well, as you know," the commander said, "we have not named suspects in this case, and we are going to continue to maintain that. What I will say is that we have an umbrella of suspicion. People have come and gone under that umbrella. They do remain under an umbrella of suspicion, but we're not ready to name any suspects."

As for Burke, who turned ten the month following his sister's death, Beckner said, "At this point, we're treating him as a witness."

That the media had picked up the scent was evident from the next question: "Can you tell us specifically why it's important to reinterview John and Patsy Ramsey and what kind of progress you're making in getting them to agree to a second interview?"

Beckner explained that many witnesses had been interviewed more than once. That happens in many cases, he emphasized. "Also understand," he added, "it's been approximately six months since we last interviewed the Ramseys. During that time, there's been a lot of investigation. We've uncovered a lot of new information. We have a lot of new questions. And they can help us answer those questions. They are significant in this case, and they have information that's important to us."

Then Beckner concluded, "We made our formal request last week and have not heard back from them. But they have indicated every willingness to cooperate and have done so during my nine weeks anyway. So I expect we'll get that done in the near future."

As anticipated during the strategy sessions with Steve Pitt, the press picked up on the theme of the Ramseys' alleged cooperation. "Can you outline or give us a sense," one reporter asked, "of how the Ramseys have been cooperative and helpful since you have taken over?"

"I can only talk about the time that I've been involved," Beckner replied. "And thus far we've made several requests, and they've honored those requests. We have several more pending and we're still waiting to hear from them."

"Is it fair to say your office is trying to establish a new relationship with the media and with the American public?" Beckner was asked.

"I'm being myself," the commander said. "This is me. And you either like it or you don't, but I'm not Tom Koby. I'm not anybody else. And this is how I interact when I interact with the media."

When the Ramseys' attorneys reviewed Beckner's press conference, they were sure a deal had been cut between Hunter and the commander to take the case to the grand jury. It now looked inevitable. They only hoped that once the case got into Hunter's hands, it would be investigated seriously.

When Fleet White heard there might be a grand jury, he understood that he would be called as a witness. White, who had been cleared as a suspect on April 16, requested copies of the statements he and his wife had made to the police during the first days of the investigation. He wanted to refresh his memory, and must have read that the Ramseys had received copies of their statements. He wanted the same consideration. In fact, unknown to the public, other witnesses' attorneys had guaranteed their clients' cooperation in exchange for copies of their early police statements.

In White's case, Mark Beckner said no. The commander didn't care what had been done in the past; his policy was different. Hunter's office had the final word, however, and agreed with Beckner's decision. White was told it would not be appropriate for him to have his statements. Unable to reconcile that decision with the treatment the Ramseys had received, White let it be known to the police and close friends that he was losing confidence in the DA's office.

GRAND JURY STRATEGY

Grand juries are valued in certain cases, such as government malfeasance, investigation of powerful public officials and prosecuting big-time drug dealers and organized crime rings. Nevertheless, the modern-day grand jury has been criticized by many as a bludgeon for prosecutors. Some critics even say its original purpose—to protect the average citizen—has been turned on its head; that it often is used to harass citizens or provide political cover for police and prosecutors in weak cases.

"I don't think the grand jury is nearly the screening device it was designed to be," said Forrest Lewis of Denver, president of the Colorado Criminal Defense Bar Association. "It's stacked very much against suspects, and very much in favor of charging people."

Given the immense amount of media coverage of the case, Ramsey attorneys argue their clients could be unfairly indicted if the case ever goes to a grand jury.

—Clay Evans
Daily Camera, December 7, 1997

★ ★ ★

In 1991 I received my summons. I had no idea what was expected of a grand juror. All I knew was that this was secretive and I couldn't talk about what was happening. That was what I thought about. It was so secretive.

We all met at the old Boulder courthouse, just off the Pearl Street Mall. Everyone was naïve when we were interviewed. What did I do for a living? Can I take a day a week off? Sure. I'd have no problem with that. I never thought I'd be appointed. I was, and I didn't mind doing my civic duty.

L.A. Law had just started, so I watched the show while waiting to be called to duty. That show put me in the mood.

Then I was notified the grand jury was needed. We met in the evening and I wasn't allowed to tell anyone what I was doing. The whole thing was frightening.

At first the deputy DA gave us an overview of the case. It was a drug case. The lives of some police officers had been endangered. Then the DA presented all the evidence and many witnesses. The witnesses had nobody to protect them; they weren't allowed an attorney.

We were allowed to question the witnesses ourselves. Sometimes I felt that we should have asked more questions. I was so intimidated. I was afraid to ask the DA some questions. I just didn't want to come off stupid. If I have any advice for a grand juror, it's that you should ask a lot more questions.

There were some witnesses who took the Fifth. They'd answer a few questions and then they'd take the Fifth. They took the Fifth again and again. They took it until the DA asked them to leave.

That made me think they were hiding something, even though we were told they had a constitutional right to take the Fifth. Just hearing someone take the Fifth has to have a negative influence on any jury. In my case, it cast doubt on the person that the DA was trying to build a case against. I even thought that maybe the DA called the witness knowing he was going to take the Fifth, that the DA was trying to plant a seed of doubt.

It was strange. I remember considering the evidence, rereading some testimony, some records, considering the testimony of the people who spoke; but the memory of the people staring right at you—taking the Fifth. I could never get away from the image of a person continually saying nothing. The doubt was there. So you go, "OK, do we disregard that person because they never said anything?"

I felt I was only seeing part of a picture. Some jurors kept saying, "Why didn't they bring up this?" Or, "Why did they bring that up in the first place? Was it because they wanted us to link this guy over here to

that one over there?" We had the feeling that games were being played.
We were being manipulated.

Someone should have been there to represent the other side, to make
sure this tool doesn't get misused.

That is why we voted unanimously not to indict. On a second case we
did indict.

—Anonymous grand juror

On December 14, Boulder's First United Methodist Church held a memorial service for JonBenét. The program included "A Christmas Message from the Entire Ramsey Family," which had also been posted on the family's Web site, which the family's press representatives maintained. It gave journalists quick access to the Ramseys' press statements and transcripts of television programs regarding the case, and the various ads and flyers the Ramseys had released.

"On the one hand, we feel like Christmas should be canceled," the message read. "Where is the joy? Our Christmas is forever tainted with the tragedy of her [JonBenét's] death. And yet the message rings clear: Had there been no birth of Christ, there would be no hope of eternal life, and hence, no hope of ever being with our loved ones again."

Local freelance writer Frank Coffman mentioned to Patsy's onetime friend Judith Phillips, whom he had met through Jeff Shapiro, the phrase *and hence* in the Christmas message. Phillips remembered that *and hence* appeared in the ransom note too: "if we monitor you getting money early, we might call you early to arrange an earlier delivery of the money and hence a [sic] earlier pick-up of your daughter."

Phillips told Steve Thomas about the similarities they had seen and Coffman told Lou Smit, who said it was a good find. He agreed with Coffman that the writer of the ransom note was educated and seemed too sophisticated to be a typical sex criminal. It sounded more like someone with business experience, who was in the habit of writing. It might even be a friend of the Ramseys, Smit thought.

Hunter was also told about the phrase *and hence* and he told Donald Foster. The Vassar professor thought it was significant. All these little things add up, he said. Hunter, who had recently found Foster erratic during their conversations, told the linguist that the police would soon be contacting him with additional writing samples. To one confidant of Hunter the DA seemed to be losing interest in Foster.

★ ★ ★

That same week, Lou Smit received a letter from John Ramsey, who gave the investigator his list of suspects in his daughter's murder: Jeff Merrick, Mike Glynn, and Jeff Marino—all of whom had once worked for him—and Bill McReynolds, who had been Santa at their Christmas party. To Smit it was clear that Ramsey was desperate for the police to check these men, because they had all but stopped looking for suspects other than him and his wife. Smit, too, was frustrated. He was eager for the case to be turned over to the DA's office, because he knew Pete Hofstrom would be a fairer arbiter of the evidence.

After the first of the year, Smit showed Ramsey's letter to Alex Hunter, who then showed it to the police. The detectives found it odd that Ramsey had written to Smit at home and that he had named Jim Marino as a suspect when Marino was appearing on television in support of the Ramseys.

As soon as the detectives finished one task, Mark Beckner moved them to the next. Now they were recanvassing the Ramseys' neighborhood, on the possibility that the duct tape and the rope had been obtained from a nearby home and the remnants returned to their original location. Detective Weinheimer asked Margaret Dillon, who lived at 756 14th Street, across the Ramseys' back alley, if she'd had any tape or white cord in her garage at the time of JonBenét's murder.

"Why, I don't have a garage," she replied.

"OK," Weinheimer said. Then he asked: "Do you have a stun gun, or a taser?"

"What's that?" she asked. "Is it something like a cattle prod?" Then he asked about Hi-Tec shoes. She knew nothing about them, either.

When the detective left, Dillon wondered why he had asked her only whether she kept duct tape and white cord in her garage. Why didn't he ask her if she had those things in her house? From his manner, she was surprised he didn't ask her if she had run across the alley and killed JonBenét. In Dillon's opinion, Weinheimer had simply wanted answers—any answers—to a short list of questions. He hadn't seemed interested in *investigating*.

On December 8, Hal Haddon learned that Lisa Ryckman of the *Rocky Mountain News* was about to break a story about the unidentified Hi-Tec shoe imprint that had been found next to JonBenét's body. Within an hour, he faxed her a letter.

HADDON, MORGAN & FOREMAN, PC
ATTORNEYS-AT-LAW

December 8, 1997

Ms Lisa Ryckman
Rocky Mountain News
400 W. Colfax Avenue
Denver, Colorado 80204

Re: Ramsey Stories

Dear Ms Ryckman:

Pat Furman [another Ramsey attorney] advises me that the
Rocky Mountain News, under your byline, intends to print
a story tomorrow which will identify a key item of evidence
in the Ramsey investigation. One other news organization
has known about this evidence for several months but did
not print it because publication of the information would
likely cause the killer to dispose of that evidence. It would
be irresponsible in the extreme for the *News* to publish this
information. We beg you not to do so.

Sincerely,
[signed]
Harold A. Haddon

Ryckman called Furman and told him that Haddon's request had been
rejected and that her story would be published as written originally.

When Alex Hunter heard that Ryckman was going to break the
story about the shoe imprint he also worried about the release of this
information. The police had so far been unable to date the imprint. They
didn't know whether the owner of the shoe was aware that the print had

been left behind or, indeed, if it was even connected to the murder. Now, with the public revelation, the owner of the Hi-Tec shoes might destroy them—even if he or she wasn't the killer. If that happened, investigators might never understand this piece of the puzzle.

Meanwhile, reporters were canvassing the Ramsey neighborhood looking for a new angle to use in their stories on the first anniversary of JonBenét's murder. Louis Sahagun of the *Los Angeles Times* interviewed Margaret Dillon, who told him that the police had asked her whether she knew if the Ramseys owned a Taser or stun gun. They had also asked her about duct tape and white nylon cord, she said. When Sahagun called Rachelle Zimmer, a Ramsey spokeswoman, to check the information, he learned that they had "known about the use of a stun gun in this murder for many months." She added, "It must now be clear to any open-minded person that this vicious crime was committed by an outsider."

On December 16, Sahagun asked Bill Wise whether a grand jury would be convened and then asked if the police were investigating the use of a stun gun in the murder. Wise had no idea what he was talking about. It was just another crazy rumor, he thought. Sahagun had gotten a virtual "no comment" from the police when he had asked them about the stun gun.

Three days later, on December 19, before Wise had time to mention the rumor to his boss, Hunter walked into his office, closed the door, and said that the next day, the *Los Angeles Times* would report that a stun gun might have been used in the murder. Hunter, who had known about Smit's stun gun theory, had gotten a call at home the night before from a writer who had been tipped and wanted to warn the DA. Wise, who knew nothing of the investigation by Smit and Ainsworth, since he had been removed at Koby's request from the daily briefings in February, hadn't thought to ask Hofstrom or DeMuth about a stun gun after Sahagun called him earlier in the week. On Saturday December 20, the Los Angeles newspaper broke the stun gun story on the front page. Ramsey attorney Hal Haddon told *The Denver Post*: "We've been told affirmatively that one [a stun gun] was used."

Over the weekend Bill Wise received many calls from reporters about the stun gun. On Monday morning, December 22, he asked Tom Faure, the coroner's chief investigator, what he knew about it. Faure told

Wise that there were two marks on JonBenét's back that could have come from that kind of device, though in retrospect, Meyer thought the marks were scratches, not abrasions from a stun gun. Nevertheless, there were two more scratches on the back of one of JonBenét's legs which were the same color as the marks on her back.

Since Mark Beckner's press conference two weeks earlier, Pete Hofstrom had encouraged him to communicate directly with the Ramseys' attorneys. On December 19, the lawyers met face-to-face with Beckner at the DA's office. Bluntly, Bryan Morgan told Beckner that he and his colleagues didn't trust the Boulder PD to conduct an objective or competent investigation, judging by the department's unprofessional conduct in the past. He hoped to see a change under Beckner's leadership. Beckner ignored the insult and got down to business. He repeated his request for a second set of formal interviews with the Ramseys and their son, Burke. In addition, he listed some items the police would need for their continuing investigation, including the clothes John and Patsy had worn during the evening of December 25 and the morning of December 26. Morgan said they would discuss the matter with their clients, and on that very professional note the meeting ended.

Meanwhile, the detectives working the Ramsey case decided that their attorneys should tour the house in order to get a better perspective, but they thought it best not to request access through the Ramseys' attorneys. There was enough bad blood on both sides to guarantee that it would be delayed or denied. They contacted an authorized representative who agreed to give them access.

With everyone gathered at the house, it was discovered that the representative's key didn't fit the lock. The detectives, embarrassed in front of their attorneys, who had come all the way to Boulder, decided to climb in through a window. Almost immediately, they noticed video cameras, installed as a security precaution, trained on them. Their illegal entry had probably been recorded. On the spot, they decided to remove the cameras and the videotapes, which they later returned on the advice of the department's legal adviser, who said: "You don't exactly have a search warrant, and you don't really have a possessory right."

★ ★ ★

Late on the night of December 21, Susannah Chase, a student at the University of Colorado in Boulder, was beaten unconscious just a few blocks from Pasta Jay's restaurant. A baseball bat was found near the scene of the crime. The press learned that there were no arrests imminent. Sheriff Epp offered his department's help to Commander Eller, whom Tom Koby had assigned to the case. Eller declined the sheriff's offer. Instead, using his authority as head of the detective division, he reassigned several detectives from the Ramsey case to the Chase investigation.

CU STUDENT DIES FROM BEATING

The death of a 23-year-old University of Colorado student has detectives once again working around the clock through the holidays to solve a brutal slaying.

After lingering in grave condition for two days, Susannah Chase was removed from life-support equipment and pronounced dead at 11:35 P.M. Monday at Boulder Community Hospital, where her Stamford, Conn., family had gathered.

Chase died unable to tell police who beat her beyond recognition and left her to die early Sunday in an alley a short distance behind her home. The police recovered a baseball bat near the bloody crime scene at 18th and Spruce streets.

Chase's death came a few days shy of the first anniversary of the murder of JonBenét Ramsey.

—John C. Ensslin
Rocky Mountain News, December 24, 1997

A few days after Chase's death, Epp realized his office still hadn't been given information about the crime or a possible killer, though his department was responsible for protecting the county, which included the city of Boulder, and there was a murderer on the loose. Eller would wait two weeks before calling a meeting with Epp's officers.

For his part, Alex Hunter couldn't understand Tom Koby's thinking. Just a week earlier, the chief had told the *Daily Camera* that dismissing Larry Mason from the Ramsey case was one of the biggest mistakes of his career. "This was one of the most painful things from start to finish on everybody involved," Koby had said. "I supported the decision that was wrong. It had terrible consequences for Larry. There is no way I can ever make that right." Then in almost the same breath, Koby put Eller in charge of Boulder's second high-profile case in less than a year, though the murder of Susannah Chase posed a more serious threat to public safety than JonBenét's killing. Everything had changed, Hunter knew, but in effect nothing had changed. A year earlier, Eller had seemed certain that the Ramsey case would be solved within a few weeks; now he seemed to believe the same thing about the Chase murder. To Hunter, it looked like a rerun. An overconfident Eller was keeping at bay everyone who offered to help him.

Just before 7:00 P.M. on December 26, Judith Phillips drove from her home on Lincoln Place to the Ramseys' former home on 15th Street. Phillips and a few friends had organized a small gathering to remember JonBenét on the first anniversary of her death.

By evening, the lights decorating the surrounding houses were washed out by the floodlights that TV camera crews had set up for their coverage of the candlelight vigil. A framed black and white photograph of a pensive JonBenét rested atop two golden angels attached to a lamppost. A burning candle and bunches of flowers rested on the front stoop. A ten-year-old girl had brought a decorative tiara and left it as a symbol of her sorrow.

"She was a sweet individual and I miss her," said Phillips, who had helped arranged the small shrine. "She will have justice."

Holiday wreaths and stuffed animals lay at the base of the lamppost beside a typed poem, "The Ballad of JonBenét," which began, "In 1990 a child was born. Her cold wealthy father ruled with scorn. Her mother did the best that she could do."

Reporters and TV crews outnumbered the thirty or so residents of Boulder who kept vigil on the bitter cold night. Some held candles; others stood with bowed heads. After they sang "Silent Night" and "Amazing Grace," the crowd dispersed and the media departed.

For the past week, local and national papers and TV stations had carried features about the case. The *Daily Camera*'s headline read, NO END IN SIGHT, and the article noted that the investigation had been suspect from the start. Reports stated that to date, the case had cost the taxpayers nearly $200,000 and the cost was expected to climb to at least half a million dollars. One story claimed the case was made up of tiny particles that had become a huge mound of evidence. Every media outlet recapped the highlights of the last twelve months. Some stations reran the Ramseys' CNN interview. Still, nobody knew for sure if there was any hard evidence that linked the Ramseys to their daughter's murder.

By now it had been leaked to the media that the DNA evidence did not tie the Ramseys to the crime, that hair and blood samples, fingernail scrapings, and fluids from the crime scene were still unidentified. The *Daily Camera* noted that palm prints and fingerprints were like snowflakes—no two were alike. Fibers that had been found in JonBenét's genital area, the white cord, the garrote, and the duct tape might yet yield some answers. The broken paintbrush, the ransom note, some pens, various handwriting samples, and a note pad may have held answers but they were also still hidden. The mystery of the shoe imprint had yet to be solved. So many unyielding puzzles, yet the police remained cautiously optimistic—perhaps defying logic.

PART FOUR

Destruction Derby

1

THE GALLUP ORGANIZATION

Princeton, NJ—The American public is skeptical that the murder of JonBenét Ramsey. . . will ever be solved. . . . Over six out of ten Americans interviewed in a November [6 though 9] Gallup poll said they had followed the case very or somewhat closely and only 10% said that they had not followed it at all.

Eighty-eight percent of those with an opinion about the murder—representing 32% of the general public—say that it was some member of the family who perpetrated the deed, with three-quarters of those citing one or both of her parents.

In December, Gallup conducted another poll, asking 1,005 adults eighteen years or older if they thought the case would be solved; 31 percent said yes, 58 percent said no, and 11 percent had no opinion.

Since Beckner's press conference the previous month, the detectives had become minor celebrities. Now that their names were connected to faces, the public could relate to them, and the department's hate mail became personal. At police headquarters, the detectives decorated their war room with letters and one area was reserved for "the letter of the day."

Dear Detectives,

Thanks for the great investigative work. Remind me to never get murdered in Boulder. Who paid you guys off.

This thing stinks. Fucking morons.

—A concerned citizen

In 1996 Alex Hunter had spent the Christmas holidays in Hawaii. This year he was in Boulder. Hunter was at his office daily, and even worked between Christmas and New Year's. He responded to calls from journalists, who wanted to know about the stun gun and the Hi-Tec shoe imprint. One writer asked how it felt when he looked back at all the criticism he and his office had received during the preceding year.

"When I was sixteen, my dad sent me on a ten-day canoe trip to Canada," Hunter told the writer. "The first stop was an island outside of Soo Look-Out, Ontario, that had the worst mosquitoes I had ever encountered in my life. The purpose of stopping at this miserable place was that the counselor wanted to make sure all of us could handle the bugs. When you went to take a leak, you even had mosquitoes on your penis. By the time that trip was over, I could roll up my sleeves and just let them bite. That's how I've felt along this year's journey."

On January 2, 1998, *The New Yorker's* fact checkers began confirming Hunter's quotes for an article that was to be published on January 12. That same day, the *New York Post* reported that JonBenét's body would be exhumed to determine if a stun gun had been used on her. The author of *The New Yorker* article asked Hunter for a comment. He said, "Every rock must be turned over, and if that means swabbing everyone's mouth or exhuming JonBenét's body, that's what the police will have to do. I don't want the public to think everything has been done if in fact, in effect, everything hasn't been done." The police said they had no plans to exhume the body.

On Monday, January 5, Hunter and Wise met to discuss the Ramsey case. Hunter told Wise that he expected Tom Koby to come to him in about three months and say, "We just don't have it. It's not there." The two men joked that they hoped Koby would still be around to say it in public. Hunter was sure Koby would also ask that a grand jury be convened. That way, he could spread the blame around. While that might be the chief's way of closing *his* file on the case, Hunter knew it would give the DA's office a chance to carry on the investigation. Then he would be able—finally—to cut Lou Smit loose. Also, the grand jury had some powers that the police and the DA didn't have. It could require witnesses to appear and answer questions and could demand certain documents and evidence. In addition, a grand jury would have its own investigators. New evidence might well come to light under the auspices of such a secret proceeding.

"Koby still doesn't seem to get it," Wise told Hunter. The chief had given the Susannah Chase case to Eller, even though Eller was leaving the department on February 28. Again, the commander wasn't cooperating with Pete Hofstrom, who was getting his information from the coroner's office. The Chase murder was as mysterious as Jon-Benét's death. No motive had been established for the killing, and the perpetrator was still at large and unknown to the police. Moreover, the threat to public safety in Boulder was escalating. Recently there had been a rash of burglaries where entry was made through unlocked doors. In the first nine months of 1997, the police had recorded 722 burglaries, of which 231 did not involve forced entry.

BOULDERITES QUERY COPS IN STUDENT DEATH

There were at least 125 victims in the savage beating death of 23-year-old University of Colorado student Susannah Chase, and they were at a meeting Monday night with Boulder police.

The residents of the Whittier neighborhood . . . erupted in anger, tears and frustration at times during the meeting, and police could do little to calm their fears. Police have interviewed more than 100 people, but the investigation has gone 15 days without a suspect being named.

Residents peppered police Detective Cmdr. John Eller with questions about evidence, suspects and similar assaults in the past two months. They even questioned the department's investigative techniques.

"We're suggesting that young white women do not walk alone after dark," Eller said. . . . "I don't want to have anymore victims."

—Dave Curtin
The Denver Post, January 6, 1998

Tom Koby called Alex Hunter on January 6 and asked to meet. At the Foundry coffee house, after some small talk about how Koby thought Beckner was getting along with Hofstrom, the chief got down to business.

"Fleet White came in to talk to me and Beckner," Koby told Hunter. "White wants you off the case. He says you leaked stuff to one of the tabloids after you met with him last year." Hunter remained silent. "He's on the warpath, and he's threatening to see the attorney general." Koby said that White refused to cooperate with the police as long as Hunter was still on the case. In one conversation with detectives, White had even teased the officers: "What would you say if I told you the Ramseys owned Hi-Tec shoes?"

Hunter had known for some time that the Whites were angry with him. Bob Grant, a member of his task force, had advised Hunter to mend his fences, but the Whites wanted access to their police statements, and Hunter and Mark Beckner had declined because they felt it would taint White's usefulness as a witness. The police believed that White might have critical evidence in the case—he had been with John Ramsey when JonBenét's body was found—but they did not want to make the same trade they'd granted the Ramseys the previous April. Some of the detectives were doubtful that White had even opened the wine cellar door when he made his first trip to the basement early that morning. For his part, White couldn't understand why Hunter had fought for the Ramseys' right to see their police statements while now Hunter was denying him the same privilege. He was also upset that in April, Hunter had softened the wording of Koby's statement intended to exonerate him of involvement in Jon-Benét's murder. The Whites felt they were being slighted by Hunter.

On December 19, the couple had met with Colorado governor Roy Romer and his chief of staff, Meg Porfido, in Denver. At the meeting, White leveled some charges against Hunter, saying he ran a timid office, wasn't aggressive enough, had problems with the police, and was hampering the police investigation. White asked the governor to assign a special prosecutor to take over the Ramsey case.

The governor called Bob Grant and Denver district attorney Bill Ritter for their opinions. Grant told Romer that Hunter was handling the case properly and explained that Hunter was restricted until he was presented with the case by the Boulder PD, which was still completing a to-do list. Only then would the law allow for removing or replacing him for improper behavior. However, in his opinion, Grant said, Hunter's past actions had no bearing on his handling of the Ramsey case.

Koby told Hunter that the governor had called him in December too. He'd told Romer that there was no basis for the Whites' request. He confirmed what Bob Grant had said—the case was still with the Boulder PD.

Meg Porfido called White and told him that the governor wouldn't intervene at this time and didn't see a need for a special prosecutor. Afterward, the Whites wrote to Romer again, repeating what they'd said at their meeting. The same day that Koby and Hunter were meeting at the Foundry, the Whites went to see the state attorney general, Gale Norton, to repeat what they had told the governor. Norton told them she had no jurisdiction over the matter, since Alex Hunter had not said he wasn't going to press charges. No one could move against Hunter until the Boulder PD had finished its investigation and handed over the case.

On Monday, January 12, 1998, this writer's article, "Justice Boulder Style," was published in *The New Yorker*. It updated readers on the status of the case and explained why Hunter had not indicted JonBenét's parents for her murder. The story discussed the Ramseys' presumption of innocence and explored Hunter's views on the case.

Pete Hofstrom told Bill Wise that the article gave the police ammunition for their case that Hunter was the source of media leaks. Hofstrom reminded Wise that to protect the flow of information from the police, he had agreed to Beckner's condition that he withhold from Hunter some evidence the police were developing. Hofstrom also told this to Hunter, and the DA accepted it. When one deputy DA heard about the condition Hofstrom had accepted, he remarked: "Pete hasn't thrown his boss under the bus; he's crawled under it willingly. Luckily for Alex, the bus wasn't moving forward."

The most extreme reaction to *The New Yorker* article came from Fleet and Priscilla White. They wrote a letter to the editor of *The Denver Post* and on January 14 delivered it personally. Because the Whites refused to allow it to be edited for length, the paper rejected it. That same afternoon, the *Daily Camera* agreed to publish it unedited.

On January 15, a reporter from the *Daily Camera* called Alex Hunter for his comments on the as yet unpublished letter. The DA, on his way to the newspaper's office to meet with Tom Koby and senior editor Barrie Hartman on an unrelated matter, told the reporter he would address the issue later in the day. At the *Camera* offices, Hunter told Koby about the Whites' letter, in which they asked the governor to appoint a special prosecutor. Koby said he wasn't surprised, knowing the Whites' state of mind.

Before leaving the newspaper office, Hunter made the rounds of its senior staff. He saw Thad Keyes, the managing editor, and Colleen

Conant, the new publisher, briefing them off the record. He also said he would have to pass on giving their reporter a comment and would release a statement later in the day.

Hunter wanted his response to be released simultaneously with the Whites' letter. Bill Wise wrote the statement, which was given to the *Daily Camera* that afternoon and faxed to the governor and the attorney general, both of whom issued statements saying that this was not the time to intervene. Chief Koby also issued a statement. In part, it said, "The Boulder District Attorney has not done anything but try and be supportive of the investigation. Whether people agree with that is another issue."

The Whites' letter, part of which is reprinted below, was published in the *Daily Camera* on January 16.

> Letter to the Editor
>
> As witnesses in the JonBenét murder investigation, we are reluctant to express our views regarding the investigation. At this time, however, we feel compelled to address matters which we feel to be of great importance.
>
> Public officials who contemplate the release of information concerning the case or desire to publicly express their opinions must be mindful [that they risk putting every aspect of the case in jeopardy]. Such statements and release of information should only serve the goals of furthering the investigation or protecting the public. There are simply no other valid reasons for making information regarding the investigation available to the public.
>
> As witnesses, we have developed confidence and trust in Boulder Police Department investigators.
>
> On the other hand, we have not developed such [positive] sentiments toward the Boulder County District Attorney. Our sentiments toward the Boulder County District Attorney are based on our personal experiences which have been augmented by the following considerations:
>
> 1. There are various relationships between the Boulder County District Attorney and members of the Boulder

and Denver legal communities which may have impaired the objectivity of the Boulder County District Attorney.

2. The Boulder County District Attorney under the leadership of District Attorney Alex Hunter has been criticized in the past for not being an aggressive prosecutor of homicide cases.

3. There appears to be an atmosphere of distrust and non-cooperation between the Boulder County District Attorney and the Boulder Police Department.

4. There is a strong impression that the Boulder County District Attorney has acted improperly by sharing evidence and other information with the attorneys and other parties not officially involved in the investigation.

5. There is a strong impression that Alex Hunter and members of his staff have acted inappropriately by giving their opinions and information regarding the investigation to various news media organizations. This impression has been strengthened recently by the statements made by District Attorney Alex Hunter appearing in the Jan. 19, 1998 issue of New Yorker magazine. What public service did Mr. Hunter envision when he made such statements and revealed details of the investigation over a period of five months to a noted journalist who had publicly announced his intention to write a book about the investigation?

At a minimum, these considerations have created the strong appearance of impropriety, professional incompetence and a lack of objectivity.

The idea of waiting for the case to be "completed" and to be "referred" to the Boulder County District Attorney presupposes that the negative effect of the presence of the Boulder County District Attorney in the investigation will somehow be mitigated in the future. It ignores the practical problem that the Boulder Police Department and relevant witnesses have no confidence in the ability of the Boulder County District Attorney to prudently handle evidence and to professionally and impartially consider a case presented to it.

We request that Governor Romer immediately intervene and remove the Boulder County District Attorney and its offices from the investigation and appoint a competent and completely independent special prosecutor who is capable of establishing and maintaining the confidence and the trust of the Boulder Police Department, witnesses to the case, and the public, whereby to maximize the likelihood of a successful conclusion to this case.

—Fleet Russell White, Jr.
Priscilla Brown White

D.A. RESPONSE TO MEDIA
RE: FLEET WHITE LETTER

We have known for some time of Mr. and Mrs. White's concerns. We understand the difficulty of being so closely linked to an investigation of such extreme complexity and duration. Unfortunately, because of Mr. and Mrs. White's status as witnesses in the case, we are unable to share with them the information and insights that might provide them the reassurance they seek. Of course Mr. and Mrs. White are well within their rights to contact the Governor's office, the Attorney General's Office, the Boulder Police Department and the media as often as they wish to share their concerns.

—The Office of the District Attorney

On January 17, Hunter and Wise attended the scheduled meeting of the metro DAs who were consulting with Hunter on the case. Since Eller would soon be out and Koby was leaving, Wise was now back in the loop.

At the meeting, Fleet White's letter and the effect of *The New Yorker* article were discussed. Hunter explained that the presumption of innocence for the Ramseys had been foremost in his thinking and that he had wanted to offer a counterweight to the media's condemnation of the Ramseys, which he considered a result of Commander Eller's view. The Ramseys' constitutional rights had to be protected, he repeated. He left the meeting with the impression that the other DAs agreed that the public was better served by the publication of his views on the matter.

Later that afternoon, Tom Koby suggested to Hunter that in the coming weeks some overture should be made to Fleet White—maybe a meeting between them, the police department, and Hunter. The DA agreed.

CITY OF BOULDER   FOR IMMEDIATE RELEASE
JANUARY 17, 1998   BOULDER PRESS RELEASE #63

The Boulder Police Department has received written communication through John and Patsy Ramsey's counsel that John and Patsy will not submit to a second interview with investigators under the reasonable conditions set by investigators. The Boulder Police Department's position in requesting the second interviews has been clear and straightforward. There are questions the police have that are related to clarifications of previous statements and questions related to information that was not available during the first interviews.

The police are still waiting to receive clothing requested from the Ramseys in Nov., 1997, and for a final decision on whether they will be allowed to interview Burke Ramsey.

In their dealings with the police, the Ramseys' attorneys had always taken the position that their clients were in fact defendants, not simply suspects, and as such should have the rights of every defendant—full access to discovery.

In the department's press release, Beckner denied the Ramseys' request to review the evidence before agreeing to more interviews. The commander said it would hamper the effectiveness of the investigation and compromise the information provided by other witnesses and potential suspects. It was also contrary to accepted investigative procedures and had not been permitted to any other person involved in the case. Chief Koby told one journalist, "The bottom line is these are people whose daughter has been killed, and we're trying to find the killer. The fact that they keep handcuffing us hinders us from successfully resolving this investigation."

The Ramseys' attorneys responded on January 23 with an open letter to Beckner, which was given to the media. They complained that the commander was negotiating through the media and that, like Eller, Beckner was after an "elimination of defenses" rather than an "objective search for the real killer." The attorneys said that the leaks about the shoe imprint and the stun gun had taken place on Beckner's watch, implying that the police had been the source. On this matter, the attorneys were disingenuous. They were the ones who had responded to the *Los Angeles Times* story about the stun gun, whose source, the article stated, was a Ramsey neighbor who had been interviewed by the police. The source of an early December *Rocky Mountain News* story about the shoe imprint was not a member of law enforcement either. More to the point, however, was something that the attorneys failed to point out in their letter: during their investigation, detectives often failed to admonish possible witnesses not to discuss their interviews with anyone.

The attorneys' letter concluded on an ominous note: "We will no longer deal with the Boulder Police Department, except to honor our previous commitments."

With John and Patsy Ramsey now living in Atlanta, it was unclear to the police whether their attorneys were consulting with the couple or acting independently. Frustrated by this, Beckner authorized Steve Thomas to approach Rev. Hoverstock and ask if he would act as a liaison between the family and the police. Hoverstock agreed, and within a few days he told the police that the Ramseys would meet with Beckner at their home in Atlanta. Beckner clarified that the meeting would be all business—he didn't "want to chat about the weather." Negotiations broke down over the scope of the questions Beckner would be allowed to ask. The police assumed that the Ramseys' attorneys had intervened.

Meanwhile, Beckner called Hunter to say that he was looking at the first week of March as a likely time for the DA to issue an arrest warrant or to convene a grand jury. Beckner had not mentioned in whose name the warrant would be written. Hunter replied that he was open to convening the grand jury but not to a fishing expedition.

Bob Grant had told Hunter he didn't have the horsepower to handle this case before a jury, and now Hunter called Bill Ritter, another member of his task force, for advice about a grand jury specialist with Colorado experience. Ritter recommended Michael Kane, a former assistant U.S. attorney now living in Mechanicsburg, Pennsylvania, and working for the Pennsylvania Department of Revenue. Ritter said he was one of the finest grand jury experts he'd ever worked with.

In mid-January, Beckner told Hunter that Donald Foster, the Vassar linguistics expert who had been working on the case with them, at Hunter's suggestion, was making some headway with his analysis. Beckner was eager to hear from Foster.

Steve Thomas had visited Foster earlier in the month, taking along hundreds of pages of writing from many different suspects, including Patsy and John Ramsey. Foster had followed the case on the Internet long before he was sought out to work on it. He had even entered some of the chat rooms and discussed the case with people like Jameson.

Foster was impressed with the detective. "I can't tell you what our theories or the evidence are," Thomas had said. "And I'm not going to prejudice your thinking." Foster found that kind of commitment to justice unusual. He had heard the same thing from Hunter when they first talked on the phone. To the professor, both men seemed dedicated to finding JonBenét's killer.

In his work, Foster always began with the assumption that no detail, however small, is irrelevant. Something as seemingly trivial as a period after the abbreviation *Mr.* can be a vitally important clue. In this example, it could suggest someone's nationality: Americans use a period after the abbreviation but British writers do not. In one murder case, Foster identified the author of a document as someone educated in India. Among other clues was the misspelling of the name Rhonda as *Rondha*. In addition to such minutiae, Foster tracked down source material such as books, TV shows, movies, or music lyrics that might have influenced the writers whose documents he analyzed.

Beckner hoped Foster would name Patsy Ramsey as the author of the ransom note, and he asked Hunter if he would consider filing a motion to admit linguistic evidence when he filed charges against Patsy. It was the first time Hunter had heard Beckner name a suspect in connection with the death of JonBenét.

The commander also suggested that if the motion was denied, the DA could dismiss the charges and jeopardy would not be attached. The DA would have lost nothing, and the police could continue the investigation, or Hunter could take the case to a grand jury. Beckner was suggesting something known as a motion in limine. If the court ruled Foster's evidence inadmissible, the DA could petition the court to dismiss the charges, a perfectly routine procedure.

Hunter told Beckner he wouldn't want to handle it that way. He considered linguistics a good investigative tool, but he did not think it would be deemed admissible in a Colorado court.★ Also, Foster had never testified in a criminal trial. They could use linguistics testimony with the grand jury, Hunter assured Beckner, since the rules of admissibility were much broader—even hearsay evidence could be heard by a grand jury. The DA told the commander he would send him Colorado's evidentiary rules concerning scientific evidence. The two men agreed to wait for Donald Foster's written report.

Beckner seemed deflated the next day when he told Hofstrom they "might not have it." Hofstrom told Hunter he saw a grand jury request coming.

John Ramsey knew there was no position for him at Lockheed Martin in the Atlanta area and that time was running out on his contract, so he looked into the ever-expanding computer business. Computers were becoming smaller and faster, but programming hadn't changed much.

In early January Ramsey traveled to Spain, to meet with José Martin, cofounder of Jaleo Software and Communicacion Integral Consultores, which controlled the rights to a program that integrated editing and high-end compositing for TV. CBC, CNN, Spain's TVE, Australia's Channels 9 and 7, and Germany's and Argentina's networks were all using the Jaleo program. In the coming months, Ramsey and his Spanish partners agreed that Ramsey would head Jaleo Technologies in the United States and sell the firm's products through dealers in Mexico, Canada, and the United States. Glen Stine, a close friend of the Ramseys, who was vice president for budget and finance at CU, would leave his job in Boulder and move his family to Atlanta to join Ramsey's new company.

★ A decade and a half ago, expert testimony about handwriting comparisons was almost universally accepted, but DNA evidence was viewed with suspicion. In the intervening years, some judges (notably Judge Richard Matsch, from the Oklahoma City bombing trials) had expressed skepticism about the scientific validity of handwriting analysis, while during the same period DNA evidence became overwhelmingly acceptable. A U.S. Supreme Court decision in 1993 made an effort to clarify the standards for the validity of scientific evidence but succeeded only in emphasizing the discretion of the trial judge to allow or disallow it. There was no way to predict whether a judge would find that a convincing scientific basis could be laid down for the kind of linguistic analysis Foster performed, and so no way to be sure that his testimony could, or could not, be used at a trial.

A day after Ramsey left for his first meeting with his future partners in Spain, Craig Lewis of the *Globe* was tipped off to the trip. He followed the family, tailing them around Madrid. He witnessed Patsy crying before a painting in the Prado museum that resembled JonBenét. When Lewis discovered that Spain might not have an extradition treaty with the United States, he found the hook for his *Globe* story. The headline read RAMSEYS FLEE TO SPAIN. The story said that the *Globe* had learned the family had plans to flee the country before a grand jury forced testimony from their son, Burke.

PARENTS TURN IN CLOTHES

More than a year after JonBenét Ramsey was murdered, her parents have turned over to Boulder police the clothing they were wearing the night before their 6-year-old daughter was found dead in their home.

Two months after police finally made the request, they received two shirts, a pair of pants and a sweater this week from John and Patsy Ramsey, according to sources. Authorities sought the clothing to compare with fibers found in the case, sources said.

Police have also requested additional interviews with John and Patsy Ramsey and to talk more with their son, Burke, now 11.

—Marilyn Robinson
The Denver Post, January 29, 1998

When the police inspected the clothes they had received—and there were more items than were reported in the press—they noticed that a red blouse of Patsy's looked brand-new, as if it had just come off the rack. The detectives were also interested in Patsy's red-and-black checkerboard-design jacket. Four fibers had been found attached to the duct tape, and they were red and black. The police lost no time in sending the clothing to the CBI for fiber analysis.

2

In the first week of February, Detectives Jane Harmer and Steve Thomas tried to patch up relations between Hunter's office and Fleet and Priscilla White. Thomas felt it was important to keep White happy since he was a material witness, and he also thought Hunter's office should not have let the situation deteriorate to the point of the Whites' campaigning for the DA's dismissal. The couple agreed to meet with Hunter, Beckner, and the detectives, and Priscilla suggested their house. A few hours before the meeting, however, Beckner told Thomas that Hunter would send Pete Hofstrom in his place. Hunter had given no explanation. Thomas broke the news to the Whites. Predictably, Fleet White wasn't happy, but he agreed to meet with Hofstrom and Beckner nonetheless. For forty-five minutes the group sat in the Whites' kitchen. Hofstrom chatted about his years as a prison guard at San Quentin. But since he couldn't speak for Hunter, nothing was resolved. Soon afterward, Thomas heard that White was now as angry with Commander Beckner as he was with Hunter. He persisted in trying to obtain the statements he had made to the police, and no one would release them to him.

Alex Hunter was wrestling with the inevitability of a grand jury. In the past, Hunter had enjoyed meeting with groups of Boulderites to ask what the public wanted from its DA. Now, while giving a talk to a group of Louisville residents, he asked how many of them had formed opinions on the Ramsey case and on what basis. All but one person said that the Ramseys were guilty, and even the holdout, Hunter felt, had an opinion about the case but pretended otherwise. Driving back to his office, Hunter wondered how he would find twelve impartial county residents for a grand jury.

On February 5, Lockheed Martin, which had bought the Ramseys' house under its employment agreement with Ramsey, sold it for $650,000 to a limited liability company owned by some friends of the Ramseys. Attorney Michael Bynum said that when the house was eventually sold, the profits would go to the JonBenét Ramsey Children's Foundation.

While the police and the DA believed that the ransom note was the most important piece of evidence against the Ramseys, the couple's attor-

472

neys believed that the house was the most important piece of evidence for a potential criminal defense of their clients. It was their position that the house should be kept in its original state so that grand jurors or trial jurors could tour it and see how an intruder might have entered and made his way through it. By July 1997, the DA's office had begun making architectural drawings of the house so that a large-scale model could be built for use during legal proceedings. Both sides knew the house would play an important role in determining who had killed JonBenét.

RAMSEY FRIENDS' PALMS CHECKED

Police investigating the murder of JonBenét Ramsey have been asking friends of the family for palm prints, indicating they have a print they can't match yet.

Police have found a palm print on the ransom note. It is unclear whether this latest request is related to that print.

The palm-print search appears to be another item in the list of investigative tasks created by Cmdr. Mark Beckner when he took over the investigation late last year.

—*Rocky Mountain News*, February 8, 1998

Carol McKinley, who had gone to work for Fox TV in January, called Dr. Henry Lee to ask how he would rate the chances that the case would ever be solved. On a scale of 1 to 10, Lee gave it a 2. It will never be solved, he said. Then he added, "I'm coming to Boulder. Alex Hunter is making my life hard. He wants me to meet with police again." That night McKinley made arrangements to fly to San Francisco, where the doctor was attending a forensics conference, to tape his statement for her network.

Hunter had been trying to get the police and Dr. Lee together for months. The detectives were reluctant, but the DA was insistent. Now that the police investigation was winding down, he wanted to make sure nothing had been overlooked. Lee said he'd make himself available during a layover at the Denver airport. Hunter told Beckner that if his detectives would attend, there would be no press conference and no grandstanding. If the story leaked, he'd tell the press that Lee was consulting with the Boulder PD and not with his staff. Beckner agreed. When Carol McKinley's report aired, Hunter discovered that only the local press was interested. He was pleased that interest in the case seemed to be abating.

The meeting took place on February 13. Hunter wanted Pete Hofstrom to come along, but the deputy would not give up his customary Friday court responsibilities. He had invested months in determining the just punishment for felons about to be sentenced, and he wanted to be the one to present his findings to the court. The Ramsey case was not yet on his docket. If Hunter was frustrated by Hofstrom's decision, he didn't show it. That kind of dedication was what he admired in Pete.

Lee met for almost six hours with Hunter, Smit, DeMuth, Beckner, and Detectives Wickman and Trujillo. Afterward, the group hastily called a press briefing for the small media contingent that had assembled at the airport.

"I need to state that I'm disappointed," Hunter said, "that we have not had more cooperation from the Ramseys in helping us get to the truth. We need to have that in order to answer questions that remain that are critical to finding out what happened in this case."

This was the first time Hunter had criticized the Ramseys in public. During the meeting with Lee, the police and the DA realized that the Ramseys' refusal to grant additional police interviews had brought the investigation to a standstill. The detectives had completed almost all the items on their to-do list. Now they needed answers that only JonBenét's parents could provide. Hunter's remark, possibly made in frustration, was a turning point in his relations with the police. The DA had now supported the department in public. It would make a big difference in his dealings with Beckner.

When Dr. Lee took his turn at the microphone, he said that after the meeting, he now gave the case a 50–50 chance of being solved.

Later in the day, Hal Haddon, one of the Ramseys' attorneys, was asked for a comment. "We do not intend to have any further dealings with the police because they are hopelessly biased," he asserted.

After the airport meeting, Hunter met with Tom Koby.

"I need to look at what we have," Koby said, referring to the evidence. "It may be that I will stand up and say the case needs to be put on the shelf, or I may recommend to you that you take it to a grand jury." Koby told the DA that he wanted some witness testimony legally preserved as soon as possible. A grand jury was the only solution Koby saw. ★ Melody Stanton, the neighbor of the Ramseys who had heard the

★ Koby's faith in the power of the grand jury to preserve testimony is questionable. In Colorado, there is little difference in admissibility between a witness's signed statement and that same witness's grand jury testimony under oath. Either one would be admissible if the witness later testified at trial and said something different. Most likely, neither one would be admissible if the witness disappeared before trial or refused to testify.

scream, was a case in point. Her interview wasn't signed or given under oath, and since the *Globe* had published her story, she'd become more and more frightened and reluctant to testify. Then there were the Ramseys' close friends—the Fernies, the Stines, and the Walkers. Some of them refused to talk to the police, and more than one detective wanted them charged with obstruction of justice. Koby and Hunter discussed granting them "use immunity" before a grand jury to get them to talk.* Finally, they wanted Burke Ramsey's testimony preserved. He was now eleven, and his memories of the events surrounding his sister's death were sure to be fading. Hunter discussed all this with the chief, though in his opinion it was not the proper use of a grand jury. If a grand jury was to be considered, he told Koby firmly, they would have to go all the way and ask for an indictment.** The grand jury could not become simply another investigative body.

TOM KOBY DEFENDS POLICE DEPARTMENT

In an unscheduled public appearance before the City Council, Koby explained that the department has been faced with an unusual number of high-intensity cases—from the non-lethal shooting of a state trooper to December's Susannah Chase murder and several suspicious transient deaths.

Among other things Koby said:

• There will be a resolution to the Ramsey case in three months.

• The Boulder County Sheriff's Department will assign officers to help Boulder police with an investigative backlog.

• Officers from the traffic division have been temporarily

---

* Use immunity assures that neither the resulting testimony nor any fruits of that testimony can be used against the person to whom it has been granted. A witness who has been granted use immunity is therefore not vulnerable to self-incrimination and must answer all questions put to him.

**There was no impropriety in what the police were suggesting. In a 1983 case that got national attention, Alex Hunter had entered into an agreement with an attorney for a suspect in the murder of Sid Wells (a student who was dating the daughter of Robert Redford) that a grand jury would investigate the crime but would not return an indictment. The grand jurors investigating the Wells homicide were not made aware of this agreement. (As reported by the *Daily Camera,* November 22, 1998, p. C1.)

moved to work 60 investigations, which is expected to result in fewer tickets for speeding and other violations. The department is not easing up on drunken driving patrols.

• To boost morale, a consultant has been brought in to provide "emotional survival" training to the top administrators. In April, the consultant will work with officers and their families.

—Julie Poppen
Daily Camera, February 18, 1998

Commander Beckner was in discussions with Jim Jenkins, an Atlanta attorney who had represented Melinda and John Andrew Ramsey since March 1997 and was now counsel for Burke Ramsey. The police were hoping to conduct a formal interview of Burke and to do it before the media got wind of it. By mid-February, Beckner and Jenkins had agreed that the interview would take place in Atlanta, at a neutral location, and that it would be videotaped and conducted by a police officer rather than a child psychologist. Most important to the police was the stipulation that John and Patsy would not be present and that neither they nor their attorneys would be provided with information about the interview. The day after they agreed, Marilyn Robinson of *The Denver Post* called Jenkins, detailed for him the position he'd taken in his discussions with Beckner, and asked for a comment on the pending interviews. Jenkins was livid. Not only had someone leaked the fact that he was talking to Beckner, but they knew everything he had said. Jenkins now believed he saw Beckner's hidden agenda—to use Burke as a weapon in the police-backed media campaign against his parents. Beckner denied Jenkins's charges. Nevertheless, that same afternoon, the lawyer called off the interview between the Boulder PD and Burke Ramsey.

FORMER RAMSEY CASE CHIEF QUITS

The former chief investigator of the widely criticized JonBenét Ramsey murder investigation will call it quits Saturday.
"I wanted to be chief. I wanted to do it my way," Eller said.
On Friday, personal belongings packed in boxes stacked in his office, Eller, characteristically wearing a pin-striped suit, talked about

his career, his family, the Ramsey case and his future.

On one side, Eller, whose smiles are few and fleeting, is a self-pro-claimed "fairly hard-nosed" cop who doesn't mind he has rattled a few cages. On the other side is a man whose all-time favorite band is Led Zeppelin, who painted a mural of sea creatures and animals at the Niwot Child and Family Advocacy center and who has expressed his sense of humor by drawing political cartoons.

—Christopher Anderson
Daily Camera, February 23, 1998

That week, twenty-four Boulder detectives took John Eller out to lunch at Dolan's restaurant. It was more like a wake than a retirement celebration. The officers had a group picture taken of themselves to make into a plaque. Eller took the floor and gave the detectives an inspirational speech of the sort Knute Rockne used to give his players before they took the field.

A week later, Steve Thomas and Eller's brother, who had come from Florida, helped Eller load two Ryder trucks with his life's belongings. On February 28, with Eller's brother in one truck and Thomas and Eller in the other, they began the four-day drive to Florida. Within a few months, Eller would return to the police academy for night courses to get his Florida law enforcement credentials.

The cross-country trip was tiring for Thomas. He couldn't under-stand why he needed so much coffee to keep awake during the drive east. He had also been having headaches for months. He knew he needed to see a doctor, but he couldn't fit an appointment into his tight schedule.

BECKNER TO TAKE COMMAND
OF DETECTIVE BUREAU

The names should be a roll call of the Boulder Police Depart-ment's best and brightest—Detective Linda Arndt, Sgt. Larry Mason, Cmdr. John Eller and Chief Koby.

Instead, the litany represents the tarnished reputations of Boul-der's men and women in blue, careers forever changed—some would even say ended—by the ghost of JonBenét Ramsey.

But Mark Beckner, the 42-year-old commander who took the reins of this city's most notorious murder investigation last fall, doesn't expect to be the next casualty.

One week from today, he'll assume command of the department's beleaguered detective bureau with eyes on the ultimate prize—one day becoming chief of police.

—Matt Sebastian
Daily Camera, February 23, 1998

On Monday, February 23, a detective on the Ramsey case returned a phone call from a writer covering the story. The writer wasn't in, so the detective left the following message:

TELEPHONE ANSWERING MACHINE MESSAGE SAVED AT 6:09 P.M.

I am sorry it has taken me so long to return your call. I just got back in town. I am simply not in a position to talk to you right now. The reason is twofold. One, I think that the defense would try and make an issue should I talk to you, however benign or innocent it may be. And secondly, the department would make the same issue with Koby's blanket gag order.

But I can tell you there are things that I have witnessed in this case that you simply would not believe. Things, in my opinion, have been unconscionable. I know this case from the inside, I guess, as well as anyone. And there are things that probably should be known at some time.

Let's just see where this is at in a couple of months. This case, this victim, which has consumed my life in every waking moment, is just too important to me to jeopardize.

By the first of March, some members of Hunter's staff thought that Lou Smit and Trip DeMuth had become fixated on the intruder theory, almost to the point of ignoring evidence that ran against it—much the same way they had accused the police of obsessively focusing on the Ramseys as the guilty parties. Hofstrom was noncommittal; he said he would only give his opinion after reviewing the entire case file. For his part, Hunter had said for months that he wanted to see convincing evidence before anyone was charged. He claimed that so far only 40 percent of the evidence he had seen pointed to the Ramseys. Since the case would soon be coming his way and his team was sure to expand, he renewed the lease on the war room for the rest of the year. They would need a secure place to work.

On March 3, Beckner met with Hofstrom and said he wanted to put about a dozen witnesses before a grand jury: Fleet and Priscilla White; John, Patsy, and Burke Ramsey; friends of the Ramseys; and various Access Graphics employees. Hofstrom explained that the commander couldn't use the grand jury as an extension of his authority. The jury didn't work for the police, and it wasn't an investigative arm or an extension of the district attorney's mandate.* Hofstrom repeated what he was sure Beckner knew: that the purpose of the grand jury was to indict if there was a question about probable cause or if the DA's office didn't want to reveal its evidence at a preliminary hearing before a judge.** Hofstrom acknowledged, however, that as part of the grand jury process, evidence could be preserved until a trial took place.

The current grand jury's term was to expire on May 30, and by that date a new jury would have to be seated. Colorado law required that the selection process and the names and addresses of jurors be made public. Though Denver DA Bill Ritter had occasionally petitioned the court for secret selection of a grand jury and had been granted his request, Hunter saw a public relations value in doing things according to the letter of the law in the Ramsey case. He welcomed the public scrutiny and an open selection process. It would help rebuild his credibility, he thought.

In early March, chief district judge Joseph Bellipanni picked April 22 as the date the selection process would begin for a new grand jury. A panel of about 150 Boulder residents would be summoned, selected from

* This statement may have resulted from Boulder County's infrequent use of grand juries and Hofstrom's consequent unfamiliarity with their workings. In fact, using a grand jury to investigate a crime is a venerable and entirely proper practice.

** In Colorado and most states, a criminal prosecution may commence without a grand jury consideration, simply by the prosecutor's creating and signing of a document called an information. In cases begun by this method, the defendant is entitled to a proceeding called a preliminary hearing, at which the prosecutor must present enough evidence to satisfy the presiding judge that there is probable cause to support the accusation. Unlike a grand jury proceeding, a preliminary hearing is usually public and is always adversarial, with defense counsel present and entitled to cross-examine and present witnesses.

When there has been an indictment, the defendant is not entitled to a preliminary hearing, on the theory that the grand jury has already made a determination of probable cause. Most defense attorneys vastly prefer their clients to be charged by information rather than by indictment, because the adversarial preliminary hearing offers them opportunities to discover portions of the prosecution's case.

motor vehicle and voter registration records. Twelve jurors and five alternates would be selected by the judge in consultation with the DA.

At about this time, Trip DeMuth told Pete Hofstrom that the DA's office still didn't have all the police department's files. For example, he was missing the detectives' handwritten notes, and typed reports were not sufficient for a thorough review of the case. Also, six of the police department's thirty binders hadn't been handed over.

On March 5, Hofstrom wrote to Commander Beckner.

THE STATE OF COLORADO
TWENTIETH JUDICIAL DISTRICT
ALEXANDER M. HUNTER
DISTRICT ATTORNEY

TO: Commander Mark Beckner
              Boulder Police Department

FROM: Peter A. Hofstrom
              Chief Trial Deputy District Attorney

SUBJECT: Possible use of the Boulder County Grand Jury in
              the JonBenét Ramsey homicide investigation.

I am writing this memorandum in response to your request that I take notice of the fact that you are considering asking the District Attorney's Office to convene the Boulder County Grand Jury and to ask the Grand Jury if they would desire to hear evidence concerning and investigate the JonBenét Ramsey homicide. The purpose of this letter is to set out my thoughts concerning the conditions precedent to such a request being considered in a meaningful and productive manner.

While this office will support the appropriate use of the Boulder County Grand Jury in this case, the following need to be received before your request of use of the Grand Jury can be evaluated and acted upon by the District Attorney's Office.

1. A written statement from you setting out the Police Department's position on the issue of whether or not there is, at this time, sufficient admissible evidence to charge an identifiable person.

2. A statement of reasons that, in your opinion, support the use of the Grand Jury at this time.
3. A list of every "reluctant" witness that the Police Department believes should be called before the Grand Jury . . . The list should include the following information regarding each person named:
    a. Has this person been interviewed by the Police in the past?
    b. If not, why not?
    c. If the person has been interviewed, how many times has he or she been interviewed?
    d. Have you attached a transcript of each interview, and a copy of each report, or witness information sheet or relevant notes for that person to the list?
    e. If not, why not?
    f. Why does the person have to be called before the Grand Jury instead of simply being interviewed by law enforcement personnel?
    g. What do you expect that this person will testify to before the Grand Jury if called to testify?
    h. Why do you expect that the person called to testify would provide the testimony referred to in g) above?
    i. What is the relevance and materiality of that testimony to the issue of whether or not there is sufficient admissible evidence to file a charge against an identifiable person in this case?
4. An appropriately organized and formatted copy of the Police Department's investigative case file.

. . . The procedure set out above will allow us to properly evaluate your request for Grand Jury involvement in the JonBenét Ramsey homicide investigation.

[signed]
Peter A. Hofstrom

The next day, Hunter told Koby he did not want to wait until his office was handed the case to receive the six missing binders. Koby told him that if he wanted support in getting the files, he should support Beckner's request for a grand jury. To Koby, Hofstrom's letter looked like an attempt to block the request for a grand jury.

Hunter was noncommittal; he said he'd have to keep his options open for now.

Indeed, Hofstrom was a stumbling block for Hunter too. He had said it might take six months to reinvestigate the entire case after they received it from the police. Hunter had told Pete there was no way he could afford to take six months. "But look at how many other cases I have," Hofstrom protested. When Koby heard about the six-month estimate, he went directly to Hofstrom. "The media is going to be all over you, like they were all over us," the chief told the deputy DA.

Bob Grant, who for a year had acted as spokesman for Hunter, said on TV that once the DA's office was handed the case, evaluation of the police files would take around thirty days.

D.A. HINTS RAMSEY CASE
HEADED FOR GRAND JURY

District Attorney Alex Hunter hinted Monday that the 15-month-old JonBenét Ramsey murder case is headed for a grand jury.

"It has been an option for a long time and it has become a matter of more serious consideration at this point in time," said Hunter, who declined to elaborate on his reasons.

"We're certainly a lot closer to making a decision [on a grand jury] than we were months ago," Beckner said Monday.

—Kevin McCullen
Rocky Mountain News, March 10, 1998

On Thursday morning, March 12, Koby and Beckner paid a visit to Hofstrom. They would respond to his letter in due course, they said, but they wanted to move the process along. Within hours, they would announce that they were asking the DA's office to submit the case to a grand jury. Hofstrom was sure the detectives' pro bono attorneys had suggested this.

"You guys don't have it," Hofstrom told Koby. "Why don't you be honest? Put it out on the table." He pointed out that if they asked for a grand jury, they would lose control of the investigation.

Beckner asked if a Boulder police detective would be used as an investigator for the grand jury. Hofstrom explained that it might be improper. Beckner said he didn't understand why and said he would consult their own attorneys about what the law required.★ A few days later, a deputy DA commented, "If the cops think they're still going to be running around investigating this case, they're wrong. It's ours now. They're out of it." Most likely, the DA's staff was unenthusiastic about involving the police in the grand jury investigation because they had little faith in the department's ability to carry out tasks properly and professionally.

CITY OF BOULDER
FOR IMMEDIATE RELEASE

March 12, 1998

Police ask District Attorney to convene a grand jury in Ramsey investigation (Ramsey Update #65).

Boulder Police Chief Tom Koby and Commander Mark Beckner today requested and recommended that the Boulder District Attorney convene a grand jury investigation into the homicide of JonBenét Ramsey. While there is still some investigation left to be done, both Chief Koby and Commander Beckner believe the investigation has progressed to the point at which the authority of a grand jury is necessary in order to complete the investigation.

The next step will be for the police to assist the District Attorney's Office in the review of case files and evidence.

THE STATE OF COLORADO
TWENTIETH JUDICIAL DISTRICT
ALEXANDER M. HUNTER
DISTRICT ATTORNEY

NEWS RELEASE
March 12, 1998

The Boulder Police Department has concluded that its investigation has not yet resulted in sufficient admissible evidence to charge anyone with the murder of JonBenét Ramsey. The

★ Under Colorado law the court supervising a grand jury may appoint an investigator to assist it, and the individual may be "an existing investigating law enforcement officer who is presently investigating the subject matter." Once appointed, the grand jury investigator may be permitted to sit in on a grand jury's proceedings. In the Sid Wells murder case, Alex Hunter's office had police detective Dave Hayes, who headed the police department's investigation of the murder, serve as the grand jury's investigator.

Department has recommended that the District Attorney have the grand jury investigate the case further.

Apparently, Beckner still believed he could use the grand jury solely as an investigative tool and interview only those witnesses the police wanted to call. Hofstrom and Hunter met with him again and explained painstakingly that once the process began, the grand jury—not the police and not the DA—was in charge. The jury could call whomever they wanted, ask to hear all the evidence, and send out their own investigators. In the midst of this conversation, Hunter realized that his own staff didn't know everything there was to know about the law pertaining to grand juries. He had been putting it off, but now it was time to hire an expert. On April 3, Hunter would call Michael Kane, the grand jury specialist Bill Ritter had recommended. Kane told Hunter he was interested and said he would respond in writing within a week.

On March 13, the day after the Boulder PD announced its request for a grand jury, attorneys Bryan Morgan and Patrick Burke paid a visit to Hunter and Hofstrom. Hunter, having heard that the Ramseys were to be the subject of a British documentary, brought up the subject. How could the Ramseys grant extensive interviews to the foreign press while they avoided the Boulder PD? Was there any hope of cooperation between the police and the Ramseys? No, said their attorneys.

By now, Hunter preferred that the Ramseys testify before a grand jury. If nothing else, it would show the public that his office had clout and meant business. He set about making his case to the couple's attorneys. The Ramseys should testify before a grand jury if called, he said, because they are their own best witnesses about their innocence. The lawyers listened in stony silence. The next day, Saturday, March 14, Morgan and Burke met with Pete Hofstrom. Hunter had left for a short vacation. The Ramseys' attorneys were seeking assurances that the DA's office would present objective evidence to a grand jury. Hofstrom told them that the office had a moral if not a legal obligation to introduce all evidence, including anything exculpatory.

In a letter dated March 16 and addressed to Hunter, the attorneys stated that they saw the case moving into "the hands of competent and unbiased professionals" and that they "welcomed it." Noting that the grand jury should be presented with an impartial view of the evidence, since the police were unable to be objective, they said, "No sane persons would continue to deal with a police department bent on scapegoating them."

Hunter and Hofstrom considered the letter a signal that the Ramseys were ready to cooperate with the DA's office and would either grant interviews when the case was turned over to the office or would testify before a grand jury if called.

Hunter hoped it wouldn't turn out to be a hollow victory. He had his fears about asking a grand jury to bring an indictment on the basis of flimsy evidence. Both the setting and the rules governing grand juries were very different from those governing courtroom proceedings, since defense attorneys were not permitted to cross-examine witnesses. Also, the grand jury could conduct its own investigation, follow all sorts of leads, and call many witnesses whose testimony might not be admissible in court. In that climate, hearing so much damning evidence and no counterarguments or alternate scenarios, the grand jury might run away and indict, and the DA's office might be left with a case that it couldn't prove in court. For those same reasons, Hunter's staff was still debating whether the case should be taken to a grand jury. Hunter warned them that it was easier not to present the case and suffer the wrath of the public than to wind up with a case they couldn't win in court. Nevertheless, taking all these factors into consideration, the inclination of most of his staff was to go ahead and convene a grand jury.

The detective who had called the writer earlier in the month called again one Saturday afternoon, from his desk at police headquarters. The journalist wasn't in, so the officer left a voice mail message. He wanted the writer to know that he cared tremendously about Jon-Benét, a little girl he had never met. He really hoped the case was moving in the direction of a grand jury.

The writer was struck by the urgency in the detective's tone. He realized that the police wanted the public to know how they looked upon their work now that the case was almost out of their hands. Though prevented from speaking to the media by the chief of police, the detective seemed nevertheless to want to reach out. He was bursting to talk about what the detectives had been through.

3

When Sherry Keene-Osborn called Alex Hunter about the grand jury announcement, she also told the DA about the British documentary that was under way. Its main thrust, she said, would be an indictment of the media, which had convicted the Ramseys in the court of public opinion. Director/producer David Mills and coproducer Michael Tracey, she said, had just finished three days of on-camera interviews with the Ramseys and their family members in Atlanta. Keene-Osborn told Hunter that she and Dan Glick were freelance consultants on the film and that *Newsweek* would get first publication rights to the story at the time the documentary aired.

By then, Mills had met with most of the Ramseys' attorneys and persuaded those who didn't want their clients to make the documentary to come around. Mills thought that Tracey's decision to hire Glick and Keene-Osborn was excellent. Since most of the *Newsweek* reporters' coverage of the case had been slanted toward the couple, it almost insured the Ramseys' cooperation. At first Keene-Osborn had been wary about the project, but then she signed on. In the intervening months, Britain's Channel 4 had backed out of the project over creative differences, and Mills was financing the film himself, at a cost of about $260,000. Tracey, Mills, Glick, and Keene-Osborn would split the profits from the broadcast rights.

When the British crew arrived in Atlanta, Keene-Osborn and Glick were shaping the questions the Ramseys would be asked. Then, just days before filming was to begin, the Ramseys' attorneys decided to place restrictions on what their clients would talk about—or could be asked about—on camera. Things got tense. David Mills reminded them of the written agreement, which stipulated that there would be no restrictions. John and Patsy broke the deadlock, saying they would be open to all questions and that their friend Susan Stine would do their makeup.

The interviews covered every aspect of their married life—the children, JonBenét's involvement in beauty pageants, rumors of sexual abuse, and a tabloid publication's assertion that John had had an affair while Patsy was ill with cancer. Ramsey admitted that he had once visited a pornographic bookshop, though not in Boulder. He denied ever having an affair. Tracey's questions covered every aspect of the day of the murder—including John's finding his daughter's body. Describing how

Barbara Fernie had led her toward JonBenét's body, Patsy cried. The couple discussed how they felt about the media and how they looked upon the mistakes they'd made with the police and the press.

Michael Tracey thought the Ramseys had been honest with him. One night while he was working on the documentary, he had a very vivid dream. JonBenét knocked on his bedroom door and woke him up. "Michael, you have to go to work now," she said. When he awoke he saw it was 6:29 A.M. He had set his alarm for 6:30.

Geraldo Rivera, Peter Boyles, and reporters for the tabloids refused to sit for Mills's cameras. Chuck Green and *The Denver Post* also passed up the invitation. However, Charlie Brennan of the *Rocky Mountain News* and Julie Hayden of Denver's ABC affiliate responded on camera to the charges that Tracey leveled against them.

When Keene-Osborn realized the scoop the filmmakers had landed with these interviews, she called contacts to see about marketing the film in the United States. Because of the agreement with the Ramseys not to air the film while a grand jury was considering the case, time was of the essence in making a deal. Mills's agent, Barry Frank, started by asking for a million dollars and creative control for his client. After long deliberations, NBC and CBS finally said no. U.S. news departments were extremely reluctant to cede editorial control. With no takers, the price dropped to $250,000, which ABC was willing to pay. Then the network retracted. England's Channel 4, after seeing some interview footage, purchased the British and non-U.S. rights, reducing Mills's financial risk. The show would air on July 9 in Great Britain, with no simultaneous broadcast in America. In time, Dan Glick's involvement in the documentary and his many TV appearances would lead other journalists to believe that he had almost become a PR rep for the Ramseys. Keene-Osborn's lower profile spared her such criticism.

Alex Hunter saw the documentzary as the Ramseys' way of trying to influence the grand jury or a potential jury. *Jury poisoning* was the term the media used. Bill Wise pointed out to one journalist that since no one had been arrested, charged, or indicted, it wasn't possible to impose sanctions for jury poisoning.

At the end of March, Donald Foster, the Vassar linguistics expert, delivered his written report to the Boulder police. It was almost a hundred pages long and concluded that Patsy Ramsey had written the ransom note. It was key evidence, Beckner told DeMuth. He went on to explain how Foster had come to his conclusion. DeMuth pointed out that it would not be admissible in a Colorado court.

"My guys think you're an asshole," Beckner said to him, "but we're going to need an asshole to fight for us." He asked DeMuth to persuade Hofstrom and Hunter to use Foster's report and conclusions as evidence before the grand jury. DeMuth remained neutral; he agreed only to discuss Foster's findings with his colleagues. Later that afternoon, Hunter, Hofstrom, and DeMuth met. They decided to draft a letter to Beckner stating that the DA's office could not accept Foster's conclusions as evidence of Patsy Ramsey's culpability.

In taking this hard line, it was likely that Hunter was buying time until his grand jury expert came on board. Only then, and with the complete case file in hand, could the DA's office decide conclusively which pieces of the puzzle would be presented.

Not long afterward, Hunter's staff reviewed Foster's report and the documents he had based his conclusions on. They discovered that many of the writing samples he used had been taken from the family's computer. However, the document files from the computer had been obtained under a search warrant that didn't extend to their use for linguistic analysis. The search warrant granted the police the right to search the hard drive and floppy discs only for child pornography downloaded from the Internet—which at the time they had believed was relevant to the case. They had not requested the right to search text files to use for a comparison to the ransom note.

Hofstrom and some other deputies thought that under the circumstances, which pointed to inadmissibility in court, the professor's report and conclusions should not be presented to the grand jury.

It was his voice in the ransom note and her hands. I can see it in my mind. She's sitting there. We need paper, we need a note. He's dictating and she's doing. Like he's almost snapping his fingers. She grabbed her notepad and her felt-tip pen. That is not her language. But the essence of her is there, like the percentages: "99% chance" and "100% chance." That is how she talked because of her cancer or how you talk when you are around someone with cancer. And the phrase "that good southern common sense of yours." John wasn't from the South, but Patsy and Nedra always teased him about being from the South.

—Linda Wilcox

★ ★ ★

CITY GOING IN-HOUSE FOR NEW CHIEF

Boulder's next police chief will be plucked from within the department in a month or two—probably before a new permanent city manager is even on board, city officials said Tuesday.

Five of Boulder's six police commanders are considering the job. They include Mark Beckner, head of the detective bureau who is overseeing the high-profile JonBenét Ramsey murder investigation; Jim Hughes, traffic commander; Dave Hayes, patrol day-shift commander; Molly Bernard, head of personnel; and Tom Kilpatrick, swing shift commander.

—Julie Poppen
Daily Camera, April 1, 1998

Later in the month, the city council changed the title police chief to director of police services. In May the city council held community meetings to find out what the citizens of Boulder wanted in a new director. In late May, the candidates made their presentations to the community, and in early June a panel composed of incoming city manager Ron Secrist, acting city manager Dave Rhodes, fire chief Larry Donner, and acting director of human resources Joann Roberts-Stacy conducted the final candidate interviews. Boulder would have a new director of police services by late June.

By the first week in April, the police had completed all but twenty-four of the seventy-two tasks on the to-do list, which left some of the detectives with nothing to do. The inactivity was wreaking havoc on Steve Thomas, who was always tired. By four o'clock in the afternoon, he could barely stay awake. He started drinking more coffee and Coke and was a bundle of nerves. He kept wondering if Hunter's office would really take the case to the grand jury. He had heard the DA say more than once that there wasn't enough evidence to prosecute the Ramseys, and Pete Hofstrom and Trip DeMuth were saying the same thing. Recently Thomas had gotten into an argument with the two of them about whether or not he'd be involved in the case if it went to the grand jury. He now avoided them whenever possible. Every time he talked to them, he felt sick to his stomach.

489

Some of the detectives hated DeMuth. They felt he always talked down to them and that he didn't know the case. They respected Hofstrom's intelligence and skills, but his gruff approach was a real turnoff. His attitude was, You guys are well paid and you get all this overtime, so get on with your work. Plus, he was the guy who had given the store away to the Ramseys' attorneys.

Hunter would soon ask Beckner to present the case officially to the DA's office. The thirty thousand pages of case files would have to be organized, summed up, and presented orally. With this in mind, Beckner and the detectives met with their pro bono attorneys, who invited the cops to use the equipment in their offices to put together their presentation. They should make it a tour of the case and use visual aids—blowups of written reports, enlargements of still pictures of the evidence, videos of the Ramseys' house, and so forth. No one was going to read thirty thousand pages, the lawyers felt.

The detectives were elated by the assignment, which gave them something concrete to do. Steve Thomas was assigned to open and close the presentation. He would present an overview of the case, including everything that had happened on December 26. Finally, he would get the chance to do something for JonBenét.

But his chronic fatigue was worsening. Some days he drank five or six cups of coffee every couple of hours and could still hardly stand on his feet. Thomas knew that something was wrong with him. He visited his doctor, who did a workup of his blood. She told him he had an autoimmune problem and that further testing would be needed. Thomas thought she was hinting he had AIDS, but he was afraid to ask if that was what she meant. For three days he waited in anguish for the results.

He learned that his body was producing antibodies that were attacking his thyroid.★ He would have to take a thyroid-replacement medicine for the rest of his life. A review of his medical history did not reveal the cause of the problem. It might be work-related, he was told. If he continued his eighteen-hour-a-day job, he would be risking his life. He was to change his environment. His job, the doctor said, was to sleep late, go to bed early, and take it easy. Thomas refused to quit the

★ The thyroid gland, situated in the neck, regulates the body's metabolic rate. Thyroid tissue is made up of millions of tiny saclike follicles that store thyroid hormone in the form of thyroglobulin, a protein containing iodine. When secreted into the bloodstream, thyroglobulin is converted to thyroxine and small amounts of other similar hormones. Sufficient dietary iodine and stimulation by the pituitary gland are necessary for proper thyroxine production. Metabolic disorders result from oversecretion or undersecretion by the thyroid gland.

department. The Ramsey case had to be presented to the DA's office, and he felt that no other detective knew it the way he did.

Thomas's mother, who had died when he was a young child, had had Addison's disease,★ he learned from his sister. His thyroid problem might be hereditary. He began to experience the side effects of his medicine. He was often sick to his stomach, but he told nobody. By the end of April, he began to regain some of his energy.

EX-MARSHAL ADMITS TO KILLING

Shaking and sometimes crying, Robin Anderson watched former Nederland Marshal Renner Forbes plead guilty Thursday to the shooting death of her 19-year-old brother, killed in Forbes' custody nearly 27 years ago.

Forbes, 69 years old and in poor health, won't serve a day in prison for the crime. Instead, he will spend the rest of his life on probation in a Northglenn nursing facility under a sentencing arrangement approved by Boulder County District Judge Morris Sandstead.

Sandstead agreed to drop a second-degree murder charge as Forbes pleaded guilty to voluntary manslaughter, which allowed him to be placed on probation instead of going to prison. The burden of caring for Forbes would create an extraordinary cost for taxpayers and Forbes' health problems are more confining than prison, said Deputy Boulder Country District Attorney Peter Hofstrom. He also suffers from seizures, chronic pain and depression and requires 24-hour health care, according to his attorney, Robert Pepin.

—Christopher Anderson
Daily Camera, April 3, 1998

On April 8, Alex Hunter received a formal letter of interest from Michael Kane, the grand jury specialist he had sought out. After reviewing Kane's letter, he knew he had the right man. Kane had studied criminal law at CU, worked in the Denver DA's office, and been cocounsel on a case in 1984 that involved the kidnap, rape, and murder of a bookkeeper by Christopher Rodriguez and his brother. It had been the first

---

★ A disease caused by partial or total failure of adrenocortical function, which is characterized by a bronzelike pigmentation of the skin and mucous membranes, anemia, weakness, and low blood pressure.

death-penalty case in Denver in over a decade, and the defendant was convicted and given a life sentence. That same year, Kane had prosecuted the Gjertsen murder case, in which a nine-year-old child had been killed in his bed at one o'clock in the morning. Kane obtained a conviction despite the absence of eyewitnesses and a murder weapon. In 1991, Kane conducted a grand jury investigation into the death of another nine-year-old, a boy who had burned to death in his mother's home in what was originally called an accident. In the end, the mother plea-bargained to third-degree murder.

On April 9, Alex Hunter told his staff that he would ask Michael Kane to join them in reviewing the Ramsey case for prosecution and presentation to a grand jury. He had concluded that there was no alternative unless the evidence clearly pointed to some other suspects than the Ramseys. It troubled him that he could not find one piece of evidence connecting the Ramseys—in their lifestyle, their personalities, or their histories—with the killing. As Dr. Lee had advised him, the only way out was a grand jury.

Hunter knew that his delay in filing charges in the Michael Grainger case would be used against him by the media. A plea agreement had finally been reached with Grainger's attorneys. Hunter's office argued before Judge Joseph Bellipanni that though Grainger had suffered a head injury, he was still responsible for his wife's death.

MAN PLEADS GUILTY TO 1995 DEATH OF WIFE

The Boulder man [Michael Grainger] charged with murdering his obese wife three years ago pleaded guilty to reckless manslaughter Wednesday acknowledging that he neglected to care for the ailing woman—but not that he killed her.

—Matt Sebastian
Daily Camera, April 9, 1998

In early May, before he handed down his sentence, Judge Bellipanni would note that Grainger refused to accept professional help. Then he sentenced Grainger to three years in prison.

On April 13, Hunter, Hofstrom, and Bill Nagel met with Judge Bellipanni to discuss the selection process for a new grand jury. Summonses would be issued to 145 people, who would then have to answer questions.

Hunter showed the judge the lengthy questionnaires used for jury selection in the Simpson and Oklahoma City bombing proceedings. The judge wanted a one-page document but agreed to two pages since this grand jury might have to hear the Ramsey case. The first page would contain general background questions; the second would raise issues that were specific to the Ramsey case. Hofstrom asked the judge to tell the prospective jurors that if the Ramsey case came before them, they might be required to meet every day. The judge said no, these people had jobs and two days a week would be sufficient. Next they discussed whether or not to keep the selection process secret. Hofstrom said he preferred a secret process, but the judge didn't. What was the point? he asked. The media would just wind up taking pictures of every license plate in the parking lot. Were they prepared to guard against this kind of thing, not just during the selection process but during the proceedings? In the judge's opinion, it was futile to try to preserve the jurors' anonymity. Hofstrom didn't press the issue, and Hunter agreed with the judge.

On April 15, attorney Bryan Morgan hand-delivered a two-page letter to Alex Hunter from John Ramsey, dated April 11, 1998. Ramsey said he was prepared to cooperate with and assist the DA and his staff in every way.

In January, Hunter had discussed with his staff the possibility of opening a channel to the Ramseys through their Atlanta counsel. The police had tried using Rev. Hoverstock as a go-between. None of their efforts had been successful. Now Ramsey seemed to be carrying the ball himself. Maybe now that he was living in Atlanta, unable to feel the pulse of events in Boulder, Ramsey was getting itchy. He was about to start a new business, and he wanted to get on with his life.

Trying to read between the lines, Hunter also wondered whether Ramsey was trying to short-circuit a grand jury or avoid appearing before one. The DA felt that Ramsey might be saying, "I'm a smart person. I may not have gotten the best advice from my attorneys, so I want to move quickly on the outstanding issues and directly with you, the DA. I trust your team, not the cops." Hunter believed the letter meant that Ramsey wasn't going to be guided solely by his attorneys. Ramsey said he was prepared to deliver not only Patsy, his older children, Burke, and his ex-wife, Lucinda, but also his friends and business associates for interviews with the DA's office. There was only one condition: the Boulder police were not to be involved.

Unknown to Hunter, Ramsey discovered during his interviews

for the documentary just how isolated from the case he had become. He learned that his attorneys and closest friends, like the Stines, had been shielding him and Patsy to such an extent that they no longer had a clear picture of what was happening. Sherry Keene-Osborn described to him a different Alex Hunter than what he had pictured. More important, Ramsey discovered that what he wanted said wasn't always being communicated to the DA or the police. After the TV crew left Atlanta, Ramsey sat down and wrote Hunter a letter.

"You can give this to him," Ramsey told Bryan Morgan, "or you can throw it away. But you can't change one word of it." The following day, Morgan met with Hunter.

In response to Ramsey's letter, Hunter told Morgan that the case was still in the hands of the police, and his office could not conduct interviews without the police at this time. Hunter told Morgan that the next day he would officially reveal that he had asked the police to make a full presentation of the case during the first week of June. Then the case would be in the DA's hands. The two men agreed to wait.

Thinking ahead, however, Morgan and Hunter agreed that Burke Ramsey's interview should be conducted first. They should work toward conducting the interviews right after the police presentation, Hunter said—the second week in June. Hunter agreed that the interviews should be held in Atlanta and said he'd have Hofstrom contact Jim Jenkins in the coming weeks.

Because Morgan was so cooperative, Hunter felt—correctly, it turned out—that John Ramsey was calling the shots.

That same afternoon, Morgan visited Hunter again, this time to discuss conditions for the interviews. He didn't want the police to be consulted and refused to allow the sessions to be videotaped. Hunter knew he would need videos if for some reason he couldn't subpoena the Ramseys again or if his office was notified that they would take the Fifth Amendment. In that case, the tapes were as good as a signed statement and could be used before a grand jury or in a trial.* Hunter reminded

* The Fifth Amendment to the United States Constitution provides that no person may be compelled to incriminate himself, and it gives all criminal defendants the option to refuse to testify at trial or before a grand jury. At a trial, the prosecutor is not allowed to call the jury's attention to the defendant's failure to take the stand, or to suggest that an innocent person would have offered some explanation for incriminating evidence. But evidence of a voluntary statement made before trial may be put before a jury, as long as the defendant was not compelled to make it and (if in custody when the statement was made) was advised of his right to remain silent.

Morgan that his client had said "no conditions" other than the absence of the police. Morgan backed down. That evening, Hunter felt that after standing out in the rain for so long, he was finally seeing sunlight.

The next day, Hunter told Beckner about Morgan's visit and Ramsey's letter. Beckner thought that Ramsey's actions were a last-minute effort to avoid the grand jury, which would soon be sworn in. Then the public would be clamoring for him and his wife to be called.

On April 22, chief district judge Joseph Bellipanni's courtroom in the Boulder County Justice Center was packed with fifty-seven potential grand jurors. Also on hand were twenty-seven reporters, who came to watch what they called "the Ramsey grand jury." Representatives from *USA Today*, *Time* magazine, *The New Yorker*, Fox TV, the *Globe*, ABC, NBC, CBS, and *The New York Times*, as well as all of Denver's and Boulder's local press, filled the courtroom and adjacent hearing room.

First the jury candidates completed the two-page questionnaire that the judge and prosecutors would use during voir dire.* The first-page questions aimed at constructing a personal profile—occupation, marital status, possible connections to law enforcement, and so on. The second page asked questions relating to the Ramsey case; for example, "Are you involved or do you know anyone who is presently involved in any current criminal investigation? (including but not limited to the investigation into the death of JonBenét Ramsey). Explain." Another question asked, "Please describe any opinions you now hold based upon what you know of the investigation into the death of JonBenét Ramsey."

After the potential jurors had completed the forms, Bellipanni turned the proceedings over to the DA.

Hunter greeted the prospective jurors with a classroom lecture tracing the grand jury process back to 1166, during the reign of England's King Henry I, as a means of finding "twelve true and lawful men" to provide a safeguard against prosecutors' abuse of their legal powers. The goal, Hunter said, was to pick people who could set any

---

*Voir dire (a corrupted pairing of the French words for *to see* and *to speak*) is the law's name for the process of questioning prospective jurors or grand jurors to determine their qualifications and eliminate the unqualified, such as those who are acquainted with the litigants or have formed fixed opinions about the matters the jury will be hearing. In trial jury selection, most jurisdictions also offer lawyers the opportunity to exercise *peremptory challenges* (to eliminate a certain number of jurors without giving a reason), and the voir dire process gives the lawyers an opportunity to amass information they will employ to exercise their peremptory challenges.

prejudices or biases aside and render impartial judgment "in any matter that my office deems appropriate."

After the break, Pete Hofstrom introduced himself.

"Ladies and gentleman, as you know, my name is Peter Hofstrom.
This is a process of asking questions to obtain information to help us
in making judgments."

Hofstrom worked his way across both rows of the jury box, sin-
gling out the candidates one by one, asking a few personal questions,
aiming to get a layer or two beneath what they'd written on the
forms. When he finished, Judge Bellipanni dismissed twenty-one
potential jurors, including Joel Ripmaster, who had handled the sale
of the Ramseys' home.

Bellipanni and Hunter's team continued after lunch with a closed-
door voir dire of the remaining candidates. Next to the judge's chambers
was a large meeting room, with windows looking toward the Flatirons
on one side and a long conference table in the center. Each prospective
juror took a turn at the head of the table, the judge to his left and
Hunter, Hofstrom, DeMuth, Maguire, Nagel, and Smit around the sides.

The judge and the DA wanted to know what they knew about
the Ramseys and the case. When the judge asked, "Are you aware of
the conflict between the district attorney and the police department?" most people answered yes. When one juror hesitated, Hunter
patted him on the arm as if to say, "It's OK." Another person said he
knew that the police hadn't turned over some evidence to the DA.
One prospective juror, Michael Morris, a photographer who had
taken pictures of Access Graphics controller Susan Richart, told the
judge that Richart had described Ramsey as a man who could get in
front of a thousand people and seem as if he was talking one on one.

Hunter wanted to know if the prospective jurors listened to Peter
Boyles or watched Geraldo Rivera. Most said no.

Could you take everything you have heard and put it aside? asked
Hofstrom. He asked the same question repeatedly in different ways.
Most said yes.

Then Hunter wanted to know if they had any theories about how
the murder took place. One juror said, "How could you not have one?"

For most prospective jurors, the questioning was over in less than
ten minutes.

At the end of the day, when the closed-door session was over,
Judge Bellipanni excused all but seventeen people. They would be the

twelve grand jurors—four men and eight women—plus five alternates—four women and one man.

Those who had been selected were photographed by the assembled media as they left the Justice Center. The foreman was James Please, of Boulder, and his assistant foreperson was Loretta Resnikoff, also of Boulder. The ten other jurors were Elizabeth Annecharico, Boulder; Michelle Czopek, Superior; Francis Diekman, Longmont; Josephine Hampton, Lafayette; Martin W. Kordas, Jr., Lafayette; Susan LeFever, Boulder; Barbara McGrath-Arnold, Boulder; Martin Pierce, Longmont; Tracey Vallad, Longmont; Jonathan N. Webb, Louisville. The alternates were Janice McCallister, Longmont; Polly Palmer, Niwot; Marcia Richardson, Boulder; Theresa Van Fossen, Broomfield; and Morton Wegman-French, Boulder.

It wasn't long before the media learned that Alex Hunter wasn't personally returning their calls and Suzanne Laurion, the DA's press representative, was becoming his point person. On April 24, Laurion had the following conversation with a writer.

LAURION: The media liaison doesn't ad-lib anymore. I used to ad-lib through answers all the time. Now I clear them with four or five people. "What is this quote doing in the paper?" It's not that people are being tyrants at all. It's more of a very conservative approach to communication. Even more conservative than in the past. And so the notion of one deputy doing an interview with someone writing an article or someone writing a book is giving people pause more than it did before. I know that sounds weird.

WRITER: You mean the answers to the questions that I asked you on the day of the grand jury selection?

LAURION: Let me go through the log from that day. I know Talkington is absolutely ready to give you an interview.* It's not him. It is really a time when everybody is zipping their lips for fear of violating the notion of "no one ought to be talking right now."

WRITER: Could you find out if Hofstrom had his coat on or off when the individual voir dire took place? Same with Hunter. Did the judge have a coat or robe?

* Tim Talkington was a deputy DA in Hunter's office whom the writer wanted to interview about the history of the DA's office.

LAURION: Just some general atmosphere?

WRITER: Correct.

Three days later Laurion called the writer back.

LAURION: Your question "Who was wearing a coat and who wasn't?"
Alex didn't want to answer that. I don't know why not. I said [to
him], "You can at least speak about your own wardrobe that day."
And he said, "I just don't want to answer that right now."

On Sunday, April 26, Steve Thomas was working at home on his part
of the police presentation. He was excited that they would finally be
making their case after sixteen months of work. He was giving it his
all, he owed it to JonBenét.

One of the most critical elements to clarify in the presentation
were the events of December 26, 1996, which Thomas was covering.
He spent several days speaking to the officers who had worked the
case that first day. Linda Arndt had been the first detective to arrive on
the scene and had then been the only detective in the house from
10:30 A.M. until JonBenét's body was found at 1:05 P.M. Arndt had
filed a lawsuit against the Boulder PD and Chief Koby for allowing
her name to be maligned but was still employed by the department
and was working on other cases. One morning Thomas stopped by
her cubicle to discuss her reports about December 26, some of which
lacked specifics as to when certain events took place.

Looking Thomas directly in the eye, she said she would not give
him or any other officer help on the Ramsey case. Thomas pulled up
a chair next to her and patiently explained that her firsthand knowledge was invaluable. He would not be able to present the events of
that day clearly and fully without her input, he said.

"Besides what is in my written reports," Arndt said, "I have forgotten everything."

"But this isn't about Koby," Thomas protested. "It's about the murder of JonBenét."

Arndt wouldn't budge. "I no longer have any memory of that
day," she said.

In his presentation, Thomas would have to say that Arndt refused
to cooperate with him and the department.

4

We have a fire drill every month at school. From my classroom we go straight out in front of the building. Last month we happened to congregate right beside the tree that's dedicated to JonBenét.

As we waited, the kids began talking among themselves and the conversation came around to JonBenét: "Well, you know she is buried right here."

That's the impression some students have, because there's a plaque, like a tombstone, beside the tree. And I said, "No, she's not. She's buried in Atlanta. This is just in memory of her." And then they started to relay some of the rumors they'd heard about her death.

"I think her dad did it," one student said. "My dad thinks that her dad did it."

I tried to steer the conversation away from the subject. The children didn't get upset that I did that. They were just being detectives, like the rest of the world.

—music teacher Yvonne Haun

Like most reporters covering the Ramsey story, Jeff Shapiro was out in the cold. The police no longer had any use for him, and everyone in Alex Hunter's office knew not to talk to him.

By chance, when the Monica Lewinsky story broke in January 1998, Shapiro was in Washington, D.C., visiting a girlfriend. Through contacts he'd established as an intern in the White House Office of Media Affairs, he got some information about Bill Clinton's paramour for the *Globe*. Next the paper sent him to Los Angeles for six weeks to track down the identity of Jodie Foster's "secret lover." He tailed some black BMWs for a while and eventually found the actress driving a car that belonged to another woman. By May, Shapiro was tired of the celebrity beat and was transferred back to Boulder. Soon he found a new police source, and developed another contact in the DA's office.

On May 30, after obtaining John Ramsey's unlisted home number, Shapiro called him in Atlanta. Ramsey himself answered the phone. After identifying himself and saying he was an investigative journalist for the *Globe*, Shaprio said he was sure Ramsey was innocent and apologized for any pain Ramsey may have suffered because of the media's reporting. Ramsey said little. Once or twice he replied, "Thank you." A week later, Shapiro called Ramsey again. This time he kept Ramsey on the phone for forty-nine minutes. Shapiro did all the talking. He apologized again and said that the media had been wrong in accusing Ramsey. Again Ramsey said little except "Uh-huh," "Yes," "No." Then Shapiro asked him if he had any theories, and Ramsey replied, "Oh, I don't have any concrete theories, no." At one point, Shapiro told Ramsey that the evidence he had found was linked in some ways to Patsy. Ramsey didn't respond. Toward the end of the conversation, however, Ramsey introduced a topic: the violent crimes that had taken place in Boulder since JonBenét's death. Mentioning an attack on a woman by a man posing as a prospective home buyer, he said, "When I saw that, I said holy mackerel." Shapiro replied that there had been many skull injuries to women. "Exactly," Ramsey said. Shapiro mentioned the red heart drawn on JonBenét's hand, and Ramsey said he had heard about it only recently. He hadn't seen the Barbie nightgown in the wine cellar, he said. Then he volunteered that he didn't know whether his daughter had been sexually assaulted or whether it was staging.

Shapiro told Ramsey, "Someone I know said, referring to you, 'This guy didn't do it. Trust me.'"

"I say that twenty-four hours a day," Ramsey replied.

It was unclear why John Ramsey stayed on the phone with Shapiro and listened to the reporter's monologue. Possibly Ramsey tape-recorded the conversation, hoping Shapiro would say something Ramsey could use in a future civil lawsuit against the *Globe*.★

Shapiro placed a third call to Ramsey, and Melinda answered. After Shapiro introduced himself, Melinda passed the phone to her father, who said he was busy and would call back. He never did. The reporter wrote Ramsey a twenty-nine-page letter saying, among other things, that he felt guilty about the type of work he was doing and that he wanted to advance himself in life. He admitted his wrongdoing and said he was considering becoming a Christian.

By the end of the year Ramsey and Shapiro were talking without the knowledge of his editors. When Melinda got married, Shapiro sent flowers. On December 23, Ramsey sent Shapiro a letter thanking him for the flowers and enclosing two books on Chistian faith that he said might be meaningful. He complimented the reporter on his

★ John Ramsey may have hoped that he could create an indelible record of Shapiro suggesting that the *Globe* had printed material harmful to the Ramseys with reckless disregard for its truth or falsity. In most American jurisdictions proof of such reckless claims, if they are not true, would subject the publisher to liability for defamation. Any statements by Shapiro would be admissible against his employer.

"good journalist skills" and even mentioned a Texas case he might look into, in which a woman on death row for killing her children might be "a victim of our flawed justice system."

On Friday, May 1, Hunter and Beckner agreed that the police would make their formal presentation of the case to the DA's office within a month. The commander told Hunter that the detectives would not name a perpetrator but would lean on linguistics and handwriting analysis to link the ransom note to Patsy Ramsey. Also, they were expecting the results of the CBI's analysis of the clothes worn by the Ramseys the night of the murder and the morning afterward. Beckner told Hunter that the presentation would be unlike any other that the police had given the DA's office. Hunter said he would bring a team of experts to listen. He would approach this with an open mind, Hunter reassured Beckner, and if there was a case, he would take it to trial. If there was any doubt, he said, he would take it to a grand jury.

They discussed where to hold the presentation. The police department's conference rooms were being used for the training of thirty new officers, and Judge Bellipanni saw a conflict of interest in using a courtroom. The next best site was the CU campus. School would be out by June 1, and some of the buildings were so large that the entire Boulder police force could fit in them. Although the presentation had to be made in complete secrecy, the location was sure to leak. Therefore, Hunter and Beckner agreed to disclose it, in order to keep the process as open to the public as possible. The Boulder PD secured the use of the Coors Events Center on the CU campus.

Hunter had called grand jury specialist Michael Kane after receiving his letter and asked the prosecutor to make himself available so that he could bone up on the case before the police department's presentation. Hunter wanted Kane's recommendation on how to proceed afterward. Kane agreed to head the prosecution through the end of 1998.

On May 5, Hunter announced that he had hired Kane, who "would assist the DA's office in making the decision of whether to present the Ramsey case to the grand jury, and to actively participate in the presentation if the grand jury is convened." When word got out, the press scrambled to find out more about him.

At forty-six, they learned, Kane had a reputation of being a "no-nonsense guy." "We called him Deputy Dog. He would bring the hammer down on cases," said Robert Judge, Kane's boss at the Pennsylvania Department of Revenue. The *Post-Gazette* in Pittsburgh said that the Ramsey case was perfect for the prosecutor: "This is where 'Twin Peaks' meets the 'X-Files.'"

For his part, Pete Hofstrom didn't mind hiring Kane. He had his own docket to worry about and, more important, had serious doubts about convening the grand jury. Nevertheless, he would reserve judgment until after the presentation, he told Hunter.

The same day Hunter announced the hiring of Kane, he and Bill Wise asked the county commissioners for an additional $156,584 to cover costs related to the Ramsey case. The previous week Wise had submitted an itemized list: $60,779 to pay Kane from May 10 through the end of the year and $38,387 for a grand jury "research prosecutor." The balance of the money would go toward cell phones, computer workstations, laptops, pagers, and a leased car. It was clear from Wise's request that a grand jury investigation was more than just a possibility.

"In no way do we expect this case to be shelved," Hunter told the three-member board. "Rather, we remain optimistic this case will be solved." The board voted unanimously to disburse the funds.

As Hunter and Wise left the commissioners' chambers in the old courthouse on Pearl Street, the DA was caught by reporters. Why all the money for another expert? Wasn't this a case of throwing good money after bad? Hunter had to admit that no one currently employed by his office was well enough versed in grand jury investigation or prosecution.

"If you have a heart problem," Hunter said, "you're going to need a heart specialist."

Like many police officers, Steve Thomas had followed the O. J. Simpson case and remembered how Simpson's attorneys had destroyed the LAPD's case by attacking their work. He feared the same thing might happen in the Ramsey case. On May 8 Los Angeles attorney Daniel Petrocelli, who had proved to a civil jury that Simpson caused the wrongful death of his ex-wife, Nicole, and Ron Goldman, was in Denver to promote his book on the subject. Thomas and his wife, Karena, went to hear him speak at the Tattered Cover bookstore.

Listening to Petrocelli talk about the case, Thomas came up with an idea. He invited Petrocelli to dinner, but the attorney already had a dinner engagement. A few weeks later the two men talked on the phone. Thomas wanted to know if an average citizen, or a member of law enforcement, could sue parents for causing a child's death—as the

Goldmans had sued Simpson for the death of their son. Could an officer like Thomas sue John and Patsy Ramsey for the death of JonBenét? Petrocelli said no. He knew of no law or previous cases that allowed someone other than a blood relative or a family member related by marriage or adoption—who had directly suffered a loss—to sue.

That same week, knowing that a grand jury was not too far off, Fleet White again requested copies of his police statements. This time Beckner decided that although White couldn't have them, he would be allowed to read them, without taking notes.

Detectives Thomas and Harmer visited the Whites to tell them of Beckner's decision. White was furious. Again he said he should be afforded the same rights that John and Patsy had been given in April 1997, when they were given copies of their prior statements. Thomas said that Beckner was immovable and the decision was final. White then said that as of that moment, his cooperation with the police was over. As the detectives left, Priscilla White gave Jane Harmer a hug, and when Thomas reached for White's hand, he was surprised to see tears in his eyes. White hugged the detective, but Thomas was sure that White had meant what he said.

Meanwhile, the city of Boulder released the police department's running costs on the Ramsey case. In 1996 the officers' overtime had amounted to $20,340.80. In 1997, overtime, travel, and investigative expenses came to $222,844.20. For the first four months of 1998, similar expenses came to $31,138.21. The district attorney's additional costs of $215,000 were not included.

Though the case was on the DA's doorstep, Pete Hofstrom told his boss that his weekly felony calendar was just as important as the Ramsey case. During the first week of May, for example, he was scheduled to make fourteen court appearances. On some Fridays, he attended hearings on a dozen pleas and sentences. For Hofstrom, it was a matter of policy that no one's life should be neglected in favor of the Ramsey case, in which the search for justice had so often been subordinated to other agendas.

By May 8, Michael Kane was at work in the Boulder Justice Center. Trip DeMuth was unhappy about reporting to an outsider but understood the need for a specialist. An avid middle-distance runner, DeMuth now added a few more miles to his weekly schedule.

Finally, Bob Grant saw the months of consultation with Hunter start to pay off. All Hunter had really needed during the last year and a half, Grant believed, was support. Now, with Michael Kane on board, Grant saw little need for additional input from the metro DAs.

One of the first pieces of advice Kane gave Hunter was that the DA's office should keep its collective mouth shut. Hunter knew that for eighteen months he had made up the rules with the media as he went along and had taken himself to the precipice—indeed, had possibly stepped over the edge. He realized that he could no longer risk having his casual remarks wind up in print. Nor could he afford to waste time talking. Abruptly, he withdrew behind a wall of silence.

The police department's position about its officers talking to the press was made clear to a writer in a conversation with one of the detectives.

DETECTIVE: I have always been unclear as I watch Beckner, Koby, and Hunter and some other people that [talk] freely through the media and journalism circles while we are threatened with beheading if we say anything.

WRITER: Look at what happened to Linda Arndt.

DETECTIVE: Yeah, a tragedy.

They changed the subject:

WRITER: The case is going to be on his [Hunter's] shoulders now.

DETECTIVE: I've got to believe that he will step up to the plate. I think the detectives at this point are just pouring their heart and souls into this presentation.

I know that Beckner is really encouraged. He wants us to come through. And Hunter is bringing all of his VIP people. I don't think that they're going to be disappointed.

I have prosecuted X number of murder cases over the years and I can say to you, I have never had a murder case with one-hundredth of the investigation that has been put into this one.

After the detective hung up, he sat quietly thinking about the presentation.

"What's wrong?" Mark Beckner said to him. "You've been so quiet lately."

"It's my medicine," the detective replied. Beckner laughed. *My medicine* was a term the detectives used when they were taking it on the chin from the DA's office.

On May 26, Hunter met with the members of his staff who would attend the police presentation including Denver DA investigator Tom Haney, who had been hired several weeks before. Haney felt like a relief pitcher coming in during the ninth inning. It would be his job to conduct any further interviews with either John or Patsy. Having spent time with the detectives and Smit and DeMuth, he could see that the police had only one opinion—namely, that the Ramseys had killed their daughter. Some on Hunter's staff, however, were more flexible. Haney felt it was definitely better to talk about evidence, interviews, and scenarios without making preconceived judgments.

Haney worried that both Steve Thomas and Lou Smit had lost their perspective. It wasn't that they were unprofessional in meetings, but they had forgotten to keep an open mind. During one meeting, Smit, Thomas, DeMuth, and the other detectives had gotten into an argument over the grate covering the broken basement window. That was when Haney said to himself, Hey, I'm not here to fight, I'm not here to referee, I'm not here to take sides. I'm here to do a job. He wondered whether Thomas and Smit shouldn't have been taken off the case earlier.

Hunter, Kane, Smit, DeMuth, and Wise met with Hofstrom to draw up a list of who would attend the police presentation from their side and came up with seventeen names.

Wise joked that they had to add two more to make a small foreign faction.

"What do you mean?" Hofstrom asked.

"I assumed that you had read the ransom note," Wise replied. "I'll get you a copy."

Meanwhile, the Boulder PD received word from the CBI about the four red and black fibers that had been found attached to the duct tape. The lab had been sent a red blouse and sweater, black pants, and a red-and-black checked jacket belonging to Patsy.

Now the CBI reported that the fibers were not consistent with the slacks or the sweater but were consistent with the jacket. The CBI could not say for sure that the fibers didn't come from some other piece of clothing made of the same material, but this important evidence would be included in the police presentation.

When the detectives began working the Ramsey case, they said to each other that they wouldn't settle for anything less than the death penalty. After the CBI's tests determined that what they had thought was semen was in fact blood, the detectives said they would accept nothing less than a conviction on a murder charge. A few months later, they would have settled for a felony conviction. By the time they met with the FBI at Quantico in September 1997, they would have considered an indictment a victory. When Eller was replaced, handcuffing would have felt like a triumph. After a solid year of working the case, they prayed for the chance at a second interview with the Ramseys. Now, eighteen months in, they were happy to have the opportunity to present the case to the DA.

On May 26, Beckner and the seven detectives began rehearsing the presentation. For almost a month they had worked in the law offices of their pro bono attorneys, Bob Miller, Richard Baer, and Daniel Hoffman. Baer's staff showed them how lawyers presented complex evidence to a jury, and the detectives organized their presentation along those lines.

The previous year, the attorneys had mediated between the DA's staff and the police. Now Steve Thomas and his colleagues hoped that after their attorneys had seen their run-though, they would call Hunter and say, "We've looked at it, and we think they've got it." The call was not made.

On Saturday, May 30, two days before the scheduled police presentation, Alex Hunter was gardening in his front yard when the phone rang at about 9:00 A.M. Hunter's nine-year-old son answered.

"This is John Ramsey," a man said. "Is Alex Hunter there?"

"Yeah, right," the boy replied. The family had received many crank calls.

When the caller was unable to convince the child that he was Ramsey, he asked to speak to an adult. "Oh, sure it is," Margie Hunter said sarcastically when her son told her that a John Ramsey was on the phone.

Unable to convince Hunter's wife, Ramsey still insisted on speaking to her husband.

"Am I supposed to drop everything I'm doing each time someone calls?" Hunter grumbled as he walked into the house. Then he found himself on the line with John Ramsey.

Ramsey wanted assurances that the interviews with him, Patsy, and Burke were going to take place in the near future. Hunter should understand, Ramsey said, that he was in charge and that if there was a problem with the arrangements, he wanted to know about it.

The DA explained that the canon of ethics prevented him from discussing the interviews or any other aspect of the case with Ramsey directly, unless his attorney approved their communications. Though Hunter had taken a call from Patsy just after his February 13, 1997, press conference, he had done no more than listen to her praise his comments on TV. Hofstrom had met with Patsy and John but always in the presence of their attorneys. Lou Smit had spoken to both Ramseys on the phone, interviewed them, and met them in person but always with their counsel, except for the chance meeting at the Ramseys' house on June 6, 1997.

John Ramsey told Hunter he would try to get his lawyers' approval for the conversation he wanted to have with the DA. Ramsey made calls to Bryan Morgan and Hal Haddon but couldn't reach either one. Frustrated, by evening he was on a plane to Denver. The next morning, he spoke to Morgan in person in a candid one-on-one session. Again, Ramsey told Morgan he would cooperate with the DA, no matter what advice he received from anyone.

That same morning, Hunter told his staff and Beckner about the phone call he'd received from Ramsey. In less than two days, a version of their phone conversation would be set in type by the *Globe*.

On June 2, the second day of the police presentation, Craig Lewis, a *Globe* reporter, called Hunter at home before 7:00 A.M. to tell him what the tabloid was about to publish.

After a long pause, Hunter replied, "This makes me think my phone is tapped." For Lewis, that was confirmation of what the *Globe* had been told. Hunter begged Lewis to hold the story for at least a week but was refused.

At that very moment, Pete Hofstrom was on the phone to Jim Jenkins, Burke Ramsey's attorney in Atlanta, about the interview Hunter's office wanted to conduct after the police presentation. Jenkins found Hofstrom straightforward, proper, and reasonable. Their conversations over the course of a few days were mostly about logistics. Hofstrom mentioned that he would use Dan Schuler, an expert with children, to conduct the interview. Schuler, a detective in his late forties from nearby

Broomfield, had degrees in psychology and guidance counseling and was known throughout Colorado for his work with young people. Jenkins said there would be no conditions placed on the interviews and that the choice of interviewer was the DA's call. They agreed on a location where the questioning could be conducted without the media finding out, and June 10 was set as the starting date for what might be a three-day interview. Hofstrom said he would personally go to Atlanta to make sure that everything went as planned. Both men were cooperative and accommodating. For his part, Hofstrom knew that if Burke's interviews went smoothly, he could look forward to pretty smooth sailing in arranging John and Patsy's for the latter part of June.

On Sunday, May 31, Bill Wise picked up Dr. Henry Lee and Barry Scheck at the Denver airport. Lee had made time to attend the presentation in the midst of his tight schedule. On Thursday he would be off to Taiwan, where a mayor, two senators, and their bodyguards had been murdered. Next stop was the Philippines, where there had been four air crashes almost back-to-back, and expert help was sorely needed. Scheck, who was working with Johnnie Cochran on a case in New Jersey, joked that Lee was on the other side of the same murder case, representing the government. But nothing, he said, would ever stand in the way of their friendship. Scheck would have to leave Boulder by noon on June 2.

On the agenda for the day was a tour of the Ramseys' house. Hunter, Scheck, Lee, Kane, and Wise had never been inside before. At the crime scene, the Ramseys' attorneys and investigators were the first to arrive: lawyers Foreman, Burke, Bynum, and investigator Armistead. Commander Beckner and Detective Sgt. Wickman pulled up just before Hofstrom, DeMuth, Haney, Smit, and Kane appeared. Before long the Ramseys' group left so that Hunter's team could be alone.

Outside, Henry Lee lifted the grate that led to the broken basement window. He climbed down into the window well to see how hard it would be to enter the house from there.

"I could do it, but I don't think Barry could," Lee teased. Then Lee inspected the ventilation duct from the boiler room that led to the front of the house.

Once inside, everyone noticed how empty the house was. The only furniture was in the caretaker's room. Some walls had been repainted, though, and the basement was clear of the clutter it had once held. Lee took out his Sherlock Holmes magnifying glass. He photographed everything against a scale card that indicated inches and centimeters. Soon he was totally absorbed in his work, measuring and asking questions.

At first several members of the team couldn't find the basement door, though they had studied floor plans. The way the door opened at the top of the basement stairs was unusual. They noticed that even in daylight, it took some time to find the light switch to the basement stairs. Its location on the wall opposite the basement door was counterintuitive—the last place you'd think of looking.

Standing in the doorway to the wine cellar, Lee first looked in quickly, exactly as Fleet White said he had done. The room was dark. There was a foot-thick concrete wall immediately to the right as he stood in the doorway, and Lee had to turn his head to the left to see inside the room. Even though a bare lightbulb hung just outside the doorway, its angle was such that light did not shine directly into the room. If you weren't looking down, you might not see the white blanket in the dark. However, when Tom Haney made the same test, he stepped a foot inside and quickly saw the blanket lying on the floor.

One observer, seeing what he called the maze of the house and the basement entrance, said that the intruder theory wasn't worth even a footnote. "Who gives a fuck if every window and every door was open in the house?" said another visitor. A stranger entering the house for the first time would need a map and a guide, he claimed.

On the theory that JonBenét had eaten the pineapple in the kitchen before she was hit on the head, the group walked every possible route from JonBenét's room to the kitchen and then to the basement. But they didn't stumble on any overlooked evidence that would solve the case.

From the house, the group went to the war room at the Justice Center, where DeMuth, Smit, Haney, and Hofstrom gave Lee and Scheck another briefing. Then Hunter invited everyone to his home for dinner. With the unobstructed view of the Flatirons in the background, it was a pleasant, relaxing evening, with very little talk about the Ramsey case.

5

On Sunday, May 31, Steve Thomas sat in his usual back pew at St. John's, reflecting on the last eighteen months and what he had learned about some of the people sitting in the rows ahead of him. He looked at the

Fernies and the other friends who had been left behind after the Ramseys moved back to Atlanta, all of them bewildered and damaged as they searched for some meaning in the events since December 1996. It was like watching a fire burn out of control and knowing you couldn't do anything about it. Thomas found peace in taking communion. Rev. Hoverstock held the detective by the shoulders and prayed over him.

Later that afternoon, Thomas and Jane Harmer visited Fleet and Priscilla White. Here were two more people who, like it or not, had been pulled into a vortex from which there seemed no escape.

On Monday morning, June 1, seventy-five members of the media showed up outside the University of Colorado's Coors Events Center to cover the first day of the Boulder Police Department's presentation of the JonBenét Ramsey case. Peter Boyles, of Denver's KHOW radio, began broadcasting live from the parking lot at 5:00 A.M. Remote vehicles from CNN, NBC, ABC, CBS, and Fox stood ready to transmit video as soon as anyone said anything on camera.

Alex Hunter and Bill Wise, accompanied by Barry Scheck and Henry Lee, arrived at 7:00 A.M. The DA answered questions shouted by reporters without breaking his stride. He had "come to listen," he said. Lee and Scheck had no comment. By 7:30 forty-one people had arrived for the presentation.

In the Events Center, the police had chosen a room designed as a lecture hall; it had tiered seats in three sections. On the right sat five rows of Boulder police officers, including case supervisor Detective Sgt. Tom Wickman and Detectives Tom Trujillo, Steve Thomas, Jane Harmer, Ron Gosage, Carey Weinheimer, and Michael Everett. Sitting above them were metro DAs Bob Grant, Bill Ritter, and Jim Peters and forensic psychiatrist Steve Pitt. Just behind them were pro bono attorneys Richard Baer, Daniel Hoffman, and Robert Miller. Chief Tom Koby sat alone in another row.

The police had arranged their voluminous files, photographs, and visual displays in the first few rows of the center section. Behind those seats, Barry Scheck and Henry Lee sat next to each other. Behind them were Alex Hunter and Bill Wise. In the top row, sitting alone, was Pete Hofstrom.

To the left was Hunter's group—Trip DeMuth, deputy DAs Pete Maguire, Bill Nagel, John Pickering, and Mary Keenan—and beside them, Tom Haney, Michael Kane, Lou Smit, and Dan Schuler, and

John Dailey and Terry Gillespie from the Colorado attorney general's office. Also present were four Boulder police commanders who had applied for the position of director of police services—Molly Bernard, Jim Hughes, Tom Kilpatrick, and Dave Hayes.

Bill Hagmaier, Mike Morrow, and Larry Ankrom from the FBI's Child Abduction and Serial Killer Unit were also there, joined by CBI personnel, including Pete Mang, Kathy Dressel, and Chet Ubowski.

In front was a podium equipped with a microphone and, behind it, a large screen.

The room was stifling; the air-conditioning wasn't working.

The Boulder PD wanted to make sure that Hunter would take the case to a grand jury. The detectives had exhausted their resources and were ready to turn the case over. The crime and its aftermath had taken a heavy toll on everyone in the department. Among the casualties were John Eller, Tom Koby, Larry Mason, and Linda Arndt. Jane Harmer had been hospitalized once, and Rick French, the first officer to respond to Patsy's 911 call, was reportedly still tortured by his failure to open the wine cellar door when he searched the house in those first minutes. What if JonBenét had still been alive? he kept asking himself.

Beckner opened by thanking everyone for coming and was soon followed by Steve Thomas, who spoke for ninety minutes, to the accompaniment of images projected on the screen behind him. He began by describing the Ramseys' life in Atlanta and Boulder. The first image he showed was JonBenét on Christmas morning with her new bike. The second, which Thomas kept on the screen for five minutes, was Patsy holding her daughter's arm, the pressure of her fingers evident on the child's skin. Thomas then moved on to the events of the day of the murder. He told the audience that Linda Arndt had "amnesia" and couldn't assist the department, though she had been the first detective on the scene and the only one present when Jon-Benét's body was found. Thomas was followed by Tom Trujillo, who discussed the autopsy findings; Michael Everett, who described the crime scene and the items collected from the house; and Carey Weinheimer, who presented the evidence about the pineapple.

The police said that JonBenét's head injury could have been caused by the flashlight they found on the Ramseys' kitchen counter, although nothing had been found on the flashlight to tie it to the crime or the injury. There was nothing on the child's scalp to suggest the pattern on the casing of the Maglite. Whatever had struck JonBenét on the head had left a triangular hole in her scalp about the size of a dime. It could have been made by the joint that connects a golf club to its shaft. John Ramsey's partial set of clubs had been discovered just paces away from where JonBenét's body was found.

Next the police presented the facts about the noose—also called a garrote by some—the rope, the type of knot, and the broken paintbrush attached to the rope that was used to strangle JonBenét. The knot on the stick and the knot on the wrist were different. The one on the wrist ligature was a "capsized square knot." The rope had been pulled through a knot and acted as a noose rather than a true garrote. The point where the rope became a noose was at the back of the neck, which suggested to some that JonBenét was lying facedown when the ligature was tied. That seemed to be consistent with the bruises on the front of her face that the coroner had noted in the autopsy.

The police did not say whether the garroting had occurred before or after the blow to the child's head. The coroner himself wasn't sure if strangulation by the noose or garroting was the sole cause of death. He had said—and the police now repeated—that death had been caused by the noose in association with a blunt cranial trauma. Though there was no expert opinion to confirm it, a reasonable person listening to the presentation could conclude that the blow to the head had probably come first.

Also unclear from the crime scene was where JonBenét had been when she suffered the blow to the head. The injury hadn't produced any bleeding to leave a trail. She could have had her skull fractured in her bedroom, the kitchen, or the basement. Nobody could be sure that the scream heard by the neighbor was JonBenét's, the police said. Sound tests indicated that a scream should also have been audible to the parents on the third floor, but whether it would have been loud enough to awaken them was unclear.

The police addressed the likelihood of staging at the crime scene. Their analysis of the ransom note indicated that it was evidence of staging. The white blanket in which JonBenét's body was enveloped and the Barbie nightgown found next to her body were strong indications of staging, as was the cord tied lightly around her wrist, the police said. All suggested compassion, caring, and emotional attachment. The FBI profile said that parents typically found it harder to dispose of a child's body than an intruder would. Listening to the presentation, one investigator theorized that the nightgown might have been bundled up together with the blanket, a gesture not unlike burying the child with her favorite stuffed animal.

Throughout the presentation, Dr. Lee took notes by hand. Scheck typed on his laptop. Pete Hofstrom had three legal pads. On one, he took notes with a blue pen; it indicated significant evidence that implicated the Ramseys. On the second pad he used a red pen, to record evidence of an intruder. The third pad, on which he used a black pen, was for inconclusive evidence. Everyone paid strict attention to the speakers. No one left until breaks were called.

Detective Harmer covered the family history of the Ramseys and the Paughs and reviewed the medical findings about JonBenét's genital injuries. Several well-known experts had concluded that the child's hymen was torn weeks or even months before her murder, Harmer said, but other experts had said the tear was recent. Broken blood vessels inside the child's vagina clearly indicated that she was penetrated that night, but there was no conclusive evidence of a sexual assault before that time. The blood stained her underpants. The state of the hymen offered clues, but they were open to interpretation. Experts were also divided over the act of penetration. Some said it occurred before she suffered the blow to the head; others thought it was part of the staging. Several experts had told the police that the microscopic piece of cellulose found in JonBenét's vagina was wood. Most likely it came from the same splintered paintbrush that had been used for the "garrote." If she was penetrated with part of the paintbrush or a finger that carried the cellulose into the body, it had probably taken place around the time of the garroting or while JonBenét was dying.

Steve Thomas presented the tape, ligature, and cord evidence. According to their best conclusions, the cord and the duct tape had probably been bought at McGuckin Hardware by Patsy Ramsey. Thomas pointed out, however, that even though Patsy had purchased items that cost the same amounts as the tape and the cord, the store's computerized sales slips did not list the name or number of the items purchased—only the prices. It was also possible that the duct tape had been purchased in Atlanta. The purchase of the items did not show intent to use them in a criminal act and, Thomas admitted, someone other than the Ramseys might have used those items in the crime.

The trace evidence lifted from the duct tape was presented. The CBI had established that the four fibers found on the duct tape were consistent with the jacket Patsy wore to the Whites' house on Christmas, which she also had on the next morning. A photograph taken at the Whites showed Patsy in the jacket. The detectives were certain of this evidence and its importance. They considered it a match.

To Henry Lee, however, the word *consistent* was not the same as a definitive match. Lee, like Scheck, thought like a defense attorney. In his mind, fibers were fibers. When confronted with evidence like this, Lee always asked himself what other garments existed that were made of the same fiber. He knew it was impossible to match a fiber to a garment the way a fingerprint or DNA could be matched to a person. The fibers found on the duct tape here might be slightly persuasive to a jury, but in Lee's opinion, they were not a smoking gun.

It was also possible that the fibers had gotten stuck to the duct tape in a secondary transfer. For example, the fibers could have been transferred to the child's blanket as Patsy tucked her daughter into bed and then could have adhered to the duct tape even if Patsy never came into contact with it. The police had found the tape on the blanket.

Listening to the presentation, Tom Haney knew that trace evidence could be strongly convincing to a jury but that a good defense attorney could explain it away, especially when the defendant lived in the house where it was found. Haney also knew it was a tedious and enormous job to identify and trace every fiber that had been found on JonBenét's blanket. They hadn't even begun the process, and he would lobby for it in the coming weeks. For example, the pubic hair found on the blanket had to be thoroughly investigated. It was decidedly odd for pubic hair to be on a child's blanket—especially one that was washed often. At first the police understood the hair to be somewhat like Melinda Ramsey's, but the match didn't rise even to the level of consistency. Only John Ramsey had been excluded as the source of the pubic hair, which meant that a lot of work still had to be done. It also could turn out to be a secondary transfer.

The police reported that they had been unable to find a match for the fibers discovered on JonBenét's labia and on her inner thighs. The fibers did not match any clothes belonging to John or Patsy. The police were stumped.

The detectives presented a long list of suspects who had been considered and dropped. Randy Simons, Kevin Raburn, Bud Henderson, Linda Hoffmann-Pugh, Joe Barnhill, and Chris Wolf had been eliminated by forensics evidence. Others, like Sandra Henderson, had ironclad alibis. By now, all but two of the thirty-two known sex offenders in the Boulder area had been cleared.

As for other suspects, Steve Thomas had told more than one observer that Bill McReynolds was not involved in the crime because he was too infirm from his then-recent heart surgery.

The results of DNA testing were inconclusive at this time, the police said. The DNA found under JonBenét's fingernails showed the possibility of contamination. Nevertheless, the police claimed that they had been able to exclude certain people by these DNA tests. This led Barry Scheck to comment, "You can't say the DNA test results are iffy and then exclude people because their DNA doesn't match. You can't have your cake and eat it." He recommended further RFLP or newer types of PCR testing. Most in the audience considered the DNA test results the weakest part of the presentation.

Fleet and Priscilla White, who were eliminated by forensics and alibi, were still the subject of some conversation. Someone asked if White's erratic behavior during JonBenét's funeral and afterward had been considered before he was cleared. Yes, the police replied. What about his continued involvement? Was it a sign of guilt? Detective Harmer pointed out that White had information that he still had not shared with the detectives. Metro DAs Bob Grant and Bill Ritter both said that since White had sat on the information for so long, its credibility was questionable, regardless of what it was.

Every ninety minutes, the audience took a break. Despite their animosity of the past eighteen months, there was now an easygoing exchange between the DA's staff and the police. Steve Thomas even joked with Barry Scheck that the attorney wasn't any friend of law enforcement. Scheck said he was more a friend than Thomas knew. Tom Koby, a lame duck as he awaited his replacement, made small talk during the breaks.

When the cops played the tape of Patsy's 911 call, Alex Hunter wrote on his legal pad, "Doesn't sound as upset as I thought." But others on his team had the opposite reaction. Then John and Patsy's statement that Burke had been asleep and knew nothing about the events of that morning was called into question when what sounded like Burke's voice could be heard on the tape—if you could be sure it was a voice, said one listener.

The police discussed the Ramseys' demeanor both before and after JonBenét's body was found. They had seemed distant from each other the entire morning, had never tried to comfort each other, and had remained physically separate. Patsy was looking around, peeking through the fingers covering her face, one police report said, while John was off by himself much of the time, out of Arndt's sight. He had even gone alone into the basement at midmorning, after which time he had become despondent, sitting alone. The Ramseys' refusal to grant formal interviews until four months after the murder was also highly suspicious, the police said.

The physical layout of the house was reviewed. It appeared that all the doors were locked that night, yet it shouldn't be forgotten that there were still several keys missing as of June 1998. There had been no indication of forced entry. The pry marks discovered on two doors had not produced evidence of splintering on the ground below, and Barbara Fernie, a close friend of Patsy's, had told the police that she had seen the pry marks before the murder and at that time they were already old.

Mike Everett discussed the spiderwebs found on outside windows and on the grate in front of the broken basement window. Spiders didn't build new webs during winter, he told the audience. He explained how little force it would take to break the web that had been found intact across the window grate.

Deliberately, it seemed, the police had organized the information to negate an intruder theory. Would an intruder have tied the cord so loosely on JonBenét's arm? Would an intruder cover her with a blanket? Would an intruder wipe off her body and redress her? Would an intruder have used Patsy's paintbrush to tighten the noose? Wouldn't an intruder have written a ransom note in advance? If he intended to write a note, wouldn't he bring paper? His own pen? Would an intruder travel easily and freely through a mazelike house? One observer later said he could almost imagine this intruder saying, "Oh, fuck! My comrades and I, in our small foreign faction, forgot to bring a pad and a pen. Shit! We forgot to bring a garrote, some rope, and duct tape. What else did we forget?"

The police listed twenty-five indications that pointed away from an intruder: Lab tests showed that the fine-line Sharpie pen with which the note was written was one that Patsy had used before. Also, the pad, the note, and the flashlight were all discovered in close proximity of each other. The pen in a cup with other Sharpies right beside the phone in the kitchen where Patsy always kept them. The detectives admitted that even though the handwriting analysis did not show definitively that Patsy had written the note, the evidence indicated that Patsy couldn't be eliminated as the author. Moreover, the police said, Donald Foster had determined—although not scientifically—that she had written and may have composed the note. Comparisons of phraseology and punctuation were shown to the audience. Of everyone interviewed, Patsy was the only one who was not eliminated as the author of the ransom note.

Possible scenarios, speculation, and conjecture about what might have taken place Christmas night in the Ramsey home came up during breaks in the presentation. The police had presented no motive or theory, but almost everyone agreed it was unlikely that a mysterious intruder, heretofore unknown, would emerge as the killer. There was speculation that perhaps JonBenét had wet her bed or soiled her clothes and that Patsy had reacted violently but had not intended to kill her. Then perhaps she and her husband had conspired to cover it up and make it look like something else.

The police listed all the reasons why the case should be presented to a grand jury. They mentioned sixteen people who should be questioned under oath on twenty different topics. Some of them had so far been uncooperative. In other cases they simply didn't know what real information, if any, people had, as with Fleet White. Also, some school, phone, and credit card records that were necessary could be obtained at this late date only by order of a grand jury.

Finally, in closing, Steve Thomas listed over a dozen reasons, in no particular order, why the police suspected the Ramseys. Some of them had been mentioned during the discussion of other categories.

1. The date engraved on JonBenét's headstone was December 25, not December 26, 1996, which indicated they knew she did not die in the early morning hours. December 25—that is, before midnight—was the earliest approximate time of death judging from the state of the pineapple found in her small intestine.

2. Sound tests conducted by the police indicated that the scream heard by Melody Stanton across the street should have been heard by the parents in their bedroom.

3. The behavior of Patsy and John after Rick French arrived at their house was not in keeping with a kidnapping but more the way people would respond after a death.

4. The phone call placed by John Ramsey to arrange for a pilot to fly his entire family to Atlanta that evening was made within thirty-five

minutes of his finding his daughter's body.

5. Prior vaginal trauma was unlikely to have been caused by a person outside the immediate family.

6. The flashlight, the writing pad, and the Sharpie pen were all found in the kitchen area. The flashlight—which may have caused the head injury—was left on the kitchen counter.

7. The ransom note was written on paper torn from a writing pad that belonged to the Ramseys.

8. The Sharpie pen used to write the note was not found close to where the pad was discovered; but in a cup next to the kitchen phone where the pen was kept.

9. The writing pad was discovered close to where the ransom note was allegedly found.

10. Patsy Ramsey had not been eliminated as the author of the ransom note.

11. The enhanced 911 tape contradicted the version of the events of that morning told by both Patsy and John Ramsey on several occasions to different police officers.

12. Patsy's statements about when she discovered that her daughter was not in her room and John's statements about what he did with his daughter after taking her to bed on December 25, 1996, were inconsistent.

13. The paintbrush used in the "garrote" was linked to Patsy.

14. The confusing layout of the home would make it difficult for a stranger to commit all the aspects of the crime and its cover-up without fear of discovery.

15. The elements used in the aftermath of the crime and its staging, such as the blanket were obtained from places in the house known to the parents.

16. When the first officer arrived at the house Patsy answered the door fully dressed and with her makeup on.

A question-and-answer session followed the presentation. All the detectives sat at a table at the front of the room. Beckner was to one side, behind the lectern. Dr. Lee maintained his usual professional demeanor, but his frustration was clear nonetheless. He would pose a question and then add, "I asked you a year ago for this information. I still don't have it." DAs Bob

Grant and Bill Ritter also remarked to each other that despite their best efforts, the police investigation seemed to have fallen short.

By the time Barry Scheck had to leave, Hunter's group was saying that there wasn't a filable case. Ritter, Peters, Grant, Lee, Scheck, and Hunter agreed. Not even close, was their verdict: 95 percent of what they had heard was already public knowledge, the remaining 5 percent wasn't enough even for a runaway grand jury to indict. They all agreed that the intruder theory, given the existing evidence, was untenable.

Daniel Hoffman, one of the lawyers working pro bono for the police, remarked to Bill Ritter during an earlier break, "Looks like they got it."

"Got what?" Ritter countered.

"Felony murder," Hoffman said confidently.

Ritter didn't see it. The felony-murder statute in Colorado allowed for a murder conviction even when the intent to kill couldn't be proved, if it could be shown that the death occurred during the commission of a felony such as arson, burglary, or sexual assault. Ritter knew that none of those secondary felonies could be proved in the Ramsey case—not even sexual assault. If JonBenét was penetrated after death, it wasn't a sexual assault; it was abuse of a corpse. But that wasn't Ritter's main reservation about Hoffman's suggestion. Even if the evidence someday proved that a sexual assault had preceded the child's death, the prosecution would still have to prove which parent was responsible for the assault. That left prosecutors with the troubling question of which parent—if indeed either parent—had knowingly caused the child's death. Until investigators could identify each parent's individual actions, two suspects meant no suspects.

After Henry Lee and Barry Scheck had left, Beckner, accompanied by the detectives who had brought the case to this juncture—Thomas, Gosage, Trujillo, Harmer, Weinheimer, Everett, and Wickman—faced the press. Standing behind the microphones, Beckner reviewed where they had been: 590 people had been formally interviewed, 1,058 pieces of physical evidence investigated, some thirty thousand pages written up for the case file, twenty-two thousand man-hours spent on the investigation, seventeen states visited, sixty-eight people studied as possible suspects, and thirty different reasons given for why the department was justified in asking that a grand jury be convened.

Then Beckner answered a reporter's question: "I have an idea who did it, yes." Nothing in his body language or words suggested that he had a mystery suspect in mind. Reporters felt they heard a door slam shut on the intruder theory.

Someone reminded Beckner that six months earlier, he had said the Ramseys were under the "umbrella of suspicion." In what way, if at all, had that changed?

"There are certainly fewer people under the umbrella of suspicion now than there were in October," Beckner said. "The umbrella is not quite so big."

Another reporter asked Beckner if the case could now be considered Alex Hunter's. Had the baton been passed? Beckner conceded that the biggest decision—whether or not to take the case to a grand jury—was now in the DA's hands. The commander pointed out that his detectives would still be working on various details of the case.

At the same time, inside the Events Center, Hunter was holding a meeting with his staff, the FBI, and the police department's pro bono attorneys.

"Now that the case is ours," Hunter told the group, "we are moving ahead with interviewing the Ramseys." He wanted to plan strategy. "The Ramseys need to fish or cut bait," Hunter said. Dan Schuler said he was going to interview Burke "properly," which seemed to some like a jab at the detectives' prior work. The FBI objected to the interviews, saying it was time to put the Ramseys under oath before a grand jury, let the threat of perjury hang over their heads. Hofstrom said that the Ramseys were cooperating; the interviews were going to take place. Most likely he thought there was no alternative but to question the Ramseys, since he didn't see a case worthy of going to the grand jury. One FBI agent said it was insane to question them now, in the presence of their lawyers, who would easily figure out what the prosecutors knew by the questions being asked. In a grand jury proceeding, the Ramseys' attorneys would not be allowed to cross-examine or raise objections. The Ramseys had been protected by their attorneys long enough.

Hunter didn't want to hear it. He was going to rely on his "trusted advisers" on this, he said.

"With no disrespect to your position as DA," said Bill Hagmaier of the FBI, "I know the grand jury is your call—"

"Yes, it's my call," Hunter said, cutting him off. "And I'll make that decision after I've considered all the alternatives—"

"But this little girl has been dead and buried for over eighteen months," Hagmaier continued in a firm voice.

Hunter turned red. "This is a political decision," he said. "It is not a police decision."

Pro bono attorney Bob Miller said to Hofstrom that the DA's office had an obligation to listen to the FBI. Trip DeMuth shouted at Miller that they *were* going to interview the Ramseys. They had made the commitment. "Don't ever raise your voice to me," Miller said pointedly.

"We've always wanted to help," Hagmaier put in, "but considering what is going on here in Boulder, there's no purpose in continuing here today."

At that point the FBI agents left. Minutes later, Pete Hofstrom walked alone to his car.

When Beckner's press conference was over, Hunter strode toward the cluster of microphones. His tough-guy expression was evident, but only briefly.

"This is the kind of weather that brings us all here," he began cheerily, gesturing toward the cloud-free skies, the brilliant late afternoon sun. "How many of you are here from out of state?"

Clutching a legal pad with his notes, Hunter told the press that he thought it made sense to take the case to a grand jury. But, he added, no final decision had been made. People should make no assumptions about what was going to happen next. Even his rough timetable—that there would be a public decision within thirty days—could change, he warned.

"We do not have enough to file a case, and we have a lot of work to do," he said. He was choosing his words much more carefully now than when he held his first press conference in February 1997.

"I will go back to my people and analyze what we heard and make sure it is sensible to ask Boulder citizens to spend the time it takes to run a grand jury."

Two days after the presentation, New York radio commentator Don Imus was talking about the first game of the NBA finals between the Chicago Bulls and Utah Jazz and said that the Bulls would have been better off to have "pulled Michael Jordan and substituted for him with Alex Hunter." A friend told Hunter he was on the verge of becoming as well known as Kenneth Starr.

6

On Wednesday, June 3, the police detectives began to transfer the voluminous case file to Hunter's office at the Justice Center. Two days later Hunter, Kane, DeMuth, Beckner, and Wickman met. Beckner said the police wanted to direct the continuation of the investigation.

"This is our case now. Stay away from it," Hunter said at the outset. "You've had eighteen months to do it yourself, and you haven't done it." Wickman remained calm as he reminded the DA that there were close to two dozen tasks still to be completed, let alone the interviews of John, Patsy, and Burke. To calm things down, Kane said that he'd come away from the presentation with the notion that there might be a case against Patsy.

Later in the afternoon, Beckner met privately with Hunter and Hofstrom to argue his position. He pointed out that it was important for the grand jury to subpoena the Ramseys' credit card and telephone records before they were interviewed. In their April interviews they had said that they had never bought duct tape or cord. Maybe the records would show otherwise. "Get the hard evidence and confront them with it," Beckner said. Hofstrom replied that they would go ahead without the records. The interviews with the Ramseys were more important. Beckner said he would tell his officers.

"Look, we've done all we can do. It's no longer our case," Beckner told his assembled officers an hour later. "Go back and resume your lives. Make your summer vacation plans. And don't worry about this case anymore."

The detectives were distraught. Some of them felt that Beckner didn't want to challenge Hunter because he was concentrating on becoming chief and believed that a street fight with the DA wouldn't help his cause.

"If this isn't our case," Gosage said to Thomas, "then there is no case." Another officer told a friend that he felt as if he'd handed over his baby to a stranger and wasn't even allowed to change its diaper anymore.

Beckner assigned Tom Wickman, the case officer, to be the liaison with Kane and the DA's office. Later, he would be sworn in as primary grand jury investigator.

★ ★ ★

On Tuesday, June 9, as agreed, Pete Hofstrom and Dan Schuler traveled to Atlanta to interview Burke Ramsey. In preparation, they consulted the FBI and the Boulder detectives and reviewed the videotape of Burke's January 8, 1997, interview. The interviews were to be conducted at a local district attorney's office and videotaped. On three consecutive days, June 10, 11, and 12, for two hours each day, JonBenét's brother would be questioned by Schuler, a police officer with a gift for talking to kids, a cop who didn't like guns and never carried one.

In Atlanta, attorney Jim Jenkins had obtained written consent from Patsy and John and made sure they understood that they would not be allowed near the interview room. John Ramsey had previously told the attorney that he wanted to cooperate fully with Hunter's staff and supply them with everything they needed.

Jenkins knew it was inappropriate to prepare Burke for the sessions. For his part, Jenkins didn't want to know what Burke had to say, and he had never attempted to discuss the events of December 25 and 26 with the boy. Jenkins told him only one thing: "The people who are coming are trying to solve the murder of your sister, and you need to help them." Then he added, "The conversations are going to be serious." The last thing Burke wanted to do, now that school was out, was to sit in a room for three days. Nevertheless, he said OK. Jenkins told the child he'd be nearby if he needed any help.

When Hofstrom and Schuler arrived, Jenkins could see that they didn't have an agenda, that they were only interested in factual and accurate information. Hofstrom still wasn't committed to one theory or another. He and Jenkins watched the sessions from another room on a video monitor. Patsy, who had brought her son, stayed elsewhere in the building.

Burke was polite and bright, but it was understandably difficult for him, because he didn't want to talk about the death of his sister. Like any child, he was defensive, which indicated that he wanted to forget the past. Within a short period of time, however, he developed a rapport with Schuler, who sensed that Burke was adjusting to the loss of his sister, had made new friends, and was doing well in school.

Each day the videotapes were taken to Jane Harmer's hotel room in Atlanta. In keeping with Hunter's agreement that the police would not be involved, Harmer wasn't allowed to observe. The tapes were shipped overnight to Boulder so that Kane and the Boulder PD detectives could make recommendations to Schuler for the next day's interview sessions.

When Schuler asked Burke if his mother and father had prepared him for their conversations, he said no.

Gently, Schuler explored whether Burke thought his sister had sometimes been a bad girl and gotten mad at people. They discussed which people she got mad at and whether she had been mean and nasty to those people. Schuler asked Burke if his mother and father ever got really mad at his sister. Burke said he didn't think so. Schuler's most important question, never asked directly, was whether JonBenét had ever done something to bring about her death. Again Burke answered no. Had she fallen and hit her head? He didn't remember her doing that.

The most delicate part of the interview was getting Burke to answer questions without revealing what the police knew. First he was asked if he ate any pineapple and when he went to bed. He didn't remember. What did he and his father talk about when they played with his Christmas gift that night? Just that it was time for bed. Then Schuler asked what had happened after Burke went to bed. Did he have any dreams? Did he hear anything in his sleep? Burke said he had heard voices, in the distance. Maybe it was a dream; maybe not. It was so long ago, he said.

Without mentioning the 911 tape, Schuler asked Burke when he got up that morning and how he awakened. He did not want the Ramseys to learn what the police knew. The plan was to confront them about the tape during their own interviews, which would probably take place later in the month.

Burke said he remembered waking up and hearing a loud conversation from down the hall or on the front stairs. Maybe his mother had come into his room, but he was sure he stayed in his bed and pretended to sleep. Even when his dad came in, he said, he pretended to be asleep. He was concerned while he pretended, he said. Burke told Schuler he was awake when his mother made the phone call. His parents might have thought he was asleep, but he wasn't, he said. When he was asked if he spoke to his parents that morning before being awakened at seven to be taken to the Whites' home, he said no. He said that he had stayed in his room the whole time. The 911 tape seemed to say otherwise. Had Burke been coached, or had his thinking changed independently since his January 1997 interview? The detectives wondered.

On the third day, Schuler asked Burke if he had any questions, anything he wanted to know. By the way, that Rolex watch you have on, Burke asked, how much did it cost?

Back in Boulder, several of the detectives watching the videotapes thought Burke's credibility hinged on one answer he gave. Schuler asked the boy how much he and his parents had talked about Jon-Benét during the last year or so. Burke said that they didn't talk much about what had happened to JonBenét. More than one detective felt that this wasn't plausible. Experience told them that any child of Burke's age was inquisitive and that he must have asked his parents about his sister's death; it would be natural for him to believe that his parents knew things he didn't. This reply of Burke's, combined with his not remembering leaving his bedroom and talking to his parents at the time of the 911 call, led the Boulder investigators to believe that some reorientation—coaching or coaxing—had taken place during the intervening period.

Later in 1998, Jim Jenkins would be asked about the 911 tape by a reporter covering the story. Burke's lawyer said that the boy's answer was not inconsistent with what one would expect a child to remember under traumatic circumstances. Jenkins suggested a scenario to the reporter: "Patsy came into Burke's room, turned on the light, saw her son was OK, and turned her attention back to her missing daughter. She rushed back downstairs, where John had gone to read the ransom note. Maybe she left the light on in Burke's room and the conversation between her and John downstairs was emotional and loud. If so, it very well could have been overheard by the boy. And if he overheard it, Burke could very well have gotten up and gone to the head of the stairs. I'm not saying that this is Burke's memory of what happened. I'm just saying that it's entirely consistent. I'm saying that Burke never told anyone he was asleep the whole morning. And I believe he was awake when the 911 call was made."

Jenkins also told the reporter that if there was any notion of Burke being a suspect, the interviews with Schuler had ruled out the possibility.

Tom Koby had attended the department's presentation of the Ramsey case to the DA's office though he had less than a month left on the job. A new director of police services would be announced shortly. On June 10, Koby sent an e-mail to city employees, friends, and business associates.

★ ★ ★

From: TOM KOBY
To: COBO1.IS.SPRINT
Date: 6/10/98 5:19pm
Subject: "What a Long Strange Trip it has Been"—Who
              said that?

If my memory serves me correctly it was the Grateful Dead.
However, knowing that I am entering into the senility time
of life, who knows for sure.

Still it has been an interesting seven years that I would enjoy
sharing with folks, excluding media types, over a few beers
next Thursday, June 18th, at the West End Tavern, 936
Pearl, from 4:30PM-7:00PM.

So stop by if you would like to, "Say Hello, I must be
going," (Phil Collins said that,) before I slip away into the
void.

Feel free to extend this invitation to anyone outside the city
who might not get this e-mail but who I might have encouraged, discouraged, pleased or abused over the last seven
years. The only requirement is that they like to drink beer
while enjoying the humor in all that we tend to make so
serious in our lives.

Two of Koby's friends couldn't make it to his going-away party. His
closest friend, Tim Honey, former city manager of Boulder, had
already sold his house and was in Budapest advising city managers in
emerging Eastern European democracies. John Eller had already
moved to Florida to look for a job as police chief in a small city.

Some forty people showed up at the party on June 18. None of
the Ramsey case detectives or police union leaders attended. Only
two reporters showed up, and Jeff Shapiro was one of them. Alex
Hunter and Phil Miller were there on behalf of the DA's office. It was
a sad affair for Hunter, who considered Tom Koby a friend. The DA
didn't have much to say that night.

★ ★ ★

CHIEF CANDIDATE SEES LACK OF CONFIDENCE

The past 18 months haven't been easy for Boulder police.

JonBenét Ramsey's unsolved murder, Susannah Chase's unsolved murder and student riots in the University Hill area have put the department in an unflattering spotlight and have caused the public to question the department's competence.

But even more troubling, said Cmdr. Tom Kilpatrick, is what is happening inside the department.

The unsolved murders, the negative attention, the riots all have exacerbated the problem, Kilpatrick said.

"But it has its roots in how we do our work, how we prioritize." To restore the confidence, Kilpatrick said, "we need to roll up our sleeves and do good work. We need to reaffirm our commitment to basic police work—how we investigate crime scenes, how we staff the street."

He acknowledges there are union-mandated constraints on supervisors, "but the chief and the union have to get together on this."

Kilpatrick . . . said working in patrol, as he does now, "is tremendously rewarding" because patrol officers interact directly with the public. "It is the essence of policing." But as a commander, he has noticed a gulf between the rank-and-file officers and management.

Management staff, he said, is too far removed from the work. Kilpatrick doesn't quarrel with the decision, made in the early '90s, to adopt a community-oriented approach to police work, in which officers are involved in programs like mentoring troubled kids, working with community groups to prevent crime, and participating in educational programs.

"With the best of intentions, we have created a monster in the minds of patrol officers and convinced them that community-oriented policing" was an obstacle to doing their jobs.

—Karen Auge
The Denver Post, June 15, 1998

John and Patsy's attorneys were now talking to Hunter's staff about scheduling their interviews. The city of Broomfield's police headquarters was chosen as the location. Simultaneous interviews could be conducted there without John and Patsy ever seeing each other in the large facility. It was important that the Ramseys not be able to consult with each other—or each other's attorneys—during the day's questioning.

Hofstrom told the couple's attorneys that the interviews would take at least three days and maybe longer. The Ramseys chose to arrive at the Jefferson County Airport, which was close to Broomfield and where a private plane could land without attracting undue attention.

Beckner and Wickman weren't told the dates and location, presumably for fear of a leak to the media. Nevertheless, the detectives could sense the interviews were imminent from the flurry of activity in the DA's office. The detectives were furious at being shut out, because they thought they were the only ones familiar enough with the case to interview the Ramseys properly. When Wickman raised the issue of the interviews, one deputy DA said, "This ain't your ball game anymore."

In the battle zone, Michael Kane emerged as the figure the detectives could communicate with. He had talked to a number of them privately and had managed to avoid offending them, even when he told them that they hadn't yet run everything into the ground. Kane understood that somewhere, deep in the recesses of some detective's brain, might lie the key to this case. For their part, when talking to Kane, the detectives understood that there was still work to be done.

Soon there would be a new list of tasks. Kane wanted to revisit Janet and Bill McReynolds, who, according to Trip DeMuth, hadn't been properly cleared. Lou Smit wanted Randy Simons, Chris Wolf, Linda Hoffmann-Pugh, and her husband to be looked at again. There were still interviews to be done with Patsy's family in Atlanta. Kane needed foot soldiers. Hofstrom and DeMuth wanted to rehire Steve Ainsworth from the sheriff's department, and he was ready to come back, to spend weekends and nights if need be, but his wife was less enthusiastic. Hunter thought of asking for help from the Colorado Springs Police Department, the El Paso County Sheriff's Office, or even the CU police. It irritated Bill Wise that the Boulder PD hadn't asked for extra help earlier. If they had, he felt, they wouldn't be months behind now.

It had become clear to Hunter as a result of the presentation how little he really knew about the case. He began to work on weekends.

Preparing for the interviews with the Ramseys, Kane and Hunter knew they would need balanced teams of interrogators and decided that Patsy and John would each be questioned by a team made up of one investigator and one lawyer. Lou Smit and Michael Kane would handle John, while Trip DeMuth and Tom Haney would take on Patsy.

Haney, a veteran detective, had conducted interviews in the front seats of police cars, while standing on corners, even while standing over dead bodies—but this case troubled him. Soon after he arrived to work for Hunter in late April, he realized that no one theory of the murder accounted for all the evidence. Whenever the puzzle seemed to be complete, there were always more than a few pieces left on the table.

Now, preparing for the new interviews, Haney studied the Ramseys' CNN interview of January 1, 1997; the transcripts of the police department's April 30, 1997 questioning, and the Ramseys' May 1, 1997, press conference in Boulder. As he reviewed them, something struck him about Patsy. Her answers were never satisfactory. A new question always emerged after she had responded to a query. Haney kept that in mind as he prepared. For his interviews, he decided to work from a broad outline rather than predesigned questions. Over the years he had learned to listen intently to interviewees' answers and to let them be his guide to follow-up questions.

Haney spent a week talking to the detectives. He knew Wickman and Gosage from the period when they had worked at the Denver PD; he'd played softball against Gosage over the years. Haney also spent time with Thomas and Trujillo, who had conducted Patsy's first police interview. Thomas's insights were particularly informative. Like Patsy, he came from down South, and that gave him an insider's understanding of her. Haney was also impressed with Thomas's thoroughness and enthusiasm despite eighteen months on the case.

Lou Smit, who was intimately familiar with the case, still thought it was solvable, though he admitted it was the most difficult one he'd ever investigated. "Look how much evidence was left behind," Smit said to Wise. "The ransom note, the garrote, the tape." What he found most disturbing was that the police had never taken the time to develop suspects, as he had been taught to do. These detectives had asked people a series of questions—such as "Where were you on Christmas?" "What's your mother's phone number?" "Was your friend with you?" Then, often after making a few phone calls and visits, they'd said thank-you and good-bye. He would have spent time finding out about the behavior of the suspect—even about the behavior of the suspects' alibi witnesses—how they related to children JonBenét's age, for example. The detectives had done that type of work on John Andrew and a few people close to the Ramseys, but once they locked onto their target, they stopped developing other suspects. Yet Smit had to admit that he didn't have a gut feeling about anyone.

In their preparation, Kane and DeMuth sought advice from Henry Lee, Steve Pitt, the FBI, and the police. As they finalized their plan, Hofstrom and Kane decided that the detectives should screen videotapes of each two hours of questioning daily and make suggestions to the interrogators before the next day's session began.

On Sunday, June 21, Steve Thomas and his wife and sisters spent Father's Day with his dad, who was in failing health. Driving home, he was troubled. He knew the Ramseys' interviews were imminent and that he would not be involved. For the first time in eighteen months, he had no goals to work toward. He felt alone and adrift, no longer involved in the battle to get justice for JonBenét.

That evening, Thomas learned that the interviews were about to begin. He didn't even know where they were being held. The next day, Monday, he went to see Lou Smit. They met in the parking lot of the Justice Center. Thomas wanted to know why the police hadn't been included in the planning. It was their case, he told Smit again and again. The investigator had to remind him that on June 2 it had become the DA's case.

"But not to let us know when and where is an insult," Thomas fumed.

"Hunter's office thinks you guys will leak it," Smit replied.

"The leaks are over at the Justice Center," Thomas protested.

"You're right. Alex Hunter is the worst," Smit answered. "I feel bad that you guys get blamed for all the leaks."

This made Thomas take a step back. "You have to go after them with hard questions," he said. "Don't softball them."

Smit said he would try.

Now Steve Thomas was certain he would no longer be consulted. Beckner had told him that he wasn't going to be sworn in as a grand jury investigator. Hunter, he was sure, would fold under pressure from the Ramseys' attorneys and use the grand jury as a device to let the Ramseys off. He could see that the case was moving away from an indictment.

Thomas was tired of hitting his head against a brick wall. He was a bundle of nerves. The twenty-seven pounds he'd lost over the last year were starting to show. He had no energy. His medication was making him sick to his stomach. That afternoon, June 22, Thomas went to see Tom Koby, who was still acting chief, and told him about his illness. He requested some vacation time. Koby suggested that he apply for a work disability. The chief said he'd go to bat for him, but when Thomas put in his claim, the city denied it, stating that his medical problem was not work-related.

His physical condition, Alex Hunter, Lou Smit's view that the Ramseys were innocent—it all infuriated him. He was sure that JonBenét's parents were involved. Nobody, he told himself, would fight for that little girl the way he was prepared to do.

That same night, June 22, Carol McKinley, on behalf of Fox News, asked Hunter's office if interviews with the Ramseys were in the works. Suzanne Laurion replied that they would eventually speak to that issue. To McKinley, the answer suggested that the interviews had already begun. She was right.

The interviews began, without restrictions. Everyone understood that the process would be open-ended. Patsy and John each had an attorney and an investigator present.

As Haney began, he knew that Patsy would be vague—it was her style, as he had discovered by watching the videotapes. In her earlier interviews she had been medicated, and it had affected her responses. Now, when she was asked if she was still taking medication, she said yes. But she said she hadn't taken anything to calm her for these interviews. Haney had been warned by Steve Thomas that Patsy would crank up the charm and could become religiously charismatic at times. Haney knew he'd have to ignore it. He wanted to look into her eyes and get direct answers. That was what he would try for.

In the first two days, Haney went through Patsy's story of what had happened on December 25 and 26. As these interviews were open-ended, Haney had the luxury of time. Photographs taken by the police at the Ramseys' house after the murder had been assembled into several thick books. Haney took Patsy through nearly all of them. She said she saw nothing really out of place except for a few things in JonBenét's room.

For the first time, she was asked about the conversation with Burke that the police had discovered on the 911 enhanced tape. She knew nothing about it, she said. Her story remained the same: Burke was asleep. When did JonBenét eat the pineapple? Again her story was the same: Her daughter had been taken directly to bed. She knew nothing about JonBenét eating any pineapple. For two days, Pasty was polite and charming. She would do anything to help find the killer of JonBenét. She repeatedly denied any involvement in her daughter's murder. "I just did my best," she kept saying. "I took her to bed, I just did my best."

At first Haney had the impression that Patsy might be acting, but she was hard to assess. She seemed to have moments of real emotion. Still, he doubted her sincerity.

The videotapes of the ongoing interviews were sent to the Boulder police headquarters twice daily, where the case detectives screened them. They thought Haney was doing a good job, considering what little he knew. Patsy often seemed to retreat into herself. She'd close her eyes as she talked, not wanting to look directly at Haney or DeMuth. Steve Thomas noted many inconsistencies in what he called "Patsy's southern belle routine." One minute Haney would be talking to a sophisticated, articulate Miss America contestant, Thomas observed, the next, she'd be trying to charm him. One moment she'd be earnest and naive; the next, she'd be chattering away as if holding court with her friends over lunch.

On the second day, Haney asked Patsy if she had talked to her husband about the previous day's interviews. "No," she said. "We didn't talk about what went on."

"You didn't talk about anything I asked you or about anything John was asked, what kind of questions he got?" Haney inquired. "You didn't say, 'How did it go, John?'"

"Yes, we did. But we never discussed what was asked," she replied.

Patsy's performance was not making a good impression on Tom Haney. On the third day, he went all-out.

What would you do if I told you we had evidence that shows you're not being truthful? he said, looking directly into her eyes.

Let's see it, Patsy said, as if she had been brought up on the streets of Brooklyn.

We're not in a position to show it to you now, Haney replied. You have lied to me, he added.

Pal, you don't want to go there. Don't start that, she snapped.

The tougher the questions became, the tougher Patsy became. Once, she raised her hand across the table in front of Haney's face and said, You're going down the wrong road.

When Haney took the offensive, Patsy Ramsey was ready for him. She had the answers, and she didn't care if he liked them or not.

When the detectives viewed the tapes of the third day, they gave Haney four stars. He'd gotten to the real Patsy, they believed. She had exhibited the hard side of her persona. A side, they believed, capable of doing harm to her daughter.

★ ★ ★

By contrast, Thomas and his fellow detectives were outraged to see Lou Smit shake John Ramsey's hand and engage him in chitchat. He was so friendly with Ramsey, it was if the two men were on the same team. Smit had his pet intruder theory written all over him. Meanwhile, when Ramsey was taken through the photos of his home, he claimed to find something out of place in almost every one. More than once, he said that what he saw in the photo was evidence that an intruder had been there. In a photo of the basement bathroom window, he pointed to a smudge on the window frame and said it looked like the dust had been disturbed. He wanted to know if the police had checked it out. In a picture of the broken basement window, he saw some messed-up dirt near the window frame, also an indication that someone might have entered the house at that point.

Looking at a photograph taken near his upstairs desk, Ramsey suddenly asked, "What's that, what's that?" Pictured was a copy of a local journal, the *Boulder Business Report.* Clearly visible on page 1A of the October 1995 issue was a story, "People vs. Profits," that featured photographs of Mary Ellen Vernon, Jirka Rysavy, Jeffrey Kohn, and Ramsey, winners of the journal's Esprit awards. Someone had drawn an X over each of the faces except Ramsey's, which had a heart around it. Startled, Ramsey said he'd never seen that in his house. He had no way to explain it, but it was something out of the ordinary, he told the investigators. He was sure it had been brought in by a stranger. That evening the police remembered that Chris Wolf, who was a suspect at one time, had worked for the newspaper. He would have to be reinterviewed.

When Ramsey was asked about JonBenét, he would introduce his remark by saying, How could I do something like that to a loving, beautiful child that I cared so much about? I didn't kill her. To the cops, it looked as if Ramsey was selling an image of himself as a father. Only rarely did he answer with a straightforward "No" or "I didn't." He seemed to ask almost as many questions during the interviews as were asked of him.

Asked whether Burke had talked to him at the time of the 911 call, he said he was sure Burke was in his room and asleep. There had been no conversation between them. Asked about the pineapple, Ramsey said that he took his daughter directly to bed and that he was sure she hadn't eaten any pineapple.

553

On the second day, Ramsey began by telling Kane and Smit that he wanted to correct a statement he'd made the previous day about the pineapple.

Last night it hit me like a brick, Ramsey said. I remembered hearing that there was an agreement between Santa and JonBenét to meet that night, he continued. If an intruder had come into her room, she would have kicked and screamed, but she knew Santa and she would have hopped out of bed and gone with him. One person who might have been able to coax his daughter downstairs to eat some pineapple without his or Patsy's knowledge was Santa—Bill McReynolds, Ramsey said. JonBenét trusted him and would have done whatever he suggested. The police should question McReynolds again. According to profilers he had hired, Ramsey said, McReynolds fit the description of a possible kidnapper. He doesn't have two nickels to rub together, he added.

Asked about the cord, Ramsey said, "It's not mine. Fleet White knows about cords, lines, and sailing." Asked about the duct tape, he replied that it was something White would own: "Fleet had some special tapes, possibly black duct tape." Asked about the stun gun, he said he didn't have one, but he knew that women from California sometimes carried them for protection. Maybe Priscilla White had one, he suggested.

Watching the videotape, Thomas was enraged that Ramsey had taken control of the questioning. The detectives screamed at the TV monitor and banged their fists on the table.

"Shut him up.""Ask him this!" they yelled. Gosage threw his remote control at the TV. "That's not the way to ask the fucking question!"

By Thursday night, June 25, the interviews were over. The twenty hours Tom Haney had spent interviewing Patsy were unlike anything he'd ever experienced. He didn't believe in the baloney about multiple personalities, but having interviewed Patsy for all those hours, he was sure that she was not who she pretended to be—ever. That was what he believed. Still, it was almost impossible to believe that she'd turned from a normal mother, which until then she had given every indication of being, into a murderer that night. Haney had never been able to come up with a motive for the killing, and now, after three days of questioning, he had not been able to find a trigger that might have set Patsy off—if she was the killer. All he knew for sure, based on his years of experience, was that the person who killed JonBenét was not afraid of discovery in the house. The ransom note alone convinced him of that. Someone had sat down after the murder and written the note. Haney was sure of it.

One deputy DA viewing the videotape felt it would be unreasonable to assume that Patsy Ramsey, out of the blue and cold-bloodedly, placed a noose around her daughter's neck and used it. Logic suggested, however, that Patsy might have hit her daughter on the head with a heavy object by accident and rendered her unconscious. Then, believing JonBenét was already dead—and unable to face the horrifying idea that the world would see her as her child's murderer—she might have set about to cover it up. If that was true, at that moment Patsy Ramsey became her daughter's killer.

Of course, the deputy DA had to admit that there were holes and unanswered questions in his theory. What was the motive that might have caused Patsy, who had never been seen so much as slapping her kids, to hit—deliberately or accidently—JonBenét on the head? If she did hit the child by accident, why not take her pulse or call 911? If Patsy was together enough to engage in a cover-up, she had to have been capable of seeking medical attention.

Over Thanksgiving break in 1994, the Ramseys went to Georgia. I was working for them as their housekeeper. They were due home on Sunday but were a day late because Atlanta was fogged in. When I came to work Monday morning, the house was flooded. It was really bad. A window in John's third-floor bathroom had been left open by a painter. Then the wind blew the shutter, which apparently hit the hot water control on the shower and turned it on. The water must have been running for three days. It destroyed the bathroom floor, ran down into John Andrew's closets and out into his room on the second floor, and all the way down into some rooms on the ground floor. It was so bad that I called Don Paugh at Access Graphics.

When John and Patsy showed up, they went straight upstairs. We were all standing in the bathroom. There was water everywhere. John was in his stocking feet; he always took his shoes off when he came into the house.

He slammed the window shut. Then he realized his socks were wet. That made him furious. He was more mad about his socks being wet than about the house being ruined. I looked into his eyes and they'd almost changed color. He was so angry. Really angry. I don't know how to explain it. It was like this light switch had come on behind his eyes. It was the last straw.

He didn't freak out, didn't throw things. It wasn't even in his voice.
But you could see the rage. You could feel it. I mean, it was powerful. I
wanted to get out of the room, but Patsy was standing between me and
the door. I'm not saying he didn't have a right to be angry. I'm just saying I
saw him angry. I saw the coldest eyes. He never said a word, but it was
right there in his face. It was palpable. You could cut it with a knife.

Patsy was freaking out. It was, "What are we going to do? We're hav-
ing the Christmas house tour . . ." He was angry, but she was in a total
panic. The flood had ruined Patsy's image of what her perfect house
should look like.

—Linda Wilcox

After the interviews were over, Hunter's staff met in his office. Some
thought the Ramseys were guilty; others were sure they were innocent.

Kane, Smit, DeMuth, and Haney found that their opinions were
divided. Smit and DeMuth thought the intruder theory was more viable
now and that no one could say for sure that the Ramseys had killed their
daughter. Tom Haney, however, couldn't see any suspects besides the
Ramseys. The door hadn't been closed on an outsider committing the
crime, he said, but he thought it was a very distant possibility.

Kane saw no alternative but to go to a grand jury. Smit didn't like
what he was hearing. He realized that Kane had made up his mind
that at least one of the Ramseys was guilty.

Hunter agreed with Kane: they would take the case to the grand jury.

They discussed how to proceed, and decided to use the Boulder
police as primary investigators. Each officer would be sworn in. The
grand jury wasn't like a courtroom trial, where the police were only
advisory witnesses. Tom Wickman would sit in during all the testimony
in the grand jury sessions. He'd be allowed to whisper in Kane's ear, "Be
sure to get this in," and "Don't forget that this cop did that." Officers
who had worked the case would be called as witnesses, and as the grand
jury moved along, Kane said, he would use the detectives as investigators
for special assignments. Haney, who had known Kane for years, knew he
would present everything, including exculpatory evidence.

But they were putting the cart before the horse with all this talk
of a grand jury. There was a lot of work to do before they got there.

The next day, Lou Smit told Hunter that his wife had recently had a
recurrence of cancer and he wanted to be by her side. They were in

their sixties, he said, and they wanted to travel before she began chemotherapy. Smit said he wouldn't leave the case but that he'd like to work out of his home in Colorado Springs, cut his time back to twenty hours a week, and come to Boulder only for weekly meetings. "I'm in this for the duration," he assured the DA.

With the Ramseys' interviews over, a full-scale public relations war broke out. The first official word of the interviews was published in the local dailies on June 25, even as they were taking place. The DA's office told the press that the interviews didn't preclude the Ramseys appearing before a grand jury and that the current questioning was part of an ongoing investigation. The same day, Beckner told one reporter that "significant" test results from the Ramseys' clothing had surfaced; he didn't say, however, that the fibers on the duct tape were found to be consistent with Patsy's jacket. In *The Denver Post*, Chuck Green noted that the Ramseys were talking now because in this interview situation, they were allowed to ask their attorneys' advice. Green also speculated that "by submitting to interviews now, they should be able to detect the direction of the investigation and anticipate what jeopardy they might be in if a grand jury summons their testimony."

Denver attorney Larry Pozner, president-elect of the National Association of Criminal Defense Lawyers, confirmed for the media that the Ramseys had given Hunter's office medical records and confidential documents that even a grand jury would be unable to obtain. "All the Ramseys ever wanted was a competent, objective set of investigators," Pozner told *The Denver Post*, "and they now believe it is in the hands of such investigators. They will cooperate fully." Pozner was speaking for the Ramseys just as Bob Grant had often spoken for Hunter's office.

Grant told one journalist, "The fact of the matter is that people who are under the umbrella of suspicion or who are suspects are more likely to wait to talk to prosecutors, because prosecutors are in a decision-making capacity and police are not."

Hal Haddon released a prepared statement, which said in part, "We have honored every request for information which has been made by the district attorney's office over the past 18 months." This outraged several members of Hunter's staff, who had made numerous requests on behalf of the Boulder PD that were never honored. Hunter, displeased by Haddon's spin, issued a statement of his own.

★ ★ ★

D.A.: RAMSEYS' HELP WAS LIMITED

Boulder District Attorney Alex Hunter on Friday disputed claims by defense lawyers that his office conducted numerous formal and informal interviews with John and Patsy Ramsey for more than a year.

Hunter also indicated the number of documents given to investigators by the couple has been limited.

His claims came a day after Ramsey attorney Hal Haddon indicated the couple had been quietly cooperating with the district attorney's office for about 18 months. . . in stark contrast to earlier reports. Haddon made the statements Thursday, after three days of investigators' intensive questioning of his clients.

Hunter told *The Denver Post* the idea of this week's interviews came April 15, when he was given a letter from John Ramsey indicating he was willing to be interviewed.

—Howard Pankratz and Karen Auge
The Denver Post, June 27, 1998

Dan Glick learned about one exchange of words during the Ramseys' interviews, and *Newsweek* published the snippet on June 28:

LOU SMIT: John, look, it was an accident. This could all be a lot easier for everybody.

JOHN RAMSEY: Look, somebody bashed my daughter's head in, Somebody strangled her. It wasn't any accident.

A few days later, freelance writer Frank Coffman spoke to Lou Smit on the phone.

"People think that because your beliefs are similar to the Ramseys' religious beliefs, you might be sympathetic to them."

"I've put just as many Christians in jail as anybody," Smit retorted.

"Don't you think the motive is difficult?" Coffman asked.

"Yes," Smit said.

"I just don't see why anybody had to kill that little girl," Coffman said.

"Yeah, really," Smit sighed.

When Coffman told a friend he thought Smit was on the Ramseys' side, his friend said, "He's just jerking your chain. He's buttering up the Ramseys so he can get close to them."

★ ★ ★

On June 23, during the Ramseys' interviews, Mark Beckner was named Boulder's new director of police services.

"Because Commander Beckner and I have worked closely on the Ramsey case this past half year," Alex Hunter told the *Daily Camera*, "I can say that we are on the way to forging the sort of cooperative relationship that will serve this community as well."

Tom Koby, who'd had his retirement accelerated, agreed to stay with the Boulder city manager's office to work on special projects. Among them was an expansion of the Restorative Justice program, which handled community-service sentencing. By year's end, however, callers would hear the following message on his voice mail: "This is Tom Koby. I don't live here anymore. Those of you I've worked with, I've enjoyed it. I wish you all well." Alex Hunter told the *Daily Camera*, "Tom Koby was a great fit for the city of Boulder. This community and what it stands for took Tom and his wife by storm. He loved Boulder."

RAMSEY COOPERATION MITIGATES SKEPTICISM

Who ever would have guessed that we would be so easy to manipulate? The Ramseys did, I suppose. Or their team of experts.

News that JonBenét's parents and her brother finally are providing long-sought insight into what happened on the night of her murder already has gone a long way toward rehabilitating the family's relationship with the public and the media.

Even some of the couple's harshest critics have been overheard discussing the return of the Ramseys' reputation.

It makes you wonder, doesn't it, how things would have gone if they'd done this from the start.

"If it were me, if it were my child, I'd want to give the police all the help I could," we all said. But the hard truth is, despite all the criticism, the Ramseys had a right to do things the way they did.

Meanwhile, it's kind of nice to think that maybe, just maybe, these two people didn't kill their 6-year-old daughter and then cover it up.

Was it too easy for the Ramseys and their team of professional mind-changers to make us go hmmm? Probably.

But they've been trying to spin this for an awfully long while. If it took the lawyers and the private investigators and the public relations people that long to find this angle, they're getting paid way too much.

—Kim Franke-Folstad
Rocky Mountain News, June 29, 1998

By the end of June, Pete Hofstrom had reviewed all the evidence and had made up his mind. Regardless of what his boss, Alex Hunter, intended, he himself would not participate in presenting the Ramsey case to the grand jury. As far as he was concerned, the evidence did not amount to probable cause against the Ramseys—or anyone else. The chief deputy DA would stand on principle: he thought it was just plain wrong to go after the Ramseys with so little hard evidence.

7

I have to fault Alex Hunter for not being willing to stand up and say, "We don't have it." He doesn't have the backbone to do what's right when he doesn't have it. In the Elizabeth Manning case, he passed it on to the judges. Now he's passing the decision on to the grand jury. I'd rather see him go on record in the Ramsey case if the evidence isn't there and be straight and say that he's not going to pursue it. After twenty-five years in office, you'd think he'd be able to take the heat himself.

A truly principled man would stand up and say, "If you don't like my conclusion, if you want to appoint a special prosecutor, go ahead—that's fine. But these are my ethics."

—Judge Murray Richtel

By the end of the first week in July, there were disagreements in the DA's office about how and when to interview the Ramseys' friends. Susan and Glen Stine were willing to come in voluntarily, as were others, now that the case was in the DA's hands. Pete Hofstrom, who was still advising Hunter, even though not directly involved in presenting the case, suggested that the staff move ahead with the interviews, but Michael Kane said that conducting them now might be a mistake. The Stines were sure to be called before the grand jury, and there the DA's office would get testimony that was unrehearsed and given under oath.

Bill and Janet McReynolds had recently returned from the East Coast to collect their personal belongings before moving permanently to Massachusetts. When asked, they came in for another interview with the DA. It took all day. Detective Dan Schuler, who had interviewed Burke Ramsey, joined Lou Smit in the questioning. The similarities between Janet McReynolds' play and JonBenét's murder were discussed at length. The investigators explored Bill McReynolds' physical ability to commit the murder—and questioned all the details of his travel to Spain, complete with several plane changes, the carrying of bags, all within ten days of the crime.

In the end Schuler said Bill McReynolds required more investigation and Smit felt that his wife had to be interviewed again.

When Steve Thomas heard of the interviews, he was outraged. In his mind, the Ramseys were destroying another person's life in their desire to avoid being charged for murder.

Steve Thomas couldn't forget the three days he had sat at police headquarters viewing the videotapes of the Ramseys' interviews each evening, exchanging ideas for the next day's session. Hunter's group had sat on the right side of the room, and the detectives who had worked the case for over eighteen months sat on the left. Haney sat with the cops.

During one of those sessions, Thomas glanced across the room and saw Alex Hunter talking on his cell phone. Here were the videotaped interviews of the most critical suspects in the most important unsolved case confronting Boulder law enforcement, and the DA couldn't give them his undivided attention? Thomas decided to resign from the Boulder Police Department. He had been weighing the pros and cons of such a move, but watching Hunter chat on his cell phone while the detectives gave their evaluations of the interviews finally tipped his internal scale. Thomas began to draft his letter of resignation.

CHASE TESTS TURN UP LITTLE

Seven months after the brutal murder of University of Colorado senior Susannah Chase, the detective investigating the slaying pledges to forge on "until all leads are exhausted."

"Do we have enough for an arrest warrant?" Kerry Yamaguchi asked. "Probably not."

But police did have enough, in recent months, to secure court-ordered saliva samples from at least two potential suspects, including one man who knew Chase and alluded to killing both her and Jon-Benét Ramsey.

Additionally, Boulder police have taken voluntary samples from at least 14 people, according to court documents recently obtained by the *Daily Camera*.

Police had hoped to match a perpetrator's DNA to semen recovered from Chase's body—semen that a Colorado Bureau of Investigation analyst said was no more than 30 hours old at the time it was recovered.

—Matt Sebastian
Daily Camera, July 23, 1998

Throughout July, as the media awaited word that the case would go to the grand jury, the DA's staff was immersed in analyzing the evidence. The results of eighteen months of work by the Boulder police, the FBI, the CBI, and other agencies took time to review, and they were generating their own material too. More than forty-six hours of interviews with John, Patsy, and Burke Ramsey still had to be transcribed and cross-indexed.

Hofstrom had prevailed over Michael Kane on one point. On July 21, Trip DeMuth had interviewed Susan Stine for five hours. She came without an attorney, and the interview wasn't tape-recorded. DeMuth dug around to see if Patsy or John had perhaps confessed to the Stines while living in their home in 1997. Absolutely not, said Susan Stine, who came off as such a staunch supporter of the Ramseys that they wondered how much weight to give her statements.

Fleet White refused to come in voluntarily to talk to Hunter's staff. That alone confirmed the need to take the case to a grand jury. But there were good reasons for holding back on an announcement.

For over a year, the Ramseys had provided the police with very little, if any, documentation. Now they were complying with most of the DA's requests, and Kane didn't want to jeopardize their chance of getting whatever they needed. As long as the DA's office didn't publicly call for a grand jury, it seemed that the Ramseys would cooperate. Nevertheless, Hunter hoped that by Labor Day he could announce that on September 15 the case would go to the grand jury. As far as Kane was concerned, the Ramseys were the target the grand jury would hear about.

Steve Thomas finished his resignation letter around July 25 but decided to wait until August 6, JonBenét's birthday, to turn it in. As the date approached, he thought about making the letter public at the same time that he presented it to Beckner. He had gotten many calls from reporters ever since rumors of his medical leave had surfaced. The most persistent caller was a female producer for ABC. On August 5, Thomas sent her a copy of his letter by FedEx. He had no idea what her reaction might be. That night he realized that when she received it the next day at around 10:30 A.M. New York time, the letter would be out of his control, so he quickly arranged to have copies delivered to Beckner, Dave Hayes, and police department attorney Bob Keatley at 9:00 A.M. Boulder time.

The next morning, ABC called to say that they wanted to videotape him. Peter Jennings would be reporting his resignation on the evening news, and they needed a face to associate with his name. Thomas agreed to let them film him at Home Depot, where he would be buying some lumber. He had been doing some home remodeling work with Todd Sears, a close friend. Sears had resigned from the department several years earlier, when Tom Koby interfered with a drug investigation he was heading.

When Mark Beckner arrived at work that morning, he found a copy of Thomas's letter: *

> Chief Beckner,
>
> On June 22, I submitted a letter to Chief Koby, requesting a leave of absence from the Boulder Police Department. In response to persistent speculation as to why I chose to leave the Ramsey investigation, this letter explains more fully those reasons.
>
> The primary reason I chose to leave is my belief that the district attorney's office continues to mishandle the Ramsey case. It became a nearly impossible investigation because of the political alliances, philosophical differences, and professional egos that blocked progress. The wrong things were done, and

---

* This letter is excerpted here. It appears in its entirety in Appendix B.

made it a matter of simple principle that I could not continue to participate as it stood with the district attorney's office.

We [detectives] conducted an exhaustive investigation, followed the evidence where it led us, and were faithfully and professionally committed to this case. We were never afforded true prosecutorial support. How were we expected to "solve" this case when the district attorney's office was crippling us with their positions? I believe they were, literally, facilitating the escape of justice.

Thomas went on to detail some of his grievances.

During the investigation, detectives would discover, collect, and bring evidence to the district attorney's office, only to have it summarily dismissed or rationalized as insignificant. The most elementary of investigative efforts, such as obtaining telephone and credit card records, were met without support, search warrants denied. The significant opinions of national experts were casually dismissed or ignored by the district attorney's office, even the experienced FBI were waved aside.

Those who chose not to cooperate were never compelled before a grand jury early in this case, as detectives suggested only weeks after the murder, while information and memories were fresh.

In a departure from protocol, police reports, physical evidence, and investigative information were shared with Ramsey defense attorneys, all of this in the district attorney's office "spirit of cooperation."

I was advised not to speak to certain witnesses, and all but dissuaded from pursuing particular investigative efforts. Polygraphs were acceptable for some subjects, but others seemed immune from such requests.

Innocent people were not "cleared," publicly or otherwise, even when it was unmistakably the right thing to do, as reputations and lives were destroyed.

There is evidence that was critical to the investigation, that to this day has never been collected, because neither search warrants nor other means were supported to do so. Not to mention evidence which still sits today, untested in the laboratory, as differences continue about how to proceed.

Then Thomas vented his frustrations about being muzzled during the investigation.

As the nation watched, appropriately anticipating a fitting response to the murder of the most innocent of victims, I stood bothered as to what occurred behind the scenes. We learned to ignore the campaign of misinformation in which we were said to be bumbling along, or else just pursuing one or two suspects in some ruthless vendetta. Much of what appeared in the press was orchestrated by particular sources wishing to discredit the Boulder Police Department. We watched the media spin, while we were prohibited from exercising First Amendment rights. Last year, when we discovered hidden cameras inside the Ramsey house, only to realize the detectives had been unwittingly videotaped, this should have rocked the police department off its foundation. Instead, we allowed that, too, to pass without challenge. The detectives' enthusiasm became simply resigned frustration, acquiescing to that which should never have been tolerated. In the media blitz, the pressure of the whole world watching, important decisions seemed to be premised on "how it would play" publicly. As it goes, "evils that befall the world are not nearly so often caused by bad men, as they are by good men who are silent when an opinion must be voiced."

I believe the district attorney's office is thoroughly compromised. When we were told by one person in the district attorney's office, months before we had even completed our investigation, that this case "is not prosecutable," we shook our heads in disbelief.

We delayed and ignored, for far too long, that which was "right" in deference of maintaining this dysfunctional relationship with the district attorney's office. Some of us bit our tongues as the public was told of this "renewed cooperation" between the police department and the district attorney's office—this at the very time the detectives and those in the district attorney's office weren't even on speaking terms.

Finally, Thomas stated his hopes, fears, and regrets.

Will there be a real attempt at justice? I may be among the last to find out. I submitted over 250 investigative reports for this case alone. I'd have been happy to assist the grand jury. But the detectives, who know this case better than anyone, were told we would not be allowed as grand jury advisory witnesses, as is common place. If a grand jury is convened, the records will be sealed, and we will not witness what goes on inside such a proceeding.

The district attorney's office should be the ethical and judicial compass for the community, ensuring that justice is served—or at least, sought. Instead, our DA has becoming [sic] a spinning compass for the media.

It is difficult to imagine a more compelling situation for the appointment of an entirely independent prosecution team to be introduced into this matter, who would oversee an attempt at righting this case.

I know that to speak out brings its own issues. I know what may occur—I may be portrayed as frustrated, disgruntled. Not so. In no way do I wish to harm this case or subvert the long and arduous work that has been done. I want justice for a child who was killed in her home on Christmas night.

There is some consolation that a greater justice awaits the person who committed these acts, independent of this system we call "justice." A greater justice awaits. Of that, at least, we can be confident.

As a now infamous author, panicked in the night, once penned, "use that good southern common sense of yours." I will do just that. Originally from a small southern town where this would never have been tolerated, where respect for law and order and traditions were instilled in me, I will take that murderous author's out-of-context advice.

Regretfully, I tender this letter, and my police career, a calling which I loved.

I recalled a favorite passage recently, Atticus Finch speaking to his daughter: "Just remember that one thing does not abide by majority rule, Scout—it's your conscience."

At thirty-six years old, I thought my life's passion as a police officer was carved in stone. I realize that although I may have to trade my badge for a carpenter's hammer, I will do so with a clear conscience. It is with a heavy heart that I offer my resignation from the Boulder Police Department, in protest of this continuing travesty.

Detective Steve Thomas #638
Detective Division
Boulder Police Department
August 6, 1998

By 9:30 A.M. Mark Beckner's secretary had left a message on Thomas's voice mail: "The chief would like you to come in and work things out." When he hadn't returned the call an hour later, internal affairs called: "Could you please come in so we can work this out."

After Craig Lewis of the *Globe* showed up at Thomas's house at 1:30 P.M. asking for an interview, he knew that the news of his letter had gotten around to the media. Thomas refused to speak to Lewis. Within hours of ABC's newscast reporting his resignation, every major media outlet called for an interview. One publication offered him over $100,000 for his first-person story. Thomas said no.

That night, he received a letter from the Boulder PD asking him to come in and surrender his badge and credentials. The letter said he would be provided with an "armed escort through the department's secure areas." Was he also going to be handcuffed? He told the department that he would only turn over his shield to Commander Dave Hayes, whom he trusted and respected. A meeting was set for 10:00 P.M. the next evening in the parking lot of a feed store in Golden, beyond Boulder's jurisdiction. Precisely on time, Thomas, in his white pickup truck, pulled up alongside an unmarked police car in the empty lot. As in a movie, under a bare lightbulb, Dave Hayes and Sgt. Mike Ready approached Thomas. They went through an inventory of everything that had to be returned to the department, down to the clip on his belt. Last was his shield. Thomas held it for a long moment, looking at his name and number. Then time was up and he handed it over. Hayes gave him a respectful nod, and they parted. As Ready and Hayes drove off, Thomas sat in his pickup.

Thomas was sure that the same egos that had run his friend John Eller out of town would want some payback from him. He braced himself, anticipating the worst.

The day after Steve Thomas's resignation became public, Governor Romer called Bob Grant.

"A lot of people have been calling me about this Thomas letter," said Romer, who mentioned he was calling from an airport. "I need some kind of response." Grant had this image of Romer running through a terminal like O. J. Simpson talking on his cell phone. Clearly, the governor was hearing from people he respected.

"What do we do?" Romer wanted to know. Grant suggested that he and the other metro DAs discuss the situation and report back to him. It sounded as if Romer wanted the four of them to say publicly that everything was still on track with the case so that the governor could say, "I'm satisfied if they are satisfied."

That same morning, Friday August 7, while Alex Hunter was touring Alaska's inland waterway with his family, Wise and Hofstrom met with Beckner and Wickman to discuss Thomas's letter. The problem, as Wise saw it, was that unlike Fleet White, who was simply an angry witness, Thomas would be taken seriously because he was a detective on the case. Wise asked Beckner to announce that Thomas's letter was misleading and untrue, but the chief refused to go public. Wise thought Beckner was afraid that his officers would back Thomas and that he himself would be faced with a no-confidence vote, as Koby had been the previous year. Finally, Beckner relented, but he would only say publicly that he did not agree with Thomas's opinion that the case could not be concluded successfully.

That same day, the *Daily Camera* printed Thomas's letter. The headline read, DETECTIVE BLASTS DA'S OFFICE. Suzanne Laurion, speaking for the vacationing Alex Hunter, said, "This letter is outrageous and is substantially false and misleading." *The Denver Post* not only headlined the story, but columnist Chuck Green told his readers: "To preserve public confidence in his office, Hunter needs to forcefully rebut Thomas's accusations—point by point." On Sunday, August 9, the paper published Green's second column on the subject:

★ ★ ★

THERE'S A BIG PROBLEM IN BOULDER

The city fathers of Boulder, including its top two law enforcement officers, have a problem.

If former Detective Steve Thomas is a reliable cop whose judgment can be trusted, then his eight-page tale of horror about the inside workings of the JonBenét Ramsey murder investigation signal a crisis in the case. There would be a problem.

But if he's not reliable, and if his scathing letter of resignation is a rambling collection of falsehoods and exaggerations, then for 18 months an untrustworthy detective played a guiding role in the most-noted crime in the city's history. That would be a problem.

So either way, there is a problem—a big, big problem—in Boulder.

At week's end, the city leadership hadn't chosen its course. The short-term strategy seemed to be to ignore the situation and hope it might go away.

That's leadership in Boulder.

Of course, it won't work. The Thomas problem won't just evaporate. One way or the other, it will dog this case 'til the end.

—Chuck Green
The Denver Post, August 9, 1998

Hunter finally called his office on Monday, August 10, from a bed and breakfast in Juneau. Wise read him Thomas's letter and told him about the meeting with Beckner. Hunter was stunned. Wise said he thought it would just go away, like Fleet White's letters, but Hunter saw that Thomas's letter was entirely different. The detective had, after all, been on the inside of the case, and if it went to trial, any defense attorney worth his retainer was sure to make good use of the letter with the jury. The DA said he'd call Wise back. When he did, Wise told him that the governor had gotten the metro DAs involved.

"Our dream team," Wise said, "is now the governor's task force." Alex Hunter understood that the DAs were no longer his trusted advisers.

That same afternoon, Monday, August 10, the metro DAs met to discuss Thomas's letter. They had to be able to talk candidly, so nobody from Hunter's office was invited. Grant, who knew the case best, thought that there was nothing troublesome in the letter from a prosecutorial perspective. What concerned the DAs, however, was that

Thomas had hit a nerve, expressing the same frustration that the public was feeling. They realized that something had to be done to restore the public's confidence in the prosecution's handling of the case.

Grant and Ritter knew that there was serious dissension within Hunter's team about taking the case to the grand jury. Grant felt that Kane needed the support of strong attorneys and that anyone who was standing in his way should be asked to leave.

The DAs called Governor Romer and told him that Hunter was making the right decisions, that the case was on target. Hunter had told them, they said, that the grand jury would meet to hear the Ramsey case on September 15. They assured the governor that Thomas's letter hadn't changed their thinking. They were, however, prepared to recommend that Hunter take on additional prosecutorial support. They hoped this would reassure the public that the case was on track.

Late Monday, Bob Grant called Hunter, who had finally arrived home. Grant told the DA what had happened in his absence and said there would be a meeting with all involved parties in Denver on Wednesday.

"I or anybody you want will be available," Hunter said. "Anytime, anywhere."

On Tuesday, August 11, Hunter, Hofstrom, and Wise met to prepare for their meeting with the metro DAs. Michael Kane was not invited to join the discussions. It was better to isolate him from these kinds of problems, they thought. He had enough on his plate with the case itself.

Wise had known the metro DAs for years, much better than Hunter. Having talked to Grant the previous day, he was sure the DAs would tell the governor that no special prosecutor was needed. Wise had suggested to Grant that he talk directly to Beckner, who would certainly say that Thomas's charges were wrong.

Wise detailed for Hunter and Hofstrom what he knew to be the truth behind Thomas's allegations. The "hidden surveillance camera" Thomas referred to was bullshit. The way Wise remembered it, the police had gone to the Ramsey house in December 1997 without the DA's permission or the Ramseys' knowledge. A representative of the Ramseys had been asked up to open up the place and he'd brought the wrong key, so the detectives had entered the house through a broken window. Once inside, the police saw the motion-activated security cameras pointed at them: They were caught making an illegal entry.

Then Thomas referred to some forensic tests that hadn't been done.

He could be talking about the mixed DNA stain on JonBenét's underwear or a test that had still not been conducted on the pubic hair found on the blanket. It had been decided to hold up on this test because it would destroy all the remaining hair, and under the law, a defendent had the right to be present when such destructive testing took place. Since the Ramseys hadn't been formally charged or named as suspects, Hunter's office had advised the police to wait before conducting the test.

In his letter, Thomas had also objected that the Boulder detectives wouldn't be used as "advisory witnesses." There was no such thing as an "advisory witness" in a grand jury proceeding. Wise believed that Thomas may not have known that Kane and Hunter were using Wickman as the primary investigator and that Wickman would be advising the DA's office during the grand jury proceedings. It was also possible that Thomas didn't know that the officers who had been at the crime scene would be called to testify before the grand jury.

When it came to the detective's motive, his illness had to be considered, Wise thought. Thomas was saying he couldn't continue being a cop and had applied for medical leave. The stress of working this case must have aggravated his thyroid condition. Yet he had to know that the prosecution's case would be damaged by his airing his views. Wise knew that everything had to be considered before anyone could pass judgment on Thomas's motives.

On Wednesday, August 12, Hunter, Wise, and Hofstrom met again—this time with the metro DAs—in a fourth-floor office at the Colorado District Attorney's Council in downtown Denver.

The DAs told Hunter that they were prepared to back him against Thomas's accusations. They recommended that Hunter not reply to specific allegations which, in their opinion were without merit. However, since the governor was now involved, a public response had to be made. The governor had the power to appoint the attorney general as a special prosecutor, they reminded Hunter. They didn't think the situation warranted that, but Grant said, "One guy can't do it by himself," referring to Michael Kane. They told Hunter that now, more than ever, his office needed solid prosecutorial support. "*We* need to make sure the case is properly presented," Grant said, "and *you* need to make sure the case is properly presented."

"It's all right to have people in your office with different opinions," Grant added, without mentioning Hofstrom, who was sitting there, by name, or Trip DeMuth or Lou Smit. "But now you need

people who are reading from the same book if not the same page."
Hofstrom listened but said nothing.

Hunter saw the handwriting on the wall: he was being told to take
help whether he needed it or not.

Then the DAs asked to talk to Hunter alone. The final decision,
Grant said, would have to be made by the elected district attorneys.
Wise and Hofstrom left the room.

Grant told Hunter that the metro DAs had backed him for eighteen months with their own reputations. Now those reputations were
also on the line. In the long run, Grant pointed out, the discussion
they were having now would have come up anyway. In fact, there was
no discussion: everyone in the room knew where this was heading.

Bill Ritter reminded Hunter of a state statute that allowed for special prosecutors to be brought in under *his* authority.* Hunter, as the
Boulder County DA, would still make the ultimate decisions about
how to proceed and whether to bring charges. Any prosecutor
brought aboard would understand that it was still Alex Hunter's case.

Ritter told Hunter that he had already made inquiries about Al
LaCabe, an attorney in the Denver office of the U.S. attorney general.
LaCabe was available. The next step, Ritter said, would be for Hunter to
make a formal request of U.S. attorney general Janet Reno in Washington
and, locally, of U.S. attorney for Denver Henry Solano, LaCabe's boss.
Ritter told Hunter that LaCabe was not only a fine prosecutor but also a
former police officer; he would get along with the Boulder detectives.
Everyone agreed that a second person would be needed—someone with
both general experience and some expertise in DNA.

The meeting lasted maybe half an hour. When it ended, Hunter said
he wanted to tell Hofstrom and Wise personally that a team would be
brought in to present the case to the grand jury and prosecute it if an
indictment was handed down. Hofstrom would no longer have to be
involved even as the DA's adviser. Soon after, Hofstrom left for Boulder.

After talking to his colleagues, Hunter returned to the room and the
governor was called and told the outcome of the meeting. Romer said he
wanted to call a press conference for that same afternoon, before the
problem got any worse. He would tell the media Thomas's letter was

* Colorado law allows for the appointment of "special deputy district attorneys" by a district attorney who requires such assistance to "properly discharge the duties of his office."
The special deputies may be drawn from the state attorney general's office, from the
offices of other district attorneys or city attorneys in the state, or from federal prosecutors
based in Colorado. C.R.S. 20-1-201.

without merit and that, to move the case along, special prosecutors were being brought in to help Hunter's office. Romer asked about the grand jury. Hunter said that for some time he had planned to begin that process on September 15. The governor was glad to have something positive to talk about: He, not Hunter, would announce the grand jury, he said.

A few minutes later, the four metro DAs walked the four blocks to the state capitol. Hunter stayed behind while the DAs met with Romer. Afterward, the governor called Hunter, who understood it was best that he not attend the press conference. The metro DAs had more credibility, so they should answer the media's questions.

Hunter and Wise then stepped into an elevator, followed by a reporter and a photographer. When the photographer started taking pictures, Wise wanted to put his hand up to the camera lens but stopped himself. It was not the image he wanted to see in the next morning's papers.

As Hunter and Wise were driving back to Boulder, Governor Romer stepped before reporters and TV cameras and announced that Alex Hunter would be convening a grand jury.

"It would not be proper to appoint a special prosecutor now," Romer added. "It would impair [the case], it would delay it." Then the governor stepped aside. The metro DAs, who were seated behind a long table, confirmed their support of Hunter and announced that outside prosecutors would be assisting Hunter in the grand jury presentation. Grant told reporters that the prosecutors would help with legwork, interview witnesses, and prepare the case for trial—and protect it from attack on appeal.

"You don't replace the prosecution team just because [the] police are not pleased with [the DA's] decisions," defense attorney Larry Pozner told the press later that afternoon. "Justice is not a pickup football game. You don't get rid of players because you don't like them."

The next morning, Wise wrote a letter to Janet Reno, requesting her assistance in obtaining the services of Al LaCabe, whom Bill Ritter had recommended as an outside prosecutor. Ritter also called Reno, whom he had worked with before. He told her how important it was to get LaCabe. Reno said she would talk to Henry Solano, LaCabe's boss.

It's the phenomenon of Steve Thomas's letter. In spite of the fact that the metro DAs and the governor said to the world, "We know all the answers to all these allegations and there is nothing there," clearly that's not the impression the world got that afternoon. They think Thomas is a fucking hero. We should have answered all his charges point by point.

A friend of mine was recently asked, "What do you think about Alex Hunter?" and the guy answered his own question. "I think the guy is really slimy. He's obviously been bought."

Our reputations have been ruined. They're fucking down the toilet. I can't spend time dwelling on the problem, because I don't know if it can be changed. I just have to live with it.

Regardless of what happens out of the grand jury, even assuming an indictment and conviction, I don't think we can salvage our reputations. I believe the outcome of the case will be treated as "in spite of mumbling, incompetent pond scum, others were brought in and took it over and salvaged something."

Coming up to this case, I had some minor recognition, and I think I had a good reputation. And it's gone. But you can imagine Hunter.

It is really sad.

—Bill Wise

When Lou Smit heard the governor's announcement, he was devastated. Now he knew there was no turning back for Hunter. Smit was, he said, tired of "yelling from the back of the truck." He was sure that the Ramseys were innocent, and he wasn't going to take part in a case brought against them. Hofstrom had always been objective, but Kane had seen Pete as an obstacle to a successful prosecution and he had now been totally isolated from the case. Smit thought the time had come for him to leave too.

Fleet White, who didn't own a computer and had resisted buying one, was spending nights at the Boulder library, researching the law. One night he bumped into Frank Coffman.

"Do you know anyone in this town who has confidence in Alex Hunter?" White asked Coffman.

Coffman didn't know how to answer. The citizens of Boulder must have had confidence in Hunter or they wouldn't have elected him for six consecutive terms.

"Don't you think Michael Kane is respectable?" Coffman replied. "Aren't you encouraged by having such a hardworking, honest, and dedicated guy in charge?"

"Oh yeah, I met Kane," White responded finally. It had taken him a few seconds to figure out who Kane was. "It doesn't matter if it's Kane, if it's you or me. I've got to keep the pressure on."

"Were you impressed?" Coffman asked.

"Not really. They should have gone to a grand jury a long time ago," White replied.

Coffman tried to figure out what was driving White. Then he realized that White had experienced something he himself hoped never to see: a six-year-old child lying murdered at his feet on the floor of his friend's living room—a child who had played with his own daughter the night before.

White had recently told one of the detectives that he would go to jail before he would testify before the grand jury. His attitude was puzzling. The proceedings were secret, he would not be cross-examined, and he would be able to tell an impartial jury what he had been unwilling to tell the police. During this period, a journalist also had a chance to meet the Whites. They had told her she could write a story about them but that she wasn't to take notes, use a tape recorder, or quote them. They talked for hours, but in the end there seemed to be nothing new to print.

A local lawyer who commented occasionally on legal affairs in the media also met with them. She, too, found their attitude illogical—they wanted closure in the case but refused to cooperate. Eventually, she concluded that the Whites, having lost confidence in the process and thinking there would never be an indictment, had reasoned that their noncooperation couldn't hurt the case. It was like stabbing a corpse: it's already dead, so you can't hurt it anymore.

On August 17, the Whites released a letter to the media in which they said they shared Steve Thomas's view about the DA's office. The grand jury had been delayed by all parties, Fleet White wrote, even the current leadership of the Boulder PD, in order to take advantage of a new statute, passed on March 21, 1997, but not going into effect until October 1, 1997, which allowed grand juries to issue reports when allegations of commission of a class 1, class 2, or class 3 felony are not proved or no indictments are handed down. Apparently, White believed that even if the grand jury was used in the case, it would issue a report rather than an indictment.

The police may have been baffled by Fleet White's behavior and his decision not to cooperate with a grand jury, but it was possible that he was consumed by one big discrepancy—the fact that he had not seen JonBenét's body when he looked into the wine cellar in the early morning of December 26, 1996, whereas John Ramsey had found her body after a similarly quick glance into the same dark room several hours later. White knew from his police contacts that the John Ramsey had suggested him as a possible suspect—and that Ramsey went so far as to speculate to Lou Smit that White's wife, Priscilla, might have owned a stun gun. Since White hadn't been given access to his previous statements to the police, he might have also wondered whether someone was hoping to trap him in inconsistencies between what he had told the police earlier and what he might say as a grand jury witness.

By the summer of 1998, the Whites seemed to have become convinced that the DA's office wanted to avoid prosecuting the Ramseys. What if, in their eagerness to absolve the Ramseys, prosecutors led the grand jury to believe that White's account of what he had—or hadn't—found that day was false? Clearly the Ramseys were trying to implicate others. Were they, with their allies in the DA's office, going to make White their scapegoat? Was it possible that the DA's office might indict him for perjury—or maybe even charge him with responsibility for JonBenét's death?

8

On August 18, returning home at about 11:00 P.M., Steve Thomas saw an unfamiliar car in his driveway and the light on in his living room. Jeff Shapiro was on his doorstep talking to his wife through the door. She was in her pajamas and frightened. Thomas told the reporter he'd crossed the line by coming to his home.

"I'm trying to help you," Shapiro said, now standing in the driveway. "The *Globe* has found a source who told them some things that you don't want made public. They hope you'll cooperate with them." Thomas said nothing.

"They need to know things about the grand jury," Shapiro said. Thomas thought the reporter was playing good cop, bad cop—the oldest trick in the book.

"They know about your mother," Shapiro continued. "We know she committed suicide."

"My mother . . . my mother . . ." Thomas said, staring at Shapiro. "You've got that all wrong." Thomas had been just seven years old when his mother became suddenly ill and died.

"I don't want to see that story run," Shapiro said. "I'm just trying to protect you."

But the way Thomas saw it, Shapiro was trying to buy him. He told the reporter to leave at once.

Three days later, a FedEx package arrived at Thomas's house. In it was a letter from Craig Lewis of the *Globe*, who requested an interview. Enclosed were pictures of Thomas's long-deceased mother and late aunt, who had died of brain cancer.

That afternoon, Thomas told his lawyer to write Shapiro and the *Globe* that any further contact with him would be met with legal action. Several days later, Thomas heard that the DA's office was floating a rumor that mental instability ran in his family.

Several months later, the FBI talked to Shapiro about the possibility that he had engaged in extortion with Thomas. Shapiro played them a tape he had recorded during a conversation with *Globe* staff, where the topic of how to go about leveraging Detective Steve Thomas had been discussed.

Thomas decided not to press charges against the *Globe* or any of its employees and the FBI dropped the investigation for the time being.

Meanwhile, Michael Kane asked Ron Gosage and Michael Everett to visit Linda Hoffmann-Pugh and show her a photograph of a knife the police had discovered at the Ramsey house just after the killing. It had been found on the counter near the microwave oven in the utility area just off JonBenét's bedroom.

Hoffmann-Pugh said it was the paring knife from the kitchen, which she had put away many times. It had a wooden handle and wasn't serrated. She said that the knife had never been used upstairs; it was always in the kitchen. Linda wondered if the knife had something to do with an intruder. Surely Patsy would never scare JonBenét with a knife. That same day, the police told her she would be called before the grand jury.

Two days later, the *National Enquirer* called her to inquire about the Barbie nightgown that had been found next to JonBenét's body. Linda mentioned to the reporter that she'd just been visited by Gosage and Everett—they had never told her to keep their visit private. The *Enquirer* reporter offered her $300 for the story of the detectives' visit. Hoffmann-Pugh turned it down. The next day, she called Craig Lewis of the *Globe*. He offered her $1,000 and came over with the money. He was sitting in her living room getting ready to take notes when David Wright of the *Enquirer* knocked on the door. When he saw Lewis in the living room, he yelled, "Don't say a word until I make you another offer!" Unable to decide what to do, Hoffmann-Pugh asked Lewis to leave. She said she'd call him the next day. Several hours later, Wright called her back. "I've just gone to the bank, and I'm on my way to your house with cash." He gave her $1,500 for the story. Now Linda Hoffmann-Pugh had enough money to pay the rent and buy her daughter Ariana some new clothes for school.

By now it was apparent to Alex Hunter that he wouldn't be able to use Al LaCabe. LaCabe's boss, Henry Solano, said the Denver U.S. Attorney's office was understaffed. Hunter withdrew his request and began to look for two prosecutors. With the grand jury start date just three weeks away, Bill Ritter recommended Mitch Morrissey, who understood DNA. From his office, Bob Grant said that he was willing to loan out Bruce Levin, his chief trial deputy.

Levin had the reputation of always doing the right thing in a case, though some of his colleagues thought he was only average. He'd been at his job for eighteen years. Unlike Pete Hofstrom, who did his own docket every week, Levin took only the cases he wanted. Nevertheless, Levin had good courtroom skills and came off as sincere and honest. Jurors seemed to like him. Few could figure out why Ritter had suggested Morrissey. He had no particular expertise in DNA, and he was considered unremarkable in the courtroom.

Meanwhile, Michael Kane was working seven days a week, totally focused and giving every minute to the job. Awake well before seven in the morning, he worked until nine in the evening and would often sleep on an air mattress in the war room when he was too tired to drive to his apartment. He had even cut his running down to three miles a day—from the Justice Center down to Folsom Avenue and then back along the Boulder Creek bike path.

Levin and Morrissey reported to work at the end of August. Neither had attended the Boulder PD's presentation, nor had they been around during the Ramseys' interviews. Kane worried whether they would get up to speed by September 15, when the grand jury proceedings were to begin.

★ ★ ★

Hunter now had a team: Kane, Levin, and Morrissey. Pete Hofstrom, who didn't want anything to do with the grand jury, took off for his yearly vacation to San Francisco to see old friends. Though Trip DeMuth still held to the intruder theory, he was important because he carried encyclopedic knowledge of the case in his head. Lou Smit, mad that the Ramseys were to be made the target of a grand jury investigation, was rarely in the office. He still thought that Bill McReynolds should be looked at again.

By now, it was likely, Kane had decided that his goal was to return an indictment and go to trial. And if the indictment was supported by the evidence, he hoped Hunter would be prepared to sign it. The attitude in the office was not "if this case reaches a courtroom" but "it will reach a courtroom."

On September 3, Steve Thomas and his wife, Karena, took off for a three-week trip across the United States. Thomas loved to travel the interstate highways, and this much-needed vacation would take them to Arkansas, Louisiana, Mississippi, and Florida, where they would visit John Eller.

Meanwhile, Hunter was adjusting to life with outside prosecutors in his midst. When one Boulderite saw the DA at the Boulder recycling center, his four-wheel-drive bursting with empty milk jugs and piles of newspapers, he thought that Hunter looked tired. The DA told his acquaintance that if anyone could do something with the Ramsey case, it was Michael Kane. It might take some time, Hunter said, maybe another six months, but Kane could do it.

Kane had been given complete autonomy in preparing the case for the grand jury. He held daily meetings with Hunter, but if they came to an impasse, Kane had the last word. Nevertheless, the final decision—whether or not to sign a true bill, also known as an indictment—would be for Hunter, the elected official, to make.* By then Kane's job would be done.

---

*The common term *indictment* is an abbreviation of the document's formal name, a bill of indictment. Ordinarily a bill of indictment is prepared for the signature of the jury foreperson by the prosecutor working with the grand jury. If the grand jury votes to indict, the foreperson signs and the indictment becomes a "true bill." If the grand jury declines to indict, the document becomes known as a "no true bill," or (more commonly) a "no bill." In the event that a prosecutor refused to sign a true bill of indictment returned by the grand jury, the indictment would not be legally sufficient as an accusation. The only remedy provided in Colorado law for this uncommon situation is contained in C. R. S. 16-5-209, which provides for the substitution of a special prosecutor in the event of a regular prosecutor's "unjustified refusal" to prosecute a crime.

Kane, Levin, and Morrissey were not new kids on the block. On many occasions, Kane had taken cases that seemed to have no answers and developed new evidence. He had acquired his reputation by going before grand juries, getting indictments, and then convincing a trial jury that the grand jury had been right in its findings. Kane got convictions.

While the three prosecutors reviewed the evidence, they handed out assignments to the Boulder PD, the Georgia Bureau of Investigation, and the Boulder County Sheriff's Office. Some interview subjects still hadn't provided saliva for DNA testing or had their palm prints taken. Tom Haney and Steve Ainsworth did some work, and so did Gosage, Harmer, and Everett.

On Sunday, September 13, Kane, Levin, and Harmer went to see Linda Hoffmann-Pugh at her home in Fort Lupton. Hoffmann-Pugh was worried that they were going to subpoena her for the grand jury. Instead, they brought with them books of photographs. For three hours, Hoffmann-Pugh was asked about the photographs, taken inside the Ramseys' house shortly after the murder, depicting furniture, clothing, and household objects. Did this garment have these stains on them? Was this ever used by JonBenét for sleepwear? Did JonBenét ever wear this shirt inside out? Did she sleep in this? What about this shirt and the thermal underwear found on the bed?

By the time they were through, Hoffmann-Pugh wondered why she hadn't been asked these questions before. Everyone knew she had been the Ramseys' full-time housekeeper for a year and a half. She had last cleaned the house on December 23, just two days before Jon-Benét was murdered.

Michael Kane did most of the talking, and everyone took notes.

First, Hoffmann-Pugh was asked about JonBenét's bedroom. The photos showed everything from her beds to her bedding, her TV, her videotapes, and her shoes. She was asked about the many hair ties scattered on the floor at the foot of the bed and in front of the closet. Hoffmann-Pugh said that wasn't normal. The ties were usually kept in a basket in the bathroom. Maybe one or two would be lying on the bathroom counter, but they were never on the *floor*, or even in the bedroom. Then there was an open drawer. The housekeeper confirmed that it was the drawer where JonBenét's panties were kept. A new pair of underwear might have been put on JonBenét that evening, or maybe the drawer was left open from the morning. They wanted to know which shampoos were used on JonBenét's hair and where she bathed. She was always bathed in Patsy's tub on the third floor, Hoffmann-Pugh told them. Burke was also bathed in Patsy's tub, but lately he had taken baths in his father's bathroom. She knew for sure, because his Legos were always at the bottom of the tub when she drained the water. Then there was a photo of the decorative curtain treatment on the wall just behind JonBenét's bed. One of the ties was undone. Could JonBenét have hidden behind the drape? The housekeeper didn't think there was enough space, but JonBenét could have drawn the fabric around her for protection. Had JonBenét tried to protect herself from someone or from something like a stun gun? Linda Hoffmann-Pugh asked herself.

They also showed her a picture of JonBenét's white thermal blanket which had many urine and brown-colored stains on it. Some of them looked like dried blood. Then they showed her a picture of JonBenét's bed, which looked strange to her. Looking at the comforter, you couldn't tell that the blanket beneath it had been pulled off. The bed looked barely disturbed. Hoffmann-Pugh knew that to pull the blanket off, you had to first remove the comforter, otherwise it would get messed up. But in the photo, it was neat. Maybe the white blanket hadn't been on the bed at all. She told the police that the blanket might have been in the washer-dryer outside JonBenét's room. Then they showed her a photograph of the dryer, with the door open. Inside, she saw JonBenét's pink-and-white-checked sheets, which she had put on the bed two days before the murder. But on JonBenét's bed in another photo were the *Beauty and the Beast* sheets.

The logical explanation, Hoffmann-Pugh said, was that JonBenét had wet the bed on either Monday, Tuesday or Wednesday night. The clean sheets had probably been put on the bed and the wet sheets, blanket, and maybe even the Barbie nightgown were put in the wash and dried. The Ramseys didn't even have a clothes hamper, she said. When they took off their dirty clothes, they would just leave them lying around. The only things that went directly into the washer were JonBenét's urine-soaked sheets and blanket, so that they wouldn't smell. Only someone who knew which washer and dryer the Ramseys used for JonBenét's sheets and blanket would know where to find the blanket if it wasn't on the bed. Just as important, the washer-dryer outside JonBenét's room was built into a cabinet. Hoffmann-Pugh speculated that whoever killed JonBenét knew where the blanket was that night and probably took it out of the dryer.

Then they showed her the picture of Patsy's paint tray—or tote, as she called it—and some paintings leaning against the wall. The photograph had been taken just outside the wine cellar, right next to where Hoffmann-Pugh's own daughter had put John Ramsey's golf clubs. But that wasn't where she'd left the tray on December 23, she said. She had put it at the foot of the stairs and didn't know who had moved it. They asked her about the bowl with pineapple that was found on the dining room table. Did she recognize the white ridged bowl with a little lip on the bottom that served as a base, about the size of a softball?

Yes, it looked familiar, she said, but it would be better to see the real bowl, since there were so many in the kitchen that looked alike. Later, thinking about it, Hoffmann-Pugh felt that it was almost as if they had been playing the game "What's wrong with this picture?"

Finally, Kane showed her a picture of the Bible that John kept on his bedroom desk. Hoffmann-Pugh knew it was always open to Psalm 118. Every time she dusted, she saw it open to the same page. She told them she often read the verse. She didn't sit down to read it, just read it standing up. Hoffmann-Pugh started to cry. She remembered that the amount of the ransom demand was $118,000, and thought about JonBenét being dead.

"That's OK," Michael Kane said, patting her on the hand. "Don't worry about it."

"We'll see you in court," said Bruce Levin.

That same Sunday, Lou Smit thought about the tunnel vision that, he believed, had set in at Hunter's office. Now that Levin and Morrissey were up to speed, they were thinking just like Kane—they wanted the grand jury to return an indictment. Smit understood that it was their job—they hadn't been brought in to evaluate the case: they were there to present it. They were hired guns. Though it wouldn't be known to the public for several weeks, Trip DeMuth had been removed from the case.

Smit gave it one last crack. He asked Hunter to wait with the grand jury, came close to begging him. Smit could see that Hunter felt the evidence wasn't quite there yet, but at the same time it was clear to him that the DA was not exactly in charge—he had been told what to do.

9

On Tuesday, September 15, the grand jury convened at the Justice Center to hear the Ramsey case. It had been 628 days since JonBenét was found murdered in her parents' basement.

The sky was cloudless and postcard-perfect as reporters and photographers gathered once again. There were representatives from all the Denver and Boulder news outlets, from TV networks—NBC, ABC, CBS, and their affiliates—and from the *National Enquirer, Globe,* and *Extra.* Few of the participants would talk, so members of the media chatted with each other as they waited for something to happen.

The grand jurors arrived shortly after 8:00 A.M., and a Boulder County sheriff escorted each one up the sidewalk, past television camera crews and still photographers, to the entrance. None of the jurors seemed upset by the photographers. As they passed the newspaper vending machines by the entrance of the building, they could see that the morning edition of the *Daily Camera* had published their Department of Motor Vehicle photos on the front page. The mug shots made them look like criminals.

The grand jury spent its first two days in Courtroom L on the second floor. On the right side of the room, with its tight-pile pale blue carpet, stood the jury box, with two tiers of high-backed, cushioned purple chairs, seven in the back row and six in the front. On the front railing of the box sat a white plastic water pitcher and two stacks of paper cups. Arranged in front of the jury box were nine royal blue, cushioned armchairs. The witness box was on the spectators' far left, at the judge's right hand. Behind the raised area where the judge would sit were two flags, the American flag on one side and the Colorado flag on the other. White paper was taped over the panes of glass on the door so that no one could see in.

Outside the courtroom, no fewer than four sheriff's deputies were on hand, to keep the press at a distance. There were enough casual exchanges between reporters and grand jurors—"How are you?" "Good morning," and the like—that a judge ordered the reporters to stand back.

The DA's position was clear: They would say as little as possible. Bill Wise told *Daily Camera* reporter Matt Sebastian, "I'm not answering any questions except to say that it's a beautiful day in Boulder." Alex Hunter—carrying a legal pad and an orthopedic seat for his back condition—also said to reporters, "It's a beautiful day."

Michael Kane's plan was to present the case in the classic way—in the order in which the police had discovered the various elements, without first presenting a history of the family or suggesting possible motives. There was none of that in this case anyway. There were only the crime, the evidence, and the targets. The grand jury would follow the events through the reports and recollections of every officer who had come into contact with the Ramseys, starting just after 5:52 A.M. on December 26, 1996, when Patsy called 911.

After a day of introduction, the grand jury heard from Rick French, Karl Veitch, Paul Reichenbach, Bob Whitson, Linda Arndt, Barry Weiss, and Larry Mason. Detective Arndt gave the grand jury an emotional account of being left alone in the Ramsey house that morning for over two hours, one law enforcement officer with the near-impossible task of supervising the distraught Ramseys and their equally distraught friends. She emphasized that her desperate calls for assistance had gone unanswered. The prosecutors were furious; it was obvious that she was attacking the investigation. Within days the grand jury was told that their job was not to investigate the investigation.

The following week, the grand jury was moved to Courtroom E, on the first floor of the Justice Center. By then, the proceedings had taken on a routine air. Pete Hofstrom, in sweater-vest, tie, and tweed jacket, would walk briskly past the grand jury room, making an exaggerated grimace at a reporter he recognized but never pausing to comment as he headed off to litigate cases that no one would ever read about in the newspaper.

In his thirty-two years as a law enforcement officer, Lou Smit had worked enough grand juries to know that "you can indict a ham sandwich if you present only one side of the case." What about all the evidence that had been found of an intruder? Smit asked himself. If Michael Kane was planning to introduce any exculpatory evidence, Smit hadn't yet seen any signs of it. He was sure the Ramseys were going to be indicted.

Smit didn't want his name associated with the case anymore. On September 19, he finished writing his letter of resignation and showed it to Pete Hofstrom and Trip DeMuth before leaving it for Hunter on September 20. He knew it wouldn't be long before the media got word of it, but it surprised him that Hunter didn't call him until three days later—to say that *The Denver Post* knew he'd resigned and wanted a copy of his letter. Hunter was calling to ask Smit's permission to release it to the press. Smit first said yes, then called Hunter back and asked him to wait a few days.

Smit's had already received a phone call from Sherry Keene-Osborn of *Newsweek*. She also asked for permission to print his letter. Smit said no. Keene-Osborn then drove all the way from Denver to Colorado Springs, where Smit lived on the west side of town, just below majestic Pikes Peak, on a tree-lined street right out of Norman Rockwell's America. Beside the door to his lovingly maintained duplex hung a wooden shingle: "The Smits—Founded 1958."

"This is the greatest case I ever worked," Smit told the *Newsweek* reporter. "For a detective it's a real puzzle—a whodunit." Keene-Osborn talked the retired detective into giving her an unsigned copy of his resignation letter. She sensed that by the time she arrived at his door, Smit's attitude was, Why quit if nobody is going to know the reasons behind it? When *Newsweek* decided not to print it in the magazine, she shared the letter with the AP, which released it on September 25, the same day that *Newsweek* put it up on its Web site.*

Sept. 20, 1998

Dear Alex:

It is with great reluctance and regret that I submit this letter of resignation. Even though I want to continue to participate in the official investigation and assist in finding the killer of JonBenet, I find that I cannot in good conscience be a part of the persecution of innocent people.

When we first met I told you that my style of approaching an investigation is from the concept of not working a particular theory, but working **the case**.

Alex, even though I have been unable to actively investigate, I have been in a position to collect, record and analyze every piece of information given to your office in the course of this investigation. At this point of the investigation "**the case**" tells me that John and Patsy Ramsey **did not** kill their

---

* The letter is abridged here. It appears in its entirety in Appendix C.

daughter, that a very dangerous killer is still out there and no one is actively looking for him.

The Boulder Police Department has many fine and dedicated men and women who also want justice for JonBenet. They are just going in the wrong direction and have been since day one of the investigation. The case tells me that there is substantial, credible evidence of an intruder and lack of evidence that the parents are involved. If this is true, they too are tragic victims whose misery has been compounded by a misdirected and flawed investigation, unsubstantiated leaks, rumors and accusations.

Alex, you are in such a difficult position. The media and peer pressure are incredible. You are inundated with conflicting facts and information, and "expert" opinions. And now you have an old detective telling you that the Ramseys did not do it and to wait and investigate this case more thoroughly before a very tragic mistake would be made. What a double travesty it could be; an innocent person indicted, and a vicious killer on the loose to prey on another innocent child and no one to stop him.

Shoes, shoes, the victim's shoes, who will stand in the victim's shoes?

Good Luck to you and your fine office and may God bless you in the awesome decisions you must soon make.

Sincerely
[signed]
Detective Lou Smit

When Bill Wise read Smit's letter, he saw it as an invitation to a defense attorney to call Smit as a star witness. Wise could not understand what evidence of an intruder Smit was talking about, but of course he wasn't a detective. Still, it was one thing to say that there was insufficient evidence to go after the Ramseys. It was quite another to conclude that the parents couldn't have done it. That really astounded Wise.

When Tom Haney read the letter, he thought the intruder theory had gotten the best of Smit and that the veteran detective had lost his objectivity. Haney knew that in every case, there was something that didn't fit. In this case, it was the shoe imprint and the palm print on the wine cellar door. Haney had debated every aspect of the case with Smit, and with all the evidence that also pointed to the Ramseys, it didn't make sense for Smit to say that they were innocent.

For his part, Bob Grant saw a fundamental difference between Thomas's letter and Smit's. Thomas had intended his to be made public; he'd had an agenda. Smit, on the other hand, had meant his letter to be private; only as an afterthought did he release it to the media. That made Smit's message weightier. If the case reached trial, no matter who the defendant was, any defense attorney would have to try to get Lou Smit as a defense witness. Not doing so would be tantamount to malpractice.

The two letters showed exactly how complicated the case was. Two experienced detectives, both with full knowledge of all the evidence, had come to opposite conclusions. That raised a question: If these two disagreed, could a grand jury ever agree on who killed JonBenét?

Hal Haddon told *The Denver Post*, "I would hope the authorities in charge of the investigation will take note of what Lou Smit said, and will devote some significant resources to finding the real killer."

"Lou Smit has been on this case for how many months now," Mark Beckner told the same paper, "and I don't recall him ever presenting any arrest warrants to the DA's office."

Reporters had barely digested Thomas's letter when they were faced with Smit's. On the morning of September 27, ABC's *20/20* released part of a report about recent developments in the Ramsey case, which the network had been working on for several weeks. A producer had called both Hunter and Beckner, requesting interviews about the recently reactivated Smika/Wells case.* Hunter and Beckner, after consulting with each other, had both declined, deciding that ABC was simply using this as a pretext to get them to talk about the Ramsey case, which neither wanted to do.

* Sidney Lee Wells, twenty-two, was murdered by a shotgun blast to the back of his head on August 1, 1983, in his Boulder apartment. Wells, a CU journalism student, had been dating Shauna Jean Redford, the daughter of actor Robert Redford, at the time. Boulder's entire detective division, then numbering sixteen officers, was assigned to the case. Thayne Smika, Wells' roommate, was arrested October 6, 1983, for first-degree murder, but he was soon released for lack of evidence and was never charged. He is currently wanted on a 1986 felony theft warrant issued in Denver. In the wake of JonBenét Ramsey's murder, the investigation into the Wells case was reactivated, in the hope that some forensic tools not available to the police fifteen years before would provide a break in the investigation. As of this writing, Smika remains the prime suspect in the Wells murder.

On the evening of September 27, Smit's letter spread like wildfire on the Internet, and *20/20* broadcast its one-hour special, hosted by Barbara Walters and Diane Sawyer. Correspondent Elizabeth Vargas pointed out: "We emphasize there may be evidence to the contrary [to what we are reporting] not available to us or different conclusions that might be drawn [from what we are reporting]. And a reminder—in law, and in fairness, all people are considered innocent until proven guilty." The report detailed Donald Foster's conclusions about Patsy's authorship of the ransom note; the enhanced 911 call with Burke's voice in the background; the four fibers found on the duct tape that seemed to match Patsy's jacket; and a time study prepared by the police, that showed how long it would take for someone to complete the murder and the cover-up while the family slept, unaware.

Vincent Bugliosi, a former Los Angeles prosecutor, told Vargas, "The strongest evidence against the Ramseys in this case is nothing that directly implicates them. [It is] the implausibility that anyone else committed these murders. But paradoxically, the strongest evidence that I've just pointed to, by its very nature, is the weakest evidence against the Ramseys." Vargas asked, "Why?" Bugliosi continued, "If we come to the conclusion that JonBenét was not murdered by an intruder, the inevitable question presents itself: which [parent] did it? A prosecutor can't argue to a jury, 'Ladies and gentlemen, the evidence is very clear here that either Mr. or Mrs. Ramsey committed this murder and the other one covered it up . . .' There is no case to take to the jury unless [the DA] could prove beyond a reasonable doubt which one [of them] did it." Later in the show, Bugliosi told Vargas, "Even if you could prove beyond a reasonable doubt that Patsy Ramsey wrote the ransom note, that doesn't mean that she committed the murder."

Steve Thomas was the featured guest on the program. He did not discuss the evidence; he only talked about why he left the case and the department.

Alex Hunter had watched *20/20* fearing the worst. The attack on him wasn't as bad as he had expected. But listening to Foster's conclusions regarding Patsy and the ransom note, he knew there was another side to that story, which the Ramseys' attorneys were sure to make public. Several months earlier, Bryan Morgan had given Hunter a copy of a letter that Foster had written to Patsy Ramsey in the spring of 1997, before he agreed to work for Hunter. The DA was aware that Foster had followed the case on the Internet from February 1997 and that he had also written to Patsy. But when Morgan told him about a second letter, which Foster wrote to Jameson, Hunter was dismayed. It seemed that first Foster had believed that Sue Bennett, known only at the time as Jameson, who ran an information Web site on the Internet, was in fact John Andrew. After corresponding with Jameson in a series of Internet bulletin board messages, Foster believed not only that Jameson was John Andrew but that John Andrew had murdered JonBenét. Foster had even gone as far as writing to Jameson, asking that he—John Andrew—confess to the murder and turn himself in.

In Foster's letter to Patsy, he had written, "I know you are innocent—know it absolutely and unequivocally. I will stake my professional reputation on it, indeed my faith in my humanity." He also said that his analysis of the note [at the time] "leads me to believe you did not write it and the police are wasting their time by trying to prove that you did." Even though Foster's spring 1997 conclusions were based only on the fragments of the ransom note that were available at the time, there was a powerful contradiction between his conclusion at the time and what he said in 1998.

"Did you think the Ramseys were going to forget about his letter?" Wise said to a reporter when word of it leaked. In his final report, Foster used strong language to state that Patsy Ramsey had written the ransom note. In the letter to Patsy claiming he was sure she didn't write it, Foster had used almost the same language.

After the *20/20* broadcast, Steve Thomas's attorney, Peg Miller, called a TV journalist and asked how her client had come across. The reporter said the press thought Thomas was the source of the leaked information about Foster, the fibers, and the unidentified palm print that had come out on the show, and some people thought that Thomas was also the source of some recent revelations about the 911 tape in the *National Enquirer*. Miller, who knew her client had not been the one to reveal any of the information, nevertheless advised Thomas to stay away from the press.

The 20/20 broadcast also caused problems for the prosecution. Hunter had so far been able to isolate Kane, Levin, and Morrissey from the media. In fact, his entire office had been avoiding the press and there were no leaks from the grand jury room. But now *20/20* had put the case in the news again. This, combined with Lou Smit's resignation, discouraged the prosecutors. The grand jurors had to be advised again not to read the papers or watch TV—not forbidden, simply advised. They were told that their decisions should be based only on what they heard in the courtroom, no matter how difficult it might be to block out what they heard or read elsewhere.

On the afternoon of Friday, October 16, Randy Simons, who had photographed JonBenét in June 1996 and whose photographs had subsequently appeared on many magazine covers throughout the world, was found walking naked along a residential street in Genoa, Colorado, a town of two hundred residents on the eastern plains, where he lived. Approached by a sheriff's deputy, Simons blurted out, "I didn't kill JonBenét." The sheriff, who had no idea who Simons was, hadn't even mentioned the subject.

Simons was taken into custody and then transferred to University Hospital in Denver. No charges were filed. When the story was reported, the Ramseys' investigators immediately interviewed Simons at the hospital. It would be a week before the Boulder police arrived to talk to the photographer. Even though Simons didn't have a good alibi for the evening of JonBenét's murder, this incident didn't provide any new information and he was released.

10

By October 27, 1998, the grand jury had been sitting for five weeks, had met ten times, and had taken one ten-day break. Coroner John Meyer and experts from the CBI presented their evaluations of the evidence, including Chet Ubowski, the handwriting expert, who had reported to the police that Patsy could not be excluded as the writer of the ransom note. He had also told Pete Mang, his boss at the CBI, that his gut told him it was her handwriting.

Alex Hunter attended every session. For the first time in his career as DA, Hunter was giving his full attention to a case. He knew that his legacy and reputation would depend on his evaluation of the evidence being presented to the grand jury. If an indictment was handed down, it would be his responsibility to sign it if he believed there was a case against either of the Ramseys. If he didn't see the evidence—well, that was a bridge Hunter might have to cross later.

The police also worried about their legacy. In November 1998, Tom Wickman asked a journalist, "Why does the media keep talking about how we screwed up?" Before the reporter could answer, Wickman said, "We've been looking outside the Ramseys since the beginning. We are doing the best we can to look at other leads and I don't know why this story keeps perpetuating." Then he suggested that they have coffee. They didn't talk about the grand jury—only about Wickman's background as a psychology major and his interest in law enforcement and how different this case would have been if the press had gone away after the first few weeks.

That evening, Jay Leno did a routine about an imaginary phone call:

> CALLER: "I'd rather not give my name. I'm a detective with the Boulder Police Department. I don't appreciate your jokes about us not being very good investigators. I just don't think it's fair."
>
> LENO: Well, I understand what you're saying but you have to admit it does seem like you're moving awful slow on this JonBenét Ramsey murder case.
>
> CALLER: There's been a murder at the Ramseys'!?! Why didn't someone tell me? I'd better get over there right now!!!

In many respects, the case was "scene-dependent"—could a person have lifted the window-well grate and climbed through the broken window to the basement? How well could someone hear from one room to another?

On October 29, the grand jury toured the Ramseys' fifteen-room house. By 9:10 A.M. some jurors were already combing the property, going in and out through the side doors on the north side of the house and in and out the front door and peering in through the windows on the ground level. Each juror carried a notepad and several pages of photocopied material.

Kane, Levin, Morrissey, Wise, and Hunter lingered in the yard while the jurors spent several hours in the house, working mostly alone, almost never speaking to one another, each moving along at his or her own speed. The house was now unfurnished, and without the aid of photographs, it was hard to visualize how it had once looked. Still, the tour was sure to have an impact on the jurors. It was, after all, the crime scene.

Before the group left, one male juror tested the drainpipes on the exterior of the house, to see how strong they were. Possibly he wondered whether the pipes could support someone trying to scale the outside of the house. Another juror looked at the duct that led from the boiler room to the front of the house. Probably the jurors had been told Lou Smit's theory about how the scream might have been heard by the neighbor but not on the third floor, by JonBenét's parents.

At 11:20 the jurors left, two hours and twenty minutes after they arrived.

As the sheriff's van pulled away from the house, Wise said to Kane, "We've got a problem. Sixteen of them went in and only fifteen came out. I think we lost one." Wise saw a momentary flicker of panic cross Kane's face before the prosecutor realized that Wise was pulling his leg.

That afternoon, the grand jury heard from Tom Trujillo, who had been sworn in as a grand jury investigator. CBI analyst Debbie Chavez was the next to give testimony. Her areas of expertise included the ink on the ransom note, the paintbrush, and Patsy's paint tray. Chavez was followed by CBI fingerprint expert George Herrera, who testified for less than an hour. Even as the grand jury was working, the police were still taking palm prints from witnesses in the hope of finding a match to the print on the wine cellar door.

Alex Hunter can just say at some point, "I've developed the evidence and I see the case." He doesn't have to wait for a grand jury to reach a verdict. He can indict and arrest his target. There are some technical problems, but it can be done.

He would have to show a good reason to do that. In my view, it would be easy for the prosecution to say, "I want this evidence you've developed to be presented at a public preliminary hearing."

A preliminary hearing, to a limited degree, is an adversarial proceeding. A defense attorney can cross-examine. There might be probable cause, but maybe there isn't a reasonable likelihood of a conviction. So maybe the DA says, "I want a judicial officer to review the evidence." And there is some public benefit in that, because all the evidence gets aired.

There's a downside and an upside. You might have a judge who is well versed in criminal law saying that some evidence is admissible at a preliminary hearing and before a grand jury but will never be admissible in a trial. Depending on the nature of the evidence, a prosecutor might want to have that unbiased judicial arbiter.

That may be the reason you take the case to a preliminary hearing.

—Bob Grant

★ ★ ★

On November 14, the grand jury met for the fourteenth time. That week the CBI leaked to a journalist that the DNA of a second person—and possibly a third person—had been discovered on JonBenét's underpants. Even though the police and the CBI had known this since February 1997, the CBI was now using a new PCR 21-band DNA testing method in the hope of finding a match. The CBI was also trying to match the foreign DNA on JonBenét's underpants with the DNA found under her fingernails. The journalist did not report the leak.

That same week, a reporter covering the case had an off-the-record lunch with an attorney connected with the Ramseys. By now, the lawyer had become so embittered that it was visible in his eyes. He said his clients were going to be a human sacrifice to the media culture that now prevailed in the world. "It's the LaBrea tar pits," he told the journalist. "You get in it, you can't get out, and you die." He was sure there was at least a 50–50 chance that his clients would be indicted. He was also sure that the majority of Americans had already convicted them. The attorney said he wasn't so sure that Patsy would survive a trial. Not that she'd commit suicide, but she might suffer a relapse of her cancer from the stress. In fact, he was surprised that Patsy, exhausted as she was, hadn't already had a relapse.

Later, a different writer had lunch with another attorney representing the Ramseys. At times, the writer raised his voice above the ambient noise of the restaurant, loud enough to be overheard from nearby tables. At 2:00 P.M., the attorney said he had to leave but suggested that the writer finish his meal, which he did. Moments later, a woman approached his table and sat in the booth where the writer's guest had been seated. She was well dressed and spoke in a soft voice.

WOMAN: I hope you don't mind. You see I'm a friend of a grand juror. This case is so complicated. I don't know if I'm allowed to talk to you or if my friend should have been talking to me.

WRITER: I'm sure she knows the law better than I. Someone must have explained it to her.

WOMAN: I don't know. It's so confusing that she has had to go to her astrologer for help.

WRITER: Is that so?

WOMAN: Do you know about that secret room the Ramseys built for $150,000? I don't know what they did in that room, the one on the ground floor.

WRITER: I didn't know.

WOMAN: And you must know about the dumbwaiter on the second floor. That's where they found some of her blond hair. Caught in the door. And you know they used chloroform on her? They think she was taken that way.

WRITER: I didn't know about the dumbwaiter.

WOMAN: I didn't know either until I was told.

With that, the woman got up and went back to her table.

"The system will put it right," John Ramsey had often said. And each time they failed, he was confident that at the next juncture, things would be put right. He had begun to think that way while waiting for their April 1997 police interviews. When those interviews failed to diminish the police's interest in him and Patsy, he waited for the next chance to put things right. A second set of interviews with the DA's office in June 1998, had changed nothing and now the grand jury was meeting and his lawyers had told him to expect Patsy to be charged, since experts were saying that she had written the ransom note. Nevertheless, Ramsey didn't lose his faith in the process.

By now his attorneys had told him that it was likely that Patsy would be charged in the murder of their daughter. He just didn't know how to tell her. Ramsey knew they would have to wait for a trial. Only then would he and Patsy be exonerated.

Like many Americans, Steve Thomas and Lou Smit, waited for the grand jury to finish hearing the case. Smit and Thomas, both intimately familiar with it, had different opinions about the meaning of the evidence. Smit hoped that the evidence would exonerate the Ramseys, while Thomas believed that it would cast enough doubt to let them off. The two detectives agreed, however, that all conclusions about the case—as well as the grand jury's verdict—hinged on six major items of evidence.

The first was the pubic hair found on the white blanket that had partly covered JonBenét's body. There was only one test—called advanced mitochondrial—that could still be done to tie the pubic hair to someone. There was so little of the hair left after the previous tests, however, that this mitochondrial test would destroy what remained. Some of the detectives believed that the hair belonged to some family member, but the couple's attorneys had objected to doing the destructive test at this time. They insisted that it should be conducted only when a suspect had been matched to other elements of the crime—and, of course, no one, including the Ramseys, had been conclusively matched to any element of the crime. It was also possible that the hair had adhered to the blanket in the Ramseys' dryer, left there by another garment on some earlier occasion.

The shoe imprint found near JonBenét's body was the second piece of evidence. Ron Gosage had compiled a list of more than six hundred people who had been in the Ramseys' house during the six months prior to JonBenét's death. He had gotten in touch with more than four hundred of those people, and not one of them had ever worn or owned that kind of Hi-Tec hiking shoe. The imprint was of the "poon"—the area on the sole at the heel where the brand name is stamped. The size of shoe couldn't be determined from the imprint, since the poon is the same size in all shoes, the better to advertise brands. Unless the detectives could match the shoe to someone who had been cleared of the crime by other means, the possibility existed that it was the killer who had left the shoe imprint.

The third piece of evidence was related to the window in the basement train room. It had been open, there was a scuff mark on the wall under it, and pieces of glass had been found on the suitcase just beneath it—possibly the result of Fleet White's visit to the basement window that morning when he picked up the broken glass from the floor under the window and replaced some of it on the windowsill. The spiderweb on the window-well grate was not conclusive proof that nobody had entered though the window opening. The sudden rise in temperature the morning after the murder allowed for a spider to come out of hibernation and spin a new web, and some people argued that the web itself was elastic enough to survive disruption.

The fourth area of evidence consisted of the unidentified palm prints—one smear of a partial print found on the ransom note and a full palm print found on the wine cellar door. The print on the note covered such a small area of a hand that it could never be matched to anyone. The print on the door had not been matched to anyone whose prints were taken for this case, and the national crime-scene fingerprint database doesn't include palm prints. Clearly, the print on the door did not belong to John or Patsy Ramsey. If it could be matched to a person who had a legitimate reason to be in the basement, it might mean nothing; but in the absence of such a match, the print was compelling evidence of an intruder.

The fifth element was the stain on JonBenét's underpants containing mixed (foreign) DNA. The first component was JonBenét's. Testing showed that the second or—possibly, third—component did not seem to match either parent or any relative, friend, playmate, or acquaintance whose DNA sample had been taken. How could the foreign DNA have gotten onto the underpants? It was possible that it belonged to the person—as yet unknown—who had killed JonBenét. It was also possible, however, that it came from a known person who had not given DNA samples and did not want to reveal that he or she had had contact with JonBenét in a manner that left DNA on her underpants. Such a person could be someone who had helped wipe JonBenét while she was on the toilet. The person might have been afraid that no truthful and innocent explanation would satisfy those who were eager to find a murderer.

The sixth element—in Lou Smit's opinion only—was the possible use of a stun gun on JonBenét. The autopsy photos seemed to show marks consistent with those left by such a device, and the marks were fresh enough to have been caused during the murder. So little support had been given to this theory, however, that nobody had tried to have JonBenét's body exhumed for the necessary testing of the skin tissue.

Not on the list but equally puzzling were the questions about the duct tape and the cord. The cord had a frayed end and had been cut, but it couldn't be determined how recently. The tape had been ripped from a roll. How recently that had taken place was also unknown. Why were all the other leftovers from the crime—such as the stick used in the "garrote," the Sharpie pen used to write the ransom note, and the writing pad—left behind and not the roll of tape and the remainder of the cord? Only the killer knew the answer to that question.

Even more mystifying, the ransom note itself showed no fingerprints or signs of handling, creasing, or damage. Patsy said she saw the three sheets of paper comprising the note spread across the entire width of a step as she descended the spiral staircase. She said she stepped over the three pages before turning around to read its contents. The pages showed no indication that they had been stepped on. This seemed plausible until the police recreated the scenario Patsy described. The detectives found it was impossible, while descending this spiral staircase, to skip any of the steps without losing one's balance and almost falling forward.

GORDON MURDER TRIAL OPENS

DAVID GORDON CHARGED WITH MARCH
SHOOTING DEATH OF LIVE-IN GIRLFRIEND

For the first time since 1992, a defendant is scheduled to enter a Boulder courtroom today and stand trial on a charge of murder.

Compared to a trio of unsolved Boulder slayings—the Sid Wells, Susannah Chase and JonBenét Ramsey homicides—the [Angela] Foulks murder has received little attention and relatively few headlines in the eight months since the 44-year-old woman was killed [by her boyfriend].

In that time, Gordon had quietly wended his way through Boulder District Court without making a deal with prosecutors.

Foulks had cocaine in her system at the time of her death, according to Boulder County Coroner John Meyer's autopsy report. "Cocaine is at the bottom of this," Gordon reportedly told detectives after his arrest.

—Matt Sebastian
Daily Camera, December 7, 1998

Four days later, a jury convicted David Gordon of first-degree murder. In Colorado a first-degree murder conviction carries a mandatory life sentence without the chance of parole.

By December 1998, Michael Kane was calling civilian witnesses. Before anyone appeared, Kane and his staff would conduct extensive interviews. Michael Archuleta and Linda Hoffman-Pugh and her husband, Merv, were called. Fleet White had probably become less paranoid; in any event, he agreed and testified twice. He was cordial with prosecutors and told the grand jury what he knew. As he left he informed one deputy DA that he was still upset at Hunter for releasing a photo of his daughter and JonBenét to a tabloid. White's accusation was without merit. The photographer had supplied the phototgraph to a third party who gave it to the paper. Barbara and John Fernie were next to testify.

Steve Thomas heard that Kane was afraid to call him, fearing an episode like Linda Arndt's testimony. Kane, according to the rumor, was conviced Thomas would attack Hunter and his office for their handling of the case. Lou Smit also wanted to testify, but he refused to meet with Kane beforehand. Nevertheless, he hoped Levin or Morrissey would convince Kane to call him regardless. Maybe then he could present the evidence he thought would clear the Ramseys.

What neither Thomas, Smit, Hunter, Eller, Hofstrom, nor anyone else connected with the investigation could explain was the use of the noose on JonBenét. The garroting did not connect to any other element of the crime. The FBI had no record of a young child being strangled with one, let alone by a parent.

After JonBenét's skull was fractured she would have slipped into unconsciousness quickly. It would have been just as easy to end her life by smothering or strangling her by hand. There was no explanation why anyone would even think of making a noose—which takes time—slip it around her neck, and use it to kill her.

Death by this method is gruesome and horrifying. It does not come quickly. The person pulling the cord and tightening the noose little by little around JonBenét's neck would not even have been able to look away. He or she would have had to eventually look into the child's face, to be sure that she was dead.

It was so merciless to that child who had once asked, "Do roses know their thorns can hurt?"

11

This has been a story of images, by turns stark, sensational, pedestrian and poignant—the images, accurate and otherwise, of the Ramseys, the police, the DA's office, the suspects, a portrait, even of one city's idea of itself. And at the center has been all the images of one little girl.

It would be not the worst, but perhaps the most unkind injustice of the many done to this child if we remembered only a small shape in a body bag or the strutting pseudo-adult of the pageant videos. I would rather close this account with an image that Patsy's sister Pam remembered vividly:

One summer in Charlevoix, JonBenét was standing on the dock bare-foot. Worried that she might get a splinter, Pam ran after her.

"You need to put shoes on," she told JonBenét.

"I don't want to," the child answered. "I want to feel the earth's life under my feet."

EPILOGUE

Throughout my research on this case, I was then, and am still convinced that neither John nor Patsy ever asked each other, "Did you cause JonBenét's death?" It is entirely possible that neither of the Ramseys ever dared to ask such a question. That way, despite the tragedy engulfing this couple, they would at least be spared the horror of the question. Even if one or both had momentary doubts, or worse—persistent doubts, I think the question was never asked. To do so would have had to place such strain on their relationship that it could surely have ended their marriage.

On the other hand, convinced or not, I still wanted to verify whether anyone I interviewed could offer some indication that the Ramseys might have questioned each other's innocence. It wasn't long, however, before I was fairly certain once again that John would never raise the subject. If he actually knew Patsy was involved in their child's death, then there was no need for discussion. If he was merely suspicious, he would still refrain. And if he doubted Patsy's word, then why ask? For how would he ever know if any answer she gave him was honest?

Soon enough I encountered all the other theories of the crime: Santa did it. John was molesting his daughter and Patsy caught them in the act. Patsy went crazy over her daughter's bed-wetting. The theories went on. Yet the more I learned about the murder from those investigating the case, the more clearly I saw, as did some of the detectives, that no one theory included all the evidence.

In fact, the more I was told by law enforcement about what they knew, the less confident I became of ever finding an answer for myself. It seems, at least so far, that some questions have no recoverable answers—and not necessarily because someone known to the police was withholding information.

What I know now with hard-earned certainty is that since I was not present when JonBenét was killed, I have to question my right to offer an explanation, a best guess, or a likely scenario of the events of

December 25–26, 1996. So, I find myself getting angry when I hear someone say, "Patsy did it because. . .," or "John did it, you see . . ." Every time I hear yet another theory, I understand all over again why I wrote this book. I came to learn that I saw it as my job to find out as much as I could and therefore create the most accurate record available for others.

If someone is ever charged with JonBenét's murder and the case comes to trial, only then will a jury have the right to pass judgment. We should not consider John and Patsy Ramsey anything less than innocent unless and until a guilty verdict is pronounced on one or both of them by twelve of their fellow citizens. I know it is hard to maintain that level of objectivity when confronted with the facts of a six-year-old's death, an exceptionally beautiful and charming six-year-old. The urge to blame someone is deep-seated. But we are obliged to remember the presumption of innocence. For, whoever may ultimately be charged with JonBenét's death is absolutely entitled to a fair chance for a fair trial— that startling notion, rooted in English common law, that holds every man and woman equal, and equally innocent, before the bar of justice.

CHARACTER LIST

Steve Ainsworth—Boulder County Sheriff's Detective assigned to assist District Attorney Alex Hunter in the investigation.

Kit Andre—Dance instructor hired by Patsy Ramsey to teach JonBenét a dance number.

Mike Archuleta—The private pilot who had been scheduled to fly the Ramsey family to Michigan the morning of Dec. 26, 1996.

Ellis Armistead—Private investigator hired by the Ramseys' lawyers.

Linda Arndt—First Boulder Police Detective to arrive at the Ramsey home after JonBenét was discovered missing.

Richard Baer—Denver attorney and advisor on the case to the Boulder Police.

Joe Barnhill—A Ramsey neighbor who knew the family well and attended their Christmas party December 23, 1996.

Mark Beckner—Boulder Police Commander who replaced Tom Koby as chief.

Dr. Francesco Beuf—JonBenét's pediatrician since she was one year old.

Richard Bjelkovig—Private pilot who works with John Ramsey's pilot, Mike Archuleta.

Peter Boyles—Denver radio talk-show host station KHOW-AM .

Charlie Brennan—Legal affairs writer for the *Rocky Mountain News*.

Diane Brumfitt—The Ramsey next-door neighbor who observed the absence of a familiar light in their house the night of the murder.

Detective Jim Byfield—Boulder Police Detective who authored the initial search warrants and affidavits.

Patrick Burke—Denver defense attorney hired to represent Patsy Ramsey.

Michael Bynum—Family friend and Boulder attorney who worked for John Ramsey's company, Access Graphics.

Brian Cabell—Southeast regional correspondent for CNN who interviewed John and Patsy Ramsey Jan. 1, 1997.

Tom Carson—Access Graphics executive.

Susannah Chase—University of Colorado student attacked in downtown Boulder Dec. 21, 1997, who died the next day. Her murder is unsolved.

Frank Coffman—Boulder artist and free-lance writer.

J. T. Colfax—Artist and body transport driver.

Marc Colin—Denver attorney who represented Sgt. Larry Mason.

Trip DeMuth—Chief trial deputy for District Attorney Alex Hunter assigned to the case in its first hours.

Jacqueline Dilson—Boulder County woman who raised concerns to police about her friend Chris Wolf.

John Douglas—Former FBI criminal profiler and consultant to the Ramseys' lawyers.

Charles Elbot—The principal at High Peaks Elementary School, where both JonBenét and Burke Ramsey were enrolled.

John Eller—The Commander of the Boulder Police Department detective division.

Robert Elmore—Longtime member of the congregation at St. John's Episcopal Church, where the Ramseys worshipped.

Jay Elowsky—Owner of Pasta Jay's restaurant, where John Ramsey was an investor.

George Epp—The Sheriff of Boulder County who made his staff and advice available to both the Boulder Police and the district attorney throughout the investigation.

Clay Evans—Staff writer and columnist for the *Daily Camera*.

Michael Everett—Among the first detectives assigned to the case.

Barbara and John Fernie—Church friends of John and Patsy Ramsey.

Donald Foster—Vassar College English professor and language/text analyst.

Rick French—First officer at the Ramseys' home following the 911 call concerning JonBenét's disappearance.

Tony Frost—Editor-in-chief of the *Globe*.

Patrick Furman—Attorney for Patsy Ramsey and a University of Colorado School of Law professor.

Scott Gibbons—A Ramsey next-door neighbor.

Daniel Glick—Special correspondent for *Newsweek*.

Mike Glynn—Former business associate of John Ramsey.

Ron Gosage—A Boulder Police detective assigned to the case.

Bob Grant—Adams County District Attorney brought in as an advisor to Boulder D.A. Alex Hunter.

Chuck Green—Columnist for *The Denver Post*.

Kristine Griffin—A teen-aged veteran of the beauty pageant world and daughter of Pam Griffin.

Pam Griffin—A seamstress who made many of JonBenét's pageant outfits.

Hal Haddon—Denver attorney who represents John Ramsey.

Bill Hagmaier—Unit chief for the FBI's National Center for the Analysis of Violent Crimes.

Tom Haney—Former Denver Police Department homicide investigator who assisted the Boulder District Attorney's office in the investigation and interrogated Patsy Ramsey.

Jane Harmer—A Boulder Police Detective assigned to the case.

Julie Hayden—Reporter for KGMH-TV—Channel 7, Denver's ABC affiliate.

Niki Hayden—Staff writer for the *Daily Camera* and member of the Ramseys' church.

Bud and Sandra Henderson—Former Ramsey business associate and former employee of Access Graphics.

Jeff Hendry—Boulder County Sheriff's Department sergeant.

Melissa Hickman—Boulder Police Detective.

Daniel Hoffman—Denver attorney, advisor on the case to the Boulder Police.

Linda Hoffmann-Pugh—Ramseys' housekeeper.

Pete Hofstrom—Chief of the felony division in the Boulder District Attorney's office.

Tim Honey—Boulder City Manager.

Rev. Rol Hoverstock—The family minister.

Karen Howard—A director of Access Graphics.

Alex Hunter—Boulder County District Attorney.

Brooke Jackson—Denver attorney who represented Boulder Police Detective Linda Arndt.

Mary Lou Jedamus—Boulder police victim assistance worker.

Jim Jenkins—Atlanta attorney representing Burke, John Andrew, and Melinda Ramsey.

Lucinda Ramsey Johnson—John Ramsey's first wife.

Michael Kane—Boulder District Attorney grand jury prosecutor.

Bob Keatley—Staff legal advisor to the Boulder Police Department.

Sherry Keene-Osborn—*Newsweek* reporter.

Tom Kelley—Denver attorney specializing in First Amendment law.

Tom Koby—Boulder Chief of Police.

Pat Korten—Veteran Washington, D.C.–based public relations pro hired by the Ramseys' lawyers.

Barbara Kostanick—Mother of a JonBenét playmate.

Suzanne Laurion—Media spokeswoman for District Attorney Alex Hunter and University of Colorado journalism professor.

Henry Lee—World renown forensics expert.

Bruce Levin—Boulder District Attorney grand jury prosecutor.

Craig Lewis—Writer for the *Globe*.

Pete Mang—Colorado Bureau of Investigation Inspector.

Gary Mann—Vice President of Lockheed-Martin's Commercial Systems Group, parent company to Access Graphics.

James Marino—Former sales representative for Access Graphics.

Larry Mason—Boulder Detective Sergeant.

Kevin McCullen—Staff writer for the *Rocky Mountain News*, Boulder bureau.

Carol McKinley—Reporter for KOA-AM Radio, Denver.

Bill and Janet McReynolds—Former journalism professor and part-time Santa Claus, and his wife, a writer.

Jeff Merrick—Longtime business associate of John Ramsey and employee of Access Graphics.

Gary Merriman—Director of Human Resources at Access Graphics.

Glenn Meyer—Tenant of the basement apartment in the Barnhills' home.

John Meyer—Forensic pathologist and elected coroner of Boulder County.

Brad Millard—Friend of John Andrew Ramsey.

Robert Miller—Denver attorney and advisor on the case to the Boulder police.

Bryan Morgan—Boulder attorney and law partner of Hal Haddon, hired to represent John Ramsey.

Grace Morlock—Boulder Police victim assistance worker.

Mitch Morrissey—Boulder District Attorney grand jury prosecutor.

Joe Mullins—News editor for the *Globe*.

Patty Novack—Ramsey family friend.

Don Paugh—JonBenét's maternal grandfather and a former Union Carbide executive.

Nedra Paugh—JonBenét's maternal grandmother.

Pam Paugh—Sister of Patsy Ramsey.

Polly Paugh—Sister of Patsy Ramsey.

Jim Peters—Arapahoe County District Attorney.

Judith Phillips—Photographer and Ramsey family friend.

Dr. Steve Pitt—Forensic psychiatrist and consultant to the Boulder Police.

Larry Pozner—Denver defense attorney, frequent media commentator on the case.

Beth Ramsey—John Ramsey's first child, a product of his marriage to Lucinda Ramsey Johnson. She died in a January 8, 1992 automobile accident.

Burke Ramsey—First child of John and Patsy Ramsey, 9 years old the night of the murder.

Jeff Ramsey—John Ramsey's brother.

John Ramsey—President and Chief Executive Officer of Access Graphics. Father of JonBenét Ramsey.

John Andrew Ramsey—Step-brother to JonBenét Ramsey and a University of Colorado sophomore.

JonBenét Ramsey—Born Aug. 6, 1990.

Melinda Ramsey—The second child of John Ramsey and Lucinda Ramsey Johnson.

Patsy Ramsey—The former Patricia Ann Paugh, mother of JonBenét Ramsey and wife to John Ramsey.

Sgt. Paul Reichenbach—Former detective working in patrol.

Murray Richtel—Retired Boulder County district criminal judge.

Bill Ritter—Denver District Attorney.

Roy Romer—Governor of Colorado.

Allison Russ—University of Colorado student, friend of John Andrew Ramsey.

Charlie Russell—Denver public relations executive hired by the Ramseys' lawyers.

Lisa Levitt Ryckman—Staff writer for the *Rocky Mountain News*.

Suzanne Savage—A former Ramsey babysitter.

Barry Scheck—A New York attorney and nationally recognized expert on DNA.

Brian Scott—Landscaper who worked for the Ramseys.

Jeff Shapiro—Free-lance researcher for the *Globe*.

Randy Simons—Pageant photographer who had taken pictures of JonBenét Ramsey.

Lou Smit—Retired El Paso County homicide investigator.

Melody Stanton—A neighbor of the Ramseys who reported hearing a child's scream the night of JonBenét's murder.

Kim Stewart—Boulder Police detective.

Glen and Susan Stine—Friends of John and Patsy Ramsey.

Dave Thomas—Jefferson County District Attorney.

Steve Thomas—Boulder Police Detective.

Tom Trujillo—Boulder Police Detective.

Chet Ubowski—Colorado Bureau of Investigation documents examiner.

Laurie Wagner—Longtime business associate of John Ramsey.

Roxanne Walker—Friend of Patsy Ramsey.

Carey Weinheimer—Boulder Police Detective.

Rod Westmoreland—Atlanta attorney and vice president of Merrill Lynch.

Fleet and Priscilla White—Ramsey friends.

Carl Whiteside—Director of the Colorado Bureau of Investigation.

Sgt. Tom Wickman—Boulder Police Detective.

Linda Wilcox—A former Ramsey housekeeper.

Bill Wise—First Assistant District Attorney for Boulder County.

Chris Wolf—Boulder journalist.

Paula Woodward—Reporter for KUSA TV—Channel 9, Denver's NBC affiliate.

Rachelle Zimmer—Denver attorney and press spokeswoman for the Ramseys.

ACKNOWLEDGMENTS

During the one and a half years I spent in Boulder researching and writing this book, over 194 people were interviewed—more than 100 face-to-face—in 571 conversations, which resulted in more than twenty-five thousand pages of transcripts.

Members of the law enforcement community helped me understand not only the Ramsey case but also the county in which they serve. Many of the interviews and conversations took place during the investigation into JonBenét's death. To protect those who supported this book, I have occasionally credited them as "a detective" or "the DA's "staff" and in other instances I have combined several law enforcement sources into one, with their permission. There are seven members of law enforcement who asked not to be credited for their assistance; their names, however, do appear in the text. "A reporter," "a journalist" or "a writer," often refers to members of the press who wished not to be named. At the request of one reporter I have used Cordwainer Bird as his pseudonym.

Patsy and John Ramsey did not grant any interviews for this book. Three of their attorneys spoke off the record a few times. Chief Tom Koby and Commander John Eller gave no formal interviews but did meet with me to discuss some aspects of the case and their lives. John Eller told me he would some day write his own book. Pete Hofstrom, in keeping with his long-standing policy on the media, granted no interviews but did chat with me on an unrelated subject. Those who wished to be credited as contributors to this work are mentioned by name.

I wish to thank Charlie Brennan, the legal affairs writer for the *Rocky Mountain News*. His knowledge of the first six months of the case was invaluable in helping me understand what had taken place before I arrived in Boulder in June 1997. I have a heartfelt debt of gratitude to Charlie.

★ ★ ★

My reporting of the Ramsey case began as an assignment from Tina Brown, former editor of *The New Yorker*. The effect of that article, published in January 1998, has been noted in this work. Without Tina's support, there might not have been a book.

As noted earlier, I did not interview Patsy or John Ramsey and did not personally speak to John Andrew, Melinda, or Burke Ramsey. Other members of the family did grant interviews to me or Charlie Brennan on several occasions.

I wish to thank the following for their invaluable contributions: Paul Danish, Charles Elbot, George Epp, Bob Grant, Pam Griffin, Linda Hoffmann-Pugh, Alex Hunter, Barbara Kostanick, Paul McCormick, Gregg McCrary, Carol McKinley, Nedra Paugh, Judith Phillips, Murray Richtel, Tom and Enid Schantz, Brian Scott, Jeff Shapiro, Marianne "Mimi" Wesson, and Bill Wise.

I would like to further thank Kit Andre, Susan Bennett, Caroline Brady, Brian Cabell, Dan Caplis, Virginia Chavez, Frank Coffman, Chuck Davis, Michael Dobersen, John Eller, Jay Elowsky, Clay Evans, John Fernie, Donald Foster, Lee Frank, David Grimm, Ken Harrell, Yvonne Haun, Julie Hayden, Niki Hayden, Bud Henderson, Jeff Hendry, Tim Honey, Jim Jenkins, Pat Korten, Suzanne Laurion, Brad Leach, Craig Lewis, Sandy Long, Janet and Bill McReynolds, Pete Mang, Gary Mann, Kurt Matthews, Kevin McCullen, Gary Merriman, Glenn Meyer, John Meyer, David Mills, Patty Novack, Karen Paget, Kevin Parker, Pam Paugh, Steve Prentup, Jay Propst, Kevin Raburn, Charlie Russell, Lysa Ryckman, Suzanne Savage, Brett Sawyer, Dick Schwarz, Randy Simons, Stephen Singular, Werner Spitz, Jane Stobie, James Thompson aka J. T. Colfax, Michael Tracey, Chet Ubowski, Laurie Wagner, Ricky Weiser, Carl Whiteside, Linda Wilcox, Mark Wilson, and Chris Wolf.

In addition, the following: Leslie Aaholm, Peter Adler, Ann Angiella, Matthew Appelbaum, Larry Arndt, Claudia Bayliff, Ann Louise Bardach, Joe Barnhill, Mark Beckner, Robert Bennett, Bob Bernard, Steve Berkowitz, Suzanne Bernhard, Clint Blackhurst, Peter Boyles, Patrick Brickman, John Buechner, Mike Butler, Leo Carrillo, Leonard Chessler,

Mary Clark, Marc Colin, Ruth Correll, Jane Cracraft, Paige Doherty, Wayne Doland, John Drexler, George Dunphy, Leslie Durgin, Robert Elmore, Nick Isenberg, Tom Faure, Mark Fix, Tim Fuller, Mike Glynn, Dale Goetz, Chuck Green, LaDonna Griego, Kristine Griffin, William Hankins, Rod Hendrick, Diane Hollis, Bill Howard, Karen Howard, Faye Johnson, Sarah Jussen, Peter Kass, Tom Kelley, Sherry Keene-Osborn, Steve Krizman, Richard Krugman, Alli Krupski, Joseph Kurtz, Al LaCabe, Phil LeBeau, Santina Leuci, William Light, Jack Logan, Karen Luebke, Joseph Maier, James Marino, Liz McDonough, Richard McLean, Kelvin McNeill, David Michaud, Jan Miller, Charlie Montgomery, Brenda Niemand, Gail Nolan, Mike Patty, Mike Phelan, Tammy Polson, Julie Poppen, Chuck Pringle, Rob Pudim, Robert Ressler, Richard Rianoshek, E. Chester Ridgway, Dave Rivers, Bill Scanlon, Todd Sears, Craig Silverman, Ray Simmon, Craig Skinner, Jim Smith, Hugh Snodgrass, John Stack, Edie Stevens, Robert Stewart, Matt Sugar, Peter Teets, Patrick Vann, Ron Walker, Roxanne Walker, Richard Woodbury, Paula Woodward, David Wright, Harry Wright, Elliott Zaret, Gene Ziemer, and Rachelle Zimmer.

The following librarians were most helpful: Charlotte Smokler, *Daily Camera*; Janet Boss, Paula Ehresman, Carol Kasel, and Janet Reeves of the *Rocky Mountain News* as were Suzanne Laurion of the District Attorney's office, Jana Petersen public information officer for the County of Boulder and media liaison Jennifer Bray for the City of Boulder.

With much admiration for the unique talents of Jason Epstein, I offer my grateful appreciation for his vital understanding and help with every aspect of this book.

The editorial assistance of Jennifer Mears, Judith McNally, and Veronica Windholz, was central to this book. Jennifer Mears, a reporter for the Associated Press, became my right hand, reviewing all the interviews and organizing the material. Her work laid the foundation for the writing. Judith McNally was my consultant during the early stages of this book. Her counsel, as in my previous book, *American Tragedy*, was invaluable. Veronica Windholz worked with me through the book's completion. Her advice and suggestions helped shape this work.

★ ★ ★

A further thanks to Marianne Wesson, who advised and drafted the majority of the legal footnotes in the book. And to Deborah Goeken of the *Rocky Mountain News*, who approved Charlie Brennan's leave of absence to work on this book.

My personal assistant Brenda Williams's commitment to this book also made it possible, and Sandy Lyon, Nickey Hernandez, and Pat Rankin aided me in Los Angeles. A special thanks to Paul Amerman, Casey Brennan, Janet Brennan, and Terry Swartz, who kept our work in order. And to my son Howard Schiller who designed the book's jacket.

My thanks to Joelle Delbourgo, Cathy Hemming, Jane Friedman, James Fox, Tim Duggan, Robin Arzt, Joseph Montebello, Patti Wolf, and Brenda Woodward at HarperCollins.

A much earned thanks to John Taylor Williams of Palmer and Dodge, who has assisted me on four book projects.

APPENDIX A

Floor Plans of the Ramseys' Boulder Home

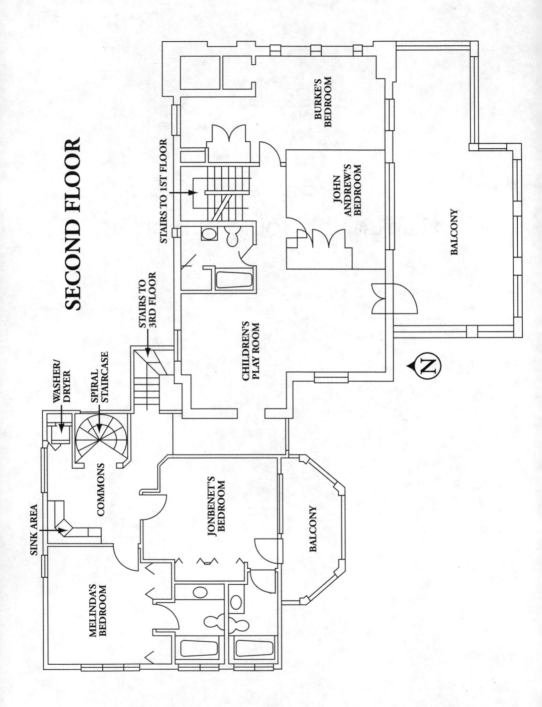

SECOND FLOOR

STAIRS TO 1ST FLOOR

STAIRS TO 3RD FLOOR

WASHER/ DRYER

SPIRAL STAIRCASE

SINK AREA

COMMONS

MELINDA'S BEDROOM

JONBENET'S BEDROOM

BALCONY

CHILDREN'S PLAY ROOM

BURKE'S BEDROOM

JOHN ANDREW'S BEDROOM

BALCONY

N

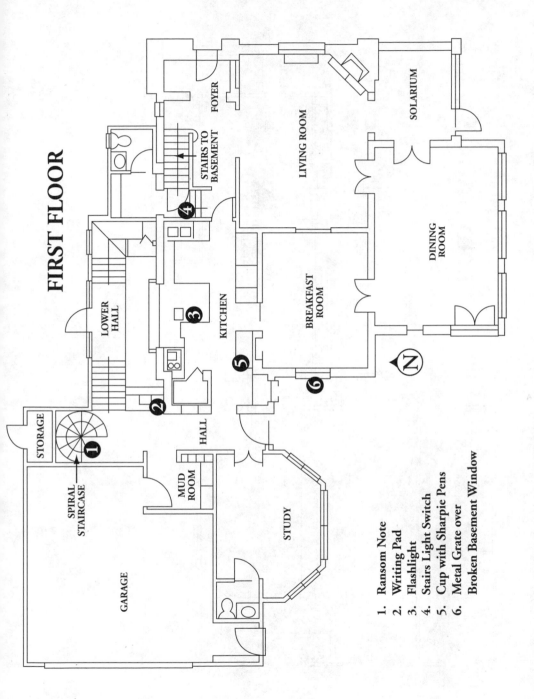

FIRST FLOOR

1. Ransom Note
2. Writing Pad
3. Flashlight
4. Stairs Light Switch
5. Cup with Sharpie Pens
6. Metal Grate over
   Broken Basement Window

THIRD FLOOR

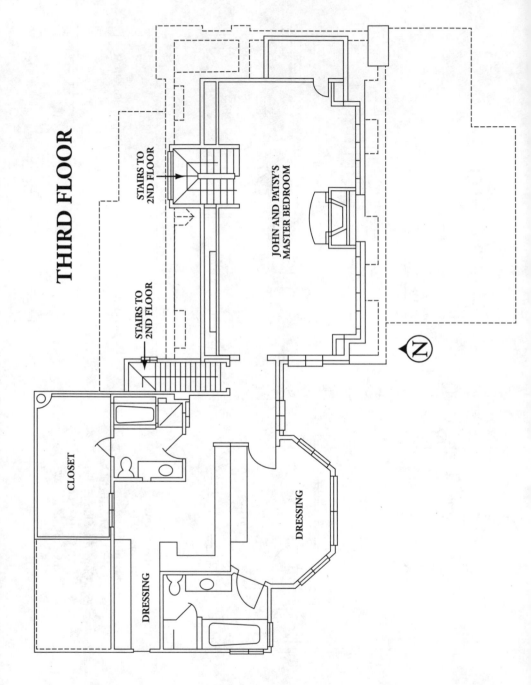

STAIRS TO
2ND FLOOR

STAIRS TO
2ND FLOOR

CLOSET

DRESSING

DRESSING

JOHN AND PATSY'S
MASTER BEDROOM

N

BASEMENT

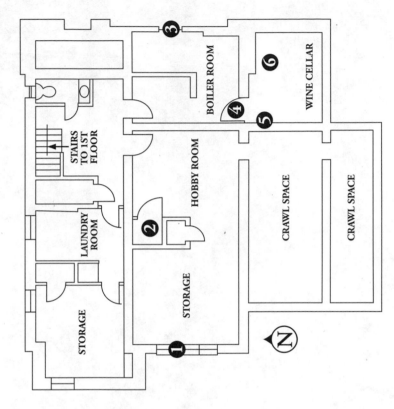

STAIRS TO 1ST FLOOR

BOILER ROOM

WINE CELLAR

HOBBY ROOM

LAUNDRY ROOM

STORAGE

STORAGE

CRAWL SPACE

CRAWL SPACE

N

1. **Broken Window**
2. **Subic Bay Plaque Found**
3. **Exposed Ventilation Duct**
4. **Approximate Position of Fleet White Looking Into Room**
5. **Approximate Position of Light Switch**
6. **JonBenet's Body**

APPENDIX B

Chief Beckner,

On June 22, I submitted a letter to Chief Koby, requesting a leave of absence from the Boulder Police Department. In response to persistent speculation as to why I chose to leave the Ramsey investigation, this letter explains more fully those reasons. Although my concerns were well known for some time, I tried to be gracious in my departure, addressing only health concerns. However, after a month of soul searching and reflection, I feel I must now set the record straight.

The primary reason I chose to leave is my belief that the district attorney's office continues to mishandle the Ramsey case. I had been troubled for many months with many aspects of the investigation. Albeit an uphill battle of a case to begin with, it became a nearly impossible investigation because of the political alliances, philosophical differences, and professional egos that blocked progress in more ways, and on more occasions, than I can detail in this memorandum. I and others voiced these concerns repeatedly. In the interest of hoping justice would be served, we tolerated it, except for those closed door sessions when detectives protested in frustration, where fists hit the table, where detectives demanded that the right things be done. The wrong things were done, and made it a matter of simple principle that I could not continue to participate as it stood with the district attorney's office. As an organization, we remained silent, when we should have shouted.

The Boulder Police Department took a handful of detectives days after the murder, and handed us this case. As one of those five primary detectives, we tackled it for a year and a half. We conducted an exhaustive investigation, followed the evidence where it led us, and were faithfully and professionally committed to this case. Although not perfect, cases rarely are. During eighteen months on the Ramsey investigation, my colleagues and I worked the case night and day, and in spite of tied hands. On June 1-2, 1998, we crunched thirty thousand pages of investigation to its essence, and put our cards on the table, delivering the case in a formal presentation to the district attorney's office. We stood confident in our work. Very shortly thereafter, though, the detectives who know this case better than anyone were advised by the district attorney's office that we would not be participating as grand jury advisory witnesses.

The very entity with whom we shared our investigative case file to see justice sought, I felt, was betraying this case. We were never afforded true prosecutorial support. There was never a consolidation of resources. All legal opportunities were not made available. How were we expected to "solve" this case when the district attorney's office was crippling us with their positions? I believe they were, literally, facilitating the escape of justice. During this investigation, consider the following.

During the investigation, detectives would discover, collect, and bring evidence to the district attorney's office, only to have it summarily dismissed or rationalized as insignificant. The most elementary of investigative efforts, such as obtaining telephone and credit card records, were met without support, search warrants denied. The significant opinions of national experts were casually dismissed or ignored by the district attorney's office, even the experienced FBI were waved aside.

Those who chose not to cooperate were never compelled before a grand jury early in this case, as detectives suggested only weeks after the murder, while information and memories were fresh.

An informant, for reasons of his own, came to detectives about conduct occurring inside the district attorney's office, including allegations of a plan intended only to destroy a man's career. We carefully listened. With that knowledge, the department did nothing. Other than to alert the accused, and in the process burn the two detectives (who captured that exchange on an undercover wire, incidentally) who came forth with this information. One of the results of that internal whistleblowing was witnessing Detective Commander Eller, who also could not tolerate what was occurring, lose his career and reputation undeservedly; scapegoated in a manner which only heightened my concerns. It did not take much inferential reasoning to realize that any dissidents were readily silenced. In a departure from protocol, police reports, physical evidence, and investigative information were shared with Ramsey defense attorneys, all of this in the district attorney's office "spirit of cooperation." I served a search warrant, only to find later defense attorneys were simply given copies of the evidence it yielded.

An FBI agent, whom I didn't even know, quietly tipped me off about what the DA's office was doing behind our backs, conducting an investigation the police department was wholly unaware of.

I was advised not to speak to certain witnesses, and all but dissuaded from pursuing particular investigative efforts. Polygraphs were acceptable for some subjects, but others seemed immune from such requests.

Innocent people were not "cleared," publicly or otherwise, even when it was unmistakably the right thing to do, as reputations and lives were destroyed. Some in the district attorney's office, to this day, pursue weak, defenseless, and innocent people in shameless tactics that one couldn't believe more bizarre if it were made up.

I was told by one person in the district attorney's office about being unable to "break" a particular police officer from his resolute accounts of events he had witnessed. In my opinion, this was not trial preparation, this was an attempt to derail months of hard work.

I was repeatedly reminded by some in the district attorney's office just how powerful and talented and resourceful particular defense attorneys were. How could decisions be made this way?

There is evidence that was critical to the investigation, that to this day has never been collected, because neither search warrants nor other means were supported to do so. Not to mention evidence which still sits today, untested in the laboratory, as differences continue about how to proceed.

While investigative efforts were rebuffed, my search warrant affidavits and attempts to gather evidence in the murder investigation of a six year old child were met with refusals and, instead, the suggestions that we "ask the permission of the Ramseys" before proceeding. And just before conducting the Ramsey interviews, I thought it was inconceivable I was being lectured on "building trust."

These are but a few of the many examples of why I chose to leave. Having to convince, to plead at times, to a district attorney's office to assist us in the murder of a little girl, by way of the most basic investigative requests, was simply absurd. When my detective partner and I had to literally hand search tens of thousands of receipts, because we didn't have a search warrant to assist us otherwise, we did so. But we lost tremendous opportunities to make progress, to seek justice, and to know the truth. Auspicious timing and strategy could have made a difference. When the might of the criminal justice system should have brought all it had to bear on this investigation, and didn't, we remained silent. We were trying to deliver a murder case with hands tied behind our backs. It was difficult, and our frustrations understandable. It was an assignment without chance of success. Politics seemed to trump justice.

Even "outsiders" quickly assessed the situation, as the FBI politely noted early on: "the government isn't in charge of this investigation." As the nation watched, appropriately anticipating a fitting response to the murder of the most innocent of victims, I stood bothered as to what occurred behind the scenes. Those inside this case knew what was going on. Eighteen months gave us a unique perspective.

We learned to ignore the campaign of misinformation in which we were said to be bumbling along, or else just pursuing one or two suspects in some ruthless vendetta. Much of what appeared in the press was orchestrated by particular sources wishing to discredit the Boulder Police Department. We watched the media spin, while we were prohibited from exercising First Amendment rights. As disappointment and frustration pervaded, detectives would remark to one another, "If it reaches a particular point, I'm walking away." But we would always tolerate it "just one more time." Last year, when we discovered hidden cameras inside the Ramsey house, only to realize the detectives had been unwittingly videotaped, this should have rocked the police department off its foundation. Instead, we allowed that, too, to pass without challenge. The detectives' enthusiasm became simply resigned frustration, acquiescing to that which should never have been tolerated. In the media blitz, the pressure of the whole world watching, important decisions seemed to be premised on "how it would play" publicly. Among at least a few of the detectives, "there's something wrong here" became a catch phrase. I witnessed others having to make decisions which impacted their lives and careers, watched the soul searching that occurred as the ultimate questions were pondered. As it goes, "evils that befall the world are not nearly so often caused by bad men, as they are by good men who are silent when an opinion must be voiced." Although several good men in the police department shouted loudly behind closed doors, the organization stood deafeningly silent at what continued to occur unchallenged.

Last Spring, you, too, seemed at a loss. I was taken aback when I was reminded of what happened to Commander Eller when he stuck his neck out. When reminded how politically powerful the DA was. When reminded of the hundreds of other cases the department had to file with this district attorney's office, and this was but one case. And finally, when I was asked, "what do you want done? The system burned down?", it struck me dumb. But when you conceded that there were those inside the DA's office we had to simply accept as "defense witnesses," and when we were reduced to simply recording our objections for "documentation purposes"—I knew I was not going to participate in this much longer.

I believe the district attorney's office is thoroughly compromised. When we were told by one person in the district attorney's office, months before we had even completed our investigation, that this case "is not prosecutable," we shook our heads in disbelief. A lot could have been forgiven, and lesser transgressions ignored, for the right things done. Instead, those in the district attorney's office encouraged us to allow them to "work their magic" (which I never fully understood. Did that "magic" include sharing our case file information with the defense attorneys, dragging feet in evidence collection, or believing that two decades of used-car-dealing-style-plea-bargaining was somehow going to solve this case?) Right and wrong is just that. Some of these issues were not shades of gray. Decisions should have been made as such. Whether a suspect's a penniless indigent with a public defender, or otherwise.

★ ★ ★

As contrasted by my experiences in Georgia, for example, where my warrant affidavits were met with a sense of support and an obligation to the victim. Having worked with able prosecutors in other jurisdictions, having worked cases where justice was aggressively sought, I have familiarity with these prosecution professionals who hold a strong sense of justice. And then, from Georgia, the Great Lakes, the East Coast, the South, I would return to Boulder, to again be thoroughly demoralized.

We delayed and ignored, for far too long, that which was "right" in deference of maintaining this dysfunctional relationship with the district attorney's office. This wasn't a runaway train that couldn't be stopped. Some of us bit our tongues as the public was told of this "renewed cooperation" between the police department and the district attorney's office—this at the very time the detectives and those in the district attorney's office weren't even on speaking terms, the same time you had to act as a liaison between the two agencies because the detectives couldn't tolerate it. I was quite frankly surprised, as you remarked on this camaraderie, that there had not yet been a fistfight.

In Boulder, where the politics, policies and pervasive thought has held for years, a criminal justice system designed to deal with such an event was not in place. Instead, we had an institution that when needed most, buckled. The system was paralyzed, as to this day one continues to get away with murder.

Will there be a real attempt at justice? I may be among the last to find out. The department assigned me some of the most sensitive and critical assignments in the Ramsey case, including search warrants and affidavits, the Atlanta projects, the interviews of the Ramseys, and many other sensitive assignments I won't mention. I criss-crossed the country, conducting interviews and investigation, pursuing pedophiles and drifters, chasing and discarding leads. I submitted over 250 investigative reports for this case alone. I'd have been happy to assist the grand jury. But the detectives, who know this case better than anyone, were told we would not be allowed as grand jury advisory witnesses, as is common place. If a grand jury is convened, the records will be sealed, and we will not witness what goes on inside such a proceeding. What part of the case gets presented, what doesn't?

District Attorney Hunter's continued reference to a "runaway" grand jury is also puzzling. Is he afraid that he cannot control the outcome? Why would one not simply present evidence to jurors, and let the jury decide? Perhaps the DA is hoping for a voluntary confession one day. What's needed, though, is an effective district attorney to conduct the inquiry, not a remorseful killer.

The district attorney's office should be the ethical and judicial compass for the community, ensuring that justice is served—or at least, sought. Instead, our DA has becoming [sic] a spinning compass for the media. The perpetuating inference continues that justice is somehow just around the corner. I do not see that occurring, as the two year anniversary of this murder approaches.

It is my belief that the district attorney's office has effectively crippled this case. The time for intervention is now. It is difficult to imagine a more compelling situation for the appointment of an entirely independent prosecution team to be introduced into this matter, who would oversee an attempt at righting this case.

Unmistakably and worst of all, we have failed a little girl named JonBenét. Six years old. Many good people, decent, innocent citizens, are forever bound by the murder of this child. There is a tremendous obligation to them. But an infinitely greater obligation to her, as she rests in a small cemetery far away from this anomaly of a place called Boulder.

A distant second stands the second tragedy—the failure of the system in Boulder. Ask the mistreated prosecution witnesses in this investigation, who cooperated for months, who now refuse to talk until a special prosecutor is established. Ask former detectives who have quietly tendered their shields in disheartenment. Ask all those innocent people personally affected by this case, who have had their lives upset because of the arbitrary label of "suspect" being attached. Ask the cops who cannot speak out because they still wear a badge. The list is long.

I know that to speak out brings its own issues. But as you also know, there are others who are as disheartened as I am, who are biting their tongues, searching their consciences. I know what may occur—I may be portrayed as frustrated, disgruntled. Not so. I have had an exemplary and decorated thirteen year career as a police officer and detective. I didn't want to challenge the system. In no way do I wish to harm this case or subvert the long and arduous work that has been done. I only wish to speak up and ask for assistance in making a change. I want justice for a child who was killed in her home on Christmas night.

This case has defined many aspects of all our lives, and will continue to do so for all of our days. My colleagues put their hearts and souls into this case, and I will take some satisfaction that it was the detective team who showed tremendous efforts and loyalties to seeking justice for this victim. Many sacrifices were made. Families. Marriages. In the latter months of the investigation, I was diagnosed with a disease which will require a lifetime of medication. Although my health declined, I was resolved to see the case through to a satisfactory closure. I did that on June 1-2. And on June 22, I requested a leave of absence, without mention of what transpired in our department since Christmas 1996.

What I witnessed for two years of my life was so fundamentally flawed, it reduced me to tears. Everything the badge ever meant to me was so fundamentally shaken, one should never have to sell one's soul as a prerequisite to wear it. On June 26, after leaving the investigation for the last time, and leaving the city of Boulder, I wept as I drove home, removing my detectives shield and placing it on the seat beside me, later putting it in a desk drawer at home, knowing I could never put it back on.

There is some consolation that a greater justice awaits the person who committed these acts, independent of this system we call "justice." A greater justice awaits. Of that, at least, we can be confident.

As a now infamous author, panicked in the night, once penned, "use that good southern common sense of yours." I will do just that. Originally from a small southern town where this would never have been tolerated, where respect for law and order and traditions were instilled in me, I will take that murderous author's out-of-context advice. And use my good southern common sense to put this case into the perspective it necessitates—a precious child was murdered. There needs to be some consequence to that.

Regretfully, I tender this letter, and my police career, a calling which I loved. I do this because I cannot continue to sanction by my silence what has occurred in this case. It was never a level playing field, the "game" was simply unacceptable anymore. And that's what makes this all so painful. The detectives never had a chance. If ever there were a case, and if ever there were a victim, who truly meant something to the detectives pursuing the truth, this is it. If not this case, what case? Until such time as an independent prosecutor is appointed to oversee this case, I will not be part of this. What went on was simply wrong.

I recalled a favorite passage recently, Atticus Finch speaking to his daughter: "Just remember that one thing does not abide by majority rule, Scout—it's your conscience."

At thirty-six years old, I thought my life's passion as a police officer was carved in stone. I realize that although I may have to trade my badge for a carpenter's hammer, I will do so with a clear conscience. It is with a heavy heart that I offer my resignation from the Boulder Police Department, in protest of this continuing travesty.

Detective Steve Thomas #638
Detective Division
Boulder Police Department
August 6, 1998

APPENDIX C

Sept. 20, 1998

Dear Alex:

It is with great reluctance and regret that I submit this letter of resignation. Even though I want to continue to participate in the official investigation and assist in finding the killer of JonBenet, I find that I cannot in good conscience be a part of the persecution of innocent people. It would be highly improper and unethical for me to stay when I so strongly believe this.

It has been almost 19 months since we talked that day in your office and you asked me to assist you in this investigation. It has turned out to be more of a challenge than either one of us anticipated. When we first met I told you that my style of approaching an investigation is from the concept of not working a particular theory, but working the case. Detectives collect and record information from many sources, analyze it, couple that with their experience and training and let "the case" tell them where to go. This process may take days, weeks or years, depending on the direction the case tells you to go. Sometimes you must investigate "many paths" in order to find the killer. It is not a political speed contest where expediency should outweigh justice, where "resolving" the case is solving the case.

Alex, even though I have been unable to actively investigate, I have been in a position to collect, record and analyze every piece of information given to your office in the course of this investigation. I believe that I know this case better than anyone does. I know what has been investigated and what hasn't, what evidence exists and what doesn't, what information has been leaked and what hasn't. I am a detective with a proven record of successful investigations. I have looked at the murder of JonBenet Ramsey through the eyes of age and experience and a thorough knowledge of the case.

At this point of the investigation "the case" tells me that John and Patsy Ramsey did not kill their daughter, that a very dangerous killer is still out there and no one is actively looking for him. There are still many areas of investigation which must be explored before life and death decisions are made.

When I was hired I had no agenda one way or the other, my allegiance was to the case, not the Police Department nor John and Patsy Ramsey. My agenda has not changed. . . . I only desire to be able to investigate the case and find the killer of JonBenet and will continue to do so as long as I am able. The chances of catching him working from the "outside looking in" are very slim, but I have a great "Partner" who I'm sure will lead the way. There is no doubt that I will be facing a great deal of opposition and ridicule in the future, because I intend to stand with this family and somehow help them through this and find the killer of their daughter. Perhaps others who believe this will also help.

The Boulder Police Department has many fine and dedicated men and women who also want justice for JonBenet. They are just going in the wrong direction and have been since day one of the investigation. Instead of letting the case tell them which way to go, they have elected to follow a theory and let their theory direct them rather than allowing the evidence to direct them. The case tells me that there is substantial, credible evidence of an intruder and lack of evidence that the parents are involved. If this is true, they too are tragic victims whose misery has been compounded by a misdirected and flawed investigation, unsubstantiated leaks, rumors and accusations.

I have worked in this profession for the past 32 years and have always been loyal to it, the men and women in it, and what it represents, because I believed that justice had always prevailed. In this case, however, I believe that justice is not being served, that innocent people are being targeted and could be charged with a murder they did not commit.

The law enforcement Code of Ethics states it very well. My fundamental duty is to "serve mankind; to safeguard lives and property; to protect the innocent against deception, the weak against oppression or intimidation, the peaceful against violence or disorder. To respect the constitutional rights of all men to liberty, equality and justice." This applies not only to JonBenet but to her mother and father as well.

★ ★ ★

I want to thank you and the others in the office for the wonderful support and treatment I have received. You have a great D.A.'s office and the men and women who work with you are some of the most honest and dedicated people I have ever met. My life has been enriched because of this memorable time together. I have especially enjoyed working closely with Peter Hofstrom and Trip DeMuth, who also have dedicated so much of their lives to this case. I have never met two more fair, honest and dedicated defenders of our system.

Alex, you are in such a difficult position. The media and peer pressure are incredible. You are inundated with conflicting facts and information, and "expert" opinions. And now you have an old detective telling you that the Ramseys did not do it and to wait and investigate this case more thoroughly before a very tragic mistake would be made. What a double travesty it could be; an innocent person indicted, and a vicious killer on the loose to prey on another innocent child and no one to stop him.

History will be the judge as to how we conducted ourselves and how we handled our responsibilities.

Shoes, shoes, the victim's shoes, who will stand in the victim's shoes?

Good Luck to you and your fine office and may God bless you in the awesome decisions you must soon make.

Sincerely

Detective Lou Smit